Trusts and Trustees

A Treatise

on the Law of

Trusts and Trustees

BY

JAIRUS WARE PERRY

SIXTH EDITION
REVISED AND ENLARGED
BY
EDWIN A. HOWES, JR.

IN THREE VOLUMES

Volume II

BeardBooks

Washington, D.C.

CONTENTS OF VOL.

CHAPTER III.

EXPRESS TRUSTS, AND HOW EXPRESS TRUSTS ARE
CREATED AT COMMON LAW, SINCE THE STATUTE OF
FRAUDS, AND IN PERSONAL PROPERTY, AND HEREIN
OF VOLUNTARY CONVEYANCES OR SETTLEMENTS IN
TRUSTS . . . . 73–111 a

CHAPTER IV.

CHAPTER V.

CHAPTER VI.

CHAPTER VII.

Trusts that arise by Equitable Construction in the Absence of Fraud

CHAPTER VIII.

CHAPTER IX.

CHAPTER X.

CHAPTER XI.

PROPERTIES AND INCIDENTS OF THE LEGAL ESTATE IN
THE HANDS OF TRUSTEES   321–355

CHAPTER XII.

CHAPTER XIII.

CHAPTER XIV.

CHAPTER XV.

POSSESSION — CUSTODY — CONVERSION — INVESTMENT OF TRUST PROPERTY, AND INTEREST THAT TRUSTEES MAY BE MADE TO PAY 438–472

CHAPTER X.

NATURE, EXTENT, AND DURATION OF THE ESTATE TAKEN BY TRUSTEES.

§ 298. IT may happen that although words of express trust are used in the grant or bequest of an estate to a trustee, yet no estate vests or remains in the trustee. This may be because only a *power* is given and no estate, as where a testator simply directs his executor to sell certain property and apply the proceeds to certain purposes instead of granting the property to the executor or trustee to sell, &c., or because the statute of

507

uses *executes* the legal estate at once in the *cestui que trust*.[1] Thus, if A. grants or bequeaths land to B. and his heirs, in trust for C. and his heirs, the trustee, B., will take nothing in the land, but the legal title, as well as the beneficial use, will vest immediately in C.;[2] for the statute of uses,[3] so called, executes the possession and the legal title in the same person to whom the beneficial interest is given. As stated in previous sections,[4] a large part of the land in England was at one time held to uses. The legal title was in one person, but upon the trust and confidence that such person would apply it to the use of some person named, or that such legal owner would permit some other person to have the possession, use, and income of the estate. This system, originating partly in fraud of the law, and partly in the necessities and convenience of the subject, became at last the source of great abuses. To remedy these abuses, the statute of uses was enacted.[5] This statute executes the use by

[1] West *v.* Fitz, 109 Ill. 425.

[2] Austin *v.* Taylor, 1 Eden, 361; Williams *v.* Walters, 14 M. & W. 166; Robinson *v.* Grey, 9 East, 1; Chapman *v.* Blissett, Cas. t. Talbot, 150; Broughton *v.* Langley, 2 Salk. 150; 2 Ld. Raym. 873; Thatcher *v.* Omans, 3 Pick. 521; Upham *v.* Varney, 15 N. H. 466; Kinch *v.* Ward, 2 Sim. & St. 409, and see Doe *v.* Biggs, 2 Taunt. 109; Shapland *v.* Smith, 1 Bro. Ch. 75, and notes; Boyer *v.* Cockerell, 3 Kan. 282; Witham *v.* Brooner, 63 Ill. 344.

[3] 27 Henry VIII. c. 10, § 1.

[4] *Ante,* §§ 3, 4.

[5] *Ante,* §§ 5, 6, 7. And see the preamble of the statute. The first section of the statute was as follows: "That where any person or persons stand or be seized, or at any time hereafter shall happen to be seized of and in any honors, castles, manors, lands, tenements, rents, services, reversions, remainders, or other hereditaments, to the use, confidence, or trust of any other person or persons, or of any body politic, by reason of any bargain, sale, feoffment, fine, recovery, covenant, contract, agreement, will, or otherwise, by any manner of means, whatsoever it be; that in every such case, all and every such person and persons, and bodies politic that have or hereafter shall have any such use, confidence, or trust in fee-simple, fee-tail, for term of life, or for years, or otherwise, or any use, confidence, or trust in remainder or reverter, shall from henceforth stand and be seized, deemed, and adjudged, in lawful seizin, estate, and possession, of and in the same honors, castles, manors, lands, tenements, rents, services, reversions, remainders, and hereditaments, with their appurtenances, to all intents, constructions, and purposes, in the law of and in such like estates as they had or shall have

conveying the possession to the use, and transferring the use into possession, thereby making the *cestui que use* complete owner of the estate, as well at law as in equity. It does not abolish the conveyance to uses, but only annihilates the intervening estate, and turns the interest of the *cestui que use* into a *legal* instead of an *equitable* estate.[1] A *use*, a *trust*, and a *confidence* is one and the same thing, and if an estate is conveyed to one person for the use of, or upon, a trust for another and nothing more is said, the statute immediately transfers the legal estate to the use, and no trust is created, although express words of trust are used.[2] So absolute is the statute that it will operate upon all conveyances in the words above stated, although it was the plain intention of the settlor that the estate should vest and remain in the first donee; for the intention of the citizen cannot control express enactments of the legislature,[3] or positive rules of property.

§ 299. The statute of uses is in force in most of the United States,[4] but where the statute is not in force either by adoption

in use, trust, or confidence of or in the same; and that the estate, title, right, and possession that was in such person or persons that were or hereafter shall be seized of any lands, tenements, or hereditaments, to the use, confidence, or trust of any such person or persons, or of any body politic, be from henceforth clearly deemed and adjudged to be in him or them, that have, or hereafter shall have, such use, confidence, or trust after such quality, manner, form, and condition as they had before, in, or to the use, confidence, or trust that was in them." Saund. on Uses, 70–82.

[1] Eustace *v.* Seamen, Cro. Jac. 696; 2 Black. Com. 333, 338; Thatcher *v.* Omans, 3 Pick. 529; Hutchins *v.* Heywood, 50 N. H. 495.

[2] Terry *v.* Collier, 11 East, 377; Right *v.* Smith, 12 East, 454; Broughton *v.* Langley, 2 Salk. 679; Ease *v.* Howard, Pr. Ch. 338, 345; Hammerston's Case, Dyer, 166 a, note; Ramsay *v.* Marsh, 2 McCord, 252; Moore *v.* Shultz, 13 Penn. St. 98; Jackson *v.* Fish, 10 Johns. 456; Parks *v.* Parks, 9 Paige, 107.

[3] Carwardine *v.* Carwardine, 1 Eden, 36; Gregory *v.* Henderson, 4 Taunt. 772. In this case the intent of the testator was loosely talked of, but it was an active trust, as pointed out by Heath, J. Doe *v.* Collier, 11 East, 377; Shapland *v.* Smith, 1 Bro. Ch. 75; 1 Sugd. Ven. 309, 314.

[4] 4 Kent, Com. 299; 1 Green. Cru. tit. 11, Use, c. 3, § 3, note. [See Kay *v.* Scates, 78 Am. Dec. 399, and note.]

or by re-enactment, and even where it is expressly repealed and a form of deed is enacted, a knowledge of the law of uses is necessary in order to understand and apply the common forms of conveyance.[1] The statute of uses, and the doctrines it established, are so interwoven with the history of every American State, and with the growth of its jurisprudence in regard to real estate, that the law of tenures is necessarily interpreted in America by the precedents established under the statute;[2] and in this branch of the law, as in all others, it is impossible to obtain a clear perception of its present state, without a full knowledge of the successive steps by which the latest development has been reached. The application of the statute has been very much modified in many of the States, but the general idea is still acted upon.[3] Mr. Washburn remarks, that it is

[1] Walk. Am. Law, 311; Helfensteine v. Garrard, 7 Ohio, 275; 2 Washb. on Real Prop. 152.

[2] 4 Kent, Com. 299–301.

[3] In Maine, a person may convey land by deed acknowledged and recorded. Rev. Stat. 1857, c. 73, § 1. [Rev. Stat. (1903), c. 75, § 1.] And a deed may be any species of conveyance, not plainly repugnant in terms, and necessary to give effect to the intention of the parties. Emery v. Chase, 5 Maine, 235. And the statute of uses is in force. Shapleigh v. Pilsbury, 1 Maine, 271; Emery v. Chase, 5 id. 232; Webster v. Cooper, 14 How. 496; Morden v. Chase, 32 Maine, 329.

In New Hampshire, the form in which lands may be conveyed is fixed by statute. Rev. Stat. But this does not exclude other known forms of conveyance at common law, and the statute of uses is in full force. Exeter v. Odiorne, 1 N. H. 232; Chamberlain v. Crane, id. 64; French v. French, 3 id. 234; Upham v. Varney, 15 id. 462; Hayes v. Tabor, 41 id. 526; Bell v. Scammon, 15 id. 394; Pritchard v. Brown, 4 id. 397; Dennett v. Dennett, 40 id. 498; Hutchins v. Heywood, 50 id. 496. [Fellows v. Ripley, 69 N. H. 410.]

In Vermont, there is a similar legislation as to the form of conveyances; but Chief-Justice Redfield held that the English statute of uses was not in force, for the reason that their court of equity could carry out the intention of parties without the help of the statute. Gorham v. Daniels, 23 Vt. 600; Sherman v. Dodge, 28 id. 26. Mr. Justice Thompson, of the United States court for the district, held the contrary. Soc. &c. v. Hartland, 2 Paine, C. C. 536. [See Atkins v. Atkins, 70 Vt. 565.]

In Massachusetts, a deed acknowleged and recorded conveys land without any other ceremony. Gen. Stat. 1860, c. 89, § 1. [Rev. Laws (1902), c. 127, § 1.] The form of deed in general use *gives, grants, bargains, sells* and

not a fair inference that the doctrine of uses would be inapplicable in any State where they are not declared not to exist,

conveys, upon a consideration, limiting the estate to the grantee and his heirs *to their use*. These words prevent a resulting use in the grantor; and it is a conveyance at common law, since the *grantee* and the *cestui que use* is the same person. But if, for any reason, it is necessary, in order to give effect to the conveyance, to construe it as operating under the statute of uses, the court will do so. Cox *v.* Edwards, 14 Mass. 492; Marshall *v.* Fish, 6 Mass. 24; Hunt *v.* Hunt, 14 Pick. 374; Wallis *v.* Wallis, 4 Mass. 135; Pray *v.* Pierce, 7 Mass. 381; Russell *v.* Coffin, 8 Pick. 143; Blood *v.* Blood, id. 80; Parker *v.* Nichols, 7 id. 111; Gale *v.* Coburn, 18 id. 397; Brewer *v.* Hardy, 22 id. 376; Thatcher *v.* Omans, 3 id. 522; Norton *v.* Leonard, 12 id. 157; Newhall *v.* Wheeler, 7 Mass. 189; Chapin *v.* Univer. Soc., 8 Gray, 580; Baptist Soc. *v.* Hazen, 100 Mass. 322; Durant *v.* Ritchie, 4 Mason, 45; Northampton Bank *v.* Whiting, 12 Mass. 104; Johnson *v.* Johnson, 7 Allen, 197. [See Carr *v.* Richardson, 157 Mass. 576; Dakin *v.* Savage, 172 Mass. 23.]

In Rhode Island, deeds of bargain and sale, lease and release, and covenants to stand seized, are recognized by statute. Rev. Stat. (1857), p. 335. [Gen. Laws (1909), c. 253, § 11.] And the statute of uses would seem to be in partial force. 1 Lomax, Dig. 188; Nightingale *v.* Hidden, 7 R. I. 132. [Fish *v.* Prior, 16 R. I. 566; Sullivan *v.* Chambers, 18 R. I. 799; Ames, Petitioner, 22 R. I. 54.]

In Connecticut, the act of acknowledging and recording a deed is held equivalent to livery of seizin. Barrett *v.* French, 1 Conn. 354. But the statute of uses is held to be part of its common law. Bacon *v.* Taylor, Kirb. 368; Barrett *v.* French, 1 Conn. 354; Bryan *v.* Bradley, 16 Conn. 474.

In New York, previous to 1827, the English statute of uses was in full force. Jackson *v.* Myers, 3 Johns. 388; Jackson *v.* Fish, 10 id. 456; Jackson *v.* Root, 18 id. 79; Jackson *v.* Cary, 16 id. 302; Jackson *v.* Dunsbagh, 1 Johns. Cas. 91; Jackson *v.* Cadwell, 1 Cow. 622. [See Brown *v.* Wadsworth, 168 N. Y. 225.] After that year, the rules of the common law were repealed; all uses and trusts were abolished, except such as were expressly authorized. Every interest in land is declared to be a legal right, and cognizable in a court of law except where it is otherwise provided. A conveyance by *grant*, *assignment*, or devise is substituted for a conveyance to uses, and future interests in lands may be conveyed by grant. 3 Rev. Stat. 15 (5th ed.); 4 Kent, 300. It has, however, been determined that if land is granted to one in fee in trust for another, the *cestui que trust* takes the estate absolutely, but subject, however, to such incumbrances as the trustee made upon the estate at the time of the conveyance, as if the trustee should give back a mortgage for the purchase-money, it would be held to be one transaction. Rawson *v.* Lampman, 1 Seld. 456. Nor have these statutes any application to securities by mortgage. King *v.* Merchants' Exchange Co., 1 Seld. 547. [The New York statutes expressly provide against passive trusts of real estate and that title shall vest at once in the person beneficially entitled.

either because no case has arisen in the courts of the State to test the question, or because a form of deed not known under

IV Consol. Laws (1909), p. 3389, § 91 *et seq.* See Wendt *v.* Walsh, 164 N. Y. 154; Jacoby *v.* Jacoby, 188 N. Y. 124; Adams *v.* Adams, 100 N. Y. S. 145, 114 App. Div. 390.]

In New Jersey, the statute of uses is substantially re-enacted. Den *v.* Crawford, 3 Halst. 107; Prince *v.* Sisson, 13 N. J. 168. [N. J. Gen. Stat. (1895), p. 877, § 119.]

In Pennsylvania, a statute declares all deeds in a prescribed form equivalent to a feoffment with livery of seizin at common law, and the statute of uses is also in full force. Opinion of the Judges, 3 Binn, 599; Welt *v.* Franklin, 1 Binn, 502; Ashhurst *v.* Given, 5 Wat. & S. 323; Sprague *v.* Woods, 4 id. 192; O'Kinson *v.* Patterson, 1 id. 395; Hurst *v.* McNeil, 1 Wash. C. C. 70; Franciscus *v.* Reigart, 4 Watts, 118. Indeed, at one time the Pennsylvania courts carried the application of the statute to an unsual extent, and held that *equitable* were converted into *legal* estates in all cases except active trusts, and even *then* if the purposes of the trust did not furnish a legitimate reason for not executing the trust in the beneficiary. Kuhn *v.* Newman, 26 Penn. St. 227; Whichcote *v.* Lyle, 28 id. 73; Bush's App., 33 id. 85; Kay *v.* Scates, 37 id. 31. But these cases were overruled, and the law restored to its former condition, in Barnett's App., 46 Penn. St. 392; Shankland's App., 47 id. 113; Earp's App., 75 id. 119; Deibert's App., 78 id. 296.

In Delaware, the statute provides that lands may be transferred by deed without livery, and that the legal estate shall accompany the use, and pass with it. Rev. Code (1852), p. 266. [Rev. Code (1893), c. 83, § 1.]

In Maryland, the English statute of uses is the foundation of their conveyances, and their rules of construction of it are nearly similar to the English rules. Lewis *v.* Beall, 4 Harr. & McH. 488; Mason *v.* Smallwood, id. 484; Matthews *v.* Ward, 10 Gill & J. 443; Cheney *v.* Watkins, 1 Harr. & J. 527; West *v.* Biscoe, 6 id. 465; Calvert *v.* Eden, 2 Harr. & McH. 331. [Rogers *v.* Sisters of Charity, 97 Md. 550; Numsen *v.* Lyon, 87 Md. 31; Hooper *v.* Felgner, 80 Md. 262; Graham *v.* Whitridge, 99 Md. 248.]

In Virginia, the statute of uses was a part of the colonial law; but it was repealed in 1792. Afterwards, in 1819, and in Rev. Code (1849), p. 502 [Va. Code (1904), § 2426], a partial substitute was adopted, by which the possession was transferred to the use only in cases of deeds of bargain and sale, lease and release, and deeds operating by way of covenant to stand seized to uses. If uses or trusts are raised by any other form of conveyance, as by devise, they remain, as before the statute of Henry VIII., mere equitable estates, not cognizable by courts of law. Bass *v.* Scott, 2 Leigh, 359; 1 Lomax, Dig. 188; 2 Matt. Dig. 34; Rowletts *v.* Daniel, 4 Munf. 473; Tabb *v.* Baird, 3 Call, 475; Duvall *v.* Bibb, id. 362. [The court of West Virginia, interpreting a statute worded precisely the same, held that it was designed only to aid those conveyances which could not pass the legal title without its aid and that a deed of bargain and sale to A., trustee for B., did

the statute of uses may have been declared by the statute of a
State sufficient to convey lands.[1]   It is true that Lord Hard-

not pass the legal title to B.   Blake *v.* O'Neal, 63 W. Va. 483; W. Va. Code
(1906), § 3033.]
   In North Carolina, the statute is similar to the statute of Virginia.   Rev.
Code (1854), p. 270; Den *v.* Hanks, 5 Ired. 30; Smith *v.* Lockabill, 76 N. C.
465. [Code of N. C. (1908), § 1584.   But it is not applied in the same way
as the Virginia statute.   See Smith *v.* Proctor, 139 N. C. 314; Webb *v.*
Borden, 145 N. C. 188; Kirkman *v.* Holland, 139 N. C. 185; Wilson
v. Leary, 120 N. C. 90.]
   In South Carolina, the statute of uses was re-enacted in terms.   2 Stat.
at Large, p. 467; Ramsay *v.* Marsh, 2 McCord, 252; Redfern *v.* Middleton,
Rice, 464; Kinsler *v.* Clark, 1 Rich. 170; Chancellor *v.* Windham, id. 161;
Laurens *v.* Jenney, 1 Spears, 356; McNish *v.* Guerard, 4 Strob. 74. [S. C.
Civ. Code (1902), § 2580; Uzzell *v.* Horn, 71 S. C. 426; Young *v.* McNeill,
78 S. C. 143; Foster *v.* Glover, 46 S. C. 522; Holmes *v.* Pickett, 51 S. C. 271.]
   In Georgia, the form of deed in general use is that of bargain and sale,
which operates under the statute of uses.   Adams *v.* Guerard, 29 Ga. 676.
[Ga. Code (1895), § 3157, provides that in an executed trust for the benefit
of a person capable of taking and managing property in his own right, the
legal title is merged immediately in the equitable interest, and the perfect
legal title vests in the *cestui*.   See also §§ 3158 and 3149; Trammell *v.* Inman,
115 Ga. 874; Thompson *v.* Sanders, 118 Ga. 928; Taylor *v.* Brown, 112 Ga.
758.]
   In Florida, there is a statute similar to the statute of Virginia, and the
statute of uses is in partial force.   Thompson's Dig., p. 178, § 4; 1 Lomax,
Dig. 188. [Fla. Gen. Stat. (1906), § 2455.]
   In Alabama, the statute of uses is part of the law of the State.   Horton
v. Sledge, 29 Ala. 478; You *v.* Flinn, 34 Ala. 411. [Ala. Civ. Code (1907),
§ 3408, provides that when a use, trust, or confidence is declared of any land
or any charge upon the same for the mere benefit of a third person the legal
title vests in the latter and not in the trustee.   Huntington *v.* Spear, 131
Ala. 414; Berry *v.* Bromberg, 142 Ala. 339; Everett *v.* Jordan, 152 Ala. 259;
Jordan *v.* Phillips, 126 Ala. 561; Edwards *v.* Bender, 121 Ala. 77.]
   In Mississippi, there is a statute similar to the statute of Virginia.   How.
& Hutch. Dig., p. 349. [See Miss. Code (1906), § 2762.]
   In Louisiana, conveyances originated under the civil law, or the code
of France.
   In Texas, a statute recognizes deeds of bargain and sale, which operate
under the statute of uses.
   In Arkansas, the mode of conveyance is by deeds of bargain and sale,
and of course the statute of uses must be a part of their law.
   In Tennessee, the statute of uses [seems to be in force.   Hughes *v.* Loan

---

[1] 2 Washburn on Real Property, 154.

wicke is reported to have said, that the statute of uses had no
other effect than to add at most three words to a conveyance;[1]

Assoc., 46 S. W. 362 (Tenn. Ch. App. 1897). See Temple v. Ferguson, 110
Tenn. 84; Hart v. Bayliss, 97 Tenn. 72.]

The statute of Kentucky is in nearly the same words as the statute of
Virginia. Rev. Stat., p. 279 (ed. 1860). [Ky. Stat. (1909), § 2057.]

In Ohio, the statute of uses was never in force, and if trusts or uses are
raised by the form of conveyance they remain unexecuted, and mere
equitable estates, cognizable only in courts of equity. Williams v. Presbyterian Church, 1 Ohio St. 497; Helfensteine v. Garrard, 7 Ham. 276;
Foster v. Dennison, 9 Ohio, 124; Walker Am. Law, 124; Thompson v.
Gibson, 2 Ohio, 439.

In Indiana, the statute of uses is enacted in substance. Rev. Stat.
(1843), p. 447; Linville v. Golding, 11 Ind. 374; Nelson v. Davis, 35 Ind.
474. [The statute at present in force goes further than the statute of uses.
Ind. Stat. Burns (1908), § 4024; Myers v. Jackson, 135 Ind. 136; Stroup
v. Stroup, 140 Ind. 179.]

In Illinois, [the statute of uses is substantially re-enacted. Hurd's
Rev. Stat. (1909), c. 30, § 3.]

In Michigan, the laws are similar to the statutes of New York. 2 Compt.
Laws (1857), p. 824; Ready v. Kearsley, 14 Mich. 228. [Mich. Comp.
Laws (1897), §§ 8829–8852.]

In Missouri, the statute of uses is re-enacted in substance. Rev. Stat.
(1845), p. 218; Guest v. Farley, 19 Mo. 147. [Mo. Annot. Stat. (1906),
§ 4589; Cornwell v. Orton, 126 Mo. 355.]

In Iowa, uses are recognized, and deeds may operate under the statute
of uses. Pierson v. Armstrong, 1 Iowa, 282.

In Wisconsin, the statute is very similar to the statute of New York,
and all uses and trusts are abolished except those specially provided for.
Rev. Stat. (1858), p. 529. [Wis. Stat. (1898), §§ 2071–2094. See Perkins
v. Burlington Land and Imp. Co., 112 Wis. 509; McWilliams v. Gough, 116
Wis. 576.]

In Minnesota, [the statute law is the same as in New York. Minn. Rev.
Laws (1905), §§ 3240–3262; Thompson v. Conant, 52 Minn. 208.]

In California, conveyances originated under the old Spanish law, and
probably the statute of uses has little or no influence upon the law of the
State. [It has been held not to be part of the law of the State. Estate of
Fair, 132 Cal. 523, 533 et seq.; Estate of Dixon, 143 Cal. 511. See also Cal.
Civ. Code, § 847 et seq.]

[Kansas Gen. Stat. (1909),§ 9706, provides that "A conveyance or devise
of lands to a trustee whose title is nominal only, and who has no power of
disposition or management of such lands, is void as to the trustee, and
shall be deemed a direct conveyance or devise to the beneficiary." It has

---

[1] Hopkins v. Hopkins, 1 Atk. 591.

Mr. Kent thinks this rather too strongly expressed, and says that the doctrine of the statute has insinuated itself deeply and thoroughly into every branch of the jurisprudence of real property.[1] It seems to have been the intention of the statutes of the various States to supply the want of livery of seizin, and to make all deeds, or other writings executed with certain formalities, equivalent to the old feoffments; therefore, any old and well-established rule of conveyancing ought not to be considered as abolished, in the absence of express provisions to that effect.

§ 300. The statute of uses at the time when it was passed had an immense effect upon the tenures of the realm. Many interests in land which had been merely equitable, and cognizable only according to the rules of equity, became at once legal interests, cognizable in courts of common law. Many persons who were seized of estates to uses, and who only could sue or be sued at law in relation to the same, ceased at once to have any title either at law or equity. Although it is probable that it was the intent of the statute to convert all uses or trusts

been held that a conveyance to grantees as trustees for others without setting forth the terms of the trust, but containing no restriction upon the trustees' power of disposition, does not come within the terms of this statute and that the trustees have a valid title. Webb v. Rockefeller, 66 Kan. 160; Boyer v. Sims, 61 Kan. 593. A similar statute in Indiana has been given a different interpretation. See Stroup v. Stroup, 140 Ind. 179.

The statute of uses has been held to be part of the common law of Colorado. Teller v. Hill, 18 Colo. App. 509; Morgan v. Rogers, 79 Fed. 577. And of Utah. Henderson v. Adams, 15 Utah, 30; Schenck v. Wicks, 23 Utah, 576.

It has been held not to be the law of Nebraska. Farmers' & Merchants' Ins. Co. v. Jensen, 58 Neb. 522.

In North Dakota and South Dakota, there are statutes practically the same as those of New York. No. Dak. Civ. Code (1905), §§ 4816–4837. Smith v. Security L. & T. Co., 8 N. D. 451. So. Dak. Civ. Code (1908), §§ 296–318.

In the District of Columbia, the statute of uses has been substantially re-enacted. D. C. Code (1905), § 1617.]

[1] 4 Kent, Com. 301.

into legal estates,[1] yet the convenience to the subject of being able to keep the legal title to an estate in one person, while the beneficial interest should be in another, was too great to be given up altogether, and courts of equity were astute in finding reasons to withdraw a conveyance from the operation of the statute.[2] Three principal reasons or rules of construction were laid down, whereby conveyances were excepted from such operation: first, where a use was limited upon a use; second, where a copyhold or leasehold estate, or personal property, was limited to uses; third, where such powers or duties were imposed with the estate upon a donee to uses that it was necessary that he should continue to hold the legal title in order to perform his duty or execute the power.[3] In all of these three instances, courts both of law and equity held that the statute did not execute the use, but that such use remained, as it was before the statute, a mere equitable interest to be administered in a court of equity. These uses, which the statute did not execute, were called trusts, and justify Mr. Cruise's language that "a trust is a use not executed by the statute of 27 Henry VIII." The statute may execute the use in regard to one party and not as to another in the same deed; for example, where land is

---

[1] 1 Green. Cruise, tit. 12, c. 1, § 1.

[2] Mr. Cruise thought that the strict construction put upon the statute by the judges in a great measure defeated its effect. Id. Mr. Blackstone is of a similar opinion. 2 Black. Com. 336. And Lord Mansfield, in Goodright v. Wells, 2 Doug. 771, said that it was not the liberality of courts of equity, but the absurd narrowness of courts of law, resting on literal distinctions, which in a manner repealed the statute of uses, and drove *cestuis que trust* into equity.

[3] Hill on Trustees, 230. See § 735, a; Farr v. Gilreath, 23 S. C. 511; Preachers' Aid Society v. England, 106 Ill. 129 (referring to the text). Where an estate is conveyed to A. for the use of B., and nothing more is said, the title is immediately vested in B. by the statute, even though express words of trust are used; but if certain duties are imposed on A., such as collection of rents, making investments, &c., which require that he should keep the estate, the trust will be an active one, and the statute will not execute it. Kellogg v. Hale, 108 Ill. 164; Howard v. Henderson, 18 S. C. 189; Hooberry v. Harding, 10 Lea (Tenn.), 392; Henderson v. Hill, 9 Lea (Tenn.), 25. [Harris v. Ferguy, 207 Ill. 534.]

conveyed to A. in trust for B. for life, contingent remainder to C., the statute may execute the life estate in B., and still leave the fee in A. for the preservation of the remainder.[1]

§ 301. The first two of these rules originated in a strict construction of the technical words used in the statute, which are, "where any person is *seized* of any lands or to the use of another." If A. grants lands to B. for the use of C. for the use of D., B. was said to be "seized" of the lands to the use of C.; and the statute immediately executed the use in C. and gave him the legal title. But C. was said not to be "seized" in lands to the use of D., but only of a *use;* therefore the use of C. for D. remained, as it was before the statute, unexecuted.[2] It remained, therefore, a mere equitable estate or trust, cognizable in a court of equity alone. Hence the maxim that a use could not be limited on a use; not that such second use was void, but the statute did not execute it, and it remained a mere equitable interest. Thus, if lands come to A. and his heirs by feoffment, grant, devise, or other assurance, to the use of B. and his heirs, to the use of C. and his heirs; or to the use of C. in fee or for life, with remainders over; or to B. and his heir in trust to permit C. and D. to receive the rents, — in all these cases the statute executes the first use only in B. and his heirs, and the legal estate is vested in him, as trustee for the parties beneficially interested.[3]

---

[1] Howard *v.* Henderson, 18 S. C. 192; Williman *v.* Holmes, 4 Rich. Eq. (S. C.) 476. [Thompson *v.* Sanders, 118 Ga. 928. See *infra*, § 309 and notes.]

[2] Tyrrell's Case, Dyer, 155 a.

[3] Durant *v.* Ritchie, 4 Mason, 65; Hurst *v.* McNeil, 1 Wash. C. C. 70; Hutchins *v.* Heywood, 50 N. H. 496; Croxall *v.* Sherard, 5 Wall. 268; Reed *v.* Gordon, 35 Md. 183; Cueman *v.* Broadnax, 37 N. J. Eq. 523; Matthews *v.* Ward, 10 G. & J. 443; Whetstone *v.* Bury, 2 P. Wms. 146; Wagstaff *v.* Wagstaff, id. 258; Att. Gen. *v.* Scott, Forrest, 138; Doe *v.* Passingham, 6 B. & Cr. 305; Jones *v.* Lord Saye & Sele, 1 Eq. Cas. Ab. 383; Marwood *v.* Darell, Ca. t. Hard. 91; Hopkins *v.* Hopkins, 1 Atk. 581; Jones *v.* Bush, 4 Harr. 1; 1 Sand. Uses, 195; 2 Black. Com. 336; Williams *v.* Waters, 14 M. & W. 166; Ramsay *v.* Marsh, 2 McCord, 252; Burgess *v.* Wheate, 1 W. Black. 160;

§ 302. So where lands are conveyed by covenant to stand seized, or by bargain and sale, or by appointment under a power, to A. and his heirs, to the use of B. and his heirs, the *legal* estate will vest in A., and B. will take only an equitable interest; for these conveyances do not operate to transfer the seizin to A.[1] They merely raise a use which the statute executes in him, and stops there. Thus, in a deed of bargain and sale, the operation is as follows: the consideration and the bargain raise a use in the bargainee which the statute executes; and thus, under a deed of bargain and sale, the bargainee obtains both the use and the legal title. But no use can be limited and executed on a use. Hence, if A. conveys land to B., to the use of C., by a deed of bargain and sale, the statute will not execute the use in C., but the legal title will remain in B. subject to a trust for C., to be administered in equity; for the consideration and bargain only raise a use in B., which the statute executes but the use in B. for C. is in the nature of a use limited upon a use, which the statute does not execute.[2] (a)

Wilson v. Cheshire, 1 McCord, 233. The statute of uses in some of the States as Virginia, speaks of uses raised by deed. Consequently, it is said that uses raised by devise are not executed, but remain trusts. Judge Lomax, however, denies this construction. 1 Lomax, Dig. 188, 196. [But see Blake v. O'Neal, 63 W. Va. 483.] In New York, the uses named in the text would be executed in the *cestui que use* by the statute of uses and trusts, and he would have the entire legal title.

[1] Johnson v. Cary, 16 Johns. 304; 1 Cruise, Dig. tit. 12, c. 1, § 9; Gilb. on Uses, 67, 347. Mr. Blackstone condemned this rule. 2 Black. Com. 336. And Lord Mansfield said that the rule grew up from the absurd narrowness of courts of common law. Goodright v. Wells, 2 Doug. 771. And Mr. Greenleaf doubts if the rule that a use cannot be limited upon a use would be generally acted upon in the United States, especially in those States which have declared by statute what formalities shall alone be necessary to pass estates. Green. Cruise, Dig. tit. 12, c. 1, § 4, n. (vol. i, p. 380); and see Davis v. Hayden, 9 Mass. 514; Flint v. Sheldon, 13 Mass. 443; Marshall v. Fisk, 6 Mass. 24.

[2] The question has been raised in Massachusetts whether land can be conveyed by deed of bargain and sale to one for the use of another, and create anything more than a trust for the last beneficiary. Stearns v.

(a) It has been held in Massachusetts and Maryland that where the
form of the deed is such that it may take effect either as a deed of bargain

§ 303. Another technical construction of the word "seized" withdrew all uses or trusts created in copyhold or leasehold estates, and all chattel interests and personal property, from the operation of the statute. The judges resolved in the 22d of Elizabeth that the word "seized" was only applicable to freeholds; consequently no one could be said to be "seized" of a leasehold or other chattel interests in real estate, or of personal property. Therefore, if A. gave leaseholds or personal property to B. for the use of C., the statute did not execute the use, but B. took the *legal* title in trust for C., which trust was not recognized at law, but only in equity.[1] So tenants by curtesy or in dower cannot stand seized to a use, for they are in by act of law in consideration of marriage and not in privity of estate; but in equity they would be held to execute any trusts charged upon their interests or estates.[2]

Palmer, 10 Met. 32; Norton *v.* Leonard, 12 Pick. 152. The general doctrine stated in the text is fully admitted, but it is claimed in answer that the deeds in general use, although in the general form of deeds of bargain and sale, are in fact, by force of the statutes, equivalent to grants or feoffments, and it is said that if deeds will not operate in the form in which they are drawn, they shall be construed to operate according to the intention of the parties. Higbee *v.* Rice, 5 Mass. 352; Pray *v.* Peirce, 7 Mass. 384; Knox *v.* Jenks, id. 494; Russell *v.* Coffin, 8 Pick. 143. The question was left undecided in Norton *v.* Leonard and Stearns *v.* Palmer, *ut supra*, but see the remarks of Chief Justice Dana, in Thatcher *v.* Omans, 3 Pick. 528. The same question may arise in other States, where their deeds are in form deeds of bargain and sale.

[1] *Ante*, § 6; Dyer, 369 a; Doe *v.* Routledge, 2 Cowp. 709; Sympson *v.* Turner, 1 Eq. Ab. 383; 2 Wooddes. Lect. pp. 295, 297; 1 Cruise, Dig., p. 354, and tit. 12, c. 1; Gilb. Ten. 182; Gilb. Uses, 67 n.; Rice *v.* Burnett, 1 Spear, Eq. 579; Joor *v.* Hodges, Spear, 593; Pyron *v.* Mood, 2 McMullan, 293. In some States, the statutes use the word "possessed" instead of the word "seized," in which case both real and personal estate and chattel interests would be transferred to the uses raised. Tabb *v.* Baird, 3 Call, 482. But this construction is controverted by Judge Lomax. 1 Lomax, Dig. 196.

[2] 1 Saunders on Uses, 86; 2 Fonbl. Eq. book 2, c. 6, § 1, and notes, p. 140.

and sale or as a feoffment, the court will construe it in such a way as to carry out the evident intention of the parties. Dakin *v.* Savage, 172 Mass. 23; Carr *v.* Richardson, 157 Mass. 576; Rogers *v.* Sisters of Charity, 97 Md. 550.

§ 304. From these instances, it will be seen that, in order to create a trust, it is necessary to prevent the legal estate from vesting in the *cestui que trust*, and it is necessary that not only the *legal* title, but the *primary use*, should vest in the trustee. Any form of conveyancing that will effect this, notwithstanding the statute, will create a trust; as if a grant or devise be made to a *trustee and his heirs*, to the *use of the trustee* and his heirs, or unto and to the use of the trustee and his heirs, the title and the primary use will both be vested in the trustee; and although there is a trust or use over to some other person, yet it will not be effected by the statute, it not being the primary use.[1] (*a*)

§ 305. The third rule of construction is less technical, and relates to special or active trusts, which were never within the purview of the statute.[2] Therefore if any agency, duty, or power be imposed on the trustee, as by a limitation to a trustee and his heirs to pay the rents,[3] or to convey the estate,[4] or if

[1] Rackham *v.* Siddall, 1 Mac. & G. 607; Doe *v.* Passingham, 6 B. & C. 305; Robinson *v.* Comyns, t. Talb. 154; Doe *v.* Field, 6 B. & Ad. 564; Att. Gen. *v.* Scott, t. Talb. 138; Hopkins *v.* Hopkins, 1 Atk. 589; Harris *v.* Pugh, 12 Moore, 577; 4 Bingh. 335; Prise *v.* Sisson, 2 Beas. 168; Eckels *v.* Stewart, 33 Penn. St. 460; Freyvogle *v.* Hughes, 56 id. 228; Dodson *v.* Ball, 60 id. 49; McMullin *v.* Beatty, 56 id. 387; Keyser's App., 57 id. 636; Koenig's App., id. 352; Bacon's App., id. 504; Goodrich *v.* Milwaukee, 24 Wis. 422.

[2] Chapin *v.* Universalist Soc., 8 Gray, 580; Exeter *v.* Odiorne, 1 N. H. 232; Mott *v.* Buxton, 7 Ves. 201; Wright *v.* Pearson, 1 Edw. 125; Wheeler *v.* Newhall, 7 Mass. 189; Norton *v.* Leonard, 12 Pick. 152; Striker *v.* Mott, 2 Palge, 387; Wood *v.* Wood, 5 id. 596.

[3] Robinson *v.* Grey, 9 East, 1; Jones *v.* Saye & Sele, 1 Eq. Cas. Ab. 383; Barker *v.* Greenwood, 4 M. & W. 429; Sympson *v.* Turner, 1 Eq. Cas. Ab. 383; Chapman *v.* Blissett, Cas. t. Talb. 145; Garth *v.* Baldwin, 2 Ves. 646; Sherwin *v.* Kenny, 16 Ir. Ch. 138; Anthony *v.* Rees, 2 Cr. & Jer. 75; Doe *v.* Hampray, 6 Ad. & El. 206; White *v.* Barker, 1 Bing. N. C. 573; Kenrick *v.* Beauclerk, 3 Bos. & P. 178; Neville *v.* Saunders, 1 Vern. 415.

[4] Ibid.; Doe *v.* Edlin, 4 Ad. & El. 582; Doe *v.* Scott, 4 Bing. 505; Mott *v.* Buxton, 7 Ves. 201. [Kirkman *v.* Holland, 139 N. C. 185; Henson *v.* Wright, 88 Tenn. 501.]

(*a*) This is otherwise in States which have patterned their statutes after those of New York. See *supra*, § 299, note.

any control is to be exercised, or duty performed by the trustee in *applying* the rents to a person's maintenance,[1] or in making repairs,[2] or to preserve contingent remainders,[3] or to raise a sum of money,[4] or to dispose of the estate by sale,[5] — in all these, and in other and like cases, the operation of the statute is excluded, and the trusts or uses remain mere equitable estates. So if the trustee is to exercise any discretion in the management of the estate, in the investment of the proceeds or the principal, or in the application of the income;[6] (*a*) or if the

See the elaborate case, Leggett *v.* Perkins, 2 Comst. 297; Brewster *v.* Striker, id. 19; Morton *v.* Barrett, 22 Maine, 261; McCosker *v.* Brady, 1 Barb. Ch. 329; Doe *v.* Biggs, 2 Taunt. 109; Wickham *v.* Berry, 53 Penn. St. 70; Manice *v.* Manice, 43 N. Y. 203; Adams *v.* Perry, id. 487; Hutchins *v.* Heywood, 50 N. H. 500; Barnett's App., 46 Penn. St. 392; Shankland's App., 47 id. 113; Ogden's App., 70 id. 501; Deibert's App., 78 id. 296; Meecham *v.* Steele, 93 Ill. 135. [Clarke's Appeal, 70 Conn. 195, 219; Hart *v.* Seymour, 147 Ill. 598.]

[1] Sylvester *v.* Wilson, 2 T. R. 444; Doe *v.* Edlin, 4 Ad. & El. 582; Vail *v.* Vail, 4 Paige, 317; Porter *v.* Doby, 2 Rich. Eq. 52; Doe *v.* Ironmonger, 3 East, 533; Gerard Ins. Co. *v.* Chambers, 46 Penn. St. 485. [Hart *v.* Bayliss, 97 Tenn. 72; Chicago Term. R. Co. *v.* Winslow, 216 Ill. 166; Simmons *v.* Richardson, 107 Ala. 697.]

[2] Shapland *v.* Smith, 1 Bro. Ch. 75; Brown *v.* Ramsden, 3 Moore, 612; Tierney *v.* Moody, 3 Bing. 3. [Matthern *v.* Rankin, 228 Ill. 318; Reynolds *v.* Reynolds, 61 S. C. 243, 249.]

[3] Biscoe *v.* Perkins, 1 Ves. & B. 485; Barker *v.* Greenwood, 4 M. & W. 431; Vanderheyden *v.* Crandall, 2 Denio, 9.

[4] Wright *v.* Pearson, 1 Eden, 119; Stanley *v.* Lennard, id. 87.

[5] Bagshaw *v.* Spencer, 1 Ves. 142; Wood *v.* Mather, 38 Barb. 473. [Johnson *v.* Lee, 228 Ill. 167; Pope *v.* Patterson, 78 S. C. 334; Perkins *v.* Burlington Land & Imp. Co., 112 Wis. 509.]

[6] Exeter *v.* Odiorne, 1 N. H. 232; Ashhurst *v.* Given, 5 W. & S. 323; Vaux *v.* Parke, 7 W. & S. 19; Nickell *v.* Handly, 10 Grat 336. [Holmes *v.* Bushnell, 80 Conn. 233; Krebs's Estate, 184 Pa. St. 222.]

(*a*) The duty of paying over the rents and profits to the beneficiary involves the duty of management and renders a trust active. Webb *v.* Borden, 145 N. C. 188; Mason *v.* Mason, 219 Ill. 609; Burbach *v.* Burbach, 217 Ill. 547; Ure *v.* Ure, 185 Ill. 216; Slater *v.* Rudderforth, 25 App. D. C. 497; Newton *v.* Jay, 95 N. Y. S. 413, 107, App. Div. 457; West's Estate, 214 Pa. St. 35; Hunt *v.* Hunt, 124 Mich. 502; Forney's Estate, 161 Pa. St. 209; McIntosh's Estate, 158 Pa. St. 528; Harbster's Estate, 133 Pa. St. 351; Webber *v.* Webber, 108 Wis. 626. Likewise

purpose of the trust is to protect the estate for a given time, or until the death of some one, or until division,[1] or until a request for a conveyance is made.[2] So if an estate is given upon a trust to sell or mortgage for the payment of debts, legacies, or annuities, or to purchase other lands to be settled to certain uses;[3] and this construction will not be affected by a power given to one of the *cestuis que trust* to control the sale of part of the estate,[4] nor by the fact that the direction for the payment of debts and legacies, out of the proceeds of the sale of the land, is only in aid of the personal property.[5]

---

[1] Posey *v.* Cook, 1 Hill (S. C.), 413; Morton *v.* Barrett, 22 Me. 261; Wood *v.* Mather, 38 Barb. 473; McCaw *v.* Galbraith, 7 Rich. L. 74; Williams *v.* McConico, 36 Ala. 22; Nelson *v.* Davis, 35 Ind. 474; McNish *v.* Guerard, 4 Strob. Eq. 66, was to the contrary upon the facts of that particular case. [Graham *v.* Whitridge, 99 Md. 248; Sanders *v.* Houston, etc., Co., 107 Ga. 49; Taylor *v.* Brown, 112 Ga. 758; McFall *v.* Kirkpatrick, 236 Ill. 281.]

[2] Walter *v.* Walter, 48 Mo. 140. [Johnson *v.* Lee, 228 Ill. 167; Dyett *v.* Central Trust Co., 140 N. Y. 54.]

[3] Curtis *v.* Price, 12 Ves. 89; Doe *v.* Ewart, 7 Ad. & El. 636, 668; Ashhurst *v.* Given, 5 W. & S. 323; Vaux *v.* Parke, 7 W. & S. 19; Keene *v.* Deardon, 8 East, 248; Bagshaw *v.* Spencer, 1 Ves. 142; Chamberlain *v.* Thompson, 10 Conn. 244; Sanford *v.* Irby, 3 B. & Al. 654; Creaton *v.* Creaton, 3 Sm. & Gif. 386; Spence *v.* Spence, 12 C. B. (N. S.) 199; Smith *v.* Smith, 11 C. B. (N. S.) 121.

[4] Chapman *v.* Blissett, Forr. 145; Naylor *v.* Arnitt, 1 R. & M. 501; Wykham *v.* Wykham, 18 Ves. 395. [Kirkman *v.* Holland, 139 N. C. 185; Pope *v.* Patterson, 78 S. C. 334.]

[5] Ibid.; Murthwaite *v.* Jenkinson, 2 B. & Cr. 257.

---

where a discretion is given to the trustee as to the time and manner of turning over the principal to the beneficiary, although he may have no discretion to withhold it indefinitely. Marshall's Estate, 147 Pa. St. 77; Krebs's Estate, 184 Pa. St. 222.

It has been held that a power given to the trustee to sell if and when he deems best prevents the statute of uses from vesting the title in the beneficiaries. Carrigan *v.* Drake, 36 S. C. 354. But in States which have statutes similar to the New York statute it seems probable that such a power alone would not be sufficient to prevent the vesting of legal title in the *cestuis*. See Drake *v.* Steele, 242 Ill. 301. As to the effect of an imperative power to sell, see *infra* § 311, note *b.*

§ 306. If, however, the trust simply is to *permit and suffer* A. to occupy the estate, or to receive the rents, the legal estate is executed in A. by the statute.[1] And a trust to hold for the use and benefit of, and to apply the rents to, the children of A., is executed in the children, notwithstanding the word "apply" is used.[2] But where the trust is "*to pay* unto" or to permit and suffer a person to receive the rents, using both expressions, the construction will be governed by the intention of the donor; and in this view the position of the words in the sentence, and the priority of the words, and the consideration whether the instrument is a deed or will, will have a material bearing upon the decision.[3] Mr. Jarman and Mr. Lewin suggest that the repugnancy would be obviated in such a case by construing the instrument to give an election or discretion to the trustees.[4]

§ 307. Although the direction may be for the trustees to *permit and suffer* another person to receive the rents, yet if any duty is imposed upon the trustees expressly or by implication, the legal estate will remain in them unaffected by the statute. (a) As if the direction is to *permit* A. to receive the net [5] rents, or the *clear* [6] rents, the trustees take the legal estate, the words *net* and *clear* implying that the trustees are to pay all charges,

---

[1] Right *v.* Smith, 12 East, 455; Wagstaff *v.* Smith, 9 Ves. 524; Gregory *v.* Henderson, 4 Taunt. 773; Warter *v.* Hutchinson, 5 Moore, 143; 1 B. & C. 721; Barker *v.* Greenwood, 4 M. & W. 429; Boughton *v.* Langley, 1 Eq. Cas. Ab. 383; 2 Salk. 679 (overruling Burchett *v.* Durdant, 2 Vent. 311); Doe *v.* Biggs, 2 Taunt. 109; Ramsay *v.* Marsh, 2 McCord, 252; Parks *v.* Parks, 9 Paige, 107; Witham *v.* Brooner, 63 Ill. 158. [Cornwell *v.* Orton, 126 Mo. 355; Byrne *v.* Gunning, 75 Md. 30.]

[2] Laurens *v.* Jenney, 1 Spears, 356.

[3] Doe *v.* Biggs, 2 Taunt. 109; Pybus *v.* Smith, 3 Bro. Ch. 340.

[4] 1 Jarm. Pow. Dev. 222, n.; Lewin on Trusts, 174 (5th Lond. ed.).

[5] Barker *v.* Greenwood, 4 M. & W. 421; Keene *v.* Deardon, 8 East, 248; Rife *v.* Geyer, 59 Penn. St. 395.

[6] White *v.* Parker, 1 Bing. N. C. 573.

(a) As where the trustee is given the duty of seeing that the taxes are paid and the property kept in re-pair. Carney *v.* Byron, 19 R. I. 283; Pugh *v.* Hayes, 113 Mo. 424.

and pay over the balance. So if, in addition to a devise in trust to preserve contingent remainders, there is a direction to *permit* A. to receive the rents and profits;[1] and so if trustees are to pay certain life annuities out of the rents, and subject to those annuities are to *permit and suffer* certain persons to receive the rents and profits.[2] So if the trustees are to exercise any control,[3] as if there is a trust to *permit and suffer* a woman to receive the rents, and that her receipts with the approbation of one of the trustees should be good.[4] (*a*)

§ 308. A mere *charge* of debts and legacies on real estate will not vest the estate in the trustees, unless there is some direction to them to raise the money and pay them, or unless there is some other implication that they are to exercise an *active trust* for the purpose.[5] (*b*) Nor does the legal estate vest in the trustees where the *charge* of the debts and legacies upon the real estate is contingent upon the insufficiency of any other fund, for in that case the trustees do not take an *immediate* vested interest;[6] but if the *charge* is made in aid of any other fund without contingency, the trustees will take immediately a

[1] Biscoe *v.* Perkins, 1 Ves. & B. 485, 489; Webster *v.* Cooper, 14 How. 499; Vanderheyden *v.* Crandall, 2 Denio, 9.

[2] Naylor *v.* Arnitt, 1 R. & M. 501.

[3] Exeter *v.* Odiorne, 1 N. H. 232.

[4] Gregory *v.* Henderson, 4 Taunt. 772; Barker *v.* Greenwood, 5 M. & W. 430.

[5] Doe *v.* Claridge, 6 Man. & Scott, 657; 1 Jarm. Pow. Dev. 224, n.; Kenrick *v.* Beauclerk, 3 B. & P. 178; Cadogan *v.* Ewart, 7 Ad. & El. 636, 668; Jones *v.* Saye & Sele, 8 Vin. 262; Creaton *v.* Creaton, 3 Sm. & Gif. 386; Collier *v.* McBean, 34 Beav. 426. [*In re* Stephens, 43 Ch. Div. 39.]

[6] Goodtitle *v.* Knott, Coop. 43; Hawker *v.* Hawker, 3 B. & Al. 537; Gibson *v.* Montfort, 1 Ves. 485.

(*a*) Or if there is a valid provision against anticipation, Ames, Petitioner, 22 R. I. 54, or a provision that the trustee take charge of the property if efforts should be made by creditors of the life beneficiary to subject the property to payment of his debts. People's Loan & Exch. Bank *v.* Garlington, 54 S. C. 413.

(*b*) Mere authority given to executors and trustees by will to pay debts does not charge them upon the testator's real estate. *In re* Head's Trustees, 45 Ch. D. 310.

legal estate.[1] So if the trustees are to demise the estate for a term, at rack-rent or otherwise, the term must come out of their interest, and the legal estate must be in them.[2] If, however, the instrument confers by construction upon the trustees a mere *power* of leasing, a good legal term may be created by the exercise of the power and without the legal estate in them.[3] So if a testator give his trustees a simple power of disposing of his estates, as that his executors or trustees, or other persons, shall sell or let or mortgage, or otherwise dispose of his estate, to pay his debts or legacies or annuities, or other charges, or where he directs his executors to raise money, no estate vests in the trustees, executors, or other persons, but it descends to the heir or the person to whom it is directed to go in the will, until it is wanted for the purposes named, and then it is divested only to the extent necessary for the purposes named. So where an estate was to remain in the hands of executors, for the use of the widow and children, until the youngest child should become twenty-one years old, the executors or trustees took no interest in the estate but a simple power.[4] Such directions are simple *powers* of disposition, which may be executed without any legal title.[5]

---

[1] Murthwaite *v.* Jenkinson, 2 B. & Cr. 357; Wykham *v.* Wykham 18 Ves. 395; and see Popham *v.* Bamfield, 1 Vern. 79.

[2] Doe *v.* Willan, 2 B. & Al. 84; Doe *v.* Walbank, id. 554; Osgood *v.* Franklin, 2 Johns. Ch. 20; Burr *v.* Sim, 1 Whart. 266; Riley *v.* Garnett, 3 De G. & Sm. 629; Brewster *v.* Striker, 2 Comst. 19; Doe *v.* Cafe, 7 Exch. 675.

[3] Doe *v.* Willan, 2 B. & Al. 84; Doe *v.* Simpson, 5 East, 162.

[4] Burke *v.* Valentine, 52 Barb. 412.

[5] Reeve *v.* Att. Gen., 2 Atk. 223; Hilton *v.* Kenworthey, 3 East, 553; Bateman *v.* Bateman, 1 Atk. 421; Fowler *v.* Jones, 1 Ch. Cas. 262; Lancaster *v.* Thornton, 2 Burr. 1027; Yates *v.* Compton, 2 P. Wms. 308; Fay *v.* Fay, 1 Cush. 94; Shelton *v.* Homer, 5 Met. 462; Bank of U. S. *v.* Beverly, 10 Peters, 532; 1 How. 134; Deering *v.* Adams, 37 Maine, 264; Jackson *v.* Schauber, 7 Cow. 187; 2 Wend. 12; Burr *v.* Sim, 1 Whart. 266; Guyer *v.* Maynard, 6 Gill & J. 420; Dabney *v.* Manning, 3 Ohio, 321; Jameson *v.* Smith, 4 Bibb, 307; Hope *v.* Johnson, 2 Yerg. 123; Bradshaw *v.* Ellis, 2 Dev. & Bat. Eq. 20. In Pennsylvania, such powers conferred upon executors pass the estate by force of a statute. Miller *v.* Meetch, 8 Penn. St. 417;

§ 309. Where a testator gave his wife an annuity, and a certain sum to his children to be paid when they arrive at twenty-one years, and appointed three persons by name, "as trustees of inheritance for the execution thereof," it was held that the trustees took the legal estate.[1] And if several trusts are created in the same instrument, some of which would be executed by the statute, and others would require the legal estate to remain in the trustees, they will take the legal estate; and this will be the case, though the trusts are limited to arise successively.[2] (a)   In all cases where an estate is given to

Chew v. Chew, 28 id. 17. [See IV N. Y. Consol. Laws (1909), p. 3389, § 93; p. 3391, § 99; Mich. Comp. Laws (1897), § 8840; Minn. Rev. Laws (1905), § 3250; No. Dak. Civ. Code (1905), § 4825; So. Dak. Civ. Code (1908), § 306; Wis. Stat. (1898), § 8840.]

[1] Trent v. Harding, 10 Ves. 495; 1 B. & P. N. C. 116; 7 East, 95; Re Hough, 4 De G. & Sm. 371; Re Turner, 2 De G., F. & J. 527.

[2] Hawkins v. Luscombe, 2 Swanst. 375, 391; Horton v. Horton, 7 T. R. 652; Blagrave v. Blagrave, 4 Exch. 570; Brown v. Whiteway, 8 Hare, 156; Stockbridge v. Stockbridge, 99 Mass. 244. But see Tucker v. Johnson, 16 Sim. 341; Leonard v. Diamond, 31 Md. 536.

(a) Thus if an estate in fee is given to trustees for the benefit of a life beneficiary with active duties to perform during the existence of the equitable life estate and to hold upon a passive trust after the latter's death, the statute of uses will operate to vest the legal title in those entitled in remainder upon the ceasing of the active duties of the trustee at the death of the life beneficiary. Hooper v. Felgner, 80 Md. 262; Numsen v. Lyon, 87 Md. 31; Graham v. Whitridge, 99 Md. 248; Smith v. Proctor, 139 N. C. 314. It should be noted that this is an entirely different question from the one which often arises in such cases, viz., whether or not the estate originally conferred upon the trustees was an estate in fee or an estate *pur autre vie.* Although the statute of uses will not operate to vest title of an estate in remainder when the persons entitled are not in being or not ascertained; Clarke v. E. Atlanta Land Co., 113 Ga. 21; Taylor v. Brown, 112 Ga. 758; Sanders v. Houston, etc., Co., 107 Ga. 49; Young v. McNeill, 78 S. C. 143; Cushman v. Coleman, 92 Ga. 772; it may operate when the *cestuis* come into being and the extent of their interests becomes certain, Mims v. Machlin, 53 S. C. 6; Henderson v. Adams, 15 Utah, 30; or upon the happening of the contingency which makes certain the beneficiaries and the extent of their interests. Uzzell v. Horn, 71 S. C. 426; Simonds v. Simonds, 199 Mass. 552. See Ames, Petitioner, 22 R. I. 54. But in such a case the trust for the intervening life estate may not

trustees to preserve contingent remainders, the statute does not execute the estate in the *cestui que trust;* [1] and in every case where the words "to the use of the trustees" are used, the statute does not execute the estate, although it is to the use of the trustees in trust for another; for the statute only executes the first use.[2]

§ 310. If an estate be given to trustees upon a trust for a married woman "for her sole and separate use," and "her receipts alone to be sufficient discharges," or if the trust be to "permit and suffer a *feme covert* to receive the rents to her separate use," the legal estate will vest in the trustees, and the statute will not execute it in the *cestui que trust.*[3] (a)   In all

[1] Laurens *v.* Jenney, 1 Spears, 365; Co. Litt. 265 a, n. 2; 337 a, n. 2.

[2] *Ante,* § 304; Keene *v.* Deardon, 8 East, 248; Whetstone *v.* St. Bury, 2 P. Wms. 146; Pr. Ch. 591; Sympson *v.* Turner, 1 Eq. Cas. Ab. 383; Hopkins *v.* Hopkins, 1 Atk. 586; Hawkins *v.* Luscombe, 3 Swanst. 376, 388.

[3] Horton *v.* Horton, 7 T. R. 652; Neville *v.* Saunders, 1 Vern. 415; Jones *v.* Saye & Sele, 1 Eq. Cas. Ab. 383; Doe *v.* Claridge, 6 C. B. 641; Hawkins *v.* Luscombe, 2 Swanst. 391; South *v.* Alleyne, 5 Mod. 63, 101; Bush *v.* Allen, id. 63; Robinson *v.* Grey, 9 East, 1; Ayer *v.* Ayer, 16 Pick. 330; Williman *v.* Holmes, 4 Rich. Eq. 475; McNish *v.* Guerard, 4 Strob. Eq. 475; Franciscus *v.* Reigart, 4 Watts, 109; Escheator *v.* Smith, 4 McCord, 452; Bass *v.* Scott, 2 Leigh, 356; Rogers *v.* Ludlow, 3 Sandf. Ch. 104; Richardson *v.* Stodder, 100 Mass. 528. [Cushing *v.* Spalding, 164 Mass. 287; Walton *v.* Drumtra, 152 Mo. 489; Schiffman *v.* Schmidt, 154 Mo. 204; Temple *v.* Ferguson, 110 Tenn. 84; Carpenter *v.* Browning, 98 Ill. 282.]

terminate. See Sanders *v.* Houston, etc., Co., 107 Ga. 49; Clarke *v.* E. Atlanta Land Co., 113 Ga. 21; Graham *v.* Whitridge, 99 Md. 248; Smith *v.* McWhorter, 123 Ga. 287.

The statute of uses cannot operate to execute a dry trust where the beneficiary has no capacity to take a legal title, as where the conveyance is in trust for a partnership described by the firm name.   Silverman *v.* Kristufek, 162 Ill. 222.

(a) It is otherwise in Georgia, where a married woman is not one of the class of persons for whom statute permits the creation of a trust, and the statutes have made her *sui juris.*   Smith *v.* McWhorter, 123 Ga. 287; Thompson *v.* Sanders, 118 Ga. 928; Tillman *v.* Banks, 116 Ga. 250; Tramwell *v.* Inman, 115 Ga. 874.   See also Snell *v.* Payne, 78 S. W. 885 (Ky. 1904); Adams' Trustee *v.* Adams, 56 S. W. 151 (Ky. 1900) where the court decreed a termination, the trustee having been given no active duties.

these cases the court will give this construction to the gift, if possible;[1] for if the statute should execute the estate in the married woman, certain rights would arise to the husband which might defeat the intention of the donor.[2] These are not the only words that will prevent the estate from vesting. Any words that show an intent to create an estate or a trust, for the sole and separate use of a married woman, will have the same effect.[3] (a) And a woman in contemplation of marriage may deed lands to another to stand seized to the sole use of the grantor, and the statute will not affect the transaction, but a trust will be created, as otherwise the intent of the parties would be defeated.[4] But it is said that if an estate is "released by deed" to A. and his heirs "upon a trust" for "the sole and separate use of the releasor," and no *active* duty is imposed upon the trustee in respect to the sole and separate estate, a common-law court will reject the sole and separate use as an estate unknown to the law; and it has been held in such case that the statute vested the estate in the *cestui que trust*.[5]

§ 310 *a*. But [in Pennsylvania] in order that an estate given to the sole and separate use of a woman may vest and remain in the trustees, it is necessary that she should be married or in immediate contemplation of marriage. (b) For if she is un-

---

[1] Ware *v.* Richardson, 3 Md. 505; Moore *v.* Shultz, 13 Penn. St. 98.

[2] Ibid.; Rice *v.* Burnett, 1 Spear, Eq. 580.

[3] Ayer *v.* Ayer, 16 Pick. 331; Kirk *v.* Paulin, 7 Vin. Ab. 95; Tyrrel *v.* Hope, 2 Atk. 558; Darley *v.* Darley, 3 Atk. 399; Hartley *v.* Hurle, 5 Ves. 540. [See *infra*, § 647 *et seq*.]

[4] Pittsfield Savings Bank *v.* Berry, 63 N. H. 109.

[5] Nash *v.* Allen, 1 Hurl. & Colt. 167; Williams *v.* Waters, 14 M. & W. 166 (see remarks on this case in Ware *v.* Richardson, 3 Md. 505); Roberts *v.* Moseley, 51 Mo. 282; Westcott *v.* Edmunds, 68 Penn. St. 34; Edmund's App., id. 24. [Woodward *v.* Stubbs, 102 Ga. 187.]

(a) But the mere fact that the person named as beneficiary is a married woman does not make the trust one for her "separate use" and for that reason outside the operation of the statute of uses. McKenzie *v.* Sumner, 114 N. C. 425; Foster *v.* Glover, 46 S. C. 522.

(b) The courts of Pennsylvania themselves admit that this limita-

married, or the estate is not given in the immediate contemplation of her marriage, it will vest in her at once by the statute
of uses; or she will have the right to call for the execution of
the trust at once, by a conveyance of the legal estate to her by
the trustee, unless there are some other provisions in the will
or purposes of the trust which render it an active trust, and
the continuance of the legal estate in the trustees necessary for
its purposes.[1] It is not necessary that the contemplation of her
immediate marriage should appear upon the face of the will or
settlement, if in fact an immediate marriage was contemplated,
and such fact was probably known to the testator or settlor.[2]
In such cases the trust will continue during the coverture of
the woman, and at the decease of her husband she will have the
right to call for a conveyance of the property as upon a termination of the trust.[3] A conveyance "in trust for B., wife of C., and
her heirs and assigns forever," creates a trust during B.'s coverture and a legal estate afterwards. If C. dies, the legal estate is
in B. and her heirs, though B. subsequently marries again.[4] (*a*)

[1] Lancaster *v*. Dolan, 1 Rawle, 231; Smith *v*. Starr, 3 Wharton, 63;
Hammersley *v*. Smith, 4 Wharton, 129; McBride *v*. Smyth, 54 Penn. St.
250; Yarnall's App., 70 id. 339; Ogden's App., id. 501; 29 Legal Int. (May,
1872) 165; Wells *v*. McCall, 64 Penn. St. 207; Springer *v*. Arundel, id. 218;
7 Phila. R. 224; Credlant's Est., id. 58.

[2] Wells *v*. McCall, 64 Penn. St. 207; Springer *v*. Arundel, id. 218.

[3] Megargee *v*. Naglee, 64 Penn. St. 211; Yarnall's App., 70 id. 339;
Freyvogle *v*. Hughes, 56 id. 230.

[4] Moore *v*. Stinson, 144 Mass. 594. [Cushing *v*. Spalding, 164 Mass.

tion upon the creation of equitable
separate estates in married women
is a peculiarity of the law of that
State. Kuntzleman's Trust Estate,
136 Pa. St. 142; Quin's Estate, 144
Pa. St. 444. *Infra*, § 652, note. As
the point involves the law peculiarly
applicable to equitable separate estates of married women, reference is
made to the chapter on that topic,
§ 652 *et seq.*, for the law in the other
States and in England.

There is the further peculiarity in

the law of Pennsylvania, that if a
trust purports to be for the separate
use of a woman who is not married
or contemplating immediate marriage, the trust will not be kept
alive by the fact that active duties
have been given to the trustee, unless it appears that these duties were
intended to be irrespective of coverture. Kuntzleman's Trust Estate,
136 Pa. St. 142.

(*a*) The fact that the person
named as beneficiary of a passive

§ 311. As stated, chattel interests in land and personal property were never within the statute of uses, and the legal title to them will remain in the trustee, until the purposes of the trust are accomplished, and until the possession of the property is in some way transferred to the person entitled to the use, or the last use.[1] But where the trust is at an end, the title is in the person entitled to the last use;[2] and a mere delivery, without other formality, gives such person full and absolute control of the property.[3] Until such delivery the law cannot recognize any equitable interests in the property.[4] If the *cestui que trust* is an infant, it is said that the trust will not be executed by delivering the property to him, because he is incapable of assenting to such transfer.[5] (a)

287; Temple *v.* Ferguson, 110 Tenn. 84; Roberts *v.* Moseley, 51 Mo. 282.]

[1] *Ante,* § 303; Harley *v.* Platts, 6 Rich. L. 315; Rice *v.* Burnett, 1 Spear, Eq. 590; Schley *v.* Lyon, 6 Ga. 530; Doe *v.* Nichols, 1 B. & Cr. 336; Slevin, *v.* Brown, 3 Mo. 176. [Ure *v.* Urè, 185 Ill. 216; Byrne *v.* Gunning, 75 Md. 30. See Guild *v.* Allen, 28 R. I. 430, 437; Martin *v.* Fort, 83 Fed. 19, 24; Matter of De Rycke, 91 N. Y. S. 159, 99 App. Div. 596.]

[2] Westcott *v.* Edmunds, 68 Penn. St. 34; Bacon's App., 57 id. 500; Dodson *v.* Ball, 60 id. 492; Barnett's App., 10 Wright, 392; Rife *v.* Geyes, 59 Penn. St. 395; Freyvogle *v.* Hughes, 56 id. 228; Deibert's App., No. 1, 83 id. 462; Schaffer *v.* Lauretta, 57 Ala. 14.

[3] Ibid.; Bringhurst *v.* Cuthburt, 6 Binn. 398; Lawrie *v.* Bankes, 4 K. & J. 142.

[4] Ibid.; Iorr *v.* Hodges, 1 Spear, Eq. 593.

[5] Harley *v.* Platts, 6 Rich. L 315. But see Lawrie *v.* Bankes, 4 K. & J. 142; White *v.* Baylor, 10 Ir. Eq. 53; Bulstrode, 184.]

trust is a minor will not prevent the statute of uses from operating to vest the estate in him. Hooper *v.* Felgner, 80 Md. 262; Thompson *v.* Conant, 52 Minn. 208. But the fact may have an important bearing upon the question whether or not the trust instrument imposes active duties on the trustee.

(a) A devise of lands to a trustee with an imperative direction to sell and to divide the proceeds among those entitled is an equitable conversion of the land and is treated as a trust of personalty so far as concerns the rights of those entitled to the proceeds. McWilliams *v.* Gough, 116 Wis. 576; Van Zandt *v.* Garretson, 21 R. I. 352. As to equitable conversion, see *infra*, § 448, note.

§ 312. In all cases where an estate is given to one for the use of another, in such manner that the statute of uses steps in and executes the estate in the *cestui que trust*, the statute executes in the *cestui que trust* only the estate that the first donee or trustee takes; that is, the statute executes or transfers the exact estate given to the trustee. Therefore, if A. give an estate to B. and his heirs for the use of C. and his heirs, the statute will execute the fee-simple in C. But if A. gives an estate to B. for the use of C. and his heirs, the statute will execute only an estate for the life of A. in C.; for that is the extent of the estate conveyed to B. by a deed in that form; that is, by a deed that has no words of inheritance in B.[1] While this is the rule in respect to estates which the statute executes, a very different rule applies to estates upon a trust or use not executed by the statute. In these cases, the extent or quality of the estate taken by the trustee is determined, not by the circumstance that words of inheritance in the trustee are or are not used in the deed or will, but by the intent of the parties. And the intent of the parties is determined by the scope and extent of the trust. Therefore, the extent of the legal interest of a trustee in an estate given to him in trust is measured, not by words of inheritance or otherwise, but by the object and extent of the trust upon which the estate is given.[2] On this principle, two

[1] Newhall *v.* Wheeler, 7 Mass. 189; Cro. Car. 231; Nelson *v.* Davis, 35 Ind. 474; Baptist Soc. *v.* Hazen, 100 Mass. 322; Idle *v.* Cooke, 1 P. Wms. 77; Doe *v.* Smeddle, 2 B. & A. 126; Chambers *v.* Taylor, 2 M. & Cr. 376; Vanhorn *v.* Harrison, 1 Dall. 137; Jackson *v.* Fish, 10 Johns. 456. Where a gift is made by deed to individuals and their "successors," without the word "heirs," in trust for or to the use of a corporation or religious society, an inheritance or succession is not created; and if the statute of uses applies to the conveyance, only a life-estate is executed in the corporation or religious society. Henderson *v.* Hunter, 59 Penn. St. 325; First Bap. Soc. in Andover *v.* Hazen, 100 Mass. 322.

[2] Cleveland *v.* Hallett, 6 Cush. 407; Gibson *v.* Montfort, 1 Ves. 485; Newhall *v.* Wheeler, 7 Mass. 189, 198; Oates *v.* Cooke, 3 Burr. 1684; Stearns *v.* Palmer, 10 Met. 32; Sears *v.* Russell, 8 Gray, 86; Gould *v.* Lamb, 11 Met. 84; Brooks *v.* Jones, id. 191; Fisher *v.* Fields, 10 Johns. 495; Doe *v.* Field, 2 B. & Ad. 564; Trent *v.* Hanning, 7 East, 99; Doe *v.* Willan, 2 B. & A. 84; 8 Vin. Ab. 262, pl. 18; Shaw *v.* Wright, 1 Eq. Cas. Ab. 176, pl. 8; Brewster *v.*

rules of construction have been adopted by courts: first, "Wherever a trust is created, a legal estate, sufficient for the purposes of the trust, shall, if possible, be implied in the trustee, whatever may be the limitation in the instrument, whether to him and his heirs or not." [1] (a) And, second, "Although a legal estate

Striker, 1 E. D. Smith, 321; Richardson v. Stodder, 100 Mass. 528; Fox v. Storrs, 75 Ala. 267; Gosson v. Ladd, 77 id. 224; West v. Fitz, 109 Ill. 425; Jourolmon v. Massengill, 86 Tenn. 82. See Henderson v. Hill, 9 Lea (Tenn.) 25; Young v. Bradley, 101 U. S. 782.

[1] Neilson v. Lagow, 12 How. 98; Sears v. Russell, 8 Gray, 86; Chamberlain v. Thompson, 10 Conn. 244; Cleveland v. Hallett, 6 Cush. 407; Payne v. Sale, 2 Dev. & Bat. Eq. 460; Nichol v. Walworth, 4 Denio, 385; Upham v. Varney, 15 N. H. 462; King v. Parker, 9 Cush. 71; Williams v. First Soc. in Cin., 1 Ohio St. 478; Hawley v. James, 5 Paige, 318; Deering v. Adams, 37 Maine, 265; Webster v. Cooper, 14 How. 499; Combry v. McMichael, 19 Ala. 751; Gill v. Logan, 11 B. Mon. 233; Powell v. Glen, 21 Ala. 468; King v. Akerman, 2 Black, 408; Ward v. Amory, 1 Curtis, C. C. 427; White v. Baylor, 10 Ir. Eq. 54; Meeting St. Bap. Soc. v. Hail, 8 R. I. 240; Nelson v. Davis, 35 Ind. 474; Kirkland v. Cox, 94 Ill. 400; Preachers' Aid Society v. England, 106 Ill. 128.

(a) This is generally true where the instrument creating the trust is a will, for in that case words of inheritance are not usually necessary to devise a fee, but the intention of the testator controls. Davies v. Jones, 24 Ch. Div. 190; Crane v. Bolles, 49 N. J. Eq. 373; People's L. & Exch. Bank v. Garlington, 54 S. C. 413 ; Bean v. Commonwealth, 186 Mass. 348; Olcott v. Tope, 213 Ill. 124; Smith v. McWhorter, 123 Ga. 287. But in a recent case in England where a trust was created by a deed of conveyance to trustees without words of inheritance, it was held that the trustees got only an estate for the life of the survivor, although it was clear from the deed that the creator of the trust intended to transfer the entire beneficial interest and did not intend that the legal title should revert to him or his heirs. In re Irwin, [1904] 2 Ch. 752. Probably the decision did not affect the rights of the *cestuis que trust*, but concerned only the title of the trustees, and the result probably was that the title, instead of descending to the heir or the representative of the surviving trustee, reverted to the heirs of the grantor charged with the same trust; for it is clear law in England, as well as in America, that words of inheritance are not necessary to transfer an equitable fee to the *cestui que trust*. If it is clear upon the face of the deed that the grantor intended to transfer the entire beneficial interest, absence of words of inheritance as to it will not prevent its passing. *In re* Irwing, [1904] 2 Ch. 752; *In re* Tringham's Trusts, [1904] 2 Ch.

may be limited to a trustee to the fullest extent, as to him and his heirs, yet it shall not be carried farther than the complete execution of the trust necessarily requires." [1]

[1] Norton *v.* Norton, 2 Sandf. 296; Williman *v.* Holmes, 4 Rich. Eq. 475; Watson *v.* Pearson, 2 Exch. 593; Blagrave *v.* Blagrave, 4 id. 569;

487; Smith *v.* Proctor, 139 N. C. 314; Holmes *v.* Holmes, 86 N. C. 205.

The rule in North Carolina prior to the statute of 1879 (see Code (1905) § 946), seems to have been in accord with *In re* Irwing. Smith *v.* Proctor, 139 N. C. 314; Allen *v.* Baskerville, 123 N. C. 126; Fulbright *v.* Yoder, 113 N. C. 456. But it has been declared the settled law in Massachusetts that where the declared purposes of the trust require a fee in the trustee, the absence of words of inheritance from the deed to him will not limit his estate to a life estate. Packard *v.* Old Colony Railroad, 168 Mass. 92; Cleveland *v.* Hallett, 6 Cush. 403; King *v.* Parker, 9 Cush. 71. And generally the American courts have taken the view that where the trust is created by deed, as well as where it is created by will, the extent of the legal interest given the trustee "is measured not only by words of inheritance or equivalent terms, but by the object and extent of the trust upon which the estate is given." Brown *v.* Reeder, 108 Md. 653; North *v.* Philbrook, 34 Me. 532; McFall *v.* Kirkpatrick, 236 Ill. 281 (*semble*); Smith *v.* McWhorter, 123 Ga. 287 (*semble*); Morffew *v.* S. F., etc., R. Co., 107 Cal. 587, 595; Carney *v.* Kain, 40 W. Va. 758, 764.

In many States the necessity of words of inheritance in deeds of conveyance has been done away with by statute.

When there are no words of inheritance used with reference to the *cestui*, and the deed does not show an intention to vest in him the entire beneficial interest and where he has no equitable right to it independently of the deed, as he would have, if he had paid the purchase money, it has been held that he gets only an equitable life estate. The fact that the legal title is conveyed to the trustee and his heirs will not enlarge the *cestui's* interest in such a case. See *In re* Tringham's Trusts, [1904] 2 Ch. 487; McElroy *v.* McElroy, 113 Mass. 509.

In cases of executory contracts to convey which equity will specifically enforce the technical requirement of words of inheritance is of little effect when the intention of the parties is clear. Phillips *v.* Swank, 120 Pa. St. 76; Dorr *v.* Clapp, 160 Mass. 538.

Wherever the form of the will or other instrument of title is not clear as to the title given the trustee, the court will apply as far as possible the general principle that the trustee's title shall be commensurate with the needs of the trust, and, so far as the rules of law permit, will enlarge or decrease the trustee's apparent title accordingly. Carney *v.* Kain, 40 W. Va. 758, 764; Morffew *v.* S. F., etc., R. Co., 107 Cal. 587, 595; Smith *v.* McWhorter, 123 Ga. 287.

§ 313. Thus courts have by construction implied an estate in the trustees, although no estate was given them in words; but, in all such cases, the trustees were required to do something that required a legal estate of some kind in them; as, where a testator gave to a married woman the rents and profits of certain lands to be paid her by his executors, it was held to be a devise of the land itself to the executors, although nothing was given them in terms, to enable them to carry out the purposes of the trust.[1] So a power given to executors to rent, lease, repair, and insure implies a legal title in them.[2]

§ 314. In the same manner, and for the same reasons, courts have enlarged or extended estates given to trustees. Thus, if A. gives an estate to B. without words of limitation, it is an estate for the life of B.; but if A. gives an estate to B. to pay certain annuities to persons named, for their lives, the trustee takes an estate for the lives of the several annuitants.[3]

Brown v. Whiteway, 8 Hare, 156; Saye & Sele v. Jones, 1 Eq. Cas. Ab. 383; 33 Bro. P. C. 113; Shapland v. Smith, 1 Bro. Ch. 75; Heardson v. Willamson, 1 Keen, 33; Player v. Nicholls, 1 B. & Cr. 142; Warter v. Hutchinson, 5 Moore, 153; 1 B. & Cr. 721; Chapman v. Blissett, Forr. 145; Doe v. Hicks, 7 T. R. 433; Nash v. Coates, 3 B. & A. 839; Ex parte Gadsden, 3 Rich. 468; Adams v. Adams, 6 Q. B. 866; Barker v. Greenwood, 4 M. & W. 429; Doe v. Claridge, 6 C. B. 641; Ware v. Richardson, 3 Md. 505; Pearce v. McClenaghan, 5 Rich. 178; Ellis v. Fisher, 3 Sneed, 231; Gardenhire v. Hinds, 1 Head, 402; Smith v. Metcalf, id. 64; Slavin v. Brown, 32 Mo. 176; Greenwood v. Coleman, 34 Ala. 150; Bryan v. Weems, 29 Ala. 423; Koenig's App., 57 Penn. St. 552; Ivory v. Burns, 56 id. 300; Wilcox v. Wilcox, 47 N. H. 488; McBride v. Smyth, 59 id. 245; West v. Fitz, 109 Ill. 425; Farmers' Nat'l Bank v. Moran, 30 Minn. 167; Davis v. Williams, 85 Tenn. 646. But see Watkins v. Specht, 7 Cold. 585; McElroy v. McElroy, 113 Mass. 509.

[1] Oates v. Cooke, 3 Burr. 1684; W. Black. 543; Bush v. Allen, 5 Mod. 63; Doe v. Woodhouse, 4 T. R. 89; Doe v. Homfray, 6 Ad. & El. 206; Doe v. Sampson, 5 East, 162; Feedey's App., 60 Penn. St. 349. [Davies v. Jones, 24 Ch. Div. 190; Bean v. Commonwealth, 186 Mass. 348; Crane v. Bolles, 49 N. J. Eq. 373.]

[2] Kellam v. Allen, 52 Barb. 605.

[3] Jenkins v. Jenkins, Willes, 656; Shaw v. Weigh, 2 Str. 798; Oates v. Cooke, 3 Burr. 1684, and other cases cited, § 313, n. 1.

§ 315. So, if land is devised to trustees without the word "heirs," and a trust is declared which cannot be fully executed but by the trustees taking an inheritance, the court will enlarge or extend their estate into a fee-simple, to enable them to carry out the intention of the donor.[1] Thus, if land is conveyed to trustees, without the word "heirs," in trust to *sell*, they must have the fee, otherwise they could not sell.[2] The construction would be the same if the trust was to sell the whole or a part; for no purchasers would be safe unless they could have the fee;[3] and a trust to convey or to lease at discretion would be subject to the same rule.[4] *A fortiori*, if an estate is limited to trustees and their heirs in trust to sell or mortgage or to lease at their discretion, or if they are to convey the property in fee, or divide it equally among certain persons; for to do any or all these acts requires a legal fee.[5] (a)

[1] Villiers *v.* Villiers, 2 Atk. 72; Cleveland *v.* Hallett, 6 Cush. 407; Fisher *v.* Fields, 10 Johns. 505; Ellis *v.* Fisher, 3 Sneed, 231; Rackham *v.* Siddall, 1 Mac. & G. 607; 2 Hall & T. 44; Deering *v.* Adams, 37 Maine, 265; Brown *v.* Brown, 12 Md. 87; Webster *v.* Cooper, 14 How. 499; Blagrave *v.* Blagrave, 4 Exch. 569; Hawkins *v.* Chapman, 36 Md. 94; Farquharson *v.* Eichelberger, 15 Md. 72; Packard *v.* Marshall, 138 Mass. 302.

[2] Gibson *v.* Montford, 1 Ves. 491; Amb. 95; Shaw *v.* Weigh, 1 Eq. Cas. Ab. 184; Bagshaw *v.* Spencer, 1 Ves. 144; Glover *v.* Monckton, 3 Bing. 113; 10 Moore, 453; Hawker *v.* Hawker, 3 B. & A. 537; Warter *v.* Hutchinson, 5 Moore, 143; 1 B. & C. 121; Watson *v.* Pearson, 2 Exch. 594; Chamberlain *v.* Thompson, 10 Conn. 244; Doe *v.* Howland, 7 Cow. 277; Jackson *v.* Robins, 16 Johns. 537; Spessard *v.* Rohrer, 9 Gill, 262. [But see *supra*, § 312, note.]

[3] Bagshaw *v.* Spencer, 1 Ves. 144; Kirkland *v.* Cox, 94 Ill. 402.

[4] Booth *v.* Field, 2 B. & Ad. 556; Keen *v.* Walbank, id. 554; Brewster *v.* Striker, 2 Comst. 19; Deering *v.* Adams, 37 Maine, 265. But see Doe *v.* Cafe, 7 Exch. 675.

[5] Bagshaw *v.* Spencer, 1 Ves. 142; Keane *v.* Deardon, 8 East, 242; Cadogan *v.* Ewart, 7 Ad. & El. 636; Tompkins *v.* Willan, 2 B. & A. 84; Keen *v.* Walbank, id. 354; Garth *v.* Baldwin, 2 Ves. 646; Booth *v.* Field, 2 B. & Ad. 564; Rees *v.* Williams, 2 M. & W. 749; Shelly *v.* Eldin, 4 Ad. & El.

(a) It is not absolutely necessary that a valid power to sell be coupled with ownership of the fee. Thus, it frequently happens that a life tenant has power to sell the fee or a trustee of a life estate has the same power as an executor without any title at all. See Luquire *v.* Lee, 121 Ga. 624; Tillman *v.* Banks, 116 Ga. 250.

§ 316. Where an estate is given to trustees in fee upon trusts that do not exhaust the whole estate, and a power is superadded which can only be exercised by the trustees conveying in fee-simple, the trustees will take the fee, and the estate conveyed by them will be sustained by the fee in them, and not by the mere power.[1] Where it is possible that the trustees may be under the necessity of exercising a power over the fee, as by mortgage, a gift to them of the fee will not be cut down;[2] and the rule is that all the trusts which trustees must execute are to be executed out of the estate given them.[3] Lord Talbot said that it was wholly a matter of intention whether the trustee should take a fee or not;[4] hence, in other cases, it has been said that if no intention appeared upon the face of the will that the trustees were to take anything beyond what was necessary for the execution of the trust, the estate, though limited to them and their heirs, would be cut down to the limit of the trust.[5] So trustees may take only a *chattel* interest in real estate, although limited to them and their heirs, as where they are to hold it in trust only for a short time to pay debts and legacies, and convey it to the *cestui que trust* when he comes of age or at a certain time;[6] and this construction will be much stronger if the fee is not

582; Creaton v. Creaton, 2 Sm. & Gif. 386; Collier v. Walters, L. R. 17 Eq. 265. [Crane v. Bolles, 49 N. J. Eq. 373; People's Loan & Exch. Bank v. Garlington, 54 S. C. 413.]

[1] Fenwick v. Potts, 8 De G., M. & G. 506; Poad v. Watson, 37 Eng. L. & Eq. 112; Watkins v. Frederick, 11 H. L. Cas. 354; Haddelsey v. Adams, 22 Beav. 266. A power of appointment superadded to a life-estate will not enlarge it into a fee; and so a power of appointment added to an estate of inheritance will not cut down the fee. Yarnall's App., 70 Penn. St. 342; Burleigh v. Clough, 52 N. H. 267.

[2] Fenwick v. Potts, 8 De G., M. & G. 506; Horton v. Horton, 7 T. R. 652; Brown v. Whiteway, 8 Hare, 156.

[3] Watson v. Pearson, 2 Exch. 593.

[4] Chapman v. Blissett, Forr. Cas. t. Talb. 145; Hawkins v. Luscombe, 2 Swanst. 375; Curtis v. Price, 12 Ves. 89; Collier v. McBean, L. R. 1 Ch. 80.

[5] Doe v. Hicks, 7 T. R. 433; Nash v. Coates, 3 B. & A. 839; Boteler v. Allington, 1 Bro. Ch. 72, is criticised in 7 T. R. 433, by Lord Kenyon; Webster v. Cooper, 14 How. 499; Beaumont v. Salisbury, 19 Beav. 198. [See Luquire v. Lee, 121 Ga. 624.]

[6] Goodtitle v. Whitby, 1 Burr. 228; Warter v. Hutchinson, 1 B. & Cr.

limited to them.[1]   The same construction as to the estate of
trustees will prevail where the limitation is to them and their
heirs, to their use and behoof forever, whether it is contained
in a deed or will.[2]   Where a gift was made to one in trust for
his wife for life, and to her heirs forever, subject to her husband's
curtesy, the trustee took an estate for the life of his wife only
and at her death the trust ceased.[3]

§ 317.   Where a testator gave all his real and personal estate
to trustees, "their executors, administrators, and assigns," in
trust to pay several annuities, sums, and legacies, on the deficiency of the personal estates out of the rents, issues, and profits
arising from the real estate, and gave the residue over, Lord
Hardwicke held that if the annual reception of the rents and
profits would satisfy the purposes of the trust, the trustees
would take only a chattel interest in the real estate; but, as
the land must be sold for the payment of the legacies, the trustees took the fee.[4]   The court, however, is always reluctant to
enlarge an estate in trustees beyond the terms of the gift; and it
will not be done unless it is necessary for the execution of the
trust.[5]   Where it is plain that the trustees are to pay all charges,
debts, legacies, annuities, or other moneys out of the rents and

721; Stanley v. Stanley, 16 Ves. 491; Badder v. Harris, 2 Dowl. & Ry. 76;
Wheedon v. Lea, 3 T. R. 41; Pratt v. Timins, 1 B. & Ald. 530; Brune v.
Martin, 8 B. & Cr. 497; Tucker v. Johnson, 16 Sim. 341; Glover v. Monckton,
3 Bing. 13; Doe v. Davies, 1 Q. B. 430; Player v. Nicholls, 1 B. & Cr. 336;
Cadogan v. Ewart, 7 Ad. & E. 136, 667.

[1] Pearce v. Savage, 45 Maine, 90; Boraston's Case, 3 Co. 19; Player
v. Nicholls, 1 B. & Cr. 336.

[2] Hawkins v. Luscombe, 2 Swanst. 375; Curtis v. Price, 12 Ves. 89;
Venables v. Morris, 7 T. R. 342; Watkins v. Specht, 7 Cold. 585.   But see
Cooper v. Kynock, L. R. 8 Ch. 402.

[3] Noble v. Andrews, 37 Conn. 346.

[4] Gibson v. Montfort, 1 Ves. 485; Amb. 93; Woodgate v. Flint, 44 N. Y.
21, n.

[5] Heardson v. Williamson, 1 Keen, 33; White v. Simpson, 5 East, 162;
Wykham v. Wykham, 3 Taunt. 316; 11 East, 458; 18 Ves. 395, 416; Ack-
land v. Lutley, 9 Ad. & El. 879; Doe v. Claridge, 6 C. B. 641.

profits of the estate, and no anticipation of the income is necessary or contemplated for that purpose, they will take a chattel
interest, or a term for years necessary for the purpose, and not
the legal inheritance;[1] and if the testator use an inartificial
word, as that the trustees are to lend the estate, they will not
take a fee.[2] A trust to preserve contingent remainders, without
limitation to heirs, will not be enlarged; for the trust does not
require an estate of inheritance.[3]

§ 318. If, however, the subject-matter of the gift to trustees
is personal estate, the whole legal interest will vest in them
without words of limitation. They may generally dispose of
personal estate absolutely, being compelled to account for it.[4]

§ 319. In England, a distinction is kept up between limitations to trustees in wills and deeds. Thus it is said that in wills
there is more room for construction to ascertain and carry into
effect the intention of testators, and that in deeds the rules of
property are carried into effect with more strictness. So it is
said, that if in a deed an estate is given to a trustee *and his
heirs*, there is no power to abridge the estate on the ground that
the purposes of the trust do not require a fee in the trustees;
and that, on the other hand, when an estate is given by deed to

---

[1] Cordall's Case, Cro. Eliz. 315; Carter *v.* Bernadiston, 1 P. Wms. 589;
Hitchens *v.* Hitchens, 2 Vern. 404; Wykham *v.* Wykham, 18 Ves. 416;
Heardson *v.* Williamson, 1 Keen, 33; Co. Litt. 42 a.

[2] Payne *v.* Sale, 2 Dev. & Bat. Eq. 455.

[3] Thong *v.* Bedford, 1 Bro. Ch. 14; Webster *v.* Cooper, 14 How. 499;
Beaumont *v.* Salisbury, 19 Beav. 198; Co. Litt. 290 b; Butl. n. viii.

[4] Dinsmore *v.* Biggert, 9 Barr, 135; Nicoll *v.* Walworth, 4 Denio, 385;
Chamberlain *v.* Thompson, 10 Conn. 244; Combry *v.* McMichael, 19 Ala.
751; Elton *v.* Shepherd, 1 Bro. Ch. 531; 2 Jarm. Pow. Dev. 631; Doe *v.*
Willan, 2 B. & Ald. 84; Smith *v.* Thompson, 2 Swan, 386; Foster *v.* Coe,
4 Lans. 59; Fellows *v.* Heermans, id. 230; and Aiken *v.* Smith, 1 Sneed,
304, held that when personalty was limited to trustees, their heirs and
executors, in trust for a married woman for life, and after her death to be
equally divided among her children or to be conveyed to her children, the
trustee took an estate for her life only, and that at her death the trust
ceased. These cases, however, are not consistent with principle or authority, and probably would not be followed.

a trustee in trust without words of inheritance, there is no authority to enlarge the estate in the trustee because the purposes of the trust seem to require a larger estate. There is a very respectable amount of authority, even in England, that an estate given to trustees and their heirs in trust, by a deed, may be restricted to an estate for the life of another, where the purposes of the trust can all be answered by such an estate in the trustee.[1] In the cases sustaining the power to abridge the legal operation of the words of inheritance in a deed, there were some further limitations of the estate, either to the trustees or to third persons, inconsistent with the idea of a fee in the trustees.[2] The authorities, however, greatly preponderate, that courts cannot look to the equitable interests given or created by a *deed*, in order to determine whether the trustee under it takes a fee or not, if there are plain words of inheritance in it. Lord Eldon said, that it appeared to him very difficult to apply the doctrine to a *deed*, and he refused thus to cut down an estate.[3] While there is this conflict of authority upon the point, whether an estate given in fee by deed to trustees can be abridged to the extent of the trust, there is said to be no authority in England that an estate given by a deed to trustees without words of inheritance can be enlarged to suit the purposes of the trust;[4] although there is one expression by Lord Hardwicke that such enlargement is within the power of the court when the circumstances require it.[5]

§ 320. In the United States, the distinction between deeds and wills, in respect to the trustees' estate, has not been kept

[1] Curtis *v.* Price, 12 Ves. 89; Venables *v.* Morris, 7 T. R. 342, 438; Doe *v.* Hicks, id. 437; Brune *v.* Martyn, 8 B. & Cr. 497; Beaumont *v.* Salisbury, 19 Beav. 198, (where the authorities were commented on); Lewis *v.* Rees, 3 K. & J. 132; Cooper *v.* Kynock, L. R. 8 Ch. 403.

[2] Ibid.

[3] Wykham *v.* Wykham, 18 Ves. 395; Colomore *v.* Tyndall, 2 Y. & J. 605; Co. Litt. 20 b; Butl. n. viii.; Dinsmore *v.* Biggert, 9 Barr, 123; Lewis *v.* Rees, 3 K. & J. 132, where the authorities are reviewed by Wood, V. C.

[4] Pottow *v.* Fricker, 6 Exch. 570; Hill on Trustees, 251. [See *In re* Irwin, [1904] 2 Ch. 752; *supra*, § 312, note.]

[5] Villiers *v.* Villiers, 2 Atk. 72.

up; and the general rule is, that, whether words of inheritance in the trustee are or are not in the *deed*, the trustee will take an estate adequate to the execution of the trust, and no more nor less.[1] Courts will abridge the estate where words of inheritance are used, if the execution of the trust does not require a fee; and so they will enlarge the estate if no words of inheritance are used in a deed.[2] In examining the cases, however, where a trust ceases upon the death of a tenant for life, or upon the death of a person for whom the property was held in trust, care must be taken that this principle is not confounded with another. Thus, where an estate is given to trustees and their heirs in trust to pay the income to A. during her life, and at her decease to hold the same for the use of her children or her heirs, or for the use of other persons named, the trust ceases upon the death of A. for the reason that it remains no longer an *active* trust; the statute of uses immediately executes the use in those who are limited to take it after the death of A., and the trustees cease to have anything in the estate, not because the court has abridged their estate to the extent of the trust, but because, having the fee or legal estate, the statute of uses has executed it in the *cestui que trust*.[3] But where the operation of the statute

[1] King *v.* Parker, 9 Cush. 71; Stearns *v.* Parker, 10 Met. 32; Gould *v.* Lamb, 11 Met. 8; Cleveland *v.* Hallett, 6 Cush. 403; Att. Gen. *v.* Federal Street Meeting House, 3 Gray, 1; Wright *v.* Delafield, 23 Barb. 498; Fisher *v.* Fields, 10 Johns. 105; Welch *v.* Allen, 21 Wend. 147; Rutledge *v.* Smith, 1 Busb. Eq. 283; Liptrot *v.* Holmes, 1 Kelly (Ga.), 390; Cooper *v.* Kynock, L. R. 8 Ch. 402. [See *supra*, § 312, note.]

[2] Neilson *v.* Lagow, 12 How. 110; North *v.* Philbrook, 34 Maine, 537; Rutledge *v.* Smith, 1 Busb. Eq. 283; Cleveland *v.* Hallett, 6 Cush. 406. See to the contrary, Miles *v.* Fisher, 10 Ohio, 1.

[3] Parker *v.* Converse, 5 Gray, 336; Greenwood *v.* Coleman, 34 Ala. 150; Churchill *v.* Corker, 25 Ga. 479. See Vallette *v.* Bennett, 69 Ill. 336. And whenever the active duties required of the trustees have been performed and the purpose of the trust ceases, having no longer any proper object to serve, the legal estate is executed in the *cestui que trust*, without further action by the court or the trustee. Stoke's App., 80 Penn. St. 337; Dodson *v.* Ball, 60 id. 492; Wells *v.* McCall, 64 id. 207; Yarnall's App., 70 id. 335; Meacham *v.* Steele, 93 Ill. 135. And this is always so when an estate of inheritance or an absolute estate is put in trust for coverture. Megargee *v.* Naglee. 64 Penn. St. 216; Lynch *v.* Swayne, 83 Ill. 336. If

of uses does not put an end to the trust, and where it is necessary to enlarge an estate although there are no words of inheritance, courts have been obliged to resort to different expedients to avoid the technical rules of law upon the subject of inheritances.[1] In those States where no technical or other words are necessary to convey a fee no difficulties arise. (a)

the trust property is to be sold and proceeds distributed to the beneficiaries, there is still an active trust, and the estate is not executed in the *cestui*. Kirkland v. Cox, 94 Ill. 402; Read v. Power, 12 R. I. 16.

[1] Williams v. First Presby. Soc., 1 Ohio St. 498; Rutledge v. Smith, 1 Busb. Eq. 283; Co. Litt. 385, 386; 1 Prest. Touchstone, 182; Rawle on Covenants, 344; Shaw v. Galbraith, 7 Penn. St. 112. [See Brown v. Reeder, 108 Md. 653.]

(a) In many States statutes have done away with the necessity of words of inheritance in all conveyances.

CHAPTER XI.

PROPERTIES AND INCIDENTS OF THE LEGAL ESTATE IN THE HANDS OF TRUSTEES.

§ 321. As a general rule, the legal estate in the hands of a trustee has at common law precisely the same properties, characteristics, and incidents, as if the trustee were the absolute beneficial owner. The legal title vests in him, together with all the appurtenances and all the covenants that run with the land.[1] The trustee may sell and devise it, or mortgage it, or it may be taken on execution. It may be forfeited, and it will escheat on failure of heirs, and so it will descend to heirs on the death of the trustee.[2] (a) All these properties and incidents attach to the legal estate at common law, whether in the hands of a trustee or of an absolute owner; but these incidents do not generally interfere with the proper execution of the trust, for all conveyances and all incumbrances made or imposed upon the estate by the trustee, for other purposes than those of the trust, or in breach of the trust, are utterly disregarded by a court of equity, whatever may be the effect of such conveyances or incumbrances in a court of common law.[3] And as the trustee may in a court of law, as a general rule, deal with the legal estate in his hands, as if he was the absolute owner, so the *cestui que trust* in a court of equity may deal with the equitable estate in him: he is the beneficial and substantial owner, and in the absence of any disability, — that is, if he is *sui juris*, — he may sell and dispose of it; and any legal conveyance of it will have in equity the same operation upon the equitable estate as a similar conveyance of the legal estate would have at law upon the legal estate.[4] While a trust for the general benefit of one

[1] Devin *v.* Henderchott, 32 Iowa, 192.

[2] Zabriskie *v.* Morris & Essex R. Co., 33 N. J. Eq. 22. [As to the effect of a conveyance known to be in contravention of the terms of the trust, see Robinson *v.* Pierce, 118 Ala. 273.]

[3] Leake *v.* Leake, 5 Ir. Eq. 366.

[4] Matthews *v.* Wardel, 10 G. & J. 443; Burgess *v.* Wheate, 1 Eden, 226; Croxall *v.* Sherard, 5 Wall. 268; Reid *v.* Gordon, 35 Md. 184; Boteler *v.* Allington, 1 Bro. Ch. 72; Campbell *v.* Prestons, 22 Grat. 396.

(a) In several States statutes have rendered all conveyances by trustees in contravention of the terms of the trust absolutely void at law. See statutes of New York, Michigan, Minnesota, North Dakota, South Dakota, Wisconsin, Montana, California, Kansas. And in several States it is part of the statutory law that the title does not descend to the heir of a trustee or pass to his personal representative. *Ibid.;* Alabama.

sui juris, not confined to maintenance, may create a transmissible interest, yet a trust for the maintenance of an imbecile son will not create a transmissible interest, although the will contains a limitation over to the issue of such son.[1] In case of a trust for the use of a married woman as if she were sole, the husband has no control over the property, and cannot of himself lease or otherwise dispose of it.[2]

§ 322. The legal estate in the hands of a trustee was subject at common law to dower and curtesy;[3] but, as those who take in dower or curtesy take by operation of law, they are subject to the same equities as the original trustee; therefore, if the widow of a trustee should take dower in a trust estate, she would take her dower subject to the same trusts that the estate was under in the hands of her husband. It would thus be of no benefit to her; and it is now understood to be the equitable rule, that a widow has no dower in the lands held by her husband as trustee, and the same observations apply to the right of curtesy in trust estates.[4] (*a*) If, however, the equitable estate meets

[1] Gray *v*. Corbit, 4 Del. Ch. 135.

[2] Panill *v*. Coles, 81 Va. 380.

[3] Bennett *v*. Davis, 2 P. Wms. 319; Noel *v*. Jevon, Freem. 43; Nash *v*. Preston, Cro. Car. 190; Casborne *v*. English, 2 Eq. Cas. Ab. 728; Hinton *v*. Hinton, 2 Ves. 631; 1 Sugd. V. & P. 358.

[4] King *v*. Bushnel, 121 Ill. 656; Derush *v*. Brown, 8 Ham. 412; Green *v*. Green, 1 id. 249; Cooper *v*. Whitney, 3 Hill, 97; Powell *v*. Monson, etc., 3 Mason, 364; Bartlett *v*. Gouge, 5 B. Mon. 152; Cowman *v*. Hall, 3 Gill & J. 398; Robison *v*. Codman, 1 Sumn. 129; Dean *v*. Mitchell, 4 J. J. Marsh. 451; Ray *v*. Pung, 5 B. & Ald. 561; Gomez *v*. Tradesmen's Bank, 4 Sandf. 102.

(*a*) This equitable rule has been so far adopted by courts of law that it is not necessary or customary for the wife of a trustee to join in the latter's conveyances for the purpose of releasing dower and homestead or for the husband of a trustee to release curtesy. Substantially, if not theoretically, therefore, there is neither dower nor curtesy in the legal estate held by a trustee. Barker *v*. Smiley, 218 Ill. 68; Gritten *v*. Dickerson, 202 Ill. 372; King *v*. Bushnell, 121 Ill. 656; Schaefer *v*. Purviance, 160 Ind. 63; Johnston *v*. Jickling, 141 Iowa, 444. See 1 Ames' Cases on Trusts, (2d ed.) 374, notes; Lewin on Trusts, (11th

the legal estate in the same holder, the equitable merges in the legal estate, and dower and curtesy will attach;[1] and so they will attach so far as there is a beneficial interest in the trustee.[2]

[1] Hopkinson v. Dumas, 42 N. H. 303.

[2] 4 Kent, 43, 46; Prescott v. Walker, 16 N. H. 343.

ed.) 241. This is true whether the trust is express or implied. Thus it has been held that a wife has no dower rights in land which her husband has entered into a valid contract to convey to another either before acquiring the legal title or contemporaneously with the deed to him, Hallett v. Parker, 69 N. H. 134; or before his marriage. Oldham v. Sale, 1 B. Mon. 76. But it has been held that an unenforceable parol trust in land held by a husband does not deprive a wife of her dower rights, and that a subsequent reconveyance by the husband in recognition of the trust does not shut out her dower rights. Bartlett v. Tinsley, 175 Mo. 319; Pruitt v. Pruitt, 57 S. C. 155. But see Johnson v. Jickling, 141 Iowa, 444.

A wife's rights to dower in partnership lands of which her husband holds a moiety of the legal title is at least subject to the "trust" upon which it is held. Brewer v. Browne, 68 Ala. 210; Ratcliffe v. Mason, 92 Ky. 190, 194; Burnside v. Merrick, 4 Met. 537, 541; Dyer v. Clark, 5 Met. 562; Young v. Thrasher, 115 Mo. 222; Sparger v. Moore, 117 N. C., 449; Parrish v. Parrish, 88 Va. 529; Martin v. Smith, 25 W. Va. 579, 584. Whether or not the wife of a partner has dower in the portion of partnership real estate in which her husband, holding legal title, has an ultimate beneficial interest, has been a subject of controversy. Under the English statute and decisions the wife of a partner has no rights of dower in the land itself, because under the implied agreement of the partners, it is equitably converted, so that no partner has an ultimate right to partition, but only a right to share in the proceeds of the land. Deering v. Kerfoot's Ex'r, 89 Va. 491; Parrish v. Parrish, 88 Va. 529; In re Music Hall Block, 8 Ont. Rep. (Can.) 225. The same is true in America wherever the court has found an actual agreement which equitably converts the land. Greene v. Greene, 1 Ohio, 535; Mallory v. Russell, 71 Iowa, 63; Galbraith v. Gedge, 16 B. Mon. 631, 636; Markham v. Merrett, 7 How. (Miss.) 437. In the absence of such an agreement, a wife has dower in her husband's ultimate share of real estate remaining unconverted after the partnership has been wound up, but whether or not she has any vested or inchoate right of dower in the partnership real estate until the extent of her husband's ultimate share has been determined has not been clearly settled. See Strong v. Lord, 107 Ill. 25; Young v. Thrasher, 115 Mo. 222; Woodward-Holmes Co. v. Nudd, 58 Minn. 236, 27 L. R. A. 340; Dawson v. Parsons, 63 N. Y. State Rep. 320; Welch v. McKenzie, 66 Ark. 251; Walling v. Burgess, 122 Ind. 299; Huston v. Neil, 41 Ind. 504; Revelsky v. Brown, 92 Ala. 522; Du Bree v. Albert, 100 Pa. St. 483, 487.

§ 323. While speaking upon this subject, it may be said that, until lately, in England, the widow of a *cestui que trust* had no dower in his equitable estate, or his equitable fee in lands.[1] A widow was not dowable of a use, and lands were frequently conveyed to uses to defeat the right of dower.[2] Thus, if a man before marriage conveyed his lands to trustees upon trust for himself and his heirs in fee, or if after marriage he purchased lands, and took the conveyance to a trustee upon a trust for himself and his heirs, his wife had no right of dower.[3] But if lands were settled on trustees upon a trust for a woman and her heirs in fee, her husband was entitled to his curtesy.[4] This anomaly grew up from an attempt to give to equitable estates the same incidents that belong to legal estates; but when it was proposed to assign dower to a widow out of her husband's equitable estate, it was found that it would disarrange so many titles and estates that the attempt was abandoned. The same inconvenience did not arise in allowing curtesy to a husband, for the reason that a wife could not convey her equitable interests without her husband joining in the act, and thus, to allow him curtesy would not affect titles to any considerable extent.[5] But by a late statute a wife is now dowable in equity of all the lands in which her husband dies possessed of a beneficiary interest.[6]

---

[1] Dixon *v.* Saville, 1 Bro. Ch. 326; Maybury *v.* Brien, 15 Pet. 38; D'Arcy *v.* Blake, 2 Sch. & Lef. 387; 2 Eq. Cas. Ab. 384; 4 Kent, 43; 1 Rop. Hus. & Wife, 354; Banks *v.* Sutton, 2 P. Wms. 716, was overruled; Park on Dow. 138. In Pennsylvania, however, a wife can have dower in both legal and equitable estates. Dubs *v.* Dubs, 31 Penn. St. 154.

[2] Wms. Real Prop. 134–136; Perkins, § 349.

[3] Co. Litt. 208 a (n. 105).

[4] D'Arcy *v.* Blake, 2 Sch. & Lef. 387; Chaplin *v.* Chaplin, 3 P. Wms. 234; Att. Gen. *v.* Scott, t. Talb. 139; Watt *v.* Ball, 1 P. Wms. 108; Sweetapple *v.* Bindon, 2 Vern. 536; Cunningham *v.* Moody, 1 Ves. 174; Dodson *v.* Hay, 3 Bro. Ch. 405.

[5] Chaplin *v.* Chaplin, 3 P. Wms. 234; Att. Gen. *v.* Scott, t. Talb. 139; Burgess *v.* Wheat, 1 Ed. 196; Dixon *v.* Saville, 1 Bro. Ch. 327; Banks *v.* Sutton, 2 P. Wms. 713; Casburne *v.* Casburne, 2 J. & W. 204; Watt *v.* Ball, 1 P. Wms. 109; D'Arcy *v.* Blake, 2 Sch. & Lef. 388.

[6] 3 & 4 Wm. IV., c. 105; 1 Spence, Eq. Jur. 505.

§ 324. The general rule in the United States is, that a wife is dowable in equity in all lands to which the husband had a complete [1] equitable title at the time of his death.[2] This rule, it is presumed, would apply in all the States where the common-law principles of dower prevail, except in Maine and Massachusetts, where a wife is not entitled to dower in her husband's equitable estates.[3] (a) The husband also in most States has

---

[1] It must be such a title as equity would enforce. Efland v. Efland, 96 N. C. 488.

[2] Shoemaker v. Walker, 2 Serg. & R. 554; Dubs v. Dubs, 31 Penn. St. 154; Reid v. Morrison, 12 Serg. & R. 18; Miller v. Beverly, 1 Hen. & M. 368; Clairborne v. Henderson, 3 id. 322; Lawson v. Morton, 6 Dana, 471; Bowie v. Berry, 1 Md. Ch. 452; Miller v. Stump, 3 Gill, 304; Hawley v. James, 5 Paige, 318; Thompson v. Thompson, 1 Jones (N. C.), 430; Gully v. Ray, 18 Ky. 113; Barnes v. Gay, 7 Iowa, 26; Lewis v. James, 8 Humph. 537; Rowton v. Rowton, 1 Hen. & M. 92; Gillespie v. Somerville, 3 St. & P. 447; Robinson v. Miller, 1 B. Mon. 93; Smiley v. Wright, 2 Ohio, 512; Davenport v. Farrar, 1 Scam. 314; Bowers v. Keesecker, 14 Iowa, 301; Peay v. Peay, 2 Rich. Eq. 409; Mershon v. Duer, 40 N. J. Eq. 333, a resulting trust in husband. [Pettus v. McKinney, 74 Ala. 108, 114; Redmond's Adm'x v. Redmond, 112 Ky. 760; Kirby v. Vantrece, 26 Ark. 368; Howell v. Jump, 140 Mo. 441, 454. Chiefly by statute. See Tenn. Code (1896), § 4139; N. J. Gen. Stat. p. 1275, § 1; Radley v. Radley, 70 N. J. Eq. 248.]

[3] Hamlin v. Hamlin, 19 Maine, 141; Reed v. Whitney, 7 Gray, 533; Lobdell v. Hayes, 4 Allen, 187. [See Hopkinson v. Dumas, 42 N. H. 296, 306; Hall v. Hall, 70 N. H. 47; Mann v. Edson, 39 Me. 25.]

(a) It has been held in Rhode Island that where property was devised to A. and his heirs in trust for D. for life with a remainder to D. on termination of his own life estate, D.'s widow had no right of dower since D. was never seized in fee, even though a court of equity might on his application have terminated the trust and vested the fee in him. Kenyon v. Kenyon, 17 R. I. 539.

Where land held in trust has been equitably converted so that the sole beneficiary is entitled only to the proceeds, his widow is not entitled to dower. Hunter v. Anderson, 152 Pa. St. 386; Phelps v. Phelps, 143 N. Y. 197. Under an Indiana statute which provides that a conveyance or devise of lands to a trustee whose title is nominal only and who has no power of disposition, vests the title in the beneficiary, it has been held that a husband has the legal title and his wife dower in land which he has purchased with his own money and has had conveyed to a trustee to hold for his benefit for life and to convey at his request or as he should appoint by will. Stroup v. Stroup, 140 Ind. 179, 185; Ind. Stat. (Burns, 1908), § 4024. But it is otherwise in New York and in Massachusetts, and the fact

curtesy in the equitable estates of his wife.[1] But the wife must be actually in possession of her equitable interest: a mere right not in possession is not enough to entitle the husband to curtesy.[2] But the husband's curtesy will not be defeated by the negligence of the trustee, as where money is directed to be laid in land in such manner that the husband would have been entitled to his curtesy, and the trustee neglected to invest the money during the life of the wife, the husband was held to be entitled to his curtesy.[3] Nor will a trust for the separate use of the wife exclude the husband's curtesy, if at her decease the estate is to go to her heirs.[4]

[1] Tillinghast v. Coggeshall, 7 R. I. 383; Nightingale v. Hidden, id. 115; Dubs v. Dubs, 31 Penn. St. 154; Alexander v. Warrance, 17 Mo. 228; Robinson v. Codman, 1 Sumn. 128; Gardner v. Hooper, 3 Gray, 404; Houghton v. Hapgood, 13 Pick. 154; Rawlings v. Adams, 7 Md. 54; and see Fletcher v. Ashburner, 1 Bro. Ch. 503, and Amer. notes; 1 Green. Cruise, 147, n.; Cushing v. Blake, 30 N. J. Eq. 689.

[2] Parker v. Carter, 4 Hare, 413; Sartill v. Robeson, 2 Jones, Eq. 510; Pitt v. Jackson, 2 Bro. Ch. 51; Morgan v. Morgan, 5 Madd. 408; 4 Kent, Com. 31.

[3] Sweetapple v. Bindon, 2 Vern. 536; Dodson v. Hay, 3 Bro. Ch. 405; Parker v. Carter, 4 Hare, 413; Casborne v. Scarfe, 1 Atk. 609.

[4] Roberts v. Dixwill, 1 Atk. 609; Hearle v. Greenbank, 3 Atk. 715; Morgan v. Morgan, 5 Madd. 408; Follett v. Tyrer, 14 Sim. 125; Bennett v. Davis, 2 P. Wms. 316; Tillinghast v. Coggeshall, 7 R. I. 383.

that his motive in not taking title himself was to prevent his wife from acquiring rights of dower is not in itself fraudulent as to her. Phelps v. Phelps, 143 N. Y. 197; Seaman v. Harmon, 192 Mass. 5. See also Nichols v. Park, 79 N. Y. S. 547, 78 App. Div. 95.

A binding executory contract to convey land upon the payment of a price has been held not to create such an equitable estate in the vendee that his widow is entitled to dower in the land upon the performance of the contract by the administrator of the vendee after the latter's death. Hall v. Hall, 70 N. H. 47. See Schaefer v. Purviance, 160 Ind. 63. But it is otherwise in Massachusetts by statute. See Reed v. Whitney, 7 Gray, 533.

When land owned by a husband has been taken by right of eminent domain, the better opinion is that the wife's inchoate right of dower does not entitle her to have any part of the money received for the land either paid to her or set aside for her benefit on the contingency of her surviving her husband. Flynn v. Flynn, 171 Mass. 312. See contra, Wheeler v. Kirtland, 27 N. J. Eq. 534.

§ 325. At common law if a person holding land committed treason or felony, he forfeited his land to the crown; and if he died without heirs, the land escheated to the crown or to his superior lord. Exactly the same incidents applied to land held in trust for another, if the trustee committed a treason or felony, or died without heirs.[1] This rule of law has been changed in England by statute.[2] At the present day the land either will not be forfeited or escheat, or the crown or superior lord will take it subject to the same equities under which the trustee held it. In the United States, either the land would not be forfeited or escheat, by reason of the failure or incapacity of the trustee or his heirs, or the State would hold it, subject to all the equities it was under in the hands of the trustee. It might not go to the State, for the reason that, if trustees are wanting, courts will appoint new trustees; and if, for any reason, the trust estate should vest in the State, care would be taken that all the rights of the *cestui que trust* should be protected. There are statutes in most of the States determining the rights of the *cestui que trust* in such cases.

§ 326. The trustee is so far clothed with the legal title and all its incidents, that he must perform all the duties of the holder of the legal estate.[3]

§ 327. Before the statute of uses, the estate of the *cestui que use* was not forfeited for crime, and did not escheat upon failure of heirs; but the feoffee to uses held the estate absolutely as his

---

[1] Burgess v. Wheat, 1 Ed. 177; 1 Bro. Ch. 123; Hovenden v. Annesley, 2 Sch. & Lef. 617; Eales v. England, Pr. Ch. 200; Pawlett v. Att. Gen., Hard. 467; Att. Gen. v. Leeds, 2 M. & K. 243; Penn v. Baltimore, 1 Ves. 453; Williams v. Lonsdale, 3 Ves. Jr. 752; Reeves v. Att. Gen., 2 Atk. 223; Geary v. Bearcroft, Cart. 67; King v. Mildmay, 5 B. & Ad. 254; Wilks's Case, Lane, 54; Scounden v. Hawley, Comst. 172.

[2] 4 & 5 Wm. IV. c. 23; 39 & 40 Geo. III. c. 88; Hughes v. Wells, 9 Hare, 749; 14 Vic. c. 60.

[3] Wilson v. Hoare, 2 B. & Ad. 350; Trinity Coll. v. Brown, 1 Vern. 441; 2 Ld. Raym. 994; Bath v. Abney, 1 Dick. 260; Carr v. Ellison, 3 Atk. 73; 1 Cru. Dig. 305.

own.[1] And the same rule was afterwards followed in regard to trusts.[2] Although it was enacted by statute that the *cestui que use* or *cestui que trust* should forfeit his equitable interest upon conviction for *treason*,[3] yet the law never went further; and if the *cestui que trust* committed a *felony*, so that he could no longer claim his equitable rights, the trustee continued to hold the lands for his own use discharged of the trusts.[4] And so it was held, after great debate in Burgess *v.* Wheat, that if the *cestui que trust* left no heirs, the trust estate of inheritance did not escheat, but that the trustee thenceforth held the estate discharged of the trust.[5] This case has been doubted,[6] but it has been followed as the law.[7] This is upon the principle, that there is no want of a tenant to the land, the trustee being clothed with all the rights of ownership against all the world except the *cestui que trust*, and those claiming under him. But this principle does not apply to chattels, where there can be no tenant, nor to leaseholds,[8] nor to an equity of redemption.[9] In the United States, trustees would hold personal property subject to the right of the State as *ultima hæres*, in case the *cestui que trust* died without heirs or next of kin; and it is conceived that they would hold real estate under the same rule.[10]

---

[1] Burgess *v.* Wheat, 1 Ed. 199, per Sir Thomas Clarke, M. R.

[2] Att. Gen. *v.* Sands, 1 Hale, P. C. 249.

[3] 33 Hen. VIII. c. 20; 1 Hale, P. C. 248.

[4] Att. Gen. *v.* Sands, 1 Hale, P. C. 249.

[5] Burgess *v.* Wheat, 1 Ed. 177; 1 Black, 123; 1 Bro. Ch. 123.

[6] Middleton *v.* Spicer, 1 Bro. Ch. 204; Fawcet *v.* Lowther, 2 Ves. 300; Sweeting *v.* Sweeting, 33 L. J. Ch. 211.

[7] Taylor *v.* Haygarth, 14 Sim. 8; 8 Jur. 185; Henchman *v.* Att. Gen., 3 Myl. & K. 485; Onslow *v.* Wallis, 1 Mac. & G. 506; 1 Hall & T. 513; Rittson *v.* Stordy, 3 Sm. & Gif. 230; Barrow *v.* Wadkin, 24 Beav. 1. [See *In re* Bacons's Will, 31 Ch. D. 460.]

[8] Middleton *v.* Spicer, 1 Bro. Ch. 201; Walker *v.* Denne, 2 Ves. Jr. 170; Barclay *v.* Russell, 3 Ves. 424; Henchman *v.* Att. Gen., 3 Myl. & K. 485; Taylor *v.* Haygarth, 14 Sim. 8; Cradock *v.* Owen, 2 Sm. & Gif. 241; Bishop *v.* Curtis, 17 Jur. 23; Powell *v.* Merritt, 22 L. J. 208; 1 Sm. & Gif. 381.

[9] Down *v.* Morris, 3 Hare, 394.

[10] McCaw *v.* Galbraith, 7 Rich. L. 75; Darrah *v.* McNair, 1 Ash. 236; Matthews *v.* Ward, 10 G. & J. 443; 4 Kent, 425; Crane *v.* Ruder, 21 Mich. 25.

§ 328. It is the duty of the trustee to defend and protect the
title to the trust estate; and, as the legal title is in him, he alone
can sue and be sued in a court of law; the *cestui que trust,* the
absolute owner of the estate in equity, is regarded in law as a
stranger.[1] (*a*) The rule is carried to the extent that the grantee
of the trustee can alone maintain an action upon the legal title,
although the conveyance to him was a breach of the trust.[2] To
protect himself, the trustee must defend the title if he is sued.
It is his duty to give the *cestui que trust* notice of a suit hostile
to his interests, and to defend the action in good faith. To act
otherwise would be a breach of trust.[3] A trustee may also
maintain an action for any trespass upon the land;[4] but if the

[1] May *v.* Taylor, 6 M. & Gr. 261; Gibson *v.* Winter, 5 B. & Ad. 96;
Allen *v.* Imlett, Holt, 641; Goodtitle *v.* Jones, 7 T. R. 47; Baptist Soc. *v.*
Hazen, 100 Mass. 322; Cox *v.* Walker, 26 Me. 504; Beach *v.* Beach, 14 Vt.
28; Moore *v.* Burnet, 11 Ohio, 334; Wright *v.* Douglass, 3 Barb. 59; Matthews *v.* Ward, 10 G. & J. 443; Mordecai *v.* Parker, 3 Dev. 425; Finn *v.*
Hohn, 21 How. 481; Hooper *v.* Scheimer, 23 How. 235; Fitzpatrick *v.* Fitzgerald, 13 Gray, 400; Chapin *v.* Universalist Society, 8 Gray, 581; Crane
v. Crane, 4 Gray, 323; Davis *v.* Charles River Railroad, 11 Cush. 506; Raymond *v.* Holden, 2 Cush. 268; Moody *v.* Farr, 33 Miss. 192; Adler *v.* Sewell,
20 Ind. 598; Western R. R. Co. *v.* Nolan, 48 N. Y. 517; Church *v.* Stewart, 27
Barb. 553; Ryan *v.* Bibb, 46 Ala. 323; Ponder *v.* McGruder, 42 Ga. 242;
Kirkland *v.* Cox, 94 Ill. 402. [Bailey *v.* Selden, 112 Ala. 593; Simmons
v. Richardson, 107 Ala. 697; Miller *v.* Butler, 121 Ga. 758; Sanders *v.* Houston Guano Co., 107 Ga. 49; McDevitt *v.* Bryant, 104 Md. 187; Attwill *v.*
Dole, 74 N. H. 300; O'Malley *v.* Gerth, 67 N. J. Law, 610; Robinson *v.*
Adams, 81 App. Div. (N. Y.) 20; 179 N. Y. 558; Butler *v.* Butler, 58 N.
Y. S. 1094; 41 App. Div. 477; Price *v.* Krasnoff, 60 S. C. 172; *In re* Kenney,
136 Fed. 451. See Birmingham, etc., Co. *v.* Louisville, etc., Co., 152 Ala.
422; Kaylor *v.* Hiller, 72 S. C. 433.]
[2] Reece *v.* Allen, 5 Gilm. 241; Taylor *v.* King, 6 Munf. 358; Canoy *v.*
Troutman, 7 Ired. 155; Cary *v.* Whitney, 48 Maine, 516; Matthews *v.*
McPherson, 65 N. C. 189; Phillips *v.* Ward, 51 Mo. 295.
[3] Mackay *v.* Coates, 70 Penn. St. 350; Warland *v.* Colwell, 10 R. I. 369.
[4] Walker *v.* Fawcett, 7 Ired. 44.

(*a*) It has been held in Alabama
that a trustee suing in equity for an
injunction against the erection of
telegraph poles on the trust property
needs to allege that the trust is an
active one, since he has no legal title
if the trust is passive. Roman *v.*
Long Distance Tel. & Tel. Co., 147
Ala. 389.

cestui que trust is in the actual possession of it, he may maintain an action for any injury done to his possession.[1] If, however, the trust is terminated by operation of law or otherwise, and the property has vested in the *cestui que trust*, he may after that time maintain an action upon the title;[2] and so if there has been a conveyance or surrender by the trustees to the *cestui que trust*,[3] or a presumption of a surrender from the fact that the purposes of the trust are all accomplished.[4] If the trustee is in possession, he must sue for all injuries to the possession, and he is the proper person to maintain the claim for damages for flowing the land under the mill acts, or for taking it for railroad purposes, turnpikes, or public highways.[5] (a)   In

[1] Cox *v.* Walker, 26 Maine, 504; Stearns *v.* Palmer, 10 Met. 32; Second Cong. Soc. North Bridgewater *v.* Waring, 24 Pick. 309. [Thomas Machine Co. *v.* Voelker, 23 R. I. 441; Cape *v.* Plymouth Church, 117 Wis. 150.]

[2] Nicoll *v.* Walworth, 4 Denio, 385; Matthews *v.* McPherson, 65 N. C. 189; Lockhart *v.* Canfield, 49 Miss. 470.

[3] Den ex d. Obert *v.* Bordine, 1 Spencer (N. J.), 394; Hopkins *v.* Ward, 6 Munf. 38; Doggett *v.* Hart. 5 Fla. 215.

[4] Ibid.

[5] Davis *v.* Charles River R. R. Co., 11 Cush. 506; Woodruff *v.* Orange, 32 N. J. 49. [See Lewin on Trusts, (11th ed.) 851; 1 Ames on Trusts (2d ed.), 255.]

(a) If the trustee refuses to bring suit against a third person to protect the trust property or to recover it when it has been improperly transferred or when he has been disseised, the *cestui* is sometimes allowed to proceed in equity against the third person joining the trustee as a party defendant. Bailey *v.* Selden, 112 Ala. 593; Robinson *v.* Adams, 81 App. Div. (N. Y.) 20; 179 N. Y. 558; Butler *v.* Butler, 58 N. Y. S. 1094, 41 App. Div. 477. See Anderson *v.* Daley, 56 N. Y. S. 511. It is necessary to allege and prove that the trustee has been requested to bring suit and has refused. *Ibid.* And even when this is the case, it is within the discretion of the court whether or not to allow this form of procedure. See Sharp *v.* San Paulo Brazilian Ry. Co., 8 Ch. 597; Yeatman *v.* Yeatman, 7 Ch. Div. 210; Meldrum *v.* Scorer, 56 L. T. 471.

A trustee is not estopped from bringing suit to recover property transferred by himself in breach of trust without consent of all the *cestuis*, Ludington *v.* Mercantile Bank, 92 N. Y. S. 454, 102 App. Div. 251; Robertson *v.* De Brulatour, 188 N. Y. 301; Clemens *v.* Heckscher, 185 Pa. St. 476; nor is a substituted trustee. Safe Deposit & Tr. Co. *v.* Cahn, 102 Md. 530; Leake *v.* Watson,

Pennsylvania, however, the action of ejectment is an equitable action, and the *cestui que trust* may maintain the suit if he is entitled to possession, or it may be maintained by the trustee.[1] In a few States there are statutes or codes which enact that parties beneficially interested in the subject-matter of the suit shall be made the parties' plaintiffs; but the right or duty of trustees, or persons holding the legal title in a fiduciary capacity, to sue is generally provided for.[2] Merely nominal trustees, as officers of a town or parish, cannot sue in their own name.[3] (a)

[1] School Dir. v. Dunkleberger, 6 Barr, 29; Presbyterian Cong. v. Johnston, 1 Watts & S. 56; Kennedy v. Fury, 1 Dall. 76; Hunt v. Crawford, 3 Pa. 426; Caldwell v. Lowden, 3 Brews. 63. [Chamberlain v. Maynes, 180 Pa. St. 39.]

[2] See Codes of New York and Ohio; McGill v. Doe, 9 Ind. 306. [See Cunningham v. Bank of Nampa, 13 Idaho, 167; Wright v. Conservative Inv. Co., 49 Or. 177; McDevitt v. Bryant, 104 Md 187; Zion Church v. Parker, 114 Iowa, 1; Pyle v. Henderson, 55 W. Va. 122; First Nat. Bank v. Hummel, 14 Colo. 259. As to whether or not the *cestuis* should be parties to suits by or against trustees, see *infra* § 873, note.]

[3] Regina v. Shee, 4 Q. B. 2; Manchester v. Manchester, 17 Q. B. 859; Queen v Commissioners, 15 Q. B. 1012; Connor v. New Albany, 1 Blackf. 88.

58 Conn. 332; First Nat. Bank v. Broadway Bank, 156 N. Y. 459, 467. And equity will take jurisdiction and give relief, although the trustee has an adequate remedy at law. Safe Dep. & Tr. Co. v. Cahn, 102 Md. 530.

The trustee is not estopped from setting up any defence which the *cestuis*, were they in person defending the action, might properly urge in their own behalf. Thus in defence to a foreclosure proceeding upon a mortgage given by himself, he is not estopped to set up that he had no power to mortgage. Wagnon v. Pease, 104 Ga. 417.

As to the duty of a trustee for the life beneficiary to protect the interests of the remainder-man in personalty, see Leake v. Watson, 58 Conn. 332.

(a) A trustee who owes his appointment to a court of another State than that in which he brings suit may nevertheless sue strangers to the trust, since he sues as legal owner, not in a representative capacity. Toronto Gen. Tr. Co. v. C. B. & Q. R. Co., 123 N. Y. 37; Pennington v. Smith, 69 Fed. 188; Iowa & Cal. Land Co. v. Hoag, 132 Cal. 627; Bradford v. King, 18 R. I. 743. But see Bangs v. Berg, 82 Iowa, 350; Hale v. Harris, 112 Iowa, 372.

§ 329. Whether the trustees are entitled to the possession, control, and management of real estate, as against the *cestui que trust*, depends upon the whole scope of the settlement, and the nature of the duties which the trustees are required to perform. A fund in trust for the sole use of a person, with power to dispose of the fund by will, does not give the *cestui* a right to recover possession of the fund from the trustee.[1] If the entire interest is vested in the trustees, and they are to manage the property, keep it insured, and pay taxes, premiums, annuities, and other charges out of the income, the court will imply that the trustees are to have the possession, and will not take it from them, unless there is some very clear intention expressed to control such directions.[2] (*a*) And the trustees may purchase whatever is necessary, and cultivate the land instead of renting it.[3] If the *cestui que trust*, or tenant for life, is a *female*, the court will continue the possession in the trustees for her protection in case of marriage.[4] So, if the trustees themselves have a beneficial interest, or a reversion or remainder after the death of the tenant for life, the court will continue the possession in them.[5] If, however, the plain intention of the settlement is that the *cestui que trust* is to have the possession, then all other

---

[1] Barkley *v.* Dosser, 15 Lea (Tenn.) 529.

[2] Tidd *v.* Lister, 3 Madd. 429; Naylor *v.* Arnitt, 1 R. & M. 501; Young *v.* Miles, 10 B. Mon. 290; Blake *v.* Bunbury, 1 Ves. Jr. 194, 514; 4 Bro. Ch. 21; Jenkins *v.* Milford, 1 J. & W. 629; Moseley *v.* Marshall, 22 N. Y. 200; Marshall *v.* Sladen, 4 De G. & Sm. 468; Matthews *v.* McPherson, 65 N. C. 189.

[3] Mayfield *v.* Kegour, 21 Md. 241.

[4] Ibid.; Weekham *v.* Berry, 55 Penn. St. 70.

[5] Ibid.

(*a*) Now, in England, the Settled Land Acts have granted such powers to and imposed such duties on tenants for life that, if the estate and trustees can be well protected by reasonable safeguards, an equitable tenant for life is to be let into possession and enabled personally to exercise these powers and discharge these duties when there is no urgent counter reason. See *In re* Wythes, [1893] 2 Ch. 369; *In re* Bagot, [1894] 1 Ch. 177; *In re* Newen, 2 id. 297; *In re* Bentley, 54 L. J. Ch. 782.

considerations must give way; as, if it is plain that the settlor intended the estate to be a place of residence for the *cestui que trust,* the intention must be carried out.[1] If the tenant for life takes a *legal* estate, subject to a charge, he will of course be entitled to the possession, so long as he discharges all incumbrances thus put upon the estate.[2] But if the tenant for life allows the annuities or other charges to fall in arrears, the trustees must take possession for the security of the annuitants, and must continue the possession until ample security is made for the future.[3] Security may be required in any case where the tenant for life is let into possession.[4]

§ 330. The trustee is entitled to the possession of all personal securities, such as bonds, notes, mortgages, and certificates of stocks, belonging to the trust estate; and he may maintain an action for their delivery, even against the *cestui que trust.*[5] All personal actions for injury to the personal property, or for its detention or conversion, such as trespass,[6] trover,[7] detinue,[8] or replevin,[9] must be brought in the name of the trustee, although

[1] Tidd *v.* Lister, 5 Madd. 432; Campbell *v.* Prestons, 22 Grat. 396.

[2] Denton *v.* Denton, 7 Beav. 388; Blake *v.* Bunbury, 1 Ves. Jr. 194; Tidd *v.* Lister, 5 Madd. 432.

[3] Ibid.

[4] Ibid.; Pugh *v.* Vaughn, 12 Beav. 517; Langston *v.* Ollivant, Coop. 33; Baylies *v.* Baylies, 1 Col. 137.

[5] Jones *v.* Jones, 3 Bro. Ch. 80; Poole *v.* Pass, 1 Beav. 600; Beach *v.* Beach, 14 Vt. 28; Gunn *v.* Barrow, 17 Ala. 743; White *v.* Albertson, 3 Dev. 241; Guphill *v.* Isbell, 8 Rich. L. 463; Presley *v.* Stribling, 24 Miss. 257; Pace *v.* Pierce, 49 Mo. 393; Ryan *v.* Bibb, 46 Ala. 343; Western R. R. Co. *v.* Nolan, 48 N. Y. 513.

[6] McRaeny *v.* Johnson, 2 Fla. 520.

[7] Hower *v.* Geesaman, 17 Serg. & R. 251; Poage *v.* Bell, 8 Leigh, 604; Coleson *v.* Blanton, 3 Hayw. 152; Guphill *v.* Isbell, 8 Rich. L. 463; Thompson *v.* Ford, 7 Ired. 418; Schley *v.* Lyons, 6 Ga. 530.

[8] Jones *v.* Strong, 6 Ired. 367; Murphy *v.* Moore, 2 Ired. Eq. 118; Chambers *v.* Mauldin, 4 Ala. 477; Parsons *v.* Boyd, 20 Ala. 112; Stoker *v.* Yelby, 11 Ala. 327; Baker *v.* Washington, 3 Stew. & P. 142; Newman *v.* Montgomery, 5 How. (Miss.) 742.

[9] Presley *v.* Stribling, 24 Miss. 527; Daniel *v.* Daniel, 6 B. Mon. 230.

the possession is in the *cestui que trust*,[1] (*a*) and although there may be a defect in the title of the trustee;[2] for the possession of the *cestui que trust* is the possession of the trustee, and in law he is not allowed to dispute the title or possession of his trustee.[3] The action of assumpsit is an equitable action, and, generally, if a promise is made to one for the benefit of another, the person for whose benefit the promise is made may bring the action; but if a promise is made to a trustee for the benefit of the *cestui que trust*, the trustee alone can sue.[4] So only those parties can sue on a contract with whom it is made, unless it is negotiable paper; therefore, substituted trustees cannot sue upon a contract made with their predecessors in the trust, but the suit must be in the names of the parties with whom it was made, for the benefit of the estate.[5] (*b*)   Generally, all notices and tenders [6] must be made to the trustees; and they must use all due diligence in prosecuting suits in favor of the estate and of the *cestui que trust*, and they must take the proper care in defending such suits; and if appeals are taken from decrees or judgments in favor of the estate, or of the *cestui que trust*, they must duly support the rights of the *cestui que trust* in whatever court the case may be carried.[7]   If the *cestui que trust* brings an action in the name of the trustee, the trustee may insist upon indemnity

[1] Jones *v.* Cole, 2 Bail. 330; Wynn *v.* Lee, 5 Ga. 236.

[2] Rogers *v.* White, 1 Sneed, 69.

[3] White *v.* Albertson, 3 Dev. 241.   [Barker *v.* Furlong, [1891] 2 Ch. 172.]

[4] Treat *v.* Stanton, 14 Conn. 445; Porter *v.* Raymond, 53 N. H. 519. [See 1 Ames on Trusts, (2d ed.) 258.]

[5] Binney *v.* Plumly, 5 Vt. 500; Ingersoll *v.* Cooper, 5 Blackf. 420; Davant *v.* Guerard, 1 Spear, 242; Wake *v.* Tinkler, 16 East, 36.

[6] Cahoon *v.* Hollenback, 16 Serg. & R. 425; Henry *v.* Morgan, 2 Binn. 497.

[7] Wood *v.* Burnham, 6 Paige, 513.

(*a*) But a *cestui* who has the right of possession may sue third persons for damages due to disturbance of his possession. Cape *v.* Plymouth Church, 117 Wis. 150; Thomas Machine Co. *v.* Voelker, 23 R. I. 441.

(*b*) The substituted trustee has of course all the rights of an assignee of a chose in action, and as such has by statute in some States been given the right to sue in his own name. See Mass. R. L. [1902] c. 173, § 4.

against the costs.[1] If the trustee collusively releases such suit
without the consent of the party beneficially interested, the
court will set aside the release.[2] So, if a trustee discharges a
debt or mortgage without payment, the court would set aside
the discharge;[3] (a) and if a trustee refuses to bring a suit, or to
allow his name to be used, equity will compel him to take such
steps as the interest of the estate and of the *cestui que trust*
requires.[4] In all such suits in the name of the trustee, a debt
due from the *cestui que trust* cannot be set off.[5] If a trustee sue

[1] Ins. Co. *v.* Smith, 11 Penn. St. 120; Annesley *v.* Simeon, 4 Madd.
390; Roden *v.* Murphy, 10 Ala. 804. [Falmouth Bank *v.* Cape Cod Canal
Co., 166 Mass. 550, 567.]

[2] Anon. Salk. 260; Bauerman *v.* Radenius, 7 T. R. 670; Legh *v.* Legh, 1
B. & P. 447; Payne *v.* Rogers, Doug. 407; Manning *v.* Cox, 7 Moore, 617;
Hickey *v.* Burt, 7 Taunt. 48; Barker *v.* Richardson, 1 Y. & J. 362; Roden
v. Murphy, 10 Ala. 804; Greene *v.* Beatty, Coxe, 142; Kirkpatrick *v.* Mc-
Donald, 11 Penn. St. 387.

[3] Woolf *v.* Bate, 9 B. Mon. 210.

[4] Blin *v.* Pierce, 20 Vt. 25; Chisholm *v.* Newton, 1 Ala. 371; Robinson
v. Mauldin, 11 Ala. 978; Welch *v.* Mandeville, 1 Wheat. 233; Parker *v.*
Kelly, 10 Sm. & M. 184; McCullum *v.* Coxe, 1 Dall. 139. [Sharpe *v.* San
Paulo Brazilian Ry. Co., 8 Ch. 597; Yeatman *v.* Yeatman, 7 Ch. Div. 210;
Meldrum *v.* Scorer, 56 L. T. 741.]

[5] Wells *v.* Chapman, 4 Sandf. Ch. 312; Campbell *v.* Hamilton, 4 Wash.
C. C. 93; Woolf *v.* Bates, 9 B. Mon. 211; Beale *v.* Coon, 2 Watts, 183;

(a) So too of a judgment binding
the trust property, if the judgment
was obtained by collusion between
the trustee and the creditor. Snelling *v.* Am., etc., Mort. Co., 107 Ga.
852. But the mere fact that the
trustee has allowed the judgment to
be entered by default is not sufficient to have it set aside in the absence of other evidence of collusion.
Sanders *v.* Houston Guano Co., 107
Ga. 49.

It has been held that the trial
judge may, of his own motion, order
a trustee, who has been joined as
defendant, to answer in his capacity

of trustee to protect the rights of the
cestui. Kaylor *v.* Hiller, 72 S. C. 433.

In an Alabama case where there
was a proceeding at law for the taking, by right of eminent domain, of
land held in trust for a railroad, the
cestui, whose defence to the taking
was that it had already devoted the
land to a public purpose, was allowed to present this defence by a
bill in equity for an injunction
against the suit at law which had
been brought against the trustee.
Birmingham, etc., Co. *v.* Louisville,
etc., R. Co., 152 Ala. 422.

for matters pertaining to the trust estate, a private debt due from the trustee cannot be set off.[1] [Under the Massachusetts statute] a trustee cannot set off against the assignee of the *cestui* a debt for money lent by him to the *cestui* before his appointment as trustee.[2]

§ 331. The trustee, being liable for a breach of the trust, if he permits any misapplication of the funds should of course have the possession and control of all personal property. So all the duties and privileges which attach to such property pertain to him. If the property consists of stocks in corporations, he may attend corporate meetings, vote, and hold office by virtue of such stock.[3] So the trustee is rated or assessed for taxes, and must see that the taxes upon the trust property are paid. The statutes of the various States determine the localities where such property shall be assessed: real estate is generally assessed in the parish, town, or county where it is situated; and personal property, either in the place of the domicil of the trustee or of the *cestui que trust*, as the statutes of a State may direct. In the absence of a statute, the law would look upon the trustee as the owner, and assess the property at his domicil.[4] (a)

§ 332. The trustee must prove a debt against a bankrupt debtor of the estate, as he is the person to receive the divi-

Tucker *v.* Tucker, 4 B. & Ad. 745; Porter *v.* Morris, 2 Harr. 509. [1 Ames on Trusts (2d ed.), 270.]

[1] Page *v.* Stephens, 23 Mich. 357. [See Ames' Cases on Trusts (2d ed.), 270.]

[2] Abbott *v.* Foote, 146 Mass. 333. [R. L. (1902) c. 174, § 6.]

[3] Matter of Barker, 6 Wend. 509; *Re* Phœnix Life Assur. Co., 2 John. & H. 279.

[4] Latrobe *v.* Baltimore, 19 Md. 13; Green *v.* Mumford, 4 R. I. 313; and see the statutes of the various States.

(a) If there are two or more trustees residing in different places the tax is divided, the trustees being treated as equal owners. Trustees *v.* Augusta, 90 Ga. 634, 20 L. R. A. 151 and note. But the matter of taxation of trust property has been largely dealt with by statute. See Mass. R. L. (1902), c. 12, § 23, cl. 5.

dend;[1] but in special cases the concurrence of the *cestui que trust* may be required, as where he may have a right to receive the payment.[2]

§ 333. In England, trustees had at common law the right to vote for local officers and for members of parliament, by virtue of the qualification conferred upon them by the trust property, if it was sufficient in amount. Statutes have, however, changed the common law, and given the right in most cases to the *cestui que trust*. In the United States, property qualifications of voters are generally abrogated.[3]

§ 334. Trustees of real or personal estate may, *at law*, sell, convey, assign, or incumber the same, as if they were the beneficial owners,[4] and each of several trustees may exercise all his rights of ownership. If the trustees are joint-tenants, each may receive the rents,[5] and each may sever the joint-tenancy by a conveyance of his share,[6] and each may collect the dividends on stocks, and on the death of one, the survivor may sell the whole estate.[7] The general power of a trustee to sell and convey the estate is co-extensive with his ownership of the legal title; and this general power over the legal title is entirely distinct from the execution of a special power given in respect to the sale of an estate. Though the trustee may thus sell, even in breach of the trust, a conveyance without consideration will not injure the *cestui que trust;* as the grantee, who is a volunteer, will hold upon the same trusts as the trustee held, and if the purchaser for a valuable consideration have notice of the trust

---

[1] *Ex parte* Green, 2 Dea. & Ch. 116.

[2] *Ex parte* Dubois, 1 Cox, 310; *Ex parte* Butler, Buck, 426; *Ex parte* Gray, 4 Dea. & Ch. 778; *Ex parte* Dickenson, 2 Dea. & Ch. 520.

[3] See 5 Ired. Eq. Appendix; 4 Kent, Com. 195.

[4] Shortz *v.* Unangst, 3 Watts & S. 55; Canoy *v.* Troutman, 7 Ired. 155. [Marx *v.* Clisby, 130 Ala. 502.]

[5] Townley *v.* Sherborne, Bridg. 35.

[6] Boursot *v.* Savage, L. R. 2 Eq. 134.

[7] Saunders *v.* Schmaelzle, 49 Cal. 59.

he will still hold the estate upon trust.[1] In New York, however,
a statute has converted the trustee's ownership of the legal title
into a power, or power in trust;[2] and where a trust is expressly
created by a written instrument, every sale in breach or contravention of the trust is declared to be absolutely void, even if the
sale is under the sanction of a court.[3] (a)   Whether a trustee
intends to convey an estate is frequently a question made upon
conveyances, and it has been determined that a general assignment of all the trustee's estates, for the benefit of his creditors,
does not pass estates held by him in trust.[4]

§ 335. As among the incidents of the trustee's legal title in
the trust estate is his power to sell it, so he may devise it by his
last will and testament. The principal question that here arises
is, whether the words of the will of a trustee embrace estates
held by him in trust, for a trust estate will not in all cases pass
by the same words as would pass the beneficial ownership; for
wherever an estate passes, not by operation of law, but by the
intention of any one, it is necessary to find the intention from
the instrument under the circumstances in which it is made;
and an intention to devise a trust estate is not so readily inferred as an intention to devise a beneficial estate. (b)   If the

[1] See ante, § 321.

[2] Anderson v. Mather, 44 N. Y. 249; New York, &c., v. Stillman, 30
N. Y. 174; Fitzgerald v. Topping, 48 N. Y. 441; Fellows v. Heermans, 4
Lans. 230; Martin v. Smith, 56 Barb. 600; Critton v. Fairchild, 41 N. Y.
289. The law is the same in Michigan. Palmer v. Wilkins, 24 Mich. 328.
See Jones v. Shaddock, 41 Ala. 262; 1 Rev. Stat. 330, § 65; Briggs v. Palmer,
20 Barb. 392; Briggs v. Davis, 20 N. Y. 15; 21 N. Y. 574. [IV Consol.
Laws (1909), p. 3392, § 105.]

[3] Cruger v. Jones, 18 Barb. 468; Lahens v. Dupasseur, 56 Barb. 256.

[4] Ludwig v. Highley, 5 Barr, 132; Abbott, Pet'r, 55 Maine, 480.

(a) Several other States have
similar statutes. Mich. Comp. Laws
(1897), § 8849; Minn. Rev. Laws
(1905), § 3259; Mont. Civ. Code
(1907), § 4549; No. Dak. Civ. Code,
(1905), § 4836; So. Dak. Civ. Code
(1908), § 317; Wis. Stat. (1898),
§ 2091; Kansas Gen. Stat. (1909),
§ 9698; Ind. Burns' Stat. (1908),
§ 4016.

(b) This question has but little
practical importance in the United
States. See infra, § 341.

trust is only a personal one, the donor using no words requiring continuance of the trust beyond the life of the immediate trustee, the estate cannot be devised by the trustee, but ceases at his death.[1]

§ 336. An assignment in general words by a trustee of all his estate for his creditors will not pass a trust estate, for the reason that the court will not presume that the trustee intended to commit a breach of trust;[2] for a similar reason it has at times been said that a devise of all a trustee's estates in general words would not operate upon estates that he held in trust, unless there appeared a positive intention that they should so pass.[3] The question was finally considered by Lord Eldon; and after a careful examination, the rule was declared to be, that "where the will contained words·large enough, and there was no expression authorizing a narrower construction, nor any such disposition of the estate as it was unlikely a testator would make of property not his own, in such case the trust property would pass."[4] Mr. Hill states the rule, "that a general devise of real estate will pass estates vested in the testator as trustee or mortgagee, unless a contrary intention can be collected from the expressions of the will, or from the purposes or limitations to which the devised lands are subjected."[5] This general rule is acted upon in the United States.[6]

---

[1] Hinckley v. Hinckley, 79 Maine, 320.

[2] Cook v. Tullis, 18 Wall. 332; Kelly v. Scott, 49 N. Y. 595; In re McKay, 1 Lowell, 345; Chase v. Chapin, 130 Mass. 128. [1 Ames' Cases on Trusts, (2d ed.) 316.]

[3] Casborne v. Scarfe, 1 Atk. 605; Strode v. Russell, 2 Vern. 625; Leeds v. Munday, 3 Ves. 348; Ex parte Sergison, 4 Ves. 147; Ex parte Bowes, cited note, 1 Atk. 605; Pickering v. Vowles, 1 Bro. Ch. 198; Att. Gen. v. Buller, 5 Ves. 340.

[4] Braybrooke v. Inskip, 8 Ves. 436; Roe v. Reade, 8 T. R. 118; Ex parte Morgan, 10 Ves. 101; Langford v. Auger, 4 Hare, 313; Linsell v. Thacher, 12 Sim. 178; Ex parte Shaw, 8 Sim. 159; Hawkins v. Obeen, 2 Ves. 559.

[5] Hill on Trustees, 283.

[6] Taylor v. Benham, 5 How. 270; Heath v. Knapp, 4 Barr, 228; Jackson v. Delancy, 13 Johns. 537; Hughes v. Caldwell, 11 Leigh, 342; Merritt v. Farmers' Ins. Co., 2 Edw. Ch. 547; Ballard v. Carter, 5 Pick. 112 ; Asay

§ 337. Notwithstanding the rule, that a trust estate will pass
by general words in a devise, unless there is something in the
will to show a contrary intention, there has continued to be a
conflict of opinion upon the propriety of the rule, and more
conflict upon its application. But a charge of debts, legacies,
and annuities upon the estate devised, or a power given to sell
it, is an indication that the testator did not intend that the
trust estate should pass under the words of his devise, for the
reason that he could not have intended that his devisee should
do that with the estate which would be a breach of trust.[1] So,
if there is a limitation of the estate in strict settlement, with a
great number of complicated conditions, contingencies, remainders, and limitations, it will not be presumed that a trustee intended to devise a dry trust in a legal title upon such
terms, and the estate will not pass under general words;[2] so if
the devise is to A. in tail with remainder over in strict settlement;[3] so a devise to a testator's nephews and neices in equal
shares as tenants in common is to a class not ascertained at the
date of the will, and will not by general words pass a trust
estate.[4] So a devise to a woman for her separate use, imports a
beneficial use, and not a dry legal estate, and the trust estate
would not pass to her under general words.[5] But a devise to a
woman, her heirs and assigns, to her and their own sole and
absolute use, passes the estate for the reason that there is noth-

v. Hoover, 5 Barr, 35; Richardson v. Woodbury, 43 Me. 206; Drane v.
Gunter, 19 Ala. 731.   [See 1 Ames' Cases on Trusts, (2d ed.) 316.]

[1] Rackham v. Siddall, 16 Sim. 297; 1 Mac. & G. 607; Hope v. Liddell,
21 Beav. 183; Life Asso. of Scotland v. Siddall, 3 De G., F. & J. 58; Wall
v. Bright, 1 Q. & W. 494; Leeds v. Munday, 3 Ves. 348; Ex parte Marshall,
9 Sim. 555; Re Morley's Trusts, 10 Hare, 293; Sylvester v. Jarman, 10 Price,
78; Roe v. Reade, 8 T. R. 118; Att. Gen. v. Buller, 5 Ves. 339; Ex parte
Morgan, 10 Ves. 101; Ex parte Brettell, 6 Ves. 577; Merritt v. Farmers'
Ins. Co., 2 Edw. Ch. 547.

[2] Braybrooke v. Inskip, 8 Ves. 434.

[3] Thompson v. Grant, 4 Madd. 438; Ex parte Bowes, cited 1 Atk. 603;
Galliers v. Moss, 9 B. & Cr. 267; Re Horsfall, 1 McClel. & Y. 292.

[4] Re Finney's Est., 3 Gif. 465.

[5] Lindsell v. Thacher, 12 Sim. 178; the case istelf, not the marginal
note.

ing inconsistent with their holding the absolute use in trust;[1] and a devise to A. and B. to be equally divided between them, as tenants in common, and their respective heirs, will pass the estate.[2] A devise of all my estates will pass trust property.[3] So a devise to A., his heirs and assigns, to and for his and their own use and benefit;[4] and a devise to A. and her heirs, to be disposed of, by her will or otherwise, as she shall think fit,[5] will pass trust property under general words, for there is no necessary breach of the trust.

338. The interest of a *mortgagee in fee* in the mortgaged land stands upon a somewhat different ground. The mortgagee has a debt due him which is the principal thing, and the mortgage is a beneficial interest in the land as security for the debt. This interest generally goes with the debt. And mortgage estates will pass by a general devise, notwithstanding a charge of debts and legacies, if the intent appears, to pass them as securities for money.[6] But if there are special trusts for sale, or other special charges annexed to the devise, inconsistent with the idea of holding the estate as security for money, it would not pass under a general devise.[7]

[1] Lewis v. Mathews, L. R. 2 Eq. 177.

[2] *Ex parte* Whiteacre, cited Lewin on Trusts, 186; 1 Saund. Uses & Tr. 359; Re Morley's Trusts, 10 Hare, 293.

[3] Braybrooke v. Inskip, 8 Ves. 425; Bangs v. Smith, 98 Mass. 273; Amory v. Meredith, 7 Allen, 397; Willard v. Ware, 10 Allen, 263; Stone v. Hackett, 12 Gray, 237.

[4] *Ex parte* Shaw, 8 Sim. 159; Bainbridge v. Ashburton, 2 Y. & C. 347; Sharpe v. Sharpe, 12 Jur. 598; *Ex parte* Brettell, 6 Ves. 577; Heath v. Knapp, 4 Barr, 228; Abbott, Petitioner, 55 Maine, 580.

[5] Ibid.

[6] *Ex parte* Barber, 5 Sim. 451; Doe v. Benett, 6 Exch. 892; Re Cantley, 17 Jur. 124; King's Mort., 5 De G. & Sm. 644; Knight v. Robinson, 2 K. & J. 503; Rippen v. Priest, 13 C. B. (N. S.) 508; Re Arrowsmith, 4 Jur. (N. S.) 1123; Mather v. Thomas, 6 Sim. 119; overruling Galliers v. Moss, 9 B. & C. 267; Sylvester v. Jarman, 10 Price, 78, and Re Cantley, 17 Jur. 124; Ballard v. Carter, 5 Pick. 112; Asay v. Hoover, 5 Barr, 35; Richardson v. Woodbury, 43 Maine, 206; Field's Mort., 9 Hare, 414, overruling Benvoize v. Cooper, 10 Price, 78, and in opposition to Doe v. Lightfoot, 8 M. & W. 553.   [7] Re Cantley, 17 Jur. 123.

§ 339. In allowing a trust estate to pass under general words of a devise, it is assumed that the testator does not intend by his devise to commit a breach of the trust. It is simply a question, whether the testator has devised, or can or should devise, a trust estate, or whether he should allow it to descend to his heir or legal representatives. It was said in Cook v. Crawford, that it was not lawful for the trustee to dispose of the estate, but that he ought to permit it to descend; that a devise did not differ from a deed *inter vivos;* and that it was only a *post mortem* conveyance.[1] On the other hand, it is said that there is a wide distinction between a conveyance and a devise. That during the trustee's lifetime there was a personal trust and confidence in his discretion, which he could not delegate; that the settlor could have reposed no confidence in the heir, for he could not know beforehand who the heir would be; that if the estate was allowed to descend, it might become vested in married women, infants, bankrupts, or persons out of the jurisdiction of the court; and that therefore it could not be a breach of trust for a trustee to devise the estate by will to persons capable of executing it, or of transferring it to other trustees.[2] Mr. Lewin concludes from these observations, that whether the devise of the trust estate is proper or not depends upon the circumstances of each case. If the heir is a fit person to execute the trust, the testator ought not to intercept the descent and pass the legal estate to another, and especially not to an unfit person. In such case the estate of the testator might be liable for the costs of restoring the trust estate to its proper channel or to proper trustees. If, however, the heir is an unfit person, as an infant, bankrupt, insolvent, lunatic, married woman, or out of the jurisdiction, it may be proper to devise the estate.[3] And this seems to be the result of the authorities.[4]

---

[1] Cook v. Crawford, 13 Sim. 98; and see Beasley v. Wilkinson, 13 Jur. 649.

[2] Titley v. Wolstenholme, 7 Beav. 435; Macdonald v. Walker, 14 Beav. 556; Wilson v. Bennett, 5 De G. & Sm. 479.

[3] Lewin on Trusts, 187, 188.

[4] Beasley v. Wilkinson, 13 Jur. 649. [See *infra,* § 341.]

§ 340. It does not follow that the devisee can execute the trust from the fact that the legal title is devised to him, nor does it follow that the heir can execute the trust from the fact that the legal title descends to him. How far either can execute the trust depends upon the intention of the settlor, to be gathered from the terms of the instrument.[1] Thus, if an estate is so vested in A. that A. alone shall *personally* execute the trust, neither the heir nor the devisee of A. could execute it, although holding the legal title.[2] As if an estate is vested in A. and his heirs upon a trust to sell, and A. devises the estate, neither the heir nor the devisee can sell: for the heir has nothing in the estate to sell, it having gone to the devisee; and the devisee has no power, he not being mentioned in the original settlement.[3] So, where property was vested in two trustees, their executors and administrators in trust, and the surviving trustee devised the property to A. and B., and appointed A., B., and C. executors, the court refused to hand over the property to A. and B., for the reason that devisees were not named as parties who could execute the trust; and the court refused to hand it over to the executors, for the reason that the legal title was given away from them; new trustees were therefore appointed to receive the property and execute the trust.[4] But where the word "assigns" is part of the limitation of the estate to trustees, as where an estate is vested in A., his heirs, executors, administrators, and *assigns* in trust, and A. devises the estate, the devisee may execute the trust, for the reason that he comes within the limitation of the persons who may take the trust property and execute the trust.[5] This principle has been

[1] Abbott, Pet'r, 55 Maine, 580.

[2] Mortimer v. Ireland, 6 Hare, 196; 11 Jur. 721; Ockleston v. Heap, 1 De G. & Sm. 640.

[3] Mortimer v. Ireland, 6 Hare, 196; 11 Jur. 721; Ockleston v. Heap, 1 De G. & Sm. 640; Cook v. Crawford, 13 Sim. 91; Stevens v. Austen, 7 Jur. (N. S.) 873; Wilson v. Bennett, 5 De G. & Sm. 475. [But see Osborne v. Rowlett, 13 Ch. Div. 774; *In re* Ingleby and Ins. Co., 13 L. R. Ir. 326.]

[4] *Re* Burtt's Est., 1 Dr. 319; Macdonald v. Walker, 14 Beav. 556.

[5] Titley v. Wolstenholme, 7 Beav. 425; Saloway v. Strawbridge, 1 K. & J. 371; 7 De G., M. & G. 594.

doubted and criticised,[1] but it seems to be acted upon in the English courts.[2]

§ 341. In New York, Michigan, Wisconsin, [Indiana, Minnesota, and Kansas] trust property, upon the death of the surviving trustee, does not descend to the heir, nor can it be devised, but it vests in the court, and will be administered by the court by the appointment of new trustees to execute the trust.[3] (a)   In the other States, the trust estate descends to the heir, or vests in the devisee, as the legal title must go somewhere in the absence of a statute, upon the death of the surviving trustee.[4] Courts in the United States do not have occasion often to consider the question, whether the heir or devisee can execute the trust, as new trustees can be appointed in any case at the desire of the parties, and, in many States, the trust property may be vested in the new trustees by an order of the court. In most

[1] Ockleston v. Heap, 1 De G. & Sm. 642.

[2] Mortimer v. Ireland, 6 Hare, 196; 11 Jur. 721; Ashton v. Wood, 3 Sm. & Gif. 436; Hall v. May, 3 K. & J. 585; Lane v. Debenham, 11 Hare, 188.

[3] Clark v. Crego, 47 Barb. 597; Hawley v. Ross, 7 Paige, 103; McCosker v. Brady, 1 Barb. Ch. 329; People v. Morton, 5 Seld. 176; McDougald v. Cary, 38 Ala. 320; Hook v. Dyer, 47 Mo. 241. This rule is confined to real property. Trusts in personal property are governed by the ordinary rules that apply to them in other States. Bucklin v. Bucklin, 1 N. Y. Dec. 242.

[4] Trusts of real estate, on the death of the trustee, vest in the heir, trusts of personalty in the executor or administrator. Schenck v. Schenck, 16 N. J. Eq. 174. [Lawrence v. Lawrence, 181 Ill. 248; Ewing v. Shannahan, 113 Mo. 188, 201; State v. Miss. Valley Trust Co., 209 Mo. 472; Hitch v. Stonebraker, 125 Mo. 128; Kirkman v. Wadsworth, 137 N. C. 453; Woodruff v. Woodruff, 44 N. J. Eq. 349; Reeves v. Tappan, 21 S. C. 1; Fisher v. Dickenson, 84 Va. 318; St. Stephen's Church v. Pierce, 8 Del. Ch. 179. See Ames' Cases on Trusts (2d ed.), 345, 346 and notes.]

(a) IV N. Y. Consol. Laws (1909), p. 2846, § 20, p. 3395, § 111; Mich. Comp. Laws (1897), § 8852; Wis. Stat. (1898), § 2094; Burns' Ind. Stat. (1908), § 4021; Minn. Rev. Laws (1905), § 3262; Kan. Gen. Stat. (1909), § 9703; see Dyer v. Leach, 91 Cal. 191. In Alabama, the title does not descend but rests in abeyance until the appointment of a new trustee. Ala. Civ. Code (1907), § 3415; Lecroix v. Malone, 157 Ala. 434.

cases, it would simply be a question whether the words of the will were comprehensive enough to pass the trust estate, or whether it had descended to the heir; and this question would be important only in determining who should make a conveyance of the trust property to the new trustees, if it became necessary that a conveyance should be made. (a)

§ 342. If an owner of real estate contracts to sell it, he becomes a trustee of the legal title for the vendee; and if he dies before conveying the legal title, it will descend to his heir or heirs, as the legal title must vest somewhere; and so he may devise it; and the heir, in case it descends, and the devisee, in case it is devised, may be called upon to convey it to the vendee.[1] In Massachusetts, there is a statute authorizing the vendor's executor or administrator to convey such estate, under the direction of the court of probate.[2]

§ 343. Trust property is generally limited to trustees, as joint-tenants; and if by the terms of the gift it is doubtful, whether the trustees take as joint-tenants, or tenants in common, courts will construe a joint-tenancy if possible, on account of the inconvenience of trustees holding as tenants in common; and, where statutes have abolished joint-tenancy, an exception is generally made in the case of trustees. And courts will not allow a process for the partition of a trust estate.[3] Therefore, upon the death of one of the original trustees, the whole estate, whether real or personal, devolves upon the survivors, and so on to the last survivor; and upon the death of the last survivor, if he has made no disposition of the estate by will or otherwise, it devolves upon his heirs if real estate, and upon

[1] Wall v. Bright, 1 J. & W. 494; Read v. Read, 8 T. R. 118.

[2] Gen. Stat. c. 117; §§ 5 and 6; Reed v. Whitney, 7 Gray, 533. [Rev. Laws (1902), c. 148, § 1.]

[3] Baldwin v. Humphrey, 44 N. Y. 609; Saunders v. Schmaelzle, 49 Cal. 59.

(a) See *supra*, § 269, and notes.

his executors or administrators if it is personal estate.[1] The title in the surviving trustee is complete, and no breaches of trust after the death of his cotrustees can be charged upon their estate;[2] nor can the representatives of his cotrustees interfere with his management of the trust estate, even if he is insolvent or unfit for the trust.[3] The *cestui que trust* alone can interfere or apply to the court for redress or relief. So all rights of action are in the surviving trustee, and he may sue in his own name or as survivor, according as the cause of an action accrued before or after the death of his cotrustees;[4] and, in case of his death, his executor or administrator may continue the action.[5] The rule is that actions must be brought in the names of the parties to the contract.[6]

§ 344. So absolute is the rule that the heir or administrator takes the trust property upon the death of the last surviving trustee, that a husband, as administrator of his wife, takes the personal property that she held in trust, but he must hold it upon the original trust.[7] In England, the heir in case of real estate in trust, or the executor in case of personal, is competent to administer and execute the trusts, but they cannot execute

[1] Whiting *v.* Whiting, 4 Gray, 236; Moses *v.* Murgatroyd, 1 Johns. Ch. 119; De Peyster *v.* Ferrars, 11 Paige, 13; Shook *v.* Shook, 19 Barb. 653; Shortz *v.* Unangst, 3 W. & S. 45; Gray *v.* Lynch, 8 Gill, 404; Mauldin *v.* Armstead, 14 Ala. 702; Powell *v.* Knox, 16 Ala. 364; Richeson *v.* Ryan, 15 Ill. 13; Stewart *v.* Pettus, 10 Mo. 755; Jenks *v.* Backhouse, 1 Binn. 91; King *v.* Leach, 2 Hare, 59; Watkins *v.* Specht, 7 Coldw. 585; Webster *v.* Vanderventer, 6 Gray, 429. [See 1 Ames on Trusts(2d ed.), 346.   Except as otherwise provided by statute.]

[2] See *post*, § 426. [*Re* Palk, 41 W. R. 28; Head *v.* Gould, [1898] 2 Ch. 250.]

[3] Shook *v.* Shook, 19 Barb. 653.

[4] Richeson *v.* Ryan, 15 Ill. 13; Wheatley *v.* Boyd, 7 Exch. 20. [Maffet *v.* Or. & C. R. Co., 46 Or. 443.]

[5] Nichols *v.* Campbell, 10 Grat. 561; Powell *v.* Knox, 16 Ala. 364; Mauldin *v.* Armstead, 14 Ala. 702.

[6] Robins *v.* Deshon, 19 Ind. 204; King *v.* Lawrence, 14 Wis. 238; Farrell *v.* Ladd, 10 Allen, 127; Childs *v.* Jordan, 106 Mass. 323.

[7] *Ante*, § 264; Kuster *v.* Howe, 3 Ind. 268.

discretionary trusts confided *personally* to the original trustee, unless the power and confidence are also confided in them by the instrument.[1] In the United States, (a) the heirs or executors will take the trust property, and they must settle the accounts of the testator in relation to the trust. They must also see that the property is protected and preserved, but they are not under any obligation to execute the trust. They may decline the office, and generally the court will appoint new trustees to succeed to the original trustees. If the heirs or executors continue to act as trustees, they will be liable for no past breaches of trust, but only for breaches that occur under their own management.[2]

§ 345. It has been before stated that a general assignment for creditors does not pass a trust estate. In such case it requires special words to vest the estate in an assignee. So an assignment in bankruptcy of all the trustee's property does not pass estates which the bankrupt holds in trust.[3] If the bankrupt by a breach of trust has converted the trust estate into other property, the *cestui que trust* may follow it into the hands of the assignee, so far as he can identify the particular property obtained by breach of the trust.[4] But if the trust property has become so amalgamated with the general mass of the bankrupt's estate that it cannot be traced or identified, the *cestui que trust* must prove his claim.[5] If an assignee should get possession of

[1] *Ante,* § 264; Mansell *v.* Mansell, Wilm. 36; Cook *v.* Crawford, 13 Sim. 91; Hall *v.* Dewes, Jac. 189; Peyton *v.* Bury, 2 P. Wms. 626; Bradford *v.* Belfield, 2 Sim. 264; Cole *v.* Wade, 16 Ves. 45; Sharp *v.* Sharp, 2 B. & A. 405. See Townsend *v.* Wilson, 1 B. & A. 608.

[2] Baird's App., 3 W. & S. 459; Schenck *v.* Schenck, 16 N. J. Eq. 174; Hill *v.* State, 2 Ark. 604.

[3] *Ante,* § 336; Scott *v.* Surman, Willes, 402. [Lowell on Bankruptcy, § 368; 1 Ames' Cases on Trusts (2d ed.), p. 392.]

[4] Taylor *v.* Plumer, 3 M. & S. 562; *Ex parte* Sayers, 5 Ves. 169. [See *infra,* § 828 and note.]

[5] *Ex parte* Dumas, 1 Atk. 232; Ryall *v.* Rolle, id. 172; Scott *v.* Surman, Willes, 403.

(a) See *supra,* § 269, note.

the trust estate, and refuse to restore it, the trustee, though a bankrupt, may maintain a suit for its restoration, or the *cestui que trust* may have a bill for the appointment of new trustees, and the conveyance of the property to them.[1]

§ 346. It is now a universal rule that all those who take under the trustee, except purchasers for a valuable consideration without notice, take subject to the trust, and they must either execute the trust themselves, or convey the property to new trustees appointed by the court. Thus the heir, executor, administrator, devisee, and the assignee by deed or in bankruptcy, are bound by the trust; so are those who take dower or curtesy in the trust estate, or a creditor who levies an execution upon it. If the trust estate is forfeited to the crown or the State, it is still subject to the trust; so if it escheats upon the failure of heirs. But a disseizor is not an *assignee* of the trustee, he holds a wrongful title of his own, adversely to the trust. The *cestui que trust* has no remedy in such case, except to procure the trustee to bring an action upon his legal title to recover the possession. The *cestui que trust* could not maintain a suit in equity to compel the disseizor to hold upon the same trusts as the trustee; for there is no privity between the disseizor and disseizee.[2] The only remedy of the *cestui que trust* is against the trustee; and if he refuses to bring an action to recover the estate, he may be removed and a new trustee appointed. (a)

§ 347. Where the legal and equitable estate in the same land becomes vested in the same person, the equitable will merge in the legal estate; for a man cannot be a trustee for himself, nor

---

[1] Winch *v.* Keely, 1 T. R. 619; Carpenter *v.* Marnell, 3 B. & P. 40.

[2] Finch's Case, 4 Inst. 85; Gilbert on Uses by Sugd. 249; Reynolds *v.* Jones, 2 Sim. & S. 206; Turner *v.* Buck, 22 Vin. Ab. 21; Doe *v.* Price, 16 M. & W. 603. But the *cestui que trust* is the beneficial owner, and the court will protect him in an entry and occupation against a stranger. Oatman *v.* Barney, 46 Vt. 594. [See Ames on Trusts (2d ed.), 373.]

(a) See *supra*, § 328 and notes.

hold the fee, which embraces the whole estate, and at the same time hold the several parts separated from the whole.[1] (a) But in order that this may be true, the two estates must be commensurate with each other; or the legal estate must be more extensive or comprehensive than the equitable. The equitable fee cannot merge in a partial or particular legal estate.[2]

[1] Wade v. Paget, 1 Bro. Ch. 363; Selby v. Alston, 3 Ves. 339; Philips v. Brydges, id. 126; Goodright v. Wells, Doug. 771; Finch's Case, 4 Inst. 85; Harmood v. Oglander, 8 Ves. 127; Creagh v. Blood, 3 Jones & L. 133; James v. Morey, 2 Cow. 246; Mason v. Mason, 2 Sandf. Ch. 433; James v. Johnson, 6 Johns. Ch. 417; Cooper v. Cooper, 1 Halst. Ch. 9; Healy v. Alston, 25 Miss. 190; Brown v. Bontee, 10 Sm. & M. 268; Lewis v. Starke, id. 128; Nicholson v. Halsey, 1 Johns. Ch. 422; Butler v. Godley, 1 Dev. 94; Hopkinson v. Dumas, 42 N. H. 306; Gardner v. Astor, 3 Johns. Ch. 53; Downes v. Grazebrook, 3 Mer. 208; Ayliff v. Murray, 2 Atk. 59; Wills v. Cooper, 1 Dutch. (N. J.) 137; Habergham v. Vincent, 2 Ves. Jr. 204. [In re Hitchins, 80 N. Y. S. 1125; Greene v. Greene, 125 N. Y. 506; Tuck v. Knapp, 85 N. Y. S. 1001; Tilton v. Davidson, 98 Me. 55; Robb v. Washington & Jefferson College, 93 N. Y. S. 92, 103 App. Div. 327; Weeks v. Frankel, 197 N. Y. 304; Clarke v. Sisters, 82 Neb. 85.]

[2] Selby v. Alston, 3 Ves. 339; Hunt v. Hunt, 14 Pick. 374; Donalds v.

(a) The fact that one of the beneficiaries becomes one of the trustees or sole trustee does not bring about merger of his equitable interest in his legal estate. Miller v. Rosenberger, 144 Mo. 292; Burbach v. Burbach, 217 Ill. 547. And where the sole life beneficiary becomes trustee, the trust for the life beneficiary does not cease; there is no merger of the equitable life estate. Losey v. Stanley, 147 N. Y. 560; Irving v. Irving, 47 N. Y. S. 1052; Spengler v. Kuhn, 212 Ill. 186; Doscher v. Wyckoff, 113 N. Y. S. 655. But see Weeks v. Frankel, 197 N. Y. 304.

Where real estate was devised to four as trustees to collect the income and divide it among themselves equally, the trust to continue until such time as all four should agree to sell or to divide the land, the proceeds or the land to be then divided among them, it has been held that there was no merger of the equitable interests in the legal estate and the court declined to decree a termination of the trust on application of less than all of the four. Harris v. Harris, 205 Pa. St. 460. But in a similar case in New York it has been held that no trust ever came into existence. Greene v. Greene, 125 N. Y. 506. See Tilton v. Davidson, 98 Me. 55; Bronson v. Thompson, 77 Conn. 214.

It has been held that where the sole beneficiary of a passive trust of chattels is put into possession, he becomes the full legal owner. Kronson v. Lipschitz, 68 N. J. Eq. 367. As to termination of the trust by decree of court in certain cases, see infra, § 920.

And there will be no merger, if it is contrary to the intention of the parties.[1] If A. should convey lands to B. in trust for C. and her heirs, and C. should be the heir of B., upon the death of B. the legal title would descend to C., and thus both the legal and equitable title would meet in C.; but if C. was a married woman, and it was plainly the intention of the grantor or settlor, to be gathered from the whole instrument, that the trust should not cease, but continue an active trust, the court would not allow the equitable estate to merge in the legal, but a new trustee would be appointed to take the legal title.[2] Of course, in law the estates will merge wherever the interests meet; but courts of equity will preserve the estates separate, where the rights or interests of the parties require it. If the trustee acquires the equitable interest by any breach of his duty, or by fraud, courts will not allow it to merge.[3] So if there are intervening heirs who would be squeezed out, the estates will not merge.[4] So if the legal estate comes to the *cestui que trust* by a conveyance which turns out to be void, there will be no merger.[5] (a) Whether charges upon an estate,

Plumb, 8 Conn. 453; James *v.* Morey, 2 Cow. 284; Goodright *v.* Wells, Doug. 771; Philips *v.* Brydges, 3 Ves. 125; Robinson *v.* Cuming, t. Talbot, 164; 1 Atk. 475; Boteler *v.* Allington, 1 Bro. Ch. 72; Buchanan *v.* Harrison, 1 Jon. & Hen. 662; Merest *v.* James, 6 Madd. 118; Habergham *v.* Vincent, 2 Ves. Jr. 204.

[1] Gardner *v.* Astor, 3 Johns. Ch. 53; James *v.* Morey, 2 Cow. 246; Mechanics' Bank *v.* Edwards, 1 Barb. S. C. 272; Starr *v.* Ellis, 6 Johns. Ch. 393; Donalds *v.* Plumb, 8 Conn. 453; Den *v.* Vanness, 5 Halst. 102; Hunt *v.* Hunt, 14 Pick. 374; Nurse *v.* Yerwarth, 3 Swanst. 608; Saunders *v.* Bournford, Finch, 424; Thom *v.* Newman, 3 Swanst. 603; Mole *v.* Smith, Jac. 490. [Ingle *v.* Vaughan Jenkins, [1900] 2 Ch. 368. See Asche *v.* Asche, 113 N. Y. 232.]

[2] Gardner *v.* Astor, 3 Johns. Ch. 53; James *v.* Morey, 2 Cow. 246; Mechanics' Bank *v.* Edwards, 1 Barb. S. C. 272; Starr *v.* Ellis, 6 Johns. Ch. 393; Donalds *v.* Plumb, 8 Conn. 453; Den *v.* Vanness, 5 Halst. 102; Hunt *v.* Hunt, 14 Pick. 374; Nurse *v.* Yerwarth, 3 Swanst. 608; Saunders *v.* Bournford, Finch, 424; Thom *v.* Newman, 3 Swanst. 603; Mole *v.* Smith, Jac. 490

[3] Spence, Eq. Jur. 572.   [4] Lewis *v.* Stark, 10 Sm. & M. 128

[5] Elliott *v* Armstrong, 2 Blackf. 208; Buchanan *v.* Harrison, 1 John. & H. 662; Brandon *v.* Brandon, 31 L. J Ch. 47.

(a) Or if he gets the legal title by mistake. *In re* Spencer, 128 Fed. 654.

as mortgages, will merge in the legal title, upon being paid off, depends upon the intention of the parties, and frequently upon the interests and equities between them.[1] If a leasehold is held by a wife in her right, but is in the occupation of her husband, and he purchases the reversion, there will be no merger.[2]

§ 348. Thus if a tenant for life pays off a charge or incumbrance upon an estate, it will be considered that, as his interest ceases with his life, he could never have intended that the charge should be extinguished, and not survive for the benefit of his representatives.[3] (a) And the same rule applies, though the tenant for life may be ultimately entitled to the reversion in fee, subject to remainders which fail.[4] Even in this case, evidence may be given that the tenant for life intended the charge to be merged and extinguished.[5] A tenant in tail in

---

[1] Hunt v. Hunt, 14 Pick. 374; Johnson v. Webster, 4 De G., M. & G. 474; Tyrwhitt v. Tyrwhitt, 32 Beav. 244; Morley v. Morley, 25 L. J. Ch. 1; Compton v. Oxenden, 2 Ves. Jr. 264; Forbes v. Moffatt, 18 Ves. 390; Horton v. Smith, 4 K. & J. 630; Tomlinson v. Steers, 3 Mer. 210; Smith v. Phillips, 1 Keen, 694; Medley v. Horton, 14 Sim. 226; Brown v. Stead, 5 Sim. 535; Parry v. Wright, 1 S. & S. 369; 5 Russ. 542; Mocatta v. Murgatroyd, 1 P. W. 193; Greswold v. Marsham, 2 Ch. Cas. 170; Garnett v. Armstrong, 2 Conn. & Laws. 458; Watts v. Symes, 16 Sim. 646; Cooper v. Cartwright, 1 John. 679. [Gresham v. Ware, 79 Ala. 192; Boardman v. Larrabee, 51 Conn. 39; Coryell v. Klehm, 157 Ill. 462; Chase v. Van Meter, 140 Ind. 321; Patterson v. Mills, 69 Iowa, 755; Keith v. Wheeler, 159 Mass. 161; Gibbs v. Johnson, 104 Mich. 120; Collins v. Stocking, 98 Mo. 290; Hayden v. Lauffenburger, 157 Mo. 88; Bassett v. O'Brien, 149 Mo. 381; Fellows v. Dow, 58 N. H. 21; Smith v. Roberts, 91 N. Y. 470; Duffy v. McGuiness, 13 R. I. 595; Thorne v. Cann, [1895] A. C. 11; Adams v. Angell, 5 Ch. Div. 634; Liquidation Estates P. Co. v. Willoughby, [1898] A. C. 321.]

[2] Clark v. Tennison, 33 Md. 85.

[3] Pitt v. Pitt, 22 Beav. 294; Burrell v. Egremont, 7 Beav. 205; Redington v. Redington, 1 B. & B. 139; Faulkner v. Daniel, 3 Hare, 217; State v. Kock, 47 Mo. 582.

[4] Wyndham v. Egremont, Amb. 753; Trevor v. Trevor, 2 Myl. & K. 675.

[5] Astley v. Milles, 1 Sim. 298.

(a) This presumption is not rebutted by the fact that the tenant for life and the remainder-man are parent and child. *In re* Harvey, [1896] 1 Ch. 137.

possession has the power to convert the estate into an absolute
fee; therefore, if he pays off an incumbrance, the presumption
is that he intended it to merge.[1] But if the estate of the tenant
in fee-simple or in tail is subject to any executory limitations
that may defeat their estate, or if they pay off the charges under
any mistake as to their title, the court would not allow the
charges to merge or become extinguished.[2] But if a person
pays or takes up the charges or incumbrances, and afterwards
the legal title should come to him, the charges would merge.[3]
So if a person, having the legal title and holding charges and
incumbrances upon the estate, conveys in fee or in mortgage,
and makes no mention of the charges or incumbrances, they
would merge as between the grantor and grantee.[4] Generally,
where the owner in fee-simple pays off a charge or incumbrance
on an estate, the presumption of law is that such charge or
incumbrance will merge;[5] but if he owns only a partial interest,
the presumption is that the charge was to be kept on foot.[6] Mere
possession of the property by the trustee or by the *cestui qui
trust* is no evidence of a merger.[7]

§ 349. Sometimes where an estate has been vested by deed or
will in trustees for a *cestui que trust*, whether it is a fee or some
lesser estate, the law will presume that the trustees have surrendered, conveyed, or assigned the estate, whatever it was, to

[1] St. Paul v. Dudley, 15 Ves. 173; Buckinghamshire v. Hobart, 3 Swanst.
199; Jones v. Morgan, 1 Bro. Ch. 206.

[2] Drinkwater v. Combe, 2 S. & S. 340; Shrewsbury v. Shrewsbury, 3
Bro. Ch. 120; 1 Ves. Jr 227; Wigsell v. Wigsell, 2 S. & S. 364; Horton v.
Smith, 4 K. & J. 624; Buckinghamshire v. Hobart, 3 Swanst. 199; Kirkham
v. Smith, 1 Ves. 528.

[3] Horton v. Smith, 4 K. & J. 624; Trevor v. Trevor, 2 Myl. & K. 675;
Wigsell v. Wigsell, 2 S. & S. 364.

[4] Tyler v. Lake, 4 Sim. 351; Johnson v. Webster, 4 De G., M. & G. 474.

[5] Hood v. Phillips, 3 Beav. 513; Pitt v. Pitt, 22 Beav. 294; Gunter v.
Gunter, 23 Beav. 571; Swinfen v. Swinfen, 29 Beav. 199; Tyrwhitt v. Tyrwhitt, 32 Beav. 244.

[6] Price v. Gibson, 2 Eden, 115; Swinfen v. Swinfen, 29 Beav. 199; Compton v. Oxenden, 2 Ves. Jr. 263; Donisthorpe v. Porter, 2 Eden, 162.

[7] Broswell v. Downs, 11 Fla. 62.

the *cestui que trust*.[1] This presumption of law is necessary for
the quieting of titles. If such presumptions could not be made,
some titles would remain forever imperfect. There might be
an outstanding legal estate, which would at any time defeat the
tenant, if there could not be a presumption of a conveyance or
surrender by the trustee to the *cestui que trust*. This presumption is somewhat different from that prescription by which one
tenant by an open, peaceable, and adverse occupation, under a
claim of right, obtains the legal title as against another person.
In such case, after a definite period of time, a grant or conveyance is presumed in favor of the tenant in occupation, though
it may be well enough understood that no such grant or conveyance was ever made. So there may be a presumption that a
trustee has conveyed to the *cestui que trust*, though such presumption may not always be founded on a belief that such
conveyance was actually made.[2] There is another difficulty
between trustees and *cestuis que trust* which does not exist
between adverse claimants of the same legal title. The titles,
of the trustee and *cestui que trust* are not adverse to each other,
and generally the possession of the *cestui que trust* is the possession of the trustee; at any rate it is generally consistent with
the legal title of the trustee. Therefore, mere length of time
as between trustee and *cestui que trust* will afford no ground for
a presumption of a conveyance or surrender from the trustee to
the *cestui que trust*,[3] as *cestuis que trust* may occupy the estate
indefinitely under a merely equitable title.

[1] England *v.* Slade, 4 T. R. 682; Wilson *v.* Allen, 1 J. & W. 611; Noel
v. Bewley, 3 Sim. 103; Cooke *v.* Salton, 2 S. & S. 154; Hillary *v.* Waller,
12 Ves. 239; Lade *v.* Holford, Bull. N. P. 110; Doe *v.* Hilder, 2 B. & A.
782; Emery *v.* Grocock, 6 Madd. 54; Townshend *v.* Champernown, 1 Y.
& J. 583; Goodtitle *v.* Jones, 7 T. R. 47; Doe *v.* Sybourn, id. 2; Moore *v.*
Jackson, 4 Wend. 59; Dutch Church *v.* Mott, 7 Paige, 77; Jackson *v.* Moore,
13 Johns. 513; 1 Green. Cruise Dig. 412; Matthews *v.* Ward, 10 Gill & J.
443; Jackson *v.* Pierce, 2 Johns. 226; Sinclair *v.* Jackson, 8 Cow. 543.

[2] Hillary *v.* Waller, 12 Ves. 252.

[3] Keene *v.* Deardon, 8 East, 263; Goodson *v.* Ellison, 3 Russ. 588; Hillary *v.* Waller, 12 Ves. 251; 1 Sugd. V. & P. 350, 470; Flournoy *v.*
Johnson, 7 B. Mon. 694; Doe *v.* Langdon, 12 Q. B. 719.

§ 350. This presumption has been discussed at length in several cases, and some difference of opinion has been expressed;[1] but it seems now to be well settled that three circumstances must concur in order to raise the presumption of a conveyance or surrender by the trustee to the *cestui que trust*: (1) It must have been the duty of the trustee to make the conveyance; (2) There must be some sufficient reason to support the presumption; (3) The presumption must be in support of a just title, and not to defeat it.

§ 351. Thus where the *cestui que trust* becomes absolutely entitled to the whole beneficial interest in the trust estate, and the active duties of the trustee have ceased, the statute of uses generally executes the legal title of the trustee to the *cestui que trust*, and he obtains the legal as well as the beneficial estate. (a) But there are cases where the active duties of the trustee having ceased, the legal title does not pass without a conveyance. In such cases it is clearly the duty of the trustee to convey the legal title to the *cestui que trust*, or to such person as he shall appoint.[2] Therefore, if the beneficial owner has been a long time in possession, dealing with the estate in every respect as his own, it will be presumed that the trustee performed his duty and conveyed the legal estate to the proper person. As where a mortgage in fee was made to a trustee for the real mortgagee, and the *cestui que trust* or real mortgagee took a conveyance of

[1] Lade v. Holford, Bull. N. P. 110; Doe v. Sybourn, 7 T. R. 2; Goodtitle v. Jones, id. 49; Doe v. Read, 8 T. R. 118; see note, 1 Green. Cruise, 410; 2 Pow. on Mort. 491. [See also M'Queen v. Meade, 28 L. T. N. S. 768.]

[2] Langley v. Sneyd, 1 S. & S. 45; Carteret v. Carteret, 2 P. Wms. 134; Angier v. Stannard, 3 Myl. & K. 571; England v. Slade, 4 T. R. 682; Goodson v. Ellison, 3 Russ. 583.

(a) The N. Y. Consol. Laws, Vol. IV, p. 3389, §§ 91-93, taking away the trustee's title, when merely nominal, and vesting it in the beneficiary, do not apply when the trustee has himself an interest in the grant, either as an individual or with others. King v. Townshend, 141 N. Y. 358. See *supra*, § 142.

the equity of redemption, and ever after dealt with the estate as if the legal fee was in him, a conveyance of the mortgage was presumed to have been made to him by the trustee.[1] There was a use of the estate in this case for one hundred years. Where lands were conveyed to trustees for a religious society, which was afterwards incorporated, it was held, after the use of the land for one hundred and forty years by the incorporated society, that a conveyance by the trustees might be presumed.[2] So where several persons conveyed to a trustee a tract of land for the purposes of a partition by the trustee conveying back to each person his share in severalty, as set forth in the deed, it was held, after an occupation of many years by each person in severalty according to the intended partition, that the trustee might be presumed to have conveyed.[3] Where the trustees are to convey upon a certain event, or at a certain time, as when a minor becomes twenty-one, the presumption will arise after a much shorter lapse of time.[4] Thus, where trustees were to convey to the testator's son immediately on his coming of age, the son became of age in 1788, and granted a long lease in 1789, the court presumed a conveyance in 1792, or only four years after the event, there being no proof of an actual conveyance. Lord Kenyon said "there was no reason why the jury should not presume a conveyance from the trustees. They were bound to make one, and a court would have compelled them to have done it if they had refused. It is rather to be presumed that they did their duty. And as to time, the jury may be directed to presume a conveyance and surrender in much less time than twenty years." [5] So where the direction to the trustee to convey applies to only a part of the estate, the court may presume a conveyance of the whole, if the circumstances require or warrant such presumption.[6]

---

[1] Noel v. Bewley, 3 Sim. 103.   [2] Dutch Church v. Mott, 7 Paige, 77.
[3] Jackson v. Moore, 13 Johns. 513.
[4] Wilson v. Allen, 1 J. & W. 611; Hillary v. Waller, 12 Ves. 239; Doe v. Sybourn, 7 T. R. 2.
[5] England v. Slade, 4 T. R. 682; Marr v. Gilman, 1 Cold. 488.
[6] Hillary v. Waller, 12 Ves. 239.

§ 352. If the estate was originally conveyed to trustees for some particular purpose, as by way of security or indemnity, or to raise an annuity or portion, or for any other purpose, as soon as the purpose is accomplished, the trustees become mere dry trustees, and it is their duty to convey the estate to the beneficial owner.[1] Where, from lapse of time joined with other circumstances, there is a moral certainty that the purposes of the trust have all been accomplished, the court will act upon the certainty, and presume a reconveyance although there is no direct proof of the fact.[2]

§ 353. Where an estate is vested in trustees upon an express trust, they must retain the legal title until the trusts are fully executed. Therefore, no conveyance will be presumed, so long as the trustees have any duties to perform; for that would be to presume a breach of trust, which will never be presumed: the fact must be proved by competent evidence.[3] In Aiken v. Smith, the court presumed that the conveyance was made at the death of the tenant for life, that being the time fixed for the conveyance, and the time when the active duties of the trustees ceased.[4]

§ 354. But there must always be sufficient reason for presuming a reconveyance or surrender by the trustee; that is, there must be some evidence of such a conveyance, or some evidence upon which the presumption of the conveyance may be founded. The mere fact that the trustee was to convey upon the execution of the trust, or upon the happening of a certain event, is not enough. There must be some circumstance from which it may

---

[1] Hillary v. Waller, 12 Ves. 239; Doe v. Sybourn, 7 T. R. 2; Cooke v. Soltau, 2 S. & S. 154; Ex parte Holman, 1 Sugd. V. & P. 509; Emery v. Grocock, 6 Madd. 54; Doe v. Wright, 2 B. & A. 710; Bartlett v. Downes, 3 B. & Cr. 616.

[2] Emery v. Grocock, 6 Madd. 54; Hillary v. Waller, 12 Ves. 252.

[3] Beach v. Beach, 14 Vt. 28; Doe v. Staple, 2 T. R. 684; Keene v. Deardon, 8 East, 248; Flournoy v. Johnson, 7 B. Mon. 694.

[4] Aiken v. Smith, 1 Sneed, 304. This case is opposed to Rees v. Williams, 2 M. & W. 749.

be reasonably concluded that he did in *fact* convey. Mere length of time is not enough. Courts have refused after the lapse of one hundred and twenty years to presume a reconveyance, when there were no intermediate transactions to give force to the length of time;[1] for the possession during all that time may not be inconsistent with the trustee's title.[2] However, great lapse of time is an important circumstance; and the fact that it was the duty of the trustees to convey is another important circumstance. Very slight circumstances added to these will be sufficient to justify a court or jury in presuming a conveyance; and a conveyance may be presumed where the estate has been dealt with by the beneficial owner in a manner in which reasonable men do not deal with their estates, unless they are the legal as well as beneficial owners.[3]

§ 355. It is further said that the purpose of the presumption must be to prevent a just title from being defeated by mere matter of form.[4] The presumption is a shield for defence and not a sword for attack, as was said of another principle of law. As the presumption was introduced for the security of estates and the protection of innocent purchasers, it cannot be set up to eject them from their estates; and therefore the presumption will be made only in favor of the person in whom the beneficial title is clearly vested for the time being, whatever may be the extent of his equitable interest.[5] So it was not allowed to be set up in favor of a defendant who showed no title but a mere naked possession, which might have been obtained by a dis-

---

[1] Goodright *v.* Swymmer, 1 Kenyon, 385; Goodson *v.* Ellison, 3 Russ. 583; Langley *v.* Sneyd, 1 S. & S. 45; Doe *v.* Lloyd, Mathews on Presumptions, 215.

[2] Ibid.; Keene *v.* Deardon, 8 East, 363; Hillary *v.* Waller, 12 Ves. 250.

[3] Garrard *v.* Tuck, 8 C. B. 248; Cottrell *v.* Hughes, 15 C. B. 532; Hillary *v.* Waller, 12 Ves. 239; Wilson *v.* Allen, 1 J. & W. 611.

[4] Lade *v.* Holford, Bull. N. P. 110; Doe *v.* Sybourn, 7 T. R. 2; Goodtitle *v.* Jones, 7 T. R. 47.

[5] Doe *v.* Cook, 6 Bing. 179; Tenney *v.* Jones, 10 Bing. 75; Bartlett *v.* Downes, 8 B. & Cr. 616; Noel *v.* Bewley, 3 Sim. 103; Wilson *v.* Allen, 1 J. & W. 611.

seizin of the beneficial owner.[1] And where two litigants both claimed to be the beneficial owners, a surrender of an outstanding legal estate or term was not presumed, lest either obtaining it should defeat the other without regard to the merits of his beneficial title.[2]

§ 356. In England, there was a system of conveyancing by which outstanding terms were made to attend the legal title and protect it. Much litigation and discussion has been had over these terms, their merging in the legal title, and their presumed surrender. They have very little importance in this country, and the statement of the law concerning them is not deemed necessary.[3]

[1] Doe v. Cook, 6 Bing. 179; England v. Slade, 4 T. R. 682; Doe v. Sybourn, 7 T. R. 2.

[2] Doe v. Wrighte, 2 B. & A. 710.

[3] See Hill on Trustees, pp. 253–263.

CHAPTER XII.

EXECUTORY TRUSTS.

§ 357. It is a fundamental proposition that equitable estates are governed by the same rules as legal estates, otherwise inextricable confusion would ensue.[1] If there was one rule on the equity side, and another on the law side of courts, there would be no certainty or uniformity of interpretation or construction. Thus at common law a grant to A. for life, remainder to the heirs of his body, vested an estate in fee-tail in A., which he could bar, and cut off the remainder. The same rule was applied to *executed* trusts. Thus if land is given to A. and his heirs in trust for B. for life, remainder to the heirs of his body, B. takes an equitable fee-tail;[2] for the same rules apply to the two species

---

[1] Frye *v.* Porter, 1 Mod. 300; Price *v.* Sisson, 2 Beas. 168; Cowper *v.* Cowper, 2 P. Wms. 753; Burgess *v.* Wheate, 1 Wm. Black. 123; Cushing *v.* Blake, 30 N. J. Eq. 689.

[2] This illustration states the law only in States where the rule in Shelley's Case, as it is called, is in force. In States where the rule is abrogated

of estate.[1] Therefore where technical words are used in the creation of an executed trust estate, they will be taken in their legal technical sense,[2] though Lord Hardwicke once added this qualification, "unless the intention of the testator or author of the trust plainly appeared to the contrary."[3] But this qualification has been time and again overruled, and it is now an established canon that a limitation in trust, perfected and declared by the settlor, shall have the same construction as in the case of an executed legal estate.[4] But while technical words receive their technical meaning in equitable as well as legal estates, technical words are not always necessary to create and limit equitable estates in fee. Thus an equitable fee may be created in a deed without the word "heirs," and an equitable entail without the words "heirs of the body," if the words used in their popular sense are equivalent to the technical words, or if the intention is sufficiently expressed and clear.[5] Thus if an estate is *devised* to A. and his heirs in trust for D. without other limitations, B. will take an equitable fee; for it is plain that B. is to take an equitable estate as large as the legal estate that passed to A. and his heirs, which is a legal fee.[6] But if an estate is conveyed by *deed* to A. and his heirs in trust for the grantor for life,

by statute, those who take in remainder under the limitation, take as purchasers; and the same rule applies to equitable estates.

[1] Noble *v.* Andrews, 37 Conn. 346.

[2] Wright *v.* Pearson, 1 Eden, 125; Bale *v.* Coleman, 8 Vin. 268; Jervoise *v.* Northumberland, 1 J. & W. 571; McPherson *v.* Snowdon, 19 Md. 197.

[3] Garth *v.* Baldwin, 2 Ves. 655.

[4] Brydges *v.* Brydges, 3 Ves. Jr. 125; Austen *v.* Taylor, 1 Eden, 367; Glenorchy *v.* Bosville, Ca. t. Talb. 19; Synge *v.* Hales, 2 B. & B. 507; Wright *v.* Pearson, 1 Eden, 125. But see Cushing *v.* Blake, 30 N. J. Eq. 389; Carter *v.* Montgomery, 2 Tenn. Ch. 216.

[5] Shep. Touch. by Preston, 106. [Smith *v.* Proctor, 139 N. C. 314; Holmes *v.* Holmes, 86 N. C. 205; McElroy *v.* McElroy, 113 Mass. 509; *In re* Irwing, [1904] 2 Ch. 752; *In re* Tringham's Trusts, [1904] 2 Ch. 487. See *supra*, § 312, note.]

[6] Moore *v.* Cleghorn, 10 Beav. 423; 12 Jur. 591; Knight *v.* Selby, 3 Man. & Gr. 92; Doe *v.* Cafe, 7 Exch. 675; Watkins *v.* Weston, 32 Beav. 238; McClintock *v.* Irving, 10 Ir. Ch. 481; Brenan *v.* Boyne, 16 Ir. Ch. 87; Betty *v.* Elliott, id. 110, n.; *Re* Bayley, id. 215.

remainder for his children, without the word "heirs," the children take an estate for life only, in analogy to the rules of law.[1]

§ 358. The rule in Shelley's Case was never a rule of intention, or of construction to reach and carry out the settlor's intention; but it was established as an absolute rule of property to obviate certain difficulties that would arise in relation to tenures, if certain persons to whom property was limited were allowed to take as purchasers, and not by descent.[2] (a)   It is notorious that the

[1] Overton v. Halliday, 14 Beav. 467; 15 id. 480; 16 Jur. 71; Lucas v. Brandreth, 28 Beav. 274; Tatham v. Vernon, 29 id. 604; Nelson v. Davis, 35 Ind. 474.

[2] Doebler's App., 64 Penn. St. 9.

(a) The rule in Shelley's Case has been abolished by statute, wholly or partly, in more than half the States, including Massachusetts, Maine, Connecticut, Rhode Island, New Hampshire, New York, Michigan, Minnesota, Wisconsin, Missouri, Mississippi, Virginia, West Virginia, Alabama, California, Washington, and Ohio. 2 Washburn's Law of Real Property (6th ed.), § 1616, note. The rule was abolished in Iowa by c. 159, Laws of 1907, but the law is not retroactive. See Brokaw v. Brokaw, 113 N. W. 469 (Iowa 1907). In many other States the application of the rule has been limited by legislation converting estates tail into life estates with remainders in fee. 1 Washburn's Law of Real Property (6th ed.), § 219, note. See Wheelock v. Simons, 75 Ark. 19; Black v. Webb, 72 Ark. 336; Albin v. Parmele, 70 Neb. 740.

Except so far as limited by statute provisions, the rule is usually held to be part of the common law in the United States. Hardage v. Stroope, 58 Ark. 303; Black v. Webb,

72 Ark. 336; Wheelock v. Simons, 75 Ark. 19; Jones v. Rees, 69 A. 785 (Del. 1908); McFall v. Kirkpatrick, 236 Ill. 281; Pease v. Davis, 225 Ill. 408; Deemer v. Kessinger, 206 Ill. 57; Taney v. Fahnley, 126 Ind. 88; Hughes v. Nicklas, 70 Md. 484; Seeger v. Leakin, 76 Md. 500; Waller v. Pollitt, 104 Md. 172; Cook v. Councilman, 109 Md. 622; Starnes v. Hill, 112 N. C. 1; Walker v. Taylor, 144 N. C. 175; Perry v. Hackney, 142 N. C. 368; Pitchford v. Limer, 139 N. C. 13; Tyson v. Sinclair, 138 N. C. 23; Garver v. Clouser, 218 Pa. St. 611; Hastings v. Engle, 217 Pa. St. 419; Shapley v. Diehl, 203 Pa. St. 566; Eby v. Shank, 196 Pa. St. 426; Gadsden v. Desportes, 39 S. C. 131; Clark v. Neves, 76 S. C. 484; Davenport v. Eskew, 69 S. C. 292; Kennedy v. Colclough, 67 S. C. 118; Lacey v. Floyd, 99 Tex. 112; Brown v. Bryant, 17 Tex. Civ. App. 454; Vogt v. Vogt, 26 App. D. C. 46; De Vaughn v. Hutchinson, 165 U. S. 566; Grant v. Squire, 2 Ont. Law Rep. 131. The rule was law in Iowa previous to the statute of 1907, c.

· rule disappointed the intention of settlors in most cases, and gave an absolute disposal of the inheritance to the first taker, where the settlor intended that such first taker should have only an estate for life.[1]   As trusts are wholly independent of tenure,

---

[1] For these reasons the rule is now abolished in many of the States by statute. The proposition of the text, however, should be read in the light of the remarks of Agnew, J., in Yarnall's App., 70 Penn. St. 340: "In regard to wills the cases show that technical phrases, as well as forms of expression decided in other cases, are not permitted to overturn the intent of the testator, when that intent is clearly ascertained to be different in the will under examination by the court. This broad principle needs no citation to support it, for it is founded on the universal rule that the intention of the testator is the guide for the interpretation of wills. The rule in Shelley's Case is only an apparent not a real exception to this statement. It sacrifices a particular intent only to give effect to the main intent· of the testator. All the authorities are agreed that this rule has no place in the interpretation of wills, and takes effect only when the interpretation has been first ascertained. Mr. Fearne, Contingent Remainders, p. 188,

159, which was expressly made not retroactive. Doyle v. Andis, 127 Iowa, 36; Ault v. Hillyard, 138 Iowa, 239; Kepler v. Larson, 131 Iowa, 438. See also Albin v. Parmele, 70 Neb. 740; Lippincott v. Davis, 59 N. J. Law, 241. For a good historical review of the rule see the opinion of Lord Macnaghten, in Van Grutten v. Foxwell, [1897] A. C. 658, 667. See also Bowen v. Lewis, 9 A. C. 890.

The rule has been extended by analogy to personalty, including leasehold estates. Hughes v. Nicklas, 70 Md. 484; Seeger v. Leakin, 76 Md. 500; Evans v. Weatherhead, 24 R. I. 502. But see contra, Jones v. Rees, 69 A. 785 (Del. 1908); Vogt v. Vogt, 26 App. D. C. 46 (semble).

In general the American cases agree with the English cases that the rule is an absolute rule of property, not a rule of construction, and in cases which come within the rule, the intention of the grantor or tes-

tator to create only a life estate in the first taker will have no effect. Hardage v. Stroope, 58 Ark. 303; Hughes v. Nicklas, 70 Md. 484; Travers v. Wallace, 93 Md. 507, 513; Lippincott v. Davies, 59 N. J. Law, 241; Perry v. Hackney,',142 N. C 368, 375; Wool v. Fleetwood, 136 N. C. 460, 469; Shapley v. Diehl, 203 Pa. St. 566, 569; Brown v. Bryant, 17 Tex. Civ. App. 454; Van Grutten v. Foxwell, [1897] A. C. 658; Evans v. Evans, [1892] 2 Ch. 173, 188. See Reilly v. Bristow, 105 Md. 326. But there seems to be some doubt on this point in some of the States. See Wescott v. Binford, 104 Iowa, 645; Doyle v. Andis, 127 Iowa, 36; Kepler v. Larson, 131 Iowa, 438; 7 L. R. A. (N. S.), 1109 and note; Granger v. Granger, 147 Ind. 95; Albin v. Parmele, 70 Neb. 740; De Vaughn v. Hutchinson, 165 U. S. 566.

584

they ought not to be affected by the rule, and a few cases have seemed to indicate that they were withdrawn from the operation of it;[1] but it is now established that the same rule shall apply to the same limitation whether it is of an equitable or a legal estate.[2] Thus the rule in Shelley's Case will be applied to a gift to A. and his heirs in trust for B. for life, and remainder to his heirs, or heirs of his body. The reason of the rule as applied to legal estates was some real or fancied difficulty concerning tenures, or to bring estates one generation sooner into commerce, or some other reason; for neither judges nor text-writers are agreed upon the original reasons of the rule. The reason of the

says, 'Nothing can be better founded than Mr. Hargrave's doctrine, that the rule in Shelley's Case is no medium for finding out the intention of the testator; that, on the contrary, the rule supposes the intention already discovered and to be a superadded succession to the heirs, general or special of the donee for life, by making such donee the ancestor *terminus* or *stirps*, from which the generation of posterity or heirs is to be accounted; and that whether the conveyance has or has not so constituted an estate of freehold, with a succession engrafted on it, is a previous question which ought to be adjusted before the rule is thought of; that, to resolve that point, the ordinary rules for interpreting the language of wills ought to be resorted to; that when it is once settled that the donor or testator has used words of inheritance according to their legal import, has applied them intentionally to comprise the whole line of heirs of the tenant for life, and has really made him the *terminus*, or ancestor by reference to whom the succession is to be regulated, then comes the proper time to inspect the rule in Shelley's Case.' In Hileman v. Bouslaugh, 1 Harris, 351, Ch. J. Gibson expresses the same idea in fewer words, thus: 'This operates only on the intention of the testator when it has been ascertained, not on the meaning of the words used to express it. The ascertainment is left to the ordinary rules of construction peculiar to wills; but when this is ascertained, is found to be within the rule, then there is but one way; it admits of no exception.'"

[1] Withers v. Allgood, cited, and Bagshaw v. Spencer, 1 Ves. 150.

[2] Garth v. Baldwin, 2 Ves. 646; Wright v. Parsons, 1 Ed. 128; Brydges v. Brydges, 3 Ves. 120; Jones v. Morgan, 1 Bro. Ch. 206; Webb v. Shaftesbury, 3 Myl. & K. 599; Roberts v. Dixwell, 1 Atk. 610; West, 536; Britton v. Twining, 3 Mer. 175; Spence v. Spence, 12 C. B. (N. S.) 199; Coape v. Arnold, 2 Sm. & Gif. 311; Noble v. Andrews, 37 Conn. 346; Cushing v. Blake, 30 N. J. Eq. 689; Sprague v. Sprague, 12 R. I. 703. [Van Grutten v. Foxwell, [1897] A. C. 658; *In re* Youmans' Will, [1901] 1 Ch. 720; McFall v. Kirkpatrick, 236 Ill. 281; Jones v. Rees, 69 A. 785 (Del. 1908) *semble*.]

application of the rule to limitations of trust estates is to preserve a uniformity of the law in relation to the two kinds of
estates in land. This leads Mr. Lewin to say, that although the
rule is not *equally applicable* to trust estates, yet it is *equally
applied*.[1] But the rule will not be applied to vest a fee or fee-
tail in the first taker, unless the word "heir" is used as a term
of succession, and not as a mere *designatio personæ*. Thus if
an estate be *devised* to A. and his heirs in trust for B. for life,
and after his decease in trust for the person who shall then be
his heir, B. takes an estate for life only, and the person thus
designated takes the estate by purchase.[2] (a)   So if the legal
estate is given to A. *in trust* for B. for life, and the legal remainder

[1] Lewin on Trusts, 88 (5th ed.).
[2] Greaves *v.* Simpson, 10 Jur. (N. S.) 609. [**Evans** *v.* Evans, [1892] 2
Ch. 173; Earnhart *v.* Earnhart, 127 Ind. 397.]

(a) It has been said that "to
bring a devise within the rule in
Shelley's Case, the limitation must
be to the heirs in fee or in tail as a
nomen collectivum for the whole line
of inheritable blood." Kuntzleman's Estate, 136 Pa. St. 142, 152;
McCann *v.* McCann, 197 Pa. St. 452.
And the following have been held
not to be within the rule: A devise
to a son and at his death "to his
next nearest blood relations." Mc-
Cann *v.* McCann, 197 Pa. St. 452.
A devise to a son for life and at his
death to his "nearest *male* heirs."
Jones *v.* Jones, 201 Pa. St. 548. A
devise to one "for and during his
life, and after his death to his lawful
heirs *born of his wife*." Thompson
v. Crump, 138 N. C. 32. See also
Ault *v.* Hillyard, 138 Iowa, 239;
Brown *v.* Brown, 125 Iowa, 218;
Gadsden *v.* Desportes, 39 S. C. 131;
Starnes *v.* Hill, 112 N. C. 1.

The word "children," used to
designate the successors in title, is

not given the same effect as the
word "heirs" for the purposes of the
rule, and excludes the operation of
the rule, Connor *v.* Gardner, 230
Ill. 258; Strawbridge *v.* Strawbridge,
220 Ill. 61; Reilly *v.* Bristow, 105
Md. 326; Hoover *v.* Strauss, 215 Pa.
St. 130; Clark *v.* Neves, 76 S. C. 484;
Brown *v.* Brown, 125 Iowa, 218; Cowell *v.* Hicks, 30 A. 1091 (N. J. Ch.
1895); in the absence of a clear intention to use the words to mean
"heirs" or "heirs of the body."
Shapley *v.* Diehl, 203 Pa. St. 566.
See Brown *v.* Brown, 125 Iowa, 218.
If the word "heirs" is used to mean
"children" it has been held that the
rule in Shelley's Case does not apply.
Stisser *v.* Stisser, 235 Ill. 207.

The word "issue" primarily
means heirs of the body, and under
the rule would create an estate tail
in the first taker unless it were
shown to mean "children." Faison
v. Odom, 144 N. C. 107; Hill *v.*
Giles, 201 Pa. St. 215.

to the heirs of B., at his decease the rule cannot apply; for the legal and equitable estate cannot so coalesce that B. can take a fee either legal or equitable.[1] (a)

§ 359. But in order that technical words may receive their legal signification, and in order that the rule in Shelley's Case may be applied to limitations of equitable estates, the trusts must be *executed* and *not executory*.[2] All trusts are *executory* in

[1] Collier v. McBean, 34 Beav. 426; L. R. 1 Ch. 81.

[2] Egerton v. Brownlow, 4 H. L. Cas. 210; Rochford v. Fitzmaurice, 2 Dr. & W. 20; 4 Ired. Eq. 384; Tatham v. Vernon, 29 Beav. 604; Bacon's App., 57 Penn. St. 504. This distinction was very early established. Bale v. Coleman, 8 Vin. 267; Stamford v. Hobart, 3 Bro. P. C. 33; Papillon v. Voice, 2 P. Wms. 471; Glenorchy v. Bosville, t. Talb. 3; Gower v. Grosvenor, Barn. 62; Roberts v. Dixwell, 1 Atk. 607; Baskerville v. Baskerville, 2 Atk. 279; Woodhouse v. Haskins, 3 Atk. 24; Read v. Snell, 2 Atk. 648; Marryat v. Townley, 1 Ves. 102. Several of these cases were decided by Lord Hardwicke; but in Bagshaw v. Spencer, 1 Ves. 152, he nearly confounded and denied the distinction. In Exel v. Wallace, 2 Ves. 233, however, Lord Hardwicke explained his meaning, and desired to have it remembered that he did not mean to say that his 'predecessors were wrong. The distinction, as stated in the text, is now firmly established both in England and the United States. Barnard v. Broby, 2 Cox, 8; Wright v. Pearson, 1 Eden, 125; Austen v. Taylor, id. 366; Stanley v. Lennard, id. 95; Lincoln v. Newcastle, 12 Ves. 227; Jervoise v. Northumberland, 1 J. & W. 570; Deerhurst v. St. Albans, 5 Madd. 233; 2 Cl. & Fin. 611; Blackburn v. Stables, 2 V. & B. 369; Douglass v. Congreve, 1 Beav. 59; 4 Bing. N. C. 1; 5 Bing. N. C. 318; Boswell v. Dillon, 1 Dru. 297; Neves v. Scott, 9 How. 211; 13 How. 268; 4 Kent, Com. 218 *et seq.*; Garner v. Garner, 1 Des. 444; Porter v. Doby, 2 Rich. Eq. 49; Dennison v. Goehring, 7 Barr, 177; Findlay v. Riddle, 3 Binn. 152; Edmondson v. Dyson, 2 Kelly, 307; Wiley v. Smith, 3 Kelly, 559; Wood v. Burnham, 6 Paige, 518; 26 Wend. 19; Imlay v. Huntington, 20 Conn. 162; Berry v. Williamson, 11 B. Mon. 251; Horne v. Lyethe, 4 H. & J. 434; Loring v. Hunter, 8 Yerg. 31; Bold v. Hutchinson, 5 De G., M. & G. 558. Lord Northington said that the words

(a) The rule in Shelley's Case does not apply where one of the estates sought to be carved out is equitable and the other legal, even when the legal estate in remainder is by operation of the statute of uses. Slater v. Rudderforth, 25 App. D. C. 497; Vogt v. Vogt, 26 App. D. C. 46; Brown v. Wadsworth, 168 N. Y. 225; West's Estate, 214 Pa. St. 35; Mannerback's Estate, 133 Pa. St. 342. But see *In re* Youmans' Will, [1901] 1 Ch. 720.

one sense of the word; that is, the trustee must have some duty, either active or passive, to perform, so that the statute of uses shall not execute the estate in the *cestui que trust*, and leave nothing in the trustee.[1] But such is not the meaning of judges when they speak of *executed* trusts, and *executory* trusts. These words refer rather to the manner and perfection of their creation than to the action of the trustee in administering the property. Thus a trust created by a deed or will, so clear and certain in all its terms and limitations that a trustee has nothing to do but to carry out all the provisions of the instrument according to its letter, is called an *executed* trust. In these trusts, technical words receive their legal meaning, and the rules applicable to legal estates govern the equitable estates thus created.[2] On the other hand, an executory trust is where an estate is conveyed to a trustee upon trust, to be by him conveyed or settled upon other trusts in certain contingencies, or upon certain events, and these other trusts are imperfectly stated, or mere outlines of them are stated, to be afterwards drawn out in a formal manner, and are to be carried into effect according to the final form which the details and limitations shall take under the directions thus given.[3] They are called *executory*, not because the trust is

"executory trusts" seemed to him to have no fixed signification. Lord King said a trust was executory where the party must come into court to have the benefit of the will. Mr. Lewin says the true criterion is, where the assistance of the court is necessary to complete the limitations, p. 89. Lord Eldon said the trust was executory where the testator had not completed the devise, but had left something to be done, so that the court must look to the intention. Jervoise *v.* Northumberland, 1 J. & W. 570. Lord St. Leonards distinguishes the two as follows: "Has the testator been what is called, and very properly called, his own conveyancer? Has he left it to the court to make out, from general expressions, what his intention is, or has he so defined that intention that you have nothing to do but to take that which is given you, and to convert them into legal estate?" Egerton *v.* Brownlow, 4 H. L. Cas. 210.

[1] Bagshaw *v.* Spencer, 1 Ves. 142; Egerton *v.* Brownlow, 4 H. L. Cas. 210; Coape *v.* Arnold, 4 De G., M. & G. 585.

[2] Wright *v.* Pearson, 1 Eden, 125; Austen *v.* Taylor, id. 367; 4 Kent, Com. 220; Jones *v.* Morgan, 1 Bro. Ch. 206; Jervoise *v.* Northumberland, 1 J. & W. 559; Boswell *v.* Dillon, 1 Dru. 291.

[3] Austen *v.* Taylor, 1 Eden, 366; Wright *v.* Pearson, id. 125; Jervoise

to be performed in the future, but because the trust instrument itself is to be moulded into form and perfected according to the outlines or instructions made or left by the settlor or testator.[1] (a)   Thus land conveyed to A. upon trust, to settle the same upon B. and C. and their issue, in the event of their marriage, is an *executory trust*.[2]   There is a conveyance or settlement to be executed by A., and the form or terms of this conveyance or settlement is to be determined by the intention of the original grantor.[3]   When this conveyance or settlement is finally determined and made, the trust becomes *executed* in the sense of the word as applicable to this distinction, and it is afterwards gov-

---

v. Northumberland, 1 J. & W. 570; Coape *v.* Arnold, 4 De G., M. & G. 585; Neves *v.* Scott, 9 How. 211; Wiley *v.* Smith, 3 Kelly, 559; Edmondson *v.* Dyson, 2 Kelly, 307; Wood *v.* Burnham, 6 Paige, 518; 26 Wend. 19; Thompson *v.* Fisher, L. R. 10 Eq. 207; Cushing *v.* Blake, 30 N. J. Eq. 689. [See Gaylord *v.* Lafayette, 115 Ind. 423, 429.]

   [1] Ibid.   [2] Ibid.   [3] Ibid.

(a) In Pillot *v.* Landon, 46 N. J. Eq. 310, 313, the distinction between executed and executory trusts is stated as follows by Garrison, J.: "The difference between executed and executory trusts depends upon the manner in which the trust is declared. When the limitations and trusts are fully and perfectly declared, the trust is regarded as an executed trust; when, on the contrary, the creator of the trust, instead of fully declaring its limitations expresses in general terms his intent, leaving the manner in which this intent is to be carried into effect substantially undeclared, the trust is regarded as executory.

"In practice the chief distinction between an executed and an executory trust lies in the fact that the former executes itself by converting its limitations into the corresponding legal estates, whereas in the latter, the court may direct that form of settlement or conveyance which will best give effect to the settlor's intention, and for this purpose may even disregard the construction the instrument would receive at law.

"In the executory trust the language of the settlor is considered mainly as a guide to aid the court in carrying into effect his imperfectly declared purposes. In the executed trust the grantor has been his own conveyancer, and the equitable interests created by the language he has employed are treated as estates. In trusts of this kind the controlling inquiry is, not intention, but legal operation, and as the court cannot alter the nature of the estates the grantor has created, it will not speculate as to those purposes which he has failed to effectuate." See also Smith's Estate, 144 Pa. St. 428, 434.

erned by all the rules of an executed trust. The difference between the two kinds of trusts is this. In *executed* trusts the rules of property govern, and not the intention of the settlor, if it is contrary to the law or rule of property.[1] Thus if, in an executed trust, an estate is given to A. in trust for B. for life, with remainder to his heirs, B. takes an equitable fee [under the rule in Shelley's Case] and may convey the equitable inheritance and exclude his heirs, although it is perfectly certain that the settlor intended that B. should take an estate for his life only.[2] But an executory trust is settled and carried into effect according to the *intention* of the settlor.[3] Thus if an estate is conveyed to A. in trust, with instructions to convey it to B. for life, with remainder to his heirs, or to convey it in trust for B. for life, with remainder to his heirs, B. takes an estate for life only, and his heirs take by purchase at his decease, if such appeared to be the intention of the original gift or grant.[4]

§ 360. In the history of executory trusts, still another distinction has been drawn, or a distinction between executory trusts created by marriage articles, and executory trusts created

[1] Choice v. Marshall, 1 Kelly, 97; Schoonmaker v. Sheely, 3 Hill, 165; Kingsland v. Rapelye, 3 Edw. 2; Brant v. Gelston, 2 John. Ca. 384. [Pillot v. Landon, 46 N. J. Eq. 310, 313.]

[2] Ibid.

[3] Wood v. Burnham, 6 Paige, 513; 26 Wend. 9; 4 Kent, Com. 219; 1 West, Ch. t. Hardwicke, 542. A mere direction to convey will not render the trust executory, if the directions are so clear, and the limitations are so certainly defined, that there is nothing· to do but to convey in accordance with them. In order that the trust may be executory, there must be some room for construction, in order to determine the intention of the settlor; that is, to determine what limitation shall be, and what shall not be, introduced into the conveyance to be made. Egerton v. Brownlow, 4 H. L. Cas. 210; Austen v. Taylor, 1 Ed. 341; Wight v. Leigh, 15 Ves. 564; Graham v. Stewart, 2 Macq. H. L. Ca. 205; Herbert v. Blunden, 1 Dr. & Walsh, 78; East v. Twyford, 9 Hare, 713; Doncaster v. Doncaster, 3 K. & J. 26; Stanley v. Stanley, 16 Ves. 491; Glenorchy v. Bosville, 1 Lead. Ca. Eq. 20, and notes; McElroy v. McElroy, 113 Mass. 509; Cushing v. Blake, 30 N. J. Eq. 689.

[4] Ibid.; Savage v. Tyers, L. R 8 Ch. 356. [See Steele v. Smith, 66 S. E. 200 (S. C. 1909).]

by wills. This is not so much a difference between two classes of executory trusts, as it is a difference between the rules that will be applied to the interpretation of *marriage articles and of wills*, in order to determine the intention of the settlor or the testator. Lord Eldon once said, that " there was no difference in the execution of an executory trust created by will, and a covenant in marriage articles; such a distinction would shake to their foundation the rules of equity." [1] But the great chancellor afterwards modified his expression.[2] And certainly there is no difference in the execution of the two trusts when it is settled what they are; but there is a difference in the construction of marriage articles and of wills in order to reach the intention of the creator of the trusts. Thus, in marriage articles, the intention of the parties to the articles is presumed to be a provision for the issue of the marriage, and such construction is given to the articles as to carry into effect this presumed intention if possible; while in construing wills, in order to settle the limitations of a trust, there is no such presumed leading intention; or, as Sir W. Grant put it, "I know of no difference between an executory trust in marriage articles and in a will, except that the object and purpose of the former furnish an indication of intention, which must be wanting in the latter. Where the object is to make a provision by the settlement for the issue of a marriage, it is not to be presumed that the parties meant to put it in the power of the father to defeat that purpose, and appropriate the estate to himself. If, therefore, the agreement be to limit an estate for life with remainder to the heirs of the body, the court decrees a strict settlement in conformity to the presumable intention. But if a will directs a limitation for life with remainder to the heirs of the body, the court has no such ground for decreeing a strict settlement." [3]

[1] Lincoln *v.* Newcastle, 12 Ves. 230; and see Turner *v.* Sargent, 17 Beav. 519; Reed *v.* Palmer, 53 Penn. St. 379.

[2] Jervoise *v.* Northumberland, 1 J. & W. 574; Townsend *v.* Mayer, 3 Beav. 443; Lassence *v.* Tierney, 1 Mac. & G. 551; Gardner *v.* Stevens, 30 L. J. Ch. 199; Crofton *v.* Davies, L. R. 4 C. B. 159.

[3] Blackburn *v.* Stables, 2 Ves. & B. 369; Bale *v.* Coleman, 8 Vin. 267;

§ 361. Thus if, in marriage articles, the real estate of the husband or of the wife is limited to the *heirs of the body* or to the *issue* [1] of the contracting parties, or either of them, or to the issue of the body, or to the issue and their heirs,[2] so that the words and limitations, taken in their legal sense, would enable the parents, or one of them, to defeat this provision for the children, equity will construe the articles to mean that the estate is limited to the parents for life, and the children will take at the decease of their parents or parent as purchasers; and equity will decree a formal settlement to be drawn in such way as to carry out this purpose.[3] If a settlement is already drawn *after* the marriage, but not in accordance with this rule, equity will correct and reform it so as to carry out this intention.[4] But if the settlement was formally drawn out before marriage contrary to this rule, the court will presume that the parties abandoned the articles, and entered into a new agreement, as expressed in the settlement.[5] If, however, a settlement before marriage is expressed on its face to be made to carry out the articles, and it does not carry them out in this respect, equity will reform it.[6] So if it can be shown in any other way that the formal settlement was intended to carry out the articles,

Strafford *v.* Powell, 1 B. & B. 25; Synge *v.* Hales, 2 B. & B. 508; Maguire *v.* Scully, 2 Hog. 113; Rochford *v.* Fitzmaurice, 1 Conn. & Laws. 173; 2 Dr. & War. 18; 4 Ir. Eq. 375; Jervoise *v.* Northumberland, 1 J. & W. 574; Deerhurst *v.* St Albans, 5 Madd. 260.

   [1] Dod *v.* Dod, Amb. 274.

   [2] Phillips *v.* James, 2 Dr. & Sm. 404.

   [3] Handick *v.* Wilkes, 1 Eq. Cas. Ab. 393; Gilb. Eq. 114; Trevor *v.* Trevor, 1 P. Wms. 622; Rochford *v.* Fitzmaurice, 1 Conn. & Laws. 173; 2 Dr. & War. 18; 4 Ir. Eq. 375; Cusack *v.* Cusack, 5 Bro. P. C. 116; Davies *v.* Davies, 4 Beav. 54; Griffith *v.* Buckle, 2 Vern. 13; Jones *v.* Langton, 1 Eq. Cas. Ab. 392; Stonor *v.* Curwen, 5 Sim. 269; Barnaby *v.* Griffin, 3 Ves. 206; Horne *v.* Barton, 19 Ves. 398; Coop. 257; 22 L. J. (N. S.) Ch. 225. [Grier *v.* Grier, L. R. 5 H. L. 688.]

   [4] Warrick *v.* Warrick, 3 Atk. 293; Sheatfield *v.* Sheatfield, Ca. t. Talb. 176; Legg *v.* Goldwire, id. 20; Burton *v.* Hastings, Gilb. Eq. 113; overruling same case, 1 Eq. Cas. Ab. 393; Briscoe *v.* Briscoe, 7 Ir. Eq. 129.

   [5] Legg *v.* Goldwire, Ca. t. Talbot, 20; Warrick *v.* Warrick, 3 Atk. 291.

   [6] Honor *v.* Honor, 1 P. Wms. 123; West *v.* Errissey, 2 P. Wms. 349; Roberts *v.* Kingsley, 1 Ves. 238.

and it does not do so, equity will reform it on the ground of mistake,[1] or if the settlement is made in the very words of the articles, and the legal effect of the words of the articles and settlement is different from the intention of the parties, the settlement will be corrected and reformed in order to carry out the exact intention of the parties.[2] If, however, there are any intervening rights, as those of an innocent purchaser without notice, his rights of course will be protected.[3] So it is established that daughters are included under the general term of *heirs* or *issue*, and that they take as purchasers.[4] And children includes grandchildren.[5] This has been held in England.[6] Of course in the United States, where primogeniture is abolished, estates will be settled upon sons and daughters equally, or upon daughters alone in default of sons. But if the children or issue of the marriage are provided for in some other way, as by portions to be raised for them in such manner that it appears that they are not intended to take as purchasers of the particular estate under the settlement, then the rule in Shelley's Case will prevail, and the parents or parent may sell the whole estate.[7] And so where there is an actual present conveyance of personal property by a marriage contract executed before marriage in

[1] Bold v. Hutchinson, 5 De G., M. & G. 568; Rogers v. Earl, 1 Dick. 294; 1 Sugd. V. & P. 143.

[2] West v. Errissey, 2 P. Wms. 349; Roberts v. Kingsley, 1 Ves. 238; Honor v. Honor, 1 P. Wms. 128; 2 Vern. 658; Powell v. Price, 2 P. Wms. 535; Gaillard v. Pardon, 1 McMul. Eq. 358; Neves v. Scott, 9 How. 197; Gause v. Hale, 2 Ired. Eq. 241; Smith v. Maxwell, 1 Hill, Eq. 101; Allen v. Rumph, 2 Hill, Eq. 1; Briscoe v. Briscoe, 7 Ir. Eq. 129.

[3] Warrick v. Warrick, 3 Atk. 291; Trevor v. Trevor, 1 P. Wms. 622; West v. Errissey, 2 P. Wms. 349. But if the purchaser have notice of the articles, they may be enforced against him. Davies v. Davies, 4 Beav. 54; Thompson v. Simpson, 1 Dr. & War. 491; Abbott v. Geraghty, 4 Ir. Eq. 15.

[4] West v. Errissey, 2 P. Wms. 349; Comyn, R. 412; 1 Bro. P. C. 225.

[5] Scott v. Moore, 1 Wins. (N. C.) Eq. 98.

[6] Burton v. Hastings, 2 P. Wms. 535; Gilb. Eq. 113; 1 Eq. Cas. Ab. 393; Hart v. Middlehurst, 3 Atk. 371; Maguire v. Scully, 2 Hog. 113; 1 Beat. 370; Marryat v. Townley, 1 Ves. 105; Phillips v. Jones, 4 Dr. & Sm. 406; 3 De G., J. & S. 72.

[7] Powell v. Price, 2 P. Wms. 535; Fearne's Con. Rem. 103.

trust for the wife, and at her death to the heirs of her body, it was held to be an executed trust, there being no further conveyances to be executed, and that the rule in Shelley's Case applied.[1]

§ 362. In England, when a married woman could not convey her interest in real estate, a strict settlement was not ordered under marriage articles that limited the *husband's* estate to the heirs of the body of the wife, for the reason that this created an entail that could not be barred without considerable difficulty; but since the Fines and Recoveries Act, this difficulty is removed.[2] Nor will the court order a strict settlement, if there is anything in the nature of the limitations, or otherwise on the face of the articles, which indicates that such was not the intention of the parties, for the reason that the rule now under discussion was established in order to carry out the intention of the parties. If, therefore, the intention of the parties appears to be in accordance with, or not contrary to, the ordinary rule, the ordinary rule will be allowed to prevail.[3]

§ 363. If personal property is agreed to be settled on the parents for life, and then to their heirs, or the heirs of their bodies, the chattels will not vest in the parents absolutely, but in the heirs when they are born;[4] and it is not necessary that they should survive their parents, or become actual heirs,[5] unless the gift is to the parents and their heirs living at the

[1] Carroll *v.* Renick, 7 Sm. & M. 799; Tillinghast *v.* Coggeshall, 7 R. I. 383.

[2] Rochford *v.* Fitzmaurice, 2 Dru. & W. 19; Highway *v.* Banner, 1 Bro. Ch. 587; Howel *v.* Howel, 2 Ves. 358; Green *v.* Ekins, 2 Atk. 477; Honor *v.* Honor, 1 P. Wms. 123.

[3] Rochford *v.* Fitzmaurice, 2 Dru. & W. 19; Highway *v.* Banner, 1 Bro. Ch. 587; Howel *v.* Howel, 2 Ves. 358; Green *v.* Ekins, 2 Atk. 477; Honor *v.* Honor, 1 P. Wms. 123; Power *v.* Price, 2 P. Wms. 535; Chambers *v.* Chambers, 2 Eq. Cas. Ab. 35; Fitzg. 127.

[4] Hodgeson *v.* Bussey, 2 Atk. 89; Barn. 195; Bartlett *v.* Green, 13 Sim. 218.

[5] Theebridge *v.* Kilburne, 2 Ves. 233.

death of the surviving parent, or there are other equivalent words.[1]

§ 364. If there is a covenant in marriage articles to settle personal property upon the same trusts, and for the same purposes, as the real estate is settled, the court will not apply the same limitations to the personal as to the real estate, for that would be to vest an absolute interest in the heirs at their birth; but the court will insert a provision making the personal property follow the course of the real estate.[2] Courts will also insert a provision that the children or issue shall take, as tenants in common, and not as joint-tenants, on account of the inconveniences of joint-tenancies, and from the presumed intention of the parties;[3] and so the court will insert other words and conditions, and vary the literal instruction of the articles in order to carry out the presumed intention, and promote a convenient settlement for the protection and security of all the parties,[4] as if the settlement is to be of all the property which the settlor might thereafter become entitled to, it will be construed to embrace only the property acquired during the marriage.[5] The

---

[1] Read v. Snell, 2 Atk. 642.

[2] Stanley v. Leigh, 2 P. Wms. 690; Gower v. Grosvenor, Barn. 63; 5 Madd. 348; Newcastle v. Lincoln, 3 Ves. 387, 394, 397; Scarsdale v. Curzon, 1 John. & H. 51. The matter referred to in the text seldom or never arises in the marriage settlements made in the United States, as primogeniture is abolished, and entails on the eldest son are seldom resorted to. But where personal chattels are made to vest under a marriage settlement in the eldest son as heir, and such son dies under age, very awkward effects follow; and, under covenants to settle personal property upon the same limitations as are applied to a settlement of real estate wherein the eldest son takes as heir, it was a matter of great discussion in the Court of Chancery and in the House of Lords, what kind of provisions ought to be inserted to protect the parents and other children in case the eldest son dies under age and without issue. Newcastle v. Lincoln, 3 Ves. 387; 12 Ves. 218.

[3] Taggart v. Taggart, 1 Sch. & Lef. 88; Rigden v. Vallier, 3 Atk. 734; Marryat v. Townley, 1 Ves. 103. Joint-tenancy is abolished by statute in most of the United States, with the exception, in some States, of gifts and grants to husband and wife.

[4] Kentish v Newman, 1 P. Wms. 234; Martin v. Martin, 2 R. & M. 507; Master v. De Croismar, 11 Beav. 184; Targus v. Puget, 2 Ves. 194.

[5] Steinberger v. Potter, 3 Green, Ch. 452.

court will not always order a formal settlement to be drawn out, but will declare the meaning and intention of the articles, and leave the parties to act upon the declaration, as if it was a formal settlement drawn out and executed by them.[1] So the court will sometimes rectify the settlement drawn under articles by a decree, without ordering a new deed to be drawn out and executed.[2]

§ 365. Marriage settlements, whether made in pursuance of articles, or under directions contained in wills, or under decrees of the court, are matters in which courts exercise the most liberal principles of equity. If a settlement is drawn up under a decree, and it is not in all respects in accordance with the decree, the court will set it aside, and order a new settlement.[3] In Grout v. Van Schoonhoven, the court ordered a new settlement, in substance that the trust should be for the wife during her life without power of anticipating the income; and upon her death for the use of her husband for life, in case he survived her; and, after the death of both, to be divided equally among all their children then living, and the descendants of such as had died leaving issue, *per stirpes;* with a power to make advances with the approbation of the trustees to the children, on their attaining full age or being married, out of the capital fund, in anticipation of the ultimate distribution, in order to set them up in the world.[4] An advance cannot be made in order that a child may put the money in his pocket, but an advance may be made to trustees under a marriage settlement for a child.[5] When there was power of advancement to a married woman, it was held that an advance to her husband to set him up in business might be allowed;[6] and so where there was power in a settlement to withdraw funds, and lay them out in the purchase of a trade for the

---

[1] Byam v. Byam, 19 Beav. 58.
[2] Tebbitt v. Tebbitt, 1 De G. & Sm. 506.
[3] Temple v. Hawley, 1 Sandf. Ch. 154.
[4] Grout v. Van Schoonhoven, 1 Sandf. Ch. 342.
[5] Roper v. Curzon, L. R. 11 Eq. 452.
[6] *In re* Kershaw's Trust, L. R. 6 Eq. 322.

benefit of husband and wife, the power may be exercised for the benefit of one after the death of the other.[1] In Imlay v. Huntington, a husband covenanted that he would pay over to certain trustees $10,000, and one-half of certain other expected moneys of his intended wife, to be held by said trustees in trust for the wife for the term of twenty years, after which time they were to convey to such persons as the wife should appoint. The marriage was consummated, and the husband received $60,000, which he continued to hold and manage as his own during the lifetime of his wife, making no payment to the trustees, and neither the trustees nor the wife requesting him to pay the sum over, or to make any settlement in pursuance of the articles. On the death of the wife, at the end of twenty years, her brothers and sisters, there being no issue of the marriage, applied to the court by bill in equity for the execution of the marriage settlement, in accordance with the articles and covenants entered into by the husband before marriage: but it was held that it was competent for the wife to discharge the husband from the fulfilment of the covenants, and to abandon the trust; that, under the circumstances of the case, the articles were abandoned by the wife and all the parties; that the wife's personal property vested absolutely in the husband; and that the wife's heirs had no right to maintain the bill for any part of her personal estate.[2]

§ 366. In executory trusts created by *wills*, no presumption arises *a priori* that a provision was intended for the children of the first taker, as in marriage settlements, and that such children were intended to take as purchasers. If the trust be " for A. and the heirs of his body," [3] or "for A. and the heirs of his body and their heirs," [4] or "for A. for life and after his decease

---

[1] Doorly v. Arnold, 18 W. R. 540.

[2] Imlay v. Huntington, 20 Conn. 146; Jones v. Higgins, L. R. 2 Eq. 538.

[3] Harrison v. Naylor, 2 Cox, 247; Bagshaw v. Spencer, 1 Ves. 151; Marshall v. Bousley, 2 Madd. 166; Robertson v. Johnston, 36 Ala. 197.

[4] Marryat v. Townley, 1 Ves. 104.

to the heirs of his body," [1] A. will be tenant in tail; and he may disappoint his heirs by barring the entail. So, where a testator directed an estate to be settled on his "daughter and her children, and, if she died without issue," remainder over, the court held that the daughter was tenant in tail; and that in a voluntary devise the court must take it as they find it, though upon like words in a marriage settlement it might be different.[2] So where a testator directed lands to be settled on his "nephew for life, remainder to the heirs male of his body, and the heirs male of every such heir male severally and successively, one after another, as they should be in seniority and priority of birth, every elder and the heirs male of his body to be preferred before the younger," it was held that, although the nephew took by a voluntary executory devise, the court must execute it in the words of the will and according to the rules of law, and that equity could not carry the words further than the same words would operate at law, and that the nephew took an estate tail. The words in this case all went upon the idea of an entail.[3] So if there is a direction that the trustees shall not give up their trust until "a proper entail was made to the heir male by them." [4] But in another similar executory trust, Lord Eldon declined to compel a purchaser to accept the title, on the ground that the entail was too doubtful to be acted upon in so grave a matter.[5] Where a testator devised real estate to his daughter, then unmarrled, in trust for her heirs, she to receive the income for her and their support and education, and, if she should die leaving no heirs, then over to her brothers and sisters, it was held that the word "income" passed the estate to the daughter, that the word "heirs" was a word of limitation, and that the

<hr />

[1] Blackburn v. Stables, 2 V. & B. 270; Seale v. Seale, 1 P. Wms. 290; Meure v. Meure, 2 Atk. 266; Robertson v. Johnston, 36 Ala. 197.

[2] Sweetapple v. Bindon, 2 Vern. 536.

[3] Legatt v. Sewell, 2 Vern. 551; McPherson v. Snowden, 19 Md. 197.

[4] Blackburn v. Stables, 2 V. & B. 367; Marshall v. Bousley, 2 Madd. 166; Dodson v. Dodson, 3 Bro. Ch. 405.

[5] Jervoise v. Northumberland, 1 J. & W. 559; Woolmore v. Burrows, 1 Sim. 512.

daughter took an estate tail.[1] In the gift of a fund the term "heirs at law" means next of kin or persons entitled under the statute of distributions relating to personal property.[2]

§ 367. In executory trusts under marriage articles, many distinctions arise upon the question, Who may enforce their specific performance, and compel the execution of the formal deed and the disposal of the property in accordance with the settlement that should have been made under the articles? Thus the general rule is, that parties, seeking a specific execution of such articles, must be those who come strictly within the reach and influence of the consideration of the marriage, or who claim through them, as the wife, or the husband, and the issue of the husband or wife, or both. As a general rule, mere volunteers, or collateral relatives of husband or wife, cannot interfere and ask for a specific performance of the articles.[3] (a) But there

[1] Allen v. Henderson, 49 Pa. St. 333.

[2] White v. Stanfield, 146 Mass. 424.

[3] Vernon v. Vernon, 2 P. Wms. 594; Edwards v. Warwick, id. 171; Osgood v. Strode, id. 245; Ithell v. Beane, 1 Ves. 215; 1 Dick. 132; Stephens v. Trueman, 1 Ves. 73; Pulvertoft v. Pulvertoft, 18 Ves. 90; 2 Kent, Com. 172, 173; Atherly on Mar. Sett. 145; Bradish v. Gibbs, 3 Johns. Ch. 550; West v. Errissey, 2 P. Wms. 349; Kettleby v. Atwood, 1 Vern. 298, 471; Williamson v. Codrington, 1 Ves. 512; Colman v. Sarrel, 1 Ves. Jr. 50; 3 Bro. Ch. 13; Ellison v. Ellison, 6 Ves. 662; Graham v. Graham, 1 Ves. Jr. 275;

(a) In Re Cameron and Wells, 37 Ch. D. 32, 37, Kay, J., said: "When any collateral takes an interest under a marriage settlement, it may be the bargain between the husband and wife that the collateral should so take; but that does not make him any the less a volunteer, because no consideration moves from him, which is the test whether the interest of the collateral is or is not that of a volunteer." It was there held that children of the husband by a former marriage, who were named as beneficiaries of the executory trust under the settlement, could not enforce the settlement as against a purchaser for value from the settlor, since such children were not parties to the consideration. It was admitted that children of a wife by a former marriage would, under the case of Newstead v. Searles (1 Atk. 265; 9 A. C. 320, n.), be treated differently, but the court considered this an exception which should not be extended.

are so many exceptions and qualifications to this rule, that a case is rarely decided upon it. The principle is, that, to bring collateral relations within the reach and influence of the consideration, there must be something over and above that flowing from the immediate parties to the marriage articles, from which it can be inferred that relatives beyond the issue were intended to be provided for, and that, if the provision in their behalf had not been agreed to, the superadded consideration would not have been given.[1] While this is the general rule, the courts seize hold of the slightest valuable consideration to give effect to the settlement in favor of collateral relatives; and it need not appear that these slight considerations were inserted in favor of distant relatives: the court will presume such to be the case.[2] The result of all the cases is, that, if from the circumstances under which marriage articles were entered into by the parties, or as collected from the face of the instrument itself, it appears to have been intended that the collateral relatives in a given event should take the estate, and a proper limitation to that effect is contained in the articles, a court of equity will enforce the trust for their benefit. Such parties are not volunteers outside the deed, but come fairly within the influence of the consideration upon which it is founded. Such consideration extends through all the limitations of the articles for the benefit of the remotest persons provided for, consistent with the rules of law.[3] But of course there is a more direct equity in favor of a wife and

Wycherly v. Wycherly, 2 Eden, 177, note; Bunn v. Winthrop, 1 Johns. Ch. 336; Gevers v. Wright, 3 Green, Ch. 330.

[1] Osgood v. Strode, 2 P. Wms. 245; Goring v. Nash, 3 Atk. 186; Hamerton v. Whitton, 2 Wils. 356; Williamson v. Codrington, 1 Ves. 512; Bleeker v. Bingham, 3 Paige, 246.

[2] Neves v. Scott, 9 How. 209; Stephens v. Trueman, 1 Ves. 73; Edwards v. Warwick, 2 P. Wms. 171.

[3] Neves v. Scott, 9 How. 210; Canby v. Lawson, 5 Jones, Eq. 32; Dennison v. Goehring, 7 Barr, 175; King v. Whitely, 10 Paige, 465. See this matter very learnedly discussed in Neves v. Scott, 9 Monthly Law Reporter, 67, Boston, June, 1846. This decision, however, was overruled in Neves v. Scott, 9 How. 98. The case was again discussed before the State court of Georgia, and the opinion of the circuit court of the district of

children.[1] So in respect to chattel interest, it has been held that a bond under seal, though voluntary, will uphold a decree for the execution of the trust in favor of those whom the obligor is under obligations to support, as wife or children; for a seal in law imports a consideration.[2] But this doctrine seems to be rejected; and it is now held that neither wife nor child can enforce a purely voluntary contract or [executory] settlement.[3]

§ 368. And where a third person — parent, agent, or friend of the parties — holds out any considerations of a pecuniary nature to induce a marriage, and articles are drawn up, and a marriage takes place, equity will compel the party holding out the inducements to make them good, or specifically perform the articles.[4]

§ 369. If, however, in an executory trust created in a will there are indications of an intention that the words "heirs of the body" shall be words of purchase and not of inheritance, they will receive that construction; that is, the intention of the testator will be carried out, if it is sufficiently clear, although the same words in an ordinary grant would create an estate tail. Thus, if there are other words in the will that indicate that the words "heirs of the body" are words of designation, and not of inheritance, such heirs will take by purchase, and the first taker

Georgia was followed. That case was in turn overruled in 13 How. 268. The judgment of the Supreme Court of the United States was, that on the face of that instrument the consideration extended to brothers and sisters; and, further, that it was an executed trust, and that they had an interest.

[1] Pulvertoft v. Pulvertoft, 18 Ves. 99.

[2] Bunn v. Winthrop, 1 Johns. Ch. 336; Minturn v. Seymour, 4 Johns. Ch. 500; Lechmere v. Carlisle, 3 P. Wms. 222; Walwyn v. Coutts, 3 Mer. 708; Antrobus v. Smith, 12 Ves. 44; Colman v. Sarrel, 1 Ves. Jr. 54; Beard v. Nutthall, 1 Vern. 427.

[3] Jefferys v. Jefferys, 1 Cr. & Phil. 138; Holloway v. Headington, 8 Sim. 325. [See supra, § 107.]

[4] Hammersley v. De Biel, 2 Cl. & Fin. 45.

of course will have only an estate for life. Thus, if the testator direct a settlement on A. for life "without impeachment of waste," [1] or with a limitation "to preserve contingent remainders," [2] or if he direct that "care be taken in the settlement that the tenant for life shall not bar the entail," [3] the superadded words show the intention to be, that the first taker shall have only an estate for life, with no power over the inheritance. So, where a gift was in trust for the separate use of a married woman for life, she alone to receive the rent, and her husband not to intermeddle, and, after her decease, to the heirs of her body, the wife took only for life, and the words "heirs of her body," were words of purchase; for if the wife takes the inheritance in tail, the husband will have curtesy, which would be contrary to the clause against his intermeddling.[4] So, where a testator directed an estate to be settled on a married woman for life for her separate use, and at her death on her *issue*, she was not tenant in tail; for there would be only an equitable estate in her, while a legal estate would vest in her issue, and the two estates could not coalesce in such manner as to make her tenant in tail.[5] So a direction to settle land on A. and the heirs of his body "as counsel shall advise," [6] or as "the executors shall think fit," [7] implies that a simple estate tail is not intended, for if it was there would be no need of the additional words. And where the trust was to settle on A. for life without impeachment of waste, remainder to his issue in *strict settlement*, the court directed the estates to be settled on A. for life, without impeachment for

----

[1] Glenorchy v. Bosville, Ca. t. Talb. 3; 1 Lead. Cas. Eq. 1, and notes.

[2] Pappillon v. Voice, 2 P. Wms. 471; Rochford v. Fitzmaurice, 1 Conn. & Laws. 158.

[3] Leonard v. Sussex, 2 Vern. 526.

[4] Roberts v. Dixwell, 1 Atk. 607; West Ca. t. Hardw. 536; Turner v. Sargent, 17 Beav. 515; Stanley v. Jackman, 5 W. R. 302; Stonor v. Curwen, 5 Sim. 264; Shelton v. Watson, 16 Sim. 542.

[5] Stonor v. Curwen, 5 Sim. 268; Verulam v. Bathurst, 13 Sim. 386; Coape v. Arnold, 2 Sm. & Gif. 311; 4 De G., M. & G. 574. And see Collier v. McBean, 34 Beav. 426.

[6] White v. Carter, 2 Eden, 366; Amb. 670.

[7] Read v. Snell, 2 Atk. 642.

waste, remainder to his sons successively in tail male, remainder to his daughters as tenants in common in tail male,
with cross-remainders in tail male, and with limitations to
trustees to preserve contingent remainders.[1]

§ 370. Where a testator devised his estate to trustees for the
term of six years, and to be then divided among his children or
their issue, and conveyances to be given therefor, and directed
that "in each deed or writing to any of my children shall be
inserted and expressed a clause limiting such grant or interest
conveyed to the grantee for life, *with remainder over to the right
heirs of such grantee, their heirs and assigns forever,*" it was held
that the deeds must be so drawn as to give the children a life-
estate only, and not a fee in their shares.[2] The same rule of
construction has been established and enforced in Georgia,[3] and
in Tennessee,[4] and has been recognized in South Carolina,[5]
Maryland,[6] and Pennsylvania.[7]

§ 371. It will be observed that "heirs of the body" and
"issue" are not synonymous terms. "Heirs" are technical
words of limitation, while the word "issue" is *prima facie* a
word of purchase; and courts have ordered a strict settlement
when the word "issue" was used, when it would probably have

---

[1] Trevor *v.* Trevor, 13 Sim. 108; 1 H. L. Cas. 239; Coape *v.* Arnold, 2
Sm. & Gif. 311; 4 De G., M. & G. 574.

[2] Wood *v.* Burham, 6 Paige, 515; affirmed on appeal, 27 Wend. 9. The
rule in Shelley's Case was in force in New York at the time, and would
have applied to this case if it had not been an executory trust. The rule
in Shelley's Case was soon after abrogated in that State, and the decision
has ceased to be important; nor is the subject-matter now under discussion
of importance in any State where the rule in Shelley's Case is abolished by
statute.

[3] Edmondson *v.* Dyson, 2 Kelly, 307; Wiley *v.* Smith, 3 Kelly, 551,
559; Neves *v.* Scott, 9 How. 197; 13 How. 2 8.

[4] Loring *v.* Hunter, 8 Yerg. 4.

[5] Garner *v.* Garner, 1 Des. 437; Porter *v.* Doby, 2 Rich. Eq. 49.

[6] Horner *v.* Lyeth, 4 H. & J. 431.

[7] Findlay *v.* Riddle, 3 Binney, 139.

been otherwise if the word "heir" had been used.[1] (a) The words "heirs of the body,"[2] and "issue,"[3] embrace daughters; for they equally answer the description and are equally the objects of bounty; and where the words are words of purchase,

[1] Meure v. Meure, 2 Atk. 265; Haddelsey v. Adams, 22 Beav. 276; Rochford v. Fitzmaurice, 2 Conn. & Laws. 158; Bastard v. Proby, 2 Cox, 6; Dodson v. Hay, 3 Bro. Ch. 405; Stonor v. Curwen, 5 Sim. 264; Horne v. Barton, G. Coop. 257; Crozier v. Crozier, 2 Conn. & Laws. 311; Ashton v. Ashton, cited in Bagshaw v. Spencer, 1 Coll. Jur. 402; McPherson v. Snowden, 19 Md. 197. Where a testator intends the estate to go to the whole body of persons, in legal succession, constituting *in law* the entire line of descent lineal, he evidently means the same thing as if he had said "issue" or "heirs of the body;" or if he intends it to go to the whole line of descent, lineal and collateral, he means the same thing as if he had used the term "heirs," which, as a word of art, describes precisely the same line of descent. Per Agnew, J., in Yarnall's App., 70 Penn. St. 340. And see Kleppner v. Laverty, 70 Penn. St. 70; Kiah v. Grenier, 1 N. Y. Sup. Ct. 388.

[2] Bastard v. Proby, 2 Cox, 6.

[3] Meure v. Meure, 2 Atk. 265; Trevor v. Trevor, 13 Sim. 108; Ashton v. Ashton, *ut supra*.

(a) The word "issue" in a deed or will, when used as a word of purchase, means, in the absence of an intention disclosed to the contrary, descendants generally. Drake v. Drake, 134 N. Y. 220, 224; Soper v. Brown, 136 N. Y. 244. But if there is a clear intention to include only children in the word, the intention will control. Chwatal v. Schreiner, 148 N. Y. 683; Jackson v. Jackson, 153 Mass. 374. In a statute "issue" may include an adopted child. Buckley v. Frasier, 153 Mass. 525.

The word "children" in a deed of gift or a will does not include grandchildren unless such intention is clearly exhibited or the word appears to have been used as synonymous with issue or descendants. Osgood v. Lovering, 33 Me. 464, 469; Williams v. Knight, 18 R. I. 333; Pride v. Fooks, 3 De G. & J. 252.

But if such intention appears it will be given effect. *Ibid.*; Edgerly v. Barker, 66 N. H. 434. For a case distinguishing between the *prima facie* meaning of "issue" and "children," see Pride v. Fooks, 3 De G. & J. 252. In a will by a testator who had no children of his own and no reasonable expectation of any, the word "children" has been held to include step-children. *In re* Jeans, 72 L. T. 835. In Connor v. Gardner, 230 Ill. 258, it was said: "The words 'sons,' 'daughters,' 'child' and 'children' are not technical legal terms to which a fixed meaning must be given regardless of the sense in which they are employed, but they are flexible and subject to construction, to give effect to the intention of the testator." For the interpretation of such words for the purposes of the rule in Shelley's Case see *supra*, § 358 and note.

the settlement, in default of sons, will be made upon daughters, as tenants in common in tail, with cross-remainders.[1] In the United States, the settlement would be made upon sons and daughters in common, with cross-remainders in default of issue, unless the direction was to settle upon some particular one of the heirs of the body or issue.

§ 372. If the limitations of an executory trust are imperfectly or defectively declared in a will, the court will rectify the limitations, and order the settlements to be made in accordance with the intention of the testator, and to be drawn up in proper form to effectuate that intention.[2] But if a testator undertake to be his own conveyancer, and himself draw up in his will all the particulars of the limitations upon which he desires his property to be settled, intending them to be final and to be carried into effect in the trusts, the court is bound by the words, as in Austen v. Taylor, where Lord Northington said that "the testator had referred no settlement to the trustees to complete, but had declared his own uses and trusts," and that there was no authority in the court to vary them.[3]

§ 373. When a testator has devised lands in strict settlement, and then devises personal chattels as *heirlooms*, to be held by, or in trust for, the parties entitled to the use of the real estate under the limitations of the settlement; or when he expresses a desire that the heirlooms should be held upon the same trusts as the real estate, — "so far as the rules of law and equity will permit," the tenant for life will have the use of the heirlooms,

[1] Marryat v. Townley, 1 Ves. 105; Meure v. Meure, 2 Atk. 265; Trevor v. Trevor, 13 Sim. 108; 1 H. L. Ca. 239; Bastard v. Proby, 2 Cox, 6; Ashton v. Ashton, in Spencer v. Bagshaw, *ut supra;* Shelton v. Watson, 16 Sim. 543.

[2] Franks v. Price, 3 Beav. 182; Doncaster v. Doncaster, 3 K. & J. 26; Rochford v. Fitzmaurice, 1 Conn. & Laws. 173; 2 Dr. & War. 21.

[3] Austen v. Taylor, 1 Eden, 368. This case, however, has been criticised. See Green v. Stephens, 19 Ves. 76; Jervoise v. Northumberland, 1 J. & W. 572. And see East v. Twyford, 9 Hare, 713; Meure v. Meure, 2 Atk. 265; Harrison v. Naylor, 2 Cox, 247.

and they will vest absolutely in the first tenant in tail, upon his birth, though he die immediately after.[1] In such cases, the court regards the trust, either as executed, or, if the trust is executory, that it has no authority to insert a limitation over in case of the tenant in tail dying under twenty-one. But such a limitation over is not illegal; and if the bequest of the heir-looms is clearly executory, and if the intention of the testator is plainly manifested that no person shall take the chattels absolutely who does not live to become possessed of the real estate, the court will execute the intention by directing the insertion of a limitation that the absolute interest of the first tenant in tail, if he should die under twenty-one, should go over to the next person in remainder.[2] And so where the absolute vesting of the chattels is coupled with the actual possession, and is therefor suspended until the death of the tenant for life, the chattels will vest in the child, who, after the death of the tenant for life, shall fulfil all the requisites of being tenant in tail in possession.[3] (a)

§ 374. If the words of a will, taken in their ordinary sense, create a *joint-tenancy*, the court cannot order a settlement giving a *tenancy in common*, as it may do under marriage articles. But in some cases, where a testator is providing for his children, or

---

[1] Foley v. Burnell, 1 Bro. Ch. 274; Vaughan v. Burslem, 3 Bro. Ch. 101; Newcastle v. Lincoln, 3 Ves. 387; Carr v. Erroll, 14 Ves. 478; Trafford v. Trafford, 3 Atk. 347; Doncaster v. Doncaster, 3 K. & J. 26; Rowland v. Morgan, 6 Hare, 463; 2 Phill. 674; Gower v. Grosvenor, Barn. Ch. 54; 5 Madd. 337, overruled; Evans v. Evans, 17 Sim. 108; Tollemache v. Coventry, 2 Cl. & Fin. 611; 8 Bligh (N. S.), 547; Stapleton v. Stapleton, 2 Sim. (N. S.), 212; Deerhurst v. St. Albans, 5 Madd. 232, overruled; Scarsdale v. Curzon, 1 John. & H. 40, where all the cases are cited and commented on.
[2] Potts v. Potts, 3 Jo. & Lat. 353; 1 H. L. Cas. 671; Trafford v. Trafford, 3 Atk. 347; Lincoln v. Newcastle, 3 Ves. 387.
[3] Scarsdale v. Curzon, 1 John. & H. 40.

(a) In a devise of plate and a leasehold house, the words "to be enjoyed with and to go with the title," do not create an executory trust or cut down the devisee's interest to a life estate. *In re* Johnston, 26 Ch. D. 538.

where a grandparent *in loco parentis* is providing for his grand-children, the court will order a settlement that will create a tenancy in common.[1] And, generally, executory trusts under wills will be construed in the same manner as marriage articles entered into after marriage.[2]

§ 375. When a settlement is directed in an executory trust, but there is no direction as to the powers to be given under it, the court cannot order the insertion of any powers,[3] except per-haps the power of leasing, which generally is an implied power to enable a party to enjoy the estate.[4] But if the executory articles or the will contain a direction to insert the "*usual powers,*" powers to lease for twenty-one years,[5] of sale and ex-change,[6] of varying the securities,[7] of appointing new trustees,[8] and (according to the nature of the property) of partition, of leasing mines, and of granting building leases, will be inserted.[9] But there is a distinction between powers for the management and enjoyment of the estate, and powers which are personally beneficial to one or more particular persons, such as powers of jointure, to charge portions, or to raise moneys for a particular purpose.[10] The court cannot therefore order these latter powers to be inserted under the direction to insert the *usual powers,* for there is no rule by which the court could be governed in reduc-

[1] Synge *v.* Hales, 2 B. & B. 499; Marryat *v.* Townley, 1 Ves. 102. But there were other circumstances in these cases that indicated a tenancy in common. McPherson *v.* Snowden, 19 Md. 197.

[2] Rochford *v.* Fitzmaurice, 1 Conn. & Laws. 158.

[3] Wheete *v.* Hall, 17 Ves. 80; Brewster *v.* Angell, 1 J. & W. 628.

[4] Woolmore *v.* Burrows, 1 Sim. 518; Fearne's P. W. 310; but see the late cases, Turner *v.* Sargent, 17 Beav. 515; Scott *v.* Steward, 27 Beav. 367; Charlton *v.* Rendall, 1 Hare, 296.

[5] Hill *v.* Hill, 6 Sim. 144; Bedford *v.* Abercorn, 1 M. & Cr. 312.

[6] Hill *v.* Hill, 6 Sim. 144; Bedford *v.* Abercorn, 1 M. & Cr. 312; Peake *v.* Penlington, 2 V. & B. 311.

[7] Sampayo *v.* Gould, 12 Sim. 426.

[8] Lindow *v.* Fleetwood, 6 Sim. 152; Sampayo *v.* Gould, 12 Sim. 426; Brewster *v.* Angell, 1 J. & W. 628.

[9] Hill *v.* Hill, 6 Sim. 145; Bedford *v.* Abercorn, 1 M. & Cr. 312.

[10] Hill *v.* Hill, 6 Sim. 144.

ing the *corpus* of the estate.[1] So if certain particular powers
are directed to be inserted, the *usual powers* will be qualified by
the direction. Thus, where it was directed that the settlement
should contain a power of leasing for twenty-one years, a power
of sale and exchange, and of appointment of new trustees, it
was held that a power of granting building leases could not be
inserted.[2] So the powers must be inserted and executed as they
are directed; as where a power was directed to be inserted of
selling and exchanging estates in one county, *and all other usual
powers*, it was held that the powers could not be extended to
estates in other counties.[3] And where a testator directed the
insertion of a power of making leases, *and otherwise according to
circumstances*, and of appointing new trustees, the court refused
to insert a power of sale and exchange, saying that, if where
nothing is expressed nothing can be implied, it is impossible,
where something is expressed, to imply more than is expressed,
especially where the will notices what powers are to be given.[4]
But under particular directions as to certain powers, and general
directions that other usual powers should be inserted, the two
directions being separate and independent of each other, it was
held that a power to appoint new trustees might be inserted.[5]
Where *proper powers* of making leases or otherwise were directed
to be reserved in the settlement to the tenants for life while
qualified to exercise them, and when disqualified to the trustees,
and a power of sale and exchange was inserted in the settlement,
Lord Eldon held that it was improperly introduced;[6] and Sir T.
Plummer gave a similar decision, on the ground that the tenant
for life ought not to have a power of sale unless it was expressly
directed, nor ought the trustees to have such a power in the
absence of an express direction.[7] But where there was a settle-

---

[1] Higginson *v.* Barneby, 2 S. &. S. 516.
[2] Pearse *v.* Baron, Jac. 158.
[3] Hill *v.* Hill, 6 Sim. 141.
[4] Brewster *v.* Angell, 1 J. & W. 625; Horne *v.* Barton, Jac. 439.
[5] Lindow *v.* Fleetwood, 6 Sim. 152.
[6] Brewster *v.* Angell, 1 J. & W. 625.
[7] Horne *v.* Barton, Jac. 437.

ment of stock with a power of varying the securities, and also a covenant to settle real estate upon the same trusts and with like powers, it was held that a power to sell and exchange was properly introduced in analogy to the power of varying the securities.[1]

§ 376. In drawing up the final deed of settlement under executory articles or a will, the intention of the settlor is to be carried out if possible. If the intention conflicts with any of the rules of law, it shall be executed so far, and as near as it can be. The doctrine of *cy près* applies to this class of executory trusts. (a) Thus, if a settlement is directed which would create a perpetuity, the court will order a settlement which shall carry the trust as far as it can extend without running counter to the rules against perpetuities. As where there was a devise to a corporation in trust to convey to A. for life, and after his death to his first son for life, and so on to the first son of such first son for life; and, in default of male issue, then to B. for life, and to his son for life after the death of B., and so as in the case of A., Lord Cowper said the attempt to create a perpetuity was vain, yet the directions should be complied with, so far as consistent with the law, and he directed that all the sons already born should take estates for life in succession, with limitations to unborn sons in tail.[2] But if the devise is such that it cannot be carried into effect, in any form approximating the intention of the testator, without contravening the law against perpetuities or remoteness, the whole trust will be void.[3]

---

[1] William *v.* Carter, Append. to Treatise on Powers, 945 (8th ed.); Elton *v.* Elton, 27 Beav. 634; Horne *v.* Barton, Jac. 437.

[2] See § 383; Humberston *v.* Humberston, 1 P. Wms. 332; 2 Vern. 737; Pr. Ch. 455; Parfitt *v.* Hember, L. R. 4 Eq. 443; Peard *v.* Kekewick, 15 Beav. 173; Lyddon *v.* Ellison, 19 Beav. 565; Williams *v.* Teal, 6 Hare, 239, and cases; Vanderplank *v.* King, 3 Hare, 1; Monypenny *v.* Dering, 16 M. & W. 418.

[3] Blagrave *v.* Hancock, 16 Sim. 371.

(a) See *infra*, § 390.

CHAPTER XIII.

PERPETUITIES AND ACCUMULATIONS.

§ 377. THAT the same rules apply to trusts as to legal estates
is further apparent from the rule against perpetuities. A perpetuity has been declared to be "an estate unalienable, though

all mankind should join in the conveyance;"[1] and an executory devise is said to be "a perpetuity as far as it goes." Again, it has been said, that "a perpetuity is when if all that have interest join, yet they cannot pass the estate."[2] These are characteristics of a perpetuity. There are other descriptions given, as that "a perpetuity is a thing odious in the law, and destructive to the commonwealth: it would stop commerce and prevent the circulation of property."[3] Others have described the rule of law as respects the period of remoteness, rather than the thing itself called a perpetuity;[4] thus, "a perpetuity is a limitation tending to take the subject out of commerce for a longer period than a life or lives in being and twenty-one years beyond, and, in the case of a posthumous child, a few months more, allowing for the term of gestation."[5] Mr. Saunders says: "A perpetuity may be defined to be a future limitation, restraining the owner of the estate from alienating the fee-simple of the property, discharged of such future use or estate, before the event is determined, or the period is arrived, when such future use or estate is to arise. If that period is within the bound described by law, it is not a perpetuity."[6] This describes the thing itself, and not the rule of law, or the length of time, which may vary. Mr. Lewis gives a fuller definition: "A perpetuity is a future limitation, whether executory, or by way of remainder, and of either real or personal property, which is not to vest, until after the expiration of, or will not necessarily vest within, the period fixed and prescribed by law for the creation of future estates and interests; and which is not destructible by the persons for the time being entitled to the property, subject to the future limitation, except with the concurrence of the individual interested under that limitation."[7] If such person is not yet in being,

---

[1] Scattergood v. Edge, Salk. 229.
[2] Washborne v. Downes, 1 Ch. Cas. 213.
[3] Duke of Norfolk's Case, 1 Vern. 164.
[4] Stanley v. Leigh, 2 P. Wms. 688.
[5] Rand. Perp. 48.
[6] Uses and Trusts, 204.
[7] Lewis on Perpetuity, 164. Jarman's Treatise on Wills contains this

as he may not be after an extended period, of course the estate cannot be conveyed, even if all the world join in the deed. (*a*)

marked sentence: "*Te teneam moriens* is the dying lord's apostrophe to his manor, for which he is forging these fetters that seem, by restricting the dominion of others, to extend his own." 1 Jar. on Wills, 226, note (ed. 1861).

(*a*) For a historical review of the cases showing the development of the rule see Gray on the Rule against Perpetuities (2d ed.), §§ 123–200. The rule is there stated as follows: "No interest is good unless it must vest, if at all, not later than twenty-one years after some life in being at the creation of the interest." *Ibid.* § 201.

It is frequently said that the purpose of the rule is to prevent restraints upon alienation of property by the creation of remote interests in it which are inalienable by nature; but, although this is undoubtedly a usual result of its operation, it seems better to regard the rule as aiming to prevent the creation of remote unvested interests rather than to prevent restraints upon alienation of the property itself or of vested interests in it. In other words, the rule against perpetuities concerns itself solely with the time for the vesting of the limitations over, not with the duration of the prior estate. See Winsor *v.* Mills, 157 Mass. 362, 365; Gray *v.* Whittemore, 192 Mass. 367; Lembeck *v.* Lembeck, 73 N. J. Eq. 427; Loomer *v.* Loomer, 76 Conn. 522; Pulitzer *v.* Livingston, 89 Me. 359; Gray on Perpetuities (2d ed.), §§ 269, 278; but see 8 Harv. Law Rev. 211; Missionary Soc. *v.* Humphreys, 91 Md. 131, criticised in Gray on Perpetuities (2d ed.), § 245 c.

If the prior estate falls with the void limitation over, its failure is not because of its long duration but because of an expressed or implied intention of the donor or testator that it should be conditional upon the validity of the limitations over, as where it is only part of a general scheme which fails because the limitations over cannot take effect. Pitzel *v.* Schneider, 216 Ill. 87; Central Trust Co. *v.* Egleston, 185 N. Y. 23; Reid *v.* Voorhees, 216 Ill. 236; Schuknecht *v.* Schultz, 212 Ill. 43. See Smith *v.* Chesebrough, 176 N. Y. 317; Landram *v.* Jordan, 25 App. D. C. 291, 302. Whenever it appears that the prior estate was intended as an independent gift or grant to take effect irrespective of the gift over, the invalidity of the latter because of remoteness has no effect upon the former. Georgia Code [1895], § 3102; Chapman *v.* Cheney, 191 Ill. 574; Nevitt *v.* Woodburn, 190 Ill. 283; Quinlan *v.* Wickman, 233 Ill. 39; Johnson's Trustee *v.* Johnson, 79 S. W. 293 (Ky. 1904); Graham *v.* Whitridge, 99 Md. 248, 282; First Universalist Society *v.* Boland, 155 Mass. 171; Matter of Mount, 185 N. Y. 162; *In re* Gage, [1898] 1 Ch. 498; Patching *v.* Barnett, 51 L. J. Ch. 74. See note to Saxton *v.* Webber (Wis.), 20 L. R. A. 509; Edgerly *v.* Barker, 66 N. H. 434; *In re* Dugdale, 38 Ch. Div. 176. And the same is true in case of a void at-

§ 378. Executory devises are a species of testamentary dispositions, allowed by courts of law, and when properly exercised, they pass the *legal* estate or interest to all persons in favor of whom the dispositions are made. They are devises to take effect at a certain time in the future, or upon a certain event, and in favor of certain persons. Limitations by way of springing or shifting uses are similar in effect, except that they are created by deeds *inter vivos*, and are based upon the statute of uses. Whenever the event happens when a shifting or springing use is to take effect, the statute of uses vests the legal seizin and ownership in the person entitled by virtue of the use. These executory devises, and shifting and springing uses, must vest in the persons intended to be benefited within the time allowed by law, or they will be declared illegal and of no effect. The same rules apply in equity to trusts. In cases of trusts the legal estate is vested in certain trustees, and their heirs; but the beneficial interest, or equitable estate, is given by the grantor, testator, or settlor to such person or persons, and upon such terms and upon such events, as he shall declare. The settlor can change and shift the beneficial enjoyment of the equitable estate from one person to another, in the future, in a manner analogous to the limitations of springing or shifting uses under the statute of uses.[1] (a) Courts of equity always take special care that future estates or interests shall not be destroyed by the present user

---

[1] Harrison *v.* Harrison, 36 N. Y. 543.

tempt to impose a restraint upon the alienation of a vested interest. Matter of Murray, 78 N. Y. S. 165, 75 App. Div. 246; Johnson's Trustee *v.* Johnson, 79 S. W. 293 (Ky. 1904).

The chief reason why the rule against perpetuities has been so often regarded as aimed against restraints upon alienation seems to be that with few exceptions restraints upon the power to alienate an interest in property can be imposed only by making the interest conditional

upon some future contingency. But attempted restraints upon power to alienate vested interests come under an entirely different rule. See *infra*, § 386 *et seq.*

(a) See Powers *v.* Bullwinkle, 33 S. C. 293; Glover *v.* Condell, 163 Ill. 566; Smith *v.* Kimbell, 153 Ill. 368; Welch *v.* Brimmer, 169 Mass. 204; Naylor *v.* Godman, 109 Mo. 543; Gray on Perpetuities (2d ed.), §§ 268, 317.

of the property; and that the limitations of future equitable interests shall not transcend the limits assigned for the limitation of similar legal interests or executory devises, and shifting and springing uses at law.

§ 379. The rule against perpetuities has been gradually established by judicial decisions, and affords a most notable instance of the nice adaptation of the principles of the common law to the decision of a question which requires at once a due regard for the rights of persons and property, and a careful consideration of these larger principles of public policy so essential to the welfare of communities and States. For public policy is opposed to the perpetual settlement of property in families in such manner that it is forever inalienable, or inalienable so long as there may be a person to take, answering the designation of some testator who died generations before. The first stand of the judges was to allow only those limitations which would take effect at the end of one life from the death of the testator.[1] This was afterwards modified to include two or more lives in being, and running at the same time, "or where the candles are all burning at once;" for it is plain that such a space of time is only one life in being, — that of the longest liver.[2] The next step was much debated; but it was finally settled, that an executory devise might be made to vest at the end of lives in being and twenty-one years after, to allow for the infancy of the next taker, who by reason of infancy could not alienate the estate.[3] The statute of 10 & 11 Wm. III., c. 16, having provided that

[1] Pells v. Brown, Cro. Jac. 590; 1 Eq. Cas. Ab. 187, c. 4 (A. D. 1621); see Snow v. Cutler, 1 Lev. 135, t. Raym. 162; 1 Keb. 151, 752, 800; 2 Keb. 11, 145, 296; 1 Sid. 153.

[2] Goring v. Bickerstaff, Pollexf. 31; 1 Ch. Cas. 4; 2 Freem. 163 (1664); 2 Harg. Jurid. Arg. 46; Lloyd v. Carew, Shower, P. C. 137; Pr. Ch. 72.

[3] Taylor v. Biddal, 2 Madd. 289; Freem. 243; 1 Eq. Cas. Ab. 188, c. 11; F. C. R. 432; Laddington v. Kime, 1 Raym. 203; Gore v. Gore, 2 W. Kel. 204; 2 P. Wms. 28; 2 Stra. 948; Scattergood v. Edge, 12 Mod. 277; Duke of Norfolk's Case, 3 Ch. Cas. 32; Ch. R. 229; 2 Freem. 72; Pollexf. 223; Massenburgh v. Ash, 1 Vern. 234; Maddox v. Staine, t. Talb. 228; 2 Harg. Jurid. Arg. 50.

children *en ventre sa mère*, born after their father's death, should
for the purposes of the limitations of estates be deemed to have
been born in his lifetime, a further extension of nine or ten
months was allowed for the period of gestation.[1] The next step
was to allow a period of nine months for gestation at the beginning of the term, as the life in being during which the term
would run might be that of a child *en ventre sa mère*.[2] Much
discussion arose upon each one of these steps.[3] For instance,
the term of twenty-one years, it was said, could not be allowed
as a term in gross, and without reference to the infancy of some
person interested in the estate; this question was not settled
until Cadell *v.* Palmer, in the House of Lords in 1833, when it
was finally determined, that twenty-one years might be allowed
as a term in gross, without reference to the infancy of any person, but that the period of nine months for gestation should be
allowed in cases only where the gestation had commenced [4] of
some persons who, if born, would take an interest in the estate.
By such steps, by imperceptible degrees, and after two cen-
turies of doubt and litigation, and unaided by legislation, the
judges framed and completed the *great rule against perpetuities*.[5]

§ 380. Thus all future legal estates which arise by way of
executory devise, conditional limitation, or shifting and spring-

[1] Stephens *v.* Stephens, Cas. t. Talb. 228; Forrest, 228; Goodtitle *v.*
Woods, Willes, 211; 7 T. R. 103 (n.); Sheffield *v.* Orrery, 3 Atk. 282; Gul-
liver *v.* Wicket, 1 Wils. 185; Bullock *v.* Stones, 2 Ves. 521; Goodman *v.*
Goodright, 2 Burr. 873.

[2] Long *v.* Blackall, 7 T. R. 100; 2 Harg. Jurid. Arg. 105; 6 Cru. Dig.
488.

[3] Davies *v.* Speed, 12 Mod. 39; 2 Salk. 675; Holt, 731; Bostock's Case,
Ley, 56; Roe *v.* Tranmer, 2 Wils. 75; Lloyd *v.* Carew, Show. P. C. 137;
Pr. Ch. 72; 2 Harg. Jurid. Arg. 36; Carwardine *v.* Carwardine, 1 Ed. 34;
Blandford *v.* Thackerell, 2 Ves. Jr. 241; 1 Sand. Uses & Tr. 198; Thellus-
son *v.* Woodford, 4 Ves. 337; Routledge *v.* Dorrill, 2 Ves. Jr. 357; Keily
v. Fowler, Wilmot, 306; Beard *v.* Westcott, 5 Taunt. 393; 5 B. & A. 801;
T. & R. 25; Bengough *v.* Edridge, 1 Sim. 173, 271.

[4] Cadell *v.* Palmer, 7 Bligh (N. S.), 202; 10 Bing. 140; 1 Cl. & Fin. 372;
1 Jarm. Wills, 222.

[5] Lewis on Perpetuity, pp. 140-162; 1 Powell on Devisees by Jar. 389,
n. [Gray on Perpetuities, (2d ed.) § 201 *et seq.*, § 411 *et seq.*]

ing uses, must vest within a life or lives in being at the death of the testator, and twenty-one years; and, in case the person in whom the estate or interest should then vest is *en ventre sa mère,* nine months more will be allowed; and all estates created as aforesaid, and so limited that they may not vest within that time, are void.[1] If the estates are created and limited by deeds *inter vivos,* the lives in being must be those persons who are living at the execution of the deed, and not at the death of the grantor or settlor.[2] And if an absolute term is taken, and no anterior term for a life in being is referred to, such absolute term cannot be longer than twenty-one years;[3] but a term of

---

[1] Proprietors of Church in Brattle Square *v.* Grant, 3 Gray, 149; Sears *v.* Russell, 8 Gray, 86; 1 Shep. Touch. 126; 4 Kent, Conn. 128 and notes; 2 Fearne, Cont. Rem. 50; Nightingale *v.* Burrell, 15 Pick. 111; 6 Cru. Dig. tit. 38, c. 17, § 23; Cadell *v.* Palmer, 1 Cl. & Fin. 372, 423; Bacon *v.* Proctor, T. & R. 31; Mackworth *v.* Hinxman, 2 Keen, 658; Ker *v.* Duncannon, 1 Dr. & War. 509; Com., &c. *v.* De Clifford, id. 245; Welsh *v.* Foster, 12 Mass. 97; Tilbury *v.* Barbut, 3 Atk. 617; Conklin *v.* Conklin, 3 Sandf. Ch. 64; Tyte *v.* Willis, Ca. t. Talb. 1; Att. Gen. *v.* Gill, 2 P. Wms. 369; Nottingham *v.* Jennings, 1 id. 25; Kampf v. Jones, 2 Keen, 756; Miller *v.* Macomb, 26 Wend. 229; Tator *v.* Tator, 4 Barb. 431; Ring *v.* Hardwicke, 2 Beav. 352; Ferris *v.* Gibson, 4 Edw. 707; Egerton *v.* Brownlow, 4 H. L. Cas. 1, 160. [Chilcott *v.* Hart, 23 Colo. 40; Georgia Code, (1895) § 3102; Post *v.* Rohrbach, 124 Ill. 600; Quinlan *v.* Wickman, 233 Ill. 39; Pitzel *v.* Schneider, 216 Ill. 87; Schuknecht *v.* Schultz, 212 Ill. 43; Merritt *v.* Bucknam, 77 Me. 253; Andrews *v.* Lincoln, 95 Me. 541; Towle *v.* Doe, 97 Me. 427; Graham *v.* Whitridge, 99 Md. 248, 274; Universalist Soc. *v.* Boland, 155 Mass. 171; Shepperd *v.* Fisher, 206 Mo. 208; Merrill *v.* Am. Baptist Union, 73 N. H. 414; Edgerly *v.* Barker, 66 N. H. 434; Kountz's Estate, 213 Pa. St. 390; Lawrence's Estate, 136 Pa. St. 354; Fitchie *v.* Brown, 211 U. S. 321; *In re* Frost, 43 Ch. Div. 246; *In re* Ashforth, [1905] 1 Ch. 535; *In re* Hancock, [1901] 1 Ch. 482; *In re* Bence, [1891] 3 Ch. 242; *In re* Dawson, 39 Ch. Div. 155; *In re* Harvey, 39 Ch. Div. 289.]

[2] Lewis on Perpetuity, 171, 172. Mr. Lewis observes an inconsistency in taking lives in being at the death of the testator, if the future interest is created by will, and lives in being at the date or execution of the deed, if such interests are created by deed. But it should be remembered that a will speaks as at the death of the testator, while a deed speaks as at the time of its execution, so that there is no inconsistency in principle. See Tregonwell *v.* Sydenham, 3 Dow. 194; 2 Jar. on Wills, 257; Ed. 1861. [*In re* Gage, [1898] 1 Ch. 498.]

[3] Crooke *v.* De Vandes, 9 Ves. 197; Palmer *v.* Holford, 4 Russ. 403;

any number of years may be taken, provided the term is so connected with some life or lives in being that the interest must vest in some person living at the death of the testator and at the time of the vesting.[1] So estates limited to take effect after an indefinite failure of issue of a living or deceased person are void, for the reason that the issue of such persons may not fail until after the term of a life or lives in being and twenty-one years has expired.[2] But a limitation over in case the heirs of A.'s body living at her death die before reaching the age of twenty-one, is not void if A. leave no heirs of her body, but it takes effect at her death.[3]

Speakman *v.* Speakman, 8 Hare, 180. [See Edgerly *v.* Barker, 66 N. H. 434; Towle *v.* Doe, 97 Me. 427; Andrews *v.* Lincoln, 95 Me. 541.]

[1] Lachlan *v.* Reynolds, 9 Hare, 796.

[2] Randolph *v.* Wendel, 4 Sneed, 646; Van Vechten *v.* Pearson, 5 Paige, 512; Van Vechten *v.* Van Vechten, 8 id. 104; Hone *v.* Van Schaick, 20 Wend. 564; Watkins *v.* Quarles, 23 Ark. 179; Campbell *v.* Harding, 2 Rus. & My. 390; Condy *v.* Campbell, 2 Cl. & Fin. 421, 427; Harrison *v.* Harrison, 36 N. Y. 543; Allen *v.* Henderson, 49 Penn. St. 233; Fisher *v.* Webster, L. R. 14 Eq. 287; Newill *v.* Newill, L. R. 7 Ch. 253; Roe *v.* Jeffery, 1 T. R. 589; Hawley *v.* James, 5 Paige, 318; 16 Wend. 61; Miller *v.* Macomb, 2 id. 229; 9 Paige, 265; Lorillard *v.* Coster, 5 id. 172; Boehm *v.* Clark, 9 Ves. 580; Black *v.* McAulay, 5 Jones, L. 375; Jackson *v.* Billinger, 18 Johns. 368; Fisk *v.* Keen, 35 Maine, 349; Bramlet *v.* Bates, 1 Sneed, 554; Jordan *v.* Roach, 32 Miss. 481; Gray *v.* Bridgforth, 33 Miss. 312; Tongue *v.* Nutwell, 13 Md. 415; Jones *v.* Miller, 13 Ind. 337; Chism *v.* Williams, 29 Mo. 288; Dodd *v.* Wake, 8 Sim. 615; Trafford *v.* Boehm, 3 Atk. 440; Ellicombe *v.* Gompertz, 3 Myl. & Cr. 127; Murray *v.* Addenbrook, 4 Russ. 407; Hayes *v.* Hayes, id. 311; Bell *v.* Phyn, 7 Ves. 453; Thackeray *v.* Sampson, 2 S. & S. 214; Cross *v.* Cross, 7 Sim. 201; Bradshaw *v.* Skilbeck, 2 Bing. N. C. 182; Budd *v.* State, 22 Md. 48; Johnson *v.* Currin, 10 Penn. St. 498; Bedford's App., 40 id. 18; Deihl *v.* King, 6 Serg. & R. 29; Eichelberger *v.* Barnitz, 17 Serg. & R. 293; Rice *v.* Satterwhite, 1 Dev. & B. Eq. 69; Postell *v.* Postell, Bail. Ch. 390; Conklin *v.* Conklin, 3 Sandf. Ch. 64; Brashear *v.* Marcy, 3 J. J. Marsh. 89; Allen *v.* Parkam, 5 Munf. 457; Mazyck *v.* Vanderhost, Bail. Ch. 48; Adams *v.* Chaplin, 1 Hill, Eq. 265; Lanesborough *v.* Fox, Ca. t. Talb. 262; Bennett *v.* Lowe, 5 Moor. & P. 485; Smith *v.* Dunwoody, 19 Ga. 237; McRee *v.* Means, 34 Ala. 378; Powell *v.* Brandon, 24 Miss. 343; Armstrong *v.* Armstrong, 14 B. Mon. 333. As to the legislation in the various States upon the failure of issue, see 2 Washburn, Real Prop. 683 (3d ed.). [See Smith *v.* Kimbell, 153 Ill. 368.]

[3] Egbert *v.* Schultz, 29 Ind. 242.

§ 381. It will be observed, that, in determining whether a particular devise is contrary to the rule against perpetuities, the inquiry is not whether the contingency upon which the estate is to vest actually occurs within the time limited by the rule, but whether it is possible that the event may not happen within the time. If it is possible that the event upon which an executory devise or shifting or springing use is to vest in some person may not happen within the time, the executory estate is void,[1] although in fact the event actually happens within the time.[1] And it must further be observed, that, if the estate is to vest in some persons within the time limited, it will not be obnoxious to the rule against perpetuities, even if such person may not be entitled to the actual enjoyment of the property; that is, the rule as to perpetuities deals with the *vesting of the title*, and not with the *actual reception of the profits of an estate*.[2] A gift may be to unborn children for life and then to an ascertained person, if the *vesting* of the estate in the latter is not postponed too long. The person who is to take must become certain within the period, the right of possession may be postponed longer. (a)

[1] *Post*, § 393; Langdon v. Simson, 12 Ves. 295; O'Neill v. Lucas, 2 Keen, 313; Moore v. Moore, 6 Jones, Eq. 132; Welch v. Foster, 12 Mass. 97; Craig v. Hone, 2 Edw. Ch. 554; Robinson v. Bishop, 23 Ark. 378; Sears v. Putnam, 102 Mass. 5. [Gray on Perpetuities (2d ed.), § 214.]

[2] Loring v. Blake, 98 Mass. 253; Murray v. Addenbrook, 4 Russ. 407; Phipps v. Kelynge, 2 V. & B. 57, n. (c); Curtis v. Lukin, 5 Beav. 147; Otis v. McLellan, 13 Allen, 339; Yard's App., 64 Penn. St. 95. [Conn. Trust Co. v. Hollister, 74 Conn. 228; Armstrong v. Barber, 239 Ill. 389; Flanner v. Fellows, 206 Ill. 136; Gray v. Whittemore, 192 Mass. 367; Stone v. Forbes, 189 Mass. 163; Hull v. Osborn, 151 Mich. 8; Gates v. Seibert, 157 Mo. 254; Lembeck v. Lembeck, 73 N. J. Eq. 427; Kountz's Estate, 213 Pa. St. 390; Shallcross's Estate, 200 Pa. St. 122; Wainwright v. Miller, [1897] 2 Ch. 255. See also Wilber v. Wilber, 165 N. Y. 451; Matter of Roberts, 98 N. Y. S. 809; 112 App. Div. 732; Wells v. Squires, 102 N. Y. S. 597; 117 App. Div. 502 (affirmed 191 N. Y. 529); Quade v. Bertsch, 72 N. Y. S. 916; 65 App. Div. 600 (affirmed 173 N. Y. 615).]

(a) A devise or bequest of either a legal or an equitable interest to a class of persons the members of which are to be determined upon contin- gencies which may by any possibility not happen within the period set by the rule for the vesting of estates, is void as to all members of the class. *Re*

Moreover, if a certain estate is to vest within the time on a contingency which actually occurs, the devise is not affected by the fact that the estate was limited to take effect at another time in the event of an alternate contingency which may be too remote.[1] (a)   If two constructions may be put upon a will, one

---

[1] Seaver v. Fitzgerald, 141 Mass. 401. [Gray v. Whittemore, 192 Mass. 367, 372; Brown v. Wright, 194 Mass. 540; In re Bowles, Page v. Page,

Whitten, 62 L. T. 391; Patching v. Barnett, 51 L. J. Ch. 74 ; In re Mervin, [1891] 3 Ch. 197; In re Gage, [1898] 1 Ch. 498; In re Bence, [1891] 3 Ch. 242; Kountz's Estate, 213 Pa. St. 390. But see Edgerly v. Barker, 66 N. H. 434, where contrary to the general rule, the court applied the cy près doctrine and gave effect to the intention of the testator up to the limit of time allowed by the rule, cutting off the excess. Thus a remainder after life interests to such grandchildren of the testator as may live to attain twenty-five years of age is void, since some of the class may be born after the death of the testator, and in that event it may not be possible to determine the share of each member of the class until more than twenty-one years after the cessation of lives in being. Re Whitten, 62 L. T. 391. As was said in In re Dawson, 39 Ch. Div 155, "The rule with regard to perpetuities is that every member of the class, where it is a question of a class gift, must of necessity take within the time allowed."

It is immaterial that as events turn out the class is actually determined within the period set by the rule, e. g., that no grandchild is born after the death of the testator. The rule acts as to possibilities at the time of the testator's death, or, in case the future estates are created by deed, at the time the deed is exe-

cuted and delivered. And in determining these possibilities the courts refuse to consider a living person as incapable of having issue. In re Dawson, 39 Ch. Div. 155; White v. Allen, 76 Conn. 185.

In case of a gift to a class to be determined in the future, e. g., to grandchildren, a distinction must be carefully drawn between postponement of their enjoyment or possession for more than twenty-one years after the death of their parent and the postponement of a vesting of their interests. If the share of each member of the class is to vest at his parent's death, the rule is not violated by a provision that the share shall not be paid to him until he attains twenty-five or until all the members of the class attain that age. Gray v. Whittemore, 192 Mass. 367, 373 et seq.; In re Turney, [1899] 2 Ch. 739. See Ogden v. McLane, 73 N. J. Eq. 159.

The rule of perpetuities does not apply to reversions, Kasey v. Fidelity Trust Co., 131 Ky. 609; First Universalist Soc. v. Boland, 155 Mass. 171; and will not prevent a trust from resulting for the heirs of the grantor upon failure of a declared trust or completion of its purpose at a time beyond the limit set by the rule for the vesting of estates. Hopkins v. Grimshaw, 165 U. S. 342.

(a) Thus where a life estate was

of which will offend against the rule against perpetuities, and the other not, the construction which will not offend against the rule will be adopted, if in other respects it can be sustained.[1] And so a will speaks, upon the subject of remoteness, from the time of the last codicil, and not from the date of the original will.[2] (a)

§ 382. The same rule applies with equal force in law and equity, and trusts and beneficial or equitable estates are subject

[1905] 1 Ch. 371; Evers v. Challis, 7 H. L. Cas. 531; Morton Trust Co. v. Sands, 195 N. Y. 28, 36; N. Y. Life Ins. & T. Co. v. Cary, 191 N. Y. 33; Schey v. Schey, 194 N. Y. 368; Perkins v. Fisher, 59 Fed. 801; Quinlan v. Wickman, 233 Ill. 39.]

[1] Martelli v. Holloway, L. R. 5 H. L. 532.

[2] Hosea v. Jacobs, 98 Mass. 65.

given to a son and on his death a further life estate to his widow and children, if he should leave any, with remainder to his children in fee; and if he should leave a widow but no children, the remainder after the widow's life estate to the issue of A. W., or failing such issue to the testator's right heirs-at-law, and the son died, never having married, A. W. having previously died leaving no issue, it was held that the gift over to the testator's right heirs was not too remote, since the life estates in the widow and children of the son were expressly made conditional on his dying leaving a widow and children or a widow alone. These conditions not happening, the gift over to testator's right heirs was direct and not after possible life estates. Brown v. Wright, 194 Mass. 540.

In a similar case, Gray v. Whittemore, 192 Mass. 367, 372, it was said, "This is not the case of a limitation expressed to be made upon one double contingency or upon the

happening of two events which the testator has not separated, but one in which the testator has himself made the distinction and separation between the two different events, either one of which, if it occurs, will exclude the existence of the other. . . . It is true, no doubt, that where the testator has made only one contingency, though depending upon a twofold event, the courts will not split this up into two contingencies, one good and the other bad, and sustain the limitation on the ground that only the good contingency has taken place." This last proposition is supported by several recent decisions of the English court. In re Hancock, [1901] 1 Ch. 482; In re Harvey, 39 Ch. Div. 289; In re Bence, [1891] 3 Ch. 242. Gray on Perpetuities (2d ed.), § 331; In re Wilcox, 194 N. Y. 288.

(a) But the period of time within which the estates must vest is reckoned from the date of the testator's death.

to the same restrictions.[1] A perpetuity will no more be toler-
ated when it is covered by a trust, than when it displays itself
undisguised in the settlement of a legal estate.[2] "If," as Lord
Guilford said, "in equity you could come nearer to a perpetuity
than thè common law admits, all men, being desirous to continue their estates in their families, would settle their estates
by way of trust, which might make well for the jurisdiction of
chancery, but would be destructive to the commonwealth."

§ 383. Therefore, the creation of a trust or equitable interest,
which may not vest in the object of the trust within the time
limited by law for the vesting of legal estates, will be nugatory.[3]
Thus where a testator devised his real estate to trustees, in
trust to apply the rents to the support of his wife, and his present and future grandchildren, during the life of the wife, and on
her death to convey the estates to all his present and future
grandchildren, as they respectively attained the age of twenty-
five years, to hold to them and their heirs as tenants in common,
it was held that the trust to convey was void, for the reason that
some of the grandchildren might not become twenty-five years
old until after the expiration of the life of the tenant for life,
and twenty-one years in addition.[4] So a testator cannot authorize his trustees to limit an estate beyond the limits of the rule
against perpetuities; but the persons appointed to take must be

---

[1] Duke of Norfolk's Case, 3 Ch. Cas. 20; 2 Ch. R. 229; 2 Freem. 72;
Pollexf. 293; Massenburgh v. Ash, 1 Vern. 254; Schutter v. Smith, 41 N. Y.
329; Knox v. Jones, 47 N. Y. 397; Burrill v. Boardman, 43 N. Y. 254.
Æquitas sequitur legem, but courts of equity have rather led the law courts
in fashioning the rules against perpetuities. [Gray on Perpetuities, (2d
ed.) § 322 et seq.; Pulitzer v. Livingston, 89 Me. 359.]

[2] Norfolk's Case, 1 Vern. 164; Humberston v. Humberston, 1 P. Wms.
332; Parfitt v. Hember, L. R. 4 Eq. 443; Sears v. Putnam, 102 Mass. 5;
Lovering v. Worthington, 106 Mass. 86.

[3] Bailey v. Bailey, 28 Hun, 603. [Andrews v. Lincoln, 95 Me. 541;
Towle v. Doe, 97 Me. 427.]

[4] Blagrave v. Hancock, 16 Sim. 374; Dodd v. Wake, 8 Sim. 615; Broughton v. James, 1 Coll. 26; 2 H. L. Cas. 406; Walker v. Mower, 16 Beav. 365;
Leake v. Robinson, 2 Mer. 363; Sears v. Russell, 8 Gray, 86.

capable of taking directly under the will.[1] (a)   So where a testator devised land to a corporation in trust to convey the same

[1] Marlborough v. Godolphin, 1 Ed. 404; Robinson v. Hardcastle, 2 T.
R. 241, 380, 781; Fonda v. Fenfield, 56 Barb. 503; Barnum v. Barnum,
26 Md. 119. But a power to change trustees does not come within the
principle. Clark v. Platt, 30 Conn. 282.

(a) A testator or grantor cannot
by grant of a power accomplish a
disposition of his property in the
future in violation of the rule against
perpetuities. Except in the case of
unlimited powers of disposal by deed
or by will, the validity of the execution of the power as regards the rule
against perpetuities depends upon
whether the attempted exercise
would, under the circumstances existing at the date of the attempted
exercise, have been valid if made at
the time the deed or will creating the
power took effect. Brown v. Columbia Finance, etc., Co., 123 Ky. 775;
Graham v. Whitridge, 99 Md. 248,
269; Genet v. Hunt, 113 N. Y. 158;
Dana v. Murray, 122 N. Y. 604;
Lewine v. Gerardo, 112 N. Y. S. 192;
Farmers' Loan & Tr. Co. v. Kip, 192
N. Y. 266; Lawrence's Estate, 136
Pa. St. 354; Boyd's Estate, 199 Pa.
St. 487; Bartlett v. Sears, 81 Conn.
34.

If the power is to appoint by deed
or will to whomever the donee
chooses, the remoteness of appointment is to be determined from the
point of time of its exercise, not from
the time of its creation. Gray on
Perpetuities (2d ed.), § 524; Rous v.
Jackson, 29 Ch. Div. 521; Genet v.
Hunt, 113 N. Y. 158. But notwithstanding this exception, the appointee takes under the instrument creating the power. In re Devon's
Settled Estates, [1896] 2 Ch. 562,

567; In re Johnson's Estate, 19 N.
Y. S. 963; Collins v. Wickwire, 162
Mass. 143; Olney v. Balch, 154
Mass. 318.

When the power is general in its
scope but its exercise is limited to be
by will of the donee, there is a difference of authority; but on principle
and by the weight of authority the
remoteness of the attempted disposition must be judged from the date
of the creation of the power. Gray
on Perpetuities (2d ed.), § 526; Lawrence's Estate, 136 Pa. St. 354; Genet v. Hunt, 113 N. Y. 158. See
contra, Rous v. Jackson, 29 Ch. 521.

A power is not void because under
it the donee "might, without depart-
ing from the express language, attempt to create an illegal estate.
The power is in legal effect to do
what is lawful and not what is unlawful." Hillen v. Iselin, 144 N. Y.
365, 378; Graham v. Whitridge, 99
Md. 248, 269; Brown v. Columbia
Finance, etc., Co., 123 Ky. 775 (semble); McClellan's Estate, 221 Pa. St.
261; Stone v. Forbes, 189 Mass. 163.
And the exercise of the power will
be upheld so far as it is valid, if the
invalid parts can be separated from
the valid. Graham v. Whitridge,
99 Md. 248, 269; Brown v. Columbia Finance, etc., Co., 123 Ky. 775
(semble). See also Lewine v. Gerardo, 112 N. Y. S. 192.

Where the trust is to sell within a
reasonable time after the death of

to A. for life, with remainder to his oldest son for life, remainder to the son's oldest son for life, and so on in an endless series, and in default of issue of A., then to B., for life, and remainder to his oldest son for life, and so on in the same manner as to the sons of A., it was held to be void and vain as a perpetuity.[1] So if any directions are given which, if complied with, must enforce a perpetuity, they will be void; as when a testator gave land to a college, and directed that the same should be leased forever to his wife's relations at two-thirds its value, it was held to be a void direction, as tending to a perpetuity.[2] (a)

[1] Humberston v. Humberston, 1 P. Wms. 332; Parfitt v. Hember, L. R. 4 Eq. 442; Floyer v. Bankes, L. R. 8 Eq. 115.

[2] Att. Gen. v. Greenhill, 9 Jur. (N. S.) 1307.

life beneficiaries and to divide the proceeds among persons, some of whom were not in being at the time the trust was created, it has been held that the trust for sale and division does not violate the rule against perpetuities, since the reasonable time, during which the sale is to be made and the trust terminated, cannot have been intended to exceed twenty-one years. In re Sudeley, [1894] 1 Ch. 334.

(a) Since the common-law rule against perpetuities concerns itself wholly with the vesting, or beginning, of legal and equitable interests, not with their duration, a provision that a trust shall continue for a time which extends or may extend beyond the limits allowed for the vesting of estates does not affect the validity of the trust if equitable interests covering the entire ownership of the property must fully vest within the proper time. Lembeck v. Lembeck, 73 N. J. Eq. 427; Armstrong v. Barber, 239 Ill. 389. See In re Daveron,

[1893] 3 Ch. 421; In re Bevan's Trusts, 34 Ch. Div. 716. Thus the common form of trust for the holding and management of real estate for unincorporated associations, the members of which are the equitable owners of the property, does not tend to violate the rule against perpetuities from the fact that the duration of the trust is not limited on lives in being and twenty-one years, since the entire equitable ownership is vested in the members of the association from the beginning. Hart v. Seymour, 147 Ill. 598; Pulitzer v. Livingston, 89 Me. 359; Howe v. Morse, 174 Mass. 491; Loomer v. Loomer, 76 Conn. 522; see Holmes v. Walter, 118 Wis. 409. Attempted restraints upon the power of the equitable owners to alienate their interests may be void, but this is under an entirely different rule. See Howe v. Morse, 174 Mass. 491, explaining Winsor v. Mills, 157 Mass. 362; Butterfield v. Reed, 160 Mass. 361, 368. As to the effect of such

§ 384. In private trusts the beneficial interest is vested absolutely in some individual or individuals who are, or within a
certain time may be, definitely ascertained; and to whom, therefore, collectively, unless under some disability, it is, or within
the allowed limit will be, competent to control, modify, or end
the trust.   Private trusts of this kind cannot be extended beyond
the legal limitations of a perpetuity, as before stated. (a)   Nor
can a settlor give his trustees a power to appoint the property
subject to a trust, to new trusts to arise at or upon the termination of the trusts created by himself. But a trust created for
charitable or public purposes is not subject to similar limitations, but it may continue for a permanent or indefinite time.[1] (b)

---

[1] Christ's Hospital v. Granger, 1 Mac. & G. 460; Att. Gen. v. Foster,
10 Ves. 344; Att. Gen. v. Newcombe, 14 Ves. 1; Fearon v. Webb. id. 19;
Walker v. Richardson, 2 M. & W. 892; Att. Gen. v. Aspinal, 2 Myl. & Cr. 622;
Att. Gen. v. Heelis, 2 S. & S. 76; Att. Gen. v. Shrewsbury, 6 Beav. 224;
Odell v. Odell, 10 Allen, 1; Gass v. Wilhite, 2 Dana, 183; Griffin v. Graham,
1 Hawks, 131; Miller v. Chittenden, 2 Iowa, 362; Philadelphia v. Girard,
45 Penn. St. 26; Yard's App., 64 id. 95. The rule is held differently under
the legislation of the State of New York. Levy v. Levy, 33 N. Y. 130;
Bascombe v. Albertson, 34 N. Y. 598; Beekman v. Bonsor, 23 N. Y. 308;
Yard's App., 64 Penn. St. 95, and see White v. Hale, 2 Cold. 77.

restraints in New York and in other
States which have provided a statutory substitute for the rule against
perpetuities, see *infra*, § 391 and
note *a*, p. 640.

(a) See note (a) *supra*, p. 623.

(b) The rule against perpetuities
"does not apply to a gift to a charity, with no intervening gift to or for
the benefit of a private person or
corporation; or to a contingent limitation over from one charity to another. But it does apply to a grant
or devise to a private person, although limited over after an immediate gift to a charity." Mr. Justice
Gray, in Hopkins v. Grimshaw, 165
U. S. 342, 355. See *In re* Tyler, [1891]

3 Ch. 252; *In re* Swain, [1905] 1 Ch.
669; First Universalist Soc. v. Boland, 155 Mass. 171; *In re* Clarke,
[1901] 2 Ch. 110; St. John v. Andrews Inst., 191 N. Y. 254; Asylum
v. Lefebre, 69 N. H. 238.

And the rule applies to a gift to a
charity limited over after a gift to
an individual, if the limitation is not
to take effect within the time allowed by the rule. *In re* Bowen,
[1893] 2 Ch. 491; Brooks v. Belfast,
90 Me. 318, 323; Merrill v. Am.
Baptist Union, 73 N. H. 414; *In re*
Swain, [1905] 1 Ch. 669; Merritt v.
Bucknam, 77 Me. 253. See *infra*,
§ 736.

§ 385. A trust to raise a sum of money out of an estate will be good if properly limited, although the trust itself upon which the money is limited after it is raised is void as being too remote. In such case, the heir will take the money as personal estate.[1] Contingent remainders of trust estates do not follow the strict rules of legal estates, but they are made to wait upon the contingency. In legal estates, the contingency must happen before the time, or the estate is gone. In the contingent remainders of equitable estates here spoken of, if the contingency may happen within the time, the estate is made to wait: if it happens, the estate vests; if it does not happen, the estate fails.[2]

§ 386. A legal estate in fee cannot be conveyed to a person with a provision that it shall not be alienated, or that it shall not be subject to the claims of creditors; (a) and so trusts cannot in general[3] be created with a proviso, that the equitable

---

[1] Ellis v. Lynch, 8 Bosw. 465; Burnly v. Evelyn, 16 Sim. 290; Tregonwell v. Sydenham, 3 Dow. 194. But see Parson v. Snook, 40 Barb. 144.

[2] Mogg v. Mogg, 1 Mer. 654; Monypenny v. Deering, 7 Hare, 568; Alexander v. Alexander, 16 C. B. 59; Hopkins v. Hopkins, 1 Atk. 581; Festing v. Allen, 12 M. & W. 279; Sayer's Trusts, L. R. 6 Eq. 319; Litt v. Randall, 3 Sm. & G. 83; Hodson v. Ball, 14 Sim. 558; Jee v. Audley, 1 Cox, 324; Church in Brattle Square v. Grant, 3 Gray, 142; Arnold v. Congreve, 1 R. & M. 209; Wilson v. Wilson, 4 Jur. (N. S.) 1076; 28 L. J. (N. S.) 95; Storrs v. Benbow, 3 De G., M. & G. 390; Cattlin v. Brown, 11 Hare, 372; Griffith v. Pownall, 13 Sim. 393; Merlin v. Blagrave, 25 Beav. 125; Greenwood v. Roberts, 15 Beav. 92; Dungannon v. Smith, 12 Cl. & Fin. 546; Seaman v. Wood, 22 Beav. 591; Vanderplank v. King, 3 Hare, 1; Webster v. Boddington, 26 Beav. 128; Curtis v. Lukin, 5 Beav. 147; Hardenburg v. Blair, 30 N. J. Eq. 42; Newark Meth. Episc. Ch. v. Clark, 41 Mich. 730.

[3] This is the rule in England and in some of our States; but the contrary is strongly held in a Massachusetts case of the year 1882. See § 827 a.

(a) In re Rossher, 26 Ch. Div. 801; Pritchard v. Bailey, 113 N. C. 521; Murray v. Green, 64 Cal. 363; Prey v. Stanley, 110 Cal. 423; Booker v. Booker, 104 N. Y. S. 21, 119 App. Div. 482; Clark v. Clark, 99 Md. 356; Female Orphan Soc. v. Y. M. C. A., 119 La. 278; Loosing v. Loosing, 122 N. W. 707 (Neb. 1909).

estate, or interest of the *cestui que trust,* shall not be alienated or charged with his debts.[1] (*a*) If it is ascertained that an interest is vested in the *cestui que trust,* the mode in which or the time when he is to reap the benefit is immaterial. The law does not allow property, whether legal or equitable, to be fettered by

[1] Snowdon *v.* Dales, 6 Sim. 524; Green *v.* Spicer, 1 R. & M. 395; Graves *v.* Dolphin, 1 Sim. 66; Brandon *v.* Robinson, 18 Ves. 429; Ware *v.* Cann, 10 B. & Cr. 433; Bradley *v.* Peixoto, 3 Ves. 324; Hood *v.* Oglander, 34 Beav. 513; Bird *v.* Johnson, 18 Jur. 976; Blackstone Bank *v.* Davis, 21 Pick. 43; Etches *v.* Etches, 3 Drew. 441; Sparhawk *v.* Cloon, 125 Mass. 262; Daniels *v.* Eldredge, id. 350.

(*a*) Restraints upon alienation of future income have been treated in many States as not necessarily inconsistent with the estate or interest granted to the beneficiary. (See *infra,* § 386 *a* and notes.) But restraints upon alienation of an equitable interest in the corpus of the estates are generally held to be void for repugnancy, except where the trust is for the separate use of a married woman. Winsor *v.* Mills, 157 Mass. 362; Cushing *v.* Spalding, 164 Mass. 287; Potter *v.* Couch, 141 U. S. 296; Seymour *v.* McAvoy, 121 Cal. 438; Johnson *v.* Preston, 226 Ill. 447; Kessner *v.* Phillips, 189 Mo. 515; *In re* Dugdale, 38 Ch. Div. 176. In Potter *v.* Couch, 141 U. S. 296, 315, the court said, citing many authorities: "The right of alienation is an inherent and inseparable quality of an estate in fee simple. In a devise of land in fee simple, therefore, a condition against all alienation is void, because repugnant to the estate devised. For the same reason, a limitation over, in case the first devisee shall alien, is equally void, whether the estate be legal or equitable. And on principle, and according to the weight of author-

ity, a restriction, whether by way of condition or of devise over, not forbidding alienation to particular persons or for particular purposes only, but against any and all alienation whatever during a limited time, of an estate in fee, is likewise void, as repugnant to the estate devised to the first taker, by depriving him during that time of the inherent power of alienation."

Attempted restraints upon alienation of absolute legal life estates and vested remainders are also void. Wool *v.* Fleetwood, 136 N. C. 460, 67 L. R. A. 444; Streit *v.* Fay, 230 Ill. 319. But it is an established rule in Kentucky that a will or deed creating an absolute estate may impose valid restraints upon alienation for a "reasonable" time. Lawson *v.* Lightfoot, 84 S. W. 739 (Ky. 1905); Kean *v.* Kean, 18 S. W. 1032, 19 S. W. 184 (Ky.); Morton's Guardian *v.* Morton, 120 Ky. 251; Stewart *v.* Brady, 3 Bush, 623; Smith *v.* Isaacs, 78 S. W. 434 (Ky. 1904).

A restraint upon power of alienation is not inconsistent with a legal title held in trust for others. Danforth *v.* Oshkosh, 119 Wis. 262, 275. See Asylum *v.* Lefebre, 69 N. H. 238.

restraints upon alienation. Therefore, when an equitable interest is once vested in the *cestui que trust*, he may dispose of it, or it may pass to his assignees by operation of law, if he becomes a bankrupt. (*a*) Thus a trust for a person's support,[1] or to pay the interest to a person for life, as the trustees may think proper,[2] or when it shall become payable,[3] or in such sums or portions, and at such times and in such manner as the trustees think best,[4] may be exercised according to the discretion of the trustees; but the bankruptcy of the *cestui que trust* puts an end to the discretion of the trustees, and vests the whole interest in the assignees; and this is so, even where the trustees were directed to pay as they should think proper, and at their will and pleasure and not otherwise, so that the *cestui que trust* should have no right, claim, or demand, other than the trustees should think proper. The court thought, in Snowdon *v.* Dales, that, taking the whole instrument together, the *cestui que trust* had a vested interest, that these directions applied only to the manner of enjoyment, and that the equitable interest vested in the assignees at his bankruptcy.[5] The test is, Would executors of the *cestui que trust* have a right to call for any arrears? if so, the assignees would have the right to call for the future income or interest.[6] (*b*)

[1] Younghusband *v.* Gisborne, 1 Coll. 400.
[2] Green *v.* Spicer, 1 R. & M. 395.
[3] Graves *v.* Dolphin, 1 Sim. 66.
[4] Piercy *v.* Roberts, 1 Myl. & K. 4.
[5] Snowdon *v.* Dales, 6 Sim. 524.
[6] *Re* Sanderson's Trust, 3 K. & J. 497.

(*a*) See Riordan *v.* Schlicher, 146 Ala. 615; McCrea *v.* Yule, 68 N. J. Law, 465; Binns *v.* La Forge, 191 Ill. 598; Jastram *v.* McAuslan, 26 R. I. 320; Bronson *v.* Thompson, 77 Conn. 214; Wenzel *v.* Powder, 100 Md. 36; Whittredge *v.* Sweetzer, 189 Mass. 45. This statement, although generally true in the absence of restraint imposed by the creator of the trust, must be qualified by the established rule in many States, that valid restraints may be imposed upon a *cestui's* power of anticipating income or of alienating it before it is due. See *infra*, § 386 *a* and notes, and § 827 *a*.

(*b*) A wide discretion given to the trustee as to the time, and manner of payment of income does not necessarily make the income inalienable,

§ 386 a. This doctrine, that the incidents of a legal title attach to an absolute equitable interest, and that an equitable estate for life in any other than a married woman carries with it the power of alienation by the *cestui que trust*, and may be taken for the payment of his debts, and that no provision which does not operate to terminate his interest can protect it from the claims of creditors, is the well-settled law of England, and has been approved and applied in many *dicta* and decisions in the United States.[1] But it has not been allowed to pass unchallenged, and there is eminent authority in the Federal and the State courts for the proposition, that the power of alienation is not a necessary incident to an equitable estate for life, and that the owner of property may, in the free exercise of his bounty, so dispose of it as to secure its enjoyment to the objects of his bounty without making it alienable by them or liable for their debts, and that this intention, clearly expressed by the founder of a trust, must be carried out by the courts.[2] (a)   In those

[1] *Ante*, § 386, cases cited; Tillinghast *v.* Bradford, 5 R. I. 205; Smith *v.* Moore, 37 Ala. 327; Hallett *v.* Thompson, 5 Paige, 583; Bramhall *v.* Ferris, 14 N. Y. 41, 44; Williams *v.* Thorn, 70 N. Y. 270; Nichols *v.* Levy, 5 Wall. 433, 441; Sellick *v.* Mason, 2 Barb. Ch. 79; McIllvaine *v.* Smith, 42 Mo. 45; Heath *v.* Bishop, 4 Rich. Eq. 46; Rider *v.* Mason, 4 Sandf. Ch. 352; Easterly *v.* Keney, 36 Conn. 18; Nickell *v.* Handley, 10 Grat. 336; Girard Life Ins. Co. *v.* Chambers, 46 Pa. St. 485; Dick *v.* Pitchford, 1 Dev. & B. Eq. 480; Mebane *v.* Mebane, 4 Ired. Eq. 131; Pace *v.* Pace, 7 N. C. 119.   And a trust made void by an illegal suspension of the power of alienation is not made valid by a power of sale in the trustee, the proceeds remaining subject to the trust.   Garvey *v.* McDavitt, 11 Hun (N. Y.), 457; Brewer *v.* Brewer, id. 147; but see Braman *v.* Stiles, 4 Pick. 460.

[2] Nichols *v.* Eaton, 91 U. S. 716; cited and approved in Hyde *v.* Woods, 94 U. S. 523; Ashhurst *v.* Given, 5 Watts & S. 323; Holdship *v.* Patterson, 7 Watts, 547; Brown *v.* Williamson, 36 Penn. St. 338; Still *v.* Spear, 45 id. 168; Shankland's App., 47 id. 113; Pope *v.* Elliott, 8 B. Mon. 56; White *v.* White, 30 Vt. 338; Campbell *v.* Foster, 35 N. Y. 361.   The argument in these cases proceeds upon the ground, that the doctrine of the English cases must rest upon the rights of creditors; and it is claimed that the

since this discretion must be exercised reasonably and does not give the trustee power to withhold all in-

come. Endicott *v.* University of Va., 182 Mass. 156.

(a) The doctrine of the English

States, however, where the doctrine of the English cases has
been adopted, these distinctions and observations must be borne

policy of the States of this Union has not been carried so far in further-
ance of creditors' rights, that creditors can have no claim upon property
which belonged to the founder of the trust, and of which he had the full
and entire right of disposing as he chose, for the benefit of the *cestui que
trust*, who parts with nothing in return, and that the intent of the donor
clearly expressed in disposing of his property for a lawful purpose must be
carried out; and the laws enacted in nearly or quite every State, exempting
property of greater or less amounts in value from liability for the payment
of debts, are relied on as showing the policy of these States. It is con-
ceded that there are, however, limitations, which public policy or general
statutes impose upon dispositions of property, such as those designed to
prevent perpetuities and accumulations in corporations, &c.   But the
owner of property is governed by the rules of law, both in the use and
enjoyment and in disposing of his property; and the doctrine in question
seems to be founded upon the rule that title to property includes the right
of alienation and liability for debts, and it seems impossible that there can
be any reason in public policy, under a free government, having for its
object the growth and development of a commercial people, for such a
limitation of the incidents of title to property, and the argument from the
exemption laws would seem to be well answered by the maxim, *expressio
unius est exclusio alterius*. Many of the American cases, where the English
doctrine has been doubted or denied, seem to have been cases of trusts
for the support and maintenance of the *cestui que trust;* and a clearly manifested intention on the part of the donor that the income of the fund shall
be devoted to that purpose may impose a duty and give a consequent power
in the trustee, either in his discretion or under the direction of the court,
to pay over the income only in such manner as shall insure its application
in accordance with the intent of the donor and protect it from the claims
of creditors and the improvidence of the beneficiary, with substantially
the same result upon the absolute character of the estate of the *cestui
que trust* as if the instrument declaring the trust had expressly provided
that the payments should be made at the discretion of the trustee, — a
result more in accordance with the rules of interpretation than a strict
adherence to a definition to the extent of defeating the accomplishment
of the benefit intended by the donor.

court, that restraints upon anticipation of income of trust property
are invalid because inconsistent with
the absolute right to the income, except where the beneficiary is a married woman, has been adopted by
the courts of Alabama, Georgia,
Kentucky, Rhode Island, Virginia,
and North Carolina. *In re* Fitzgerald, [1903] 1 Ch. 933; Robertson *v.*
Johnston, 36 Ala. 197; Jones *v.*
Reese, 65 Ala. 134; Gray *v.* Obear,
54 Ga. 231; Bland's Adm'r *v.* Bland,
90 Ky. 400; Cecil's Trustee *v.* Rob-

in mind. If the absolute equitable interest is in the *cestui que trust*, it goes to his assignees or creditors in case of insolvency.

ertson, 105 S. W. 926 (Ky. 1907); Ratliff's Ex'rs *v.* Commonwealth, 101 S. W. 978 (Ky. 1907); Hubbard *v.* Hayes, 98 S. W. 1034 (Ky. 1907); Hutchinson *v.* Maxwell, 100 Va. 169; Honaker Sons *v.* Duff, 101 Va. 675; Young *v.* Easley, 94 Va. 193; Pace *v.* Pace, 73 N. C. 119 (modified by N. C. Code, (1905) § 1588). See also to a similar effect Conn. Gen. Stat. (1902), §§ 837–840; Holmes *v.* Bushnell, 80 Conn. 233; Honnett *v.* Williams, 66 Ark. 148, 153 (*dictum*).

The increasing weight of authority in America favors the rule that provisions against alienation or anticipation of income to which a beneficiary is absolutely entitled are not inconsistent with any estate granted to him and not against the policy of the law. Provisions against anticipation or alienation of income not due and payable or against liability to claims of creditors of the beneficiary have been held valid in the following States: California: — Seymour *v.* McAvoy, 121 Cal. 438. Maine: — Roberts *v.* Stevens, 84 Me. 325; Tilton *v.* Davidson, 98 Me. 55, 58. Maryland: — Smith *v.* Towers, 69 Md. 77; Brown *v.* Macgill, 87 Md. 161; Jackson Sq. Ass'n *v.* Bartlett, 95 Md. 661. Massachusetts: — Munroe *v.* Dewey, 176 Mass. 184; Huntress *v.* Allen, 195 Mass. 227; Slattery *v.* Wason, 151 Mass. 266; Nickerson *v.* Van Horn, 181 Mass. 562. Mississippi: — Leigh *v.* Harrison, 69 Miss. 923. Missouri: — Lampert *v.* Haydel, 96 Mo. 439; Kessner *v.* Phillips, 189 Mo. 515. Pennsylvania: — Seitzinger's Estate, 170 Pa. St. 500, 514; Board of Char-

ities *v.* Lockard, 198 Pa. St. 572. Tennessee: — Jourolman *v.* Massengill, 86 Tenn. 84, 100. Texas: — Patten *v.* Herring, 9 Tex. Civ. App. 640; McClelland *v.* McClelland, 37 S. W. 350 (Tex. Civ. App. 1896); Wood *v.* McClelland, 53 S. W. 381 (Tex. Civ. App. 1899); Monday *v.* Vance, 92 Tex. 428 (*semble*). Vermont: — Barnes *v.* Dow, 59 Vt. 530. West Virginia: — Guernsey *v.* Lazear, 51 W. Va. 328; Talley *v.* Ferguson, 64 W. Va. 328. For *dicta* to the same effect in Illinois and Iowa, see Steib *v.* Whitehead, 111 Ill. 247; Bennett *v.* Bennett, 217 Ill. 434; King *v.* King, 168 Ill. 273; Olsen *v.* Youngerman, 136 Iowa, 404; Meek *v.* Briggs, 87 Iowa, 610. See also Hackley *v.* Littell, 150 Mich. 106; Castree *v.* Shotwell, 73 N. J. Eq. 590. None of these States goes to the extent of holding that a *cestui's* interest in the corpus of trust property, if he has an interest, can be made inalienable, except in case of married women. The American doctrine rests upon the ground that a right to receive income of a trust fund is not necessarily an interest in the fund itself. The limitations upon the American doctrine are stated as follows in Kessner *v.* Phillips, 189 Mo. 515, 524: "In order to have a spendthrift trust certain prerequisites must be observed: first, the gift to the donee must be only of the income. He must take no estate whatever, have nothing to alienate, have no right to possession, have no beneficial interest in the land, but only a qualified right to support, and an equitable interest only in the income;

And it may be said that, if an absolute equitable interest is given to a *cestui que trust;* no restraints upon alienation can be im-

second, the legal title must be vested in a trustee; third, the trust must be an active one, not a mere dry trust which may be executed under the statute of uses."

There are statute provisions in several States authorizing such restraints by the creator of the trust. Cal. Civ. Code, § 867; Blackburn *v.* Webb, 133 Cal. 420; No. Dak. Codes, (1905) § 4834; So. Dak. Code, (1908) § 315. No. Car. Code, (1905) § 1588 (applying to income not exceeding $500 per year payable to a relative of the trustor). See also Ga. Code, (1895) § 3149, as interpreted by Sinnott *v.* Moore, 113 Ga. 908; Moore *v.* Sinnott, 117 Ga. 1010. See Ariz. Stat., (1901) § 4232. Some States have statutes which provide that a person beneficially interested in the income of property held in trust cannot assign his right to future income unless the trust instrument provides that he shall have the right. N. Y. Real Property Law, (1909) § 103, Consol. Laws (1909), p. 3392; Personal Property Law (1909), § 15, ibid. p. 2844; Matter of Kirby, 100 N. Y. S. 155, 113 App. Div. 705; Stringer *v.* Barker, 96 N. Y. S. 1052, 110 App. Div. 37, Bergmann *v.* Lord, 194 N. Y. 70; Kan. Gen. Stat. (1909), § 9697; Minn. R. L. (1905), § 3257; Wis. Stat. (1898), § 2089; Burns' Ind. Stat. (1908), § 4015; Caldwell *v.* Boyd, 109 Ind. 447; Mont. Civ. Code (1907), § 4547.

In several States statutes have been interpreted to exclude creditors of a beneficiary from reaching income of a trust fund when the trust "has been created, or the fund so

held in trust has proceeded from some person other than the debtor." N. Y. Code, § 1879; Everett *v.* Peyton, 167 N. Y. 117; Keeney *v.* Morse, 75 N. Y. S. 728, 71 App. Div. 104; see Ullman *v.* Cameron, 92 App. Div. (N. Y.), 91; Hurd's Ill. Rev. Stat. (1908) c. 22, § 49; Binns *v.* La Forge, 191 Ill. 598; Mich. Comp. Laws (1897), § 436; N. J. Gen. Stat. (1895), p. 390, § 91; Stout *v.* Apgar, 69 N. J. Eq. 337; Linn *v.* Davis, 58 N. J. Law, 29; Castree *v.* Shotwell, 73 N. J. Eq. 590. In Illinois and New Jersey the statutes have been interpreted to exclude creditors from the *cestui's* interest in the *corpus.* See *supra.*

In States where there are such statutes, it is frequently provided that in case of a trust to receive income with no valid direction for accumulation, the surplus of income over what is necessary for the support and education of the beneficiary shall be liable to the claims of his creditors. N. Y. Real Prop. Law, 1909, § 98, IV Consol. Laws, 1909, p. 3391; Wetmore *v.* Wetmore, 149 N. Y. 520; Everett *v.* Peyton, 167 N. Y. 117; Dittmar *v.* Gould, 69 N. Y. S. 708, 60 App. Div. 94; Williams *v.* Thorn, 70 N. Y. 270; Mich. Comp. Laws (1897), § 8841; Spring *v.* Randall, 107 Mich. 103; Cal. Civil Code, § 859; Magner *v.* Crooks, 139 Cal. 640; Minn. Rev. Laws (1905), § 3251; No. Dak. Codes (1905), § 4826; So. Dak. Code (1908), § 307. See also Conn. Gen. Stat. (1902), § 839.

In States which permit restraints on alienation of income, the inten-

posed. But a trust may be so created that no interest vests in the *cestui que trust;* consequently, such interest cannot be alien-

tion of the creator of the trust to impose such a restraint need not be express, but may often be gathered from the circumstances and the nature of the interest given to the beneficiary. Barnes v. Dow, 59 Vt. 530; Berry v. Dunham, 202 Mass. 133; Slattery v. Wason, 151 Mass. 266; Lampert v. Haydel, 96 Mo. 439; Roberts v. Stevens, 84 Me. 325; Tilton v. Davidson, 98 Me. 55, 58; Leigh v. Harrison, 69 Miss. 923; Steib v. Whitehead, 111 Ill. 247; Bennett v. Bennett, 217 Ill. 434; Patten v. Herring, 9 Tex. Civ. App. 640; Seymour v. McAvoy, 121 Cal. 438; Castree v. Shotwell, 73 N. J. Eq. 590; Talley v. Ferguson, 153 W. Va. 328; Mattison v. Mattison, 53 Or. 254. See Conn. Gen. Stat. (1902), §§ 837–840.

It has been held that where the sole beneficiary of an attempted spendthrift trust has been given, by the terms of the trust, power to direct a disposal of the principal fund for his own benefit and so to bring about a termination of the trust at will, his creditors can reach his interest in the trust property, since he is practically the equitable owner. Morgan's Estate, 223 Pa. St. 228; Ullman v. Cameron, 92 App. Div. (N. Y.) 91.

In all jurisdictions restraints on alienation are invalid as to the *cestui's* creditors when the trust property was his own before the settlement. Egbert v. De Solms, 218 Pa. St. 207; Kene v. Hill, 92 N. Y. S. 805, 102 App. Div. 370; Newton v. Jay, 95 N. Y. S. 413, 107 App. Div. 457; Schenck v. Barnes, 156

N. Y. 316; Raymond v. Harris, 82 N. Y. S. 689, 84 App. Div. 546; Pacific National Bank v. Windram, 133 Mass. 175; Jackson v. Von Zedlitz, 136 Mass. 342. See Ames' Cases, (2d ed.) p. 400; Hackley v. Littell, 150 Mich. 106. It has been held in several cases that the principle applies with equal force where a married woman has attempted to create a spendthrift trust for her separate use. Brown v. Macgill, 87 Md. 161; Jackson v. Von Zedlitz, 136 Mass. 342; Pacific Nat. Bank v. Windram, 133 Mass. 175; Stewart v. Madden, 153 Pa. St. 445; Ghormley v. Smith, 139 Pa. St. 584. See 12 Harvard Law Rev. 53. Section 19 of the Married Women's Property Act of 1882 seems to have provided for the same result in England. See Birmingham, etc., Soc. v. Lane, [1904] 1 K. B. 35.

A creditor of the settlor who has settled property in trust for his own benefit as to the income with power of appointment as to the principal, cannot reach the corpus of the trust property in default of an appointment, provided of course the settlement was not made to defraud creditors. Crawford v. Langmaid, 171 Mass. 309. Although the exercise of the general power of appointment may make the corpus liable for the payment of the appointer's debts, it is not so liable in default of appointment, and the creditors cannot compel its exercise. Crawford v. Langmaid, 171 Mass. 309. See also Bailey v. Worster, 103 Me. 170.

The validity of an attempted

ated, as where property is given to trustees to be applied in their discretion to the use of a third person, no interest goes to the third person until the trustees have exercised this discretion. So if property is given to trustees to be applied by them to the support of the *cestui que trust* and his family, or to be paid over to the *cestui que trust* for the support of himself and the education and maintenance of his children. In short, if a trust is created for a specific purpose, and is so limited that it is not repugnant to the rule against perpetuities and is in other respects legal, neither the trustees, not the *cestui que trust*, nor his creditors or assignees, can divest the property from the appointed purposes.[1] (a)   Any conveyance, whether by operation of law or

[1] Rife *v.* Geyer, 59 Penn. St. 393; Wells *v.* McCall, 64 id. 207; White *v.* White, 30 Vt. 342; Clute *v.* Bool, 8 Paige, 83; Bramhall *v.* Ferris, 14 N. Y. 44; Doswell *v.* Anderson, 1 P. & H. (Va.) 185; Raikes *v.* Ward, 1 Hare, 445; Crockett *v.* Crockett, id. 451; Wetmore *v.* Truslow, 51 N. Y. 338; Graff *v.* Bonnett, 31 N. Y. 9; Locke *v.* Mabbett, 3 Court of App. Dec. 68; Blackstone Bank *v.* Davis, 21 Pick. 42; Etches *v.* Etches, 3 Drew. 441; Genet *v.* Beekman, 45 Barb. 382; Chase *v.* Chase, 2 Allen, 101; Loring *v.* Loring, 100 Mass. 340; Cole *v.* Littlefield, 35 Me. 439. See *ante,* § 117, and notes.

restraint on alienation is to be determined by the law of the locality where the property has its *situs.* Spindle *v.* Shreve, 111 U. S. 542, *In re* Fitzgerald, [1903] 1 Ch. 933. See Robb *v.* Washington & Jefferson Coll., 185 N. Y. 485. The same is true of the rights and remedies of creditors. Keeney *v.* Morse, 75 N. Y. S. 728, 71 App. Div. 104.

(a) It has been held in a jurisdiction which does not favor spendthrift trusts that a direction to trustees to "use part of the income and of said estate as may be necessary to provide for and comfortably maintain" the *cestui*, gives the *cestui* an interest which his creditors can reach. Ratliff's Ex'rs *v.* Commonwealth, 101 S. W. 978 (Ky. 1907). And where the trustee was directed to "apply" the income to

the use of the *cestui*, it has been held that the *cestui's* interest was alienable, since in such a case the cestui is absolutely entitled to the whole income. Huntington *v.* Jones, 72 Conn. 45. But see Meek *v.* Briggs, 87 Iowa, 610. See also Ames' Cases on Trusts, (2d ed.) p. 405.

A distinction has been made between the gift of the whole or a definite part of the income of a trust fund for the support of a beneficiary and a mere right to support out of the income. In the former case it has been held that the beneficiary has an alienable interest, the words "for support" being construed as merely stating the reason for the gift and not necessarily showing an intention to limit the beneficiary's power of alienation or anticipation. Slattery *v.* Wason,

by the act of any of the parties, which disappoints the purposes of the settlor by divesting the property or the income from the purposes named, would be a breach of the trust. Therefore it may be said, that the power to create a trust for a specified purpose does, in some sort, impair the power to alienate property.

§ 386 b. In the cases referred to in the last section, it will be perceived that the trust may be for a particular purpose, and that purpose may not be exclusively for the benefit of the primary *cestui que trust;* as where an estate was vested in trustees by a marriage settlement in trust to apply the annual produce thereof "for the *maintenance and support of A. B., his wife and children,*" it was held that the wife and children were to be supported, and that A. B. was entitled to the surplus after their support, and that such surplus would go to his assignees in case of his bankruptcy:[1] but when the trustees have an arbitrary power of applying such part of an income as they see fit to support of a *cestui que trust,* and for no other purpose, it was held that nothing passed to his assignees.[2] And so if the trustees

[1] Page v. Way, 3 Beav. 20.

[2] Twopenny v. Peyton, 10 Sim. 487; Re Sanderson's Trust, 3 K. & J. 497; Lord v. Bun, 2 Y. & C. Ch. 98; Holmes v. Penney, 3 K. & J. 90. [Weymyss v. White, 159 Mass. 484; King v. King, 168 Ill. 273; Murphy v. Delano, 95 Me. 229; Nat. Bank v. Nashville Trust Co., 62 S. W. 392 (Tenn. Ch. App. 1901). And he has no interest which his creditors can reach. Nickerson v. Van Horn, 181 Mass. 562; Stone v. Westcott, 18 R. I. 685; Meek v.

151 Mass. 266; Jastram v. McAuslan, 26 R. I. 320. In a case of the latter kind it has been said that "when the right is given for a support out of a fund which is given to another, the right is in its nature inalienable, and the intention of the donor that it shall not be alienated is presumed." Slattery v. Wason, 151 Mass. 266. See also Barnes v. Dow, 59 Vt. 530; Holmes v. Bushnell, 80 Conn. 233.

Where the interest of a bene-

ficiary in the income is not a separable interest as where the trustee is directed to expend the income for the benefit of a *cestui* and his family, he has no interest which his creditors can reach, or which he acting alone can assign. Brooks v. Raynolds, 59 Fed. 923. Talley v. Ferguson, 64 W. Va. 328. But all the beneficiaries could unite to transfer the interest of all of them. See Stern Bros. v. Hampton, 73 Miss. 555.

are to apply the money to the support of one and his wife and children, nothing tangible can pass to the assignees;[1] but if the power is not arbitrary, but is imperative on the trustees to pay over the income for the support of the *cestui que trust* and another person or persons, the assignees are entitled to take a part upon the insolvency of one, or the whole in the event of the death of the others.[2]

§ 387. There is a further exception to the general rule, that an equitable interest, without the right to alienate, cannot be created; and that is in the case of trusts created for married women. It is not unusual to create trusts for married women, and give such women all the rights of unmarried women over their separate equitable interests, and at the same time to insert a clause against their anticipating the income, by which means they are unable to assign or transfer it, or in any way receive any benefit from the property, except by receiving the income, as it becomes due and payable.[3]

§ 388. But though a settlor cannot put a restraint upon alienation, or exclude the rights of creditors, he may settle property upon another in such manner that it cannot be alienated, and creditors and assignees cannot take it. But in such case the *cestui que trust* must lose the use of the property in case of his bankruptcy. Thus A. may settle property upon B. until alienation or bankruptcy, with a limitation over to C. upon either event. Or A. may give real or personal estate to B. with a *proviso*, that, on alienation or bankruptcy, it shall shift over to

Briggs, 87 Iowa, 610; Chambers *v.* Smith, 3 A. C. 795; *Re* Bullock, 64 L. T. 736.]

[1] Godden *v.* Crowhurst, 10 Sim. 642; Kearsley *v.* Woodcock, 3 Hare, 185; Wallace *v.* Anderson, 16 Beav. 533; Hall *v.* Williams *et al.*, 120 Mass. 344.

[2] Rippon *v.* Norton, 2 Beav. 63; Wallace *v.* Anderson, 16 Beav. 533; Perry *v.* Roberts, 1 Myl. & K. 4.

[3] Pickering *v.* Coates, 10 Phila. 65; Ash *v.* Bowen, id. 96. See this matter stated *post*, chap. on Trusts for Married Women, §§ 670, 671.

C.¹ (a) But a clause divesting the property upon *alienation* alone, will embrace only the voluntary acts of the party, and

¹ Muggeridge Trusts, Johns. Ch. (Eng.) 625; Kearsley *v.* Woodcock, 3 Hare, 185; Joel *v.* Mills, 3 K. & J. 458; Large's Case, 2 Leon. 82; Churchill *v.* Marks, 1 Coll. 441; Sharpe *v.* Cossent, 20 Beav. 470; Shee *v.* Hale, 13 Ves. 404; Lewes *v.* Lewes, 6 Sim. 304; Cooper *v.* Wyatt, 5 Madd. 482; Lockyer *v.* Savage, 2 Stra. 947; Yarnold *v.* Moorhouse, 1 R. & M. 364; Stephens *v.* James, 4 Sim. 499; *Ex parte* Oxley, 1 B. & B. 257; Rochford *v.* Hackman, 9 Hare, 475; *Ex parte* Hinton, 14 Ves. 598; Stanton *v.* Hall, 2 R. & M. 175; Hall *v.* Williams, 120 Mass. 344; Nichols *v.* Eaton, 91 U. S. 716. [Olsen *v.* Youngerman, 136 Iowa, 404; Cherbonnier *v.* Bussey, 92 Md. 413; Metcalfe *v.* Metcalfe, [1891] 3 Ch. 1; Bull *v.* Ky. Nat. Bank, 90 Ky. 452, 458; Bottom *v.* Fultz, 124 Ky. 302. Compare with Bland's Adm'r *v.* Bland, 90 Ky. 400; Cecil's Trustee *v.* Robertson, 105 S. W. 926 (Ky. 1907).]

(a) The foundation of the power to restrain alienation in this way "rests upon the fact that there remains or is vested in some one a valid remainder or reversion, whose estate in possession is contingent upon some event which defeats the precedent estate, and who is entitled to take advantage of the prohibited act or use." Conger *v.* Lowe, 124 Ind. 368.

It has been held that a provision that upon bankruptcy or whenever the *cestui* shall cease to be entitled to income for his own personal use, his absolute right to it shall be forfeited and his trustees shall thereafter have an "uncontrolled discretion" to apply all or such part of the income for his benefit, accumulating the surplus for his children, has the effect of putting income beyond the reach of the *cestui's* trustee in bankruptcy. *Re* Bullock, 64 L. T. 736. In a trust to pay income to A. during life "or until he shall assign, charge or incumber," it has been held that forfeiture provision is retroactive in effect and includes past acts creating an incumbrance

unknown to the creator of the trust. West *v.* Williams, [1898] 1 Ch. 488. But where an equitable fee is given, an attempted limitation to others, in case the donee should commit or suffer any act in consequence of which he would be deprived of the right to the beneficial enjoyment has been held to be void for repugnancy; but it was said that such a limitation over would not have been repugnant to a life estate. *In re* Dugdale, 38 Ch. Div. 176. See also Thomas *v.* Thomas, 87 L. T. 58; Potter *v.* Couch, 141 U. S. 296, 315. In the first cited case it was said, " The result is that a limitation, by way of use or in a will, to A. until he attempts to alien, and on that event to B. and his heirs is valid, A. taking an estate of freehold which only endures by the terms of the limitation until the attempted alienation, and B. taking a contingent remainder. But a limitation to A. and his heirs, but if he attempts to alien, to B. in fee, is an invalid gift over. So also where the limitation is to A. and 'his heirs' until he

will not apply to transfers by operation of the law, as by bank-ruptcy,[1] unless it was intended that the clause should have so wide a signification.[2] Nor will a power to confess judgment be a voluntary act of alienation, unless it was within the contempla-tion of the parties;[3] nor will the marriage of a woman be an alienation of her *choses in action*.[4] So if there is a clause against anticipation, an assignment of arrears already accrued, and not of future income, is good.[5] An assignment in general words will not embrace property which would be forfeited by such assignment.[6]

§ 389. If a testator devises his real estate in strict settlement, and then gives his personal estate to such tenant in tail as first attains the age of twenty-one, if the tenant in tail is not of age

[1] Lear *v.* Leggett, 2 Sim. 479; 1 R. & M. 690; Wilkinson *v.* Wilkinson, G. Coop. 259; 3 Swanst. 528; Whitfield *v.* Prickett, 2 Keen, 908. [*Re* Harvey, 60 L. T. 710.]

[2] Cooper *v.* Wyatt, 5 Madd. 482; Dommett *v.* Bedford, 6 T. R. 684.

[3] Avison *v.* Holmes, 1 John. & H. 530; Barnet *v.* Blake, 2 Dr. & Sm. 117.

[4] Bonfield *v.* Hassell, 32 Beav. 217.

[5] *Re* Stulz Trusts, 4 De G., M. & G. 404; 1 Eq. R. 334.

[6] *Re* Waley's Trust, 3 Eq. R. 380. And as to the general effect of pro-ceedings in insolvency and bankruptcy, and of annulling the proceedings, see Lloyd *v.* Lloyd, 1 W. N. 307; Pym *v.* Lockyer, 12 Sim. 394; Brandon *v.* Aston, 2 Y. & C. Ch. 24; Churchill *v.* Marks, 1 Coll. 441; Townsend *v.* Early, 34 Beav. 23; Martin *v.* Margham, 14 Sim. 230; Graham *v.* Lee, 23 Beav. 388.

attempts to alien, and thereupon to B. and his heirs."

Such limitations over upon at-tempted alienation or upon the happening of any other contingency, are void within the rule against per-petuities unless the contingency must happen, if at all, within the period allowed by the rule for the vesting of estates. See Thomas *v.* Thomas, 87 L. T. 58; First Univer-salist Soc. *v.* Boland, 155 Mass. 171.

Where the settlor has made him-self the beneficiary of an interest in the property, as of a right to the income, a provision that it shall cease upon his subsequent bank-ruptcy is treated as an attempt to defraud creditors even though the settlor was solvent at the time of the settlement; and even subsequent creditors have a right to have the debtor's interest applied to payment of their claims.   Mackintosh *v.* Pogose, [1895] 1 Ch. 505; *In re* Johnson, [1904] 1 K. B. 134; Hig-ginbottom *v.* Holme, 19 Ves. 88; Murphy *v.* Abraham, 15 Ir. Ch. 371; *infra*, § 555, note.

at the testator's death, the event may never occur, and the trust is void. But if the personal property is given upon trusts that correspond to the settlement of the real estate, with a proviso that it should not vest absolutely in any tenant in tail unless he attained twenty-one, the trust is good.[1]

§ 390. Thus where trusts are complete in themselves, or are what are termed executed trusts, courts will not mould, alter, or put any peculiar construction on them, in order to avoid or evade the rule against perpetuities. The ordinary rules of construction will be adhered to without regard to the consequences of avoiding trusts that are illegal.[2] But in cases of executory trusts, where trustees are directed to settle a formal deed of trust upon terms which are faintly and incompletely sketched, another rule will be applied. If from the articles or will it appears that a perpetuity was intended, that must be the end of the trust, whether executed or executory. But if the direct object of the limitations suggested in the articles is not the creation of a perpetuity, and if the remoteness is confined to some of the distant links only in the chain of limitations, equity, in decreeing the settlement, will carry into effect the general intention, especially if the expression of that intention clearly indicates that the limitations are to be carried out so far as the law allows.[3] (a)

---

[1] Gosling v. Gosling, 1 De G., J. & S. 1, 17, Am. ed. Perkins, note 1; s. c. L. R. 1 H. L. 279; Lincoln v. Newcastle, 12 Ves. 218; Dungannon v. Smith, 12 Cl. & Fin. 546; Scarsdale v. Curzon, 1 John. & H. 40.

[2] Blagrave v. Hancock, 16 Sim. 371.

[3] Ante, § 376; Bankes v. Le Despencer, 10 Sim. 576; 7 Jur. 210; 11 Sim. 508; Lincoln v. Newcastle, 3 Ves. 387; 12 Ves. 218; Phipps v. Kelynge, 2 V. & B. 57, n.; Woolmore v. Burrows, 1 Sim. 512; Dorchester v. Effingham, 10 Sim. 587, 588, n.; 3 Beav. 180; Kampf v. Jones, 2 Keen, 756; Tregonwell v. Sydenham, 3 Dow, 194; 1 Jar. on Wills, 235; n.; see argument of Sir Edward Sugden in Bengough v. Edridge, 1 Sim. 226, 227; Mogg v. Mogg, 1 Mer. 654; 1 Jar. on Pow. Dev. 414, and note; Trevor v. Trevor, 13 Sim. 108; 1 H. L. Cas. 239; Tennent v. Tennent, Drury, 161; Boydell v. Golightly, 14 Sim. 346; White v. Briggs, 15 Sim. 17; Vanderplank v. King, 3 Hare, 5;

(a) In Edgerly v. Barker, 66 N. H. 434, this principle was applied to an executed trust.

§ 391. In some of the States, legislation has been had whereby the period within which estates must vest is shortened. Thus in Alabama[1] estates may be given to wife and children, or children only, severally successively, and jointly, and to the heirs of the body of the survivor, if they come of age, and in default thereof over. But gifts to others than wife and children must vest within the term of three lives in being, and ten years thereafter. In Connecticut,[2] no estate can be given by deed or will to any person or persons, except such as are in being, or to the immediate issue or descendants of such as are in being at the time of making the deed or will. (a) In New York,[3] Michigan,[4] Minnesota,[5] and Wisconsin,[6] the absolute power of alienation cannot be suspended, by any limitation or condition, for a

Monypenny v. Deering, 7 Hare, 568; 2 De G., M. & G. 145; 16 M. & W. 418; Hare v. Pew, 25 Beav. 335; Humberston v. Humberston, 2 Vern. 737; 1 P. Wms. 332; Pr. Ch. 455; Deerhurst v. St. Albans, 5 Madd. 232; Jervoise v. Northumberland, 1 J. & W. 559; Blackburn v. Stables, 2 V. & B. 367; Rowland v. Morgan, 2 Phill. 763; Parfitt v. Hember, L. R. 4 Eq. 443.

[1] Code 1852, § 1309. [Civil Code (1907), § 3417.]

[2] Comp. Stat. 1854, p. 630, § 4.

[3] 2 Rev. Stat. (4th ed.) 133, §§ 15–20; Knox v. Jones, 47 N. Y. 398; Wood v. Wood, 5 Paige, 596; Amory v. Lord, 5 Seld. 503; Schutter v. Smith, 41 N. Y. 328; Gott v. Cook, 7 Paige, 531; Van Vechten v. Van Vechten, 8 Paige, 104. [Real Property Law, 1909, § 42 et seq. IV Consol. Laws (1909), p. 3381; Personal Property Law, 1909, § 11, ibid. p. 2840.]

[4] Comp. Laws, 1857, c. 85, §§ 15–26. [Comp. Laws, 1897, §§ 8796, 8797, 8789, 8910, 8911.]

[5] Comp. Stat. 1859, c. 31, §§ 15–26. [Rev. Laws, 1905, §§ 3203–3205, 3319.]

[6] Rev. Stat. 1858, c. 83, §§ 15–26. [Statutes 1898, § 2039 as amended by c. 511 of 1905, §§ 2038, 2040, 2152, 2153, two lives and twenty-one years. Neither the statute nor the common-law rule applies to personalty. Danforth v. Oshkosh, 119 Wis. 262; Becker v. Chester, 115 Wis. 90.]

(a) This provision in the statutes of Connecticut was repealed by chapter 249, Acts of 1895, leaving no statutory rule. The result seems to be that the common-law rule applies as to wills and deeds coming into operation since 1895; but the repeal had no retroactive effect, and the law as it existed previous to 1895 still controls as to interests created previous to that time. Tingier v. Chamberlin, 71 Conn. 466; Security Co. v. Snow, 70 Conn. 288; Cody v. Staples, 80 Conn. 82. See White v. Allen, 76 Conn. 185; Bates v. Spooner, 75 Conn. 501; Loomer v. Loomer, 76 Conn. 522.

longer period than the continuance of two lives in being at the creation of the estate, except that a contingent remainder in fee may be limited on a prior remainder in fee to take effect in the event that the persons to whom the first remainder is limited shall die under the age of twenty-one years, or upon any other contingency by which the estate of such persons may be determined during their minority. Successive limitations of estates for life are not valid except to persons in being at the time of their creation. And if a remainder is limited on more than two successive estates for lives in being, all the subsequent successive estates are void; and upon the death of those two persons the remainder will take effect as if no other life-estate had been created. No remainder can be created for the life of a person other than the grantee or devisee of such estate, unless such remainder is in fee; nor can a remainder be created upon such an estate in a term of years, unless it is for the whole residue of the term. If more than two lives are named, the remainder takes effect upon the death of the two persons first named, in the same manner as if no other persons had been named or lives introduced. A contingent remainder cannot be limited on a term for years, unless the contingency òn which it is limited is such that it must vest during the continuance of two lives in being at the creation of such remainder, or at the termination of such term of years. Thus a limitation to A. for life, remainder to B. for life, remainder to C. and D., and the survivor of them, is within the statute, and void as to C. and D. as a limitation upon more than two lives in being.[1]   If the power of alienation is suspended for an indefinite period, the trust is void.[2] (a)

---

[1] Arnold v. Gilbert, 5 Barb. 190.

[2] Donaldson v. American Tract Soc., 1 N. Y. Sup. Ct. Add. 15; Leonard v. Bell, 1 N. Y. Sup. Ct. 608; Kiah v. Grenier, id. 388.

(a) These provisions of the New York statutes have been interpreted as a modification of the rule against perpetuities. The statute is violated not only by attempts to place restraints upon vested interests, but by attempts to create either vested or future estates which from their nature or by some statute are inalienable for a period which by any

§ 392. In Ohio,[1] no estate can be limited to any person or persons, except they are in being, or to the immediate descend-

[1] Rev. Stat. 1854, c. 42, § 1.   [Bates' Annot. Stat. (5th ed.) § 4200.]

possibility may last beyond the duration of two lives in being at the time of their creation. Such attempted estates are void even before the time set for their vesting. *In re* Wilcox, 194 N. Y. 288. This is true of estates which may not vest within the duration of two lives in being, because an unvested estate is inalienable. Dana *v.* Murray, 122 N. Y. 604; *In re* Wilcox, 194 N. Y. 288. The same is true of a trust to pay income which may continue beyond the duration of two lives in being at the time of its creation, because another statute has made the interest of a beneficiary of such a trust inalienable. Underwood *v.* Curtis, 127 N. Y. 523; Fowler *v.* Ingersoll, 127 N. Y. 472; Brown *v.* Quintard, 177 N. Y. 75; Herzog *v.* Title Guarantee & Tr. Co., 177 N. Y. 86; People's Trust Co. *v.* Flynn, 94 N. Y. S. 436, 106 App. Div. 78; Matter of Trotter, 104 App. Div. 118 (affirmed, 182 N. Y. 465); Robb *v.* Washington & Jefferson College, 185 N. Y. 485; Whitefield *v.* Crissman, 108 N. Y. S. 110, 123 App. Div. 233; Farmers' Loan & Trust Co. *v.* Kip, 192 N. Y. S. 266.

The fact that the trustee has power of sale will not save the trust if the interest of the beneficiaries is inalienable for a period which may extend beyond the duration of two lives in being. *In re* Wilcox, 194 N. Y. 288. On the other hand, a restraint upon the trustee's power to sell for a time which may exceed the statutory limit violates the stat-

ute even when the interests of the beneficiaries are alienable. See *In re* Walkerly, 108 Cal. 627.

The two lives which mark the possible suspension of absolute alienable ownership are not necessarily those of the persons interested. Schermerhorn *v.* Cotting, 131 N. Y. 48; Bird *v.* Pickford, 141 N. Y. 18. A child *en ventre sa mère* at the time of a testator's death has been held to be a life in being within the meaning of the statute. Cooper *v.* Heatherton, 73 N. Y. S. 14, 65 App. Div. 561. The fact that the person who is to take on the termination of the two lives in being is a minor, and for that reason incapable of alienating his interest in the property, does not affect the validity of a gift to him. Quade *v.* Bertsch, 72 N. Y. S. 916, 65 App. Div. 600 (affirmed 173 N. Y. 615). See Estate of Campbell, 149 Cal. 712.

In States which have a statute provision similar to that of New York a similar interpretation has been given the statute. Brown *v.* Columbia Finance, etc., Co., 123 Ky. 775; Fidelity Trust Co. *v.* Lloyd, 78 S. W. 896 (Ky. 1904); Phillips *v.* Heldt, 33 Ind. App. 388; Casgrain *v.* Hammond, 134 Mich. 419; Niles *v.* Mason, 126 Mich. 482; Torpy *v.* Betts, 123 Mich. 239; Campbell-Kawannanakoa *v.* Campbell, 152 Cal. 201; *In re* Walkerly, 108 Cal. 627; Estate of Campbell, 149 Cal. 712. But not all of them have statutes restraining the alienation of a *cestui's* right to income. See John-

ants of such as are in being at the time of making of the deed or will. In Mississippi,[1] fees-tail are prohibited, and converted into fees-simple; and estates may be limited in succession to two donees in being, and to the heirs of the body of the remainder-man, and in default thereof to the heirs of the donor in fee. In Indiana,[2] the power of selling lands cannot be suspended, by any limitation or condition, longer than the continuance of any number of specified lives in being at the time of the creation of the estate; except that contingent remainders in fee may be limited on a prior remainder in fee, to take effect in the event that the person or persons to whom the first remainder is limited

---

[1] Code, 1857, c. 38, § 1, art. 3; see Jordan v. Roach, 32 Miss. 481. [Code (1906), § 2765; Banking Co. v. Field, 84 Miss. 646.]

[2] Rev. Stat. 1852, p. 238, § 40. [Burns' Stat. (1908), § 3998.]

son's Trustee v. Johnson, 79 S. W. 293 (Ky. 1904).

In Minnesota, Michigan, and Wisconsin the statutes forbidding restraints or alienation, though similar in form to the New York statute, do not apply to personalty. In Minnesota and Michigan it has been held that the common-law rule against perpetuities applies to personalty. In re Tower's Estate, 49 Minn. 371; Toms v. Williams, 41 Mich. 552, 569. In Wisconsin it has been held that neither the statute nor the common-law rule applies to personalty, Becker v. Chester, 115 Wis. 90; Danforth v. Oshkosh, 119 Wis. 262; Dodge v. Williams, 46 Wis. 70; see In re Adelman's Will, 138 Wis. 120; Holmes v. Walter, 118 Wis. 409; with the result that whenever a trustee has power to convert real estate and to hold the proceeds invested as personalty there is no unlawful restraint upon alienation, and no rule of remoteness applies to the beneficial interests. Ibid.

It has been held that the Cali-fornia statute provisions apply to all kinds of property. In re Walkerly, 108 Cal. 627, 656–658.

The New York court has held in several cases that the validity of a bequest of personal property with respect to the rule against perpetuities is to be determined by the law of the testator's domicile. Cross v. U. S. Trust Co., 131 N. Y. 330; Dammert v. Osborn, 140 N. Y. 30, 141 N. Y. 564. To the same effect see Penfield v. Tower, 1 N. D. 216. But the New York court has also upheld a bequest of personalty by a resident of that State, in trust to pay life annuities to seven persons, since the trust funds were to be paid over to a Pennsylvania corporation and there administered. Robb v. Washington and Jefferson Coll., 185 N. Y. 485. Although the trust would have been invalid under New York law because the interests of the annuitants are inalienable, the court seemed to be of opinion that this invalidity was cured because the interests were alienable in Pennsylvania.

shall be under the age of twenty-one years, or upon any other contingency by which the estate of such person or persons may be determined during their minorities. In Kentucky,[1] the absolute power of alienation cannot be suspended by limitations or conditions for a longer period than during a life or lives in being and twenty-one years and ten months. So, in Iowa,[2] alienation cannot be suspended for a period longer than lives in being and twenty-one years. In Arkansas [3] and Vermont,[4] their constitutions declare that a perpetuity shall not be allowed. What is a perpetuity in those States would necessarily, in the absence of legislation, be determined by the common-law rule. So it is conceived that the common law prevails in those States. In all the other States, except perhaps Louisiana, where the rules of property were derived from the civil law or the code of France, and California, (a) where they were derived from the Spanish

---

[1] Rev. Stat. c. 80, § 34. [Stat. of Ky. (1909) § 2055; Brown v. Columbia Finance, etc., Co., 123 Ky. 775; Fidelity Trust Co. v. Lloyd, 78 S. W. 896 (Ky. 1904); Johnson's Trustee v. Johnson, 79 S. W. 293 (Ky. 1904).]

[2] Code, 1851, p. 1191. [Code, 1897, § 2901; Meek v. Briggs, 87 Iowa, 610, 618; Phillips v. Harrow, 93 Iowa, 92, 106.]

[3] Const. art. 2, § 19.

[4] Const. pt. 2, § 36; Gen. Stat. 1863, pp. 25, 446.

(a) Statute provisions similar to and evidently taken from the New York statutes have been enacted in California, Montana, North Dakota, and South Dakota, with the exception that the limit is "lives in being." Cal. Civ. Code, §§ 715, 716; Mont. Civ. Code (1907), §§ 4463–4465, 4492 ; No. Dak. Civ. Code (1905), §§ 4744–4746, 4771, 4772, 4872, 4873; So. Dak. Civ. Code, §§ 224–226, 251, 252, 353, 354.

The common-law rule was recognized in the following recent cases. Cribbs v. Walker, 74 Ark. 104, 120; Chilcott v. Hart, 23 Colo. 40; Quinlan v. Wickman, 233 Ill. 39; Keyes v. Northern Trust Co., 227 Ill. 354 ;

Dwyer v. Cahill, 228 Ill. 617; Hill v. Gianelli, 221 Ill. 286; Pitzel v. Schneider, 216 Ill. 87; Schuknecht v. Shultz, 212 Ill. 43; Eldred v. Meek, 183 Ill. 26; Keeler v. Lauer, 73 Kan. 388; Towle v. Doe, 97 Me. 427; Andrews v. Lincoln, 95 Me. 541; Robinson v. Bonaparte, 102 Md. 63; Graham v. Whitridge, 99 Md. 248, 274; Gray v. Whittemore, 192 Mass. 367; Brown v. Wright, 194 Mass. 540; Howe v. Morse, 174 Mass. 491; Shepperd v. Fisher, 206 Mo. 208; Edgerly v. Barker, 66 N. H. 434; Ogden v. McLane, 73 N. J. Eq. 159; Lembeck v. Lembeck, 73 N. J. Eq. 427; Stephens v. Dayton, 220 Pa. St. 522; Kountz's Estate, 213 Pa. St. 390;

laws, the common-law rules as to perpetuities are in force, and trusts that are contrary to these rules are void.

§ 393. Intimately connected with this matter is the rule against accumulations. Trusts for accumulation must be strictly confined within the limits of the rule against perpetuities. It has been seen that a settlor may restrain the alienation of property for a life or lives in being and twenty-one years; and, in case the beneficiary is then *en ventre sa mère*, an addition of nine months may be made to the term. In analogy to this rule, a settlor may prevent the beneficial enjoyment of property for the same length of time, by directing an accumulation of the interest, income, rents, or profits.[1] If a trust for accumulation may possibly exceed this limit, it is wholly void, and it cannot be cut down to the legal limit. (*a*)

§ 394. The above is the rule where there are no statutes to control it. Trusts, by which the vesting, alienation, or enjoyment of property is postponed beyond the legal period, are considered as contrary to public policy, and therefore void; and as

[1] Fosdick *v.* Fosdick, 6 Allen, 43; Hooper *v.* Hooper, 9 Cush. 122; Thorndike *v.* Loring, 15 Gray, 391; Boughton *v.* James, 1 Coll. 26; 1 H. L. Cas. 406; Southampton *v.* Hertford, 2 V. & B. 54; Marshall *v.* Holloway, 2 Swanst. 432; Curtis *v.* Luken, 5 Beav. 147; Brown *v.* Stoughton, 14 Sim. 369; Scarisbrooke *v.* Skelmersdale, 17 Sim. 187; Turvin *v.* Newcome, 3 K. & J. 16; Craig *v.* Craig, 3 Barb. Ch. 76; Mathews *v.* Keble, L. R. 1 Eq. 467; L. R. 3 Ch. 691; Killam *v.* Allen, 52 Barb. 605; Dutch Reform Church *v.* Brandon, id. 228; White *v.* Howard, id. 294; Hillyard *v.* Miller, 10 Barr, 326.

Lawrence's Estate, 136 Pa. St. 354; Loyd *v.* Loyd, 102 Va. 519; Starcher Bros. *v.* Duty, 61 W. Va. 371, 373; Fitchie *v.* Brown, 211 U. S. 321 (Hawaii). See Georgia Code (1895), § 3102.

(*a*) An accumulation for more than twenty-one years may legally take place by operation of law. Bryan *v.* Collins, 16 Beav. 14, 17. As where the person who becomes entitled after accumulation of some years is an infant whose parent is capable of supporting him. A direction to apply rents or income in payment of a specified sum to a designated person is not a direction to accumulate. Rogers' Estate 179 Penn. St. 602.

In New York, directions to accumulate rents, except during the minority of legatees, are void by statute.

courts cannot substitute legal directions in the place of illegal provisions in a will, the whole fails if there is an illegal gift for accumulation. The period during which accumulation might go on was found to be inconvenient in case a settlor availed himself of all its terms. Thus Mr. Thellusson, by an ingenious and skilful use of these legal limitations, constructed a will by which a fortune of £600,000 was left to accumulate for some person to come into existence in the future, answering a certain description, while mere pittances were given to his children and grandchildren then in being. It was calculated that accumulations might go on under this will from seventy-five to one hundred years, and that the gross accumulation would amount to a sum from £32,000,000 to £100,000,000, according to the time during which it might accumulate. The will was most carefully considered and discussed in all the courts, but it was found to be drawn carefully within the law, and all its provisions were sustained.[1] Thereupon Parliament interfered, and passed a statute, usually called the Thellusson Act, which curtailed the period during which accumulations might be directed.[2] This act established four alternate periods during which accumulations might be made: (1) The life of the settlor; (2) Twenty-one years from the death of the settlor; (3) The minority or minorities of any persons living at the death of the settlor; (4) During the minority or minorities of any person or persons who, if of full age, would be entitled under the limitations to the income which is directed to be accumulated. (a)

[1] Thellusson v. Woodford, 4 Ves. 227; 11 Ves. 112; 4 Kent, Com. 285.
[2] Stat. 39 and 40 Geo. III. c. 98.

(a) The Accumulations Act of 1892 (55 and 56 Vict. c. 58) limits the choice to the fourth period, if there is a direction to accumulate for the purchase of land only. See In re Danson, 13 Rep. 633. It has been held that the Thellusson Act does not prevent accumulations for the purpose of improvements which are in the nature of repairs. Vine v. Raleigh, [1891] 2 Ch. 13, 26; In re Mason, [1891] 3 Ch. 467. As to the exception in favor of "portions," see In re Stephens, [1904] 1 Ch. 322. See also In re Heathcote, [1904] 1 Ch. 826.

§ 395. It has been determined that these four periods are alternative, and not cumulative, and that accumulations must be confined to one of them.[1] If the accumulation does not begin until several years after the testator's death, it must cease at the end of twenty-one years from his death,[2] excluding the day of his death.[3] The act further directs, that any accumulation directed contrary to its provision shall be void. By these words accumulations directed contrary to the statute are not wholly void, as at common law, but only the excess beyond the time allowed by the statute is void.[4] Mr. Lewis calls this a " rule of construction entirely novel." [5] It is also said, that the act is one of restraining force, and cannot give validity to trusts for accumulation, which are in themselves void, as transgressing the common-law limits of a perpetuity. Thus a direction to accumulate beyond the time allowed by the statute, but within the time allowed by the common law, will be good for the actual time allowed by the statute, and void only for the excess; but a direction to accumulate, beyond the rule of common law against perpetuity, is wholly void notwithstanding the statute. Consequently, in England a trust for accumulation may verge *almost* upon the outside of the limit of a perpetuity, and yet be

[1] Ellis v. Maxwell, 3 Beav. 587; Rosslyn's Trust, 16 Sim. 391; Wilson v. Wilson, 1 Sim. (N. S.) 288.   [Jagger v. Jagger, 25 Ch. Div. 729; Re Errington, 76 L. T. 616.]

[2] Nettleton v. Stephenson, 3 De G. & Sm. 366; Att. Gen. v. Poulden, 3 Hare, 355; Webb v. Webb, 2 Beav. 493; Shaw v. Rhodes, 1 Myl. & Cr. 135.

[3] Toder v. Sansom, 1 Brown, P. C. 468; Lester v. Garland, 15 Ves. 248; East v. Lowndes, 11 Sim. 434. And the day of the death was excluded by the rules of the common law, independently of the statute. Toder v. Sansom, ut supra.

[4] Griffiths v. Vere, 9 Ves. 127; Palmer v. Holford, 4 Russ. 403; Langdon v. Simson, 12 Ves. 295; Rosslyn's Trust, 16 Sim. 391; Freke v. Lord Carbery, L. R. 16 Eq. 461. There are a great number of cases upon this construction, but they are not important in America. The reader can see 1 Jarm. on Wills, 286; Hill on Trustees, 394; Lade v. Holford, Amb. 479; Eyre v. Marsden, 2 Keen, 564; 4 Myl. & Cr. 231; Marshall v. Holloway, 3 Swanst. 432; Southampton v. Hertford, 2 V. & B. 61; Haly v. Dannister, 4 Madd. 277.

[5] Lewis on Per. 593.

void only for the excess beyond the time established in the statute; but if a trust for accumulation transcends in the slightest degree the boundary of a perpetuity, it is wholly void, and will fail without regard to the actual course of events.[1]

§ 396. If a good bequest is made to a devisee, subject to an illegal or void direction to accumulate, as where such direction is independently engrafted upon the devise, and can be stricken out without destroying the substantial form of the gift, the gift may be held to be good, but the direction to accumulate void.[2] But where the gift is limited to take effect *after* a prescribed period of accumulation, and out of the accumulated fund, as part of the subject-matter of the gift, and such period of accumulation is illegal or too remote, the gift itself will fail, as the form of the gift in such case is of the substance of it.[3] If the gift and all its accumulations are of necessity to vest in some person absolutely, in such manner that he will have a right to call for the fund, and stop the accumulations within the legal period, the bequest will be good, although such persons should allow the accumulations to go on as directed;[4] that is, the same rule applies as in the case of perpetuities. The law concerns itself with the possibilities of an illegal accumulation, and not with the fact, whether a person, having an absolute vested right to a fund, allows it to go on accumulating in accordance with a void direction.[5]

[1] Lewis on Per. 593, 594; Hargrave, Accum. 91, 110; 1 Pow. on Devi. by Jarm. 419; 2 Prest. Abst. 183. [See Smith *v.* Cuninghame, 13 L. R. Ir. 480.]

[2] Haxtum *v.* Corse, 2 Barb. Ch. 506; Craig *v.* Craig, 3 Barb. Ch. 76; Martin *v.* Margham, 14 Sim. 230; Williams *v.* Williams, 4 Selden, 525; Phelps *v.* Pond, 23 N. Y. 69; Kilpatrick *v.* Johnson, 15 N. Y. 322; Hawley *v.* James, 5 Paige, 318; Philadelphia *v.* Girard, 45 Penn. St. 1.

[3] Amory *v.* Lord, 5 Selden, 403.

[4] Phipps *v.* Kelynge, 2 Ves. & B. 57, n., 63, 62; Tregonell *v.* Sydenham, 3 Dow. 194; Lewis on Per. 640; Conner *v.* Ogle, 4 Md. Ch. 443; Saunders *v.* Vautier, 4 Beav. 115; Cr. & Phil. 240; Oddie *v.* Brown, 4 De G. & J. 179; Bateman *v.* Hotchkin, 10 Beav. 426; Bacon *v.* Proctor, T. & R. 31; Briggs *v.* Oxford, 1 De G., M. & G. 363; Williams *v.* Lewis, 6 H. L. Cas. 1013.

[5] *Ante*, § 181.

§ 397. When a direction to accumulate is void for a part of the term, the income during such void part will belong to the heir or next of kin, or to the residuary legatee. Mr. Jarman has pointed out the destination of such income as follows: (1) Where there is a present gift in possession, and the direction for accumulation is merely to govern the mode of enjoyment, the result is to give those entitled the present income, the same as if the direction had not been given.¹ (2) Where the trust for accumulation is grafted upon an estate where vesting is deferred or made contingent until after the period of accumulation, the statute by stopping the accumulation does not hasten the vesting or the possession, and the income goes to the residuary legatee or the heir, according as it is personal or real estate, until the vesting or possession of the estate is matured. But where the residue is not given absolutely, but only for life or years, the interest upon a legacy thus directed to be accumulated beyond the legal period goes into the residue of the estate as capital.² (3) Where a residue is directed to be accumulated, the income, when its accumulation becomes illegal, will go to the heir or next of kin, according as the property may be real or personal estate.³ (a)   (4) The income of the accumulations follows the

¹ Trickey v. Trickey, 3 Myl. & K. 560; Clulow's Trust, 5 Jur. (N. S.) 1002; 28 L. J. Ch. 696; Combe v. Hughes, 11 Jur. (N. S.) 194; 1 Jarm. on Wills, 292; Hawley v. James, 5 Paige, 318.

² Jones v. Maggs, 9 Hare, 605; Macdonald v. Brice, 2 Keen, 276; Eyre v. Marsden, id. 574; Ellis v. Maxwell, 3 Beav. 587; Nettleton v. Stephenson, 3 De G. & Sm. 366; Barrington v. Liddell, 10 Hare, 429; Att. Gen. v. Poulden, 3 Hare, 555; Crawley v. Crawley, 7 Sim. 427; Morgan v. Morgan, 4 De G. & Sm. 175; Hull v. Hull, 24 N. Y. 647; 1 Jarm. on Wills, 292. [But see In re Phillips, 49 L. J. Ch. 198.]

³ Skrymsher v. Northcote, 1 Swanst. 566; Macdonald v. Bryce, 2 Keen, 276; Pride v. Fooks, 2 Beav. 437; Elborne v. Goode, 14 Sim. 165; Wilson v. Wilson, 1 Sim. (N. S.) 288; Bourne v. Buckton, 2 Sim. (N. S.) 91; Oddie

(a) See St. John v. Andrews Inst., 191 N. Y. 254; Duncklee v. Butler, 56 N. Y. S. 491, 38 App. Div. 99; Weinmann's Estate, 223 Pa. St. 508. As to the disposition of surplus income legally accumulated when there is no express direction as to whom it is to go, see Brown v. Wright, 168 Mass. 506; Farley v. Bucklin, 16 R. I. 378.

same rule as the accumulation.[1] These are substantially the same rules that apply to the distribution of income which is illegally directed to be accumulated at common law.

§ 398. In New York,[2] Michigan,[3] Wisconsin,[4] and Minnesota,[5] the common-law rules in relation to accumulations are changed by statutes, which are substantially the same in each State. In those States accumulations may be directed by deed or will, during the minority of one or more persons, to commence with the creation of the estate out of which the accumulation is to be made, and to end with the minority of the persons named. If there is a direction for an accumulation for a longer period, the excess only is void. (a) In Alabama,[6] accumulations

v. Brown, 4 De G. & J. 179; Halford v. Stains, 16 Sim. 488; Wilde v. Davis, 1 Sm. & G. 475; Eyre v. Marsden, 2 Keen, 564; 4 Myl. & Cr. 431; Edwards v. Tuck, 3 De G., M. & G. 40; Burt v. Sturt, 10 Hare, 415; 1 Jarm. on Wills, 292.

[1] Crawley v. Crawley, 7 Sim. 427; O'Neill v. Lucas, 2 Keen, 316; Morgan v. Morgan, 4 De G. & Sm. 175; 20 L. J. Ch. 441; 1 Jarm. on Wills, 292.

[2] Rev. Stat. (4th ed.) p. 135; [Real Property Law, 1909, § 62, IV Consol. Laws (1909), p. 3384; Personal Property Law, 1909, § 16, IV Consol. Laws (1909), p. 2844]; Craig v. Craig, 3 Barb. Ch. 76; Killam v. Allen, 52 Barb. 605; Hawley v. James, 5 Paige, 480; Hull v. Hull, 24 N. Y. 647; Robinson v. Robinson, 5 Lansing, 167; Williams v. Williams, 8 N. Y. 358; Kilpatrick v. Johnson, 15 N. Y. 322; Haxtun v. Corse, 2 Barb. Ch. 508; Lang v. Ropke, 5 Sandf. S. C. 363; Meserole v. Meserole, 1 Hun, 66; Pray v. Hedgeman, 27 Hun, 603.

[3] Comp. Laws, 1857, c. 85, §§ 15–26. [Comp. Laws, 1897, § 8819.]

[4] Rev. Stat. 1858, c. 83, §§ 15–26. [Statutes, 1898, § 2061. Limit for charities, twenty-one years.]

[5] Comp. Stat. 1859, c. 31, §§ 15–26. [Rev. Laws, 1905, § 3226.]

[6] Code, 1852, § 1310. [Civ. Code, 1907, § 3410.]

(a) Several other States have adopted the provisions of the New York statute. Cal. Civ. Code, §§ 723–725; Mont. Civ. Code (1907), §§ 4469–4470; No. Dak. Code'(1905), § 4749; So. Dak. Civ. Code (1908), § 229; Burns' Ind. Stat. (1908), § 9724, applying only to income from personalty. Illinois has adopt- ed the four periods of the Thellusson Act. Rev. Stat. (1908), c. 30, § 155, enacted in 1907. In Wisconsin it has been held that the statute does not apply to income of personalty. Scott v. West, 63 Wis. 529, 573 et seq. It has been held in New York that an accumulation for the benefit of an unborn child, though valid for

can go on only for ten years, unless they are for the benefit of a minor child in being at the creation of the trust, or at the death of the testator, in which case they may continue during its minority. In Pennsylvania,[1] trusts for accumulation cannot be created for a longer term than the life or lives of the grantor or testator, and the term of twenty-one years from the death of such grantor or testator, and if these limits are exceeded, the excess is void. In the other States, the common-law rules, as before stated, are supposed to prevail. The rule in regard to accumulation is analogous to the rules in regard to the vesting of executory estates. At common law, the same rule prevails in both cases. In many of the States, the rules regulating the vesting of such estates have been altered by statutes. Whether the modification of those rules by statute, without reference to the rule as to accumulations, would also alter the rule as to accumulations in those States does not seem to have been considered.

§ 399. Where there are no statutes regulating accumulations, a direction to accumulate a fund for a charity, for a term beyond the common-law limit, does not vitiate the gift for the charity,[2]

---

[1] Purd. Dig. 1861, p. 853, § 9. [Brightly's Purdon's Dig. (12th ed.) p. 1833, § 9. Exception in favor of trusts for charities. See Weinmann's Estate, 223 Pa. St. 508.]

[2] Odell v. Odell, 10 Allen, 1; but see Hillyard v. Miller, 10 Penn. St. 326;

the period of its minority, is invalid for the period preceding its birth. U. S. Trust Co. v. Soher, 178 N. Y. 442. Under the statute a direction to accumulate for the purpose of paying off existing mortgages on the trust property is invalid. Hafner v. Hafner, 71 N. Y. S. 1, 62 App. Div. 316 (affirmed 171 N. Y. 633); Kirk v. McCann, 101 N. Y. S. 1093, 117 App. Div. 56; Hascall v. King, 162 N. Y. 134. It has been held that where a trustee is charged with the duty of paying annuities, the statute

does not prevent him from holding a reasonable reserve of accumulated surplus income for the purpose of providing for a possible deficiency of income. Spencer v. Spencer, 56 N. Y. S. 460 (App. Div.). Similarly, it has been held in Pennsylvania that a temporary withholding of income for the purpose of providing a reserve fund in the interest of judicious management, is not forbidden by the statute. Spring's Estate, 216 Pa. St. 529.

although no limit has been determined by courts during which an accumulation for a charity may be permitted. It is probable that courts would take care that no extraordinary or extravagant term for accumulation should be allowed for a future and prospective good. But where there are statutes against accumulations, charities will be governed by the same rules unless they are specially excepted.[1] (a)

§ 400. In Bassil v. Lister,[2] it was determined that a direction of a testator that premiums on policies of insurance should be paid out of his estate, upon the lives of his sons during their lives, was not a direction for an accumulation within the prohibition of the statute. The case is severely criticised in Jarman on Wills;[3] but it would seem, that it would not be illegal for a testator to direct the premiums to be paid upon a life policy, if the primary object of such a direction is not accumulation, but security or safety. The question cannot arise, however, in the absence of statutory provisions upon the subject of accumulations; for it can be an accumulation for one life only in being at the time, and such an accumulation is legal by the rules of the common law.

Philadelphia v. Girard, 45 id. 1. [St. Paul's Church v. Att. Gen., 164 Mass. 188, 203; Codman v. Brigham, 187 Mass. 309; Brigham v. Brigham Hospital, 134 Fed. 513; In re Swain, [1905] 1 Ch. 669. See contra, Brooks v. Belfast, 90 Me. 318, 323.]

[1] Martin v. Margham, 14 Sim. 230.

[2] Bassil v. Lister, 9 Hare, 177.

[3] 1 Jarm. 294–297.

(a) See Wharton v. Masterman, [1895] A. C. 186, where it was held that a legatee, whether an individual or a corporation, for whose sole benefit an accumulation is directed may terminate it.

CHAPTER XIV.

GENERAL PROPERTIES AND DUTIES OF THE OFFICE OF TRUSTEE.

§ 401. A TRUSTEE, having accepted a trust, cannot renounce it. If any one undertakes an office for another, he is bound to discharge its duties, and he cannot free himself from liability by mere renunciation. He must be discharged by a court of equity, or by a special power in the instrument of trust, or by the consent of all parties interested in the estate, if they are *sui juris:* if all the parties are not *sui juris*, recourse must be had to a court of equity, in the absence of any provisions in the instrument of trust.[1] Nor can a party qualify his own acts. Where he is named trustee or executor, and acts in behalf of certain parties in the management of the estate, he cannot protest that he is not acting generally, and that he will not be responsible for any mismanagement. On the contrary, if he so acts, and his coexecutors accept the trust, and commit a *devastavit*, he

---

[1] *Post*, §§ 920–922; Doyle *v.* Blake, 2 Sch. & Lef. 245; Chalmer *v.* Bradly, 1 J. & W. 68; Read *v.* Truelove, Amb. 417; Manson *v.* Baillie, 2 Macq. H. L. Cas. 80; Switzer *v.* Skiles, 3 Gilm. (Ill.) 529; Diefendorf *v.* Spraker, 6 Seld. 246; Shepherd *v.* McEvers, 4 Johns. Ch. 136; Matter of Jones, 4 Sandf. 615; Cruger *v.* Halliday, 11 Paige, 314; Courtenay *v.* Courtenay, 3 Jo. & Lat. 529. [Speakman *v.* Tatem, 48 N. J. Eq. 136.]

will be equally responsible.[1] Even if a trustee gives a bond for
the due execution of the trust, and in a suit upon the bond is
obliged to pay the full amount, he is not discharged from the
trust, nor does the trust property vest in him beneficially. He
is still a trustee, and must account for the trust property, and
all the income and profits. Courts of equity, however, in such
cases have power to do equity; and the trustee would not be
ordered to convey the trust property without repayment to him
of the money paid out on his bond.[2] Until the trustee has been
discharged, the *cestui que trust* may require the due execution of
the trust; and where the trustee will not take proper steps to
enforce a claim against a debtor, he may file a bill against the
trustee for the execution of the trust and to obtain the proper
order for using the trustee's name or for obtaining a receiver to
use the trustee's name.[3] Trustees will be held to great strictness in their dealings with the estate, but courts will treat them
leniently when they act in good faith.[4] A trustee is bound to
exercise ordinary care and judgment, and it is no excuse for
him that he did not possess them; by accepting a trust, whether
gratuitous or not, he undertakes that he does possess and will
exercise them.[5] (a)

§ 402. The office of trustee is one of personal confidence, and
cannot be delegated. If a person takes upon himself the management of property for the benefit of another, he has no right
to impose that duty on others, and if he does he will be responsi-

[1] Lowry *v.* Fulton, 9 Sim. 123; Doyle *v.* Blake, 2 Sch. & Lef. 231; Read
v. Truelove, Amb. 417; Urch *v.* Walker, 3 Myl. & Cr. 702; Van Horn *v.*
Fonda, 5 Johns. Ch. 403.

[2] Moorcroft *v.* Dowding, 2 P. Wms. 314. See Barker *v.* Barker, 14
Wis. 131; Saunders *v.* Webber, 39 Cal. 287.

[3] Sharpe *v.* San P. Ry. Co., L. R. 8 Ch. 597.

[4] Crabb *v.* Young, 92 N. Y. 56.

[5] Hun *v.* Cary, 82 N. Y. 65.

(a) "Trustees are not bound to   Per Kekewich, J., in Budgett *v.*
do anything dishonest or immoral   Budgett, [1895] 1 Ch. 202, 215.
for the sake of their *cestui que trust*."

654

ble to the *cestui que trust*, to whom he owes the duty.[1] Therefore, if a trustee confides his duties or the trust fund to the care
of a stranger,[2] or to his attorney,[3] or even to his cotrustee or
coexecutor,[4] he will be personally responsible. But, before this
responsibility can arise, the trustee must have accepted the
office. Where a person named executor received a bill by post,
and passed it over to a coexecutor who had accepted the trust,
it was held that the act might be considered as the act of a
stranger, and did not impose any responsibility.[5] So where a
coexecutor collected money, and paid it to a banker, who was
also his coexecutor, and whom the testator employed as his
banker, he was held excused for trusting the same person as his
coexecutor whom the testator trusted as his banker.[6]

[1] Turner *v.* Corney, 5 Beav. 517; Taylor *v.* Hopkins, 41 Ill. 442.

[2] Adams *v.* Clifton, 1 Russ. 297; Kilbee *v.* Sneyd, 2 Moll. 199; Hardwick *v.* Mynd, 1 Anst. 109; Venables *v.* Foyle, 1 Ch. Cas. 2; Douglass *v.*
Browne, Mont. 93; *Ex parte* Booth, id. 248; Walker *v.* Symonds, 3 Swanst.
79, n. (a); Char. Corp. *v.* Sutton, 2 Atk. 405; Wilkinson *v.* Parry, 4 Russ.
272; Hulme *v.* Hulme, 2 Myl. & K. 682; Black *v.* Irwin, Harp. L. 411; Berger
v. Duff, 4 Johns. Ch. 368; Pearson *v.* Jamison, 1 McLean, 199; Newton *v.*
Bronson, 3 Kern. 587; Andrew *v.* N. Y. Bible Soc., 4 Sandf. 156; Niles *v.*
Stevens, 4 Denio, 399; Beekman *v.* Bonsor, 23 N. Y. 298; Whittlesey *v.*
Hughes, 39 Mo. 13; Graham *v.* King, 50 Mo. 22; Howard *v.* Thornton, id.
291; Bales *v.* Perry, 51 Mo. 449.

[3] Chambers *v.* Minchin, 7 Ves. 196; Griffiths *v.* Porter, 25 Beav. 236;
Ingle *v.* Patridge, 32 Beav. 661; 34 Beav. 411; Bostock *v.* Floyer, L. R.
1 Ch. 26; *Ex parte* Townsend, 1 Moll. 139; Ghost *v.* Waller, 9 Beav. 497;
Turner *v.* Corney, 5 Beav. 115; Sinclair *v.* Jackson, 8 Cow. 582. [See
infra, §§ 409, 441, as to liability for loss due to employment of agents.]

[4] Langford *v.* Gascoyne, 11 Ves. 333; Clough *v.* Bond, 3 Myl. & Cr.
497; Eaves *v.* Hickson, 30 Beav. 136; Davis *v.* Spurling, 1 R. & M. 66;
Anon., Mos. 35, 36; Harrison *v.* Graham, 1 P. Wms. 241, n. (y); Kilbee
v. Sneyd, 2 Moll. 200; Marriott *v.* Kinnersley, Tam. 470; Thompson *v.*
Finch, 22 Beav. 316; 8 De G., M. & G. 560; Dines *v.* Scott, T. & R. 361;
Cowell *v.* Gatcombe, 27 Beav. 568; Trutch *v.* Lamprell, 20 Beav. 116;
Ex parte Winnall, 3 D. & C. 22; Berger *v.* Duff, 4 Johns. Ch, 368. [Stong's
Estate, 160 Pa. St. 13. See *infra*, §§ 415–419.]

[5] Balchen *v.* Scott, 2 Ves. Jr. 678.

[6] Churchill *v.* Hobson, 1 P. Wms. 241; Chambers *v.* Minchin, 7 Ves.
198. And see 1 P. Wms. 241, n. (y). [See Duckworth *v.* Ocean Steamship
Co., 98 Ga. 193; Dover *v.* Denne, 3 Ont. L. Rep. 664; Bermingham *v.* Wilcox, 120 Cal. 467.]

§ 403. So trustees are not responsible, if they follow the directions of the settlor. Thus, where a testator recommended his
executors to employ a person who had been his own agent and
clerk, and they employed him to collect moneys, and he became
insolvent, it was held that, as the testator pointed out the agent
to whom certain business might be delegated, the executors
were not liable for the loss, if they used due diligence to recover
the money.[1] So if an executor pays over money which he has no
right to retain. Thus a testator appointed A., B., and C. his
executors, and authorized A. to sell real estate for certain purposes. A. employed B. as his agent to sell the real estate; B.
sold the estate and paid the money over to A., who misapplied
it; and it was held that B. received the money, not as executor,
but as agent of A., and as A. had authority to sell, he had a
right to the money, and that B. could not retain it, and was not
responsible for it.[2]

§ 404. But there are circumstances where the trustees must
employ agents. Lord Hardwicke said: "There are two sorts of
necessity, *legal* necessity and *moral* necessity. As to the first a
distinction prevails. Where two *executors* join in giving a discharge for money, and only one of them receives it, they are
both answerable for it; because there is no necessity for both to
join in the discharge, the receipt of either being sufficient; but
if *trustees* join in giving a discharge and one receives, the other
is not answerable, because his joining in the discharge was
necessary. *Moral* necessity is from the usage of mankind, if the
trustee acts prudently for the trust, as he would have done for
himself, 'and according to the usage of business;' as if a trustee
appoint rents to be paid to a banker at that time in credit, but
who afterwards breaks, the trustee is not answerable. So in the
employment of stewards and agents; for none of these cases are
on account of necessity, but because the persons acted in the

[1] Kilbee *v.* Sneyd, 2 Moll. 199; Doyle *v.* Blake, 2 Sch. & Lef. 239.

[2] Davis *v.* Spurling, 1 R. & M. 64; Tam. 199; Keane *v.* Roberts, 4 Madd.
332, 356; Crisp *v.* Spranger, Nels. 109.

usual method of business." [1]   Other cases have held that "necessity includes the usual course of business," [2] as in employing a
broker in making investments of a class usually so made. [3]   But
the agent must not be employed out of the scope of his regular
business. [4]   Where an executor in London remitted money to an
executor in the country to pay debts there due, it was held to
be a *necessary* transaction in the course of business, and the
executor in London was not responsible for the loss of the
money by his coexecutor in the country. [5]   So, where A. and B.
were assignees of a bankrupt, and B. signed dividend checks
and delivered them to B. for his signature, and for delivery to
the creditors, and they were stolen from B. and negotiated at
the bank, it was held that A. was not responsible for the loss, as
he had delegated the checks to B. in the necessary course of
the business. [6]   So a trustee is not called upon, in the ordinary course of business, to take security from the agent
or other person whom he employs. [7]   One trustee may employ his cotrustee as his agent, or one trustee may act for

---

[1] *Ex parte* Belchier, Amb. 219.

[2] Bacon *v.* Bacon, 5 Ves. 335; Clough *v.* Bond,'3 Myl. & Cr. 497; Joy *v.*
Campbell, 1 Sch. & Lef. 341; Chambers *v.* Minchin, 7 Ves. 193; Langford
v. Gascoyne, 11 Ves. 335; Davis *v.* Spurling, 1 R. & M. 66; Munch *v.* Cockerell, 5 Myl. & Cr. 214; Hawley *v.* James, 5 Paige, 487; May *v.* Frazer, 4
Litt. 391; Telford *v.* Barney, 1 G. Greene (Iowa), 575; Blight *v.* Schenck,
10 Barr, 285; Lewis *v.* Reed, 11 Ind. 239; Mason *v.* Wait, 4 Scam. 132.
[See Donaldson *v.* Allen, 182 Mo. 626; *In re* De Pothonier, [1900]
2 Ch. 529; Lord De Clifford's Estate, [1900] 2 Ch. 707; Finlay *v.* Merriman, 39 Tex. 56; *In re* Weall, 42 Ch. Div. 674; *In re* Brier, 26 Ch. Div.
238.]

[3] Speight *v.* Gaunt, 22 Ch. D. 727, 9 App. Cas. 1. [Shepherd *v.* Harris,
[1905] 2 Ch. 310.]

[4] Fry *v.* Tapson, 28 Ch. D. 268. [Robinson *v.* Harkin, [1896] 2 Ch.
415; McCloskey *v.* Gleason, 56 Vt. 264.]

[5] Joy *v.* Campbell, 1 Sch. & Lef. 341; Barrings *v.* Willing, 4 Wash. C.
C. 251; Jones's App., 8 Watts & S. 147; State *v.* Guilford, 15 Ohio, 593;
Deaderick *v.* Cantrell, 10 Yerg. 254; Thomas *v.* Scruggs, id. 401; Maccubbin
v. Cromwell, 7 G. & J. 157.

[6] *Ex parte* Griffin, 2 G. & J. 114; Wackerbath *v.* Powell, Buck, 495;
2 G. & J. 151.

[7] *Ex parte* Belchier, Amb. 220.

657

the whole, within the scope of those duties where an agent may be employed.[1] (a)

§ 405. It was held in one case, that assignees were responsible for the loss of money by an attorney employed by them to collect debts due the estate, on the ground that there was no *necessity* for them to allow the attorney to receive a shilling of the money except the costs, as he could not give a valid receipt for the same;[2] and Lord Eldon was cited as an authority for this. Mr. Lewin questions this case, and says that trustees must not allow money to remain in the hands of an attorney, but that the authorities are doubtful which say that money may not pass through the hands of an attorney in the ordinary course of business. The case is authority, however, thus far, that attorneys cannot sign receipts for trustees, and if they authorize them so to do, the trustees will be responsible as for the acts of an agent improperly appointed.[3]

§ 406. If money is to be transmitted to a distant place, a trustee may do so through the medium of a responsible bank, or he may take bills from persons of undoubted credit, payable at the place where the money is to be sent; but the bills must be taken to him *as trustee:* if he neglects these precautions he will be responsible for any loss.[4]

---

[1] *Ex parte* Rigby, 19 Ves. 463; Abbott *v.* American Hard Rubber Co., 33 Barb. 579; Sinclair *v.* Jackson, 8 Cow. 543; Webb *v.* Ledsom, 1 K. & J. 385; Leggett *v.* Hunter, 19 N. Y. 445; Bowers *v.* Seeger, 3 Watts & S. 222. [Ubhoff *v.* Brandenburg, 26 App. D. C. 3; Shepherd *v.* Harris, [1905] 2 Ch. 310.]

[2] *Ex parte* Townsend, 1 Moll. 149; Anon. 12 Mod. 560; *Re* Fryer, 3 K. & J. 317. [See *infra,* § 409 and note.]

[3] Lewin on Trusts, 208.

[4] Wren *v.* Kirton, 11 Ves. 380; *Ex parte* Belchier, Amb. 219; Routh *v.*

(a) If a testator empowers his trustees to appoint a factor to the estate who may be one of themselves, but directs them to require annual accounts, the trustees are guilty of gross negligence if they do not call for such accounts. Carruthers *v.* Carruthers, [1896] A. C. 659.

§ 407. It is said that there is a difference in the rule, as applied to executors in a court of law and a court of equity. Thus, in a court of law, an executor will be charged with all the assets that come to his hands to be administered, and he must discharge himself by showing a legal administration of all of them; and he cannot discharge himself at law by showing that he intrusted them to another in the ordinary course of business; that he used due caution and prudence, and reposed a reasonable confidence in such other person; and that the assets were lost without negligence or default on his part. Such a state of facts would not sustain a plea of *plene administravit* in a court of law. But a court of equity would adjust the account of the executor upon equitable principles.[1] A court of probate, in taking the account, would also act upon equitable principles.[2]

§ 408. If a trust is of a *discretionary* nature, the trustee will be responsible for all the mischievous consequences of the delegation, and the exercise of the discretion will be absolutely void in the substitute.[3] Nor can a *discretionary* trust be delegated to a cotrustee.[4] Where a sum of money was given to three trustees to be distributed in charity in their *discretion*, and they divided it into three parts, and each took control of a third, Lord Hardwicke said: "I am of opinion that the trustees could not divide the charity into three parts, and each trustee nominate a third absolutely, because the determination of the propriety of every object was left by the testator to the discretion of *all* the executors." [5]

Howell, 3 Ves. 566; Massey *v.* Banner, 1 J. & W. 247; Knight *v.* Plymouth, 1 Dick. 120; 3 Atk. 480. [See Dunn *v.* Dunn, 137 N. C. 533.]

[1] Cross *v.* Smith, 7 East, 246; Jones *v.* Lewis, 2 Ves. 241; Poole *v.* Munday, 103 Mass. 174; Upson *v.* Badeau, 3 Bradf. Sur. 13.

[2] Ibid.

[3] Alexander *v.* Alexander, 2 Ves. 643; Att. Gen. *v.* Scott, 1 Ves. 413; Wilson *v.* Dennison, Amb. 82; 7 Bro. P. C. 296; Bradford *v.* Belfield, 2 Sim. 264; Hitch *v.* Leworthy, 2 Hare, 200; Doe *v.* Robinson, 24 Miss. 688; Singleton *v.* Scott, 11 Iowa, 589; Person *v.* Jamison, 3 McLean, 69, 197.

[4] Crewe *v.* Dicken, 4 Ves. 97.

[5] Att. Gen. *v.* Gleg, 1 Atk. 356; *ante*, § 287.

§ 409. But it must be observed that the appointment of an attorney, proxy, or agent is not necessarily a delegation of the trust. The trustee must act at times through attorneys or agents, and if he determines in his own mind how to exercise the discretion, and appoints agents or instruments to carry out his determination, he cannot be said to delegate the trust, even though deeds or other instruments are signed by attorneys in his name. (a) So, if he gives instructions to his attorneys and agents how to act, it cannot be said to be a delegation of the trust.[1]

[1] Att. Gen. v. Scott, 1 Ves. 413; Ex parte Rigby, 19 Ves. 463; Ord v. Noel, 5 Madd. 498; Sinclair v. Jackson, 8 Cow. 582; Hawley v. James,

(a) Thus a trustee with a discretionary power of sale, having exercised this discretion as to the time and terms of sale, may delegate to an agent the execution and delivery of the deed. Smith v. Swan, 2 Tex. Civ. App. 563; Keim v. Lindley, 30 A. 1063, 1074 (N. J. Ch. 1895); 54 N. J. Eq. 418 (on appeal.) Similarly, when the donee of a power of appointment by will executes it by devising the property to executors with directions to sell and divide the proceeds among the appointees in certain named shares, it has been held that nothing had been delegated but a ministerial duty. McNeile's Estate, 217 Pa. St. 179; Papin v. Piednoir, 205 Mo. 521.

A trustee who has used reasonable care in the selection of his agents for the performance of ministerial duties and who has been reasonably prudent in his supervision of the acts of the agent is not required to make good to the trust estate a loss or damage caused by the negligence or dishonesty of the agent, provided the duties delegated were such as the trustee could properly delegate. The standard of reasonable conduct in such cases is the care which "an ordinarily prudent man would exercise in the management of his own property." Donaldson v. Allen, 182 Mo. 626, 650; Speight v. Gaunt, 9 App. Cas. 1, 22 Ch. Div. 727; see also § 441 and note. But a trustee who has "unnecessarily" turned trust funds over to an agent for management is liable to make good the loss due to the latter's dishonesty. Low v. Gemley, 18 Can. Sup. 685.

In the English case of Speight v. Gaunt, 9 App. Cas. 1, where trust funds had been embezzled by a broker employed by the trustees, the rule was stated to be, "that although a trustee cannot delegate to others the confidence reposed in himself, nevertheless, he may in the administration of the trust funds avail himself of third parties, such as bankers, brokers, and others, if he does so from a moral necessity, or in the regular course of business. If a loss to the trust fund should be occasioned thereby, the trustee will be exonerated unless some negligence or default of his had led to that result."

§ 410. It has been before stated that a sale or devise of the trust estate by the trustee will not be a delegation or communication of a discretionary trust to the vendee or devisee, unless the original instrument of trust contemplated and authorized such an act by vesting the trust or power annexed to the estate in the trustee and his assigns or devisees.[1]

§ 411. Where a settlor vests his property in several cotrustees, they all form, as it were, one collective trustee; therefore they must perform their duties in their joint capacity,[2] even in making a purchase.[3] In law there is no such person known as an *acting* trustee apart from his cotrustees. All who accept the office are acting trustees. If any one trustee who has accepted refuses to join in the proposed act, or is incapable, the others cannot proceed without him, but an application must be made to the court.[4] (a) So, if trustees bring suits, or defend suits in court,

5 Paige, 487; Newton *v.* Bronson, 3 Kern. 587; Blight *v.* Schenck, 10 Barr, 285; *Ex parte* Belchier, Amb. 219; Bacon *v.* Bacon, 5 Ves. 335; Clough *v.* Bond, 3 Myl. & Cr. 497; Lewis *v.* Reed, 11 Ind. 239; Mason *v.* Wait, 4 Scam. 132; Powell *v.* Tuttle, 3 Comst. 396; Bales *v.* Perry, 51 Mo. 449.

[1] *Ante,* § 340; Saunders *v.* Webber, 39 Cal. 287.

[2] Smith *v.* Wildman, 37 Conn. 384; White *v.* Watkins, 23 Mo. 423; *Ex parte* Griffin, 5 G. & J. 116; Shook *v.* Shook, 19 Barb. 63; De Peyster *v.* Ferrers, 11 Paige, 13; Franklin *v.* Osgood, 14 Johns. 560; Cox *v.* Walker, 28 Maine, 504; Hill *v.* Josselyn, 13 Sm. & M. 597; Crewe *v.* Dicken, 4 Ves. 97; Fellows *v.* Mitchell, 1 P. Wms. 83; 2 Vern. 516; Churchill *v.* Hobson, id. 241; Chambers *v.* Minchin, 7 Ves. 198; Leigh *v.* Barry, 3 Atk. 584; Belchier *v.* Parsons, Amb. 219; *Ex parte* Rigby, 19 Ves. 463; Webb *v.* Ledsam, 1 K. & J. 385; Latrobe *v.* Tiernan, 2 Md. Ch. 480; Vandever's App., 8 Watts & S. 405; Sinclair *v.* Jackson, 8 Cow. 544; Ridgeley *v.* Johnson, 11 Barb. 527; Austin *v.* Shaw, 10 Allen, 552; King *v.* Stone, 6 Johns. Ch. 323; Powell *v.* Tuttle, 3 Comst. 396; Sherwood *v.* Read, 7 Hill, 431. [Winslow *v.* B. & O. R. Co., 188 U. S. 646; Ubhoff *v.* Brandenburg, 26 App. D. C. 3; Hosch Lumber Co. *v.* Weeks, 123 Ga. 336; Carr *v.* Hertz, 54 N. J. Eq. 127, 700; Tarlton *v.* Gilsey, 37 A. 467 (N. J. Ch. 1897); Poole *v.* Anderson, 80 Md. 454; 1 Ames on Trusts (2d ed.) 512 n.]

[3] Holcomb *v.* Holcomb, 3 Stockt. 281.

[4] Smith *v.* Wildman, 37 Conn. 384; Doyley *v.* Sherratt, 2 Eq. Cas. Ab. 742; *Re* Cong. Church *v.* Smithwick, 1 W. N. 196; Scruggs *v.* Driver, 31

(a) It seems well to note an important difference between cases where a trustee ignores his cotrustee in attempts to dispose of or bind

they must act jointly, (*a*) and they should all employ the same counsel. If they sever in their defence and incur extra costs, they might be compelled to bear them personally.

§ 412. A receipt for money, in the absence of special directions in the instrument of trust, must be signed by all the trustees, or it will be invalid.[1] Where the trustees are numerous, the court generally inserts an order that moneys may be paid to two or more.[2] This rule is, however, relaxed in the United States; and it has been held that payment of a mortgage to one of two trustees is a valid payment.[3] So all the trustees must join in proving a debt against a bankrupt;[4] but, under special circumstances, the court may order the proof to be made by one

Ala. 274; Matter of Wadsworth, 2 Barb. Ch. 381; Matter of Mechanics' Bank, id. 446; Burrill *v.* Sheil, 2 Barb. 457; Wood *v.* Wood, 5 Paige, 596; Davis *v.* McNeil, 1 Ired. Eq. 344; Matter of Van Wyke, 1 Barb. Ch. 565; Guyton *v.* Shane, 7 Dana, 498; Ridgeley *v.* Johnson, 11 Barb. 527; *Ex parte* Belchier, Amb. 219. [Fritz *v.* City Trust Co., 76 N. Y. S. 625, 72 App. Div. 532 (affirmed 173 N. Y. 622)].

[1] Walker *v.* Symonds, 3 Swanst. 63; Hall *v.* Franck, 11 Beav. 519.

[2] Att. Gen. *v.* Brickdale, 8 Beav. 223.

[3] Bowers *v.* Seeger, 8 Watts & S. 222.

[4] *Ex parte* Smith, 1 Dea. 191; M. & A. 506; *Ex parte* Phillips, 2 Dea. 334.

trust property and cases where he assumed to act as agent for his co-trustees, since the necessary participation of all the trustees may be by agency of one. The attempted disposal in cases of the former kind is entirely nugatory. Thus a lease of trust property signed by only one of two trustees is inoperative and cannot be ratified, since it does not purport to bind the other joint tenant. Winslow *v.* B. & O. R. Co., 188 U. S. 646. The same is true of an assignment of a bond and mortgage by less than the whole number of trustees. Fritz *v.* City Trust Co., 76 N. Y. S. 625, 72 App. Div. 532 (affirmed 173 N. Y. 622); Hosch Lumber Co. *v.* Weeks, 123 Ga. 336; Tarlton *v.* Gilsey, 37 A. 467 (N. J. Eq. 1897). But if the attempted disposal is made in the names of all, it becomes a question whether or not the trustee who acted or signed was properly authorized to act as agent for his cotrustees, or, in the absence of original authority, whether or not the cotrustees have ratified or adopted the act. Ubhoff *v.* Brandenburg, 26 App. D. C. 3.

(*a*) McGeorge *v.* Bigstone Gap. Imp. Co., 88 F. R. 599.

or more, even when payment must be made to all the trustees.[1] A different rule prevails in regard to bank stocks, for the bank recognizes only the legal title, and at law one joint-tenant may receive moneys; so one trustee may receive dividends upon public stocks,[2] or the rents of real estate, unless the tenant has had notice not to pay to one;[3] but all the trustees must join in conveying such stocks or in executing a conveyance of land,[4] or pledging the trust property.[5] A deed of land executed by one trustee does not convey his share, as in the case of ordinary joint-tenants.[6] Where a deed was executed by two of three trustees, the burden was put upon the purchaser to prove that the other trustee was dead.[7] It has been said, however, that in a case of necessity, and after considerable time, the concurrence of a cotrustee may be presumed in some transactions.[8] A banker may require checks to be signed by one only, or by all the trustees. But if trustees place money at a banker's in such manner that one of their number can withdraw it in his sole name, all the trustees will be liable in case of a loss under such an arrangement.[9] (a)

§ 413. In the case of a public trust, where there are several trustees, the act of the majority is held to be the act of the whole

[1] Ibid.

[2] Williams v. Nixon, 2 Beav. 472.

[3] Williams v. Nixon, 2 Beav. 472; Townley v. Sherborne, Bridg. 35; Gouldsworth v. Knight, 11 M. & W. 337; Husband v. Davis, 1 C. B. 645. See Webb v. Ledsam, 1 K. & J. 385; Mendes v. Guedalla, 2 John. & H. 259. [Dyer v. Riley, 51 N. J. Eq. 124.]

[4] Ibid.; Morville v. Fowle, 144 Mass. 109, 113. [Hosch Lumber Co. v. Weeks, 123 Ga. 336.]

[5] Ham v. Ham, 58 N. H. 70.

[6] Sinclair v. Jackson, 8 Cow. 543. [Chapin v. First Univ. Soc., 8 Gray, 580.]

[7] Ridgeley v. Johnson, 11 Barb. 527; Learned v. Welton, 40 Cal. 339; Burngarner v. Coggswell, 49 Mo. 259. [See supra, § 411, note a.]

[8] Vandever's App., 8 Watts & S. 405.

[9] Townley v. Sherborne, Bridg. 35.

(a) But see infra, § 415, note, as to exceptions in case of the business "necessity" of such an arrangement.

number;[1] but the act of the majority must be strictly within the sphere of their power and duty.[2] When a special power is given to trustees, it cannot be exercised by a majority only: all must join.[3] If a settlement declares that, on the death or resignation of a trustee, the surviving trustees shall appoint his successor, all the surviving trustees must join in the appointment.[4] Where the trustees are numerous, as in the case of a charity, the court may direct that a majority shall form a quorum. Private trusts, where the rule prevails that all must join, cannot be affected by these principles, or by any agreements that may be made by the parties.[5] But an instrument of trust may contain express directions that the trust shall be administered according to the will of the majority of the trustees, in which case the minority will be compelled to give effect to the determinations of the majority.[6] (a) So if the power is given to either of two trustees.[7] So trustees are bound to concur in every merely ministerial act necessary for the execution of the trust; and if they refuse, they may be compelled by order of the court. But where it is a mere matter of personal discretion, the court cannot interfere, unless a cotrustee refuses to act from a corrupt or selfish motive.[8] But a majority of trustees cannot

[1] Wilkinson v. Malin, 2 Tyr. 544; Perry v. Shipway, 1 Gif. 1; 4 De G. & J. 353; Att. Gen. v. Shearman, 2 Beav. 104; Att. Gen. v. Cuming, 2 Y. & C. Ch. 139; Younger v. Welham, 3 Swanst. 180; Att. Gen. v. Scott, 1 Ves. 413; Wilson v. Dennison, Amb. 82. [See Bank v. Mt. Tabor, 52 Vt. 87.]

[2] Ward v. Hipwell, 3 Gif. 547; Sloo v. Law, 3 Blatch, 66, 459.

[3] Re Cong. Church v. Smithwick, 1 W. N. 196.

[4] Ibid.

[5] Swale v. Swale, 22 Beav. 585; State v. Lord, 31 L. J. Ch. 391.

[6] Att. Gen. v. Cumings, 2 Y. & C. Ch. 139; Taylor v. Dickinson, 15 Iowa, 483.

[7] Taylor v. Dickinson, 15 Iowa, 486.

[8] Clarke v. Parker, 19 Ves. 1; Tomlin v. Hatfield, 12 Sim. 167; Goulds-

(a) In New Hampshire it has been provided by statute that, "When more than one trustee is required to execute a trust, a majority of the trustees shall be competent to act in all cases, unless the instrument or authority creating the trust shall otherwise provide." Laws of 1901, c. 2; Ladd v. Ladd, 74 A. 1045, (N. H. 1909).

deprive one of their number of his right and interest in the trust property.[1]

§ 414. A *bare authority*, committed to several persons, ceases upon the death of one; but if the authority is coupled with an interest, it passes to the survivors.[2] The committee of a lunatic's estate are mere protectors without any interest, and the death of one extinguishes the office.[3] An executorship survives, for the joint executors have an interest in the estate.[4] So testamentary guardianship survives, as such guardians have an authority over the estate.[5] So cotrustees have an authority coupled with an interest in the legal title of the estate, and the office is impressed with the quality of survivorship.[6] If land is given to two trustees in trust to sell, and one dies, the other may sell, as he holds the legal title in the land, and the office of trustee.[7] (a) Otherwise, the precaution taken by a settlor to guard

worth *v.* Knight, 11 M. & W. 337; Burrill *v.* Sheil, 2 Barb. 457; Matter of Mechanics' Bank, id. 446.

[1] Meth. Ep. Church *v.* Stewart, 27 Barb. 553.

[2] Co. Litt. 113 a; Eyre *v.* Shaftsbury, 2 P. Wms. 108, 121, 124; Att. Gen. *v.* Gleg, 1 Atk. 356; Amb. 584; Mansell *v.* Vaughn, Wilm. 49; Butler *v.* Bray, Dyer, 189 b; Peyton *v.* Bury, 2 P. Wms. 628. See § 286. [See *infra,* § 491 *et seq.*]

[3] *Ex parte* Lyne, t. Talb. 143.

[4] Adams *v.* Buckland, 2 Vern. 514; Hudson *v.* Hudson, t. Talb. 129.

[5] Eyre *v.* Shaftsbury, 2 P. Wms. 102. But if joint guardians are appointed by the court, the death of one destroys the guardianship. Bradshaw *v.* Bradshaw, 1 Russ. 528; Hall *v.* Jones, 2 Sim. 41.

[6] Hudson *v.* Hudson, t. Talb. 129; Co. Litt. 113 a; Att. Gen. *v.* Gleg, Amb. 585; Billingsley *v.* Mathew, Toth. 168; Gwilliams *v.* Rowell, Hard. 204; Stewart *v.* Peters, 10 Mo. 755; Butler *v.* Bray, Dyer, 189 b; Dominick *v.* Sayre, 3 Sandf. 555; Belmont *v.* O'Brien, 2 Kern. 394; De Peyster *v.* Ferrers, 11 Paige, 13; Moses *v.* Murgatroyd, 1 Johns. Ch. 119; Shook *v.* Shook, 19 Barb. 653; Gregg *v.* Currier, 36 N. H. 200; Powell *v.* Knox, 16 Ala. 364; Parsons *v.* Boyd, 20 Ala. 112; Leggett *v.* Hunter, 19 N. Y. 445; Aubuchon *v.* Lory, 23 Mo. 99; Barton *v.* Tunnell, 5 Harr. 182; Smith *v.* McConnell, 17 Ill. 135; Hopper *v.* Adee, 3 Duer, 235; Britton *v.* Lewis, 8 Rich. Eq. 271.

[7] Warburton *v.* Sandys, 14 Sim. 622; Watson *v.* Pearson, 2 Exch. 594;

(a) So too where only one of the three named as trustees qualifies. Draper *v.* Montgomery, 95 N. Y. S. 904, 108 App. Div. 63.

his estate, by increasing the number of trustees, would be futile; for the death of one of them might result in defeating his whole trust. Where the trust was to raise £2000 out of the testator's estate, by sale or otherwise at the discretion of the trustees, who should invest the same in their own names upon trust, one of the trustees died and the other sold; and Vice-Chancellor Wood held that the survivor could make a good title. He said: "I find a clear estate in the vendor, and a clear duty to perform. Is it to be said that the sale is a breach of trust, because the co-trustee is dead? If I were to lay down such a rule, it would come to this, that when an estate is vested in two or more trustees, to raise a sum by sale or mortgage, you must come into this court on the death of one of the trustees." [1] The survivorship of the trust will not be defeated, because the settlement contains a power for restoring the original number of trustees by new appointment,[2] unless there is something in the instrument that specially manifests such an intention.[3] Where an act of Parliament declared that "survivors should, and they were thereby required" to appoint new trustees, the court expressed an opinion that the clause was not imperative, but simply directory.[4]

§ 415. The general rule is, that one trustee shall not be responsible or liable for the acts or defaults of his cotrustee. This rule was established in the time of Charles the First, after very great consideration and consultation by the judges in the case of Townley v. Sherborne,[5] wherein it was resolved "that

Att. Gen. v. Litchfield, 5 Ves. 825; Att. Gen. v. Cumings, 2 Y. & C. Ch. 139; Stater v. Wheeler, 9 Sim. 156. [See infra, § 491 et seq.]

[1] Lane v. Debenham, 11 Hare, 188; Hind v. Poole, 1 K. & J. 383.

[2] Doe v. Godwin, 1 D. & R. 259; Att. Gen. v. Cuming, 2 Y. & C. Ch. 139; Jacob v. Lucas, 1 Beav. 436; Warburton v. Sandys, 14 Sim. 622; Hall v. Dewes, Jac. 193; Att. Gen. v. Floyer, 2 Vern. 748; Townsend v. Wilson, 1 B. & A. 608.

[3] Foley v. Wontner, 2 J. & W. 245; Jacob v. Lucas, 1 Beav. 436.

[4] Doe v. Godwin, 1 D. & R. 259. And see Att. Gen. v. Locke, 3 Atk. 166; Stamper v. Millar, id. 212; Rex v. Flockwood, 2 Chit. 252.

[5] Townley v. Sherborne, Bridg. 35; 3 Lead. Cas. Eq. 718, and notes; Bowers v. Seeger, 8 Watts & S. 222; Sinclair v. Jackson, 8 Cow. 543; Van-

where lands or leases were conveyed to two or more upon trust, that one of them receives all or the most part of the profits, and after dyeth or decayeth in his estate, his cotrustee shall not be charged or compelled in chancery to answer for the receipts of him so dying or decayed, unless some practice, fraud, or evil dealing appear to have been in them to prejudice the trust; *for they being by law joint-tenants*, or tenants in common, every one by law may receive either all or as much of the profits as he can come by; it is no breach of trust to permit one of the trustees to receive all or the most part of the profits; it falling out many times that some of the trustees live far from the lands, and are put in trust out of other respects than to be troubled with the receipt of the profits. But his lordship and the said judges did resolve, that if, upon the proofs or circumstances, the court should be satisfied that there had been any *dolus malus*, or any evil practice, fraud, or ill intent in him that permitted his companion to receive the whole profits, he should be charged though he received nothing." And the same doctrine has been acted upon from that day to this.[1] Connivance, co-operation, permission, acquiescence, or participation will bring liability;[2] and ignorance of the default of a cotrustee if it results from neglect is no excuse, as where one trustee collects a fund and keeps it without reinvestment, the other trustees may be liable.[3] (*a*)

dever's App., 8 Watts & S. 405. And see Leigh *v.* Barry, 3 Atk. 584; Anon. 12 Mod. 560; Taylor *v.* Benham, 5 How. 233; Ochiltree *v.* Wright, 1 Dev. & B. Eq. 336; Ray *v.* Doughty, 4 Blackf. 115; Jones's App., 8 Watts & S. 143; Peters *v.* Beverly, 10 Peters, 532; 1 How. 134; Taylor *v.* Roberts, 3 Ala. 86; State *v.* Guilford, 18 Ohio, 509; Latrobe *v.* Tiernan, 2 Md. Ch. 480; Worth *v.* McAden, Dev. & B. Eq. 109; Boyd *v.* Boyd, 3 Grat. 114; Glenn *v.* McKim, 3 Gill, 366; Stell's App., 10 Penn. St. 149; Banks *v.* Wilkes, 3 Sandf. Ch. 99. And see Royall *v.* McKenzie, 25 Ala. 363.

[1] Ibid. [Bruen *v.* Gillet, 115 N. Y. 10; Purdy *v.* Lynch, 145 N. Y. 462; Fesmire's Estate, 134 Pa. St. 67, 83; Graham's Estate (No. 1), 218 Pa. St. 344; Colburn *v.* Grant, 16 App. D. C. 107; 181 U. S. 601; Litzenberger's Estate, 85 Hun, 512; Laurel County Court *v.* Trustees, 93 Ky. 379.]

[2] Hinson *v.* Williamson, 74 Ala. 180; Knight *v.* Haynie, id. 542.

[3] Richards *v.* Seal, 2 Del. Ch. 266. [Fesmire's Estate, 134 Pa. St. 67, 83.]

(*a*) In the administration and management of the affairs of a trust it is usually impracticable for every trustee to actually participate in

§ 416. In the same case of Townley *v.* Sherborne, it was determined that if the trustees joined in signing a receipt for

every act. To some extent they may delegate to each other the merely ministerial duties of management, and each is entitled to rely upon the honesty and prudence of the other unless he has notice of facts which should lead him to distrust the other. On the other hand, a trustee cannot escape the responsibility for the proper management and the safety of the trust property by remaining passive and allowing his cotrustee to have the control and management of the property. A trustee's liability for losses due to the dishonesty or culpable mismanagement of his co-trustee must depend largely upon the circumstances of each case, and, except where he has delegated some positive duty requiring the exercise of his discretion, depends upon whether or not he has acted in the matter with the caution and prudence which a reasonable man would exercise in the conduct of his own affairs. He is neither "an insurer of the trust funds against the possibility of loss, nor a surety for his co-trustee." Fesmire's Estate, 134 Pa. St. 67, 83; Bermingham *v.* Wilcox, 120 Cal. 467; *In re* Gasquoine, [1894] 1 Ch. 470.

Liability for acts of his cotrustee in which he has not participated and which he has not sanctioned rests upon neglect of some duty which has made the loss possible. Graham's Estate, 218 Pa. St. 344; Colburn *v.* Grant, 16 App. D. C. 107; 181 U. S. 601; Barroll *v.* Foreman, 88 Md. 188; Bruen *v.* Gillet, 115 N. Y. 10; Dover *v.* Denne, 3 Ont. L. Rep. 664; Shepherd *v.* Harris, [1905] 2 Ch. 310;

Speight *v.* Gaunt, 9 App. Cas. 1. See also *infra*, § 848.

Where funds for investment have come into the hands of one trustee, the other has the duty of seeing for himself that they have been properly invested, and if he fails to do so he is liable for a loss made possible by his negligence. He is not protected in taking the cotrustee's word that he has properly invested the funds. Thompson *v.* Finch, 8 De G., M. & G. 560; Bermingham *v.* Wilcox, 120 Cal. 467; Beatty's Estate, 214 Pa. St. 449; Fesmire's Estate, 134 Pa. St. 67, 83; Strong's Estate, 160 Pa. St. 13; Robinson *v.* Harkin, [1896] 2 Ch. 415. So also of neglect to ascertain whether or not a co-trustee has properly deposited to the credit of the trust account a large sum which has been paid to him. Wynne *v.* Tempest, [1897] W. N. 43.

It is sometimes said that a trustee who "unnecessarily" does any act by which trust funds are transferred from the joint possession of all to the sole possession of one is responsible for a resulting misappropriation by the latter, but the word "unnecessarily" is not to be taken in its literal sense. It has been said that an act "is unnecessary when done outside the usual course of business pertaining to the subject," and that "the true question is, taking into consideration all the facts and circumstances, has the trustee employed such prudence and diligence in the discharge of his duties as in general men of average prudence and discretion would under like circumstances employ in their

money, they should each be responsible for it.[1] (*a*)   But where
the administration of a trust is vested in several trustees, they

[1] Townley *v.* Sherborne, Bridg. 35; Spalding *v.* Shalmer, 1 Vern. 303;
Sadler *v.* Hobbs, 2 Bro. Ch. 114; Bradwell *v.* Catchpole, cited 3 Swanst.
78, note (a); Fellowes *v.* Mitchell, 2 Vern. 516.

own affairs?" Purdy *v.* Lynch, 145
N. Y. 462. In the cited case where
three trustees had the duty of paying
out trust funds to a large number of
beneficiaries and two of them allowed the third to have the custody
of the funds and intrusted him with
paying them out, the court, applying
the foregoing test, held that the two
were not liable for misappropriations of the one to whom they had
left control.

Similar language was used in
Shepherd *v.* Harris, [1905] 2 Ch. 310,
where the dishonest trustee, who was
a broker, obtained exclusive control
of the trust funds in the course of
his employment as a broker in the
sale of certain trust securities for the
purpose of purchasing certain others.
As the usual business precautions
were taken and as the defaulting
trustee was a broker of good standing at the time, the innocent trustee
was held not to be liable. See also
In re Gasquoine, [1894] 1 Ch. 470.

Allowing a cotrustee to have the
custody of non-negotiable securities
and to collect and pay over the income to the persons entitled has been
held not such negligence as will render a trustee liable to make good the
default of the cotrustee in paying
over the income. Dyer *v.* Riley, 51
N. J. Eq. 124; Fesmire's Estate, 134

Pa. St. 67, 83. See also Colburn *v*
Grant, 16 App. D. C. 107, 181 U.
S. 601.

It has been held that a trustee
who has no cause to suspect that his
cotrustee is dishonest, is not liable
for the latter's misappropriation of
unregistered negotiable bonds which
were kept in a place of deposit to
which either trustee had access without the other. *In re* Halstead, 89
N. Y. S. 806, 95 N. Y. S. 1131. But
the innocent trustee has been held
liable to make good his cotrustee's
misappropriations of such securities
when, after receiving notice of a
misuse of the securities and compelling their return to the place of deposit, he took no steps to prevent a
similar misuse, other than to exact a
promise from the delinquent trustee.
Matter of Howard, 97 N. Y. S. 23,
110 App. Div. 61 (affirmed 185 N. Y.
539); *In re* Adams' Estate, 221 Pa.
St. 77. See also Matter of Westerfield, 63 N. Y. S. 10, 48 App. Div.
542. And the negligence in such a
case has been held to be a "willful"
breach of trust. Matter of Howard,
ubi supra.

It has also been held that a trustee is negligent in allowing a cotrustee an opportunity to collect a
note after the latter has become insolvent. Darnaby *v.* Watts, 21 S.

(*a*) In view of later decisions it
seems doubtful if much should usually turn upon mere receipt of the

trust funds. See Purdy *v.* Lynch,
145 N. Y. 462; Bruen *v.* Gillet, 115
N. Y. 10; see also note *a*, § 415.

must all join in signing a receipt for the principal or capital sum of the trust fund, and it is now established that a trustee who joins in the receipt for *conformity*, but without receiving any of the money, shall not be answerable for the misapplication of the money by his cotrustee who receives it; as it would be tyranny to punish a trustee for an act which the nature of his office compelled him to do.[1]   But in such case the burden is on the trustee to prove that his acknowledgment of the receipt of the money was merely for conformity, and that in fact he received none of the money, and that his cotrustee received it all.[2]   If there is

[1] *In re* Freyer, 3 K. & J. 317; Brice *v.* Stokes, 11 Ves. 324; 3 Lead. Cas. Eq. 730; Harden *v.* Parsons, 1 Eden, 147; Westley *v.* Clarke, id. 359; Heaton *v.* Marriott, cited Pr. Ch. 173; *Ex parte* Belchier, Amb. 219; Leigh *v.* Barry, 3 Atk. 584; Fellowes *v.* Mitchell, 1 P. Wms. 81; Gregory *v.* Gregory, 2 Y. & C. 316; Sadler *v.* Hobbs, 2 Bro. Ch. 117; Chambers *v.* Minchin, 7 Ves. 198; Shipbrook *v.* Hinchinbrook, 16 Ves. 479; Harrison *v.* Graham, 3 Hill's MS. 239, cited 1 P. Wms. 241; Carsey *v.* Barsham, cited 1 Sch. & Lef. 344; Anon. Mose. 35; *Ex parte* Wackerbath, 2 G. & J. 151; Kip *v.* Deniston, 4 Johns. 23; Jones's App., 8 Watts & S. 147; Irwin's App., 35 Penn. St. 294; Sterrett's App., 2 Penn. 419; Wallis *v.* Thornton, 2 Brock. 434; Monell *v.* Monell, 5 Johns. Ch. 283; Deaderick *v.* Cantrell, 10 Yerg. 264; Aplyn *v.* Brewer, Pr. Ch. 172; Churchill *v.* Hodson, 1 P. Wms. 241; Att. Gen. *v.* Randell, 7 Bacon, Ab. 184; Murrell *v.* Cox, 2 Vern. 173; Terrell *v.* Mathews, 11 L. J. (N. S.) Ch. 31; McMurray *v.* Montgomery, 2 Swanst. 374; Griffin *v.* Macauley, 7 Grat. 476; Worth *v.* McAden, 1 Dev. & B. Eq. 199; Stowe *v.* Bowen, 99 Mass. 194.

[2] Brice *v.* Stokes, 11 Ves. 324; Scurfield *v.* Howes, 3 Bro. Ch. 95, note (8); Chambers *v.* Minchin, 7 Ves. 186; Monell *v.* Monell, 5 Johns. Ch. 394; Hall *v.* Carter, 8 Ga. 388; Manahan *v.* Gibbons, 19 Johns. 427; Martindale *v.* Picquot, 3 K. & J. 317; Cottam *v.* Eastern Counties Ry. Co., 1 John. & H. 243.

W. 333 (Ky. 1893).   The rule is stated as follows in the last cited case: "Although it is a well-established general rule that one trustee is not responsible for the waste of his cotrustee, it is equally well settled that if the trustee connives at the waste or misappropriation of his cotrustee or has reason to believe that he will waste or misappropriate the trust estate, or that his condi- tion has so changed as to make it unsafe for him to control the estate, it is the duty of the trustee, upon being informed of these conditions, to take prompt action to secure the estate against the apprehended waste or misappropriation; for it is well settled that a trustee is responsible for all loss by his associate, caused by his actual or constructive negligence or connivance."

no evidence upon this point, all the trustees who join in signing the receipt will be held responsible *in solido*, on the ground
that the acknowledgment in the receipt is *prima facie* evidence
of the facts stated.[1] At law the receipt is *conclusive* evidence
and estops the trustee from denying that he received any of the
money;[2] but a court of equity rejects estoppels, and pursues the
actual truth, and will determine and decree according to the
verity and justice of the fact.[3] But if a trustee, signing a receipt, receives any part of the money, and it does not appear how
much, he will be answerable for the whole; as, where he mixes
his corn with another's heap, he must lose the whole.[4]

§ 417. It was said in Townley *v.* Sherborne,[5] that individuals
are sometimes joined in a trust, where it is not expected that
they are to take an active part in its management; and it is well
settled that each of several trustees is not bound to take upon
himself the active management of every part of a trust; and it
seems that the management of the whole may be left to any one
of the number.[6] So trustees may apportion their duties among
themselves, as where one of two guardians accepted the trust,
saying he would take care of the real estate, but would have
nothing to do with receiving and disbursing money, which
duties the other guardian assumed, it was held that the former
was not answerable for the defaults of the latter.[7] It sometimes

---

[1] Ibid.; Westley *v.* Clarke, 1 Eden, 359; Maccubbin *v.* Cromwell, 7 G. &
J. 157; Hengst's App., 24 Penn. St. 413. The answer of the trustee in
chancery would not be sufficient evidence unless responsive to the bill.
Monell *v.* Monell, 5 Johns. Ch. 283; Maccubbin *v.* Cromwell, 7 Gl. & J.
157. But as parties are now witnesses, the rule is not very important.

[2] Harden *v.* Parsons, 1 Eden, 147.

[3] Ibid.; Fellowes *v.* Mitchell, 1 P. Wms. 83.

[4] Ibid.

[5] Bridg. 35.

[6] Ray *v.* Doughty, 4 Blackf. 115; Ochiltree *v.* Wright, 1 Dev. & B. Eq.
336; State *v.* Guilford, 18 Ohio, 500. [Colburn *v.* Grant, 16 App. D. C.
107; 181 U. S. 601; Graham's Estate (No. 1), 218 Pa. St. 344; Purdy *v.*
Lynch, 145 N. Y. 462; Fesmire's Estate, 134 Pa. St. 67, 83; Duckworth *v.*
Ocean Steamship Co., 98 Ga. 193; Dover *v.* Denne, 3 Ont. L. Rep. 664.]

[7] Jones's App., 8 Watts & S. 143. But see Gill *v.* Att. Gen., Hardr. 314.

happens that the convenience or necessities of business require
the trust funds to be in the hands of one trustee. If a loss happens from the default of such trustee, the others will not be held
to answer. As where a bond is to be collected by one trustee, or
money is put in the hands of one to be paid away; or where a
fund was given to three trustees, one in London and two in
Cornwall, to build an almshouse in London, it was held that the
fund was properly in the hands of the trustee in London, and
that during the construction of the almshouse the others were
not answerable for the loss of part of it by his insolvency.[1] The
same rule applies where the shares of a company are required
to be in the name of a single individual;[2] and so where the
settlor appoints one of the trustees to perform certain acts, or
make certain sales, or receive certain moneys.[3] But if trustees
expressly agree to be answerable for each other, courts will hold
them to their agreement.[4] So this power to apportion the
duties of the trust, or the rule that a trustee not receiving the
money shall not be liable for the defaults of his cotrustees, does
not excuse him for not exercising a general superintendence and
care over the trust, or for not intervening, if the fact come to
his knowledge that the fund is unsafe, or that it ought not
longer to remain under the control of the other trustee.[5] Even

[1] Att. Gen. v. Randell, 2 Eq. Cas. Ab. 742; 7 Bacon, Ab. 184; Clough
v. Bond, 3 M. & Cr. 497; Townley v. Sherborne, Bridg. 35; 3 Lead. Cas.
Eq. 718, notes; Ex parte Griffin, 2 G. & J. 114; Bacon v. Bacon, 5 Ves. 331;
Hovey v. Blakeman, 4 id. 596; Williams v. Nixon, 2 Beav. 472; Curtis v.
Mason, 12 L. J. (N. S.) Ch. 442; Broadhurst v. Balguy, 1 N. C. C. 28;
Hanbury v. Kirkland, 3 Sim. 265. But see Cowell v. Gatchcombe, 27 Beav.
568.

[2] Consterdine v. Consterdine, 31 Beav. 331.

[3] Davis v. Spurling, 1 R. & M. 64; Paddon v. Richardson, 7 De G., M.
& G. 563; Birls v. Betty, 6 Madd. 90.

[4] Leigh v. Barry, 3 Atk. 583; Brazer v. Clark, 5 Pick. 96; Towne v.
Ammidown, 2 Pick. 535.

[5] Clark v. Clark, 8 Paige, 153; Evans's Est. 2 Ash. 470. [Matter of
Howard, 97 N. Y. S. 23, 110 App. Div. 61 (affirmed 185 N. Y. 539); In re
Adams's Estate, 221 Pa. St. 77; Darnaby v. Watts, 21 S. W. 333 (Ky.
1893). Even when he has been excluded from the management and control
of the trust property with the consent of the cestui. Matter of Westerfield,
63 N. Y. S. 10, 48 App. Div. 542.]

a direct provision in the deed of settlement, that trustees shall not be liable for the defaults of their cotrustees, does not excuse them from this general care and superintendence, and from the duty of intervening, if they hear any fact tending to call for their intervention; nor will it justify them in paying over the money to the sole credit of one trustee; and generally it will not authorize them to do any acts which would be a breach of trust, if such clause was not in the deed or will.[1] While one trustee is not liable for the defaults of cotrustees which he has not the means of preventing or guarding against, yet he must exercise due care in the approval of or acquiescence in the acts of his associates.[2] If the trustees join in accounting, and hold themselves out, in joint accounts, as acting together and as jointly liable, they will be estopped to deny their joint liability to those who have acted on a knowledge of such accounts; and this would be almost conclusive evidence of a joint liability in all cases.[3] So, if the will makes them all liable for the acts of each, or contemplates the joint action and joint liability of all, they cannot excuse themselves if they accept the trust.[4]

§ 418. Though a trustee may join in a receipt without receiving any of the money, and may not be liable or answerable for

[1] Mucklow v. Fuller, Jac. 198; Williams v. Nixon, 2 Beav. 472; Leigh v. Barry, 3 Atk. 584; Dawson v. Clark, 18 Ves. 254; Underwood v. Stevens, 1 Mer. 712; Hanbury v. Kirkland, 3 Sim. 265; Langston v. Olivant, Coop. 33; Brumridge v. Brumridge, 27 Beav. 5; Rehden v. Wesley, 29 id. 213; Drosier v. Brereton, 15 id. 221; Fenwick v. Greenwell, 10 id. 418; Pride v. Fooks, 2 id. 430; Sadler v. Hobbs, 2 Bro. Ch. 114; Bone v. Cook, McClel. 168; 13 Price, 332; Clough v. Dixon, 8 Sim. 594; 3 M. & Cr. 490; Dix v. Burford, 19 Beav. 409; Litchfield v. White, 3 Selden, 438; Wilkins v. Hogg, 3 Gif. 116; 10 W. R. 47; Worral v. Harford, 8 Ves. 8; Moyle v. Moyle, 2 R. & M. 170; Munch v. Cockerell, 9 Sim. 339; 5 M. & Cr. 178; Macdonnel v. Harding, 7 Sim. 176. [Matter of Howard, 97 N. Y. S. 23, 110 App. Div. 61 (affirmed 185 N. Y. 539).] But a testator can draw the indemnity clause so broad that cotrustees will not be liable even for gross negligence. Wilkins v. Hogg, 3 Gif. 116; 10 W. R. 47.   [2] Earle v. Earle, 93 N. Y. 104.

[3] Hengst's App., 24 Penn. St. 413; Clark's App., 18 id. 175; Duncommun's App., 17 id. 268.

[4] Burrill v. Sheil, 2 Barb. 457; Contee v. Dawson, 2 Bland, 264; Wood v. Wood, 5 Paige, 596; Weigand's App., 28 Penn. St. 471.

it, yet he may be responsible for the whole, though he receives none; thus, if knowing that his cotrustee has no character or credit, and is unfit to manage the trust funds, he suffers the money to be received by him, or to remain in his hands, he will be answerable, as if he receives it 'himself, on the ground that he has committed a breach of trust in not using due care and diligence; [1] and the same rule will apply if he suffers the money to remain in the hands of his cotrustee, however competent and responsible, longer than is necessary.[2] (a) It is also the duty of the trustee to ascertain the actual facts, and not rely upon the bare assertion of his cotrustee, in relation to the condition of the trust fund.[3] Thus, where two trustees allowed their cotrustee to open a box at their banker's in which were stocks and bonds, and he converted some of the trust property to his own use, but assured his cotrustees that all was right, they were held to answer for the loss, because they had not taken the pains to ascertain the facts, but had relied upon the assertion of their

---

[1] Clark v. Clark, 8 Paige, 153; Wyman v. Jones, 4 Md. Ch. 500; Elmendorf v. Lansing, 4 Johns. Ch. 562; Ringgold v. Ringgold, 1 H. & G. 11; State v. Guilford, 15 Ohio, 593; Pim v. Downing, 11 Serg. & R. 71; Evans's Est., 2 Ash. 470; Jones's App., 8 Watts & S. 147. But the circumstances must be such as would put a reasonable man upon his guard in relation to his own property. Jones's App., 8 Watts & S. 147; Lincoln v. Wright, 4 Beav. 427; Lockwood v. Riley, 1 De G. & J. 464. [Darnaby v. Watts, 21 S. W. 333 (Ky. 1893); In re Adams's Estate, 221 Pa. St. 77.]

[2] Brice v. Stokes, 11 Ves. 319; Re Freyer, 3 K. & J. 317; Gregory v. Gregory, 2 Y. & C. 313; Bone v. Cook, McClel. 168; Thompson v. Finch, 22 Beav. 316; Lincoln v. Wright, 4 Beav. 427.

[3] Thompson v. Finch, 22 Beav. 316; 8 De G., M. & G. 560; Hanbury v. Kirkland, 3 Sim. 265; Bates v. Underhill, 3 Redf. (N. Y.) 365. [Bermingham v. Wilcox, 120 Cal. 467; Beatty's Estate, 214 Pa. St. 449; Fesmire's Estate, 134 Pa. St. 67, 83; Robinson v. Harkin, [1896] 2 Ch. 415.]

(a) The same is true of securities which can be negotiated by one trustee without the knowledge of the other. In re Adams's Estate, 221 Pa. St. 77; Matter of Howard, 97 N. Y. S. 23,110 App. Div. 61 (affirmed 185, N. Y. 539). It would seem that the word "necessary" is used in the sense of "advantageous and prudent." Purdy v. Lynch, 145 N. Y. 462; In re Halstead, 89 N. Y. S. 806; Dover v. Denne, 3 Ont. L. Rep. 664.

cotrustee.[1] So trustees must ascertain the condition of the funds at all times within which a reasonable man should ascertain the condition of his own property; as where a mortgage to three trustees had been paid off, and the money came to the hands of one, and was invested in bills and notes of the East India Company payable in two years, and these were paid into the hands of the same trustee to whom the mortgage had been paid, and the acting trustee asked to have the money remain in his hands on a mortgage to be given; and it so remained for a year, no mortgage being executed, the other trustees taking no active steps for several years to know the actual condition of the trust fund; this was held to be a breach of trust, and they were decreed to make good the loss.[2] A trustee is bound to inquire and ascertain for what purpose a cotrustee desires the money; what investments he proposes to make, and what securities he proposes to take, and he must take pains to see that the proposed investments are actually made.[3] If a trustee performs his duty in these respects, and his cotrustee, in spite of these precautions, squanders or wastes the fund, he will not be answerable therefor. So if the cotrustee gets possession of the trust fund by a fraud or crime, the others will not be liable.[4] But if a trustee receive any portion of the funds from a transaction, he must personally see to the application of them: he cannot pass them over to his cotrustee for investment or distribution; and if he do so, he will be personally responsible for the acts and defaults of such cotrustee.[5]

[1] Mendes v. Guedalla, 2 John. & H. 259.

[2] Walker v. Symonds, 3 Swanst. 1. See Thompson v. Finch, 22 Beav. 326.

[3] Hanbury v. Kirkland, 3 Sim. 265; Broadhurst v. Balguy, 1 Y. & C. Ch. 16; Thompson v. Finch, 22 Beav. 326. [Fesmire's Estate, 134 Pa. St. 67, 83; Beatty's Estate, 214 Pa. St. 449; Stong's Estate, 160 Pa. St. 13; Bermingham v. Wilcox, 120 Cal. 467; Thompson v. Finch, 8 De G., M. & G. 560.]

[4] Cottam v. Eastern Counties R. R. Co., 1 John. & H. 243; Mendes v. Guedalla, 2 John. & H. 259; Barnard v. Bagshaw, 9 Jur. (N. S.) 220; 3 De G., J. & S. 355; Trutch v. Lamprell, 20 Beav. 116; Baynard v. Woolley, id. 583; Griffiths v. Porter, 25 Beav. 236; Eager v. Barnes, 31 Beav. 579; Margetts v. Perks, 34 L. J. Ch. 109.

[5] Sterrett's App., 2 Penn. 219; Clark's App., 18 Penn. St. 175; Nyce's

§ 419. In the original case of Townley *v.* Sherborne, it was determined that if there was any *dolus malus*, or any evil practice, or fraud, or ill intent in him that permitted his companion to receive the whole fund, *he* should be charged that received nothing.[1] Thus, if one trustee stands by and sees his cotrustee misemploy or misapply the money;[2] or acquiesces in the wrongful use of the money by his cotrustee;[3] or if a trustee acquiesces in his cotrustee's retaining the money in his hands unnecessarily;[4] or if he connives at a breach of trust by his cotrustee;[5] or conceals such breach;[6] or makes any misrepresentation respecting the investment of the fund;[7] or if he does any act to put the money out of his own control and into the sole power of his cotrustee, as by joining in a conversion of the property and allowing his cotrustee to receive and retain the proceeds exclusively;[8] or if he makes over the trust fund exclusively to his cotrustee;[9] or executes a power of attorney to him;[10] or

App., 5 Watts & S. 254; Commonwealth *v.* McAlister, 28 Penn. St. 480; Deaderick *v.* Cantrell, 10 Yerg. 263; McMurray *v.* Montgomery, 2 Swanst. 374; Hughlett *v.* Hughlett, 5 Humph. 453; Mumford *v.* Murray, 6 Johns. Ch. 1; Ray *v.* Doughty, 4 Blackf. 115; Worth *v.* McAden, 1 Dev. & B. Eq. 199; Graham *v.* Davidson, 2 Dev. & B. Eq. 155; Sparhawk *v.* Buell, 9 Vt. 41; Edmonds *v.* Grenshaw, 14 Peters, 166.

[1] Townley *v.* Sherborne, Bridg. 35; Mucklow *v.* Fuller, Jac. 198.

[2] Williams *v.* Nixon, 2 Beav. 475.

[3] Booth *v.* Booth, 1 Beav. 125; Dix *v.* Burford, 19 Beav. 409.

[4] Lincoln *v.* Wright, 4 Beav. 427; James *v.* Frearson, 1 N. C. C. 370; Evans's Est., 2 Ash. 470; Pim *v.* Downing, 11 Serg. & R. 71; Styles *v.* Guy, 1 H. & Tw. 523; 1 Mac. & Gor. 422; 16 Sim. 230; Scully *v.* Delany, 2 Ir. Eq. 165; Egbert *v.* Butter, 21 Beav. 560; West *v.* Jones, 1 Sim. (N. S.) 205.

[5] Boardman *v.* Mosman, 1 Bro. Ch. 68.   [6] Ibid.

[7] Bates *v.* Scales, 12 Ves. 402.

[8] Sadler *v.* Hobbs, 2 Bro. Ch. 114; Chambers *v.* Minchin, 7 Ves. 198; Hanbury *v.* Kirkland, 3 Sim. 265; Clough *v.* Bond, 3 M. & Cr. 496; Scurfield *v.* Howes, 3 Bro. Ch. 90; Shipbrook *v.* Hinchinbrook, 11 Ves. 252; Brice *v.* Stokes, id. 319; Underwood *v.* Stevens, 1 Mer. 713; Bradwell *v.* Catchpole, 3 Swanst. 78, n.; Williams *v.* Nixon, 2 Beav. 472; Broadhurst *v.* Balguy, 1 N. C. C. 16; Curtis *v.* Mason, 12 L. J. (N. S.) Ch. 443.

[9] Keble *v.* Thompson, 3 Bro. Ch. 111; Langford *v.* Gascoyne, 11 Ves. 333; French *v.* Hobson, 9 Ves. 103; Joy *v.* Campbell, 1 Sch. & Lef. 341; Moses *v.* Levi, 3 Y. & C. 359.

[10] Harrison *v.* Graham, 1 P. Wms. 241, n.; Hewett *v.* Foster, 6 Beav.

signs a draft or order, or assigns a mortgage, enabling his co-trustee to deal with the investments exclusively;[1] or if he suffers the trust fund to be invested in the sole name of his cotrustee;[2] or to be paid into bank to his sole credit,[3] — in all these cases there is an actual or constructive breach of trust, which renders all the trustees liable for any loss; and so if a trustee does not collect a debt due to the estate from his cotrustee.[4] In all cases, if a trustee becomes aware of any fact tending to show that his cotrustee is committing a breach of trust, or if he learns any fact endangering the trust fund, he must communicate it to his cotrustees or make application to the court,[5] and take active measures to protect the fund, or he will be personally liable for its loss. If a trustee himself receives the trust fund or part of it, and pays it over to his cotrustee, who wastes it, he will be liable for it;[6] and so if he permits his cotrustee to receive money, having notice that it will be misapplied, or if he is guilty of any negligence or want of reasonable care.[7]

§ 419 a. If the trust instrument gives the *cestui* a right to appoint one to whom the trustee shall convey, this power cannot be exercised by will, for the will takes effect only at the death

259; Monell *v.* Monell, 5 Johns. Ch. 283; Pim *v.* Downing, 11 Serg. & R. 66; Duncommun's App., 17 Penn. St. 268.

[1] Sadler *v.* Hobbs, 2 Bro. Ch. 114; Broadhurst *v.* Balguy, 1 Y. & C. C. C. 16.

[2] Walker *v.* Symonds, 3 Swanst. 58.

[3] Clough *v.* Bond, 3 M. & Cr. 490.

[4] Mucklow *v.* Fuller, Jac. 198; Candler *v.* Tillett, 22 Beav. 254.

[5] Wayman *v.* Jones, 4 Md. Ch. 506; Chertsey *v.* Market, 6 Price, 279; Powlet *v.* Herbert, 1 Ves. Jr. 297; Franco *v.* Franco, 3 Ves. 75; Walker *v.* Symonds, 3 Swanst. 71; Brice *v.* Stokes, 11 Ves. 319; Olive *v.* Court, 8 Price, 166; Att. Gen. *v.* Holland, 2 Y. & C. 699; Booth *v.* Booth, 1 Beav. 125; Williams *v.* Nixon, 2 Beav. 472; Blackwood *v.* Burrows, 2 Conn. & Laws. 477; Holcomb *v.* Holcomb, 2 Beas. 413; Crane *v.* Hearn, 26 N. J. Eq. 378.

[6] Mumford *v.* Murray, 6 Johns. Ch. 1; Monell *v.* Monell, 5 Johns. Ch. 283; Clark *v.* Clark, 8 Paige, 153; Ringgold *v.* Ringgold, 1 H. & G. 11; Glenn *v.* McKim, 3 Gill, 366; Evans's Est., 2 Ash. 470; Graham *v.* Austin, 2 Grat. 273; Graham *v.* Davidson, 2 Dev. & B. Eq. 155. [But see *supra,* § 417.]

[7] Schenck *v.* Schenck, 1 Green, Ch. 174.

of the *cestui*, and that very event terminates the relation of trust between the trustee and *cestui*.[1] This reasoning seems very flimsy, and likely to produce injustice if applied to cases where the facts are different from those in the above case, where the title was held to have passed by the will itself, though not by the trustee's deed in pursuance of the will.

§ 420. In a few cases, it has been held that, if trustees join in executing a power of sale, and one receive the money, all must be held answerable, if it is lost by the one that receives it.[2] These decisions have been founded upon the rule, that all the trustees who join in any transaction must be responsible for carrying it through. But they ignore the other rule, that a power must be strictly executed by all the persons to whom it is given, and that if a trustee joins in the power, and signs receipts for conformity, but receives none of the money, omits no duty, and does no act tending to a breach of the trust, he will not be held for a loss occasioned by a breach of trust by the other trustees. The great preponderance of authority is, that a sale under a power is not different from the execution of a receipt for the trust moneys.[3] If, however, a proper investment of the money received under a sale is once made, the liability of a non-acting trustee ceases under all the cases.[4] If a trustee renounces the trust, he, of course, cannot be liable for a breach of the trust by the other trustees, unless the trust fund

[1] Bradstreet *v.* Kinsella, 76 Mo. 63.

[2] Spencer *v.* Spencer, 11 Paige, 299; Ringgold *v.* Ringgold, 1 H. & G. 11; Maccubbin *v.* Cromwell, 7 G. & J. 157; Deaderick *v.* Cantrell, 10 Yerg. 263; Wallace *v.* Thornton, 2 Brocken. 434; Hauser *v.* Lehman, 2 Ired. Eq. 594.

[3] See *ante*, § 416, note; Griffin *v.* Macauley, 7 Grat. 476; Atcheson *v.* Robertson, 3 Rich. Eq. 132; Kip *v.* Deniston, 14 Johns. 23; Jones's App., 8 Watts & S. 147; Boyd *v.* Boyd, 3 Grat. 114. But if a trustee not only join in the execution of the power, but in receiving the money, he must keep it in the joint names of the trustees until invested; and he cannot pay it over to his cotrustee without being responsible for it if lost. Ringgold *v.* Ringgold, 1 H. & G. 11; Glenn *v.* McKim, 3 Gill, 366.

[4] Glenn *v.* McKim, 3 Gill, 366.

is in some manner in his hands, and is misapplied by him.[1] So the estate of a deceased trustee cannot be liable for a breach of trust by a surviving trustee, after the decease of a cotrustee.[2] (a) A distinction has been attempted between discretionary trusts and directory trusts as follows: it has been said, that, in discretionary trusts, that is, where the funds may be invested or employed according to the discretion of the trustees, a non-acting trustee will not be responsible for a misapplication of the fund by a cotrustee, unless he is guilty of some fraud or negligence that amounts to a breach of trust, upon the principles before stated;[3] but where a will is peremptory that certain investments shall be made by the trustees, all the trustees will be liable if the directions of the will are not carried out.[4] But these directory trusts may be executed by a part of the trustees, and the others may join for *conformity*, without doing more than is absolutely necessary to accomplish the trust, and therefore these trusts fall within the rule, that a trustee who signs receipts for *conformity*, and does no more, is not liable for a breach of trust by his cotrustee.[5] But if the will expressly provide for the joint action and responsibility of the executors or trustees, it will be binding upon all those who assume the trust, and render them all liable for any loss through the default of one.[6]

§ 420 *a*. Where there are two trustees, and the management of the trust is left to one, and the acting trustee commits a

[1] Claggett *v.* Hall, 9 G. & J. 80.

[2] Brazer *v.* Clark, 5 Pick. 96; Towne *v.* Ammidown, 20 Pick. 535. [Graham's Estate (No. 1), 218 Pa. St. 344; *Re* Palk, 41 W. R. 28.]

[3] Deaderick *v.* Cantrell, 10 Yerg. 264; Thomas *v.* Scruggs, id. 400.

[4] Ibid.

[5] *Ante*, § 416, note.

[6] Weigand's App., 28 Penn. St. 471; Wood *v.* Wood, 5 Paige, 596; Contee *v.* Dawson, 2 Bland, 264; Burrill *v.* Sheil, 2 Barb. 457.

(a) If trustees have resigned with the certainty that their successors will commit a breach of trust which they themselves had refused to do, it has been intimated that they will be liable for the loss if the facts show that their resignation was for that purpose. Head *v.* Gould, [1898] 2 Ch. 250.

breach of trust, the passive trustee is not entitled to indemnity from the acting trustee, unless there are some special circumstances, as where the acting trustee is solicitor for the trust, or has derived a personal benefit from his breach of trust.[1] (a)

§ 421. Following the rule as to cotrustees, executors are generally liable only for their own acts, and not for the acts of their coexecutors.[2] But while cotrustees may not be liable for money

[1] Bahin v. Hughes, 31 Ch. D. 390.   [See In re Linsley, [1904] 2 Ch. 785.]

[2] Hargthorpe v. Milforth, Cro. Eliz. 318; Anon. Dyer, 210 a; Went. Ex. 306; Williams v. Nixon, 2 Beav. 472; Peters v. Beverly, 10 Peters, 532; 1 How. 134; Sutherland v. Brush, 7 Johns. Ch. 17; White v. Bullock, 20 Barb. 91; Douglas v. Satterlee, 11 Johns. 16; Banks v. Wilkes, 3 Sandf. Ch. 99; Moore v. Tandy, 3 Bibb, 97; Fennimore v. Fennimore, 2 Green, Ch. 292; Call v. Ewing, 1 Blackf. 301; Williams v. Maitland, 1 Ired. 92; Kerr v. Kirkpatrick, 8 Ired. Eq. 137; Clarke v. Blount, 2 Dev. Ch. 51; Clarke v. Jenkins, 3 Rich. Eq. 318; Knox v. Pickett, 4 Des. 190; Kerr v. Water, 19 Ga. 136; Charlton v. Durham, L. R. 4 Ch. 433; McKim v. Aulbach, 130 Mass. 481. [Cocks v. Haviland, 124 N. Y. 426; Nanz v. Oakley, 120 N. Y. 84.]

(a) Although the liability of a trustee to the *cestuis* for breaches of trust which were committed by his cotrustee without his actual participation is not that of a surety, cases sometimes arise where one trustee, though equally liable to the *cestuis*, is entitled to indemnity from the guilty cotrustee, e. g., where one trustee has appropriated trust funds to his own use without the knowledge of the other, who, however, is liable, because his neglect of duty gave the other his opportunity. Bahin v. Hughes, 31 Ch. Div. 390.

A proper case for indemnity may arise also where a trustee unwittingly participated in a breach of trust through his reliance upon the advice of a solicitor trustee in a matter wherein the latter could be expected to have special knowledge. In re Linsley, [1904] 2 Ch. 785. See also McCartin v. Traphagan, 43 N. J. Eq. 323, 334. *Supra*, § 420 a.

But in general the courts will not give indemnity on the ground that one trustee was more active in the breach than the others or was more to blame than the others. Cases cited *supra*. A reason that is sufficient to entitle a trustee to indemnity from a cotrustee would usually be sufficient to relieve him from all liability to the *cestui* for the breach.

As to a trustee's right to indemnity from a *cestui* who has received the entire benefit of the breach of trust, see *infra*, § 848 and note. As to contribution among trustees who are jointly liable, see *infra*, § 848.

which they did not receive, although they joined in the receipt, coexecutors are always liable if they join in the receipts. (a) The reason is this: trustees *must* join in many acts, they having for the most part a joint power, while executors have a several power, over the estate. Each executor has an independent right over the personal property of his testator: he may sell it, and receive the purchase-money, and give receipts in his own name. If, therefore, an executor joins his coexecutor in signing a receipt, he does an unmeaning act, unless he intended to render himself jointly answerable for the money; and so the courts hold, that if an executor joins in giving a receipt for money he shall be answerable, whether he received any of it or permitted his coexecutor to receive the whole.[1] So, if an executor joins in executing a power of sale, given in the will, he will be responsible for the appropriation of the proceeds, though his coexecutor received all the money.[2] An attempt has been made

[1] Aplyn v. Brewer, Pr. Ch. 173; Murrill v. Cox, 2 Vern. 560; *Ex parte* Belchier, Amb. 219; Leigh v. Barry, 3 Atk. 584; Harrison v. Graham, 1 P. Wms. 241; cited Darwell v. Darwell, 2 Eq. Cas. Ab. 456; Gregory v. Gregory, 2 Y. & C. 316; Hall v. Carter, 8 Ga. 388; Monell v. Monell, 5 Johns. Ch. 283; Monahan v. Gibbons, 19 Johns. 427; Sterrett's App., 2 Penn. 219; Jones's App., 8 Watts & S. 143; Johnson v. Johnson, 2 Hill, Eq. 290; Clarke v. Jenkins, 3 Rich. Eq. 318. [See Fesmire v. Shannon, 143 Pa. St. 201.]

[2] Ochiltree v. Wright, 1 Dev. & B. Eq. 336; Hauser v. Lehman, 2 Ired. Eq. 594; Mathews v. Mathews, 1 McMul. Eq. 410; Johnson v. Johnson, 2 Hill, Eq. 277; Murray v. Montgomery, 2 Swanst. 374; Deaderick v. Cantrell, 10 Yerg. 263.

(a) "At the present day, executors and administrators hold the assets of the estate in a fiduciary capacity. Their rights and liabilities, in respect of the fund in their hands, are very like those of trustees. But this way of regarding them is somewhat modern." Judge Holmes, in an article in 9 Harv. L. Rev., p. 42, which reviews instances of this change in the law. "The executor originally was nothing but a feoffee to uses. The heir was the man who paid his ancestor's debts and took his property. The executor did not step into the heir's shoes, and come fully to represent the person of the testator as to personal property and liabilities until after Bracton wrote his great treatise on the Laws of England." Ibid., in 12 Harv. L. Rev. 446. See also Walker v. Walker's Ex'r, 88 Ky. 615, 625; 3 Williams on Executors, (Am. ed.) 395, note.

to break down these distinctions between executors and trustees, and to establish the rule, that no intention to be jointly answerable can be inferred from the mere fact of signing a receipt without receiving any part of the money either separately or jointly.[1] And it appears now to be well settled, that if the joint receipt is purely nugatory, and no funds pass upon it into the hands of either executor, a coexecutor will not be liable.[2] So far the doctrine of Lord Northington in Westerly v. Clarke has been agreed to, though the case itself seemed to go further.[3] Lord Harcourt, in Churchill v. Hobson,[4] started another distinction, that executors who joined in the receipt were liable to creditors, though they did not receive the money, while they were not liable to legatees or heirs; but this distinction has no standing in a court of equity, whatever may be the rule at law, and is now overruled.[5]

§ 422. If an executor does any act to transfer the property into the exclusive control of a coexecutor, and thus enables his coexecutor to misapply the same, he will be liable;[6] as if

---

[1] Westerly v. Clarke, 1 Ed. 537; 1 Dick. 329; Candler v. Tillett, 22 Beav. 257; Harden v. Parsons, 1 Ed. 147; Churchill v. Hobson, 1 P. Wms. 241, n.; Stell's App., 10 Penn. St. 152; McNair's App., 4 Rawle, 145; Ochiltree v. Wright, 1 Dev. & B. Eq. 336; Doyle v. Blake, 2 Sch. & Lef. 242; McKim v. Aulbach, 130 Mass. 481.

[2] Westerly v. Clarke, 1 Ed. 537; Scurfield v. Howes, 3 Bro. Ch. 94; Hovey v. Blakeman, 4 Ves. 608; Chambers v. Minchin, 7 Ves. 198; Brice v. Stokes, 11 Ves. 319; 3 Lead. Cas. Eq. 557, 558.

[3] Scurfield v. Howes, 3 Bro. Ch. 94; Hovey v. Blakeman, 4 Ves. 608; Chambers v. Minchin, 7 Ves. 198; Brice v. Stokes, 11 Ves. 325; 3 Lead. Cas. Eq. 725–759; Walker v. Symonds, 3 Swanst. 64; Shipbrook v. Hinchinbrook, 16 Ves. 479; Joy v. Campbell, 1 Sch. & Lef. 341; Doyle v. Blake, 2 id. 242.

[4] 1 P. Wms. 241; Gibbs v. Herring, Pr. Ch. 49; Harden v. Parsons, 1 Eden, 147.

[5] Sadler v. Hobbs, 2 Brown, Ch. 117; Doyle v. Blake, 2 Sch. & Lef. 239.

[6] Townshend v. Barber, 1 Dick. 356; Moses v. Levi, 3 Y. & C. 359; Candler v. Tillett, 22 Beav. 263; Clough v. Dixon, 3 Myl. & Cr. 497; Dines v. Scott, T. & R. 361; Edmonds v. Crenshaw, 14 Pet. 166; Sparhawk v. Buell, 9 Vt. 41; Adair v. Brimmer, 74 N. Y. 539. [In re Osborn, 87 Cal. 1; Walker v. Walker, 88 Ky. 615.]

he joins in drawing [1] or indorsing [2] a bill or note, or delivers or assigns securities to his coexecutor to enable him to receive the money alone,[3] or if he gives him a power of attorney,[4] or does any other act that enables his coexecutor to misapply the money; and so it was held, "that, if by agreement between the executors, one be to receive and intermeddle with such a part of the estate, and the other with such a part, each of them will be chargeable for the whole, because the receipts of each are pursuant to the agreement made betwixt both." [5] Probably the case would not now be followed, but it illustrates the principle.

§ 423. But if the act is such that it is absolutely necessary that the executors should all join in it, their liability will be put upon the same ground as the liability of trustees joining; as, if it is necessary that they should indorse a bill in order to collect it,[6] or that they should join in transferring stock.[7] But even if the act is indispensable, it is still the duty of the executor to see that it is consistent with a due execution of the trust,[8] and he must not rely upon the representations or assertions of his coexecutor, as to its necessity. He must use due diligence and make due investigations to ascertain if the representations are true; [9] as where the debts should have been long paid in the ordinary course of administration a coexecutor applied to the other to join in a sale of stocks to pay the debts, and the executor

[1] Sadler v. Hobbs, 2 Bro. Ch. 114.

[2] Hovey v. Blakeman, 4 Ves. 608.

[3] Candler v. Tillett, 22 Beav. 236.

[4] Doyle v. Blake, 2 Sch. & Lef. 231; Lees v. Sanderson, 4 Sim. 28; Kilbee v. Sneyd, 2 Moll. 200.

[5] Gill v. Att. Gen., Hardw. 314; Moses v. Levi, 3 Y. & C. 359; Lewis v. Nobbs, L. R. 8 Ch. D. 591.

[6] Hovey v. Blakeman, 4 Ves. 608.

[7] Chambers v. Minchin, 7 Ves. 197; Shipbrook v. Hinchinbrook, 11 Ves. 254; 16 Ves. 479; Terrell v. Mathews, 1 Mac. & G. 434, n.; Murrill v. Cox, 2 Vern. 570; Scurfield v. Howes, 3 Bro. Ch. 94; Moses v. Levi, 3 Y. & C. 359.

[8] Ibid.; Underwood v. Stevens, 1 Mer. 712; Bick v. Motley, 2 Myl. & K. 312; Williams v. Nixon, 2 Beav. 472; Hewett v. Foster, 6 Beav. 259.

[9] Ibid.

inquired and learned that there were debts to be paid, but it afterwards appeared that the coexecutor had the money to pay the debts in his own hands; the executor who joined in conveying the stocks was held for the default of his coexecutor, on the ground of negligence in not knowing how the assets in the hands of the coexecutor were disposed of, and how it happened that the debts remained unpaid.[1]

§ 424. So an executor will be called upon to make good the loss of money that he allows to remain two years or any other unreasonable time in the hands of his coexecutor;[2] but he will not be called upon to repay that part which he can show that his coexecutor actually expended in the execution of the trust.[3] So, if an executor neglects for an unreasonable time to insist upon the payment of a debt to the estate due from his coexecutor, he will be liable to pay the debt himself.[4] (a)

§ 425. The same rules that apply to the powers and liabilities of coexecutors apply also to the powers and liabilities of joint administrators. There is one *dictum* that the liability of joint administrators is like the liability of cotrustees,[5] but it is well settled that the liability of joint administrators and coexecutors is identical.[6]

[1] Shipbrook v. Hinchinbrook, 11 Ves. 254; Bick v. Mathews, 3 Myl. & K. 312; Clark v. Clark, 8 Paige, 152.

[2] Scurfield v. Howes, 3 Bro. Ch. 91; Styles v. Guy, 1 Mac. & G. 422; 1 H. & Tw. 523; Egbert v. Butter, 21 Beav. 560; Lincoln v. Wright, 4 Beav. 427.

[3] Shipbrook v. Hinchinbrook, 11 Ves. 252; 16 Ves. 477; Williams v. Nixon, 2 Beav. 472; Kilbee v. Sneyd, 2 Moll. 213; Underwood v. Stevens, 1 Mer. 172; Brice v. Stokes, 11 Ves. 328; Hewett v. Foster, 6 Beav. 259.

[4] Styles v. Guy, 1 Mac. & G. 422; 1 H. & Tw. 523; Egbert v. Butter, 21 Beav. 560; Scully v. Delany, 2 Ir. Eq. 165; Candler v. Tillett, 22 Beav. 257; Carter v. Cutting, 5 Munf. 223.

[5] Hudson v. Hudson, 1 Atk. 460.

[6] Willand v. Fenn, 2 Ves. 267, cited; Murray v. Blatchford, 1 Wend. 583; O'Neall v. Herbert, 1 McMul. Eq. 495.

(a) An executor cannot escape liability for loss due to failure to call in loans on personal security by leaving the matter in the hands of his coexecutor. Stong's Estate, 160 Pa. St. 13.

§ 426. It must be borne in mind, that in the United States, administrators, executors, guardians, and a large class of trustees, are appointed by judges of probate, surrogates, ordinaries, or officers exercising a similar jurisdiction. All trustees appointed under wills, proved and recorded in probate courts, are appointed by decrees of the court in the same manner as executors. In many cases, a bond with sureties is required as a prerequisite to an appointment and qualification to act, unless such bond is expressly waived by the testator or the *cestui que trust.* This bond generally runs to the judge or some officer for the use and protection of those beneficially interested in the estate. If it is a joint bond, executed by all the joint administrators, guardians, coexecutors or cotrustees, it is in the nature of an agreement to be answerable for each other's acts and defaults. The remedy for a breach of trust in such cases is a suit upon the bond in the name of the proper person for the benefit of those interested, against all the joint makers and sureties of the bond; and any breaches of trust, committed by either or all of the trustees, may be given in evidence, and a judgment against all will be rendered, although the breach of trust was committed by one alone.[1] This joint liability of all the cotrustees under a joint bond results from the nature of the bond, and from the technical nature of an action at law for a breach of the bond by a breach of the trust. If, however, one of the coexecutors or cotrustees dies and a breach of trust is committed by the survivor after his death, the estate of the deceased executor cannot be made liable for the breach of the trust.[2] It will be seen at once, that very few of the rules heretofore stated in relation to

---

[1] Ames *v.* Armstrong, 106 Mass. 35; Hill *v.* Davis, 4 Mass. 137; Brazer *v.* Clark, 5 Pick. 96; Towne *v.* Ammidown, 20 Pick. 535; Newcombe *v.* Williams, 9 Met. 525; Sparhawk *v.* Buell, 9 Vt. 41; Boyd *v.* Boyd, 1 Watts, 368; Bostick *v.* Elliott, 3 Head, 507; Braxton *v.* State, 25 Ind. 82; Jeffries *v.* Lawson, 39 Miss. 791; Gayden *v.* Gayden, 1 McMul. Eq. 435; Hughlett *v.* Hughlett, 5 Humph. 453; Clarke *v.* State, 6 G. & J. 288; South *v.* Hay, 3 Mon. 88; Anderson *v.* Miller, 6 J. J. Marsh. 568; Morrow *v.* Peyton, 8 Leigh, 54; Babcock *v.* Hubbard, 2 Conn. 539.

[2] Brazer *v.* Clark, 5 Pick. 96; Towne *v.* Ammidown, 20 Pick. 535.

the liabilities of executors or trustees for the acts and defaults of their coexecutors or cotrustees have any bearing upon the liability of cotrustees who have given a joint bond for the faithful execution of the trust. The statutes of many of the States, however, provide that separate bonds with sureties may be taken from each of the administrators, executors, guardians, or trustees, as the case may be. And where separate bonds are taken from each of the executors or trustees, the liability of the executor or trustee for the acts and defaults of his coexecutor or cotrustee would be governed by the rules and principles hereinbefore stated.[1] But if they sign a joint bond, they are jointly liable.[2]

§ 427. Trustees hold a position of trust and confidence. The legal title of the trust property is in them, and generally its whole management and control is in their hands. At the same time the beneficiaries of the trust may be women, or children, or persons incompetent to protect their own interests. For these reasons, to protect the weak and helpless on the one hand, and to prevent trustees from using their position and influence for their own gain, and to prevent them from hazarding the trust property upon what they may think to be profitable speculations, on the other, they are not allowed to make any profit from their office. They cannot use the trust property, nor their relation to it, for their own personal advantage. All the power and influence which the possession of the trust fund gives must be used for the advantage and profit of the beneficial owners, and not for the personal gain and emolument of the trustee. No other rule would be safe; nor would it be possible for courts to apply any other rule, as between trustee and *cestui que trust*.[3] (a)

[1] McKim v. Aulbach, 130 Mass. 481.
[2] Ames v. Armstrong, 106 Mass. 18.
[3] Burgess v. Wheate, 1 Ed. 226; Docker v. Somes, 2 Myl. & K. 664; O'Herlihy v. Hedges, 1 Sch. & Lef. 126; Bentley v. Craven, 18 Beav. 75;

(a) A trustee will not be allowed to retain for himself a profit made   from his dealings with trust property, although he is able to show that the

This rule is so stringent that Lord Eldon once sent a case to a master to inquire whether the privilege of sporting on the trust

Gubbins v. Creed, 2 Sch. & Lef. 218; *Ex parte* Andrews, 2 Rose, 412; Hamilton v. Wright, 9 Cl. & Fin. 111; Middleton v. Spicer, 1 Bro. Ch. 205; Sherrard v. Harborough, Amb. 165; *Re* Shrewsbury School, 1 Myl. & Cr. 647; Martin v. Martin, 12 Sim. 579; Cooke v. Cholmondeley, 3 Drew. 1; Hawkins v. Chappell, 1 Atk. 621; Johnson v. Baber, 22 Beav. 562; 6 De G., M. & G. 439; Parshall's App., 65 Penn. St. 233; Ellis v. Barber, L. R. 7 Ch. 104; Sloo v. Law, 3 Blatch. C. C. 457; Williams v. Stevens, L. R. 1 P. C. 352.

profit was not made at the expense of the trust. Jarrett v. Johnson, 216 Ill. 212; Bay State Gas Co. v. Rogers, 147 Fed. 557. But see, *contra*, Heckscher v. Blanton, 66 S. E. 859 (Va. 1910). Thus where a trustee of property which his duty as trustee required him to insure joined an underwriters' association and by reason of his membership received a commission on insurance premiums paid by him on the trust property, he was required to turn his commission over to the trust, although the insurance premiums were no larger because of his commissions. White v. Sherman, 168 Ill. 589. But with respect to such commissions he is a debtor, not a trustee, and the *cestui* is not entitled to trace them into property which the trustee has purchased and claim it as belonging to the trust. Lister v. Stubbs, 45 Ch. Div. 1.

Where one of two cotrustees received a bonus upon an investment which resulted in a loss to the trust estate, he was obliged to make good the loss on the investment, and also to turn over the bonus to the trust estate. *In re* Smith, 44 W. R. 270.

A trustee may retain for himself remuneration as director of a corporation when his election as director was due to his ownership of shares of stock as trustee. *In re* Dover Coalfield Extension, [1907] 2 Ch. 76; [1908], 1 Ch. 65. See *contra*, *In re* Francis, 74 L. J. Ch. 198. The distinction between these two cases lies in the fact that the commissions in the former case were paid to the trustee in a matter wherein he acted for the trust, while in the latter case his remuneration as director was for services rendered entirely to the corporation. See also Whitney v. Smith, 4 Ch. 513, where a solicitor obtained employment in a matter disconnected with the trust because of his position as trustee. In Matter of Hirsch, 116 App. Div. 367 (affirmed 188 N. Y. 584), the opinion was expressed that it was improper conduct for a trustee who had been elected president of a corporation by reason of his ownership of stock held in trust, to allow the directors to vote him a large increase of salary over that which the former president had drawn.

The same principle applies to agents and partners. Thus an agent to buy or sell cannot retain for himself a commission or bonus, paid entirely by the other party to the transaction. Williamson v. Krohn, 66 Fed. 655.

estate could be let for the benefit of the *cestui que trust;* if not, he thought the game should belong to the heir; the trustee might appoint a game-keeper for the preservation of game for the heir, but he ought not to keep up a lodge for his own pleasure.[1] So where a trustee retired from the office in consideration that his successor paid him a sum of money, it was held that the money so paid must be treated as a part of the trust estate, and that the trustee must account for it, as he could make no profit, directly or indirectly, from the trust property or from the position or office of trustee.[2] If a trustee joins in betraying the trust for private gain, he will have to bear any loss that may fall on him by the dishonesty of his confederates. The law will not aid him against them. It will not unravel a tangled web of fraud for the benefit of one through whose agency the web was woven and who has himself become enmeshed therein.[3] Trustees may be enjoined from carrying out a contract made for their own benefit.[4] But where one holds a trust for the support of another, the trustee may supply goods from his store at a fair price. This is not dealing with the trust for his private gain.[5]

§ 428. A trustee, executor, or assignee cannot buy up a debt or incumbrance to which the trust estate is liable, for less than is actually due thereon, and make a profit to himself; but such purchase inures for the benefit of the trust estate, and the creditors, legatees, and *cestuis que trust* shall have all the advantage of such purchase.[6] But if a trustee buys up an outstanding debt

---

[1] Webb *v.* Shaftesbury, 7 Ves. 480; Hutchinson *v.* Morritt, 3 Y. & C. 47.

[2] Sugden *v.* Crossland, 3 Sm. & Gif. 192.

[3] Farley *v.* St. Paul M. & M. Rd., 4 McCrary, (U. S.) 142.

[4] Sloo *v.* Law, 3 Blatch. C. C. 457.

[5] Cogbill *v.* Boyd, 77 Va. 450.

[6] Robinson *v.* Pett, 3 P. Wms. 251, n. (a); Pooley *v.* Quilter, 4 Drew. 184; 2 De G. & J. 327; Morret *v.* Paske, 2 Atk. 54; Dunch *v.* Kent, 1 Vern. 241; Darcy *v.* Hall, id. 49; *Ex parte* Lacey, 6 Ves. 628; Anon. 1 Salk. 155; Fosbrooke *v.* Balguy, 1 Myl. & K. 226; Carter *v.* Horne, 1 Eq. Cas. Ab. 7; Schoonmaker *v.* Van Wyke, 31 Barb. 457; Matter of Oakley, 2 Edw.

for the benefit of the *cestuis que trust*, and they refuse to take it or to pay the purchase-money, they cannot afterwards, when the purchase turns out to be beneficial, claim the benefit for themselves.[1] Nor can the trustee make any contract with the *cestui que trust* for any benefit, or for the trust property, nor can he accept a gift from the *cestui que trust*.[2] The better opinion, however, is, that a trustee may purchase of the *cestui que trust*, or accept a benefit from him, but the transaction must be beyond suspicion; and the burden is on the trustee to vindicate the bargain or gift from any shadow of suspicion, and to show that it was perfectly fair and reasonable in every respect, and courts will scrutinize the transaction with great severity.[3] So, if a trustee buys the trust property at private sale or public auction, he takes it subject to the right of the *cestui que trust* to have the sale set aside, or to claim all the benefits and profits of the sale for himself.[4]

478; Herr's Est., 1 Grant's Cas. 272; Quackenbush *v.* Leonard, 9 Paige, 334; Slade *v.* Van Vechten, 11 Paige, 21; Barksdale *v.* Finney, 14 Grat. 338; King *v.* Cushman, 41 Ill. 31. [Baugh's Ex'r *v.* Walker, 77 Va. 99. See Bush *v.* Webster, 72 S. W. 364 (Ky. 1903). *Supra*, § 195, note *b*.]

  [1] Barwell *v.* Barwell, 34 Beav. 371.

  [2] Vaughton *v.* Noble, 30 Beav. 34; Baxter *v.* Costin, 1 Busb. Eq. 262; Andrews *v.* Hobson, 23 Ala. 219; Mason *v.* Martin, 4 Md. 124; Green *v.* Winter, 1 Johns. Ch. 26; Spindler *v.* Atkinson, 3 Md. 409; Wiswall *v.* Stewart, 3 Ala. 433. [Avery *v.* Avery, 90 Ky. 613.]

  [3] *Ex parte* Lacey, 6 Ves. 626; Scott *v.* Davis, 1 Myl. & Cr. 87; Coles *v.* Trecothick, 9 Ves. 234; Morse *v.* Royal, 12 Ves. 372; Dunlop *v.* Mitchell, 10 Ohio, 17; Harrington *v.* Brown, 5 Pick. 519; Bolton *v.* Gardner, 3 Paige, 273; Ames *v.* Downing, 1 Bradf. 321; Lyon *v.* Lyon, 8 Ired. Eq. 201; Pennock's App., 14 Penn. St. 446; Bruch *v.* Lantz, 2 Rawle, 392; Stuart *v.* Kissam, 2 Barb. 493; Jones *v.* Smith, 33 Miss. 215; Soller *v.* Chandler. 26 Miss. 154; Herne *v.* Meeres, 1 Vern. 465; Smith *v.* Isaac, 12 Mo. 106; *ante* § 195.

  [4] Beeson *v.* Beeson, 9 Barr, 279; Patton *v.* Thompson, 2 Jones, Eq. 285; Mason *v.* Martin, 4 Md. 124; Spindler *v.* Atkinson, 3 Md. 409; Davoue *v.* Fanning, 2 Johns. Ch. 252; Iddings *v.* Bruer, 4 Sandf. Ch. 222; Hendricks *v.* Robinson, 2 Johns. Ch. 283; Evertson *v.* Tappan, 5 id. 497; Smith *v.* Lansing, 22 N. Y. 530; Ames *v.* Downing, 1 Bradf. 321; Andrews *v.* Hobson, 23 Ala. 219; Charles *v.* Dubois, 29 Ala. 367; Wiswall *v.* Stewart, 32 Ala. 433; Bellamy *v.* Bellamy, 6 Fla. 62; Schoonmaker *v.* Van Wyke, 31 Barb. 457. [*Supra*, § 195, n.]

§ 429. Trustees cannot make a profit from the trust funds committed to them, by using the money in any kind of trade or speculation, nor in their own business; nor can they put the funds into the trade or business of another, under a stipulation that they shall receive a *bonus* or other profit or advantage. In all such cases, the trustees must account for every dollar received from the use of the trust-money (a) and they will be absolutely responsible for it if it is lost in any such transactions. (b) By this rule, trustees may be liable to great losses

(a) Smelting Co. *v.* Reed, 23 Colo. 523.

(b) He becomes an insurer of the fund with at least simple interest and must make good any loss, accidental or otherwise. Bangor *v.* Beal, 85 Me. 129; *Re* Hodges' Estate, 66 Vt. 70; Ward *v.* Tinkham, 65 Mich. 695. He incurs the same liability when he deposits money in the bank or invests in his own name as an individual. White *v.* Sherman, 168 Ill. 589.

When the misappropriated trust funds have been so mingled with funds of the trustee that their increase and income cannot be determined, it is usual to impose upon him a charge of interest at not less than the legal rate, and at a rate as much larger as may be necessary to give to the trust all the estimated increase and income of the misappropriated funds. (See cases cited *infra*, this note.) His liability with respect to income upon misappropriated trust funds is to make up to the trust the income which the trust funds would have earned if they had been properly invested, and to turn over to the trust all the actual profit or income in excess of this amount. General Proprietors *v.* Force, 72 N. J. Eq. 56. (See also cases cited *infra*, this note.) The charge of simple

interest at the legal rate usually brings to the trust more than the funds would have earned if properly invested as trust funds should be, but it is reasoned that the most lenient view of such a transaction is that the trustee is a borrower of the trust funds and as such should pay the legal rate. Bangor *v.* Beal, 85 Me. 129; Society *v.* Pelham, 58 N. H. 566; Stanley's Estate *v.* Pence, 160 Ind. 636; Conn. *v.* Howarth, 48 Conn. 207; Erie School District *v.* Griffith, 203 Pa. St. 123; White *v.* Ditson, 140 Mass. 351, 362; Young's Estate, 97 Iowa, 218; Wolfort *v.* Reilly, 133 Mo. 463.

Simple interest in excess of the legal rate or compound interest is imposed, not for the purpose of punishing the trustee for his breach of trust, but for the purpose of giving to the trust the increase and profits earned by the trust funds. Hazard *v.* Durant, 14 R. I. 25; Cook *v.* Lowry, 95 N. Y. 103; Kane *v.* Kane's Adm'r, 146 Mo. 605; Perrin *v.* Lepper, 72 Mich. 454, 551, 555; Lehman *v.* Rothbarth, 159 Ill. 270; *In re* Davis, [1902] 2 Ch. 314; Forbes *v.* Allen, 166 Mass. 569; Forbes *v.* Ware, 172 Mass. 306; *In re* Ricker's Estate, 14 Mont. 153, 29 L. R. A. 622 and note; Hughes *v.* The People,

while they can receive no profit; and the rule is made thus
stringent, that trustees may not be tempted from selfish mo-

111 Ill. 457; *In re* Eschrich, 85 Cal.
98; *In re* Clary, 112 Cal. 292. See
also Vyse *v.* Foster, 8 Ch. 309, 335.
But see Page's Ex'r *v.* Holman, 82
Ky. 573. In Forbes *v.* Ware, 172
Mass. 306, the conclusion of the
court is summed up as follows: "In
other words, the principle of liability is accountability for what has
been received, or ought to have been
received, or must be presumed to
have been received, and not punishment for a breach of duty."

Where the trustee has used trust
funds in his own business, the court
will not usually give to the trust a
definite share of the profits, but will
charge the trustee with interest
at a rate based to some extent upon
the size of the profits earned in the
business if the rate of return is larger
than simple interest at the legal rate.
Faulkner *v.* Hendy, 103 Cal. 15; *In
re* Thompson, 101 Cal. 349; Page's
Ex'r *v.* Holman, 82 Ky. 573. But
where the business itself is partly the
property of the trust estate a definite
share of the profits should be given
to the trust. This is frequently the
case where a surviving or solvent
partner continues the business on
his own account. Perrin *v.* Lepper,
72 Mich. 454, 551; Jones *v.* Dexter,
130 Mass. 380. See Byrne *v.* Mc-
Grath, 130 Cal. 316.

It has been held that where persons borrow trust funds with notice
that the loan to them is a breach of
trust, the rate of interest charged is
not based upon the earnings of the
trust funds. In other words the
principle that the trustee shall not
be permitted to gain a profit from

the use of trust funds has no application to such borrowers. Stroud *v.*
Gwyer, 28 Beav. 130; Dent *v.*
Slough, 40 Ala. 518; Rau *v.* Small,
144 Pa. St. 304. See 30 Am. Law
Reg. (N. S.), 569. But when the
trustee lends to a partnership of
which he is a member the principle
applies to the extent that his share of
profits is increased by use of the
trust funds. See *In re* Davis, [1902]
2 Ch. 314; Hankey *v.* Garratt, 1 Ves.
Jr. 236; Docker *v.* Somes, 2 Myl. &
K. 655; 30 Am. Law Reg. (N. S.) 569.
On the question of liability of the
trustee's copartners in such cases,
see *infra*, § 846 and note.

If misappropriated trust funds
can be traced and identified their entire increase and income belong to
the trust. Hazard *v.* Durant, 14 R.
I. 25. Thus where a trustee used
trust funds to pay all the premiums
on a policy of insurance upon his
life, it has been held that the entire
proceeds of the policy belonged to
the *cestui.* Holmes *v.* Gilman, 138
N. Y. 369. See also Byrne *v.* Mc-
Grath, 130 Cal. 316. But see *In re*
Ricker's Estate, 14 Mont. 153, 29
L. R. A. 622.

Where it appears that an article of
property or a parcel of land has been
purchased with a fund of which the
trust funds form only a small part,
it has not been clear from the cases
whether the *cestui* is entitled to a
share in the property itself, if it has
increased in value, or is confined to
his lien upon the property for the
principal of the trust funds which
have gone into it and an equitable
share of the increase, as income upon

tives to embark the trust fund upon the chances of trade and speculation.[1] If a trustee charge a bonus in his account for his skill and services in conducting the business of the trust, it will be set aside.[2]

§ 430. All persons who stand in a fiduciary relation to others must account for all the profits made upon moneys in their hands by reason of such relation.[3] Thus partners stand in a fiduciary relation to each other, and if a partner, instead of winding up the partnership affairs, when for any reason he ought to do so, continues to use the partnership property in business, and makes a profit thereon, he must account for it.[4]

[1] Docker v. Somes, 2 Myl. & K. 664; Willett v. Blanford, 1 Hare, 253; Cummins v. Cummins, 6 Ir. Eq. 723; Wedderburn v. Wedderburn, 2 Keen, 722; 4 Myl. & Cr. 41; 22 Beav. 84; Townend v. Townend, 1 Gif. 201; Parker v. Bloxam, 20 Beav. 295; Manning v. Manning, 1 Johns. Ch. 527; Brown v. Ricketts, 4 id. 303; In re Thorp, Davies, 290; William v. Stevens, L. R. 1 P. C. 352; Blauvelt v. Ackerman, 20 N. J. Eq. 141; Durling v. Hammer, id. 220; Pluman v. Slocum, 41 N. Y. 53; Frank's App., 5 Penn. St. 190.

[2] Barrett v. Hartly, L. R. 2 Eq. 789.

[3] Hawley v. Cramer, 4 Cow. 717; Richardson v. Spencer, 18 B. Mon. 450; Thorp v. McCullum, 1 Gil. (Ill.) 615; Van Epps v. Van Epps, 9 Paige, 237; Ackerman v. Emot, 4 Barb. 626.

[4] Bentley v. Craven, 18 Beav. 75; Parsons v. Hayward, 31 Beav. 199; Crawshay v. Collins, 15 Ves. 226; Brown v. De Tastet, Jac. 284; Wedderburn v. Wedderburn, 2 Keen, 722; 4 Myl. & Cr. 41; 22 Beav. 84. [Perrin v. Lepper, 72 Mich. 454, 551.] A partner who receives the partnership property on a resale from the purchaser at public auction, by a secret arrangement between them, is bound to account as if no sale had been made, although his copartner was a bidder at the auction sale. Jones v. Dexter, 130 Mass. 380.

the investment. In New Jersey it has been held that the cestui has the option of claiming the land subject to the trustee's lien for the amount of his own money used in the purchase and improvement, or of claiming a lien for the amount of trust funds put into the land. Bohle v. Hasselbroch, 64 N. J. Eq. 334. See also Rochfoucauld v. Boustead, [1898] 1 Ch. 550. Other recent cases seem inclined to confine the cestui to an equitable lien upon the property into which the trust funds are traced. Humphreys v. Butler, 51 Ark. 351; Lehman v. Rothbarth, 159 Ill. 270; In re Ricker's Estate, 14 Mont. 153, 29 L. R. A. 622, and note; Bresnihan v. Sheehan, 125 Mass. 11. See also 19 Harv. Law Rev. 511 (article by Prof. J. B. Ames).

But in making up the accounts, courts will make a just allowance for time, skill, and other elements of success in conducting the business.[1] If a trader has trust funds in his hands, not in a fiduciary character, but through a breach of trust by a trustee, he is liable only for interest.[2] Agents, guardians, directors of corporations, officers of municipal corporations, and all other persons clothed with a fiduciary character, are subject to this rule.[3] (a)

§ 431. So if persons, standing in such a relation to an estate, obtain advantages in respect to it, those who succeed to the estate shall have the advantages which are thus obtained.[4] As where a mortgagee had purchased the right of dower of the widow of a deceased mortgagor, the heir of the mortgagor, upon a bill to redeem, was held to have the right to take the purchase of the dower at the price which the mortgagee had paid.[5] So an heir cannot hold an incumbrance for more than he gave for it, against the creditors of the ancestor's estate,[6] and it is conceived that the same rule applies to a devisee.[7] But if the heir or devisee is himself an incumbrancer at the death of the ancestor,

[1] Docker v. Somes, 2 Myl. & K. 662; Willett v. Blanford, 1 Hare, 253; Brown v. De Tastet, Jac. 284.

[2] Strowd v. Gwyer, 28 Beav. 130; Townend v. Townend, 1 Gif. 210; Simpson v. Chapman, 4 De G., M. & G. 154; Macdonald v. Richardson, 1 Gif. 81; Brown v. De Tastet, Jac. 284; Chambers v. Howell, 11 Beav. 6; Ex parte Watson, 2 V. & B. 414. [Dent v. Slough, 40 Ala. 518; Rau v. Small, 144 Pa. St. 304. See 30 Am. Law Reg. (N. S.) 569.]

[3] Morret v. Paske, 2 Atk. 52; Powell v. Glover, 3 P. Wms. 251; Great Luxembourg Ry. Co. v. Magnay, 23 Beav. 640; 25 Beav. 586; Chaplin v. Young, 33 Beav. 414; Bowes v. Toronto, 11 Moore, P. C. C. 463; Docker v. Somes, 2 Myl. & K. 665.

[4] Baldwin v. Bannister, cited 3 P. Wms. 251; Dobson v. Land, 8 Hare, 220; Arnold v. Garner, 2 Phill. 231; Mathison v. Clarke, 3 Drew. 3.

[5] Ibid.

[6] Lancaster v. Evors, 10 Beav. 154; 1 Phill. 354; Morret v. Paske, 2 Atk. 54; Long v. Clopton, 1 Vern. 464; Brathwaite v. Brathwaite, id. 334; Darcy v. Hall, id. 49.

[7] Long v. Clopton, 1 Vern. 464; Davis v. Barrett, 14 Beav. 542.

(a) Namely, the rule applicable to trustees.

he may buy in a prior, but not a subsequent, incumbrance, and hold it for the whole amount due. The court considers him, in buying such a prior incumbrance, not as heir or devisee, but as an incumbrancer or stranger; and so if, as such prior incumbrancer, he obtains a prior incumbrance by the bounty or gift of another, he shall hold such bounty or gift for the benefit of his own incumbrance, and there is no reason why he should hold it for the benefit of the creditors of the ancestor.[1] So the heir or devisee may hold a prior incumbrance for full value, though bought for less, against a subsequent incumbrancer.[2] So, if one of several joint purchasers of an estate buy in an incumbrance for less than its face, he shall hold it for his copurchasers at the same price he paid.[3] And the opinion has been expressed, that a tenant for life holds the same relation toward the remainder-man; and if such tenant buy in an incumbrance upon the estate for less than its face, he cannot claim from the remainder-man more than he gave.[4]

§ 432. The rule that trustees can make no profit out of the estate is carried so far in England that they can receive no compensation for their services. In the United States, trustees are entitled to reasonable compensation. But both in England and the United States, a trustee can receive no indirect profit from the estate by reason of his connection with it. Thus a trustee cannot be appointed *receiver* with a salary,[5] nor would he be

---

[1] Davis *v.* Barrett, 14 Beav. 542; Darcy *v.* Hall, 1 Vern. 49; Anon. 1 Salk. 155.

[2] Davis *v.* Barrett, 14 Beav. 542.

[3] Carter *v.* Horne, 1 Eq. Cas. Ab. 7. [Morrison *v.* Roehl, 215 Mo. 545. See *supra*, § 195, note.]

[4] Hill *v.* Brown, Dr. 433. [Downing *v.* Hartshorn, 69 Neb. 364; Keller *v.* Fenske, 123 Wis. 435; First Cong. Church *v.* Terry, 130 Iowa, 513; Griffith *v.* Owen, [1907] 1 Ch. 195. See also Magness *v.* Harris, 80 Ark. 583; Blair *v.* Johnson, 215 Ill. 552; Crawford *v.* Meis, 123 Iowa, 610; Boon *v.* Root, 137 Wis. 451; Lewis *v.* Wright, 148 Mich. 290; *supra*, § 195, note.]

[5] Sutton *v.* Jones, 15 Ves. 584; Morison *v.* Morison, 4 Myl. & Cr. 215; Sykes *v.* Hastings, 11 Ves. 363; —— *v.* Jolland, 8 Ves. 72; Anon., 3 Ves. 515.

appointed without compensation except under peculiar circumstances; for it is his duty to superintend and watch over the receiver.[1] The same reasons do not apply for excluding a dry trustee.[2] If trustees are factors,[3] or brokers,[4] or commission agents,[5] or auctioneers,[6] or bankers,[7] or attorneys, or solicitors,[8] they can make no charges against the trust estate for services rendered by them in their professional capacity to the estate of which they are trustees. They may employ the services of such agents, if necessary, and pay for them from the estate; but if they undertake to act in such capacities themselves for the estate, they can receive no compensation. (a) This rule is so

[1] Sykes v. Hastings, 11 Ves. 363.
[2] Sutton v. Jones, 15 Ves. 587.
[3] Scattergood v. Harrison, Mos. 128.
[4] Arnold v. Garner, 2 Phill. 231.
[5] Sheriff v. Aske, 4 Russ. 33.
[6] Mathison v. Clarke, 3 Drew. 3; Kirkman v. Booth, 11 Beav. 273.
[7] Crosskill v. Bower, 1 Dr. & Sm. 319.
[8] Pollard v. Doyle, 1 Dr. & Sm. 319; Moore v. Frowd, 3 Myl. & Cr. 46; Frazer v. Palmer, 4 Y. & C. 515; York v. Brown, 1 Col. C. C. 260; Broughton v. Broughton, 5 De G., M. & G. 160; In re Sherwood, 3 Beav. 338; Douglass v. Archbutt, 2 De G. & J. 148; Harbin v. Darby, 28 Beav. 325; Morgan v. Homans, 49 N. Y. 667; Gomley v. Wood, 9 Ir. Eq. 418; Binsse v. Paige, 1 Keyes, 87; 1 N. Y. Decis. 138. [Clarkson v. Robinson, [1900] 2 Ch. 722. See contra, Perkins's Appeal, 108 Pa. St. 314.]

(a) In the United States, where trustees are allowed compensation for care, custody, management, and other ordinary services, it is usual to allow them reasonable compensation also for extraordinary services, i. e., services of a nature not usually required of a trustee and for which he would have had the right to employ another person. Turnbull v. Pomeroy, 140 Mass. 117, 118; Willis v. Clymer, 66 N. J. Eq. 284; Perkins's Appeal, 108 Pa. St. 314; Jarrett v. Johnson, 216 Ill. 212; Morris v. Ellis, 62 S. W. 250 (Tenn. Ch. App. 1901); infra, §§ 917–919, and notes. See also Matter of Froelich, 107 N. Y. S. 173, 122 App. Div. 440. "When it is once admitted that a trustee may be paid for ordinary services, it is hard not to admit also that there may be circumstances under which he may be allowed an additional sum for extraordinary services which it was not his duty to render." Holmes, J., in Turnbull v. Pomeroy, 140 Mass. 117, 118.

On similar principles a surviving partner, who is not usually entitled to compensation for services in winding up the affairs of the partnership has been allowed compensa-

strict, that if the trustee has a partner, and employs such part-ner, no charge can be made by the firm;[1] but if the trustee is excluded from all participation in the compensation, the part-ner of the trustee may be paid like any other person for similar services.[2] In one case where several trustees were made defend-ants, one of them, being a solicitor, conducted the defence, and was allowed his full costs, it not appearing that the costs were increased by such conduct.[3] This case is put upon the ground that the services were rendered under the eye of the court, and there could be no danger of collusion; but the case is not ap-proved in England, and has not been followed.[4] In the United States, a trustee has been refused compensation as solicitor, for professional services rendered by himself for himself as trus-tee, on the ground that no man can make a contract with himself.[5]

§ 433. Under no circumstances can a trustee claim or set up a claim to the trust property adverse to the *cestui que trust*.[6]

[1] Collin v. Carey, 2 Beav. 128; Lincoln v. Winsor, 9 Hare, 158; Chris-tophers v. White, 10 Beav. 523; Lyon v. Baker, 5 De G. & Sm. 622; Manson v. Baillie, 2 Macq. (H. L.) 80. [See *contra*, Turnbull v. Pomeroy, 140 Mass. 117; Thayer v. Badger, 171 Mass. 279.]

[2] Clack v. Carlon, 7 Jur. (N. s.) 441; Burge v. Burton, 2 Hare, 373.

[3] Cradock v. Piper, 1 McN. & G. 664; 1 Hall & T. 617; overruling Bain-brigge v. Blair, 8 Beav. 588.

[4] Lyon v. Baker, 5 De G. & Sm. 622.

[5] Mayer v. Galluchet, 6 Rich. Eq. 2; Jenkins v. Fickling, 4 Des. 470; Edmonds v. Crenshaw, Harp. 232. [See note *a*, *supra*.]

[6] Att. Gen. v. Monro, 2 De G. & Sm. 163; Stone v. Godfrey, 5 De G., M. & G. 76; Frith v. Curtland, 2 Hem. & M. 417; Pomfret v. Winsor, 2 Ves. 476; Kennedy v. Daley, 1 Sch. & Lef. 381; *Ex parte* Andrews, 2 Rose, 412; Conry v. Caulfield, 2 B. & B. 272; Newsome v. Flowers, 30 Beav. 461; Shields v. Atkins, 3 Atk. 560; Langley v. Fisher, 9 Beav. 90; Reece v. Frye,

tion for necessary services which lay outside his duty as surviving part-ner. Vanduzer v. McMillan, 37 Ga. 299; Starr v. Case, 59 Iowa, 491, 503; Thayer v. Badger, 171 Mass. 279.

In some States it is expressly pro-vided by statute that trustees shall receive compensation for such ser-vices in addition to that allowed for their ordinary services. *Infra*, §§ 917–919 and notes.

Nor can he deny his title.[1] If a trustee desires to set up a title to the trust property in himself, he should refuse to accept the trust. But if a claim is made upon him by a third person, adverse to the *cestui que trust*, he may decline to deliver over the property to his *cestui que trust* until the title is determined, or he is indemnified or secured against the consequences,[2] or he may pay the fund into court,[3] and if he neglects to do so, and thus makes a suit necessary, he will recover only such costs as he would have been entitled to if he had paid the money into court.[4] A trustee must assume the validity of the trust under which he acts, until it is actually impeached, although he may have some suspicion that there may have been fraud or collusion in the appointment and settlement.[5] (*a*) So, if a trustee obtains a knowledge of facts that would defeat the title of his *cestui que trust*, and give the property over to another, he is not justified in morals in communicating such facts to such other person. His duty is to manage the property for his *cestui que trust*, and not to keep his conscience, or betray his title or interests; [6] and he can make no admissions prejudicial to the rights of his *cestui que trust*,[7] nor can he use his influence to defeat the purposes of the trust as declared by the creator of it.[8] (*b*)

1 De G. & Sm. 279; Benjamin *v.* Gill, 45 Ga. 110. [Ownes *v.* Ownes, 23 N. J. Eq. 60. As to purchase of incumbrance or adverse interest see *supra*, § 195, note.]

  [1] Von Hurter *v.* Spergeman, 2 Green, Ch. 185. [Associate Alumni *v.* General Theol. Seminary, 49 N. Y. S. 745.]

  [2] Neale *v.* Davies, 5 De G., M. & G. 258.

  [3] Gunnell *v.* Whitear, L. R. 10 Eq. 664.

  [4] Ibid.; Weller *v.* Fitzhugh, 22 L. T. (N. S.) 567.

  [5] Beddoes *v.* Pugh, 26 Beav. 407; Reid *v.* Mullins, 48 Mo. 344.

  [6] Lewin, 234.

  [7] Thomas *v.* Bowman, 30 Ill. 34; 29 Ill. 426.

  [8] Ellis *v.* Barker, L. R. 7 Ch. 104.

(*a*) A party to a contract, who seeks to be relieved therefrom, and relies upon its illegality or want of consideration, may be estopped from setting up such a defence, and a trustee who has accepted and entered upon the administration of the trust, cannot allege the invalidity of his appointment as a reason for not accounting for the trust property. Harbin *v.* Bell, 54 Ala. 389; Saunders *v.* Richard, 35 Fla. 28, 42.

(*b*) Where a creditor of the *cestui* is seeking to reach the latter's inter-

§ 434. In England, a trustee, being in possession of real estate in trust, may profit from his trust if the *cestui que trust* dies without heirs; for, as the trustee is tenant in possession, there is no such failure of a tenant as to cause an escheat; and the trustee thenceforth holds the lands for his own use, there being no *cestui que trust* to call him to an account.[1] This is a benefit to the trustee; but it arises rather from an absence of right in others, than from an affirmative right in himself. But if he is not in possession, or if he has need of the assistance of a court of equity to enforce his rights, the court will not act;[2] though it is said, that having the legal title, which a court of law must recognize, he can obtain all the rights which a court of law must give.[3] But if the *cestui que trust* devise the estate to another upon trusts that fail, the trustee must pass over the estate to the devisee, for the reason that the trustee can have no advantage from trusts that so fail, and he has no equity against the devisee to keep the estate.[4]

§ 435. Upon this rule of law in England, several questions were started in the case of Burgess *v.* Wheate,[5] which are rather curious than practical in this country; as, for instance, if a purchaser should pay the money in full for land, and die without heirs, before he obtained a conveyance, could the vendor keep both land and purchase-money?[6] Again, if a mortgagor in

[1] Burgess *v.* Wheate, 1 Eden, 177, 186, 216, 256; Taylor *v.* Haygarth, 14 Sim. 8; Daval *v.* New River Co., 3 De G. & Sm. 394; Cox *v.* Parker, 22 Beav. 168; Barrow *v.* Wadkin, 24 Beav. 9; Att. Gen. *v.* Sands, Hard. 496.
[2] Burgess *v.* Wheate, 1 Eden, 212; Onslow *v.* Wallis, 1 McN. & G. 506; Williams *v.* Lonsdale, 3 Ves. Jr. 752.
[3] King *v.* Coggan, 6 East, 431; 2 Smith, 417; King *v.* Wilson, 10 B. & C. 80.
[4] Onslow *v.* Wallis, 1 McN. & G. 506; Jones *v.* Goodchild, 3 P. Wms. 33.
[5] 1 Eden, 177.
[6] Ibid. 212.

est in the trust property, the trustee cannot safely waive any of the neces-   sary legal steps. Kutz *v.* Nolan, 224 Pa. St. 262.

fee should die without heirs, could a mortgagee in fee keep the whole estate, for the reason that there was no person having a right to redeem?[1] Of course the equity of redemption would be assets for the payment of the debts of the mortgagor.[2] But if there were no debts, could the mortgagee keep a large estate for a small debt?[3] Another question was raised, whether a trust in such cases might not result to the grantor.[4] No answers have been given to these questions by decided cases, and as they were put more than a century ago, it is not probable that a case will arise requiring their judicial determination.

§ 436. In the United States, if a *cestui que trust* should die without heirs, the trustee could not hold for his own beneficial use; but he would hold for the State as *ultima hæres* where all other heirs fail.[5]

§ 437. Where a *cestui que trust* of chattel dies without heirs, the trustee can take no benefit; for the beneficial use in such chattel will go as *bona vavantia* to the crown or State. So, if the *cestui que trust* makes a will and appoints an executor, but makes no further disposition of his personalty, the executor will take for the State; for the executor can take no beneficial interest unless the will expressly gives it to him.[6]

§ 437 *a*.[7] Payment of a trust debt by crediting the trustee's individual account is not good.[8] A trustee may in good faith

---

[1] Ibid. 210.

[2] Beale *v.* Symonds, 16 Beav. 406; Downe *v.* Morris, 3 Hare, 394.

[3] 1 Eden, 236, 256.

[4] 1 Eden, 185.

[5] McCaw *v.* Galbraith, 7 Rich. L. 75; Matthews *v.* Ward, 10 G. & J. 443; Darrah *v.* McNair, 1 Ashm. 236; Ringgold *v.* Malott, 1 Harr. & John. 299; 4 Kent, 425; 1 Cruise, Dig. 484; Crane *v.* Reeder, 21 Md. 25.

[6] Middleton *v.* Spicer, 1 Bro. Ch. 201; Taylor *v.* Haygarth, 14 Sim. 8; Russell *v.* Clowes, 2 Col. C. C. 648; Powell *v.* Merritt, 1 Sm. & Gif. 381; Cradock *v.* Owen, 2 Sm. & Gif. 241; Read *v.* Steadham, 26 Beav. 495; Cane *v.* Roberts, 8 Sim. 214.

[7] See §§ 815 *a*, 815 *b*.

[8] Maynard *v.* Cleveland, 76 Ga. 52.

compromise a doubtful debt due the trust estate, and a fraud committed by him upon others is admissible to show his zeal for the interests of the estate.[1] But a compromise of a debt due from the trust by which an advantage is gained, as where a legatee accepted $1100 for a $3000 legacy, inures to the benefit of the trust estate, and the trustee cannot transfer the whole gain to *one* of the *cestuis*.[2] A trustee to sue for and recover certain property may make a fair and judicious compromise by which the title is secured to the *cestui*.[3] Church trustees cannot, by their acts, create any lien on the trust property unless they have express authority for so doing.[4] A trustee can be held personally for materials ordered by him for the trust estate, and on contracts made by him in its behalf, unless there be a special agreement to look only to the trust, and this even though the trustees acted under order of the court, this being merely a security to the trustee that he shall be indemnified out of the trust funds.[5] (a) But the mere fact of want of authority in a

[1] Id. 68 *et seq.*
[2] Mitchell *v.* Colburn, 61 Md. 244.
[3] Caldwell *v.* Brown, 66 Md. 293.
[4] Trustees First M. E. Church *v.* Atlanta, 76 Ga. 181.
[5] Gill *v.* Carmine, 55 Md. 339; Hackman *v.* MaGuire, 20 Mo. App. 286; People *v.* Abbott, 107 N. Y. 225; Kedian *v.* Hoyt, 33 Hun, 145. [Dantzler *v.* McInnis, 151 Ala. 293; Johnson *v.* Leman, 131 Ill. 609; Hussey *v.* Arnold, 185 Mass. 202; McGovern *v.* Bennett, 146 Mich. 558; Truesdale *v.* Philadelphia Tr. Co., 63 Minn. 49; Koken Iron Works *v.* Kinealy, 86 Mo. App. 199; Blewitt *v.* Olin, 14 Daly, 351; Mitchell *v.* Whitlock, 121 N. C. 166; Fehlinger *v.* Wood, 134 Pa. St. 517; Neal *v.* Bleckley, 51 S. C. 506; McIntyre *v.* Williamson, 72 Vt. 183; Taylor *v.* Davis, 110 U. S. 330, 334; Brazier *v.* Camp, 63 L. J. Q. B. 257.]

(a) A trustee is likewise personally liable to third persons for his *torts* either of misfeasance or of nonfeasance in failing to keep the trust property in repair, irrespective of his right to reimbursement. Baker *v.* Tibbetts, 162 Mass. 468; Shepard *v.* Creamer, 160 Mass. 496; Odd Fellows Hall Ass'n *v.* McAllister, 153 Mass. 292; O'Malley *v.* Gerth, 67 N. J. Law, 610; Gillick *v.* Jackson, 83 N. Y. S. 29; Norling *v.* Allee, 13 N. Y. S. 791. See Brown *v.* Wittner, 59 N. Y. S. 385, 43 App. Div. 135. *In re* Raybould, [1900] 1 Ch. 199; Prinz *v.* Lucas, 210 Pa. St. 620. And also for the *torts* of his agents. Blewitt *v.* Olin, 14 Daly (N. Y.) 351. As

trustee to bind the estate will not make him personally liable in cases of executory contract where the facts show that no such

to the liability of trustees of charitable funds for *torts* of employees and agents, see *infra*, §. 747, note.

He may undoubtedly relieve himself from personal liability upon his contracts for the benefit of the trust by a special provision in the contract. Packard v. Kingman, 109 Mich. 497; Mitchell v. Whitlock, 121 N. C. 166; Kohen Iron Works v. Kinealy, 86 Mo. App. 199; Hussey v. Arnold, 185 Mass. 202. But description of himself as trustee is not sufficient. Taylor v. Davis, 110 U. S. 330, 335; Connally v. Lyons, 82 Tex. 664; McIntyre v. Williamson, 72 Vt. 183; McGovern v. Bennett, 146 Mich. 558; Tuttle v. First Nat. Bank, 187 Mass. 533. Thus it has been held that a trustee with authority to mortgage who describes himself in the mortgage note as trustee and puts the word "trustee" after his signature is nevertheless personally liable upon the note. Hall v. Jameson, 151 Cal. 606. But a description of himself in the contract as trustee is doubtless some evidence of an agreement with the other party that he shall not be personally liable. See Crate v. Luippold, 43 N. Y. S. 824, 13 App. Div. 617.

Most courts do not recognize a liability of a trustee in his representative capacity. Johnson v. Leman, 131 Ill. 609; Shepard v. Creamer, 160 Mass. 496; Truesdale v. Philadelphia Trust Co., 63 Minn. 49; Hampton v. Foster, 127 Fed. 468. But see Yerkes v. Richards, 170 Pa. St. 346; Prinz v. Lucas, 210 Pa. St. 620;

Scheibeler v. Albee, 99 N. Y. S. 706, 114 App. Div. 146; Ferrier v. Trépannier, 24 Can. Sup. 86.

A trustee's liability as stockholder for calls, etc., is a personal one, but, in most States has been limited by statute to the trust property. See U. S. Rev. Stats., § 5152, as to national banks; Pauly v. State Loan & Trust Co., 165 U. S. 606; Hampton v. Foster, 127 Fed. 468; Fowler v. Gowing, 152 Fed. 801, holding that in New York an action against a trustee stockholder in an insolvent bank must be brought against him as trustee.

As to the rights of creditors to resort to the trust property, see *infra*, § 815 *b*, and note.

A substituted trustee is of course not personally liable for the *torts* of his predecessor or for the latter's contracts for the benefit of the trust estate unless he assumes them, and his acceptance of the trust is not in itself an assumption of the previous trustee's obligations. Foote v. Cotting, 195 Mass. 55; U. S. Trust Co. v. Stanton, 139 N. Y. 531.

It has been held by a divided court that three cotrustees who continued the business of the testator under a firm name for the benefit of the trust estate were not copartners since they were not beneficially interested in the business, and that a retiring cotrustee had no duty of giving notice of his retirement to those having credit dealings with the business. Failing to give notice of his retirement he was nevertheless held not to be liable on contracts with a prior dealer who did not know

701

liability was intended by either of the parties.[1] A trustee with absolute control can give a license for his life to a railway company to use the land for a roadbed.[2] A trustee cannot go beyond the purposes of the trust deed and bind the estate.[3]

§ 437 *b*. Though "trustee" be added to the signature of a note or bond it may be mere *descriptio personæ*, and the obligation individual.[4] And, on the other hand, although the signature of a receipt be merely that of the trustee as an individual, the receipt may be really given as trustee and bind the *cestuis*.[5] A note, though not signed as trustee, will, as between the *cestui* and the trustee, be the obligation of the former if the debt was properly incurred for its benefit.[6]

---

[1] Michael *v.* Jones, 84 Mo. 578. [Fehlinger *v.* Wood, 134 Pa. St. 517, 523.]

[2] Tutt *v.* R. R. Co., 16 S. C. 365.

[3] Pracht & Co. *v.* Lange, 81 Va. 711.

[4] Cruselle *v.* Chastain, 76 Ga. 840; Bowen *v.* Penny, id. 743. [Hall *v.* Jameson, 151 Cal. 606.]

[5] Thomassen *v.* Van Wyngaarden, 65 Iowa, 689.

[6] Bushong *v.* Taylor, 82 Mo. 660.

he had retired. Noyes *v.* Turnbull, 54 Hun, 26, 130 N. Y. 639. See also   Wells-Stone Co. *v.* Grover, 7 N. D. 460, 41 L. R. A. 252.

CHAPTER XV.

POSSESSION — CUSTODY — CONVERSION — INVESTMENT OF TRUST
PROPERTY, AND INTEREST THAT TRUSTEES MAY BE MADE TO
PAY.

703

§ 470.   When he improperly changes an investment.
§ 471.   When compound interest will be imposed, and when other rules will be applied.
§ 472.   Rule where an accumulation is directed.

§ 438. THE first duty of a trustee, after his appointment and qualification to act, is to secure the possession of the trust property and to protect it from loss and injury. Until possession is properly taken by the trustee the grantor is entitled to the profits of the estate.[1] If the trust property is an equitable interest or estate, he must give notice to the holder of the legal title; and if he cannot have the legal title transferred to himself, he must take such steps that no incumbrances can be put upon it by the settlor or assignor. If the trust fund consists in part of notes, bonds, policies of insurance, and other similar *choses in action*, notice should be given to the promisors, obligors, or makers of the instruments. This is the general rule in England and in many of the United States.[2] (*a*) In some

[1] Frayser *v.* Rd. Co., 81 Va. 388.

[2] Jacob *v.* Lucas, 1 Beav. 436; Wright *v.* Dorchester, 3 Russ. 49, n.; Timson *v.* Ramsbottom, 2 Keen, 35; Forster *v.* Blackstone, 1 Myl. & K. 297; Roofer *v.* Harrison, 2 K. & J. 86; Loveredge *v.* Cooper, 3 Russ. 30; Dearle *v.* Hall, id. 1; Meux *v.* Dell, 1 Hare, 73; Stocks *v.* Dobson, 4 De G., M. & G. 11; Voyle *v.* Hughes, 2 Sm. & Gif. 18; Ryall *v.* Rowles, 1 Ves. 348; 1 Atk. 165; Dow *v.* Dawson, 1 Ves. 331; 3 Lead. Cas. Eq. 612; Jones *v.* Gibbons, 9 Ves. 410; Thompson *v.* Spiers, 13 Sim. 469; Waldron *v.* Sloper, 1 Drew. 193; *Ex parte* Boulton, 1 De G. & J. 163; Pierce *v.* Brady, 23 Beav. 64; Martin *v.* Sedgwick, 9 Beav. 333; Evans *v.* Bicknell, 6 Ves. 174; Dunster *v.* Glengall, 3 Ir. Eq. 47; Forster *v.* Cockerell, 9 Bligh (N. S.), 332, 3 Cl. & Fin. 456; Feltham *v.* Clark, 1 De G. & Sm. 307; *In re* Atkinson, 2 De G., M. & G. 140; Mangles *v.* Dixon, 18 Eng. L. & Eq. 82; Brashear *v.* West, 7 Pet. 608; Stewart *v.* Kirkland, 19 Ala. 162; Cummings *v.* Fullam, 13 Vt. 134; Northampton Bank *v.* Balliet, 8 Watts & S. 311; Bean *v.* Simpson, 4 Shep. 49; Phillips *v.* Bank of Lewistown, 18 Penn. St. 394; Laughlin *v.* Fairbanks, 8 Mo. 367; Campbell *v.* Day, 16 Vt. 358; Barney *v.* Douglass, 19 Vt. 98; Ward *v.* Morrison, 25 Vt. 593; Loomis *v.* Loomis, 2 Vt. 201; Adams *v.*

(*a*) In these jurisdictions an assignment of a *cestui's* interest in personalty or income takes effect as between assignees at the date of notice to the trustee. Lambert *v.* Morgan, 110 Md. 1; Low *v.* Bouverie, [1891] 3 Ch. 82; *In re* Wyatt, [1892] 1 Ch. 188; Stephens *v.* Green, [1895] 2 Ch. 148.

States, however, it is held that an assignment of a *chose in action* is complete in itself when the assignor and assignee have completed the transfer, and that notice to the debtor is not necessary in order to make the assignment valid as against third persons, or attaching creditors, or subsequent assignees without notice.[1] But it seems to be agreed in all the cases, that, if the debtor without notice and in *good faith* pays the debt to the assignor, it will be a good payment, and discharge him from further liability;[2] but if he should pay after notice he would still be

Leavens, 20 Conn. 73; Van Buskirk *v.* Ins. Co., 14 Conn. 145; Foster *v.* Mix, 20 Conn. 395; Bishop *v.* Halcomb, 10 Conn. 444; Woodbridge *v.* Perkins, 3 Day, 364; Judah *v.* Judd, 5 Day, 534; Murdock *v.* Finney, 21 Mo. 138; Cladfield *v.* Cox, 1 Sneed, 330; Fisher *v.* Knox, 13 Penn. St. 622; Judson *v.* Corcoran, 17 How. 614. But see Beavan *v.* Oxford, 6 De G., M. & G. 507; Kekewich *v.* Manning, 1 De G., M. & G. 176; Clack *v.* Holland, 24 L. J. 19; Barr's Trusts, 4 K. & J. 219; Scott *v.* Hastings, id. 633; Bridge *v.* Beadon, L. R. 3 Eq. 664; *In re* Brown's Trusts, L. R. 5 Eq. 88; Lloyd *v.* Banks, L. R. 4 Eq. 222; 3 Ch. 488. [Low *v.* Bouverie, [1891] 3 Ch. 82; *In re* Wyatt, [1892] 1 Ch. 188; Stephens *v.* Green, [1895] 2 Ch. 148; *Re* Patrick, 39 W. R. 113; Graham Paper Co. *v.* Pembroke, 124 Cal. 117; Lambert *v.* Morgan, 110 Md. 1; Houser *v.* Richardson, 90 Mo. App. 134; Jack *v.* National Bank, 17 Okla. 430; Phillips's Estate, 205 Pa. St. 525; Dillingham *v.* Traders' Ins. Co., 120 Tenn. 302. See also Goldthwaite *v.* Nat. Bank, 67 Ala. 549, 554; Tison *v.* People's Sav. & L. Ass'n, 57 Ala. 323, 331; Duke *v.* Clark, 58 Miss. 465, 474; Williams *v.* Donnelly, 54 Neb. 193; Starr *v.* Haskins, 26 N. J. Eq. 414; Tate *v.* Security Co., 63 N. J. Eq. 559, 561; Ga. Code (1895), § 3077; 1 Ames' Cases on Trusts (2d ed.), 326.]

[1] Sharpless *v.* Welch, 4 Dall. 279; Bholen *v.* Cleveland, 1 Mason, 174; Dix *v.* Cobb, 4 Mass. 508; Wood *v.* Partridge, 11 Mass. 488; Warren *v.* Copelin, 4 Met. 594; Littlefield *v.* Smith, 17 Me. 327; Corser *v.* Craig, 1 Wash. C. C. 24; United States *v.* Vaughn, 3 Binn. 394; Muir *v.* Schenk, 3 Hill, 228; Talbot *v.* Cook, 7 Mon. 438; Maybin *v.* Kirby, 4 Rich. Eq. 105; Stevens *v.* Stevens, 1 Ashm. 590; Beckwith *v.* Union Bank, 5 Seld. 211; Conway *v.* Cutting, 50 N. H. 408; Garland *v.* Harrington, 51 N. H. 409. [Columbia Finance & Tr. Co. *v.* First Nat. Bank, 116 Ky. 364, 375; Putnam *v.* Story, 132 Mass. 205, 211; Whittredge *v.* Sweetzer, 189 Mass. 45; Thayer *v.* Daniels, 113 Mass. 129; Central Trust Co. *v.* West India Imp. Co., 169 N. Y. 314, 323; Fairbanks *v.* Sargent, 104 N. Y. 108, 116; Niles *v.* Mathusa, 162 N. Y. 546, 552; Downer *v.* So. Royalton Bank, 39 Vt. 25; Tingle *v.* Fisher, 20 W. Va. 497; Quigley *v.* Welter, 95 Minn. 383 (*semble*). See 1 Ames' Cases on Trusts (2d ed.), 326.]

[2] Reed *v.* Marble, 10 Paige, 509; Mangles *v.* Dixon, 18 Eng. L. & Eq. 82; 1 Mac. & G. 446; 3 H. L. Cas. 739, and cases before cited; Stocks *v.* Debson, 4 De G., M. & G. 11.

liable to the assignee.[1] Under all circumstances, it is safer to give notice to the debtor, whether the courts of a State hold notice necessary or not. If the assignor receive the money of the debtor after the assignment, he will hold the money in trust for the assignee.[2] These general rules concerning notice do not apply to equities in real estate.[3] Trustees should also insist upon possession of all the notes, bonds, policies, and other obligations for the payment of money being delivered to them; for if negligent in this respect, and suits and costs arise, they might be made responsible personally.[4] So, if there are debts or securities already due and payable to the trust estate, the trustees must proceed to collect them. (a) If any loss happens to the estate from any delay, they would be responsible,[5] and they may accept payment even before the debts are due.[6] Where it is important for the trustees to give notice of an assignment to them, notice to one of several obligors is notice to all: so notice to one of several of a society of underwriters is suffi-

[1] Brashear v. West, 7 Pet. 608, and cases before cited; Judson v. Corcoran, 17 How. 414.

[2] Ellis v. Amason, 2 Dev. Eq. 273; Fortesque v. Barnett, 3 Myl. & K. 36.

[3] Wilmot v. Pike, 5 Hare, 14; Etty v. Bridges, 2 Y. & Col. 486; Ex parte Boulton, 1 De G. & J. 163; Webster v. Webster, 31 Beav. 393; Stevens v. Venables, 30 id. 625; Barr's Trusts, 4 K. & J. 219; Van Rensalaer v. Stafford, Hopk. Ch. 569; 9 Cow. 316; Poillon v. Martin, 1 Sandf. Ch. 569.

[4] Fortesque v. Barnett, 3 Myl. & K. 36; Meux v. Bell, 1 Hare, 82; Evans v. Bicknell, 6 Ves. 174; Knye v. Moore, 1 S. & S. 65; Lloyd v. Banks, L. R. 4 Eq. 222; 3 Ch. 488.

[5] Caffrey v. Darbey, 6 Ves. 488; McGachen v. Dew, 15 Beav. 84; Tebbs v. Carpenter, 1 Madd. 298; Waring v. Waring, 3 Ir. Eq. 335; Platel v. Craddock, C. P. Coop. 481; Wiles v. Gresham, 2 Drew. 258; Grove v. Price, 26 Beav. 103; Rowley v. Adams, 2 H. L. Cas. 725; Macken v. Hogan, 14 Ir. Eq. 220; Mucklow v. Fuller, Jac. 198; Powell v. Evans, 5 Ves. 839; Lowson v. Copeland, 2 Bro. Ch. 156; Caney v. Bond, 6 Beav. 486; Cross v. Petree, 10 B. Mon. 413; Wolfe v. Washburn, 6 Cow. 261; Waring v. Darnall, 10 G. & J. 127; Hester v. Wilkinson, 6 Humph. 215; Garner v. Moore, 3 Drew. 277; Neff's App., 57 Penn. St. 91.

[6] Mills v. Osborne, 7 Sim. 30.

(a) They have implied power to employ attorneys for the purpose. Vilas v. Bundy, 106 Wis. 168.

cient; and if the obligors compose a corporation, there must be
notice to the directors or trustees of the corporation.[1] So, if
notice to trustees is necessary in any case, notice to one is
sufficient.[2]

§ 439. There is no fixed time within which *executors* are to
get in the *choses in action* of the testator. They must use due
diligence; and what is due diligence depends upon the existing
facts in every case, and a large discretion must necessarily be
vested in the executor.[3] If there is property that cannot be
kept without great expense, it should be sold forthwith. If the
testator's establishment is expensive, it should be broken up
within a reasonable time; and, under special circumstances, two
months were held to be reasonable.[4] If there are shares or
stocks in corporations, the executors must exercise a sound
discretion to sell in the most advantageous manner, and at the
most advantageous time. In the case of some Crystal Palace
shares owned by a testator, a sale within a year was held to be
the exercise of a reasonable discretion, although it was claimed
that they ought to have been sold within two months.[5] So,
where a large part of an estate consisted of Mexican bonds,
which the testator directed to be converted "with all convenient speed," it was held that these words added nothing to the
implied duty of every executor to convert such property with
all reasonable speed; that a conversion in the course of the
second year was proper and reasonable; that if executors were
bound to sell at once without reference to the circumstances,
there would often be a great sacrifice of property, and therefore
that executors were bound to exercise a *reasonable discretion,*

---

[1] Timson *v.* Ramsbottom, 2 Keen, 35; Meux *v.* Bell, 1 Hare, 88; *Re*
Styan, 1 Phill. 155; Smith *v.* Smith, 2 Cr. & Mee. 31; Duncan *v.* Cham-
berlayne, 11 Sim. 123.

[2] Greenhill *v.* Willis, 4 De G., F. & J. 147.

[3] Waring *v.* Darnall, 10 G. & J. 127; Hughes *v.* Empson, 22 Beav. 188.

[4] Field *v.* Pecket, 29 Beav. 576.

[5] Hughes *v.* Empson, 22 Beav. 138; Bate *v.* Hooper, 5 De G., M. & G.
338; Wilkinson *v.* Duncan, 26 L. J. (N. S.) Ch. 495.

according to the circumstances of each case.[1] But generally
stock should be sold within the year allowed for the settling of
a testator's estate, and a delay beyond this time may render
the executors or trustees liable for the loss, although they act
in good faith, and although some of the trustees became of age
only a short time before the sale.[2] If, however, it is clear that
the trustees have a discretion to sell or not according to their
judgment, the case will be governed by the intention and not be
the general rule.[3]

§ 440. Personal securities change from day to day; and as the
death of the testator puts an end to his discretion in regard to
them, unless he has exercised it in his will, the executor or
trustee will become personally liable, if he does not get in the
money within a reasonable time.[4] He must not allow the assets
to remain out on personal security,[5] (a) though it was a loan
or investment by the testator himself.[6] It is not enough for
the executor to apply for payment through an attorney: he

[1] Buxton v. Buxton, 1 M. & C. 80; Prendergast v. Lushington, 5 Hare,
171; Hester v. Wilkinson, 6 Humph. 215; Waring v. Darnall, 10 G. & J.
127.
[2] Sculthorpe v. Tiffer, L. R. 13 Eq. 238; Grayburn v. Clarkson, L. R.
3 Ch. 605.
[3] Mackie v. Mackie, 5 Hare, 70; Wrey v. Smith, 14 Sim. 202; Sparling
v. Parker, 9 Beav. 524.
[4] Bailey v. Young, 4 Y. & Col. Ch. 226; Will's App., 22 Penn. St. 330;
Mucklow v. Fuller, Jac. 198; Tebbs v. Carpenter, 1 Madd. 297.
[5] Lowson v. Copeland, 2 Bro. Ch. 156; Caney v. Bond, 6 Beav. 486;
Att. Gen. v. Higham, 2 Y. & Col. Ch. 634; Hemphill's App., 18 Penn. St.
303.
[6] Powell v. Evans, 5 Ves. 839; Bullock v. Wheatley, 1 Col. C. C. 130;
Tebbs v. Carpenter, 1 Madd. 298; Clough v. Bond, 3 Myl. & Cr. 496; Hemphill's App., 18 Penn. St. 303; Pray's App., 34 id. 100; Barton's App., 1 Pars.
Eq. 24, is overruled; Kimball v. Reading, 11 Foster, 352. In England,
bank stock must be converted. Mills v. Mills, 7 Sim. 509; Howe v. Dartmouth, 7 Ves. 150; Price v. Anderson, 15 Sim. 473. [As to continuation of
the testator's investments, see *infra*, § 465 and notes.]

(a) Unless so directed or authorized by the creator of the trust. Denike v. Harris, 84 N. Y. 89, reversing
s. c. 23 Hun, 213.

must follow the collection actively by legal proceedings,[1] unless he can show that such proceedings would have been futile and vain.[2] An executor must take the same steps when his *coexecutor* is a debtor to the estate, even if the testator has been in the habit of depositing or lending money to the coexecutor as to a banker.[3] Executors are not justified in dealing with a testator's money as he dealt with it himself, nor may they trust all the persons that he trusted. Nor will a direction in the will "to call in securities not approved by them" excuse executors from not calling in personal securities; for such direction refers to the different kinds of securities sanctioned by law and the court, and not to all investments outside the sanctions of the law.[4] If the executors are to get in the money "whenever they think proper and expedient," they will be liable for the fund if they allow it to remain uncollected out of kindness or regard for the tenant for life, and not upon an impartial judgment for the best interest of all the parties.[5] If the outstanding debt is secured by a real mortgage, it ought not to be called in, if it is safe, until it is wanted in the course of the administration.[6] But pains should be taken to ascertain whether the security is safe.[7] If the mortgage security is not adequate, the executor or trustee must insist upon payment, even where the *cestui que trust* is to consent to every change of investment, and he refuses to consent; for nothing will justify conduct that endangers the

[1] Lowson *v.* Copeland, 2 Bro. Ch. 156; Horton *v.* Brocklehurst, 29 Beav. 511; Paddon *v.* Richardson, 7 De G., M. & G. 563; Wolfe *v.* Washburn, 6 Cow. 261.

[2] Clack *v.* Holland, 19 Beav. 262; Hobday *v.* Peters, 28 id. 603; Alexander *v.* Alexander, 12 Ir. Eq. 1; Maitland *v.* Bateman, 16 Sim. 233, and note; Walker *v.* Symonds, 3 Swanst. 71; East *v.* East, 5 Hare, 343; Ratcliff *v.* Wynch, 17 Beav. 217; Ball *v.* Ball, 11 Ir. Eq. 370; Styles *v.* Guy, 16 Sim. 232; Billing *v.* Brogden, 38 Ch. D. 546.

[3] Styles *v.* Guy, 1 Mac. & G. 428; 1 Hall & Tw. 523; Egbert *v.* Butter, 21 Beav. 560; Candler *v.* Tillett, 22 Beav. 257; Mucklow *v.* Fuller, Jac. 198.

[4] Styles *v.* Guy, 1 Mac. & G. 428; Scully *v.* Delany, 2 Ir. Eq. 165.

[5] Luther *v.* Bianconi, 10 Ir. Ch. 194.

[6] Orr *v.* Newton, 2 Cox, 274; Howe *v.* Dartmouth, 7 Ves. 150; Robinson *v.* Robinson, 1 De G., M. & G. 252.

[7] Ames *v.* Parkinson, 7 Beav. 384.

fund.[1] (*a*) But if the fund is safe on a security sanctioned by the court and selected by the testator, it might be a breach of trust to call it in, and allow it to remain unproductive, or to invest it anew.[2] But if trustees are ordered by the court to call in securities, and they neglect to do so, they will be liable for any loss that occurs.[3] So, if trustees compromise a debt due from a bankrupt estate, they must show that the bankrupt would have obtained his discharge, and that it was impossible to get the whole debt, or they will be liable for the loss.[4] If the trustee himself owes the estate, he must treat his indebtedness as assets collected, and if he becomes bankrupt, he must prove the debt against himself, or he will be liable, even if he gets his discharge.[5] But in the United States bankrupts are not discharged from any liabilities which they are under in a fiduciary capacity. (*b*)

§ 441. It was observed in Harden *v.* Parsons,[6] that no man can require, or with reason expect, that a trustee should manage

[1] Harrison *v.* Thexton, 4 Jur. (N. S.) 550.

[2] Orr *v.* Newton, 2 Cox, 276.

[3] Davenport *v.* Stafford, 14 Beav. 338.

[4] Wiles *v.* Gresham, 2 Dr. 258; 5 De G., M. & G. 770. Lord Justice Turner expressed a doubt, whether the trustees should have been charged, without further inquiry. Bacot *v.* Hayward, 5 S. C. 441. [See *infra,* § 482, as to power to make advantageous compromises.]

[5] Orrett *v.* Corser, 21 Beav. 52; Prindle *v.* Holcombe, 45 Conn. 111; Ipswich Manuf. Co. *v.* Story, 5 Met. 310; Chenery *v.* Davis, 16 Gray, 89; Hazelton *v.* Valentine, 113 Mass. 472; Pettee *v.* Peppard, 120 Mass. 523. The acceptance of the trust requires him to treat an indebtedness for which he was previously responsible as assets collected. Stevens *v.* Gaylord, 11 Mass. 269; Ips. Manuf. Co. *v.* Story, 5 Met. 310; 18 Pick. 236; 1 Allen, 531; 10 Cush. 176; 120 Mass. 523.

[6] 1 Eden, 148.

(*a*) But see *In re* Medland, 41 Ch. Div. 476, holding that there is no absolute rule that the investment must be called in, but that such a matter must be dealt with as a practical one for the safety of the fund. See also *In re* Chapman, [1896] 2 Ch. 763; *infra,* § 466, note.

(*b*) The exact wording of the U. S. Bankruptcy Law of 1898, § 17, is: debts which "were created by his fraud, embezzlement, misappropriation, or defalcation while acting as an officer or in any fiduciary capacity."

another's property with the same care and discretion as his own. But this is neither sound morality nor good law. A trustee must use the same care for the safety of the trust fund, and for the interests of the *cestui que trust*, that he uses for his own property and interests.[1] And even this will not be sufficient if he is careless in his own concerns; for a trustee must in all events use such care as *a man of ordinary prudence uses in his own business of a similar nature*.[2] Thus, where a trustee had £200 of his own money, and £40 of trust-money, in his house, and he was robbed by his servant, he was not held responsible.[3] And where a trustee deposited articles with his solicitor, to be passed over to a party entitled to them, and the articles were stolen, the trustee was not held responsible.[4] But if a trustee employs an agent, and the agent steals or appropriates the property intrusted to him, the trustee will be held responsible; that is, the trustee is not responsible for the crimes of strangers, but he is responsible for the criminal acts of agents employed by himself about the trust fund,[5] (a) and for any loss that may

[1] Morley v. Morley, 2 Ch. Cas. 2; Jones v. Lewis, 2 Ves. 241; Massey v. Banner, 1 J. & W. 247; Att. Gen. v. Dixie, 13 Ves. 534; *Ex parte* Belchier, Amb. 220; *Ex parte* Griffin, 2 G. & J. 114; Taylor v. Benham, 5 How. 233; King v. Talbott, 50 Barb. 453; 40 N. Y. 86; Miller v. Proctor, 20 Ohio St. 444; Neff's App., 57 Penn. St. 91; King v. King, 37 Ga. 205; Campbell v. Campbell, 38 Ga. 304; Roosevelt v. Roosevelt, 6 Abb. (N. Y.) N. Cas. 447; Gould v. Chappell, 42 Md. 466; Carpenter v. Carpenter, 12 R. I. 544; Davis v. Harmon, 21 Grat. 194.

[2] Woodruff v. Snedecor, 68 Ala. 442.

[3] Morley v. Morley, 2 Ch. Cas. 2. [To same effect see Stevens v. Gage, 55 N. H. 175; Carpenter v. Carpenter, 12 R. I. 544.]

[4] Jones v. Lewis, 2 Ves. 240; Foster v. Davis, 46 Mo. 268.

[5] Bostock v. Floyer, L. R. 1 Eq. 28; Hopgood v. Parkin, L. R. 11 Eq. 74.

(a) In view of later decisions the proposition in the text cannot be considered a correct statement of the law. Of the two cases cited as authority, Hopgood v. Parkin has been discredited by subsequent English decisions, and Bostock v. Floyer has been construed to hold merely that misapplication of trust funds by an agent renders the trustee liable where he has unnecessarily entrusted the agent with the custody of trust funds. Speight v. Gaunt, 22 Ch. Div. 727, 761; *Re* Partington, 57 L. T. 654, 661.

Although a trustee cannot prop-

fall upon the estate by the forgery of a signature upon which he pays money.[1]

[1] Eaves v. Hickson, 30 Beav. 136.

erly delegate his trust to an agent, "he is justified in employing qualified persons as agents when in so doing he follows the ordinary course of business of a like nature," and when "according to the usual and regular course of such business moneys payable or receivable ought to pass through the hands of such agents, the course may be properly followed by the trustees, though the moneys are trust moneys." Rochfort v. Seaton, [1896] 1 Ir. R. 18; Speight v. Gaunt, 9 App. Cas. 1, 5; 22 Ch. Div. 727; McCloskey v. Gleason, 56 Vt. 264; Finlay v. Merriman, 39 Tex. 56. If the employment of agents is reasonably necessary for the performance of the duties of the trust, and the trustee selects persons who are apparently honest and properly qualified and uses reasonable supervision over them, he is not responsible for their lack of intelligence or dishonesty. In re Weall, 42 Ch. Div. 674; Jobson v. Palmer, [1893] 1 Ch. 71; Lord De Clifford's Estate, [1900] 2 Ch. 707; Carpenter v. Carpenter, 12 R. I. 544.

Thus a trustee may properly employ agents to collect sums due the estate, and is not responsible for losses of collections due to dishonesty or insolvency of such persons, if he took proper care in appointing them and exercised reasonable supervision over them. In re Brier, 26 Ch. Div. 238; Finlay v. Merriman, 39 Tex. 56. Similarly where trust funds have been lost through embezzlement by a broker employed by

trustees to purchase certain securities, and the usual business precautions were taken, they have been held not to be responsible for the loss. Speight v. Gaunt, 9 A. C. 1. But where the trustee was negligent in selecting his broker and unnecessarily put the trust funds into his custody, he was held to be liable for the loss due to the broker's dishonesty. Robinson v. Harkin, [1896] 2 Ch. 415. And where the trustee has not exercised proper supervision ove his agent and has unnecessarily given him the opportunity to misappropriate the trust funds, he is liable for the loss. McCloskey v. Gleason, 56 Vt. 264.

Where a loss of trust funds was due to the failure of a solicitor, employed by the trustees, to see that a certain assignment was properly executed, it was held that the trustees were not liable, since this was a matter in which they must necessarily rely upon solicitors. Rochfort v. Seaton, [1896] 1 Ir. R. 18. But a trustee cannot properly delegate the responsibility of choosing proper investments to a solicitor or a broker, even when the latter is a cotrustee. Re Partington, 57 L. T. 654, 661; Cowper v. Stoneham, 68 L. T. 18; Hanscom v. Marston, 82 Me. 288. And he cannot properly leave the trust funds in the hands of a solicitor or other agent while he is seeking a proper investment. Speight v. Gaunt, 9 App. Cas. 1, 5; Bostock v. Floyer, 1 Eq. 26.

Although a trustee may properly

§ 442. Several trustees, residing in different places, cannot all have the custody of the same articles; therefore it is said that articles of plate, which pass by delivery, and stocks and bonds, payable to the bearer, with coupons to be cut off for the interest, should be deposited at a responsible banker's.[1]

§ 443. A trustee may deposit money temporarily in some responsible bank or banking-house;[2] and if he acted in good faith and with discretion, and deposited the money to a trust account, he will not be liable for its loss, as where the bank failed in consequence of war;[3] but he will be liable for the money in case of a failure of the bank, or for its depreciation, if he deposits it to his *own credit*, and not to the separate account of the trust estate,[4] even though he had no other funds in bank, and told the officers at the time of deposit that the funds were held by him in trust.[5] So if he allows another person to draw

[1] Mendes *v.* Guedalla, 2 John. & H. 259. [*In re* De Pothonier, [1900] 2 Ch. 529.]

[2] Rowth *v.* Howell, 3 Ves. Jr. 565; Jones *v.* Lewis, 2 Ves. 241; Adams *v.* Claxton, 6 Ves. 226; *Ex parte* Belchier, Amb. 219; Att. Gen. *v.* Randall, 21 Vin. Ab. 534; Massey *v.* Banner, 1 J. & W. 248; Horsley *v.* Chaloner, 2 Ves. 85; France *v.* Woods, Taml. 172; Dorchester *v.* Effingham, id. 279; Freme *v.* Woods, id. 172; Wilks *v.* Groome, 3 Dr. 584; Johnston *v.* Newton, 11 Hare, 160; Swinfen *v.* Swinfen, 29 Beav. 211. [Law's Estate, 144 Pa. St. 449; Baer's Appeal, 127 Pa. St. 360.]

[3] Douglas *v.* Stephenson's Ex'r, 75 Va. 749. [Moore *v.* Eure, 101 N. C. 11; Atterberry *v.* McDuffee, 31 Mo. App. 603, 611.]

[4] Wren *v.* Kirton, 11 Ves. 377; Fletcher *v.* Walker, 3 Madd. 73; Macdonnell *v.* Harding, 7 Sim. 178; Mathews *v.* Brise, 6 Beav. 239; Massey *v.* Banner, 1 J. & W. 241; see remarks on this case in Pennell *v.* Deffell, 4 De G., M. & G. 386, 392; School Dis. Greenfield *v.* First National Bank, 102 Mass. 174; Mason *v.* Whitehorn, 2 Cold. 242.

[5] William's Adm'r *v.* Williams, 55 Wis. 300. [*In re* Arguello, 97 Cal. 196;

deposit trust funds in a bank of good standing for a reasonable time pending investment or distribution and may properly deposit in a bank the securities in which he has invested trust funds, he has been held to be liable to replace the loss caused by misappropriations by the cashier of a bank whom he has requested to purchase certain bonds and to place them on deposit in the bank for him, when he has not taken the precaution to find out for himself that the bonds have been purchased and placed on special deposit in his name. Key *v.* Hughes' Ex'r, 32 W. Va. 184.

upon the fund and misapply the money; [1] so if he deposits the money in such manner that it is not under his own exclusive control, as where money is deposited in bank so that it cannot be drawn without the concurrence of other persons, the trustee will be liable for the failure of the bank, on the principle that it is the duty of the trustee to withdraw the money from the bank upon the slightest indication of danger or loss, and he cannot perform this duty promptly if he is clogged by the necessity of procuring the concurrent action of other persons.[2] (a) So he will be liable if he keeps money in bank an unreasonable length of time, or where it is his duty to invest the fund in safe securities,[3] or to pay it over to newly appointed trustees,[4] or into court; [5] or if, having no occasion to keep a balance on hand for the purposes of the trust, he lends the money to the bank on interest upon personal security, that being a security not sanctioned by the court.[6]

§ 444. Trustees may leave money in the custody of third persons when it is necessary in the course of business, as where money is left in the hands of an auctioneer as agent of both parties on a sale or purchase; [7] and during the negotiation of

Booth v. Wilkinson, 78 Wis. 652; O'Connor v. Decker, 95 Wis. 202; Milmo's Succession, 47 La. Ann. 126, 127; McCollister v. Bishop, 78 Minn. 228. 1 Ames on Trusts, (2d ed.) 481–484, notes.]

[1] Ingle v. Partridge, 32 Beav. 661; 34 id. 411.

[2] Salway v. Salway, alias White v. Baugh, 2 R. & M. 215; 9 Bligh, 181; 3 Cl. & Fin. 44; overruling same case, 4 Russ. 60.

[3] Moyle v. Moyle, 2 R. & M. 710; Johnston v. Newton, 11 Hare, 169. [Hetfield v. Debaud, 54 N. J. Eq. 371; Stambaugh's Estate, 135 Pa. St. 585; Whitecar's Estate, 147 Pa. St. 368; Young's Estate, 97 Iowa, 218; Dick's Estate, 183 Pa. St. 647.]

[4] Lunham v. Blundell, 4 Jur. (N. S.) 3.

[5] Wilkinson v. Bewick, 4 Jur. (N. S.) 1010.

[6] Darke v. Martyn, 1 Beav. 525. [Baer's Appeal, 127 Pa. St. 360. Held otherwise in Hunt, Appellant, 141 Mass. 515.]

[7] Edmonds v. Peake, 7 Beav. 239. [See supra, § 441, note.]

(a) But it has been held no impropriety for a trustee to enter into an agreement with the sureties on his bond to deposit trust funds at a certain bank. McCollister v. Bishop, 78 Minn. 228.

an investment, the trustees may buy exchequer bills;[1] but if they leave the exchequer bills undistinguished in the hands of a banker or broker, they will be liable for the loss of the money.[2] But if trustees deposit money in bank to their own credit;[3] or if they leave it for an unreasonable time, as a year after the testator's death and after all debts and legacies are paid;[4] or if they place their papers and receipts in the hands of their solicitor, so that he can receive their money and misapply it;[5] or if the money is so paid into bank that it may be drawn out upon the check of one trustee and misapplied;[6] or if they neglect to sell property when it ought to have been sold,[7] or suffer money to remain upon personal security,[8] or upon an unauthorized security;[9] or if the money is left improperly or unadvisedly in the hands of a coexecutor or cotrustee, so that he has an opportunity to misapply it, — all the trustees will be responsible for any loss that may occur to the trust fund.[10] (a) So trustees are liable for the attorneys and solicitors whom they employ; as where they employ a solicitor to examine the title to a proposed mortgage, and they are misled by him in such manner that a loss occurs to the estate, they are liable to make it good.[11] (b)

[1] Mathews v. Brise, 6 Beav. 239.

[2] Ibid.

[3] Massey v. Banner, 1 J. & W. 241; Wren v. Kirton, 11 Ves. 377; Mason v. Whitehorn, 2 Cold. 242. [Supra, § 443.]

[4] Ibid.

[5] Ghost v. Waller, 9 Beav. 497; Rowland v. Witherden, 3 Mac. & G. 568.

[6] Clough v. Bond, 3 Myl. & Cr. 490; Clough v. Dixon, 8 Sim. 594. [Unless reasonable business necessity justifies such a course, supra, § 415, note.]

[7] Phillips v. Phillips, Freem. Ch. 11.

[8] Powell v. Evans, 5 Ves. 839; Tebbs v. Carpenter, 1 Madd. 290.

[9] Hancom v. Allen, 2 Dick. 498 and n.; Howe v. Dartmouth, 7 Ves. 137.

[10] Langford v. Gascoyne, 11 Ves. 333; Shipbrook v. Hinchinbrook, Id. 252; 16 Ves. 478; Underwood v. Stevens, 2 Mer. 712; Hardy v. Metropolitan Land Co., L. R. 7 Ch. 429.

[11] Hopgood v. Parkin, L. R. 11 Eq. 74; Bostock v. Floyer, L. R. 1 Eq. 26.

(a) As to a trustee's liability for the *devastavit* or other breach of trust committed by a cotrustee, see *supra*, § 415, note a.

(b) Later authorities have limited the scope of the two cases cited above so that the text needs considerable qualification. In cases where

§ 445. In one case it was said, that an executor would not be liable if he had placed money in bank under the control of a coexecutor. The money was entered on joint account, but the individual checks of the coexecutors could draw it out. This was held to be the ordinary and reasonable course of business.[1] If, however, there is any fraud, collusion, or wilful default, or gross neglect, or if the executor has any reason to interfere, and does not put a stop to the mismanagement of his coexecutor, he will be held liable.[2] The case of Kilbee v. Sneyd, however, is so doubtful on this point, and contrary to authority, that it would be unsafe to act upon it.[3]

§ 446. Trustees and executors have a reasonable time to wind up a testator's estate, and make investments; and they may, without responsibility, keep the money in a reliable bank for one year after the death of the testator;[4] (a) but if they draw the money out of bank, and make any irregular investment, or lend it to another bank on interest, they will be responsible for the loss of the money, even if the will directs that the trustees shall not be responsible for losses by a banker; the construction of such direction being that the trustees shall not be liable for loss of money deposited with a banker in the ordinary manner.[5]

---

[1] Kilbee v. Sneyd, 2 Moll. 186.

[2] Ibid. 203, 213.

[3] Clough v. Dickson, 8 Sim. 594; 3 Myl. & Cr. 490; Gibbons v. Taylor, 22 Beav. 344; Ingle v. Partridge, 32 Beav. 661; 34 Beav. 411.

[4] Johnston v. Newton, 11 Hare, 160; Swinfen v. Swinfen, 29 Beav. 211; Wilks v. Groome, 3 Dr. 584.

[5] Rehden v. Wesley, 29 Beav. 213.

the employment of or reliance upon attorneys and solicitors is reasonably necessary, trustees are not liable to make good losses due to the default or carelessness of the agent, when he has been trusted or relied upon no further than was reasonably necessary. Supra, § 441, note; Rochfort v. Seaton, [1896] 1 Ir. R. 18.

(a) There seems to be no rule that trustees and executors may retain the trust funds uninvested for a year and no more. They must act with reasonable diligence in view of all the circumstances. See Dick's Estate, 183 Pa. St. 647; Dorris v. Miller, 105 Iowa, 564; Howard v. Manning, 65 Ark. 122; In re Clark's Estate, 39 N. Y. S. 722; In re Muller, 52 N. Y. S. 565.

§ 447. The trustee must not mingle the trust fund with his own. (a) If he does, the *cestui que trust* may follow the trust property, and claim every part of the blended property which the trustee cannot identify as his own.[1]

§ 448. There may be express trusts for conversion; that is, to sell the trust fund, as it exists at the time of the testator's decease, and convert the same into some other kind of property or investment; (b) and there may be an express trust to allow

---

[1] Lupton v. White, 15 Ves. 432, 440; Chedworth v. Edwards, 8 Ves. 46; White v. Lincoln, id. 363; Fellowes v. Mitchell, 1 P. Wms. 83; Gray v. Haig, 20 Beav. 219; Leeds v. Amherst, id. 239; Mason v. Morley, 34 Beav. 471, 475; Cook v. Addison, L. R. 7 Eq. 470; Morrison v. Kinstra, 55 Miss. 71. [Fant v. Dunbar, 71 Miss. 576.]

(a) Nor with funds of a third person. Westover v. Carman's Estate, 49 Neb. 397.

(b) Under the generally recognized doctrine of equitable conversion an imperative direction to a trustee or to a donee of a power of sale, to change the form of the property has the effect of determining the nature of the beneficial interests as if the actual conversion had been made as directed at the moment their interests were created. Allen v. Watts, 98 Ala. 384; Burbach v. Burbach, 217 Ill. 547; Boland v. Tiernay, 118 Iowa, 59; Brown Banking Co. v. Stockton, 107 Ky. 492; Snover v. Squire, 24 A. 365 (N. J. Ch. 1892); Matter of Russell, 168 N. Y. 169; Duckworth v. Jordan, 138 N. C. 520, 525; Williamson's Estate, 153 Pa. St. 508; Thomman's Estate, 161 Pa. St. 444; Howell v. Mellon, 189 Pa. St. 169; Petition of Holder, 21 R. I. 48; Martin v. Moore, 49 Wash. 288; Lynch v. Spicer, 53 W. Va. 426, 430; Handley v. Palmer, 91 Fed. 948. See also cases cited *infra*. See Lackey's Estate, 149 Pa. St. 7. Thus if a testator has directed trustees under his will or his executor to sell his real estate, the interests of those entitled under his will are treated as personalty and the trust is treated as a trust of personalty from the beginning, although the actual conversion does not take place at once. Harrington v. Pier, 105 Wis. 485. Likewise an imperative direction to convert personalty into real estate makes the interests of those entitled real estate. McFadden v. Hefley, 28 S. C. 317; Phillips v. Ferguson, 85 Va. 509; *In re* Cleveland's Settled Estates, [1893] 3 Ch. 244. A discretion given to the trustee to postpone the actual conversion does not postpone the time of the equitable conversion, provided the actual conversion is to take place some time at all events. Bates v. Spooner, 75 Conn. 501, 508; Burbach v. Burbach, 217 Ill. 547; Lambert v. Morgan, 110 Md. 1, 29; Crane v. Bolles, 49 N. J. Eq. 373; Underwood v. Curtis, 127 N. Y. 523; Russell v. Hilton, 80 N.

the *cestuis que trust* the use and enjoyment of the *specific* property devised. Both of these forms of trust must be strictly executed,

Y. S. 563, 80 App. Div. 178; *In re* Hosford, 50 N. Y. S. 550; Severns's Estate, 211 Pa. St. 65; Tasker's Estate, 215 Pa. St. 267; Att. Gen. *v.* Dodd, [1894] 2 Q. B. 150.

Where a trustee is given mere authority to convert in his discretion without the imperative duty of doing so there is no equitable conversion. Ness *v.* Davidson, 49 Minn. 469; Condit *v.* Bigalow, 64 N. J. Eq. 504, 507; Matter of Tatum, 169 N. Y. 514; Matter of Coolidge, 85 App. Div. (N. Y.) 295; Matter of Bingham, 127 N. Y. 296; Carberry *v.* Ennis, 76 N.Y. S. 537, 72 App. Div. 489; Penfield *v.* Tower, 1 N. D. 216; Cooper's Estate, 206 Pa. St. 628; Sauerbier's Estate, 202 Pa. St. 187; Taylor *v.* Haskell, 178 Pa. St. 106; Solliday's Estate, 175 Pa. St. 114; Ingersoll's Estate, 167 Pa. St. 536; Becker's Estate, 150 Pa. St. 524; Bennett *v.* Gallaher, 115 Tenn. 568; Bedford *v.* Bedford, 110 Tenn. 204; Wayne *v.* Fouts, 108 Tenn. 145, 148. Actual conversion in the exercise of such a discretionary power converts the interests of the beneficiaries. Matter of McKay, 77 N. Y. S. 845, 75 App. Div. 78. But mere changes in investments for convenience of management do not convert the interests of those entitled. Gray *v.* Whittemore, 192 Mass. 367; Henszey's Estate, 220 Pa. St. 212. See also Hovey *v.* Dary, 154 Mass. 7.

An imperative direction to convert upon the happening of a contingency which may never occur does not accomplish equitable conversion until the happening of the contingency. Ford *v.* Ford, 70 Wis.

19. Likewise of a direction to convert if and when requested by the *cestuis.* Wheless *v.* Wheless, 92 Tenn. 293; Meade *v.* Campbell, 34 S. E. 30 (Va. 1899). To a similar effect see Pyott's Estate, 160 Pa. St. 441. But an imperative direction to convert upon request of life beneficiaries, or after their death at a time left to the discretion of the trustees, accomplishes equitable conversion of the interests of the remainder-men, since the conversion is to take place some time at all events. Att. General *v.* Dodd, [1894] 2 Q. B. 150.

Where the actual conversion is mandatory but is postponed to the happening of a future event, as, *e. g.*, the death of the life tenant, it has been held by some courts that there is no equitable conversion until the happening of the future event. Sayles *v.* Best, 140 N. Y. 368; Liveright *v.* Sternberger, 115 N. Y. S. 349, 131 App. Div. 13; Williams *v.* Lobban, 206 Mo. 399. But other courts have held that the equitable conversion dates from the beginning. Lash *v.* Lash, 209 Ill. 595; Beaver *v.* Ross, 140 Iowa, 154; Duckworth *v.* Jordan, 138 N. C. 520.

If it is clear from the whole will that the testator intended that conversion should be made at all events, an imperative direction to convert is frequently implied. Clarke's Appeal, 70 Conn. 195; Davenport *v.* Kirkland, 156 Ill. 169; Boyce *v.* Kelso Home, 107 Md. 190; Harris *v.* Ingalls, 74 N. H. 339; Roy *v.* Monroe, 47 N. J. Eq. 356; Crane *v.* Bolles, 49 N. J. Eq. 373; Matter of

and generally no question arises upon them. But a question sometimes arises from the situation and character of the prop-

Gantert, 136 N. Y. 106; Merritt v. Merritt, 53 N. Y. S. 127, 32 App. Div. 442; Keim's Estate, 201 Pa. St. 609; Severns's Estate, 211 Pa. St. 65; Fahnestock v. Fahnestock, 152 Pa. St. 56; Mustin's Estate, 194 Pa. St. 437; Marshall's Estate, 147 Pa. St. 77; McFadden v. Hefley, 28 S. C. 317; Williams v. Williams, 135 Wis. 60; Benner v. Mauer, 133 Wis. 325, 329; Dodge v. Williams, 46 Wis. 70; Att. Gen. v. Dodd, [1894] 2 Q. B. 150. See Reid v. Clendenning, 193 Pa. St. 406. In Becker v. Chester, 115 Wis. 90, 118, it was said: "When the execution of the scheme of the testator would be impossible, or attended with such difficulties that it would be unreasonable to suppose that its execution was contemplated by him without the conversion of real estate into personal property, a direction for such conversion will be deemed imperatively expressed in the will by necessary implication, to the same effect as if expressed in words; and the realty so directed to be converted will be deemed impressed with the character of personal property from the time of the death of the testator."

In Matter of Tatum, 169 N. Y. 514, it was said: "In order that a court shall be justified in so construing the will of a decedent as to effect a change in the apparent character of his estate, and in regulating its final distribution, the equivalent of such a direction should be found in the general scheme of the will, when the only power given to sell the real estate is discretionary. Unless the purpose of

the testator will fail without conversion, equity will not presume it. There should be an implication of a direction to convert, so unequivocal and so strong as to leave no substantial doubt in the mind. Indeed, conversion, to be decreed, must be so necessary, as that, without it, the provisions of the will would be rendered unreasonable and incapable of a just and effective operation." Matter of Coolidge, 85 App. Div. (N. Y.) 295, affirmed 177 N. Y. 541.

The general rule has been stated as follows in Pennsylvania: "To work a conversion of real estate into personalty, there must be either (a) a positive direction to sell; or (b) an absolute necessity to sell in order to execute the will; or (c) such a blending of realty and personalty, by the testator, in his will, as to clearly show that he intended to create a fund out of both real and personal estate, and to bequeath the same as money." Darlington v. Darlington, 160 Pa. St. 65, 70; Reid v. Clendenning, 193 Pa. St. 406; Hunt's Appeal, 105 Pa. St. 141.

An imperative direction to convert accomplishes equitable conversion only to the extent required to accomplish the manifest purpose for which conversion was directed; and, if the actual conversion will not accomplish the purpose for which it was directed or is unnecessary, there is no equitable conversion, and the property passes to those entitled in its original form. Trask v. Sturges, 170 N. Y. 482, 489; Jones v. Kelly, 170 N. Y. 401; Phillips v. Ferguson,

erty, and the relations of the *cestuis que trust* to it, whether the trustee is to convert the property into another form, or allow the *cestuis que trust* to enjoy it *in specie:* that is, the court is left to infer or imply, from the construction of the instrument, the character of the property and the relations of the *cestuis que trust*, whether it was the intention of the testator that the property should be converted, or whether the beneficiaries should take the use of it specifically, according to the terms in which

85 Va. 509; McHugh *v.* McCole, 97 Wis. 166; and cases cited *infra.* Thus a trust for sale which is invalid because of the rule against perpetuities does not work an equitable conversion. Goodier *v.* Edmunds, [1893] 3 Ch. 455. Where conversion of realty was directed upon the death of the life tenant for the purpose of division between two daughters, and both daughters died before the life tenant, it was held that, the purposes for which conversion had been ordered having ceased to exist, the property resumed its original character. Painter *v.* Painter, 220 Pa. St. 82. See also Rudy's Estate, 185 Pa. St. 359; *In re* Richerson, [1892] 1 Ch. 379.

Where the purpose for which a sale of land was directed does not entirely consume the proceeds, the surplus will be treated as real estate so far as necessary to determine who is entitled. Harris *v.* Achilles, 114 N. Y. S. 855, 129 App. Div. 847; Canfield *v.* Canfield, 62 N. J. Eq. 578; Moore *v.* Robbins, 53 N. J. Eq. 137; James *v.* Hanks, 202 Ill. 114; Fifield *v.* Van Wyck, 94 Va. 557; Harrington *v.* Pier, 105 Wis. 485, 492. And where a testator directs land to be sold "the conversion will, unless a contrary intention distinctly appears, be deemed to have been directed merely for the purposes of

the will, and consequently if these purposes fail or do not require it, it will in equity be considered land and be given to the heir." *In re* Alabone's Estate, 72 A. 427, (N. J. Prerog. 1909); Moore *v.* Robbins, 53 N. J. Eq. 137.

Where the trustee or executor sells land under a decree of court and not under any direction in the will or trust instrument, the proceeds are treated as real estate until they reach the hands of those beneficially entitled. Smith *v.* Smith, 174 Ill. 52, 59; Chapin, Petitioner, 148 Mass. 588. In case the beneficial owner is an infant, the proceeds retain the character of real estate until he becomes of age. Wetherill *v.* Hough, 52 N. J. Eq. 683; Merriam *v.* Dunham, 62 N. J. Eq. 567; Major *v.* Hunt, 64 S.C.97; Findley *v.*Findley, 42 W. Va. 372, 378; Matter of McMillan, 110 N. Y. S. 622, 126 App. Div. 155. Conversely, where under order of court an infant's personalty is used in the purchase of land, his interest will be treated as personalty during his minority. Matter of Bolton, 159 N. Y. 129.

As to the effect of an option to purchase given by a decedent see Smith *v.* Loewenstein, 50 Ohio St. 346; Adams *v.* Peabody Coal Co., 230 Ill. 469; *In re* Isaacs, [1894] 3 Ch. 506; *In re* Pyle, [1895] 1 Ch. 724.

it is given. All such cases must be determined by their own facts and the construction of the instrument under which the trust exists.[1]

§ 449. A court of equity has authority to decree the conversion of a trust fund from personal to real estate, or, *vice versa*, where such conversion is not contrary to the will of the donor expressly or impliedly, and is for the interest of the *cestui*.[2] The general rule is, that where the testator gives his persona property, or the residue of his personal property, or the interest of his personal property,[3] in trust, or directly to several persons in succession,[4] and the property is of such a nature that it grows less valuable by time, as where it is leaseholds or annuities, or where the property is wasted or consumed in the use of it, the court implies an intention that such property shall be converted into a fixed and permanent form, so that the beneficiaries may take the use and income of it in succession. Accordingly, in England, such property is converted into the investments allowed by law; and in the United States it must be converted into safe investments, according to the rules in force in the State where the trust is to be administered; and if the trustees fail to do so in a reasonable time, they will be guilty of a breach of trust.[5]

§ 450. The court presumes an intention that perishable property shall be converted, where several persons are to enjoy it in succession; not so much from the actual fact of such an inten-

---

[1] Hidden v. Hidden, 103 Mass. 59.

[2] *Ex parte* Jordan, 4 Del. Ch. 615.

[3] Howe v. Dartmouth, 7 Ves. 137; Cranch v. Cranch (cited id. 142, 147; Litchfield v. Baker, 2 Beav. 481; Crowley v. Crowley, 7 Sim. 427; Sutherland v. Cook, 1 Col. C. C. 498; Johnson v. Johnson, 2 Col. C. C. 441); Fearns v. Young, 9 Ves. 549; Benn v. Dixon, 10 Sim. 636; Oakes v. Strachey, 13 Sim. 414. [*In re* Game, [1897] 1 Ch. 881; Blake v. O'Reilly, [1895] 1 Ir. R. 479; Porter v. Baddeley, 5 Ch. D. 542; Rowlls v. Bebb, [1900] 2 Ch. 107.]

[4] House v. Way, 12 Jur. 959.

[5] Bate v. Hooper, 5 De G., M. & G. 338; see *post*, Chap. XVII.   [1 Ames' Cases on Trusts (2d ed.), 491, note.]

tion, as from its being a convenient means of adjusting the rights of those who are to enjoy the property in succession. [1] (a) This presumption is made, unless a contrary intention is indicated upon the face of the will. The later authorities give effect to slighter indications than the older cases.[2] The object of the rule is to secure a fair adjustment of the rights of all the *cestuis que trust* in succession; for if the property would greatly depreciate in value in the hands of the first taker, the remainder-man might fail to receive the benefit intended to be given to him; the court, therefore, orders the perishable property to be converted into a permanent fund, unless a contrary intention is indicated in the will. So, if property, not liable to waste, but bearing a high rate of interest, and subject to great risk, is given to one person for life, and to another in remainder, the beneficiary in remainder may call for a conversion of the stocks or bonds into a less hazardous and more permanent investment, that their interests may be better protected; [3] but the court will not call in real securities without directing an inquiry whether it is necessary for the safety or benefit of all parties.[4] On the other hand, the court applies the same principles to the protection of the first taker or tenant for life; and so, if there are reversionary interests that may not fall in and become beneficial to the tenant for life, but may come into the possession of the

[1] Cape *v.* Bent, 5 Hare, 35; Pickering *v.* Pickering, 4 Myl. & Cr. 303; Hinves *v.* Hinves, 2 Hare, 611; Prendergast *v.* Prendergast, 3 H. L. Cas. 195; see Cotton *v.* Cotton, 14 Jur. 950.

[2] Morgan *v.* Morgan, 14 Beav. 82; Craig *v.* Wheeler, 29 L. J. Ch. 374; Mackie *v.* Mackie, 5 Hare, 77; Wightwick *v.* Lord, 6 H. L. Cas. 217; Blann *v.* Bell, 5 De G. & Sm. 658; 2 De G., M. & G. 775; Burton *v.* Mount, 2 De G. & Sm. 383; Howe *v.* Howe, 14 Jur. 359; 2 Spence, Eq. Jur. 42, 554.

[3] Thornton *v.* Ellis, 15 Beav. 193; Blann *v.* Bell, 5 De G. & Sm. 658; 2 De G., M. & G. 775; Wightwick *v.* Lord, 6 H. L. Cas. 217.

[4] Howe *v.* Dartmouth, 7 Ves. 150.

(a) Since the topic of this and the following section deals with the conflicting rights of life-beneficiary and remainder-men rather than with the actual conversion by the trustees, it seems best to confine the notes upon the topic to later sections which deal more particularly with the rights of life-beneficiaries and those entitled in remainder. *Infra*, § 548 *et seq.* and notes.

remainder-man, the court may order the reversions to be sold, and the purchase-money to be invested, so that the tenant for life may have the income for life.[1] And if the trustees have a discretion as to the time of sale, which the court cannot control, and they sell when the reversion falls in, the court will give the tenant for life the difference between the actual price for which the reversion sold, and its estimated value one year after the testator's death.[2] (a)

§ 451. (b) On the other hand, an intention may be implied from the form or terms of the gift, that the property is to be enjoyed by the *cestuis que trust in specie;* as, if there is a *specific gift* of leaseholds or of stocks, the specific legatee will take the rents and dividends of the specified property.[3] A general direction to pay rents to the tenant for life, after the mention of leaseholds, is a specific devise;[4] but it is still a matter of doubt upon the authorities, whether such a direction, unconnected with any mention of the leaseholds, is a specific devise or not.[5]

---

[1] Ibid.; Fearns *v.* Young, 9 Ves. 549; Dimes *v.* Scott, 4 Russ. 200. [Rowlls *v.* Bebb, [1900] 2 Ch. 107.]

[2] Wilkinson *v.* Duncan, 23 Beav. 469.

[3] Vincent *v.* Newcombe, Younge, 599; Lord *v.* Godfrey, 4 Madd. 455; Pickering *v.* Pickering, 4 Myl. & Cr. 299; Hubbard *v.* Young, 10 Beav. 205; Harris *v.* Poyner, 1 Dr. 181; Mills *v.* Mills, 7 Sim. 501; Dunbar *v.* Woodcock, 10 Leigh, 628; Harrison *v.* Foster, 9 Ala. 955; Hale *v.* Burrodale, 1 Eq. Ca. Ab. 461; Bracken *v.* Beatty, 1 Rep. in Ch. 110; Evans *v.* Iglehart, 6 G. & J. 171; Alcock *v.* Sloper, 2 Myl. & K. 702; Pickering *v.* Pickering, 2 Beav. 57.

[4] Blann *v.* Bell, 2 De G., M. & G. 775; Crowe *v.* Crisford, 17 Beav. 507; Hood *v.* Clapham, 19 Beav. 90; Marshall *v.* Brenner, 2 Sm. & Gif. 237; Elmore's Trusts, 6 Jur. (N. S.) 1325.

[5] Goodenough *v.* Tremamondo, 2 Beav. 512; Hunt *v.* Scott, 1 De G. &

(a) The equitable income is now reckoned as if the actual conversion had taken place at the date of the testator's death. Edwards *v.* Edwards, 183 Mass. 581; Kinmonth *v.* Brigham, 5 Allen, 270; *In re* Hill, 50 L. J. Ch. 551; *In re* Goodenough, [1895] 2 Ch. 537; Rowlls *v.* Bebb, [1900] 2 Ch. 107. As to this point and as to other questions regarding the adjustment of the rights of life beneficiary and remainder-man, see *infra,* § 548 *et seq.* and notes.

(b) See *infra,* § 548 *et seq.* and notes.

A mere direction to pay dividends is not a specific devise of the stocks.[1] But a bequest of the "interest, dividends, or income of all moneys or stock, and of all other property yielding income at the testator's death," has been held to be specific, and the trustees could not convert.[2] If the devise is specific, the direction to vary the securities will not affect the rights of a specific legatee, for such direction is only for the protection of the trust fund.[3] A debt due to a testator is not devised specifically, although it is embraced in the residue of an estate specifically devised, as it is in no sense in the nature of an investment, and is therefore to be converted.[4] And if a testator use any expression implying that leaseholds or stocks or other property are not to be converted, as if he names a time for the sale of them, as at or after the death of the tenant for life, the trustees will have no power to convert the property until the time arrives.[5] But where a testator gave to his wife the whole of the interest arising from his property, both real and personal, during her life, and at her decease to be disposed of as therein directed,

Sm. 219; Wearing v. Wearing, 23 Beav. 99; Pickup v. Atkinson, 4 Hare, 624; Craig v. Wheeler, 29 L. J. Ch. 374; Vachell v. Roberts, 32 Beav. 140; Harvey v. Harvey, 5 Beav. 134; Att. Gen. v. Potter, id. 164.

[1] Neville v. Fortescue, 16 Sim. 333; Blann v. Bell, 2 De G., M. & G. 775; Sutherland v. Cook, 1 Col. C. C. 503; Hood v. Clapham, 19 Beav. 90.

[2] Boys v. Boys, 28 Beav. 436.

[3] Lord v. Godfrey, 4 Madd. 455; Llewellyn's Trusts, 29 Beav. 171; Morgan v. Morgan, 14 Beav. 72.

[4] Holgate v. Jennings, 24 Beav. 630. There is some doubt upon the principles of this case.

[5] Collins v. Collins, 2 Myl. & K. 703; Vaughan v. Buck, 1 Phill. 78; Lichfield v. Baker, 13 Beav. 451; Harris v. Poyner, 1 Dr. 180; Chambers v. Chambers, 15 Sim. 190; Daniel v. Warren, 2 Y. & Col. Ch. 290; Rowe v. Rowe, 29 Beav. 276; Alcock v. Sloper, 2 Myl. & K. 699; Hind v. Selby, 22 Beav. 373; Bowden v. Bowden, 17 Sim. 65; Burton v. Mount, 2 De G. & Sm. 383; Skirving v. Williams, 24 Beav. 275; Hinves v. Hinves, 3 Hare, 609; Harvey v. Harvey, 5 Beav. 134; Bethune v. Kennedy, 1 Myl. & Cr. 114; Hunt v. Scott, 1 De G. & Sm. 219; Pickering v. Pickering, 2 Beav. 31; 4 Myl. & Cr. 289; Prendergast v. Prendergast, 3 H. L. Cas. 195; Hood v. Clapham, 19 Beav. 90; Neville v. Fortescue, 16 Sim. 333; Howe v. Howe, 14 Jur. 359.

it was held that the trustees must convert, as there was no indication that she should enjoy any of the property *in specie*.[1]

§ 452. After a trustee has reduced the trust fund to possession, and has secured the proper custody, and after he has converted so much of the property as was necessary to sell for money, his next duty is to invest the proceeds. It is one of the most important of the duties of trustees to invest the trust fund in such manner that it shall be safe, and yield a reasonable rate of income to the *cestui que trust*. If there are directions in the instrument of trust as to the time, manner, and kind of investment, the trustees must follow the direction and power so given them. The creator of a trust may specify the kind of investment and what security may be taken, or he may dispense with all security.[2] In the absence of such directions and powers, the trustees must be governed by the general rules of the court, or by the statutes and laws of the State in which the trust is to be executed. If there are no directions in the instrument, nor rules of court, nor statutory provisions in relation to investments, they must be governed by a sound discretion and *good faith*.[3] They must not have speculation in view, but rather a permanent investment, considering both the probable income and the probable safety of the capital.[4] A trustee should clearly indicate the investments he makes on behalf of the trust. If he invests apparently in his private capacity and after loss claims it was a trust transaction, he opens himself to suspicion of maladmin-

---

[1] Benn *v.* Dixon, 1 Phill. 76; Thornton *v.* Ellis, 15 Beav. 193; Morgan *v.* Morgan, 14 Beav. 92; Blann *v.* Bell, 2 De G., M. & G. 775; Hood *v.* Clapham, 19 Beav. 90; Lichfield *v.* Baker, 13 Beav. 481.

[2] Denike *v.* Harris, 84 N. Y. 89.

[3] As a general rule investments by executors and testamentary trustees, which take the funds beyond the jurisdiction of the court, will not be sustained, and the trustee makes such investments at the peril of being held responsible for the safety of investment. This rule is not inflexible, but the circumstances must be very unusual to justify the exception to it. Cruiston *v.* Olcott, 84 N. Y. 339.

[4] Emery *v.* Batchelder, 78 Me. 233. [Mattocks *v.* Moulton, 84 Me. 545; Hart's Estate, 203 Pa. St. 480; Matter of Hall, 164 N. Y. 196.]

istration.[1] A trustee ought not as a rule to invest in second mortgages.[2] Trustees ought to invest in government or State securities, or in bonds and mortgages on unincumbered real estate. The rule is not inflexible, but subject to the higher rule that the trustees are always to employ such care and diligence in the trust business as careful men of discretion and intelligence employ in their own affairs.[2] In Rhode Island, neither statute nor rule of court fixes any special class of investments for trust funds, and trustees are therefore only required to be prudent, having regard to the income and the permanence and safety of the investment.[4] Any loss occasioned by his negligence he must bear.[5] It is the duty of trustees having funds for investment to *keep* them invested, and if they retain trust-moneys uninvested beyond a reasonable time, six months being usually allowed, they are *prima facie* liable for interest.[6] Voluntary investments must not be made by a trustee beyond the jurisdiction of the court having charge of the trust, except in case of necessity for the saving of the fund. If he does so, the investment is at his peril of loss.[7] (a) Where a trustee invested in a confederate bond which perished on his hands, he was held not liable, having acted in good faith and with due discretion according to the

---

[1] State *v.* Roeper, 82 Mo. 57.   [White *v.* Sherman, 168 Ill. 589; *Re* Hodges' Estate, 66 Vt. 70; Estate of Cousins, 111 Cal. 441, 447; Coffin *v.* Bramlett, 42 Miss. 194.]

[2] Com'rs of Somerville *v.* Johnson, 36 N. J. Eq. 211; Tuttle *v.* Gilmore, id. 617.

[3] Mills *v.* Hoffman, 26 Hun, 594.

[4] Peckham *v.* Newton, 15 R. I. 321.

[5] Cogbill *v.* Boyd, 77 Va. 450.

[6] Lent *v.* Howard, 89 N. Y. 169. [Young's Estate, 97 Iowa, 218; Hetfield *v.* Debaud, 54 N. J. Eq. 371; Stambaugh's Estate, 135 Pa. St. 585; Whitecar's Estate, 147 Pa. St. 368.   But see *In re* Wiley, 91 N. Y. S. 661, 98 App. Div. 93.]

[7] Ormiston *v.* Olcott, 84 N. Y. 339. [McCullough *v.* McCullough, 44 N. J. Eq. 313; Pabst *v.* Goodrich, 133 Wis. 43.]

(a) In Massachusetts the court has expressed disapproval of such investments, but has declined to lay down any arbitrary rule against them. Thayer *v.* Dewey, 185 Mass. 68. See also Gouldey's Estate, 201 Pa. St. 491.

lights of the time of investing.[1] The test of liability is whether or no the trustees have acted as prudent men would have acted in the management of their own property.[2]

§ 453. There is one rule that is universally applicable to investments by trustees, and that rule is, that trustees cannot invest trust-moneys in personal securities. If trustees have a discretion as to the kind of investments, it is not a sound discretion to invest in personal securities.[3] Lord Hardwicke said, that "a promissory note is evidence of a debt, but no security for it." [4] Baron Hothman observed, that "lending on personal credit for the purpose of a larger interest was a species of gam-

---

[1] Waller v. Catlett, 83 Va. 200. [Finch v. Finch, 28 S. C. 164; Franklin v. McElroy, 99 Ga. 123; Baldy v. Hunter, 98 Ga. 170; 171 U. S. 388; compare Lamar v. Micou, 112 U. S. 452.]

[2] Godfrey v. Faulkner, 23 Ch. D. 483. [Rae v. Meek, 14 App. Cas. 558; Re Somerset, [1894] 1 Ch. 231; Dickinson, Appellant, 152 Mass. 184; Gilbert v. Kolb, 85 Md. 627; Mattocks v. Moulton, 84 Me. 545; Matter of Hall, 164 N. Y. 196; Hart's Estate, 203 Pa. St. 480; In re Allis's Estate, 123 Wis. 223; Pabst v. Goodrich, 133 Wis. 43.]

[3] Walker v. Symonds, 3 Swanst. 62; Darke v. Martin, 1 Beav. 525; Terry v. Terry, Pr. Ch. 273; Adye v. Feuilleteau, 1 Cox, 24; Vigrass v. Binfield, 3 Madd. 62; Harden v. Parsons, 1 Eden, 149, note (a); Anon. Lofft, 492; Keble v. Thompson, 3 Bro. Ch. 112; Wilkes v. Steward, G. Coop. 6; Clough v. Bond, 3 Myl. & Cr. 496; Pocock v. Reddington, 5 Ves. 799; Collis v. Collis, 2 Sim. 365; Blackwood v. Borrowes, 2 Conn. & Laws. 477; Watts v. Girdleston, 6 Beav. 188; Graves v. Strahan, 8 De G., M. & G. 291; Fowler v. Reynal, 3 Mac. & G. 500; Smith v. Smith, 4 Johns. Ch. 281; Nyce's Est., 5 Watts & S. 245; Soyer's App., 5 Penn. St. 377; Willes's App., 22 id. 330; Gray v. Fox, Saxton, Ch. 259; Harding v. Larned, 4 Allen, 426; Clark v. Garfield, 8 Allen, 427; Moore v. Hamilton, 4 Fla. 112; Spear v. Spear, 9 Rich. Eq. 184; Barney v. Saunders, 16 How. 545, 546. But see Knowlton v. Brady, 17 N. H. 458. Taking notes for a loan without security is negligence, and renders the trustee responsible if the debtor becomes insolvent. Judge of Probate v. Mathes, 60 N. H. 433. [Dufford v. Smith, 46 N. J. Eq. 216; In re Blauvelt's Estate, 20 N. Y. S. 119; Nobles v. Hogg, 36 S. C. 322; Baer's Appeal, 127 Pa. St. 360; Matter of Myers, 131 N. Y. 409; Simmons v. Oliver, 74 Wis. 633; In re Roach's Estate, 50 Or. 179. But see Hunt, Appellant, 141 Mass. 515, holding that a loan to a bank in good standing was prudent.]

[4] Walker v. Symonds, 3 Swanst. 81, note (a), citing Ryder v. Bickerton.

ing." [1] Lord Kenyon said, that "no rule was better established than that a trustee could not lend on mere personal security, and it *ought to be rung in the ears* of every one who acted in the character of trustee." [2] It makes no difference that there are several joint promisors; [3] nor that the loan is to a person to whom the testator loaned money on his personal promise; [4] nor will personal sureties justify the loan. [5] There must be express authority in the instrument of trust to authorize a loan on personal promises. [6] Loose, general expressions, leaving the nature of the investments to the trustees, will not justify such loans. [7] All the terms and conditions of a loan, to be made on personal security, must be strictly complied with; as, if a loan is authorized to a husband, upon the written consent of the wife, such consent must be had in the required form; [8] and a subsequent assent will not save the trustees from responsibility. [9] An authority to loan on personal security will not justify the trustees in lending to one of themselves; [10] nor will it justify them

---

[1] Adye *v.* Feuilleteau, 1 Cox, 25.

[2] Holmes *v.* Dring, 2 Cox, 1; Wynne *v.* Warren, 2 Heisk. 118; Dunn *v.* Dunn, 1 S. C. 350. A trustee, investing in personal securities, continues responsible for them after a transfer to his successor, until they are paid or legally invested. For those that are paid he is relieved from responsibility, although the money may never be received by the trust estate. *In re* Foster's Will, 15 Hun (N. Y.), 387.

[3] Ibid.; Clark *v.* Garfield, 8 Allen, 427.

[4] Styles *v.* Guy, 1 Mac. & G. 423. [Dufford *v.* Smith, 46 N. J. Eq. 216.]

[5] Watts *v.* Girdleston, 6 Beav. 188. [Simmons *v.* Oliver, 74 Wis. 633.]

[6] Forbes *v.* Ross, 2 Bro. Ch. 430; 2 Cox, 113; Child *v.* Child, 20 Beav. 50.

[7] Pocock *v.* Reddington, 5 Ves. 799; Wilkes *v.* Stewart, G. Coop. 6; Mills *v.* Osborne, 7 Sim. 30; Wynne *v.* Warren, 2 Heisk. 118. [See *infra*, § 460, note.]

[8] Cocker *v.* Quayle, 1 R. & M. 535; Pickard *v.* Anderson, L. R. 13 Eq. 608; Forbes *v.* Ross, 2 Bro. Ch. 430.

[9] Bateman *v.* Davis, 3 Madd. 98.

[10] Forbes *v.* Ross, 2 Bro. Ch. 430; 2 Cox, 113; —— *v.* Walker, 5 Russ. 7; Stickney *v.* Sewell, 1 Myl. & Cr. 814; Francis *v.* Francis, 5 De G., M. & G. 108; De Jarnette *v.* De Jarnette, 41 Ala. 708.

in lending to a relation, for the purpose of accommodating him.¹ (*a*)

§ 454. So, in the absence of express authority, the employ-ment of trust funds in trade or speculation, or in a manufacturing establishment, will be a gross breach of trust.² (*b*) However ad-vantageous such an investment may appear, the trustee invest-ing the funds in such undertakings will be compelled to make good all losses, and to account for and pay over all profits.³ (*c*)

¹ Ibid.; Langston *v.* Ollivant, G. Coop. 33; Cock *v.* Goodfellow, 10 Mod. 489; Fitzgerald *v.* Pringle, 2 Moll. 534.

² Munch *v.* Cockerell, 5 Myl. & Cr. 178; Kyle *v.* Barnett, 17 Ala. 306; Flagg *v.* Ely, 1 Edm. (N. Y.) 206; King *v.* Talbott, 40 N. Y. 96; 50 Barb. 453; Tucker *v.* State, 72 Ind. 242. [Warren *v.* Union Bank, 157 N. Y. 259, 268.] And parol request by testator to trustee to carry on the business for the benefit of his family is inadmissible to prove authority. Raynes *v.* Raynes, 51 N. H. 201.

³ French *v.* Hobson, 9 Ves. 103; Brown *v.* De Tastet, Jac. 284; Cook *v.* Collingridge, id. 607; Crawshay *v.* Collins, 15 Ves. 218; 2 Russ. 325; Feath-erstonhaugh *v.* Fenwick, 17 Ves. 298; Docker *v.* Somes, 2 Myl. & K. 655; Wedderburn *v.* Wedderburn, 2 Keen, 722; 4 Myl. & Cr. 41; Martin *v.* Ray-born, 42 Ala. 648.

(*a*) Authority to lend to a certain named partnership does not author-ize a loan to a partnership of the same name and conducting the same business after the death or retire-ment of one or more members. *In re* Tucker, [1894] 1 Ch. 724; Smith *v.* Patrick, [1901] App. Cas. 282.

Trustees having a power with the consent of the tenant for life, to lend on personal securities, may lend on such securities to the tenant for life himself if they are satisfied that the loan will be repaid. *In re* Laing's Settlement, [1899] 1 Ch. 593, con-troverting Lewin on Trusts, (10th ed.) 335. See 11th ed., 343.

(*b*) Thus a trustee properly hold-ing an investment in shares of a na-tional bank has no right to continue the investment in the business after the bank has surrendered its charter and the stockholders have voted to continue the business as a partner-ship. Penn *v.* Fogler, 182 Ill. 76. As to investment in shares of a business corporation, see *infra*, §§ 455, 456.

(*c*) He must make good not only all losses to the corpus of the trust fund, *Re* Massingberd's Settlement, 60 L. T. 620; *Re* Walker, 62 L. T. 449; Head *v.* Gould, [1898] 2 Ch. 250; but all losses of income, as well. Matter of Myers, 131 N. Y. 409; *In re* Harmon's Estate, 61 N. Y. S. 50, 45 App. Div. 196.

Ordinarily the gain on one un-authorized investment cannot be used to offset the loss on another, but if all the investments can be con-

The law discourages all such use of trust funds, by rendering it certain that the trustee shall make no profit from such investments, and that he shall be responsible for all losses. And if a trustee stands by, and sees his cotrustee employ the funds in that manner, he will be equally liable.[1] The same rule applies if the trustees simply continue the trade or business of the testator.[2] It is their duty to close up the trade, withdraw the fund, and invest it in proper securities at the earliest convenient moment; and the same rule applies although the trustees may have been the business agents or partners of the testator.[3] Nor will a power "to place out at interest, or other way of improvement," authorize the employment of the money in a trading concern.[4] In one case the direction was to "employ" the money, and it was thought that it savored of trade, and might be employed in that manner;[5] but it would not be safe for trustees to rely upon that case as an authority, even if their trust instrument contains a similar direction. If the settlor authorize his trustees to continue the fund in a trading firm, it will be a breach of trust, if the trustees allow the fund to remain after a change in the firm, as by the death or withdrawal of one of the partners.[6] If the

---

[1] Booth v. Booth, 1 Beav. 125; Ex parte Heaton, Buck. 386; Bates v. Underhill, 3 Redf. (N. Y.) 365. [Supra, § 415 and notes.]

[2] Ibid.; Kirkman v. Booth, 11 Beav. 273. In some cases, an executor is bound to complete the contracts of the testator. Collinson v. Lister, 20 Beav. 356.

[3] Wedderburn v. Wedderburn, 2 Keen, 722; 4 Myl. & Cr. 41. [In re Smith, [1896] 1 Ch. 171; Eufaula Nat. Bank v. Manasses, 124 Ala. 379.]

[4] Cock v. Goodfellow, 10 Mod. 489.

[5] Dickinson v. Player, C. P. Coop. 178 (1837, 1838).

[6] Cummins v. Cummins, 3 Jo. & Lat. 64; 8 Ir. Eq. 723. [Smith v. Pat-

sidered as parts of one transaction, the *cestui* will not be allowed to affirm those which are profitable and to disaffirm those which have resulted in a loss. English v. McIntyre, 51 N. Y. S. 697; In re Porter's Estate, 25 N. Y. S. 822. See In re Smith, 44 W. R. 270.

Where the life beneficiary has

shut himself out from objecting to the misuse of trust funds, as where he himself has used them up through the negligence of the trustee, the latter, although liable to replace the principal, is entitled to the income, even after the bankruptcy of the life beneficiary. Fletcher v. Collis, [1905] 2 Ch. 24.

trustees are directed to continue the testator's trade, they can invest none of his general assets in the business.   They are confined to the fund already embarked in the trade.[1]   If the trustees act in good faith in continuing the testator's business under such directions in a will, they will not be liable for any loss;[2] but they must act in good faith and without collusion or interested motives. So trustees are not bound to continue the capital in such trade, and they ought not to do so against their judgment.[3] But if all the *cestuis que trust* are *sui juris*, and capable of acting for themselves, and they desire an executor, administrator, or trustee to continue the business of the testator a few months, in order to preserve it for his son, and the executor acts in accordance with their request, and uses his best skill and judgment in the conduct of the trade, he will be allowed for the loss in his accounts.[4] (a)

§ 455. In England, trustees cannot invest the trust fund in the stock or shares of any bank or private or trading corpora-

rick, [1901] A. C. 282; *In re* Tucker, [1894] 1 Ch. 724; *Re* Webb, 63 L. T. 545.]

[1] McNeille *v.* Acton, 4 De G., M. & G. 563; 17 Jur. 104. And the court will keep separate the trade property, and apply it exclusively to the purposes of the trade. Owen *v.* Delamere, 15 Eq. Cas. 139; *Ex parte* Richardson, 3 Madd. 138; *Ex parte* Garland, 10 Ves. 120. [Gallagher *v.* Ferris, 7 L. R. Ir. 489; *In re* Johnson, 15 Ch. Div. 548.]

[2] Paddon *v.* Richardson, 7 De G., M. & G. 563. [*In re* Crowther, [1895] 2 Ch. 56.]

[3] Murray *v.* Glasse, 23 L. J. Ch. 124.

[4] Poole *v.* Munday, 103 Mass. 174.

(a) A power expressly given to trustees to postpone the sale of the testator's business as long as they should deem it expedient, carries with it by implication, authority to carry on the business on behalf of the trust. *In re* Crowther, [1895] 2 Ch. 56. In the cited case the trustees carried on the business for twenty-two years. See also Sand-

ers *v.* Houston Guano, etc., Co., 107 Ga. 49.

As to the remedies of trade creditors against the trustees and against the trust property where the trustee continues the business, see *infra*, § 815 *b* and note.

As to power of assignees for the benefit of creditors to continue the assignor's business, see *infra*, § 598, note.

tion; for the capital depends upon the management of the directors, and is subject to losses.[1] (a)   It is apparent, that a manufacturing or trading corporation may lose its whole capital in the prosecution of its business strictly within the terms of its charter.[2]   Lord Eldon said of bank stock, that "it is as safe, I trust and believe, as any government security; but it is not government security, and therefore this court does not lay out or leave property in bank stock, and what this court will decree it expects from trustees and executors."[3]   By Lord St. Leonards' Act, 22 & 23 Vict. 35, trustees, not forbidden by the instrument of trust, are authorized to invest in Bank of England or Ireland or East India stock.   This act was held not to authorize an investment in these stocks of trust funds settled before the passage of the act.[4]   By 23 & 24 Vict. c. 38, the original act was made retrospective, and the courts of chancery were authorized to issue general orders, from time to time, as to the investment of funds subject to its jurisdiction, either in three per cent consolidated or reduced, or new bank annuities, or in such other stocks, funds, or securities as the court shall think fit; and trustees, having power to invest trust funds in government securities, or upon railway stocks, funds, or securities, may invest in the stocks, funds, or securities which may be designated by the general order of the court.   In pursuance of the statute, a general order was issued in 1861, as follows: "Cash

---

[1] Haynes v. Reddington, 1 Jo. & Lat. 589; 7 Ir. Eq. 405; Clough v. Bond, 3 Myl. & Cr. 496; Powell v. Cleaver, 7 Ves. 142, n.

[2] Trafford v. Boehm, 3 Atk. 440; Mills v. Mills, 7 Sim. 501; Hancom v. Allen, 2 Dick. 499, n.; 7 Bro. P. C. 375; Emelie v. Emelie, id. 259; Peat v. Crane, 2 Dick. 499, n.; Clough v. Bond, 3 Myl. & Cr. 496.

[3] Howe v. Dartmouth, 7 Ves. 150; Band v. Fardell, 7 De G., M. & G. 633; King v. Talbott, 40 N. Y. 86.

[4] Re Miles's Will, 5 Jur. (N. S.) 1266; Dodson v. Sammell, 6 Jur. (N. S.) 137; 1 Dr. & Sm. 575. The Vice-Chancellor held the other way in Page v. Bennett, 2 Gif. 117; Simson's Trusts, 1 John. & H. 89; Mortimer v. Picton, 4 De G., J. & S. 166, 179. [See 56 and 57 Vict. c. 53.]

(a) A trustee's field of investment in England has been extended by statute. See Trustee Act of 1893, 56 and 57 Vict. c. 53, as interpreted by In re Smith, [1896] 2 Ch. 590.

under the control of the court may be invested in bank stock, East India stock, exchequer bills, and £2 10s. annuities, and upon freehold and.copyhold estates, respectively in England and Wales, as well as in consolidated £3 per cent annuities, reduced £3 per cent annuities, and new £3 per cent annuities." There are also provisions in the act by which trustees may apply to the court for leave to change their investments into those now allowed by the act and the court; but the act does not apply where the fund is settled specifically and there is no power of varying the securities.[1] Courts may give directions as to investments by trustees by decrees in particular suits, or by the promulgation of general orders or rules of court.[2] (a) It is said that the public policy in England of compelling trustees to invest trust funds in government funds originated largely in the necessities of the government, and the public advantage of creating a market and demand for government securities.[3]

§ 456. The English rule, in relation to investments of trust funds in bank stock and shares in trading and manufacturing corporations, prevails in New York and Pennsylvania.[4] It is agreed, that trustees cannot invest trust funds in trade, nor directly in manufacturing, nor in business generally, nor in personal securities, unless there is an authority contained in the instrument of trust. The reasoning is, that trustees cannot use the trust fund in carrying on a private manufacturing estab-

[1] Ward's Settlement, 2 John. & H. 191; *Ex parte* Great No. Ry. Co., L. R. 9 Eq. 274; *In re* Wilkinson, id. 343.

[2] Wheeler *v.* Perry, 18 N. H. 307. [Drake *v.* Crane, 127 Mo. 85.]

[3] Brown *v.* Wright, 39 Ga. 96.

[4] Ackerman *v.* Emott, 4 Barb. 626; Hemphill's App., 18 Penn. St. 303; Worrall's App., 22 id. 44; Morris *v.* Wallace, 3 id. 319; Nyce's Est., 5 Watts & S. 254. [See also White *v.* Sherman, 168 Ill. 589; Penn *v.* Fogler, 182 Ill. 76; *In re* Allis's Estate, 123 Wis. 223; Simmons *v.* Oliver, 74 Wis. 633.]

(a) But where the creator of the trust has directed that the funds be invested in a specified security and in no other, the court will not direct or authorize an investment in other securities, so long as the required investment is possible. Ovey *v.* Ovey, [1900] 2 Ch. 524.

lishment, nor in the business of private bankers, nor in under-
writing, nor in trade and commerce, and that there is no difference in principle between carrying on such enterprises themselves
with the trust fund, or lending it to other individuals to do so on
their personal security, and buying shares or stocks in such
business corporations carried on by other private individuals, or
by the trustees themselves, as officers or agents. Perhaps these
are the only States in which the strict English rule is holden.
In Maryland, investments in bank stock, gas stock, etc., are
good.[1] In Massachusetts, it is held that trustees may invest in
bank stocks, and in the shares of manufacturing and insurance
corporations,[2] or in the notes of individuals secured by such
stocks and shares as collateral securities,[3] or in certificates of deposit issued by a National Bank.[4] The court justifies this rule in
an elaborate opinion, affirming that such stocks are subject to no
greater fluctuations than government securities; that they are as
safe as real securities, which may depreciate in value, or the
title fail; that claims against such corporations can be enforced
at law,[5] while government funds can only be enforced by suppli-
cating the sovereign power; and that government securities have
hitherto been so limited in amount that it was impossible for the
trust funds of the country to be invested in that manner. The
last reason no longer exists. There are now national, state,
county, town, and city bonds in sufficient amounts to absorb all
trust funds seeking investment, and it is not to be denied that
such investments are more permanent and safe. It may be

[1] McCoy v. Horwitz, 62 Md. 183.
[2] Harvard Coll. v. Amory, 9 Pick. 446.
[3] Lovell v. Minot, 20 Pick. 116; Brown v. French, 125 Mass. 410.
[4] Hunt, Appellant, 141 Mass. 515, 523.
[5] It is said that loans by the city of Boston always command a higher
premium in the market than the loans of the Commonwealth. The difference in part is said to be that the city of Boston can be sued upon its
contracts, and a judgment against it can be satisfied by seizing, upon an
execution, any property of any citizen within the municipal limits; while
no suit can be maintained against the State, but everything depends upon
the good faith and honor of the legislature in supplying the means of
payment.

admitted, that great public emergencies and national dangers have an unfavorable effect upon the value of public securities; but such emergencies and dangers have the same effect upon the stocks of private corporations. In addition to these depressing influences, the capital of such companies runs the risks and chances of trade, business, and speculation. Calamities that depress public credit seldom occur, while the risks of trade are constant. It would seem to be the wiser course to withdraw the funds, settled for the support of women, children, and other parties who cannot exercise an active discretion in the protection of their interests, as much as possible from the chances of business. It may be said, that settlors may always do this by directing in what manner the funds settled by them shall be invested. But it would seem to be wiser for the court to establish the safest rule in the absence of special directions, and leave it to the settlor, if he prefers, to direct a less safe investment.[1]

[1] A large number of cases have been adjudged in the late confederate States, involving the legality of investments by trustees in the bonds and securities of the confederacy. No new principles have been so established that it is necessary to alter the text; but for convenience the principal cases are noted in this place. Under § 34 of the act of Nov. 9, 1861, of Alabama, which authorized trustees to invest in confederate bonds, or to receive payment in confederate notes, it was held that trustees were justified in making such investments previous to the re-establishment of the authority of the United States. Watson v. Stone, 40 Ala. 451; Dockey v. McDowell, 41 Ala. 476. But a guardian was held liable to account for the cash in full, who received payment in confederate notes after the re-establishment of such authority. Where a trustee procured an *ex parte* order to invest in confederate bonds, he was held liable for the loss. Snelling v. McCreary, 14 Rich. Eq. 291. Where a trustee received payment of a debt due to the trust fund, in the currency in common use, and reinvested it in securities which became worthless by the result of the war, he was not held liable for the loss. Campbell v. Miller, 38 Ga. 304. To the same effect is Brown v. Wright, 39 Ga. 96, which contains an able statement of the policy of the English government in directing trust funds to be invested in public securities.

In Virginia, commissioners who collected money by order of the court in confederate notes, and held a balance subject to contested liens until it became worthless, were held not liable for the loss. Davis v. Harman, 21 Grat. 200. And substantially the same rule was held in Dixon v. McCue, 21 Grat. 374. In Morgan v. Otey, 21 Grat. 619, it was held that payments

§ 457. The power to lend on mortgage was doubted or denied, until Lord St. Leonards' act, unless there was an express power in the instrument of trust, or a decree of the court. Lord Harcourt, Lord Hardwicke, and Lord Alvanley appeared to have thought that a trustee or executor might invest the money in *well-secured real estates*.[1] But Lord Thurlow said, that in *latter* times the court had considered it improper to invest any part of

should be made in the currency of the day. See Kraken *v.* Shields, 20 Grat. 377. In Walker *v.* Page, 21 Grat. 637, it was held that a sale of infant's lands for confederate money was valid at the time it was made, and that further development of events did not vitiate it. In Myers *v.* Zetelle, 21 Grat. 733, it was held that an agent or trustee who in *good faith* sold property, and invested the proceeds in confederate securities, at a time when no other investments were open to him, was protected from loss. And see Bird *v.* Bird, 21 Grat. 711; Beery *v.* Irick, 22 Grat. 614; Campbell *v.* Campbell, id. 649; Colrane *v.* Worrel, 30 Grat. 434.

In State *v.* Simpson, 65 N. C. 497, it was held that a guardian who collected in money which was well secured to his ward, and invested the same in confederate bonds, was guilty of *laches*, and was liable for the loss. See Alexander *v.* Summey, 66 N. C. 578. An agent or trustee is authorized to receive payment of debts in the currency received by prudent business men for similar purposes. Baird *v.* Hall, 67 N. C. 230. See Wooten *v.* Sherrard, 68 N. C. 334.

In Creighton *v.* Pringle, 3 S. C. 78, a trustee was held guilty of a breach of trust in investing in confederate bonds. Cureton *v.* Watson, 3 S. C. 451. But see Hinton *v.* Kennedy, id. 459.

If a trustee, acting in *good faith*, receive funds in bank-notes which are depreciated, he will be protected if such notes were the only money attainable. Barker *v.* McAuley, 4 Heisk. 424.

When a trustee kept the identical money received by him, he was allowed to turn it over to the person entitled to receive it, without loss to himself; but if he has not kept it, he will be charged with the nominal sums collected by him. Saunders *v.* Gregory, 3 Heisk. 507.

In Texas, trustees could not receive confederate money in discharge of obligations to them. Turner *v.* Turner, 36 Tex. 41. And see Scott *v.* Atchison, id. 76; Kleberg *v.* Bond, 31 Tex. 611; Woods *v.* Toombs, 36 Tex. 85; Turpin *v.* Sanson, id. 142; McGar *v.* Nixon, id. 289; Lacey *v.* Clements, id. 661.

In the Supreme Court of the United States payment to an agent or trustee in anything but lawful money of the United States, or bank-notes of the current value of their face, is held invalid. Ward *v.* Smith, 7 Wall. 451; Horn *v.* Lockhart, 17 Wall. 570; McBurney *v.* Carson, 99 U. S. 567.

[1] Brown *v.* Litton, 1 P. Wms. 141; Lyse *v.* Kingdon, 1 Coll. 188; Knight *v.* Plymouth, 1 Dick. 126; Pocock *v.* Reddington, 5 Ves. 800.

a lunatic's estate upon private security.[1] Sir John Leach refused
to allow an infant's money to be invested in that manner, and
expressed surprise that any precedent could be found to the
contrary.[2] In a late case, the trustees invested in mortgages at
the request of the tenant for life, and to procure a higher rate
of interest, and they were held liable for the loss; but the case
did not go to the full extent of deciding that trustees could not
invest on *real securities*, for the reason that they had consulted
the interests of the tenant for life, at the expense of those of the
remainder-man, but the court did not favor mortgages.[3] If
trustees are directed to invest in public funds, of course they
cannot invest in mortgages.[4] Previous to the acts before mentioned,[5] courts did not sanction mortgages;[6] but the practice is
now relaxed, and a loan upon freeholds of inheritance to the
extent of two-thirds of their value may be allowed.[7] But the
rule of two-thirds is not inflexible. It may be improper to loan
even two-thirds of the present value; as, where the value depends
upon the chances of trade or business, and where the property
consists of houses liable to deterioration.[8] So it may not be a
breach of trust under certain circumstances to loan more than
two-thirds.[9] (a) Trustees ought not to lend on a second mort-

[1] *Ex parte* Calthorpe, 1 Cox, 182; *Ex parte* Ellice, Jac. 234.

[2] Norbury *v.* Norbury, 4 Madd. 191; Widdowson *v.* Duck, 2 Mer. 494;
Ex parte Fust, 1 C. P. Coop. (t. Cott.) 157, n. (e); *Ex parte* Franklyn, 1
De G. & Sm. 531; *Ex parte* Johnson, 1 Moll. 128; *Ex parte* Ridgway, 1
Hog. 309.

[3] Raby *v.* Ridehalgh, 7 De G., M. & G. 108.

[4] Pride *v.* Fooks, 2 Beav. 430; Waring *v.* Waring, 3 Ir. Ch. 331.

[5] *Ante*, § 455.

[6] Barry *v.* Marriott, 2 De G. & Sm. 491; *Ex parte* Franklyn, 1 De G.
& Sm. 531.

[7] Stickney *v.* Sewell, 1 Myl. & Cr. 8; Norris *v.* Wright, 14 Beav. 307;
Macleod *v.* Annesly, 16 Beav. 600.

[8] Ibid.; Phillipson *v.* Gatty, 7 Hare, 16; Drosier *v.* Brereton, 15 Beav.
221; Stretton *v.* Ashmall, 3 Dr. 9; 3 De G. 26; 24 L. J. Ch. 277; Farrar *v.*
Barraclough, 2 Sm. & Gif. 231. [Rae *v.* Meek, 14 A. C. 558.]

[9] Jones *v.* Lewis, 3 De G. & Sm. 471. This case was reversed on appeal.
See Lewin on Trusts, 263 (5th ed.).

(a) In some States statutes have
provided that the real estate must be
at least double the amount of the
mortgage. N. H. Pub. St. (1901), c.

gage, though it might not be a breach of trust in all cases to do so;[1] and so they ought to have a power of sale inserted in the deed, although it might not be a breach of trust to neglect it.[2]

§ 458. There can be no doubt that mortgages on real estate are considered proper investments in the United States, and perhaps they are the only investments which are not objection-

[1] Norris v. Wright, 14 Beav. 291; Drosier v. Brereton, 15 Beav. 221; Robinson v. Robinson, 11 Beav. 371; 1 De G., M. & G. 247; Waring v. Waring, 3 Ir. Eq. 337; Lockhart v. Reilly, 1 De G. & J. 476; Nance v. Nance, 1 S. C. 209. [In re Blauvelt's Estate, 20 N. Y. S. 119; Taft v. Smith, 186 Mass. 31.]

[2] Farrar v. Barraclough, 2 Sm. & Gif. 231.

198, § 11, c. 178, § 9; N. J. Laws of 1899, ch. 103. Mr. Loring states that this is the usual margin of security required. Loring's Trustee's Handbook, (3d ed.) p. 116. See 1 Ames, Cases on Trusts, (2d ed.) 485, n. By statute in New York the value of the real estate must exceed the amount of the mortgage by at least 50 per cent, IV N. Y. Consol. Laws (1909), p. 2847, § 21. In In re Somerset, [1894] 1 Ch. 231, Kekewich, J., referring to Speight v. Gaunt, 9 A. C. 1, and Learoyd v. Whiteley, 12 id. 727, said in substance: When there is no actual breach of trust, trustees are simply judged by the rule that they are to exercise ordinary care and prudence in the discharge of their duties. Their liability, as regards any particular transaction, is not increased by reason of the fact that one of their number is skilled in the business with which the transaction is concerned. As regards investments in mortgages, it is the duty of the trustees to decide for themselves, and to exercise their own judgment,

as to the sufficiency of the securities, even though a surveyor, solicitor, or other trusted agent, has expressed to them his opinion on the subject. There is no absolute rule respecting the choice of securities falling within the strict limits of authorized investments, or the amount proper to be advanced against any particular security. In this case it was said to be wrong for the trustee to advance a sum largely in excess of what was otherwise right because it was believed that the mortgagor was personally good for the loan.

In Learoyd v. Whiteley, 12 App. Cas. 727, 733, and in In re Salmon, 42 Ch. Div. 351, 367, the court, without attempting to lay down any fixed rule, expressed the opinion that where the mortgage security is agricultural land the margin of value should not be less than one-third the value of the land, and where the land derives its value from buildings erected on it or from use in trade, the margin of value should not be less than one-half.

able in some one of the States. In the absence of public funds to an amount hitherto sufficient to absorb the money to be invested by trustees, different rules have been established in the several States, but mortgages upon estates of inheritance, taken with proper caution as to the amount and the title, have been named in all the States as proper and safe investments; so that the question in the United States is whether the security is in fact what it is called, security upon real estate. A loan to a company owning coal lands and a canal, to a much greater value than its debts, the interest on the loan being a preferred claim upon the income, was held to be substantially on real estate;[1] but an investment in the stock of a similar company, which stock was not preferred, was held to be a breach of trust.[2] An investment in railway bonds, secured by a mortgage of the road-bed, franchise, and other property, is not real security, though real estate is covered by the mortgage; for the method of enforcing such a bond is very different from the ordinary manner of foreclosing a mortgage, and whether such a bond can be enforced at all depends upon the concurrent will of so many bondholders, that, at best, it is only nominal real estate.[3] London Dock stock and sewer bonds are not real security.[4] It is not a breach of trust to leave funds in turnpike bonds, secured by a mortgage of the tolls and real estate of the company, as they had been invested by the testator.[5] Under the right of the trustees to invest trust funds in real securities, they cannot convert the funds into real estate by taking the legal title absolutely to themselves in trust; and if they do so, the *cestui que*

[1] Twaddell's App., 5 Penn. St. 15.

[2] Worrall's App., 21 Penn. St. 508.

[3] Mant *v.* Leith, 15 Beav. 524; Allen *v.* Gaillard, 3 S. C. 279. It is not sufficient for a trustee to say, in defence of an investment, that it is on real security. There are other things to be considered, the nature of the property and other matters. The property, though sufficient, may be involved in litigation. *Per* Master of Rolls in Mant *v.* Leith. [See Clark *v.* Anderson, 13 Bush, (Ky.) 111, 119.]

[4] Robinson *v.* Robinson, 11 Beav. 371.

[5] Robinson *v.* Robinson, 21 L. J. Ch. 111; 1 De G., M. & G. 247; Miller *v.* Proctor, 20 Ohio St. 444.

trust may elect to take the land, or the trust-money and inter-est;[1] though a direction to invest in *productive real estate* was held to justify the purchase of dwelling-houses, or the purchase of a right of dower in order to render the property more pro-ductive.[2] If a testator has already invested in mortgages, a trustee may make such further advances of money as are neces-sary to secure the first investment. No general rule can be stated; but the trustee in such case must make a careful investi-gation and exercise a sound discretion, or his advances will not be allowed in case of a loss.[3] And so a guardian, in case of a grave emergency, may buy in land for the minor to save a cer-tain loss;[4] so an administrator may buy in the land of a debtor to his estate to save the debt.[5] (a) Such an investment is a mere temporary expedient, and is to be treated as personal estate.[6] A loan of trust funds on real mortgage does not change

[1] Mathews *v.* Heyward, 2 S. C. 239; Ouseley *v.* Anstruther, 10 Beav. 456; Royer's App., 11 Pa. St. 36; Kaufman *v.* Crawford, 9 Watts & S. 131; Bonsall's App., 1 Rawle, 273; Bellington's App., 3 Rawle, 55; Ringgold *v.* Ringgold, 1 H. & G. 11; Morton *v.* Adams, 1 Strob. Eq. 72; Heth *v.* Rich-mond, &c., Co., 4 Grat. 482; Eckford *v.* De Kay, 8 Paige, 89; Winchelsea *v.* Nordcliffe, 1 Vern. 134. And if a mortgage is given back, the mortgagor, if he have notice of the misapplication of the trust fund, cannot enforce his mortgage until the fund has first been replaced. Mathews *v.* Heyward, 2 S. C. 239.

[2] Parsons *v.* Winslow, 16 Mass. 368.

[3] Collinson *v.* Lister, 20 Beav. 356.

[4] Bonsall's App., 1 Rawle, 273; Royer's App., 11 Penn. St. 36.

[5] Bellington's App., 3 Rawle, 55.

[6] Oeslager *v.* Fisher, 2 Penn. St. 467.

(a) A trustee with no authority to purchase land may be authorized by court to buy in on foreclosing a mortgage investment where this course is necessary to protect the trust estate from loss. *In re* Bellah, 8 Del. Ch. 59; *In re* Baker, 8 Del. Ch. 355.

It has been held that a trustee who was directed to hold and invest a certain fund of personalty as a re-serve fund to guard against losses by shrinkage in value of certain trust real estate, had authority to contrib-ute over $20,000, from the fund, by way of donation towards the build-ing of a hotel on neighboring prop-erty when the effect of having the hotel there was to increase greatly the value of the trust real estate. Drake *v.* Crane, 127 Mo. 85. But this seems to be an exceptional case.

the character of the funds, nor constitute an investment in real estate.[1] The court may order an investment of accumulations, or of the principal fund temporarily in real estate, with a declaration that it shall continue personalty;[2] and so a court may order an investment in real estate generally, where no other way is pointed out in the trust instrument.[3] Where a trustee or guardian is obliged to take land subject to a mortgage, the trustee becomes personally liable to pay off the mortgage, to protect the interest of the *cestui que trust*. In such case, the guardian or trustee may have the possession of the estate or the management of the trust fund, in order to secure himself for the advancement so made.[4] But there must be an urgent necessity to justify such a proceeding. If a trustee is authorized to invest in real estate, stock, or securities, he cannot mortgage the trust fund in order to raise money to invest in such manner, nor invest in machinery for the use of the *cestui que trust*.[5] (a) In all cases the trustee ought to exercise high diligence in ascertaining the valuation, situation, condition, and productiveness of the real estate or other property upon which it is proposed to make a loan of the trust-money; for he will be liable for the loss if he is guilty of any negligence in this respect.[6]

§ 459. In a few States, there are statutes authorizing trustees to invest in a particular manner, and excusing them from respon-

[1] Milhous *v.* Dunham, 78 Ala. 48.

[2] Webb *v.* Shaftesbury, 6 Madd. 100.

[3] *Ex parte* Calmes, 1 Hill, Eq. 112.

[4] Woodward's App., 38 Penn. St. 322.

[5] Rider *v.* Sisson, 7 R. I. 341. [See **Warren** *v.* **Pazolt**, 203 Mass. 328, 349, 351.]

[6] Budge *v.* Gummon, L. R. 7 Ch. 721; Smethurst *v.* Hastings, 30 Ch. D. 490; Olive *v.* Westerman, 34 Ch. D. 70; Whiteley *v.* Learoyd, 33 Ch. D. 347. [Gilbert *v.* Kolb, 85 Md. 627; *In re* Roach's Estate, 50 Or. 179.]

(a) It has been held that a trustee who has been authorized to invest in real estate but who has been given no express power of mortgage, may give back a valid mortgage for part of the purchase price. Hannah *v.* Carnahan, 65 Mich. 601. A second mortgage given by the trustee subsequently for an advance of money was held to be void. Ibid.

sibility if their investments are made in good faith in the prescribed securities. (*a*)   Thus in Pennsylvania,[1] an executor,
guardian, or trustee may apply to the Orphans' Court, and the
court may direct an investment in the stocks or public debt of
the United States, of the State, or of the city of Philadelphia, or
in real securities, or in the stock of the incorporated districts of
Philadelphia County, of Pittsburg and Alleghany, and the water-
works of Kensington, Philadelphia County.   But it has been held
that trustees are not confined to these funds; that the acts are
for their benefit; that they can elect other kinds of investment,
but will be responsible for losses.[2]   In New York, there does not
appear to be any legislation on the subject; but trustees are
bound by the rules of the court to invest in real securities, or
government bonds, or in the State loan, or in loans of the New
York Life Insurance and Trust Company.[3]   (*b*)   In New Jersey,
a statute authorized an investment to be made upon an application to the court, but does not establish any particular
funds.   (*c*)   In Gray *v.* Fox, the court laid down the rule that
investments must be made in government stocks, or in real
security.[4]   In Maryland, there is neither statute nor rule of

[1] Acts 1832, 1838, 1850, 1852.   [Brightly's Purdon's Dig. of Pa. St.
(1894), p. 593, §§ 121, 122, 123; Pa. Const. § 69.]

[2] Barton's Est., 1 Pars. Eq. 24; Worrall's App., 9 Barr, 108; Twaddell's
App., 5 Penn. St. 15.

[3] Ackerman *v.* Emott, 4 Barb. 626; and see Smith *v.* Smith, 4 Johns.
Ch. 281, 445; King *v.* Talbott, 40 N. Y. 86, 97.   This case contains a full
discussion of the law in New York. Hun *v.* Cary, 82 N. Y. 65.

[4] Gray *v.* Fox, Saxton, 259; Lathrop *v.* Smalley, 23 N. J. Eq. 192; Corliss *v.* Corliss, id.

(*a*) See these statutes collected
in Loring's Trustee's Handbook (3d
ed.), 117; 1 Ames on Trusts (2d ed.),
486, n.; and 9 L. R. A. 279, 280, n.;
Clark *v.* Beers, 61 Conn. 87.

(*b*) For legislation in New York,
see IV Consol. Laws (1909), p. 2847,
§ 21; I id. p. 155, § 146.

(*c*) By Laws of New Jersey, 1899,
c. 103, trustees are authorized to
investment in mortgages on security of real estate worth twice the
amount loaned, bearing interest between 3% and 6%, in bonds of the
United States and of the State of
New Jersey, and in certain municipal bonds. By Laws of 1903, c. 146,
the field of investment is extended
to include securities authorized for
savings banks.

court to guide the trustees. The courts do not approve of changes in investments, unless express power is given in the instrument of trust; as where a testator gave certain stocks in trust without direction to vary the security, and the trustee disposed of the stocks and invested the money in other securities, he was ordered to replace the entire sum in the same stocks, although the number of shares were increased by the change.[1] In Maine, New Hampshire, (a) Vermont, Michigan, and Missouri, the courts may, upon application, direct trustees as to the manner of investment, but no special investments are pointed out.[2] If trustees invest according to the direction of the courts, they are not responsible for any loss. In Georgia, if trustees invest in the stocks, bonds, or other securities, issued by their own State, or in such other securities as shall be ordered by the court, they will be exempt from loss.[3] In Mississippi, an investment in bank stocks is allowed.[4] In States where there are no statutes nor rules of court regulating investments, trustees are bound to act in good faith and with a sound discretion in investing trust-

[1] Murray v. Feinour, 2 Md. Ch. 418; Evans v. Iglehart, 6 Gill & J. 192; Gray v. Lynch, 8 Gill, 405; Hammond v. Hammond, 2 Bland, 306. [See Hunt v. Gontrum, 80 Md. 64; Lowe v. Convention, 83 Md. 409.]

[2] Knowlton v. Brady, 17 N. H. 458. It is impossible to cite the statutes of all the States. Practising attorneys will of course know the legislation of their own States.

[3] [Ga. Code, (1895) § 3180. Any other investment must be under order of the court, or else at the risk of the trustee.] Brown v. Wright, 39 Ga. 96.

[4] Smyth v. Burns, 25 Miss. 422. These rules and regulations are established for the protection of trustees: so long as they in good faith confine their investments to those allowed by law, they are protected from loss. Stanley's App., 8 Penn. St. 432; Twaddell's App., 9 id. 108; Seidler's Est., 5 Phila. 85; Barton's Est., 1 Pars. Eq. 24; Johnson's App., 43 Penn. St. 431; Morris v. Wallace, 3 id. 319; McCahan's App., 7 id. 56; Hemphill's App., 18 id. 303; Rush's Est., 12 id. 378; Nyce's Est., 5 Watts & S. 254.

(a) In New Hampshire a statute prescribes investment in mortgages upon security of real estate worth at least double the amount of the loan, or in savings banks incorporated in New Hampshire, or in banks of the United States, of the State of New Hampshire, or of certain municipal corporations. N. H. Pub. St. [1901], c. 198, § 11; c. 178, § 9. See also c. 178, § 8.

money; and if they so act they are not responsible for any loss that may happen.[1] (a)   But to invest in mere personal securities is not a sound discretion anywhere.[2] Nor is it a sound discretion for trustees to subscribe trust funds to new enterprises, as for the stock of new manufacturing, insurance, or railroad corporations, when the undertaking must, in the nature of things, be experimental; and it will not excuse the trustee that he subscribes his own money to such enterprises, as it is permitted to him to speculate with his own money if he sees fit.[3]

[1] Clark v. Garfield, 8 Allen, 427. [Peckham v. Newton, 15 R. I. 321; Emery v. Batchelder, 78 Me. 233; Massey v. Stout, 4 Del. Ch. 274, 288. See also Citizens' Nat. Bank v. Jefferson, 88 Ky. 651, 659; Durrett's Guardian v. Commonwealth, 90 Ky. 312.]

[2] Ante, § 453.

[3] Kimball v. Reading, 31 N. H. 352; Ihmsen's App., 43 Penn. St. 471.

(a) The Massachusetts rule, as laid down in Harvard College v. Amory, 9 Pick. 446, and followed in many subsequent decisions, is that trustees should "observe how men of prudence, discretion, and intelligence manage their own affairs, not in regard to speculation, but in regard to the permanent disposition of their funds, considering the probable income, as well as the probable safety of the capital invested." Thayer v. Dewey, 185 Mass. 68; Taft v. Smith, 186 Mass. 31; Green v. Crapo, 181 Mass. 55; Pine v. White, 175 Mass. 585, 590. In applying the rule, in Dickinson, Appellant, 152 Mass. 184, 187, the court said: "A trustee, whose duty it is to keep the trust fund safely invested in productive property, ought not to hazard the safety of the property under any temptation to make extraordinary profits. Our cases, however, show that trustees in this Commonwealth are permitted to invest portions of trust funds in dividend-paying stock and interest-bearing bonds, of private business corporations, when the corporations have acquired, by reason of the amount of their property, and the prudent management of their affairs, such a reputation that cautious and intelligent persons commonly invest their own money in such stocks and bonds as permanent investments." In this case the trustees having invested about $3500, between one-fourth and one-fifth of the total trust fund, in the stock of the Union Pacific Railroad in 1881, then a comparatively new road running largely through an unsettled country, invested $2500 of the funds in the same stock. The last investment was held not a prudent investment, although the first investment was allowed. An important consideration with the court seems to have been that so large a proportion of the trust fund was put into this somewhat risky investment. For a similar decision on very similar facts, see Davis, Appellant, 183 Mass. 499. See also Warren v. Pazolt, 203 Mass. 328, 345 et seq.

§ 460. The instrument of trust frequently contains directions respecting the investment of the trust funds. If the directions are so general that they do not point to any particular class or classes of investments, the trustees must invest in those securities that are sanctioned by the court; as, if the trust is to invest in "good and sufficient security," the court will sanction no security not allowed by its rules and orders.[1] If the trustee is to invest at his "discretion," he cannot invest in personal securities.[2] (a) The powers and directions given in the instrument

[Randolph v. E. Birmingham Land Co., 104 Ala. 355; Aydelott v. Breeding, 111 Ky. 847; Matter of Hall, 164 N. Y. 196; Mattocks v. Moulton, 84 Me. 545.]

[1] Booth v. Booth, 1 Beav. 125; Trafford v. Boehm, 3 Atk. 440; De Manneville v. Crompton, 1 V. & B. 259; Wilkes v. Steward, Coop. 6; Ryder v. Bickerton, 3 Swanst. 80, n.; Nance v. Nance, 1 S. C. 209; Womack v. Austin, id. 421. [Clark v. Clark, 50 N. Y. S. 1041; Caspari v. Cutcheon, 110 Mich. 86.]

[2] Ibid.; Pocock v. Reddington, 5 Ves. 794; Wormley v. Wormley, 8 Wheat. 421; 1 Brock. 339; Langston v. Ollivant, Coop. 33.

(a) The creator of the trust may extend the field of investments into which the trustee may properly put the trust money, either by designating certain investments or by general words. Bartol's Estate, 182 Pa. St. 407; In re Allis's Estate, 123 Wis. 223; In re Smith, [1896] 1 Ch. 71. But unless the language of the trust instrument is mandatory, a trustee making investments within the extended field is not relieved from the responsibility of exercising the care and prudence which a reasonable man would exercise in making permanent investments for the purpose of insuring a steady income. Gilbert v. Kolb, 85 Md. 627; Rae v. Meek, 14 App. Cas. 558; Hutton v. Annan, [1898] A. C. 289; In re Turner, [1897] 1 Ch. 536; In re Sharp, 45 Ch. Div. 286, 289.

A trustee who has been expressly directed or authorized by the trust instrument to invest at his discretion, or as he may think proper or best, must exercise the care and prudence usual with investors who are seeking to place their funds where they will be reasonably sure of the ultimate return of their principal and of a reasonable rate of income. He must not speculate for the purpose of increasing the principal nor invest in hazardous enterprises or upon security of speculative value for the purpose of getting an extra large income. His duty is to be measured by the usual conduct of a man of ordinary prudence making permanent investments of his own savings outside of ordinary business risks. Hart's Estate, 203 Pa. St. 480; In re Allis's Estate, 123 Wis. 223; Pabst v. Goodrich, 133 Wis. 43; Matter of Hall, 164 N. Y. 196; Mattocks v.

must be strictly followed;[1] thus a power to invest in bank stocks or lots of land will not authorize an investment in the loan of

[1] Wood v. Wood, 5 Paige, 596; Burrill v. Sheil, 2 Barb. 457; Womack v. Austin, 1 S. C. 421; Sanders v. Rogers, id. 452; Ihmsen's App., 43 Penn. St. 471.

Moulton, 84 Me. 545. In States where the field of investments proper for trustees is fixed by statute or by rule of court, the effect of giving a trustee discretion in the choice of investments is to give him practically the same authority that trustees usually have under the Massachusetts rule without such an express authorization. Matter of Hall, 164 N. Y. 196.

An authority to trustees to invest in such "securities as may in their judgment be best" does not relieve them of the duty of investigating as to the safety of the particular investment into which they put the funds. Hart's Estate, 203 Pa. St. 480. It is not a reasonable exercise of their discretion to risk the trust funds in the stock of a new enterprise, Matter of Hall, 164 N. Y. 196; Mattocks v. Moulton, 84 Me. 545 ; or in a mortgage upon security which proper investigation would have shown to be insufficient in value, Gilbert v. Kolb, 85 Md. 627; or upon security of property of a speculative value. Rae v. Meek, 14 App. Cas. 558; In re Harmon's Estate, 61 N. Y. S. 50, 45 App. Div. 196. Nor can they properly expend trust funds in the opening and operation of mines in leasehold mining property which was part of the original trust property, Shinn's Estate, 166 Pa. St. 121; or in the purchase of mining lands. Butler v. Butler, 164 Ill. 171.

In jurisdictions which follow the

Massachusetts rule as to investments generally by trustees, words in the trust instrument expressly authorizing the trustee to invest according to his discretion do not usually change his duty of prudence and watchfulness for the safety of both principal and income. Mattocks v. Moulton, 84 Me. 545; Davis, Appellant, 183 Mass. 499, 502. As to whether a discretion in the choice of investments will pass to a surviving trustee or to a substituted trustee, see infra, § 505,note a.

A trustee's acceptance for himself of a commission from the corporation in whose shares he invests trust funds is inconsistent with an honest exercise of judgment, and renders him liable to account to the trust for the commission or bribe and also to make good any loss upon the investment. In re Smith, [1896] 1 Ch. 71. In the cited case an innocent cotrustee who did not know of the commission and honestly considered the investment a good one, was held not to be liable.

A direction to invest in such "securities" as the executors "may think proper," has been held not to authorize investment in shares, not fully paid up, of an unincorporated bank. Murphy v. Doyle, 29 L. R. Ir. 333; In re Kavanagh, 27 L. R. Ir. 495. The decision in the cited cases was based partly at least upon the finding that these shares were not "securities" within the meaning

the United States.[1] A power to loan on *real securities* does not justify a loan upon railroad bonds secured by mortgage of the road;[2] nor does a power to loan upon mortgage authorize an investment in railroad mortgage bonds.[3] A power to invest in "good and sufficient securities in Virginia and Maryland," authorizes a loan upon town securities.[4] A direction to invest "in any public stocks or securities bearing an interest," embraces a coal and navigation company, that being within the popular meaning of the testator.[5] If there is a direction to invest trust funds in real securities in a foreign jurisdiction, the court will allow the investment;[6] but if no such power is given, such investment will not be allowed.[7] Where trustees were authorized in their discretion to invest in a dwelling-house for the daughter of the testator, and she was married and went to reside in a foreign jurisdiction, it was held, that they might invest in a dwelling-

---

[1] Banister *v.* McKenzie, 6 Munf. 447.

[2] Mortimore *v.* Mortimore, 4 De G. & J. 472; Mant *v.* Leith, 15 Beav. 525; Harris *v.* Harris, 29 Beav. 107; King *v.* Talbott, 50 Barb. 453; 40 N. Y. 86; Allen *v.* Gaillard, 1 S. C. 279; Bromley *v.* Kelly, 39 L. J. Ch. 274.

[3] Ibid.

[4] McCall *v.* Peachy, 3 Munf. 288. But if such securities are greatly depreciated, it would be a breach of trust to invest in them. Trustees, &c., *v.* Clay, 2 B. Mon. 386.

[5] Rush's Est., 12 Penn. St. 375. See Hemphill's App., 18 Penn. St. 303.

[6] Burrill *v.* Sheil, 2 Barb. 457.

[7] Rush's App., 12 Penn. St. 375. [McCullough *v.* McCullough, 44 N. J. Eq. 313; Pabst *v.* Goodrich, 133 Wis. 43. In Massachusetts the court has expressed disapproval of such investments, but has declined to lay down any arbitrary rule against them. Thayer *v.* Dewey, 185 Mass. 68. See also Gouldey's Estate, 201 Pa. St. 491.]

---

of the trust instrument. But it has been held in a later English decision that the word "securities" used in the will of a general broker was intended to include shares of stock in corporations. *In re* Rayner, [1904] 1 Ch. 176.

Under the English Judicial Trustees Act of 1896 (59 and 60 Vict., c. 35), § 3, a trustee who seeks relief for loss on investments which are in breach of trust has the burden of proof to show that he acted, not only honestly, but also reasonably. *In re* Stuart, [1897] 2 Ch. 583; *In re* Turner, [1897] 1 Ch. 536; *Re* Barker, 46 W. R. 296.

house at the place of her residence, although it was in a foreign jurisdiction.[1] But where they were authorized to invest in bonds, debentures, or other securities, or the stocks or funds of any colony or foreign country, they were not allowed to invest in railway bonds, though guaranteed by a foreign government.[2] As before stated, all these powers are strictly construed; as, if the trustees are authorized to loan £3000 on personal securities, and they lend £5000, it is a breach of trust;[3] and if the power is to loan on bond, they cannot loan on a promissory note.[4] If the trustees may loan the trust fund to the husband, with the consent of the wife, they cannot allow the loan to continue if the husband becomes bankrupt; and they will be guilty of a breach of trust, if they do not use due diligence in calling in the loan, or in collecting such dividends as may be coming. An entire change of circumstances may change their duty, although the wife may still desire that her husband should have the use of the money.[5] Generally, where the trustees are required to invest the fund in a particular manner, with the approbation of any person, such requirement becomes imperative upon the request of such person.[6] So, if any formalities are prescribed as to the investment, they must be strictly complied with; as, where the written consent of a wife is a prerequisite to a loan to her husband, a verbal consent will not relieve the trustees from the consequences of a breach of trust, if they act on such verbal consent.[7] A subsequent consent is not sufficient where a previous consent was contemplated;[8] nor is it enough for a wife to join the husband in a petition for an order that a loan be made

[1] Amory v. Green, 13 Allen, 413.

[2] In re Langdale's Settlement, Trust, L. R. 10 Eq. 39.

[3] Payne v. Collier, 1 Ves. Jr. 170.

[4] Greenwood v. Wakeford, 1 Beav. 576.

[5] Wiles v. Gresham, 2 Drew. 258; 24 L. J. Ch. 264; Langston v. Ollivant, Coop. 33; and see Boss v. Goodsall, 1 N. C. C. 617; Burt v. Ingram, Lewin on Trusts, 339 (4th ed.).

[6] Cadogan v. Essex, 2 Dr. 227; McIntire v. Zanesville, 17 Ohio St. 352.

[7] Cocker v. Quayle, 1 R. & M. 535; Hopkins v. Myall, 2 R. & M. 86; Kellaway v. Johnson, 5 Beav. 319.

[8] Bateman v. Davis, 3 Madd. 98; Adams v. Broke, 1 N. C. C. 627.

to him.[1] If the trustees go beyond the prescribed limits, neither good faith nor care nor diligence, if they can accompany a departure from the direction of the instrument of trust, will protect them if a loss occurs.[2] If it is impossible for them to invest according to the directions, they must invest in the securities prescribed by the law or by the court, or in the safest class of securities.[3]

§ 461. A direction to invest in good freehold security must be strictly complied with;[4] (a) an authority to invest in ground rents authorizes an investment in redeemable ground rents, that being the kind of ground rent in the place where the investment is to be made;[5] a power to invest in good private security does not authorize the trustees to use the funds themselves.[6] Where stock is settled on a husband and wife for life, with remainder to the children, with a power to vary the securities for greater interest, the trustees cannot purchase an annuity for one of the tenants for life.[7] If, however, the existing securities are unsafe, and it is proper to call in the money and reinvest it, trustees may make a temporary investment in safe funds until an investment can be advantageously made in the securities directed by the testator.[8] If the direction is to invest in land or any other

[1] Norris v. Wright, 14 Beav. 291; Fitzgerald v. Pringle, 2 Moll. 534; Dunne v. Dunne, 1 S. C. 350.

[2] Ackerman v. Emott, 4 Barb. 626; Spring's App., 71 Penn. St. 11; Ringgold v. Ringgold, 1 H. & G. 25; Cloud v. Bond, 3 Myl. & Cr. 490.

[3] McIntire v. Zanesville, 17 Ohio, 352.

[4] Wyatt v. Wallace, 8 Jur. 117; 1 Coop. 155, n.

[5] Ex parte Huff, 2 Barr, 227.

[6] Westover v. Chapman, 1 Col. C. C. 177; Forbes v. Ross, 2 Bro. Ch. 430; 2 Cox, 113; ante, § 453.

[7] Fitzgerald v. Pringle, 2 Moll. 534.

[8] Sowerby v. Clayton, 3 Hare, 430; 8 Jur. 597; Mathews v. Brice, 6 Beav. 329; Ex parte Chaplin, 3 Y. & C. 397; Knott v. Cottee, 6 Beav. 77; Brownley v. Kelly, 39 L. J. Ch. 272.

(a) Thus authority to purchase freeholds does not include the purchase of an equity of redemption. Worman v. Worman, 43 Ch. Div. 296.

security, it will be implied that the settlor intended the investment to be made in land if it could be done advantageously, and
the alternative part of the direction is to be followed only in
case an investment cannot be made in land; and this construction will be followed unless there is some other controlling consideration in the instrument.[1]   And if trustees are authorized to
lend on mortgage to *three persons*, they cannot lend to *two* of
them, although they get the entire interest in the estate; nor can
they lend to the *three* without the mortgage at the time, although
they get the security in two years after.   It is no excuse to say
that the delay did not occasion the loss.   The conclusive answer
is, that they committed a breach of trust in not obeying the
power, and they must make good the loss.[2]   And so trustees
cannot let money on a mortgage to one of themselves.[3]   Under
a power to loan on mortgage they may continue existing mortgages, if safe.[4]

§ 462.   A trustee must invest the trust funds in his hands, in
the manner directed, within a *reasonable time*, although no direction is given in the deed or will as to the time or manner of
investment.   If he neglects for an unreasonable time to make
the investment, he may be charged with interest; and if any
loss or damage occurs to the *cestui que trust* from the delay, the
trustee must make it up.[5]   What is a reasonable time depends

[1] Earlom *v.* Saunders, Amb. 340; Cookson *v.* Reay, 5 Beav. 32; Cowley *v.* Hartstonge, 1 Dow, 361; Hereford *v.* Ravenhill, 5 Beav. 51; Fowler
v. Reynal, 3 Mac. & G. 500; 2 De G. & Sm. 749.

[2] Earlom *v.* Saunders, Amb. 340; Cookson *v.* Reay, 5 Beav. 32; Cowley *v.* Hartstonge, 1 Dow, 361; Hereford *v.* Ravenhill, 5 Beav. 51; Fowler
v. Reynal, 3 Mac. & G. 500; 2 De G. & Sm. 749.

[3] Stickney *v.* Sewall, 1 Myl. & Cr. 8; —— *v.* Walker, 5 Russ. 7; Fletcher
v. Green, 33 Beav. 426; Francis *v.* Francis, 5 De G., M. & G. 108; Crosskill
v. Bower, 32 Beav. 86; De Jarnette *v.* De Jarnette, 41 Ala. 708.

[4] Angerstein *v.* Martin, T. & R. 239; Ames *v.* Parkinson, 7 Beav. 379.

[5] Lyse *v.* Kingdom, 1 Coll. 184; Bates *v.* Scales, 12 Ves. 402; Ryder *v.*
Bickerton, 3 Swanst. 80; Trafford *v.* Boehm, 3 Atk. 440; Lomax *v.* Pendleton, 3 Call, 538; Garniss *v.* Gardner, 1 Edw. Ch. 128; Schieffelin *v.* Stewart,
1 Johns. Ch. 620; Chase *v.* Lockerman, 11 G. & J. 185; Armstrong *v.* Miller,
6 Ham. 118; Handly *v.* Snodgrass, 9 Leigh, 484; Aston's Est., 5 Whart.

upon circumstances. When the trustees were directed to invest in the purchase of land with *all convenient speed*, a year was held to be a reasonable time.[1] But where the trustees are directed to invest in *freehold securities*, they will not be charged with interest until it has been shown that they could have invested according to the direction; for it is not always practicable to procure such securities.[2] So a year from the testator's death was considered a reasonable time within which to make an investment in United States stock.[3] On the other hand, the Supreme Court of the United States allowed three months as a reasonable time within which to invest capital sums of a trust fund paid in to a banker, and charged the trustee for the sum lost by the failure of the banker after that time.[4] In other cases, six months have been allowed as a reasonable time within which to invest trust funds; and trustees have been charged with interest when they kept the money uninvested for a longer time.[5] But where the trustees make no effort to invest the money, they may be charged with interest from a period earlier than six months.[6] Where a trustee or executor is directed to invest a legacy *immediately in stock*, and he retains the sum for the period of one year or more, or for an unreasonable time, and the price of the stock rises, he will be ordered to purchase as

228; *In re* Thorp, Davies, 290; Shipp *v.* Hettrick, 63 N. C. 329; Owen *v.* Peebles, 42 Ala. 338. [Stambaugh's Estate, 135 Pa. St. 585; Whitecar's Estate, 147 Pa. St. 368; Hetfield *v.* Debaud, 54 N. J. Eq. 371; Young's Estate, 97 Iowa, 218. But see *In re* Wiley, 91 N. Y. S. 661, 98 App. Div. 93.]

[1] Parry *v.* Warrington, 6 Madd. 155; Johnson *v.* Newton, 11 Hare, 160.

[2] Wyatt *v.* Wallis, 1 Coop. 154, n.; 8 Jur. 117.

[3] Cogswell *v.* Cogswell, 2 Edw. Ch. 231. This was in analogy to the payment of legacies, which may be done in one year; a trustee with ready money ought to invest with more promptness.

[4] Barney *v.* Saunders, 16 How. 543.

[5] Dunscomb *v.* Dunscomb, 1 Johns. Ch. 508; Manning *v.* Manning, id. 527; Merrick's Est., 2 Ash. 485; Worrall's App., 23 Penn. St. 44; Armstrong *v.* Walkup, 12 Grat. 608; Hooper *v.* Savage, 1 Munf. 119; Frey *v.* Frey, 2 C. E. Green, 72.

[6] Ringgold *v.* Ringgold, 1 H. & G. 11; Witmer's App., 87 Penn. St. 120. Two months not an unreasonable allowance of time for reinvestment.

much stock as could have been purchased at the time the fund ought to have been invested.[1] Where trustees were directed to invest in the funds, and they paid the money into a banker's with directions to invest in bank annuities, which the banker neglected to do, and the trustees made no inquiry for five months, they were held, after the failure of the banker, for the money or the stock at the option of the *cestui que trust*.[2] Trustees and guardians are held to a stricter rule in relation to investments than executors acting as trustees, for trustees and guardians generally take an estate ready to be invested; and trustees will be held to a stricter rule in relation to capital sums, than in relation to current income from interest, dividends, rents, and other smaller sums; thus in Barney *v.* Saunders,[3] before cited, three months were held as a reasonable time within which trustees ought to have invested capital sums paid into the banker's, and they were held responsible for the loss of capital after that time by the failure of the banker, while they were not held liable to replace small sums paid into the same banker's from the rents, interest, and dividends upon the same estate. An executor will not in general be charged with interest for not investing before the expiration of a year from the testator's death.[4] A year is a reasonable time within which an executor may call in the testator's estate and pay off his liabilities; and it is necessary, during that time, that the executor

---

[1] Byrchall *v.* Bradford, 6 Madd. 235; Pride *v.* Fooks, 2 Beav. 430; Watts *v.* Girdlestone, 6 Beav. 188; Clough *v.* Bond, 3 Myl. & Cr. 496; Robinson *v.* Robinson, 1 De G., M. & G. 256; Phillipson *v.* Gatty, 7 Hare, 516. [See *Re* Massingberd's Settlement, 60 L. T. 620; *Re* Walker, 62 L. T. 449.]

[2] Challen *v.* Shippam, 4 Hare, 555.

[3] Barney *v.* Saunders, 16 How. 545; Lomax *v.* Pendleton, 3 Call, 538.

[4] But where it is the duty of executors within a reasonable time to separate a legacy from the estate, and to invest it to accumulate, or for the support and maintenance of the legatee, neglect to do so makes them chargeable with legal interest; and they will not be allowed to limit their liability by showing the rate of interest received upon the general fund, nor be excused by the fact that it was for the interest of the residuary legatee to have the funds kept together. Fowler *v.* Colt, 25 N. J. Eq. 202. [See Dick's Estate, 183 Pa. St. 647.]

should keep the money on hand. In most States an executor is allowed that time by statute; and he is exempt from suit by creditors during that year. After that time, if an executor keeps money in his hands without any apparent reason, except for the purpose of using it, it becomes a breach of trust or negligence; and the court may charge him with interest, or with the principal sum if lost.[1] So an executor will be charged with interest during the year, if he receives interest by loaning or using the money.[2]

§ 463. Trustees ought not to mix trust-money with other moneys, and take a joint mortgage for the whole, for this would be to complicate the trust with the rights of strangers; (a) nor should a mortgage in such case be taken in the name of a common trustee, for that would be a delegation of the rights of the trustee;[3] but where the trust fund was very small, it was held to be proper for a trustee to put some of his own money with it in order to loan it to the best advantage on a mortgage.[4] (b) Trustees must personally see to it that the security

[1] Forbes v. Ross, 2 Cox, 115; Flanagan v. Nolan, 1 Moll. 85; Moyle v. Moyle, 2 R. & M. 710; Johnson v. Newton, 11 Hare, 160; Hughes v. Empson, 22 Beav. 181; Johnston v. Prendergast, 28 Beav. 480; Williamson v. Williamson, 6 Paige, 300; Dillard v. Tomlinson, 1 Munf. 183; Carter v. Cutting, 5 Munf. 224; Minuse v. Cox, 5 Johns. Ch. 441; Cogswell v. Cogswell, 2 Edw. Ch. 231. [Young's Estate, 97 Iowa, 218; *In re* Estate of Danforth, 66 Mo. App. 586, 590.]

[2] Lund v. Lund, 41 N. H. 359; Stearns v. Brown, 1 Pick. 530; Wyman v. Hubbard, 13 Mass. 232; Griswold v. Chandler, 5 N. H. 499; Mathes v. Bennett, 21 N. H. 199; Wendell v. French, 19 N. H. 205; Chambers v. Kerns, 6 Jones, Eq. 280. [Westover v. Carman's Estate, 49 Neb. 397; Matter of Myers, 131 N. Y. 409; Dorris v. Miller, 105 Iowa, 564.]

[3] Lewin on Trusts, 268.

[4] Graves's App., 50 Penn. St. 189.

(a) Trustees should not ordinarily mingle funds of different trusts in one investment, even though the different trusts were established by the same will. McCullough v. McCullough, 44 N. J. Eq. 313, 316.

(b) But he should take the mortgage as trustee, not in his individual name. Re Hodges' Estate, 66 Vt. 70. See Dunn v. Dunn, 137 N. C. 533.

is forthcoming upon parting with the money;[1] as, where they allowed their solicitors to receive the money upon representations that the mortgage was ready, and there was no mortgage, and the solicitors misapplied the money, the trustees were held to make up the loss.[2] When the money is paid in to a banker or broker for investment, the trustees must see that the investment is made at once, and the securities taken in the proper form, or they will be liable for any loss that may happen;[3] or where money is suffered to remain in the hands of third persons unnecessarily, and a loss happens, the trustees must make it up.[4] So, if the trustee pays the money into a bank in his own name, and not in the name of the trust, he will be responsible for the money in case of the failure of the bank.[5] But as between the trustee, his representatives, and the *cestui que trust* the *cestui que trust* may follow the money into the hands of the banker. If it is a simple account, not complicated by mixture with deposits of the trustee's own moneys and withdrawals, it is a simple debt which the *cestui que trust* may claim to be held and applied to the trust; but the deposit of the trustee's own money, and the withdrawal of part by checks, will not defeat the right of the *cestui que trust*. (a) If anything of the trust fund remains in the hands of the banker under this rule, it will be applied to

---

[1] Cogbill *v.* Boyd, 77 Va. 450. [Key *v.* Hughes's Ex'rs, 32 W. Va. 184.]

[2] Rowland *v.* Witherden, 3 Mac. & G. 568; Hanbury *v.* Kirkland, 3 Sim. 265; Broadhurst *v.* Balguy, 1 N. & C. Ch. 16; Ghost *v.* Waller, 9 Beav. 497; 13 Beav. 336.

[3] Challen *v.* Shippam, 4 Hare, 555; Byrne *v.* Norcott, 13 Beav. 336. [Key *v.* Hughes's Ex'rs, 32 W. Va. 184.]

[4] Barney *v.* Saunders, 16 How. 543; Anon. Lofft, 492; Fletcher *v.* Walker, 3 Madd. 73; Moyle *v.* Moyle, 2 R. & M. 701; Macdonnell *v.*Harding, 7 Sim. 178; Massey *v.* Banner, 4 Madd. 419; 1 J. & W. 241; Lowry *v.* Fulton, 9 Sim. 115; Mathews *v.* Brice, 6 Beav. 239; Munch *v.* Cockerell, 9 Sim. 115; Johnson *v.* Newton, 11 Hare, 160.

[5] Ibid.; Wren *v.* Kirton, 11 Ves. 377; Pennell *v.* Deffell, 4 De G., M. & G. 392; *Ex parte* Hilliard, 1 Ves. Jr. 89; Rocke *v.* Hart, 11 Ves. 61; Freeman *v.* Fairlee, 3 Mer. 39; Jenkins *v.* Walter, 8 G. & J. 218; Luken's App., 7 Watts & S. 48; Stanley's App., 8 Penn. St. 131; Royer's App., 11 id. 36. [Coffin *v.* Bramlitt, 42 Miss. 194. See *supra*, § 443.]

(a) See *infra*, § 828, note.

the purposes of the trust.[1] This is a rule for the protection of the *cestui que trust* in case of the failure or bankruptcy of the trustee. But it does not affect the general rule before stated, that where a trustee deposits the trust-money in his own name, or mixes the money with his own, he must pay interest for it, and be responsible for the principal, in case of the failure of the banker or of any other loss.[2]

§ 464. Trustees cannot use trust-moneys in their business, nor embark i tin any trade or speculation;[3] nor can they disguise the employment of the money in their business, under the pretence of a loan to one of themselves,[4] nor to a partnership of which they are members;[5] nor can the money be loaned on security to be reloaned back to the trustee, or by the trustee at

---

[1] Pennell *v.* Deffell, 4 De G., M. & G. 392; Frith *v.* Cortland, 2 Hem. & M. 417; 34 L. J. Ch. 301; Kip *v.* Bank of N. Y. 10 Johns. 65; Kennedy *v.* Strong, id. 289; School, &c., *v.* Kirwin, 25 Ill. 73; McAllister *v.* Commonwealth, 30 Penn. St. 536; Morrison *v.* Kinstra, 55 Miss. 71.

[2] Mumford *v.* Murray, 6 Johns. Ch. 1; Kellett *v.* Rathbun, 4 Paige, 102; Jacot *v.* Emmett, 11 Paige, 142; De Peyster *v.* Clarkson, 2 Wend. 77; Garniss *v.* Gardner, 1 Edw. Ch. 128; Spear *v.* Tinkham, 2 Barb. Ch. 211; Merrick's Est., 2 Ash. 485; Dyott's Est., 2 Watts & S. 565; Beverleys *v.* Miller, 6 Munf. 99; Diffenderffer *v.* Winder, 3 G. & J. 341; Peyton *v.* Smith, 2 Dev. & B. Eq. 325; Jameson *v.* Shelly, 2 Humph. 198; Kerr *v.* Laird, 27 Miss. 544; *In re* Thorp, Davies, 290.

[3] Tebbs *v.* Carpenter, 1 Madd. 304; Lee *v.* Lee, 2 Vern. 548; Adye *v.* Feuilleteau, 1 Cox, 24; Piety *v.* Stace, 4 Ves. 622; Docker *v.* Somes, 2 Myl. & K. 655; Palmer *v.* Mitchel, id. 672, n.; Miller *v.* Beverleys, 4 Hem. & M. 415; *In re* Thorp, Davies, 290; Manning *v.* Manning, 1 Johns. Ch. 527; Brown *v.* Ricketts, 4 Johns. Ch. 303. At one time it was held that executors might employ money in their trade, especially if they were solvent, and if the assets were generally, and not specifically, bequeathed. Grosvesnor *v.* Cartwright, 2 Ch. Cas. 212; Linch *v.* Cappey, id. 35; Brown *v.* Litton, 1 P. Wms. 140; Ratcliffe *v.* Graves, 2 Ch. Cas. 152; Bromfield *v.* Wytherly, Pr. Ch. 505; Adams *v.* Gale, 2 Atk. 106; Child *v.* Gibson, id. 603; but Mr. Lewin says that Lord North overruled above forty cases, and a twenty years' practice, in Ratcliffe *v.* Graves, 1 Vern. 196; Newton *v.* Bennett, 1 Bro. Ch. 361; Adye *v.* Feuilleteau, 1 Cox, 25; Lewin on Trusts, 255, 276. [St. Paul Trust Co. *v.* Kittson, 62 Minn. 408. See *supra*, § 429, n.]

[4] Townend *v.* Townend, 1 Gif. 201.

[5] Kyle *v.* Barnett, 17 Ala. 306. [Matter of Myers, 131 N. Y. 409.]

a profit.[1]   If a trustee makes such use of the money, he will be
responsible for all loss, and he may be compelled to pay the
highest rate of interest; (a) or the *cestui que trust* may follow
the money, and insist upon all the profits made by such use; and
if the trustee is a trader or business man, he will be presumed to
use and employ the money in his business if he deposits it
in bank in his own name; for such business men must generally
keep some money in bank for the purposes of their credit, and
such trust-money answers the purpose as if it was their own.[2]
If the trust fund is employed in business, the whole increase
will belong to the fund; but if the trustee is also one of the
beneficiaries, he will be entitled to his share, and it will go to
his representatives upon his death.[3]   Where an executor bought
stock in his own name with the trust fund, and the stock rose
in price, it was held that he was liable for the market-price of
the stock at the time of the decree.   If the investment is profitable, the *cestuis que trust* are entitled to the profits; if disastrous,
they are entitled to interest on the money; and if the investment
has been made with funds of the estate mingled with funds of
the executor in various stocks, and the funds of the estate cannot be traced and identified in any particular stocks, the *cestuis que trust* are entitled to select the most profitable stocks.[4]

§ 465.   There is said to be a distinction between an original
investment improperly made by trustees, and an investment

[1] Ratcliffe *v.* Graves, 2 Ch. Cas. 152; 1 Vern. 196.
[2] Treves *v.* Townshend, 1 Bro. Ch. 284; Moons *v.* De Bernales, 1 Russ.
301; *In re* Hilliard, 1 Ves. Jr. 90; Sutton *v.* Sharp, 1 Russ. 146; Rocke *v.*
Hart, 11 Ves. 61; Brown *v.* Southhouse, 3 Bro. Ch. 107; Lamb's App., 58
Penn. St. 142. [See also *supra*, § 429, note.]
[3] Hook *v.* Dyer, 47 Mo. 24.
[4] Norris's App., 71 Penn. St. 106. [See *In re* Oatway, [1903] 2 Ch.
356; City of Lincoln *v.* Morrison, 64 Neb. 822; Putnam *v.* Lincoln Safe Dep.
Co., 104 N. Y. S. 4; 118 App. Div. 468; Bromley *v.* Cleveland, etc., R. Co.,
103 Wis. 562. As to what is sufficient identification of the trust funds, see
infra, § 828, and note (a).]

(a) As to a trustee's use of trust   sulting liability, see *supra*, § 429,
funds in his own business and his re-   note.

made by the testator himself, and simply continued by a trustee;[1] but it is a distinction that cannot be safely acted upon. If a testator gives any directions in his will to continue his investments already made, trustees must of course follow such directions; and if they follow them in good faith, they will not be liable for any losses, unless they are negligent in failing to change an investment, when it ought to be changed to save it; (a) for it cannot be supposed that the direction of a testator to continue a certain investment relieves the trustees from the ordinary duty of watching such investment, and of calling it in when there is imminent danger of its loss by a change of circumstances. If no directions are given in a will as to the conversion and investment of the trust-property, trustees to be safe should take care to invest the property in the securities pointed out by the law. It is true that a testator during his life may deal with his property according to his pleasure, and investments made by him are some evidence that he had confidence in that class of investments; but, in the absence of directions in the will, it is more reasonable to suppose that a testator intended that his trustees should act according to law. Con-

---

[1] Powell v. Evans, 5 Ves. 841; Clough v. Bond, 3 Myl. & Cr. 496; Harvard Col. v. Amory, 9 Pick. 446; Thompson v. Brown, 4 Johns. Ch. 628; Knight v. Plymouth, 3 Atk. 480; 1 Dick. 120; Rowth v. Howell, 3 Ves. 565; Wilkinson v. Stafford, 1 Ves. Jr. 41; Vez v. Emery, 5 Ves. 144; Barton's Est., 1 Pars. Eq. 24; Murray v. Feinour, 2 Md. Ch. 418; Brown v. Campbell, Hopkins, 233; Smith v. Smith, 4 Johns. Ch. 283; See 11 Amer. Law Reg. 208 (N. S.), April, 1874; Pierce v. Bowker, 130 Mass. 262, where a trustee in good faith continued an investment in railroad stock originally made by his testator, until, gradually falling in value, it became worthless.

(a) Where a testator has authorized his executors to continue his own investments, it has been held that they have no authority to carry on margin purchases of stocks which the testator had made before his death, since such a venture is not an investment, but a speculation. Matter of Hirsch, 116 N. Y. App. Div. 367 (affirmed 188 N. Y. 584).

Where a testator by express words authorized, but did not require, three trustees to continue certain investments which they would not, under the law or under any direction in the will, have had authority to make, it was held that any one of the three could bring about a sale of the investments against the wishes of the other two. Re Roth, 74 L. T. 50.

sequently, in States where the investments which trustees may make are pointed out by law, the fact that the testator has invested his property in certain stocks, or loaned it on personal security, will not authorize trustees to continue such investments beyond a reasonable time for conversion and investment in regular securities.[1] But in States where there are no fixed funds or securities in which trustees shall invest, the fact that a testator has invested his property in particular stocks, shares of corporations, mortgages, or other securities, thus indicating his confidence in such investments, will go far to justify the trustees in continuing them.[2] So trustees, in the usual course of dealing, may take notes on short time for small sums of rent due their estate, that having been the usual course of dealing with the tenants by the testator.[3] Taking all the cases together, it would appear to be a settled principle that trustees are not justified, in the absence of express or implied directions in the will, in continuing an investment permanently, made by the testator, which they would not be justified themselves in making. (a) The principle probably has this qualification, that if a

[1] Hemphill's App., 18 Penn. St. 303; Pray's App., 34 id. 100, overrules the case of Barton's Est., 1 Pars. Eq. 24; Kimball v. Reading, 11 Foster, 352. [Babbitt v. Fidelity Tr. Co., 72 N. J. Eq. 745.]

[2] Harvard Coll. v. Amory, 9 Pick. 446. [Peckham v. Newton, 15 R. I. 321.]

[3] Smith v. Smith, 4 Johns. Ch. 283.

(a) In Connecticut, trustees are authorized by statute to continue investments made by the creator of the trust, unless otherwise ordered by the court, so long as in the exercise of reasonable prudence they deem a change unnecessary, even when the investment is not within the class authorized by law for trustees. Conn. Gen. St. (1902), § 255; Beardsley v. Bridgeport, etc., Asylum, 76 Conn. 560. For a similar provision see N. J. Laws of 1899, ch. 103; Babbitt v. Fidelity Trust Co., 72 N. J. Eq. 745.

The rule that a trustee must convert and reinvest the proceeds of investments which are not in the class authorized by law does not apply to a trust created by a voluntary declaration of trust by way of gift, the donor making himself trustee. Thus where in New York an owner of shares of stock in a national bank made a voluntary declaration of trust without consideration for

trustee continue such investment in good faith, and a loss happens, he would be held to replace the original sum only, without interest.[1]

§ 466. Except upon emergency, to protect the fund from depreciation, or to convert wasting securities to those of a permanent character, or investments in securities that are not authorized by law into such as are allowed, trustees may not sell or vary specific securities given in trust, nor securities left by a testator in which he has himself invested the funds.[2] (a)

---

[1] Lowson v. Copeland, 2 Bro. Ch. 157; Tebbs v. Carpenter, 1 Madd. 298.

[2] Angell v. Dawson, 2 Y. & C. 316; Flyer v. Flyer, 3 Beav. 550; Neville v. Fortescue, 16 Sim. 333; Boys v. Boys, 28 Beav. 436; Murray v. Feinour, 2 Md. Ch. 418; Ward v. Kitchen, 30 N. J. Eq. 31; Crackelt v. Bethune, 1 Jac. & W. 566; Witter v. Witter, 3 P. Wms. 100; Hammond v. Hammond, 2 Bland, 306. But where the trustee has performed, without authority, an act which, at the time it was done, was obviously for the benefit of all concerned, and which upon proper application would have been ordered, his act will be ratified, and held of the same validity as if previously ordered. Gray v. Lynch, 8 Gill, 405. Where trustees under a will exceeded their power by buying real estate with trust funds, and continued to buy and sell, at first with a profit, but ultimately with a loss of a large part of the fund, no lack of good faith being found, they were held liable for the amount of the trust fund before the first purchase of real estate only, with interest from the time the beneficiary should have received the income. Baker v. Disbrow, 3 Redf. (N. Y.) 348. [See Massey v. Stout, 4 Del. Ch. 274, 288; Emery v. Batchelder, 78 Me. 233.]

---

the benefit of his children, and the bank afterwards became insolvent, it was held that the trustee was not personally liable to make good the loss suffered by the *cestuis.* Fowler v. Gowing, 152 Fed. 801.

(a) Trustees usually have implied, if not express, authority to change trust investments whenever the safety of the trust fund or good management requires. Citizens' Nat. Bank v. Jefferson, 88 Ky. 651; Hays v. Applegate, 101 Ky. 22. But see Branch v. De Wolf, 28 R. I. 542. And even when a trustee has no authority to change investments, it is part of his duty to apply to court for authority when the safety of the trust fund requires that a change be made. Johns v. Herbert, 2 App. D. C. 485. See Stone v. Clay, 103 Ky. 314.

When after a proper investment on the security of a mortgage, the real estate falls in value below what is regarded as safe for trust investments, the course of the trustee must be guided by circumstances. If the mortgage is overdue, there is no absolute rule that he must fore-

Nor can they change the character of the investments from realty to personalty, or *vice versa*, without special authority.[1] And if, without authority, trustees change investments properly made for others improper or unauthorized by law, they may be required to replace the securities sold, and also to invest any profits which may have accrued in the same securities;[2] or the *cestui que trust* may elect to take the money with interest upon it.[3] And even if trustees have express power to vary the securities, they will not be allowed to do so capriciously, or without some apparent object;[4] and they ought not to sell out an investment without having in view an immediate reinvestment: if they do so, they may be held to pay the loss that may occur.[5] If an

---

[1] *Post*, § 602 *et seq.*; Quick *v.* Fisher, 9 N. J. Eq. 802.

[2] Powlett *v.* Herbert, 1 Ves. Jr. 297; Evans *v.* Inglehart, 6 Gill & J. 192. In such cases of unauthorized varying the securities the trustee takes upon himself the burden of proving entire *bona fides*, and that there was reasonable ground to believe that the fund would be benefited; and if this can be shown the courts will sustain his action. Washington *v.* Emery, 4 Jones (N. C.), 32; Cornwise *v.* Bourgum, 2 Ga. Dec. 15.

[3] Forrest *v.* Elwes, 4 Ves. 497; Fowler *v.* Reynall, 2 De G. & Sm. 749; 3 Mac. & G. 500.

[4] Brice *v.* Stokes, 11 Ves. 324; De Manneville *v.* Crompton, 1 V. & B. 359; Fowler *v.* Reynall, 3 Mac. & G. 500.

[5] Hanbury *v.* Kirkland, 3 Sim. 265; Broadhurst *v.* Balguy, 1 Y. & C. Ch. 16; Watts *v.* Girdlestone, 6 Beav. 190.

---

close or press the personal claim against the mortgagor. The question is a practical one for the trustee to determine under all the circumstances with view to what seems best for the interest of the *cestuis*. *In re* Chapman, [1896] 2 Ch. 763; *In re* Medland, 41 Ch. Div. 476.

Where a trustee sells a proper investment *for the purpose* of putting the proceeds into an unauthorized investment, the *cestui* has the option of requiring him to replace the proceeds or of requiring him to replace the original investment, together with the income which it would have produced if it had been retained. *Re* Walker, 62 L. T. 449; *Re* Massingberd's Settlement, 60 L. T. 620.

Thus if the securities in which the funds were originally invested have risen in value since the change the trustee may be required to make up this difference as well as any loss of funds put into the new investment, or if the former have fallen in value the *cestui* may elect to take the actual proceeds. And this is true even when the trustee had authority to sell for a proper purpose. *Re* Walker, 62 L. T. 449.

investment in a particular fund or stock is directed by a testa-tor, it cannot be varied except by the consent of all the parties interested; and if there are parties not *sui juris*, or not in being, the court itself will not order a change.[1] Where an investment was not to be varied without the consent of the testator's wife, and she waived the provisions of the will, her consent was still held necessary.[2] In those States where there are no stocks, funds, or securities, prescribed by law, or by the order of court, in which trustees must invest in order to be safe, and invest-ments are once made by trustees in safe and proper securities, or where investments are left by the testator in such securities, the courts will be very adverse to a change, and will not allow one, except for some very controlling motive. The reason is, that where there is no rule governing investments by trustees, except that they shall act in good faith and upon a sound dis-cretion, courts are very averse to change proper investments once made, and select others by so very indefinite a rule.[3] (a)

§ 467. If trustees make an improper investment with the knowledge, assent, and acquiescence, or at the request of the *cestui que trust*, they cannot be held to make good the loss, if one happens;[4] but the *cestuis que trust*, to be affected by such

---

[1] Wood v. Wood, 5 Paige, 596; Trans. University v. Clay, 2 B. Mon. 386; Contee v. Dawson, 2 Bland, 264; Deaderick v. Cantrell, 10 Yerg. 263; Burrill v. Sheil, 2 Barb. 457; Personeau v. Personeau, 1 Des. 521; Lamb's App., 58 Penn. St. 142.

[2] Plympton v. Plympton, 6 Allen, 178.

[3] Murray v. Feinour, 4 Md. Ch. 418.

[4] Booth v. Booth, 1 Beav. 125; Langford v. Gascoyne, 11 Ves. 333; Nail v. Punter, 5 Sim. 355; Farrar v. Barraclough, 2 Sm. & G. 231; Broad-hurst v. Balguy, 1 Y. & C. Ch. 16; Raby v. Ridehalgh, 7 De G., M. & G. 104; Walker v. Symonds, 3 Swanst. 64; Munch v. Cockerell, 5 Myl. & Cr. 178; Poole v. Munday, 103 Mass. 174; Brice v. Stokes, 11 Ves. 319. [Mat-

(a) But the matter of changing investments has been said to be "one of those discretionary powers that the court will not control, fur-ther than to see that it exercised *bona fide* and with ordinary pru-dence." Massey v. Stout, 4 Del. Ch. 274, 288; Emery v. Batchelder, 78 Me. 233.

consent or acquiescence, must be *sui juris*, and capable of acting for themselves;[1] if, therefore, they are married women, or minor children, or other persons incapacitated, or under disability, they cannot be bound by any alleged acquiescence, nor by their urgent requests,[2] although a married woman may acquiesce in the investment of trust property, given to her sole and separate use, in such manner that she cannot afterwards complain of the investment as improper.[3] But in order that the *cestuis que trust* may be bound by their acquiescence in an improper investment, there must be, on their part, full knowledge of all the facts and circumstances;[4] and the trustee must be free from all suspicion of misrepresentation or concealment.[5] The remainder-man cannot acquiesce in an investment, until his interest falls into possession, so as to be bound.[6] If the improper investment has been made, at the request of the tenant for life, and such tenant has received an increased income by reason of the improper investment, such increased income can be recovered back from the tenant for life.[7] But if the

---

ter of Hall, 164 N. Y. 196; Phillips *v.* Burton, 52 S. W. 1064 (Ky. 1899); *In re* Somerset, [1894] 1 Ch. 231. See *infra*, §§ 849–851, as to consent, acquiescence, or ratification of *cestui* in case of a breach of trust.]

[1] Buckeredge *v.* Glasse, 1 Cr. & Phil. 135.

[2] Walker *v.* Symonds, 3 Swanst. 69; Hopkins *v.* Myall, 2 R. & M. 86; Ryder *v.* Bickerton, 3 Swanst. 80, n.; March *v.* Russell, 3 Myl. & Cr. 31; Nail *v.* Punter, 5 Sim. 556; Kellaway *v.* Johnson, 5 Beav. 319; Bateman *v.* Davis, 3 Madd. 98; Cocker *v.* Quayle, 1 R. & M. 535; Murray *v.* Feinour, 2 Md. Ch. 422; Barton's Est., 1 Pars. Eq. 47; Kent *v.* Plumb, 57 Ga. 207.

[3] Mant *v.* Leith, 15 Beav. 524; Brewer *v.* Swirles, 2 Sm. & G. 219; Sherman *v.* Parish, 53 N. Y. 483. But she may maintain a suit to correct the irregularity, although she cannot claim anything as for a breach of the trust. Ibid.

[4] Munch *v.* Cockerell, 5 Myl. & Cr. 178; Montford *v.* Cadogan, 17 Ves. 489. And they must be apprised of the effect of their legal rights. Adair *v.* Brimmer, 74 N. Y. 539. [White *v.* Sherman, 168 Ill. 589.]

[5] Burrows *v.* Walls, 5 De G., M. & G. 233; Underwood *v.* Stevens, 1 Mer. 712; Walker *v.* Symonds, 3 Swanst. 1. [Nichols, Appellant, 157 Mass. 20; McKim *v.* Glover, 161 Mass. 418.]

[6] Bennett *v.* Colley, 5 Sim. 181; 2 Myl. & K. 225; Brown *v.* Cross, 14 Beav. 105.

[7] Dimes *v.* Scott, 4 Russ. 195; Mehrtens *v.* Andrews, 3 Beav. 72; Howe

tenant for life protested against the illegal investment, and desired the trustees to make a proper investment, the increased income from the illegal investment cannot be recovered back.[1] In all cases the assent to an illegal investment must be so formal that the trustees are justified in acting upon it. If it is a mere expression that a certain investment would be safe, without any intention that the trustees should act upon it, the *cestui que trust* will not be bound.[2] (a)   So an assent to a particular investment cannot justify a subsequent mismanagement of the investment.[3]   And acquiescence by the *cestui que trust* will not be presumed from mere lapse of time, if he has done nothing to acknowledge it, or has received no benefit.[4]   Any party whose rights are endangered by an improper or unauthorized investment may apply to the court for redress;[5] but if the investment was made by mistake, or has been corrected, the trustees will not be removed, or they will not be deprived of the funds.[6]

§ 468. It is difficult to lay down any general rule that is equitable and applicable to all cases, as to the interest that trustees shall pay upon trust funds in their hands. In England, if trustees suffer money to remain in their own hands, or in the hands of third persons, or in bank for an unreasonable time, in addition to their liability for its loss during such delay, they

v. Dartmouth, 7 Ves. 150; Mills *v.* Mills, 7 Sim. 101; Pickering *v.* Pickering, 4 Myl. & Cr. 289; Holland *v.* Hughes, 16 Ves. 114; Hood *v.* Clapham, 19 Beav. 90; M'Gachen *v.* Dew, 15 Beav. 84; Raby *v.* Ridehalgh, 7 De G., M. & G. 104; Band *v.* Tardell, id. 628; Stewart *v.* Sanderson, L. R. 10 Eq. 26.   [See also Fletcher *v.* Collis, [1905] 2 Ch. 24; Chillingworth *v.* Chambers, [1896] 1 Ch. 685.]

[1] Bate *v.* Hooper, 5 De G., M. & G. 358; and see Turquand *v.* Marshall, L. R. 6 Eq. 112; Hood *v.* Clapham, 19 Beav. 90.

[2] Nyce's App., 5 Watts & S. 254.

[3] Lockhart *v.* Reilly, 39 Eng. L. & Eq. 135.

[4] Phillipson *v.* Gatty, 7 Hare, 516.

[5] Bromley *v.* Kelly, 39 L. J. Ch. 274.   [6] Ibid.

(a) An assent to an investment outside the proper field does not relieve the trustee from the duty of investigating as to its safety. *In re* Salmon, 42 Ch. Div. 351.

will be charged with interest at the rate of four per cent: but if the trustees are grossly negligent or corrupt, or improperly call in the money from a proper investment, and suffer it to lie idle, or if they use it in trade or speculation, or invest it in improper places, the court will charge them with interest at the rate of five per cent; (a) and, in certain special cases of misconduct, the court will order annual or semi-annual rests, for the purpose of charging them with compound interest. In the United States there is no law by which different rates of interest can be applied to different degrees of negligence or misconduct; and the only question here is, whether simple or compound interest shall be imposed. (b)   The general rules, so far as they can be

(a) *In re* Davis, [1902] 2 Ch. 314; Vyse *v.* Foster, 8 Ch. 309, 335; Ames' Cases on Trusts, (2d ed.) 496, n., 498, n.

(b) Trustees are not charged with interest on uninvested trust funds in their hands, where the funds have not earned interest, unless they have negligently failed to invest or have used the funds for their own benefit, or have detained the funds beyond the time when they ought to have turned them over to the *cestuis*. Griffith's Estate, 147 Pa. St. 274; Williams *v.* Haskins, 66 Vt. 378; *In re* Nesmith, 140 N. Y. 609.

The best considered cases base a charge of interest and the amount of such interest upon one of three theories, according to the circumstances of the case: (1) Making up to the trust estate income which the trust funds ought to have made or would probably have made, if they had been properly invested in accordance with the trustee's duty. (2) Giving to the trust estate all the income, profits, or benefits which the trustee has actually received from his use of the trust funds. (3) Giving to the

trust estate the same rate of interest charged against a person who detains or borrows money of another without a special contract as to interest, *i. e.*, simple interest at the legal rate. Howard *v.* Manning, 65 Ark. 122; Forbes *v.* Ware, 172 Mass. 306; Bangor *v.* Beal, 85 Me. 129; General Proprietors *v.* Force, 72 N. J. Eq. 56. See 1 Ames' Cases on Trusts (2d ed.), 482, 484, 496 and notes. See also cases cited *infra*, this note.

Cases where the trustee has simply detained in his hands trust funds which he ought to have paid over, but has not used them for his profit, fall within the first or the third class, whichever is most advantageous to the *cestui*. *In re* Estate of Danforth, 66 Mo. App. 586, 590; Weisel *v.* Cobb, 118 N. C. 11. Since trust funds when properly invested do not usually yield 6 % interest, compound interest at 6 % or a higher rate in cases of this class would usually be excessive on the theory of making up what the trust funds ought to have produced. Forbes *v.* Ware, 172 Mass. 306, 309. Accord-

drawn from all the cases, are as follows: (1) If a trustee retains balances in his hands which he ought to have invested, or delays for an unreasonable time to invest, or if he mingles the money

ingly when the legal rate is as high as 6 % the interest charged against a trustee in such cases would be simple interest at the legal rate.

Cases where the trustee has merely failed to earn an income for the trust, by neglect of his duty to invest or by making improper investments, fall within the first class. He must make good any loss of principal and any deficiency of income which his failure of duty or other breach of trust has caused. Howard *v.* Manning, 65 Ark. 122; Dick's Estate, 183 Pa. St. 647; *In re* Muller, 52 N. Y. S. 565, (6 % simple). When he has improperly changed from an authorized investment to one which was unauthorized he may be charged not only with loss of principal and of income which the fund would have earned but with profits which would have come to the principal of the fund through a subsequent rise in value of the securities which he has improperly sold. *Re* Walker, 62 L.T. 449; *Re* Massingberd's Settlement, 60 L. T. 620.

Cases where the trustee has used the trust fund for his own profit or in his own business would usually come within the second or third class. He should be charged at least simple interest at the legal rate, and as much more as may be necessary to take from him all the income, profit, or other pecuniary benefits he may have received from his use of the funds. Forbes *v.* Ware, 172 Mass. 306; *In re* Thompson, 101 Cal. 349; Conn. *v.* Howarth, 48 Conn. 207; Cook *v.* Lowry, 95 N. Y. 103.

The charge of simple interest at the legal rate in such a case is based upon the reasoning that the most lenient view of such a transaction is to regard the trustee as a borrower of the trust funds without a special agreement as to interest. Conn. *v.* Howarth, 48 Conn. 207; Stanley's Estate *v.* Pence, 160 Ind. 636; Young's Estate, 97 Iowa, 218; Bangor *v.* Beal, 85 Me. 129; White *v.* Ditson, 140 Mass. 351, 362; Wolfort *v.* Reilly, 133 Mo. 463; Society *v.* Pelham, 58 N. H. 566; Erie School District *v.* Griffith, 203 Pa. St. 123; Page's Ex'r *v.* Holman, 82 Ky. 573; *Re* Hodges' Estate, 66 Vt. 70; Matter of Myers, 131 N. Y. 409; Westover *v.* Carman's Estate, 49 Neb. 397.

The better opinion is that compound interest or a high rate of interest should not be imposed upon a trustee as a penalty. Forbes *v.* Ware, 172 Mass. 306; Forbes *v.* Allen, 166 Mass. 569; Kane *v.* Kane's Adm'r, 146 Mo. 605; Perrin *v.* Lepper, 72 Mich. 454, 556; Hazard *v.* Durant, 14 R. I. 25; General Proprietors *v.* Force, 72 N. J. Eq. 56; Lehman *v.* Rothbarth, 159 Ill. 270; Hughes *v.* People, 111 Ill. 457. See Vyse *v.* Foster, 8 Ch. 309, 335. But see Eastman *v.* Davis, 68 Vt. 225; Page's Ex'r *v.* Holman, 82 Ky. 573.

As to the liability of trustees to turn in to the trust all benefits or profits from use of trust property, see *supra*, § 429 and note.

with his own, or uses it in his private business,[1] or deposits it in bank in his own name, or in the name of the firm of which he was a member, or neglects to settle his account for a long time, or to distribute or pay over the money when he ought to do so,[2] he will be liable to pay simple interest at the rate established by law as the legal rate in the absence of special agreements.[3]

[1] Cool v. Jackman, 13 Brad. (Ill.) 560; Lehmann v. Rothbarth, 111 Ill. 185; Society v. Pelham, 58 N. H. 566; the trustee must pay interest from the time of diverting the fund.

[2] Judd v. Dike, 30 Minn. 385; Pickering v. De Rochemont, 60 N. H. 179; Lyons v. Chamberlin, 25 Hun, 49. [Mades v. Miller, 2 App. D. C. 455.]

[3] Burdick v. Garrick, L. R. 5 Ch. 241; Blogg v. Johnson, L. R. 2 Ch. 225; Berwick v. Murray, 7 De G., M. & G. 843; Treves v. Townshend, 1 Bro. Ch. 384; Forbes v. Ross, 2 Bro. Ch. 430; Piety v. Stace, 4 Ves. 620; Ashburnham v. Thompson, 13 Ves. 402; Bates v. Scales, 12 Ves. 402; Pocock v. Reddington, 5 Ves. 794; Sutton v. Sharp. 1 Russ. 146; Crackelt v. Bethune, 1 J. & W. 122; Att. Gen. v. Solly, 2 Sim. 515; Heathcote v. Hulme, 1 J. & W. 122; Brown v. Sansome, 1 McC. & Y. 327; Westover v. Chapman, 1 Coll. 177; Robinson v. Robinson, 1 De G., M. & G. 247; Jones v. Foxall, 15 Beav. 392; Saltmarsh v. Barrett, 21 Beav. 349; Knott v. Cottee, 16 Beav. 77; Rocke v. Hart, 11 Ves. 58; Lincoln v. Allen, 4 Bro. P. C. 553; Younge v. Combe, 4 Ves. 101; Dawson v. Massey, 1 Ball & B. 231; Hicks v. Hicks, 3 Atk. 274; Perkins v. Boynton, 1 Bro. Ch. 375; King v. Talbott, 40 N. Y. 86; Nelson v. Hagerstown Bank, 27 Md. 53; Cook v. Addison, L. R. 5 Ch. 466; Duffy v. Duncan, 35 N. Y. 187; Young v. Brush, 38 Barb. 294; Owen v. Peebles, 42 Ala. 338; Wistar's App., 54 Pa. St. 60; Newton v. Bennett, 1 Bro. Ch. 359; Littlehales v. Gascoigne, 3 Bro. Ch. 73; Franklin v. Firth, id. 433; Longmore v. Broom, 7 Ves. 124; Trimleston v. Hammil, 1 Ball & B. 385; Tebbs v. Carpenter, 1 Madd. 290; Mousley v. Carr, 4 Beav. 49; Hoskins v. Nichols, 1 N. C. C. 478; Beverleys v. Miller, 6 Munf. 99; Diffenderffer v. Winder, 3 G. & J. 341; Mumford v. Murray, 6 Johns. Ch. 1; Jacot v. Emmett, 11 Paige, 142; Kellett v. Rathbun, 4 Paige, 102; De Peyster v. Clarkson, 2 Wend. 77; Garniss v. Gardner, 1 Edw. Ch. 128; Spear v. Tinkham, 2 Barb. Ch. 211; Manning v. Manning, 1 Johns. Ch. 527; Brown v. Rickett, 4 id. 303; Williamson v. Williamson, 6 Paige, 298; Dunscomb v. Dunscomb, 1 Johns. Ch. 508; Minuse v. Cox, 5 Johns. Ch. 448; Cogswell v. Cogswell, 2 Edw. Ch. 231; Gray v. Thompson, 1 Johns. Ch. 82; Armstrong v. Miller, 6 Ohio, 118; Astor's Est., 5 Whar. 228; Merrick's Est., 2 Ash. 285; Worrall's App., 23 Penn. St. 44; Graves's App., 50 id. 189; Hess's Est., 69 id. 454; Peyton v. Smith, 2 Dev. & B. Eq. 325; Jameson v. Shelly, 2 Humph. 198; Dyott's Est., 2 Watts & S. 655; In re Thorp, Davies, 290; Carr v. Laird, 27 Miss. 544; Lomax v. Pendleton, 3 Call, 538; Handy v. Snodgrass, 9 Leigh, 484; Dillard v. Tomlinson, 1 Munf. 183; Carter v. Cutting, 5 Munf. 223; Wood v. Garnett, 6 Leigh, 271; Miller

This rule is subject to the qualification that trustees cannot make any advantage to themselves out of the trust fund; and if they make more than legal interest, they shall pay more, as, if they make usurious loans, they shall be charged with all their gains from the use of the money.[1] If the trustee cannot show what amount of interest he has received, he shall be charged with legal interest from the time when the regular investment ought to have been made.[2] There may be an exception to the rule, that a deposit of the trust-money in bank in the name of the trustee, or a mixing of the trust fund with his own, will impose a liability of legal interest. There must be some element of a breach of trust in the transaction, or a breach of duty.[3] If therefore the sums are small, and the trustee receives no credit or profit from the act, or if the act was accidental, or beneficial to the *cestui que trust*, legal interest will not be imposed upon the trustee; [4] or if the trustee was a member of a firm of bankers, and he deposited with the firm in his name as trustee, he will not be charged with interest, although the firm made a profit from the deposit.[5] The proper mode of taking the account of trustees is to treat all the income of the trust received during the current year as unproductive, and to charge against the income of the current year all the disbursements, including the compensation

v. Beverleys, 4 Hem. & W. 415; Chase *v.* Lockerman, 11 G. & J. 185; Ringgold *v.* Ringgold, 1 H. & G. 11; Arthur *v.* Marster, 1 Harp. Eq. 47; Rowland *v.* Best, 2 McCord, Ch. 317; Lyles *v.* Hattan, 6 G. & J. 122; Griswold *v.* Chandler, 5 N. H. 497; Lund *v.* Lund, 41 N. H. 355; Turney *v.* Williams, 7 Yerg. 172; Williams *v.* Powell, 16 Jur. 393; Dornford *v.* Dornford, 12 Ves. 127; Wright *v.* Wright, 2 McCord, Ch. 185; Knowlton *v.* Bradly, 17 N. H. 458; McKim *v.* Hibbard, 142 Mass. 422. [White *v.* Ditson, 140 Mass. 351; Forbes *v.* Ware, 172 Mass. 306; *Re* Hodges' Estate, 66 Vt. 70; Matter of Myers, 131 N. Y. 409; *In re* Estate of Danforth, 66 Mo. App. 586, 590.]

 [1] Barney *v.* Saunders, 16 How. 543; Oswald's App., 3 Grant, 300; Martin *v.* Rayborn, 42 Ala. 468.

 [2] Bentley *v.* Shreve, 2 Md. Ch. 219; Rapalje *v.* Hall, 1 Sandf. Ch. 339.

 [3] McKnight *v.* Walsh, 23 N. J. Eq. 136; 24 N. J. Eq. 492.

 [4] Rapalje *v.* Hall, 1 Sandf. Ch. 399; Graves's App., 50 Penn. St. 189; Bond *v.* Abbott, 42 Ala. 499.

 [5] Hess's Est., 69 Penn. St. 454. [Dick's Estate, 183 Pa. St. 647.]

or commissions of the trustees for the same year, and to strike
a balance, upon which, as a general rule, interest is to be allowed,[1] but in such a way as not to compound it.[2] If, however,
these balances are too small to invest, or for any reason the
trustees might equitably keep them on hand, interest will not
be allowed upon them until the balances so accumulate as to
be properly invested, or until the trustees ought to invest them.[3]
Of course, as soon as a trustee properly pays the fund into
court, his liability for interest ceases.[4] But so long as any litigation is pending over the fund, and the money is not brought
into court, the trustee is bound to keep it invested, and he is
liable for legal interest.[5] But a guardian is not liable to interest
while the settlement of his account is pending.[6]

§ 469. (2) If a trustee is directed and bound to invest in a
particular stock or fund within a certain time, or within a reasonable time, and he neglects to make the investment as directed, the *cestui que trust* has his election to take the money and

---

[1] Boynton *v.* Dyer, 18 Pick. 1; Pettus *v.* Clawson, 4 Rich. Eq. 92; Jones
v. Morrall, 2 Sim. (N. S.) 241; Clarkson *v.* De Peyster, 2 Wend. 78; Vanderheyden *v.* Vanderheyden, 2 Paige, 288; Luken's App., 47 Pa. St. 356;
Reynolds *v.* Waker, 29 Miss. 250; Roach *v.* Jelks, 40 Miss. 754; Crump *v.*
Gerack, id. 765.

[2] Rowland *v.* Best, 2 McCord, Ch. 317; Jordon *v.* Hunt, 2 Hill, Eq. 145;
Walker *v.* Bynum, 4 Des. 555; Powell *v.* Powell, 10 Ala. 900; Shephard
v. Stark, 3 Munf. 29 ; Burwell *v.* Anderson, 3 Leigh, 348 ; Garrett
v. Carr, 3 id. 407; Campbell *v.* Williams, 3 Mon. 122; Jones *v.* Ward, 10
Yerg. 160. See Eliott *v.* Sparrell, 114 Mass. 404.

[3] Rapalje *v.* Hall, 1 Sandf. Ch. 399; Woods *v.* Garnett, 6 Leigh, 271;
Graves's App., 50 Penn. St. 189; Luken's App., 47 id. 356. Trustee is generally chargeable with interest to be computed from the first day of January
following his receipt of the funds. Livingston *v.* Wells, 8 S. C. 347.

[4] January *v.* Poyntz, 2 B. Mon. 404; Yundt's App., 13 Penn. St. 575;
Lane's App., 24 id. 487; Younge *v.* Brush, 38 Barb. 294; Brandon *v.* Hoggatt,
32 Miss. 335.

[5] Ibid. [But see Dorris *v.* Miller, 105 Iowa, 564.]

[6] Yader's App., 45 Penn. St. 394. But a trustee who retained funds in his
hands, making a claim to them as his compensation, which he failed to
establish, was charged with interest from the time he ought to have paid
them. Jenkins *v.* Doolittle, 69 Ill. 415.

legal interest thereon, or so much stock as the money would
have purchased at the time when the investment ought to have
been made, and the dividends thereon.[1] It has been held in
some cases, that if trustees were directed to invest in *stocks, or
in real estate*, and they neglected to do either, the *cestui que
trust* might have the amount of stocks that could have been
purchased, and the dividends thereon.[2] On the other hand, it
has been held, and is now established in such case, that, as the
trustees might have invested in real securities, and such real
securitiestmight have been of less value than the original fund,
the *cestui que trust* can have only the money and legal interest
thereon, and cannot claim the amount of stocks that might have
been purchased.[3] If trustees are directed to invest a certain
fund separately, they will be liable for losses occurring by
reason of neglecting this provision.[4] In Wisconsin, it has been
held that if a trustee is directed to invest in United States bonds
or in real estate security, the interest which he might have
obtained upon proper real estate security is the measure of his
liability for failure to invest the fund.[5]

§ 470. (3) If the trust fund was properly invested, according
to the direction of the trust instrument, or according to law,
and the trustee improperly converts the fund into money and
neglects to invest it, or invests it improperly, or uses it in trade,
business, or speculation, the *cestui que trust* may, at his electoni,
take the diivdends or interest which the fund would have produced if the investment had been suffered to remain where it

[1] Shepherd *v.* Mauls, 4 Hare, 504; Robinson *v.* Robinson, 1 De G., M.
& G. 256; Byrchall *v.* Bradford, 6 Madd. 235; Vyse *v.* Foster, 8 Ch. 334;
Ihmsen's App., 43 Penn. St. 471; Blauvelt *v.* Ackerman, 20 N. J. Eq. 141;
Darling *v.* Hammer, id. 220; McElhenny's App., 46 Penn. St. 347.

[2] Hockley *v.* Bantock, 1 Russ. 141; Watts *v.* Girdlestone, 6 Beav. 188;
Ames *v.* Parkinson, 7 Beav. 379; Ouseley *v.* Anstruther, 10 Beav. 456.

[3] Marsh *v.* Hunter, 6 Madd. 295; Shepherd *v.* Mauls, 4 Hare, 500;
Robinson *v.* Robinson, 1 De G., M. & G. 256; Phillipson *v.* Gatty, 7 Hare,
516; Rees *v.* Williams, 1 De G. & Sm. 314.

[4] Wilmerding *v.* McKesson, 103 N. Y. 329.

[5] Andrew *v.* Schmitt, 64 Wis. 664.

was properly made; or he may take legal interest on the fund; or he may take all the profits that have been made upon the fund.[1] If the *cestui que trust* elects to take the profits, he must take them during the whole period, subject to all the losses of the business: he cannot take profits for one period and interest for another.[2]

§ 471. (4) If the trustee improperly changes an investment, and refuses to reinvest the money in a legal manner; or if he refuses to invest the fund in the first instance; or if he uses the fund in trade, business, or speculation; or makes an improper or illegal investment, — the *cestui que trust* may have the income that would have accrued from the proper investment; or he may have simple interest at the legal rate;[3] or he may take all the profits of the trade or business, or other investment or employment of the money, and if the trustee refuse to account for the profits arising from his use of the money, or if he has so mingled the money and the profits with his own money and profits that he cannot separate and account for the profits that belong to the *cestui que trust*, the *cestui que trust* may have legal interest computed with annual rests, in order to compound it.[4] (*a*) And sometimes even biennial rests will be allowed in computing

---

[1] Jones *v.* Foxall, 15 Beav. 392; Robinett's App., 36 Penn. St. 174; Saltmarsh *v.* Barrett, 31 Beav. 349; Kyle *v.* Barnett, 17 Ala. 306; Barney *v.* Saunders, 16 How. 543; Brown *v.* De Tastet, Jac. 284; Cook *v.* Collingridge, id. 607; Crawshay *v.* Collins, 15 Ves. 218; 2 Russ. 325; Featherstonhaugh *v.* Fenwick, 17 Ves. 298; Docker *v.* Somes, 2 Myl. & K. 655; Wedderburn *v.* Wedderburn, 2 Keen, 722; 4 Myl. & Cr. 41; Norris's App., 71 Penn. St. 125. [See *supra*, § 429, note.]

[2] Heathcote *v.* Hulme, 1 J. & W. 122.

[3] Cogbill *v.* Boyd, 79 Va. 1, and cases in next note; Seguin's App., 103 Penn. St. 139.

[4] Jones *v.* Foxall, 15 Beav. 392; Raphael *v.* Boehm, 11 Ves. 92; 13 Ves. 407; 1 Madd. 167; Saltmarsh *v.* Barrett, 31 Beav. 349; Walker *v.* Woodward, 1 Russ. 107; Heighington *v.* Grant, 5 Myl. & Cr. 258; 2 Phill. 600; Williams *v.* Powell, 15 Beav. 461; Walrond *v.* Walrond, 29 Beav. 586; Stackpole *v.* Stackpole, 4 Dow. P. C. 209; Eliott *v.* Sparrell, 114 Mass. 404; State *v.* Howarth, 48 Conn. 207; Cook *v.* Lowry, 95 N. Y. 103.

(*a*) See *supra*, § 468, note.

the compound interest where the trustee has used the fund in his own business.[1] There has been considerable conflict of opinion and authority upon the matter of compounding interest against a trustee. Lord Cranworth said, that a trustee might as well be charged with more principal than he had received as to be charged with more interest.[2] In another case, it was said in England that a trustee would be charged with more than four per cent interest:[3] (1) when he *ought* to have received more; (2) when he *did* receive more; (3) when he is *presumed* to receive more; and (4) when he is estopped to say he did not receive more.[4] Compound interest was allowed in one case where the trustee held the fund after the minor *cestui* came of age without making any arrangement with the child or explaining to him his rights.[5] The burden is on the trustee to show that he made no profits, or received no benefit from the money;[6] and if he refuses to account or to show the amount of profits received, the court will give compound interest, in order that it may be certain that the *cestui que trust* gets the profits of the trade or business in which the trustee has employed the money.[7]

[1] Page's Ex'r *v.* Holman, 82 Ky. 573.

[2] Att. Gen. *v.* Alford, 4 De G., M. & G. 851.

[3] Penney *v.* Avison, 3 Jur. (N. S.) 62.

[4] Att. Gen. *v.* Alford, 4 De G., M. & G. 851; Norris's App., 71 Penn. St. 106. [Forbes *v.* Ware, 172 Mass. 306.]

[5] Emmet *v.* Emmet, 17 Ch. D. 142.

[6] Knott *v.* Cottee, 16 Beav. 77; 16 Jur. 752; Swindall *v.* Swindall, 8 Ired. Eq. 286; Ringgold *v.* Ringgold, 1 H. & G.'11; Diffenderffer *v.* Winder, 3 G. & J. 311; Schieffelin *v.* Stewart, 1 Johns. Ch. 620; Bryant *v.* Craige, 12 Ala. 354; Hodge *v.* Hawkins, 1 Dev. & B. Eq. 566;·Hugh *v.* Smith, 2 Dana, 253; Karr *v.* Karr, 6 Dana, 3; Smith *v.* Kennard, 38 Ala. 695; McElhenny's App., 61 Penn. St. 188. Annual rests were allowed in Harland's Acct., 5 Rawle, 329; Livingston *v.* Wells, 8 S. C. 347; the question was left open in Dietterich *v.* Heft, 3 Penn. St. 91; McCall's Est., 1 Ash. 357; Pennypacker's App., 41 Penn. St. 44, and rests were wholly rejected in Graves's App., 50 Penn. St. 189.

[7] Knott *v.* Cottee, 16 Beav. 77; 16 Jur. 752; Swindall *v.* Swindall, 8 Ired. Eq. 286; Ringgold *v.* Ringgold, 1 H. & G. 11; Diffenderffer *v.* Winder, 3 G. & J. 311; Schieffelin *v.* Stewart, 1 Johns. Ch. 620; Bryant *v.* Craige, 12 Ala. 354; Hodge *v.* Hawkins, 1 Dev. & B. Eq. 566; Hugh *v.* Smith, 2 Dana, 253; Karr *v.* Karr, 6 Dana, 3; Smith *v.* Kennard, 38 Ala. 695; McElhenny's App., 61 Penn. St. 188. Annual rests were allowed in Harland's Acct., 5

To justify the compounding of interest, there must be a wilful breach of duty,[1] and not simple neglect; there must be some special and peculiar circumstances.[2] Compound interest will not be given against negligent trustees where the facts do not indicate a withdrawal of the funds from their legitimate channels of accumulation, or a realization by the trustees of profits on the assets.[3] If the money is simply used in business, and it appears that the profits were not equal to the interest, annual rests will not be made.[4] It appears now to be the settled doctrine, that compound interest will not be given as a penalty for a breach of trust, nor will it be given for an employment of the money in the course of trade, if the profits made in the trade can be clearly ascertained, and are less than legal interest, or less than five per cent; but if nothing appears as to the profits, the courts will presume that the ordinary profits of trade are made, or five per cent in England and the legal interest in the United States. And if the interests or profits of the fund are retained in the trade, instead of being paid out, it will be presumed that the trustees made a similar rate of interest or profit upon the sum retained in trade, and therefore annual rests will be made, and compound interest given; not as punishment or

Rawle, 329; Livingston v. Wells, 8 S. C. 347; the question was left open, Dietterich v. Heft, 3 Barr, 91; McCall's Est., 1 Ash. 357; Pennypacker's App., 41 Penn. St. 44, and rests were wholly rejected in Graves's App., 50 Penn. St. 189. [See Forbes v. Ware, 172 Mass. 306; Lehman v. Rothbarth, 159 Ill. 270; Hughes v. The People, 111 Ill. 457; Forbes v. Allen, 166 Mass. 569; Perrin v. Lepper, 72 Mich. 454, 551; Kane v. Kane's Adm'r, 146 Mo. 605; In re Ricker's Estate, 14 Mont. 153, 29 L. R. A. 622, note; Cook v. Lowry, 95 N. Y. 103; Hazard v. Durant, 14 R. I. 25. In re Davis, [1902] 2 Ch. 314.]

[1] Hughes v. People, 111 Ill. 457; Wilmerding v. McKesson, 103 N. Y. 329.

[2] Garniss v. Gardner, 1 Edw. Ch. 128; Ackerman v. Emott, 4 Barb. 626; Tebbs v. Carpenter, 1 Madd. 290; Fay v. Howe, 1 Pick. 528 and n.; Clemens v. Caldwell, 7 B. Mon. 171; Fall v. Simmons, 6 Ga. 272; Kennan v. Hall, 8 Ga. 417; Cartledg v. Cutliff, 21 Ga. 1.

[3] Ames v. Scudder, 83 Mo. 189.

[4] Utica Ins. Co. v. Lynch, 11 Paige, 521; Kyle v. Barnett, 17 Ala. 306; Ringgold v. Ringgold, 1 H. & G. 11; Myers v. Myers, 2 McCord, Ch. 214; Wright v. Wright, id. 185; Johnson v. Miller, 33 Miss. 553.

penalty, but because the fund and the income employed in trade are presumed to produce that amount of income, interest, or profit.[1] The trustee must seek out the *cestui que trust* to pay the income to him, or he must pay interest upon it. So, where a trustee receives property and sells it, he must account for the proceeds. And if he refuses, he will be charged with the highest value that can be sustained by the evidence.[2] But a mere payment into bank to the general account of the trustee is not such an employment of the money as to justify compound interest.[3] A trustee is accountable for all interest and profits *actually* received by him from the trust fund, and for all which he *might have obtained by due diligence and reasonable skill.*[4]

§ 472. If a trustee is directed to make a certain investment, and to accumulate the income, and he neglects or refuses so to do, the *cestui que trust* is entitled to compound interest, upon all the authorities. If, by the instrument of trust, interest is to be added to principal semi-annually, semi-annual rests will be made; otherwise annual rests will be made,[5] or an inquiry will be directed to ascertain what would have been the amount of the accumulation if the directions had been followed, in order to

---

[1] Jones *v.* Foxall, 15 Beav. 388; Burdick *v.* Garrick, L. R. 5 Ch. 233. See the matter of compound interest elaborately discussed by Mr. Justice Scarburgh in Ker *v.* Snead, 11 Law Rep. 217, Boston, Sept. 1848; and Wright *v.* Wright, 2 McCord, Eq. 200-204; McKnight *v.* Walsh, 23 N. J. Eq. 136; 24 id. 498; Lothrop *v.* Smalley, 23 id. 192. [See *supra*, § 429, note *b*.]

[2] McKnight *v.* Walsh, 23 N. J. Eq. 136; Burdick *v.* Garrick, L. R. 5 Ch. 233.

[3] Norton's Estate, 7 Phila. 484.

[4] Cruce *v.* Cruce, 81 Mo. 676.

[5] Raphael *v.* Boehm, 11 Ves. 92; 13 Ves. 407, 590; Dornford *v.* Dornford, 12 Ves. 127; Knott *v.* Cottee, 16 Beav. 77; Pride *v.* Fooks, 2 Beav. 430; Byrne *v.* Norcott, 13 Beav. 336; Stackpole *v.* Stackpole, 4 Dow. P. C. 209; Brown *v.* Southouse, 3 Bro. Ch. 107; Karr *v.* Karr, 6 Dana, 3; Bowles *v.* Drayton, 1 Des. 489; Hodge *v.* Hawkins, 1 Dev. & Bat. 564; Wilson *v.* Peake, 3 Jur. (N. S.) 155; Brown *v.* Sansome, 1 McCle. & Yo. 427; Lesley *v.* Lesley, 1 Dev. 117; Fitham *v.* Turner, 23 L. T. (N. S.) 345; Court *v.* Robarts, 6 Cl. & Fin. 64; Townsend *v.* Townsend, 1 Gif. 201.

charge the trustee with the amount.[1] And where a trustee was ordered by the court to invest a sum in controversy, and he neglected to do so, he was ordered to bring the whole sum into court with compound interest.[2] Interest may be allowed against a trustee, although the bill does not pray for it.[3] If a trustee improperly withholds money as a commission, he may be made to pay compound interest on it.[4]

[1] Brown v. Sansome, 1 McCle. & Yo. 427.

[2] Latimer v. Hansom, 1 Bland, 51; Winder v. Diffenderffer, 2 Bland, 166; McKnight v. Walsh, 23 N. J. Eq. 136; 24 id. 498; Lathrop v. Smalley, 23 id. 192.

[3] Blogg v. Johnson, L. R. 2 Ch. 225.

[4] McKnight v. Walsh, 23 N. J. Eq. 136.

CONTENTS OF VOLUME

CHAPTER XVI.

CHAPTER XVII.

Trustees of the Dry Legal Title ; to Preserve
Contingent Remainders ; of Terms Attendant ;
of Freeholds ; and of Leaseholds 520–538

CHAPTER XVIII.

Powers and Duties of Trustees as between Tenant for Life and Remainder-man 539–556

CHAPTER XIX.

CHAPTER XX.

TRUSTS UNDER ASSIGNMENTS FOR CREDITORS ; TRUSTS
   UNDER DEEDS FOR PARTICULAR CREDITORS ; AND
   TRUSTS UNDER POWER OF SALE MORTGAGES . . 585–602 *gg*

CHAPTER XXI.

CHAPTER XXII.

CHAPTER XXIII.

CHAPTER XXVI.

Rights and Duties of Third Persons in Relation to the Trust, and their Duty of Seeing to the Application of the Purchase-Money .... 788–815 c

CHAPTER XXVII.

CHAPTER XXVIII.

THE STATUTE OF LIMITATIONS, LAPSE OF TIME, AND PUBLIC POLICY AS AFFECTING TRUSTS 854–872

CHAPTER XXIX.

CHAPTER XXX.

CHAPTER XXXI.

ALLOWANCES AND COMPENSATION TO TRUSTEES . . . 904–919

CHAPTER XXXII.

LAW OF TRUSTS.

CHAPTER XVI.

POWERS.

§ 473. WHERE an express trust is created, certain powers are conferred upon the trustees to be executed by them. These powers are divided in the first instance into *general* and *special* powers. General powers are those which, by construction of law, are incident to the *office* of trustee. Every trustee must have them, whether they are named or not in the instrument creating the trust, in order that he may perform the duties imposed upon him. Special powers are such special directions and authority as the settlor gives to his trustees in order to carry out his special purposes in instituting the trust. Special powers are again divided into mere naked powers, — to be exercised by trustees at their sole discretion, and according to their own judgment, and to be forever discharged and obsolete, if the trustees do not see fit to execute them, — and powers in the nature of a trust. These latter powers are sometimes coupled with an interest, and sometimes not. But if they are in the nature of a trust, they are imperative on the trustees, and must be executed. If the trustees neglect or refuse to execute them, or die without performing them, courts of equity will execute them, or compel them to be executed. In considering this subject, the rules governing mere naked powers, and powers in the nature of a trust, will first be stated. The nature of general powers, and the rules that regulate their performance, will next be noticed. Special powers, and the rules applicable to them, will then be discussed, and the time when, and the persons by whom, they may be executed. It must be observed, that, in all cases, powers must be construed according to the intention of the party creating them, if such intention is compatible with the rules of law; and such intention must be determined from the instrument.[1]

§ 474. It must be observed, in the first instance, that whatever powers may be possessed by trustees, whether general or special, if the trust is before the court and a *decree* has been made, the powers of the trustees are thenceforth so far changed that they must have the sanction of the court for all their acts.[2] They cannot begin nor defend any suit without leave of the court;[3] they cannot sell,[4] nor make repairs,[5] nor make investments,[6] nor pay debts without consulting the court.[7] But there must be a *decree* in the case; for if there is nothing before the court but a bill, it may be dismissed at any time, and the authority of the trustees left as it was before the bill was filed.[8] Even in the case of a mere bill, the trustees ought to consult the court in important matters, and before incurring large expenses.[9] But even after a decree, which brings all the matters of the trust into the jurisdiction of the court, the trustees must

[1] Guion *v.* Pickett, 22 Miss. 77; Kerr *v.* Verner, 66 Penn. St. 326.

[2] Mitchelson *v.* Piper, 8 Sim. 64; Shewen *v.* Vanderhorst, 2 R. & M. 75; 1 R. & M. 347; Wartman *v.* Wartman, Taney, 362.

[3] Jones *v.* Powell, 4 Beav. 96; Lewin on Trusts, 425. See Abell *v.* Brown, 55 Md. 217. [Abell *v.* Abell, 75 Md. 44, 64.]

[4] Walker *v.* Smalwood, Amb. 676; Annesley *v.* Ashurst, 3 P. Wms. 282.

[5] Anon. 10 Ves. 104.

[6] Widdowson *v.* Duck, 5 Mer. 494.

[7] Mitchelson *v.* Piper, 8 Sim. 64; King *v.* Roe, L. J. May, 1858; Irby *v.* Irby, 24 Beav. 525; Jackson *v.* Woolly, 12 Sim. 18.

[8] Cafe *v.* Bent, 3 Hare, 249; Neeves *v.* Burrage, 14 Q. B. 504.

[9] Att. Gen. *v.* Clack, 1 Beav. 467; Cafe *v.* Bent, 3 Hare, 249; Talbott *v.* Marshfield, L. R. 4 Eq. 661.

not neglect the duties imposed upon their office; for if they should allow a policy of insurance to expire for want of care, they would be responsible.[1]   And they should still collect the personal assets, and prevent them from wasting, and they may give receipts for moneys paid them.[2]

§ 475.   In a court of *law*, the trustee is the absolute owner of the estate, and he can exercise all the powers of ownership; he can sue and be sued,[3] even though the *cestui que trust* is dead,[4] and must act in many respects as the owner; and so he must be treated by others as the sole proprietor; but in equity the *cestui que trust* is the owner, and the question in equity is, how far the trustee can act without exceeding his powers, and rendering himself responsible to the *cestui que trust*.   If the trust is a simple or passive one to allow the beneficiary to occupy and enjoy the estate, the trustee has no power or duty to perform, except at the instance of the *cestui que trust*.   In trusts of a more particular and active kind, the general power of the trustee is limited to the exact performance of the duty imposed upon him.   The duty and power given in such trusts must be strictly performed.   There is no room for discretion or divergence from the particular directions contained in the instrument, as where money was left to a trustee to be laid out in lands, he had no discretion to purchase land with a part of the moneys, and to expend the remainder in repairs and improvements.[5]

§ 476.   But there are *circumstances* where a trustee *must* exercise the discretionary powers of an absolute owner, otherwise great loss might happen to the estate.   The exigencies of

[1] Garner v. Moore, 3 Drew. 277.   [2] Lewin on Trusts, 426.
[3] Harrison v. Rowan, 4 Wash. C. C. 202.
[4] Slevin v. Brown, 32 Mo. 176.
[5] Bostock v. Blakeney, 2 Bro. Ch. 653; Caldecott v. Brown, 2 Hare, 145; Wormley v. Wormley, 8 Wheat. 421; Coonrod v. Coonrod, 6 Ohio, 114; Locke v. Lomas, 5 De G. & Sm. 326; Pinnell v. Hallett, 2 Ves. 276; Lewis v. Hill, 1 Ves. 275; Supp. Ves. Sr. 344; Ringgold v. Ringgold, 1 Har. & Gil. 11; Booth v. Purser, 1 Ired. Eq. 37; Beatty v. Clark, 20 Cal. 11.

the moment may demand immediate action. The *cestuis que trust* may be numerous and scattered, or under disability, or not in existence, so that their sanction cannot be obtained, or cannot be obtained without great inconvenience. The alternative of applying to the court may be attended with considerable or disproportionate expense, and perhaps delay, so that the opportunity is gone and lost forever. It is therefore evident that it is for the interest of the *cestuis que trust* that the trustee should have a reasonable discretionary power to be exercised in emergencies, though no such power is given in the instrument of trust.[1] And so it is a rule of equity that a trustee may safely do that, without a decree of the court, which the court, on a case made, would order or decree him to do.[2] But there is always danger that courts may not view the matter in the same light as the trustee, and so fail to sanction by decree what he has taken the responsibility of doing under a supposed necessity.[3] It is said in some cases, that, if it is doubtful what ought to be done under the circumstances and the terms of the trust, the trustee may give notice to the beneficiary that he intends to act in a certain manner, and unless the *cestui que trust* interferes to prevent it, the court will not hold the trustee responsible if the act turns out disadvantageous.[4] Trustees may waive all matters of mere form which save circuity, trouble, and expense.[5] Generally a trustee cannot prejudice the *cestui* by his admissions, declarations, or negligence.[6] If, however, he lets the statute of limitations run, the *cestui* is affected.[7]

[1] Ward *v.* Ward, 2 H. L. Cas. 784, note to Rowley *v.* Adams; Angell *v.* Dawson, 3 Y. & C. Ex. Eq. 317; Forshaw *v.* Higginson, 8 De G., M. & G. 827; Darke *v.* Williamson, 25 Beav. 622; Harrison *v.* Randall, 9 Hare, 407.

[2] Hutton *v.* Weems, 12 Gill & J. 83; Co. Litt. 171 a; Bath *v.* Bradford, 2 Ves. 590; Hutcheson *v.* Hammond, 3 Bro. Ch. 145; Lee *v.* Brown, 4 Ves. 369; Cook *v.* Parsons, Pr. Ch. 185; Inwood *v.* Twyne, 2 Eden, 153; Terry *v.* Terry, Gilb. 11; Shaw *v.* Borrer, 1 Keen, 576.

[3] Forshaw *v.* Higginson, 3 Jur. (N. S.) 476.

[4] Life Association *v.* Siddall, 3 De G., F. & J. 74.

[5] Pell *v.* De Winton, 2 De G. & J. 20.

[6] Calwell's Ex'r *v.* Prindle's Ad., 19 W. Va. 604.

[7] See § 863.

§ 476 a. As trustees hold the legal title for the benefit of third persons, and as the law forbids them from making any profit to themselves from their management of, or dealing with, the trust fund, so the law protects them from loss if they act according to law in good faith. And in all cases of doubt [1] as to what the law is, and what their conduct ought to be under it, they are entitled to instruction and direction from the court.[2] (a) The advisory jurisdiction will not be exercised in

[1] There must be some doubt or obscurity to entitle a trustee to apply to a court for directions. *In re* Brewer, 43 Hun, 597.

[2] Wiswell *v.* First Cong. Church, 14 Ohio St. 31; Tillinghast *v.* Coggshall, 7 R. I. 383; Att. Gen. *v.* Moore, 19 N. J. Eq. 503; Woodruff *v.* Cook, 47 Barb. 304; Goodhue *v.* Clark, 37 N. H. 551; Crosby *v.* Mason, 32 Conn. 482; Reynolds *v.* Brandon, 3 Heisk. 593; Pet'rs of Baptist Church, 51 N. H. 424; Wheeler *v.* Berry, 18 N. H. 307; Talbot *v.* Radnor, 3 Myl. & K. 252; Goodson *v.* Ellison, 3 Russ. 583; Knight *v.* Martin, 1 R. & M. 70; Taml. 237; Angier *v.* Stannard, 3 Myl. & K. 566; Curteis *v.* Candler, 6 Mod. 123; Campbell *v.* Horne, 1 Y. & C. Ch. 664; Gardiner *v.* Downes, 22 Beav. 397; Merlin *v.* Blagrave, 25 Beav. 137; Taylor *v.* Glanville, 3 Madd. 176; Loring *v.* Steineman, 1 Met. 207; Grimball *v.* Cruse, 70 Ala. 534; State *v.* Netherton, 26 Mo. App. 414; Little *v.* Thorne, 93 N. C. 72.

(a) In England and in most of the States it is within the jurisdiction of courts of equity to protect trustees by instructions as to their powers and duties in specific instances and as to the interests of beneficiaries in specified property when there are such reasonable doubts that the trustees are not fully protected in acting on the advice of competent lawyers. Stephenson *v.* Norris, 128 Wis. 242; Greely *v.* Nashua, 62 N. H. 166; Traphagen *v.* Levy, 45 N. J. Eq. 448; Read *v.* Citizens' St. R. Co., 110 Tenn. 316; Curtin *v.* Krohn, 4 Cal. App. 131. See also cases cited *infra*, this note.

But it has been held that the equity courts of Pennsylvania have not this advisory power. Morton's Estate, 201 Pa. St. 269; Jacoby's Estate, 201 Pa. St. 442.

The cases in which the advisory jurisdiction has been properly invoked by bills for instructions have usually been for interpretation of doubtful language in the trust instrument or for the determination of the rights or shares of persons beneficially interested, *e. g.*, whether funds in the hands of trustees should be treated as income or as principal. Grimball *v.* Cruse, 70 Ala. 534; Beardsley *v.* Bridgeport, etc., Asylum, 76 Conn. 560; Orr *v.* Yates, 209 Ill. 222, 227; Bailey *v.* Worster, 103 Me. 170; Graham *v.* Whitridge, 99 Md. 248; Heald *v.* Heald, 56 Md. 300; Kelley *v.* Snow, 185 Mass. 288; Edwards *v.* Edwards, 183 Mass. 581; Welch *v.* Adams, 152 Mass. 74; Hyde *v.* Wason, 131 Mass. 450; Dozier *v.* Dozier, 183 Mo. 137; Mersman *v.* Mersman, 136 Mo.

construing a will where the estate devised is a legal one and the questions raised are also purely legal.[1]   A trustee should

[1] Alsbrook v. Reid, 89 N. C. 151.

256; Traphagen v. Levy, 45 N. J. Eq. 448; Lembeck v. Lembeck, 73 N. J. Eq. 427; Greene v. Smith, 17 R. I. 28; Read v. Citizens' St. R. Co., 110 Tenn. 316; McDonald v. Jarvis, 64 W. Va. 62. See Holland Trust Co. v. Sutherland, 177 N. Y. 327, and dissenting opinion.

The purpose of this advisory jurisdiction assumed by courts of equity is not to provide a substitute for the usual legal advisers, but to protect trustees in the class of cases where the advice of competent lawyers is not sufficient protection, because of the doubtful meaning of the trust instrument or because of uncertainty as to the proper application of the law to the facts of the case. Clay v. Gurley, 62 Ala. 14; Vaccaro v. Cicalla, 89 Tenn. 63.

There must also be a real need that the trustee's doubts be solved. Thus ordinarily the courts will not instruct a trustee as to the proper distribution of a fund which has not come into his hands or when the time for distribution is indefinite or far in the future. Stapylton v. Neeley, 44 Fla. 212; Heald v. Heald, 56 Md. 300, 307; Woods v. Fuller, 61 Md. 457; Quincy v. Attorney Gen., 160 Mass. 431; Putnam v. Collamore, 109 Mass. 509; Greeley v. Nashua, 62 N. H. 166; Tuttle v. Woolworth, 62 N. J. Eq. 532; Ogden v. McLane, 73 N. J. Eq. 159; O'Cain v. O'Cain, 51 S. C. 348. See also Warren v. Warren, 72 A. 960 (N. J. Ch. 1909); Strawn v. Trustees, 240 Ill. 111. As was

stated in Griggs v. Veghte, 47 N. J. Eq. 179, the right to instructions does not extend "to the solution of problems which do not present themselves as requiring any action by the trustee; or where the events which must control the rights of parties and the duties of the trustee have not transpired and are yet uncertain; or which should properly be submitted to some other tribunal; or which are so clear as to admit of no question. The court should be called on to decide and direct, not to counsel and advise."

The Rhode Island court has declined to instruct trustees as to their powers and duties with respect to land situated in Massachusetts and controlled by the law of the latter State. Thayer v. Fairchild, 25 R. I. 509.

Upon a bill for instructions properly brought the courts are inclined to allow costs and reasonable counsel fees to all necessary parties out of the property as to which there were doubts. See Bailey v. Worster, 103 Me. 170; Bowditch v. Soltyk, 99 Mass. 136; Deane v. Home for Aged Colored Women, 111 Mass. 132. But it has been held in Wisconsin that a counsel fee cannot properly be allowed to a guardian ad litem except out of the interest of his ward. Stephenson v. Norris, 128 Wis. 242. See also Estate of Cole, 102 Wis. 1, 12; Burney v. Atkinson, 54 S. W. 998 (Tenn. Ch. App. 1899).

The cestuis que trust would usually, if not always, be necessary

781

not render a fictitious account in probate in order to settle doubtful rights, but should ask instructions by a suit in equity.[1] Whenever a case occurs which justifies the proceedings, trustees, by a bill setting forth the facts and joining the proper parties, may ask the court for instructions as to their duties under the circumstances in which they, or the trust funds, are placed. Such instructions and orders, obtained without collusion or fraud, and followed in good faith, will protect trustees from loss, whatever may be the event.[2] It would be a harsh rule to hold the trustee for an error of the court.[3] (a)

§ 477. A trustee, with power to manage real estate for a person absolutely entitled, but incapable from infancy or otherwise of giving any directions, may make repairs; but he cannot go beyond the necessity of the case, at the peril of having his expenses disallowed.[4] If there is a legal tenant for life and remainder over, the tenant for life cannot commit waste, and must not suffer the buildings to fall into decay;[5] but whatever may be the rights or liabilities of a legal tenant for life, the trus-

---

[1] Lincoln v. Aldrich, 141 Mass. 342.

[2] Loring v. Steineman, 1 Met. 207; Tucker v. Horneman, 4 De G., M. & G. 395; Rowland v. Morgan, 13 Jur. 23; Westcott v. Culliford, 3 Hare, 274; Turner v. Frampton, 2 Coll. 336; Merlin v. Blagrave, 25 Beav. 134; Boreham v. Bignall, 8 Hare, 134; Lee v. Delane, 1 De G. & Sm. 1; and see post, § 928.

[3] Frazer's Ex'rs v. Page, 82 Ky. 73.

[4] Bridge v. Brown, 2 Y. & C. Ch. 181; Att. Gen. v. Geary, 3 Mer. 513; Sohier v. Eldredge, 103 Mass. 345; Kearney v. Kearney, 3 Green, Ch. 59; Herbert v. Herbert, 57 How. (N. Y.) Pr. 333.

[5] Powys v. Blagrave, 4 De G., M. & G. 458; Harnett v. Maitland, 16 M. & W. 257.

---

parties to a bill for instructions. *In re* Aldrich's Will, 81 Vt. 308.

(a) The fact that a beneficiary becomes sole trustee of the estate does not invalidate the trust; but if empowered by the will to sell or mortgage the real estate, his interest is such that he can exercise such power only under the control of the court. Irving v. Irving, 47 N. Y. S. 1052; Losey v. Stanley, 147 N. Y. 560; Rogers v. Rogers, 111 N. Y. 228.

tee of an equitable tenant for life cannot interfere with the possession of the equitable tenant for not repairing, unless he is
clothed with the special power of managing the life estate.[1] In
other respects, the equitable and legal rights of tenants for life
and remainder-men, and trustees for tenants for life and remainder-men, are the same. Thus trustees of the life-estate
may cut timber for repairs as against the remainder-man, if
the tenant for life will consent that income shall be applied for
the purpose of using the timber for repairing; for timber cannot be cut to be sold, nor to pay for the labor of repairing.[2]
The repairs by a tenant for life are his own act, however beneficial to the remainder-man, and he cannot charge anything
upon the inheritance for them;[3] nor will a court direct any im-
povements to be made.[4] The court said in one case, that there
might be an exception to this rule; as where a fund was directed
to be laid out in lands, and there was already a settled estate
to the same uses, it might be more beneficial to apply part of
the fund to prevent buildings on the settled estate from going
to destruction, than to apply the whole fund to the purchase of
new lands;[5] but it would be an extraordinary case which would

---

[1] Powys v. Blagrave, Kay, 495; 4 De G., M. & G. 458; Re Skingley, 3
M. & G. 221; Gregg v. Coates, 23 Beav. 33. [In re Cartwright, 41 Ch. Div.
532; In re Hotchkys, 32 Ch. Div. 408; In re Courtier, 34 Ch. Div. 136;
infra, § 552.]

[2] Co. Litt. 53 b, 54 b; Gower v. Eyre, Coop. 156; Marlborough v. St.
John, 5 De G. & Sm. 181. When a power to cut timber for necessary repairs
is given, the trustees may cut timber on one part of the estates for repairs
on another part; and may sell timber, when cut, to pay for timber of the
same species, to be applied in repairs, so long as they do not cut more on
the whole property than the repairs on the whole property require. Att.
Gen. v. Geary, 3 Mer. 513. [As to rights of the tenant for life with respect
to timber, see infra, §§ 541 and 546, and notes.]

[3] Hibbert v. Cooke, 1 S. & S. 552; Caldecott v. Brown, 2 Hare, 144;
Bostock v. Blakeney, 2 Bro. Ch. 653; Hamer v. Tilsley, Johns. 486; Dent
v. Dent, 30 Beav. 363. [Moore v. Simonson, 27 Or. 117; Chilvers v. Race, 196
Ill. 71.]

[4] Nain v. Majoribanks, 3 Russ. 582.

[5] Caldecott v. Brown, 2 Hare, 145; Re Barrington's Estate, 1 John.
& H. 142.

move the court to create the exception.[1] (a) Where the trust
deed requires the trustees to manage the estate according to

[1] Dunne v. Dunne, 3 Sm. & Gif. 22; Dent v. Dent, 30 Beav. 363.

(a) In this country trustees have
in general the power and duty of
maintaining the trust property in
good repair so far as the income
from the property is sufficient for
the purpose. This is especially true
as to property which is in the nature
of an investment for producing
income, and a direction to trustees
to pay the income, rents, or profits
to a life beneficiary will be construed
to mean net income unless the
creator of the trust clearly had a
different intention. Disbrow v.
Disbrow, 61 N. Y. S. 614, 46 App.
Div. 111 (affirmed 167 N. Y. 606);
Smith v. Keteltas, 70 N. Y. S. 1065,
62 App. Div. 174; Stevens v. Melcher, 152 N. Y. 551; Berry v. Stigall,
125 Mo. App. 264; Withingham v.
Schofield's Trustee, 67 S. W. 846,
68 S. W. 116 (Ky. 1902); In re Parr,
92 N. Y. S. 990; Little v. Little,
161 Mass. 188. Doubtless the same
would usually be true with regard
to property which has been specifically devised after the termination
of the trust, if the trustee has been
given the control and management
of the property. In such a case
there is a strong natural presumption that the creator of the trust intended he should keep the property
in repair. As to property held by
the trustee as security, see Wood-
ard v. Wright, 82 Cal. 202.

Where the trustee permits the
life beneficiary to occupy the premises, it has been held to be his duty
to see that the latter makes all
repairs which are needed to main-

tain the property in as good condition as it was at the beginning of
the trust, or when the trustee acquired it. Whittingham v. Schofield's Trustee, 67 S. W. 846 (Ky.
1902).

Where, as is frequently the case
in England, an estate is conveyed
or devised to trustees merely as to
the legal title, the whole right to
possession, management, and income being given to the equitable
life tenant, the trustees have no
duty to repair and usually no right
to use income from other trust
property for the purpose of making
repairs. In re Baring, [1893] 1 Ch.
61; In re Hotchkys, 32 Ch. Div. 408.
See also In re Cartwright, 41 Ch.
Div. 532.

As to the right of the trustee to
use principal of the trust estate to
pay for repairs when the income is
insufficient, or to pay for improvements or alterations of a permanent
nature which are not properly
chargeable against income to which
a life beneficiary is entitled, there
has been much debate. Formerly
the tendency of the courts seems to
have been to treat a trustee as a
life tenant is treated in such cases,
and not to allow him to pay for
or to reimburse to himself out of
principal the expense of permanent
improvements upon the trust property, however great the benefit to
the property, unless the authority
to use principal for that purpose
was clearly given, or unless the expenditure was necessary to save

their "best judgment," it is for them to decide what repairs shall be made, and whether they shall be permanent or tempo-

the trust property from destruction or irreparable loss. Estate of Cole, 102 Wis. 1; *Re* Lord de Tabley, 75 L. T. 328; *In re* Teissier's Settled Estates, [1893] 1 Ch. 153.

American decisions show a strong tendency to modify the effect of this strict rule, by implying from the terms of the trust instrument authority to use principal not only for the preservation of the trust property but for improvements and alterations which cannot properly be paid for from income, whenever such expenditures are a good investment of trust funds. The position of a trustee to whom is given the management of the trust property is materially different from that of a life tenant, for the trustee represents both the life tenant and the remainder-man. The interests of both can be conserved and promoted best by giving to him the right and duty of making outlays on account of either interest in the exercise of his best judgment. Recent American decisions show an inclination on the part of the courts to hold that the right of managing the trust real estate includes by implication authority to make such improvements and alterations, to be paid for out of principal, as are wise and reasonable for conservative investors in real estate. See Jordan *v.* Jordan, 192 Mass. 337; Warren *v.* Pazolt, 203 Mass. 328, 345; Little *v.* Little, 161 Mass. 188, 194; Stevens *v.* Melcher, 152 N. Y. 551; Smith *v.* Ketaltas, 70 N. Y. S. 1065, 62 App.

Div. 174. But see Estate of Cole, 102 Wis. 1; *In re* Miller, 62 N. J. Eq. 764, 67 N. J. Eq. 431; Booth *v.* Bradford, 114 Iowa, 562. Thus it has been held that a trustee who had been given express authority to lease, mortgage or sell, had power to mortgage unproductive city property for the purpose of raising money to build on the land. Boon *v.* Hall, 78 N. Y. S. 557, 76 App. Div. 520. The court in that case said, "The Procrustean rule of the common law against expenditures of this kind has been relaxed somewhat, due probably to the rapid growth in cities, and the necessity of covering vacant property with buildings."

In Warren *v.* Pazolt, 203 Mass. 328, 345, where trustees had torn down several income producing buildings and had erected an office building, it was said, "We have no doubt that a trustee under a Massachusetts trust would be justified in tearing down an old building owned by the trust and erecting a new one in its place when a prudent business man would do so to secure a fair return by way of income, and at the same time to maintain the *corpus* of the portion of the principal so invested intact, having regard to the relation which such an investment, when made, would have to the amount of the principal of the trust fund as a whole." But the court was of opinion that the investment under discussion was unauthorized because it was too large a proportion of the trust property, amounting to approximately

rary. Temporary repairs of trust property are chargeable to the income, and not to the principal.[1] A trust to "receive and pay over rents and profits, beyond necessary expenses" gives power to repair and make valid contracts for that purpose.[2]

§ 478. Superintendents of public works and similar *quasi* trustees may apply the funds under their control in opposing legislation which would operate injuriously to the interests confided to them. Lord Cottenham said that "every trustee is to be allowed the reasonable and proper expenses incurred in protecting the property committed to his care." So they have a right to protect it from indirect and probable injuries;[3] but

[1] Veazie v. Forsaith, 76 Maine, 173. [*Infra*, § 552.]

[2] Cheatham v. Rowland, 92 N. C. 343. [See Att. Gen. v. Brecon, 10 Ch. D. 204; Reg. v. White, 11 Q. B. D. 309.]

[3] Bright v. North, 2 Phill. 220; Queen v. Norfolk Comm'rs, 15 Q. B.

$850,000 when the whole estate totaled $920,000.

In England the Settled Estates Acts have given trustees authority to expend the principal of personalty held in trust upon alterations and repairs of a permanent nature which are needed to put the real estate into tenantable condition where it is to be let, and upon reasonable improvements, such as rebuilding, to the extent of one half the rental value of the property improved. Conway v. Fenton, 40 Ch. Div. 512; *In re* Calverley's Settled Estates, [1904] 1 Ch. 150; *In re* Keck's Settlement, [1904] 2 Ch. 22; *In re* Legh's Settled Estates, [1902] 2 Ch. 274; *Re* Lord de Tabley, 75 L. T. 328; *In re* Teissier's Settled Estates, [1893] 1 Ch. 153.

Even when the trustee has no authority to make such expenditures from the principal of trust funds as an investment, the courts will authorize repairs and improve-

ments which are necessary to preserve the trust property from destruction or from irreparable damage. *In re* Thomas, [1900] 1 Ch. 319; *In re* Courtier, 34 Ch. Div. 136; Booth v. Bradford, 114 Iowa, 562; Conway v. Fenton, 40 Ch. Div. 512. See also Estate of Cole, 102 Wis. 1; Pennington v. Metropolitan Museum, 65 N. J. Eq. 11; *Re* Lord de Tabley, 75 L. T. 328.

When a trustee is without authority to incumber the property to pay for repairs or improvements, a contractor who has furnished material and labor upon the property acquires no mechanics' lien. Hall v. Bullock's Trustee, 97 S. W. 351 (Ky. 1906).

As to what expenditures in the nature of repairs and improvements are properly chargeable to income and what to principal, see *infra*, § 522.

these *quasi* trustees cannot apply the funds of an existing undertaking for the purpose of obtaining larger powers from the
legislature, at least without the consent of all parties interested.[1]

§ 479. An executor is allowed a reasonable time to close up
the testator's establishment. In one case a period of two
months was not considered too long.[2] In most States the time
that the testator's family may remain in his house, and use the
provisions and other materials on hand, is fixed by statute.

§ 480. An executor or a trustee may appropriate a legacy
without suit where the appropriation is such as the court would
have directed;[3] and the trustee may expend money for the protection, safety, and support of a *cestui que trust* who is incapable
from any cause of taking care of himself, but the better way is
to apply to the court.[4]

§ 481. An executor may waive the statute of limitations,
by which a debt due from his testator before his death is barred,
and if he pays such debt it will be allowed in his accounts.[5] But
in most States there are statutes which limit the time of bringing actions against executors and administrators for debts due
from the deceased person. In England, there is a decree of administration. After the action is barred against the executor

549; Att. Gen. *v.* Andrews, 2 McN. & G. 225; Att. Gen. *v.* Eastlake, 11
Hare, 205.

[1] Att. Gen. *v.* Andrews, 2 McN. & G. 225; Vance *v.* East Lancashire
R. Co., 3 K. & J. 50; Att. Gen. *v.* Guardians of Poor, &c., 17 Sim. 6; Att.
Gen. *v.* Norwich, 16 Sim. 225; Stevens *v.* South Devon R. Co., 13 Beav. 48.

[2] Field *v.* Peckett, 29 Beav. 576.

[3] Hutcheson *v.* Hammond, 3 Bro. Ch. 145, 148; Cooper *v.* Douglas, 2
Bro. Ch. 231; Green *v.* Pigot, 1 Bro. Ch. 103; Sitwell *v.* Bernard, 6 Ves.
543; Att. Gen. *v.* Manners, 1 Price, 411; Hill *v.* Atkinson, 2 Mer. 45; Webber
v. Webber, 1 S. & S. 311; 2 Wms. Ex'rs, pp. 861–864.

[4] Duncombe *v.* Nelson, 9 Beav. 211; Chester *v.* Rolfe, 4 De G., M. &
G. 798; *Ex parte* Price, 2 Ves. 407; Williams *v.* Wentworth, 5 Beav. 325;
Wentworth *v.* Tubb, 1 Y. & C. Ch. 171; Barnsley *v.* Powell, Amb. 102.

[5] Stahlschmidt *v.* Lett, 1 Sm. & Gif. 415; Hill *v.* Walker, 4 K. & J. 166;
Hunter *v.* Baxter, 3 Gif. 214; Dring *v.* Greetham, 1 Eq. R. 442.

by statute, or by decree of administration, he must plead the statute bar at his peril; and if he should pay after all actions were barred against him by statute, decree of administration, or otherwise, he would pay upon his own responsibility.[1]

§ 482. A trustee may generally, acting in *good faith*, release or compound a debt due to his trust estate.[2] But if he releases or compromises a debt without sufficient reason or justification, or if he sells a debt for a grossly inadequate consideration, when by proper diligence more could have been realized, he will be answerable for it in his accounts.[3] (*a*) In many States there are statutes authorizing executors, administrators, guardians, and trustees to refer or compromise all claims due to and from the estates which they represent. Such statutes are constitutional,[4] and courts will ratify and confirm such compromises.[5]

§ 483. Trustees who hold an equity of redemption in lands mortgaged for more than their value may release the equity

---

[1] Alston *v.* Trollope, L. R. 2 Eq. 205; Dring *v.* Greetham, 1 Eq. R. 442; Fuller *v.* Redman, 26 Beav. 614; Shewen *v.* Vanderhorst, 1 R. & M. 347; 2 R. & M. 75; Briggs *v.* Wilson, 5 De G., M. & G. 12; 2 Eq. R. 153; *Ex parte* Dewdney, 15 Ves. 496; Pool *v.* Dial, 10 S. C. 440; Bacot *v.* Hayward, 5 S. C. 441.

[2] Blue *v.* Marshall, 3 P. Wms. 381; Ratcliffe *v.* Winch, 17 Beav. 216; Forshaw *v.* Higginson, 8 De G., M. & G. 827.

[3] Jevon *v.* Bush, 1 Vern. 342; Gorge *v.* Chansey, 1 Ch. R. 125; Wiles *v.* Gresham, 5 De G., M. & G. 770; *Re* Alexander, 13 Ir. Ch. 137.

[4] Clark *v.* Cordis, 4 Allen, 466.

[5] Zambaco *v.* Cassanetti, L. R. 11 Eq. 439.

(*a*) 1 Ames on Trusts (2d ed.), 494, n. A trustee of a naked legal trust cannot, without the assent of the beneficiary, compromise or yield a right already accrued to the trust. Bizzell *v.* McKinnon, 121 N. C. 186.

When a deed of trust is given to secure bonds, the trustee cannot release until the bonds are surrendered for cancellation; it is not suffi-cient that the bonds were delivered to a third person in escrow for surrender upon the performance of a condition never performed. Chicago, &c., Land Co. *v.* Peck, 112 Ill. 408. This does not apply when the debtor and all the creditors agree that the security may be released. Pearce *v.* Bryant Coal Co., 121 Ill. 590.

of redemption to avoid the costs of a foreclosure suit, where
such suit will lie, and where costs would be imposed upon them
as defendants.[1] If a trustee is a mortgagee, he would not be
justified in releasing part of his security for the convenience of
the mortgagor merely, nor unless there was some advantage to
be gained to the *cestui que trust* or the trust estate.[2]

§ 484.   Trustees of lands must of course have a general
power to lease them, otherwise they could obtain no income;
but they must make reasonable leases. (*a*)   In one case a lease

---

[1] Lewin on Trusts, 423 (5th ed.)   [2] Ibid.

(*a*) The power of managing the
trust property usually includes
power to give leases upon terms and
for a time which are reasonable.
Such leases will bind the trust property so long as the trust continues.
Hutcheson *v.* Hodnett, 115 Ga. 990.
In re Hubbell Trust, 135 Iowa, 637;
Corse *v.* Corse, 144 N. Y. 569, 572;
In re Odell's Estate, 4 N. Y. S.
463; *In re* James, 64 L. J. Ch. 686.
See also, *infra*, § 528.   But if the
lease is unreasonable as to time
or as to its other terms, equity may
interfere to protect the interests
of the *cestuis*, always having due
regard for the equitable rights
of *bona fide* lessees.   Hutcheson *v.*
Hodnett, 115 Ga. 990.

Whether or not a lease given for
a reasonable term is binding on the
remainder-man in case the trust
terminates before the end of the
term, has not been clearly settled.
The nature of the trustee's legal
estate at the time of the lease is
given has an important bearing.
If the trustee's original legal estate
is for the life of another or for a
term of years, the legal effect of
a lease seems to be limited to his

legal estate, and it has no binding
effect upon the remainder-men after
the termination of the trust unless
his power to lease is construed to
be a power over the property in addition to his powers as legal owner
of a life estate.   *In re* Hubbell
Trust, 135 Iowa, 637. See Edghill
v. Mankey, 79 Neb. 347 (case of a
lease by a life tenant).   In cases
of this kind the weight of authority
is to the effect that the lease is not
binding upon the remainder-men
after the termination of the trust,
Bergengren *v.* Aldrich, 139 Mass.
259; Gomez *v.* Gomez, 147 N. Y.
195; Matter of McCaffrey, 50 Hun,
371; Matter of City of N. Y. (110th
St.), 81 N. Y. S. 32, 81 App. Div.
27; *In re* Armory Board, 60 N. Y. S.
882; Weir *v.* Barker, 93 N. Y. S.
732, 104 App. Div. 112; Standard
Metallic Paint Co. *v.* Prince M'f'g
Co., 133 Pa. St. 474; Hutcheson *v.*
Hodnett, 115 Ga. 990; see also
Wood *v.* Patteson, 10 Beav. 541;
In re Shaw's Trusts, 12 Eq. 124.
But see Shannon *v.* Bradstreet, 1
Sch. & Lef. 52; Clarke *v.* Moore, 1
Jon. & Lat. 723; Lowe *v.* Swift, 2
B. &. B. 529, 535; IV N. Y. Consol.

for ten years was allowed.[1] Trustees have a general power of leasing, if the lease does not exceed the quantity of estate that

[1] Naylor v. Arnitt, 1 R. & M. 501; Bowes v. East London, &c., Jac. 324; Drohan v. Drohan, 1 B. & B. 185; Middleton v. Dodswell, 13 Ves. 268. [See In re Shaw's Trusts, L. R. 12 Eq. 124; Fitzpatrick v. Waring, 11 L. R. Ir. 35; Butler v. Topkis, 63 A. 646 (Del. Ch. 1906).]

Laws, (1909) p. 3393, § 106; English Settled Land Act of 1882, § 36; unless the trustee has been given express power to make leases which shall bind the remainder-men. Taussig v. Reel, 134 Mo. 530.

If the trustee has a fee simple estate, the lease is binding at law after the termination of the trust, and the consequent vesting of the fee in the remainder-men either by his conveyance or by operation of the statute of uses. Any relief given to the remainder-men must be by the intervention of equity. In re Hubbell Trust, 135 Iowa, 637. As to the attitude of equity in cases of this kind, there is very little authority. In the case of In re Hubbell Trust, 135 Iowa, 637, the court treats reasonableness as the test, and lays down the following general rules for the guidance of trustees: "(1) The trustee may lease for such reasonable terms as are customary and essential to the proper care of and to procure a reasonable income from the property. (2) Such terms should not, save on showing of reasonable necessity to effectuate the purposes of the trust, extend beyond the period the trust is likely to continue. (3) Should they extend unreasonably beyond such period, the excess only will be void. (4) Only upon a showing of such reasonable necessity, when not given such power by the instrument creating the trust, will the trustees

be authorized to bind the estate so as to effectually deprive those ultimately entitled thereto of the property itself." And later in the opinion the court says, "In determining what terms are reasonable much necessarily depends on the nature of the property, the customs of the locality, and the conditions of the estate and the probable period of the trust." In this case the trustees had the fee, and the period of the trust was the duration of seven lives and for twenty-one years after the death of the last survivor. The court refused to confirm a lease for 99 years, suggesting that the trustees might properly have given a lease for twenty-one years with rights of renewal at the end of each term until the termination of the trust. The case contains an examination of practically all the authorities upon the point.

In England the Settled Land Act of 1882, § 6, gave to tenants for life power to give ordinary leases for terms not exceeding 21 years, building leases for terms not exceeding 99 years, and mining leases for terms not exceeding 60 years. See Boyce v. Edbrooke, [1903] 1 Ch. 836; Middlemas v. Stevens, [1901] 1 Ch. 574. § 106, of the New York Real Property Law, IV Consol. Laws (1909), p. 3393, provides that trustees to hold for the life of a beneficiary may lease for five years or less without application to court,

is in them, and is a reasonable one. In case of charitable trusts the general rule is that the trustees should lease only for years, but even a perpetual lease will not be set aside in a collateral attack unless clearly unreasonable or detrimental to the beneficiaries; and the lessees who have in good faith made valuable improvements will be protected in equity if the lease is set aside.[1] In the case of farming lands, husbandry leases only can be made: in England, such leases never exceed ten years.[2] Probably there is no such general custom in this country. But if it is a simple trust, and the *cestui que trust* is in possession, the trustee can do nothing without the consent of the beneficiary.

§ 485. A trustee may reimburse himself for money advanced in good faith for the benefit of the *cestui que trust*, or for the protection of the property, or for his own protection in the management of the trust. (*a*) It is a rule that the *cestui que trust* ought to save the trustee harmless where the trustee has honestly, fairly, and without possibility of gain to himself, paid out money for the benefit of the *cestui que trust*. And a trustee who accepts office at the request of a *cestui que trust* is entitled

[1] Richmond *v*. Davis, 103 Ind. 449.
[2] Att. Gen. *v*. Owen, 10 Ves. 560.

and that the court may authorize longer leases. See Weir *v*. Barker, 93 N. Y. S. 732, 104 App. Div. 112.

It has been held that a court of equity may authorize a lease for 99 years on the same grounds on which it may authorize a sale where the trust instrument has given no such power, viz., the necessity of preserving the trust estate for the main purposes of the trust. Denegre *v*. Walker, 214 Ill. 113; Marsh *v*. Reed, 184 Ill. 263.

As to the effect of authorization of a lease by the court with all parties

in interest represented, see Gomez *v*. Gomez, 147 N. Y. 195.

(*a*) Anderson *v*. Kemper, 116 Ky. 339; Winslow *v*. Young, 94 Me. 145; Western Union Tel. Co. *v*. Boston Safe Dep. & Tr. Co., 104 Fed. 580; Dantzler *v*. McInnis, 151 Ala. 293; Johnson *v*. Leman, 131 Ill. 609.

Even when the trust is subsequently set aside as invalid. Beck *v*. Kinealy, 89 Mo. App. 418.

As to rights of creditors by way of substitution to the trustee's right of indemnity, see *infra*, § 815 *b*, note.

to be indemnified by the *cestui* against all loss which may accrue in the proper administration of the trust.[1] (*a*)

§ 486. The trustees or managers of a trading company or partnership have no power in *any case* to borrow money beyond the capital prescribed in the deed of settlement, and bind the company or its members.[2] And where the trustees borrow money, without special authority conferred by the deed, for launching and enlarging the business, and make themselves personally liable, they have no remedy against the other members of the company.[3] But if the trustees incur expenses and debts, within the scope of their authority, and in the ordinary business of the company, or borrow money to pay for such expenses or debts, the company are in equity liable to pay or contribute to the payment of such debts.[4] (*b*)

[1] Balch *v.* Hyham, 2 P. Wms. 453; Jervis *v.* Wolferstan, 18 L. R. Eq. 18; Snyder's app., 72 Mo. 253. [Hobbs *v.* Wayet, 36 Ch. Div. 256.]
[2] Burmester *v.* Norris, 6 Exch. 796; Ricketts *v.* Bennett, 4 C. B. 688; Hawtayne *v.* Bourne, 7 M. & W. 595; Hawken *v.* Bourne, 8 M. & W. 703.
[3] *In re* Worcester Corn Exch. Co., 3 De G., M. & G. 180; *Ex parte* Chippendale, 4 De G., M. & G. 43; Australian, &c. Co. *v.* Mounsey, 4 K. & J. 733.
[4] Ibid.; Tramp's Case, 29 Beav. 353; Hoare's Case, 30 Beav. 225.

(*a*) In Hardoon *v.* Belilios, [1901] A. C. 118, the court had to consider the liability of the beneficiary, who was not the creator of the trust, to reimburse the trustee of shares of stock in a banking company for calls upon the stock in excess of the value of the shares. It was held that where the beneficiary is *sui juris* the trustee's right to indemnity against liability incurred by his retention of the trust property is not limited to the trust property but extends further and imposes upon the beneficiary a personal obligation, enforceable in equity, to indemnify his trustee, and the latter need not prove any request from the *cestui* to incur such liability. But see Fraser *v.* Murdoch, 6 A. C. 855; *In re* Earl of Winchilsea's Policy Trusts, 39 Ch. Div. 168.

(*b*) In Warren *v.* Pazolt, 203 Mass. 328, 349, it was held that trustees with power to sell the trust property and to change investments had no implied power to borrow money for the purpose of paying beneficiaries whose shares had become due, and that notes given by the trustees for this purpose should not have been paid out of the trust property. But it was held that, to avoid selling bonds and other securities at a disadvantageous time, they had authority to

§ 487. A trustee would probably be justified in insuring the property, and in case of loss the insurance money would belong to the *cestui que trust;* [1] but where there is a tenant for life entitled to the income, it would be safer to have such tenant's consent before paying the premium out of his income.[2] (*a*) A mortgagee cannot insure at the expense of the mortgagor without a special stipulation to that effect; and if he insures without such stipulation, he cannot charge the premiums to the mortgagor in his accounts.[3] If a lessor and a lessee insure on their own accounts, neither can claim anything under the policy of the other.[4] So, if a tenant for life insures out of the income, the remainder-man can claim no benefit from the policy. (*b*) If, however, a common carrier insures property in his hands as a carrier, and there is a loss, he holds the proceeds, after defraying his charges, in trust for the owners of the property, even although such owners might not be able to recover of him for the loss of the property.[5]

---

[1] Lerow *v.* Wilmarth, 9 Allen, 382. [Bridge *v.* Bridge, 146 Mass. 373; Stevens *v.* Melcher, 152 N. Y. 551.]

[2] See *post*, § 553; *Ex parte* Andrews, 2 Rose, 412; Fry *v.* Fry, 27 Beav. 146. If an annuity and a policy on the life of *cestui que vie* are made the subject of a settlement, it is implied that the trustees shall pay the premiums out of the income. Darcy *v.* Croft, 9 Ir. Ch. 19.

[3] Dobson *v.* Land, 8 Hare, 216; Phillips *v.* Eastwood, Llo. & Goo. t. Sugd. 289; *Ex parte* Andrews, 2 Rose, 412.

[4] Duncombe *v.* Nelson, 9 Beav. 211; Chester *v.* Rolfe, 4 De G., M. & G. 798.

[5] Lauderdale, &c. *v.* Glyn, 1 El. & El. 612.

borrow for a short time on security of the property they contemplated selling, the loan to them with interest to be repaid out of the proceeds of the security when it should be sold. Interest paid on such temporary loans to them was held to be a proper charge in their accounts.

(*a*) That a trustee should pay insurance premiums out of income, see Bridge *v.* Bridge, 146 Mass. 373; Stevens *v.* Melcher, 152 N. Y. 551; *In re* Earl of Egmont's Trusts, [1908] 1 Ch. 821.

(*b*) See Gaussen *v.* Whatman, 93 L. T. 101; Spalding *v.* Miller, 103 Ky. 405; *infra*, § 553 and note. But see Welch *v.* London Assurance Co., 151 Pa. St. 607; Green *v.* Green, 50 S. C. 514; Clyburn *v.* Reynolds, 31 S. C. 118.

§ 488.   As there are legal estates and equitable estates, so there are legal powers and equitable powers. Legal powers operate upon the legal estate, and are cognizable in courts of law; equitable powers affect the equitable estate alone, and are exclusively cognizable in courts of equity. Thus, if land is given to A. for life, remainder to B. and his heirs, and a power is given to C. in such manner as to operate under the statutes of uses, the execution of the power conveys the legal estate, and the common law will notice it. But if lands are limited to the use of A. and his heirs, in trust for B. for life, remainder in trust for C. and his heirs, and a power not operating under the statute of uses is given, either to the trustee or the *cestui que trust*, the execution of the power will have no effect at law. It will only convey an equitable or beneficial interest, and can be recognized only in equity.[1]

§ 489.   An equitable power, like a legal power, may be appendant to an interest in the estate, and grow out of it, or it may be simply a collateral power given to some person who has no interest whatever in the estate, legal or equitable. Thus a testator gave an estate to his sister and her heirs in trust, to settle it upon such descendants of the donor's mother as she should think fit. The sister married, and it became a question whether she could execute the power under coverture. But Lord Hardwicke held, "that it was a naked equitable power, not coupled with any beneficial interest, and that a *feme covert* can execute such naked power."[2]   But where a donor gave a legal estate to trustees in trust for an *infant feme covert* for life, and to permit her by deed or writing to dispose of the estate as she should think fit, and the donor died leaving the *infant feme covert* his heir-at-law, and she, during her infancy and coverture, executed the power, — Lord Hardwicke held this to be bad, as she had the trust in equity for life, and the trust of the inheritance, as the heir-at-law of the donor, therefore the whole

---

[1] Lewin on Trusts, 427.

[2] Godolphin *v.* Godolphin, 1 Ves. 21; *ante*, § 49.

equitable inheritance was in her, and this was a power over her own inheritance, and neither infants nor married women can execute a power coupled with an interest.[1] (a)

§ 490. Courts have treated powers as either *strict* or simply *directory*. *Strict* powers are such as are to be executed only under the exact circumstances prescribed in the instrument of trust, and in the exact manner and in favor of the particular class of persons named.[2] *Directory* powers are monitory only, and may be executed with some degree of latitude; as where an advowson was vested in trustees, to present a fit person within *six months* of the incumbent's decease, the direction was held to be monitory, and that the power might be executed after that time had elapsed.[3] So, when *six* trustees were empowered, when reduced to *three*, to appoint others, and all died but one, this power was held to be simply directory, and that one might fill the vacancies.[4] Where a power was given to sell with all convenient speed, and within *five years* after the testator's decease, these words were held to be directory only, and that a sale and a good title could be made after that time.[5] And when twenty-five trustees were appointed with a direction that when reduced to fifteen the vacancies should be filled, the court held that the trustees were at *liberty* to fill the vacancies when

[1] Hearle *v.* Greenbank, 1 Ves. 298; Blithe's Case, Freem. 91; Penne *v.* Peacock, For. 43.

[2] Loring *v.* Blake, 98 Mass. 253; Hall *v.* Culver, 34 Conn. 403; Beatty *v.* Clark, 29 Cal. 11; Boorum *v.* Wells, 4 Green, Ch. 87.

[3] Att. Gen. *v.* Scott, 1 Ves. 413; Shalter's App., 43 Penn. St. 83.

[4] Att. Gen. *v.* Floyer, 2 Vern. 748; Att. Gen. *v.* Bishop of Litchfield, 5 Ves. 825; Att. Gen. *v.* Cuming, 2 Y. & C. Ch. 139 ; Foley *v.* Wontner, 2 J. & W. 245.

[5] Smith *v.* Kenney, 33 Tex. 283; Pearce *v.* Gardner, 10 Hare, 287; Cuff *v.* Hall, 1 Jur. (N. S.) 973; Shalter's App. 43 Penn. St. 83.

(a) In *In re* D'Angibau, 15 Ch. Div. 228, it was held that an infant could exercise a power of appointment over property when he had no interest of his own in the property that would be affected or disposed of by such exercise of the power.

reduced to only seventeen, and that they would be compelled to exercise the power when reduced to fifteen.[1] Again, when powers are coupled with an interest in an estate, a substantial compliance with the directions in executing the powers will be sufficient.[2]

§ 491.   Although powers may be given to trustees in the same words which are used in giving them an estate, yet different rules of construction will apply to the gift. Thus, if an estate is given to A. and B. and their heirs, A. and B. may convey it to strangers, and the survivor, where joint-tenancy is not abolished, may devise it; but if a power is given to A. and B. and their heirs, it can neither be assigned by both, nor devised by the survivor.[3] Thus, where a *mere naked* power was given to A. and B. and their heirs, Lord Chief-Justice Wilmot said: "It was equivalent to saying, the power is to be executed by consent of both while they live; but when one dies, that consent shall devolve on the heir; the heir of the dead trustee shall consent, as well as the surviving trustee. One may abuse the power. I will supply the loss of one by his heir, and the loss of both by the heirs of both."[4] But where the estate itself is given to A. and B. and their heirs in trust, with certain powers appendant, the power is an essential part of the trust, and passes to the survivor.

§ 492.   In one case, a naked power of sale was given to *three trustees and their heirs*, to preserve contingent remainders. The money was to be paid into the hands of the trustees, the survivors or survivor of them, and the executors, administrators, or assigns of such survivor. New trustees were to be appointed as often as one or more of the trustees died. One trustee died, and the Court of Queen's Bench determined that

---

[1] Doe *v.* Roe, Anst. 86.
[2] Rowe *v.* Becket, 30 Ind. 154; Rowe *v.* Lewis, id. 163.
[3] Cole *v.* Wade, 16 Ves. 46.
[4] Mansell *v.* Vaughn, Wilmot, 50.

the survivors could not execute the power.[1] Lord Eldon was
dissatisfied with the judgment, and said, Did the court "consider that the two surviving trustees and the heir of the deceased trustee were to act together? for it was one thing to say
that the survivors should not act until another was appointed,
and a different thing to say that the heir of the deceased trustee
could act in the meantime." [2] But his Lordship felt himself
bound by the authority, and refused to compel a purchaser to
take a title under similar circumstances.[3] It will be noticed,
that, in this case, the estate itself was not in the trustees; if it
had been, the survivors would have had an interest and could
have executed the power: for it has been held, that where an
estate was devised to three trustees and their respective heirs,
upon the trust that they and their respective heirs should sell,
the word "respective" was surplusage, and that the survivors
could make a title.[4]

§ 493. A power limited to "executors" or "sons-in-law"
may be exercised by the survivors, so long as the plural number remains; [5] and if the power is limited to a number of trustees,
it may reasonably be concluded, that whether they have any
estate or not, *i. e.*, whether the power is an adjunct to the trust,
or collateral to it, it may be exercised by the surviving trustees.
A power given to "executors" will, if annexed to the office of
executor, be continued to the single survivor.[6] So a power

[1] Townsend *v.* Wilson, 1 B. & A. 608; 2 Madd. 261; Cooke *v.* Crawford,
13 Sim. 91.

[2] Hall *v.* Dewes, Jac. 193; Jones *v.* Price, 11 Sim. 557.

[3] Hall *v.* Dewes, Jac. 189.

[4] Jones *v.* Price, 11 Sim. 557; Hewett *v.* Hewett, 2 Eden, 332; Amb.
208.

[5] 1 Sugd. Pow. 128 (8th ed.).

[6] 1 Sugd. Pow. 128, Howell *v.* Barnes, Cro. Car. 382; Brassey *v.* Chalmers, 4 De G., M. & G. 528, reversing same case in 16 Beav. 231; Colsten
v. Chandos, 4 Bush, 666. [Bredenburg *v.* Bardin, 36 S. C. 197; Dick *v.*
Harby, 48 S. C. 516; Fitzgerald *v.* Standish, 102 Tenn. 383   But it is
otherwise if the power is not annexed to the office. Dillard *v.* Dillard,
97 Va. 434, 440.]

given to "trustees" will, as annexed to the estate and office, be exercisable by a single survivor;[1] (a) but it cannot be exercised by one trustee in the lifetime of the other who has not effectually renounced the trust.[2] (b)   If a power is communicated to the *trustees* for the time being, it cannot be exercised by a *single* trustee.[3]   Where there was a trust for sale, but no sale was to be made without the consent of the testator's sons and daughters, and there were seven sons and daughters, and one died, it was held that a sale with the consent of the survivors was too

---

[1] Lane v. Debenham, 11 Hare, 188; Colsten v. Chandos, 4 Bush, 666; Re Bernstein, 3 Redf. (N. Y.) 20.

[2] Lancashire v. Lancashire, 2 Phill. 664; 1 De G. & Sm. 28. [As to express provision that a majority may execute the power and as to lunacy of a trustee, see Bascom v. Weed, 105 N. Y. S. 459.]

[3] Ibid. [Coleman v. Connolly, 242 Ill. 574.]

(a) The same is true where the donees who survive are benficially interested in the subject of the power, unless there is something to show that the donor intended there should be no survival. Easy Payment Property Co. v. Vonderhide, 123 Ky. 352.

Where a power is to be exercised only upon the approval of two or more who are beneficially interested, the approval of the survivors or survivor of those whose approval is a condition precedent is ordinarily sufficient, provided they continue to have a beneficial interest in the exercise of the power. IV N. Y. Consol. Laws (1909), p. 3407, § 174. But the death of all of those whose approval is made a condition precedent ordinarily puts an end to the power. Peirsol v. Roop, 56 N. J. Eq. 739; Gulick v. Griswold, 160 N. Y. 399; Wells v. Brooklyn, etc., R. Co., 106 N. Y. S. 77, 121 App. Div. 491.

(b) Where the same person is

named as executor and trustee and powers are given to him which are evidently designed to be in aid of the trust, they will be held to attach to the office of trustee and not to the office of executor in case it happens that the two offices become separated.   Lahey v. Kortright, 132 N. Y. 450; Pollock v. Hooley, 67 Hun, 370.   Thus where a power of sale for reinvestment was given to the person named as executrix and trustee, and she renounced her executorship, it was held that the power of sale remained in her as trustee and did not pass to an administrator c. t. a.   Mordecai v. Schirmer, 38 S. C. 294; Casselman v. McCooley, 73 N. J. Eq. 253.   In a case where the executor-trustee had power to sell as executor but not as trustee it was held that after he had turned the property over to himself as trustee he had no power of sale.   Gibney v. Allen, 156 Mich. 301.

doubtful a title to be specifically enforced.[1] But where trustees had power to sell, with the consent of a majority of the
testator's children then living, and all the children were dead,
it was held that the trustees could execute the power by a sale,
and make a good title.[2]

§ 494. Where powers are confided to trustees "and their
heirs," and not "assigns," they cannot be exercised by persons
claiming by assignment under the trustees or their heirs.[3] (a)
So they cannot be exercised by a "devisee" of the original trustee,
for a devise is an assignment;[4] if the word "assigns" is added
to the limitation to the trustees, the devisees can execute such
part of the trusts as may be delegated to third persons.[5]

§ 495. When a discretionary legal power is expressly given
to A. and his assigns, the assignee or devisee of A., or any one
claiming under him by operation of law as heir or executor,
may execute the power.[6] As where a power in a mortgage is
limited to the mortgagee, his heirs, executors, administrators,
and assigns, the power goes along with and is annexed to the
security, and the power can be executed by all those to whom

[1] Sykes v. Sheard, 2 De G., J. & Sm. 6; Alley v. Lawrence, 12 Gray, 374.
[2] Leeds v. Wakefield, 10 Gray, 514; Williams v. Williams, 1 Duvall, 221.
[3] Bradford v. Belfield, 2 Sim. 264.
[4] Cooke v. Crawford, 13 Sim. 91. See Midland Counties Ry. Co. v.
Westcombe, 11 Sim. 57; Titley v. Wolstenholme, 7 Beav. 425; Mortimer
v. Ireland, 6 Hare, 196; Ockleston v. Heap, 1 De G. & Sm. 640; Beasley v.
Wilkinson, 13 Jur. 649; Wilson v. Bennett, 20 L. J. Ch. 279; Macdonald
v. Walker, 14 Beav. 556; 2 Jarm. on Wills, 716; 1 Greenl. Cruise, 407; Re
Burtt's Est., 1 Drew. 319.
[5] Lane v. Debenham, 11 Hare, 188; Saloway v. Strawbridge, 1 K. & J.
371; 7 De G., M. & G. 594.
[6] How v. Whitfield, 1 Vent. 338; 1 Freem. 476; Montague v. Dawes,
14 Allen, 369.

(a) If real estate is devised to
trustees and "their heirs" (without
"assigns") in trust for sale, the
trust is not personal, but is annexed to the fee taken by the trustees, so that it can be exercised by
the surviving trustee's devisees. Osborne to Rowlett, 13 Ch. D. 774;
but see In re Morton & Hallett,
15 id. 143.

any interest in the estate may come, whether heir, executor, administrator, or assignee.¹ When a mortgage is made to A. and B., their heirs and assigns, to secure a joint advance, the power and security are coupled together and go to the survivor, who may execute the power by sale or otherwise.² But if an estate is vested in a trustee upon trust, that he, his heirs, executors, administrators, or "assigns," shall sell, &c., the word "assigns" will not authorize the trustee to assign the estate to a stranger;³ nor, if assigned, can the stranger execute the power.⁴

§ 496. Where the power is matter of personal confidence in the trustee, it cannot be extended beyond the express words and clear intention of the donor; so if a power, indicating personal confidence, is given to a trustee and his *executors*, and the executor of the trustee dies, his executor, or the executor of the executor, who by law in England is executor both of the trustee and his executor, cannot execute the power.⁵ Still less could the executor of the executor of the trustee execute such power in this country; for if an executor dies before completing his trust, an executor *de bonis non* must be appointed. (a)

§ 497. A discretionary power to four trustees and the *survivors* of them cannot be executed by the last survivor; for, though the power may generally be held to survive, an inten-

---

¹ See *ante*, § 199; Saloway *v.* Strawbridge, 1 K. & J. 371; 7 De G., M. & G. 594.

² Hind *v.* Poole, 1 K. & J. 383.

³ Lewin on Trusts, 431; Cooke *v.* Crawford, 13 Sim. 98.

⁴ Ibid.; Mortimer *v.* Ireland, 11 Jur. 721; 6 Hare, 196; Wilson *v.* Bennett, 5 De G. & Sm. 495; Stevens *v.* Austen, 7 Jur. (N. S.) 873; Burtt's Est., 1 Drew. 319; Titley *v.* Wolstenholme, 7 Beav. 425; Ockleston *v.* Heap, 1 De G. & Sm. 542; Ashton *v.* Wood, 3 Sm. & Gif. 436; Hall *v.* May, 3 K. & J. 585; Hardwick *v.* Mynd, 1 Anst. 109, is not law.

⁵ Cole *v.* Wade, 16 Ves. 44; Stile *v.* Thompson, Dyer, 210 a; Sugd. Pow. 129 (8th ed.).

(a) But see Reeves *v.* Tappan, 21 S. C. 1.

tion to the contrary, if it can fairly be inferred, will control. The settlor may be supposed to have said, "I repose confidence in any two of the trustees jointly, but in neither one of them individually." [1] (a) But if the power is to four trustees, and the *survivor* of them, it may well be urged that on the death of one, the power may still be exercised by the survivors; for the settlor has said that he reposes confidence in the four jointly, and in each one of them individually.[2]

§ 498. If a power is given to trustees, to be exercised during the *continuance* of the trust, it cannot be exercised after the time when the trust ought to have ceased, though, from the delay of the trustees, it happens that the trust has not in fact been executed.[3] If the powers are not confined to the continuance of the trust, yet they will cease when the objects of the trust have been fully exhausted, and not before.[4] (b) If there is no direction as to the continuance of the trust, the powers will

[1] Hibbard *v.* Lamb, Amb. 309; Eaton *v.* Smith, 2 Beav. 236.

[2] Crewe *v.* Dicken, 4 Ves. 97.

[3] Wood *v.* White, 2 Keen, 664; the matter of fact was charged in this case on appeal in 4 Myl. & Cr. 460.

[4] Wolley *v.* Jenkins, 23 Beav. 53; Mortlock *v.* Buller, 10 Ves. 315; Wheete *v.* Hall, 17 Ves. 86; Lantsbery *v.* Collier, 2 K. & J. 709; McWhorter *v.* Agnew, 6 Paige, 111; Moore *v.* Shultz, 13 Penn. St. 101; Salisbury *v.* Bigelow, 20 Pick. 174; Huckabee *v.* Billingsby, 16 Ala. 417; Hetzel *v.* Hetzel, 69 N. Y. 1; Brown *v.* Meigs, 11 Hun (N. Y.), 203.

(a) But in Sweet *v.* Schliemann, 88 N. Y. S. 916, 95 App. Div. 266, where power of sale was given to two trustees "and the *successors* of them, one having failed to qualify and the other having died, it was held that the power vested in a single substituted trustee.

(b) Power to sell usually ends when the trust ends, but if it affirmatively appears that it was the intention of the testator that the trustees should have a power of sale after the trust in other respects has terminated, such power may be exercised after the termination of the trust. Heard *v.* Read, 171 Mass. 374; Dodson *v.* Ashley, 101 Md. 513; Parker *v.* Seeley, 56 N. J. Eq. 110; Corse *v.* Chapman, 153 N. Y. 466, 473; Mimms *v.* Delk, 42 S. C. 195. As where it was intended that the trustee should divide among several who were entitled in remainder. *In re* Sudeley, [1894] 1 Ch. 334.

subsist till the end of the trust, although there may be delay by the trustees in making the conveyances directed by the settlor.[1] If the trust continues as to part of the property, but has ceased as to part, the power will remain, and can be exercised over the whole,[2] unless there is a clear direction to the contrary.[3] As where an estate was vested in trustees, one-half in trust for A. for life, remainder to her children at twenty-one, and the other half in trust for B. for life, remainder to her children at twenty-one, with power to the trustees to sell during the continuance of the trust, and the children of one had arrived at twenty-one, and the trust had determined as to their share, it was held that the trustees had power to sell the whole under the terms of the settlement; it being necessary that the trustees should have the right to sell the whole, in order to preserve the trust for the full benefit of the other half.[4]

§ 499. A power of sale, whether a common-law or equitable power, or taking effect under the statute of uses, can be exercised only by the persons to whom it is expressly given.[5] If a power of sale or any other power is given to two or more persons by name, with no words of survivorship, and one dies, or refuses to act, the others cannot execute the power.[6] (a) But

[1] Wood v. White, 4 Myl. & Cr. 460; Bolton v. Jacks, 6 Rob. (N. Y.) 166; Cresson v. Ferree, 70 Penn. St. 446.

[2] Trower v. Knightley, 6 Madd. 134; Taite v. Swinstead, 26 Beav. 525.

[3] Wood v. White, 4 Myl. & Cr. 460.

[4] Trower v. Knightley, 6 Madd. 134; Taite v. Swinstead, 26 Beav. 525; Jefferson v. Tyrer, 9 Jur. 1083; Re Cooke, 4 Ch. D. 454; Re Brown, L. R. 10 Eq. 349.

[5] 1 Sugd. Pow. 141, 144 (6th ed.); Boston Franklinite Co. v. Condit, 4 Green, Ch. 395.

[6] Ibid. [Hadley v. Hadley, 147 Ind. 423, 429, a naked power.]

(a) This statement should be confined to naked powers given to several jointly, and even then if a surviving donee is beneficially interested in the exercise of the power, the *prima facie* presumption is that the donor intended the power to continue in him alone by survival. *Supra*, § 493, and note. If the power is attached to the office of trustee or executor, it will continue in the survivor in the absence of expressed

where the power is given to the *trustees as a class*, or to the office of trustee, whether their names are mentioned or not, the power will continue and can be exercised as long as there are more trustees than one, although there are no words of survivorship.[1] In the United States, a power given to executors or trustees, as such, to sell real estate may be exercised so long as a single donee survives; and so, if land is given to trustees to sell, the trustees are joint-tenants, and the survivor will have the freehold, and may exercise the power of sale, it being a power coupled with an interest.[2] And only the acting

---

[1] Ibid.; Co. Litt. 113 a, n. 2; In Matter of Bull, 45 Barb. 334.

[2] Peter *v.* Beverley, 10 Pet. 532; 1 How. 134; Shelton *v.* Homer, 5 Met. 466; Treadwell *v.* Cordis, 5 Gray, 388; Gibbs *v.* Marsh, 2 Met. 252; Wells *v.* Lewis, 4 Met. (Ky.) 269; Bonifaut *v.* Greenfield, Cro. Eliz. 80; Franklin *v.* Osgood, 2 Johns. Ch. 19; Zeback *v.* Smith, 3 Binn. 69; Davoue *v.* Fanning, 2 Johns. Ch. 254; Muldrow *v.* Fox, 2 Dana, 79; Hunt *v.* Rousmaniere, 2 Mason, 244; Wood *v.* Sparks, 1 Dev. & Bat. 389; Burr *v.* Sim, 1 Whart. 266; Niles *v.* Stevens, 4 Denio, 399; Coykendall *v.* Rutherford, 1 Green, Ch. 360; Putnam Free School *v.* Fisher, 30 Maine, 526; Jackson *v.* Burtis, 14 Johns. 391; Robertson *v.* Gaines, 2 Humph. 367; Miller *v.* Meetch, 8 Barr,

or implied intention that it should not do so. *Supra*, § 493. And when a power of sale or a similar power is given to persons who are named as trustees or executors there is a natural *prima facie* presumption of an intention that the power should survive the death, resignation, or removal of one or more of those named as donees. N. Y. Code of Civil Procedure, § 2642; Rankine *v.* Metzger, 74 N. Y. S. 649, 69 App. Div. 264 (affirmed, 174 N. Y. 540); Draper *v.* Montgomery, 95 N. Y. S. 904, 108 App. Div. 63; Sweet *v.* Schliemann, 88 N. Y. S. 916, 95 App. Div. 266; Haggart *v.* Ranney, 73 Ark. 344; Hunter *v.* Anderson, 152 Pa. St. 386; Lippincott *v.* Wikoff, 54 N. J. Eq. 107.

It has been pointed out that lunacy of one of several trustees does not have the same effect as death or resignation. He still continues to be a trustee, and it is the duty of his cotrustees to ask for his removal. Bascom *v.* Weed, 105 N. Y. S. 459.

When the surviving trustee is the sole life beneficiary, it has been held in New York that she is incompetent to execute the trust. Losey *v.* Stanley, 147 N. Y. 560, 569; Haendle *v.* Stewart, 82 N. Y. S. 823, 84 App. Div. 274; Hilton *v.* Sowenfield, 104 N. Y. S. 942; Weeks *v.* Frankel, 112 N. Y. S. 562. See *contra*, Davis *v.* Davis, 112 S. W. 948 (Tex. Civ. App. 1908). But the fact that the surviving trustee or a substituted trustee is one of the beneficiaries does not disqualify her. Sweet *v.* Schliemann, 88 N. Y. S. 916, 95 App. Div. 266.

executors or trustees need join in executing such powers.[1] In many States, statutes have been enacted which authorize the survivor of several executors to execute even naked powers given by will. A grave question has arisen upon these statutes, whether they extend to the execution of discretionary powers given to trustees, or whether they are confined to powers connected with the administrative functions of executors.[2] In general, it would be a question as to the intention of the donor, whether the powers given should be executed by all the trustees named, or any one or more of them; or whether it was the intention that successors or others connected with the trust should have and execute the powers conferred; in other words, the question is, whether the donor reposed a personal trust and confidence in the trustees appointed, or whether he reposed the power in whomsoever might in fact fill the office of trustee.[3] (a)

417; Sharp v. Pratt, 15 Wend. 610; Wardwell v. McDowell, 31 Ill. 364; Golder v. Bressler, 105 Ill. 419; Jackson v. Given, 16 Johns. 167; Jackson v. Bates, 14 id. 391; Jackson v. Ferris, 15 id. 391; Watson v. Pearson, 2 Exch. 594, n.; Cadogan v. Ewart, 7 Ad. & El. 636; Taylor v. Morris, 1 Comst. 341; Tainter v. Clark, 13 Met. 220; Warden v. Richards, 11 Gray, 277; Gould v. Mather, 104 Mass. 283; Parker v. Sears, 117 Mass. 513; Collier v. Grimsey, 36 Ohio St. 17. This matter is regulated in several States by statutes which cannot be cited, but which the reader will consult in his own State. In some States, if one of several trustees has been discharged after acceptance, the court must fill the vacancy before the trustees can execute the power. Matter of Van Wyck, 1 Barb. 565.

[1] In Matter of Bull, 45 Barb. 334; Hutchins v. Baldwin, 7 Bosw. 236.

[2] In Kentucky, South Carolina, and Mississippi, it is held that they do not extend to discretionary powers, but are confined to the functions of the executors in settling up estates. Woodbridge v. Watkins, 3 Bibb, 350; Clay v. Hart, 7 Dana, 1; Brown v. Hobson, 3 A. K. Marsh, 381; Mallet v. Smith, 6 Rich. Eq. 22; Bartlett v. Southerland, 2 Cush. (Miss.), 401. In New York, the statute was held to apply to powers to be executed by trustees generally. Taylor v. Morris, 1 Comst. 341. And see Chanet v. Villeponteaux, 3 McCord, 29; Wood v. Sparks, 1 Dev. & Bat. 389.

[3] Granville v. McNeile, 13 Jur. 252; 7 Hare, 156; Affleck v. James, 17 Sim. 121; Shelton v. Homer, 5 Met. 462; Ross v. Barclay, 18 Penn. St. 179; Pratt v. Rice, 7 Cush. 209; Cole v. Wade, 17 Ves. 27; Lorings v. Marsh,

(a) See infra, §§ 503, 505.

§ 500. As general rule, administrators with the will annexed are clothed only with the ordinary duties and powers

6 Wall. 337; Fontain *v.* Ravnell, 17 How. 369; Gibbs *v.* Marsh, 2 Met. 252.
Where the language of the will clearly indicates an intention on the part of
the testator to convert realty into personalty, as where the proceeds of
the sale are directed to be distributed or applied by the executor or trustee,
or the produce of the real estate is blended in a common fund with the personalty in the scheme provided for the settlement of the estate, there is
no room for doubt upon this question, and the cases hold that the power to
sell is attached to the office, and may be executed by the acting executors
or trustees, or by the survivor of them. Bonifaut *v.* Greenfield, Cro. Eliz.
80; Tylden *v.* Hyde, 2 S. & S. 238; Forbes *v.* Peacock, 11 Sim. 152; Gray *v.*
Henderson, 71 Penn. St. 368; Dorland *v.* Dorland, 2 Barb. 63; Sharp *v.*
Pratt, 15 Wend. 610; Meakings *v.* Cromwell, 2 Sandf. 512; Putnam Free
School *v.* Fisher, 30 Maine, 523; De Saussure *v.* Lyons, 16 Rich. 492; Lockhart *v.* Northington, 1 Sneed, 318; Going *v.* Emery, 16 Pick. 111; Alley
v. Lawrence, 12 Gray, 373; Warden *v.* Richards, 11 Gray, 277; Terre *v.* Am.
Board, 53 Vt. 171. To effect a conversion by power of sale, the will or
deed must order sale absolutely for all purposes, irrespective of contingencies or discretion. Anewalt's App., 42 Penn. St. 414; Bleight *v.* Bank,
10 id. 131; Henry *v.* McCloskey, 9 Watts, 145; Wright *v.* Trustees, &c.,
1 Hoff. 203; Dominick *v.* Michael, 4 Sandf. 274; Evans *v.* Kingsbury, 2
Randolph, 120. The principle deduced from the decisions seems to be,
that a power of sale of the realty, with a direction to distribute the proceeds
as personalty, makes an equitable conversion of the realty, and the estate
takes the character of personalty from the date of the death of the testator,
whether for the payment of debts or legacies, or other purposes of trust
declared. And it is said the cases upon this subject seem to depend upon
the question whether the testator meant to give the quality to *all intents*,
or only so far as respected the particular purposes of the will; for unless the
testator has sufficiently declared his intention, not only that realty shall
be converted into personalty for the particular purposes of the will, but
that the produce of the real estate shall be taken as personalty whether such
purposes take effect or not, so much of the real estate, or the produce thereof,
as is not effectually disposed of by the will at the time of the testator's
death (whether from the silence or inefficacy of the will or from subsequent
lapse) will result to the heir. Cruse *v.* Barley, 3 P. Wms. 21. And in
Ackroyd *v.* Smith, 1 Bro. Ch. 503, the Master of the Rolls says: "I used
to think that when it is necessary for any purpose of the testator's disposition to convert land into money, the undisposed money would be personalty; but the cases prove the contrary." Wheldale *v.* Partridge, 5 Ves. 388.
Where the power of sale is discretionary, no conversion of realty into personalty takes place until a sale is actually made. Peterson's App., 88 Penn.
St. 397; Gest *v.* Flock, 1 Green, Ch. 108; Cook *v.* Cook, 20 N. J. Eq. 375.
In order to work a conversion, an actual sale, either immediately, or in the

of administrators, and they can exercise none of the powers given to executors or trustees, in reference to the real estate, unless such powers are specially conferred upon them by the terms of the will.[1] (a) This rule has been altered by statute in

future, or upon the happening of some contingency, must be directed in terms or by necessary implication. Christler *v.* Meddis, 6 B. Mon. 35; Haggard *v.* Rout, id. 247. And see Wms. Exrs., 6 Am. Ed. p. 656 *et seq.* and notes, for full statement and citations. [For a note on the topic of equitable conversion, see *supra*, § 448, note *b*, p. 717 *et seq.*]

[1] Tainter *v.* Clark, 13 Met. 224; Moody *v.* Vandyke, 4 Binn. 31; Dunning *v.* National Bank, 6 Lans. 296; Moody *v.* Fulmer, 3 Grant, 17; Waters *v.* Margerum, 60 Penn. St. 39, 44; Drury *v.* Natick, 10 Allen, 169; Evans *v.* Chew, 71 Penn. St. 47; Conklin *v.* Egerton, 21 Wend. 430; Greenough *v.* Welles, 10 Cush. 571; Lucas *v.* Doe, 4 Ala. 679; Hall *v.* Irwin, 2 Gilm. 180; Hunt *v.* Holden, 2 Mass. 168; Knight *v.* Loomis, 30 Maine, 208; Wills *v.* Cowper, 2 Ohio, 124; Jackson *v.* Potter, 4 Wend. 672; Roome *v.* Phillips, 27 N. Y. 357; McDonald *v.* King, Coxe, 432; Armstrong *v.* Park, 9 Humph. 195; Drane *v.* Bayliss, 1 id. 174; Ashburn *v.* Ashburn, 16 Ga. 213; Smith *v.* McConnell, 17 Ill. 135; Kidwell *v.* Brumagim, 32 Cal. 436; Brown *v.* Hobson, 3 A. K. Marsh, 380; Vardeman *v.* Ross, 36 Tex. 111. In such cases

(a) When the same person is named as both executor and trustee, a power given to him as executor cannot be exercised by him as trustee after his executorship has come to an end, and similarly a power given to him in his capacity of trustee cannot be exercised by him as executor when he does not qualify as trustee. Goad *v.* Montgomery, 119 Cal. 552; Gibney *v.* Allen, 156 Mich. 301. See also Poole *v.* Anderson, 80 Md. 454. The point becomes of especial importance when for any reason the offices become separated, as by his death and the appointment of one person as administrator *de bonis non* and another person as substituted trustee. In such a case neither can exercise the powers which were attached exclusively to the office of the other. Varick *v.* Smith, 67 N. J. Eq. 1.

Whether in such a case a power is attached to the office of executor, and so passes to the administrator *de bonis non*, or is attached to the office of trustee and so passes to the substituted trustee, is a question of the intention of the testator. Frequently this intention must be gathered from the purpose for which the power was given. Sweet *v.* Schliemann, 88 N. Y. S. 916; 95 App. Div. 266; Greenland *v.* Waddell, 116 N. Y. 234; Joralemon *v.* Van Riper, 44 N. J. Eq. 299.

Sometimes a power given to a person named as executor and trustee will not pass to either an administrator *de bonis non* or a substituted trustee, as where the power was intended to be a personal discretion. *Infra,* § 503 and notes; § 505.

several States, but the statutes have been held not to apply to discretionary trusts or personal confidences,[1] but only to the general functions of executors in settling estates.[2]   A power of

a trustee should be specially appointed to execute the powers which may not be exercised by administrators with the will annexed, and the heirs at law or *cestuis que trust* should be parties to the proceedings. Roome *v.* Phillips, 27 N. Y. 357. [Hinson *v.* Williamson, 74 Ala. 180; Mordecai *v.* Schirmer, 38 S. C. 294; Lahy *v.* Kortright, 132 N. Y. 450; Greenland *v.* Waddell, 116 N. Y. 234.]

[1] Comm'rs *v.* Forney, 3 Watts & S. 357; Hester *v.* Hester, 2 Ired. Eq. 330; Smith *v.* McCrary, 3 id. 204; Drayton *v.* Grimke, 1 Bail. Eq. 392; Brown *v.* Armistead, 6 Rand. 594; Owens *v.* Cowan's Heirs, 7 B. Mon. 156; Moody *v.* Fulmer, 3 Grant, 17. [See Reeves *v.* Tappan, 21 S. C. 1.]

[2] Brown *v.* Hobson, 3 A. K. Marsh. 381; Woolridge *v.* Watkins, 3 Bibb, 350; Conklin *v.* Egerton, 21 Wend. 430; 25 id. 224; Montgomery *v.* Milliken, 5 Sm. & M. 188; Tainter *v.* Clark, 13 Met. 220; Ross *v.* Barclay, 18 Penn. St. 179; Bailey *v.* Brown, 9 R. I. 79. The cases upon this point are somewhat conflicting, — the result in some cases of different language of the statute, and in others of difference of opinion as to the power of an administrator *cum testamento annexo*. In Conklin *v.* Egerton, *ubi supra*, in an elaborate discussion of the subject, it is held that the power given to the executors to sell the real estate, and divide the proceeds among devisees to whom the estate was given by a previous clause of the will, cannot be executed by an administrator *cum testamento annexo*, notwithstanding the statute enactment that "in all cases where letters of administration *cum testamento annexo* shall be granted, the will of the deceased shall be observed and performed; and the administrators of such shall have the rights and powers, and be subject to the same duties as if they had been named executors in the will." So in Dominick *v.* Michael, 4 Sandf. 274. But the judgment in Conklin *v.* Egerton seems to have been affirmed upon another ground in the Court of Appeals, Egerton *v.* Conklin, 25 Wend. 237; while the doctrine in question was left undetermined, Chancellor Walworth saying that his opinion had been that it was the intention by the statute to subtitute the administrator *cum testamento annexo* in the place of the executor as to all trusts of the will, both real and personal, and suggesting that if the doctrine of the court was law, some further legislation was needed, as it would be impossible to carry out the intentions of testators. And in Roome *v.* Phillips, 27 N. Y. 363, the doctrine is acquiesced in, with an intimation that if it had been a new question the result might have been different. And in Elstner *v.* Fife, 32 Ohio St. 371, under statute of that State, it is held that the power of the executors ceased upon their resignation, but an administrator *de bonis non cum testamento annexo* may execute the power. See also, in Virginia, Brown *v.* Armistead, 6 Rand. 594; in North Carolina, Hester *v.* Hester, 2 Ired. Eq. 330; and in Kentucky, Galley *v.* Panther, 7 Bush, 167; and Dilworth *v.* Rice, 48 Mo. 124. And in Penn-

sale in a mortgage given to the mortgagee, his executors, administrators, or assigns, may be executed by any of the personal representatives of the mortgagee who have the duty of

sylvania, power to sell the residue for the purpose of distributing the proceeds among the beneficiaries passes under the statute to the administrator *de bonis non cum testamento annexo.* Jackman v. Delafield, 85 Penn. St. 381; Cornell v. Green, 10 Serg. & R. 14; Allison v. Wilson, 13 Serg. & R. 330. And a discretionary power of sale for the purpose of distributing the estate as personalty may be exercised by the administrator *cum testamento annexo,* where the executors and trustees renounce the trust. Wyman v. Carter, L. R. 12 Eq. 309. The early cases and some of the later ones, notably the case of Conklin v. Egerton, *ubi supra,* and Tainter v. Clark, 13 Met. 220, maintain the distinction between the duties of executors *qua* executors for the ordinary purposes of administration, and their duties under powers conferred upon them outside of the ordinary duties of administration; and hold these latter powers to be either a personal confidence in the persons named executors, or powers to them as trustees, which, being in form, when granted to more than one, joint powers, must, by the common law, be exercised jointly, and so could not pass to the survivor; while as to the ordinary duties of executors in the administration of estates, such as might qualify in the office possessed all authority given by the will to the persons named as executors. The statute of 21 Henry VIII. c. 4, seems to have been adopted to enable these powers to be conveniently combined with the duties of executors, and gave to those who should qualify under the will the full power, although others nominated by the will should disclaim; restricting the application of this statute to the cases embraced by it, where some failed to qualify, it would still have been impossible for the survivor of several qualifying executors to exercise such a power. But the courts, carrying out the principle of the statute, held that the powers to convert realty could be exercised by the survivor of several qualifying executors, thus treating the power as a part of the executorship, — "an incident of the administration," it is called in a recent case, — rather than as a distinct power. Gould v. Mather, 104 Mass. 286; Meakings v. Cromwell, 1 Seld. 136; Bogert v. Hestell, 4 Hill, 492; Smith v. Claxton, 4 Madd. 484. In view of these decisions, and of the cases which hold a power of sale by implication in the executors where no person is designated to exercise it, in cases where the proceeds from the sale are directed to be applied by an executor, *post,* § 501, note, it seems to follow that where there is an intent shown by the will to convert realty and to apply or distribute the proceeds by the hand of the executor, the power of sale must be considered a part of the scheme of administration of the estate; and as such, intended by the testator to be exercised by whomsoever should lawfully be charged with the duty of administering, whether he be designated executor or administrator *cum testamento annexo.* Blake v. Dexter, 12 Cush. 559. [See note *a, supra;* § 264, note *a,* p. 461, vol. 1.]

settling his estate.[1]   A husband cannot exercise a power given to his wife.[2]

§ 501.   If a power of sale is created by a will without stating by whom it is to be exercised, but the proceeds of the sale are directed to be applied or distributed by an executor, trustee, or other person, such executor, trustee, or other person will by implication take the power of selling, unless there is some other intention to be gathered from the whole will.[3]   If the will gives a power of sale to pay debts and legacies, or for distribution, without stating by whom the sale is to be made, the executor takes the power by implication.[4]   But if there is a power of sale, but no person is named to execute the power, and there is no purpose of the sale but a mere division of the estate, the executors cannot exercise the power; and if they sell and purchase themselves, they cannot be compelled to complete the purchase.[5]   A devise to three children in fee, to be divided or sold as two of the three children could agree, conferred no power of

---

[1] Doolittle v. Lewis, 7 Johns. Ch. 48.

[2] May's Heirs v. Frazer, 4 Litt. 391.

[3] Newton v. Bennett, 1 Bro. Ch. 135; Bentham v. Wiltshire, 4 Madd. 44; Blatch v. Wilder, 1 Atk. 420; Elton v. Harrison, 2 Swanst. 276, n.; Tylden v. Hyde, 2 S. & S. 238; Forbes v. Peacock, 11 Sim. 152; Ward v. Devon, cited id. 160; Patton v. Randall, 1 J. & W. 189; Curtis v. Fulbrook, 8 Hare, 28: Watson v. Pearson, 2 Exch. 580; Gosling v. Carter, 1 Coll. 644; Doe v. Hughes, 6 Exch. 223; Lippincott v. Lippincott, 4 Green, Ch. 121; Jones's App., 5 Grant, 19.   [Sweeney v. Warren, 127 N. Y. 426; Drake v. Paige, 127 N. Y. 569; Taber v. Willetts, 37 N. Y. S. 233, 1 App. Div. 285 (affirmed 153 N. Y. 663); Lesser v. Lesser, 32 N. Y. S. 167.   See Bradt v. Hodgdon, 94 Me. 559.]

[4] Ibid.; Bogert v. Hertell, 4 Hill, 492; Meakings v. Cromwell, 2 Sandf. 512; 1 Selden, 136; Dorland v. Dorland, 2 Barb. 63; Gray v. Henderson, 71 Pa. St. 368; and see Dunning v. National Bank, 6 Lans. 296; Davoue v. Fanning, 2 Johns. Ch. 254; Houck v. Houck, 5 Penn. St. 273; Silverthorn v. McKinster, 12 id. 67; Lloyd v. Taylor, 2 Dallas, 223; Putnam Free School v. Fisher, 30 Maine, 523; Foster v. Craige, 2 Dev. & B. Eq. 209; Robertson v. Gaines, 2 Humph. 378; Magruder v. Peter, 11 Gill & J. 217; Peter v. Beverley, 10 Peters, 532; 1 How. 134; Lockhart v. Northington, 1 Sneed, 318.

[5] Drayton v. Drayton, 2 Des. 250, n.; Shoolbred v. Drayton, id. 246.

sale on any one.[1] And so where an estate was conveyed to a trustee in trust for a corporation, to be conveyed by him under the direction of the directors, and upon his failure to convey, they to appoint other trustees by deed, a deed signed by the president and directors conveyed no estate, though it recited that they were the successors of the trustee.[2] If an estate is given to the executor for life, to be sold at his death, he can neither sell the land, nor devise the power to *his* executor.[3]

§ 502. If a power is given to several trustees, and one of them refuses to accept, the power may be exercised by the continuing trustee or trustees.[4] Even where the testator desired the remaining trustee to fill the vacancy caused by refusal of the other, and instead of doing so he acts alone, sales and deeds and other acts of such remaining trustee are valid.[5] If the power is not given to the trustees by name, but to the office, and one disclaims, there can be no doubt that the acting trustees can execute the power.[6]

§ 503. A power, though appendant to an estate, is not so appendant that it goes with the estate in every transfer made by the trustee, or in every devolution by course of law.[7] But

---

[1] Geroe v. Winter, 1 Halst. Ch. 655.

[2] Bumgarner v. Coggswell, 49 Mo. 259.

[3] Walter v. Logan, 5 B. Mon. 516. In many of the States, there are statutes which give directions as to who shall exercise powers of sale. And see Carroll v. Stewart, 4 Rich. 200.

[4] See *ante*, § 499; Crewe v. Bicken, 4 Ves. 97; Granville v. McNeile, 7 Hare, 156; Hawkins v. Kemp, 3 East, 410; Cooke v. Crawford, 13 Sim. 96; Adams v. Taunton, 5 Madd. 435; Bayly v. Cummings, 10 Ir. Eq. 410; Sands v. Nugee, 8 Sim. 130. [Haggart v. Ranney, 73 Ark. 344; Draper v. Montgomery, 95 N. Y. S. 904, 108 App. Div. 63; Rankine v. Metzger, 74 N. Y. S. 649, 69 App. Div. 264 (affirmed 174 N. Y. 540). See Coleman v. Connolly, 242 Ill. 574.]   [5] Bailey, Pet'r, 15 R. I. 60.

[6] Worthington v. Evans, 1 S. & S. 165; Boyce v. Corbally, t. Plunk. 102; Clarke v. Parker, 19 Ves. 1; Welles v. Lewis, 4 Met. (Ky.) 269; White v. McDermott, I. R. 7 C. L. 1.

[7] Cole v. Wade, 16 Ves. 47; Crewe v. Dicken, 4 Ves. 97; Burtt's Est., 4 Drew. 319; Wilson v. Bennett, 5 De G. & Sm. 475; Hardwick v. Mynd, Anst. 109, is not law.

where the estate is transferred to trustees duly appointed under a power, the transferees take the estate and office together, and can exercise the power. But where the court appoints new trustees, it cannot communicate arbitrary or discretionary powers to them,[1] unless the instrument of trust confers such powers upon the trustees for the time being, or they are annexed to the office.[2] If a power is given to a trustee, his heirs and assigns, and a new trustee is appointed, and a vesting order made, the new trustee may execute the power under the word "assigns." But statutes in England, and in many of the States, now give new trustees the same power as the old. (a) Under

[1] Doyley v. Att. Gen., 2 Eq. Ca. Ab. 194; Fordyce v. Bridges, 2 Phill. 497; Newman v. Warner, 1 Sim. (N. S.) 457; Cole v. Wade, 16 Ves. 44; Hibbard v. Lambe, Amb. 309.

[2] Bartley v. Bartley, 3 Drew. 384; Brassey v. Chalmers, 4 De G., M. & G. 528; Byam v. Byam, 19 Beav. 66; Bailey v. Brown, 9 R. I. 79; Burdick v. Goddard, 11 R. I. 516.

(a) The courts frequently have occasion to determine whether a power to be exercised in the discretion of a trustee is personal to the trustee named in the trust instrument or passes to a substituted trustee upon the death, removal, renunciation or resignation of the former. The determination depends entirely upon the intention of the creator of the trust, for if he intended that the exercise of the power should rest solely upon the personal judgment or discretion of the trustee whom he has named, the court cannot vest the power in a successor. Mercer v. Safe Dep. Co., 91 Md. 102, 118; Kennard v. Bernard, 98 Md. 513; Lowe v. Convention, 83 Md. 409; Dodge v. Dodge, 109 Md. 164; French v. Northern Trust Co., 197 Ill. 30, 39; U. S. Trust Co. v. Poutch, 130 Ky. 241.

When the power is given to the trustee "and his successor" or to "the trustee for the time being," there usually is no doubt of the intention that it shall pass with the office to a substituted trustee. Godfrey v. Hutchins, 28 R. I. 517; Luquire v. Lee, 121 Ga. 624; In re Cunningham, [1891] 2 Ch. 567. In the absence of such words, the courts seek to determine the intention of the creator of the trust, not only from the words of the trust instrument, but from all the circumstances which tend to show his intention. Each case must to a very large extent depend upon its own facts. Cases cited infra.

When the power is ministerial in its nature and one which is usually given to a trustee to enable him to carry out the trust properly, such as a power of sale for the purpose of changing investments, the courts incline to hold that it is attached to the office of trustee and is intended to continue as long as the

811

some of these statutes a new trustee may come in and prosecute a suit begun by his predecessors, without recourse to a bill

trust, however extensive may have been the discretion given. Kennard v. Bernard, 98 Md. 513; Safe Deposit & Tr. Co. v. Sutro, 75 Md. 361; Dodge v. Dodge, 109 Md. 164; Lahy v. Kortright, 132 N. Y. 450; Reeves v. Tappan, 21 S. C. 1; Dick v. Harby, 48 S. C. 516; Bradford v. Monks, 132 Mass. 405. But see Hinson v. Williamson, 74 Ala. 180; Luquire v. Lee, 121 Ga. 624; Snyder v. Safe Dep. & Tr. Co., 93 Md. 225; Lowe v. Convention, 83 Md. 409.

When the trustee has been given the discretion to determine the amount and times of payment of income to the beneficiary, the courts are somewhat less inclined to hold that the discretion was intended to be attached to the office of trustee, unless it appears from the circumstances that the main purpose of the trust will be defeated by holding that the discretion was a personal confidence in the named trustee. For cases holding that the power attached to the office, see French v. Northern Trust Co., 197 Ill. 30; Cutter v. Burroughs, 100 Me. 379; Matter of Wilkin, 183 N. Y. 104; Button v. Hemmens, 86 N. Y. S. 829, 92 App. Div. 40; Willis v. Alvey, 69 S. W. 1035 (Tex. Civ. App. 1902); Osborne v. Gordon, 86 Wis. 92. For cases holding that the power was a personal confidence, see Benedict v. Dunning, 97 N. Y. S. 259, 110 App. Div. 303; Smith v. Floyd, 108 N. Y. S. 775, 124 App. Div. 277. And when power has been given to terminate the trust by turning over the entire property to the beneficiary or to make pay-

ments of principal to him from time to time, the courts are still less inclined to hold that the power was intended to pass to a substituted trustee. French v. Northern Trust Co., 197 Ill. 30, 39; Dillingham v. Martin, 61 N. J. Eq. 276; Security Co. v. Snow, 70 Conn. 288; Whitaker v. McDowell, 72 A. 938 (Conn. 1909); Benedict v. Dunning, 97 N. Y. S. 259, 110 App. Div. 303; Smith v. Floyd, 108 N. Y. S. 775, 124 App. Div. 277; Dillard v. Dillard, 97 Va. 434, 440. But see Cutter v. Burroughs, 100 Me. 379; Mercer v. Safe Dep. Co., 91 Md. 102, 118; Hayes v. Robeson, 29 R. I. 216; Stanwood v. Stanwood, 179 Mass. 223.

In Sells v. Delgado, 186 Mass. 25, it was held that a power to pay over the principal of the trust to the beneficiary upon the latter's majority if in the trustee's discretion he "deem it prudent or advantageous," passed to a substituted trustee. The court was of opinion that a discretionary power would pass to a substituted trustee unless the words of the deed or will "clearly indicate that the donor placed special confidence in the donee, so that the element of personal choice or selection is found." A similar rule has been applied in Rhode Island in regard to a discretion as to making and changing investments. Smith v. Hall, 20 R. I. 170; Blakely, Petitioner, 19 R. I. 324. In the English case of In re Smith, [1904] 1 Ch. 139, the result of the authorities and statutes is stated as follows: "Every power given to

of revivor.[1] A release by one trustee to the others, with an intention of disclaiming, will operate as a formal disclaimer.[2]

§ 504. Though an assignment of the trust estate will not transfer a power to the assignee, neither will the power remain in the assignor; for if the settlor intended the estate and the power to be coupled together, their severance will intercept the execution of the power. (a) As where an estate is given to A. and his heirs in trust, with a power to be executed by A. and his heirs, and A. sells the estate in his lifetime or devises it by his will, the heir of A. cannot execute the power; for the heir is

[1] Murray v. Dehon, 102 Mass. 11; Mass. Gen. Stat. Ch. 100, § 9. [Rev. Laws (1902), c 147, §§ 5, 6.]

[2] Nicloson v. Wordsworth, 2 Swanst. 372; Hussey v. Markham, Finch, 258; Sharp v. Sharp, 2 B. & Ald. 405; Urch v. Walker, 3 Myl. & Cr. 702; Richardson v. Hulbert, 1 Anst. 65.

trustees which enables them to deal with or affect trust property is *prima facie* given them *ex officio* as an incident of their office, and passes with the office to the holders or holder thereof for the time being; whether a power is so given *ex officio* or not depends in each case on the construction of the document giving it, but the mere fact that the power is one requiring the exercise of a very wide discretion is not enough to exclude the *prima facie* presumption, and little regard is now paid to such minute differences as those between 'my trustees,' 'my trustees A. and B.,' and 'A. and B. my trustees'; the testator's reliance on the individuals to the exclusion of the holders of the office for the time being must be expressed in clear and apt language." The rule of interpretation set forth in the foregoing cases seems not yet to have been adopted by the courts of other jurisdictions, except possibly where the power given is one which is usually incidental to the management of trust property. Cases cited *supra*, this note.

(a) A trustee with power of sale cannot execute the power after he has been removed from or has resigned his office; Kenady v. Edwards, 134 U. S. 117; and a substituted trustee who has been expressly made subject to the control and order of the court cannot convey without an order from the court. Kenady v. Edwards, *ubi supra*.

Where a trustee was given power to sell upon the request of the life beneficiary and the latter incumbered his interest and also became bankrupt, it was held that the power might be exercised upon the consent of the beneficiary, the trustee in bankruptcy and the incumbrancer. *In re* Bedingeld & Herring's Contract, [1893] 2 Ch. 332.

no heir as to this estate.[1] But in charities it frequently happens that the estate or fund may vest in one set of donees, and the power of selecting the *cestuis que trust* may exist in another.[2]

§ 505. The survivorship of the estate carries with it survivorship of such powers as are annexed to the trust.[3] But a mere personal power given to A., B., and C. cannot be exercised by the survivors, if one die. If, however, an *equitable* power is annexed to the trust, and forms an integral part of it, as if an estate is vested in three trustees upon a trust to sell, there, as the power is coupled with an interest, and the interest survives, the power also survives.[4] And this is as old as Lord Coke, who says "If a man deviseth land to his executors to be sold, and maketh two executors, and one dieth, yet the survivor may sell the land, because as the estate, so the trust shall survive; and so note the diversity between a bare trust and a trust coupled with an interest." [5] At the present day, a trust, that is, a power imperative, whether a bare power or a power coupled with an interest, would equally be carried into execution in courts of equity; for the maxim now is, that "the trust or power imperative is the estate." And it is well settled that, even in trusts reposed in trustees by name, the survivor, *if he takes the estate* with a duty annexed to it, can execute the power; and the rule of survivorship now applies not only to trusts, or powers imperative which are construed as trusts, but also to such discretionary powers as are annexed to the office of trustee, and are intended to form an integral part of it.[6] But powers merely

[1] Wilson *v.* Bennett, 5 De G. & Sm. 475; Burtt's Est., 1 Drew. 319; Cole *v.* Wade, 16 Ves. 27.

[2] *Ex parte* Blackburn, 1 J. & W. 297; Hibbard *v.* Lambe, Amb. 309.

[3] See *ante*, §§ 499, 502.

[4] Lane *v.* Debenham, 11 Hare, 188; Peyton *v.* Bury, 2 P. Wms. 628; Eyre *v.* Shaftesbury, id. 108; Mansell *v.* Vaughn, Wilm. 49; Butler *v.* Bray, Dyer 189 b; Byam *v.* Byam, 19 Beav. 58; Co. Litt. 112 b, 113 a; Flanders *v.* Clarke, 1 Ves. 9; Potter *v.* Chapman, Amb. 100; Jones *v.* Price, 11 Sim. 557.

[5] Co. Litt. 113 a, 181 b.

[6] Lane *v.* Debenham, 11 Hare, 188; Hall *v.* May, 3 K. & J. 185; War-

arbitrary and independent of the trust, and not an integral part of it, are governed by the rules applicable to ordinary powers; as where the trustees by name have power to revoke the limitations, and change the property into a different channel, the discretion is evidently intended to be personal, and not annexed to the estate or office.[1]

§ 506. An unlimited power, to be exercised during successive estates tail, is not invalid for remoteness, for such power may be destroyed with the estate tail.[2] A power, collateral to a limitation in fee, has been supported where it was exercised by sale within the limits prescribed against perpetuities.[3] But how far the execution of such an unlimited power for an indefinite period, and beyond the limits of a perpetuity, could be supported, is not clearly settled.[4] (a) Where a testator devised an estate to trustees in trust for his brother's first

burton v. Sandys, 14 Sim. 622; Foley v. Wontner, 2 J. & W. 246; Doe v. Godwin, 1 D. R. 259; Townsend v. Wilson, 1 B. & Ald. 608; Jacob v. Lucas, 1 Beav. 436. [Haggart v. Ranney, 73 Ark. 344; Lippincott v. Wikoff, 54 N. J. Eq. 107; Sweet v. Schliemann, 88 N. Y. S. 916, 95 App. Div. 266; Rankine v. Metzger, 74 N. Y. S. 649, 69 App. Div. 264; Hunter v. Anderson, 152 Pa. St. 386.]

[1] Lane v. Debenham, 11 Hare, 192; Hazel v. Hogan, 47 Mo. 277; Hazel v. Woods, id. 298.

[2] Biddle v. Perkins, 4 Sim. 135; Powis v. Capron, id. 138, n.; Waring v. Coventry, 3 Myl. & K. 249; Wallis v. Freestone, 10 Sim. 225.

[3] Boyce v. Hanning, 2 Cr. & Jer. 334.

[4] 2 Sugd. Pow. 495.

(a) A trust for sale is invalid if not limited to take effect within the period of a life in being and twenty-one years after; but this does not invalidate a trust in the same instrument until the sale is made. Goodier v. Johnson, 18 Ch. D. 441; Goodier v. Edmunds, [1893] 3 Ch. 455. Discretion given by will to trustees to sell if and when they think fit is treated as inconsistent with an intention that the property should be sold at the testator's death. In re Pitcairn, 65 L. J. Ch. 120. Such a power may be exercised even after the death of the tenant for life, if so intended, and if then exercised within a reasonable time, it is not within the rule against perpetuities. In re Sudeley, [1894] 1 Ch. 334. On the application of the rule against perpetuities to powers of appointment, see supra, § 383, note.

and other sons successively in fee, so that the estate and interest of each should go to his next brother on his dying without issue under the age of twenty-one, and if all died without issue under that age, then in trust for the person who should be his next heir, and the trustees had power to sell the estate at their discretion at any time after his decease, it was held that a purchaser must take the estate, as the title was good, and the power did not contravene the rule against perpetuities.[1]

§ 507. Some powers are entirely discretionary; that is, it is left entirely to the judgment of the trustees whether they will execute them at all or not; as where the trustees are authorized or directed to do a certain act, or to abstain from it, "if they think fit"[2] or "proper,"[3] or "at their discretion;"[4] or the power may be imperative, and the discretion of the trustees be confined to the time, manner, and place of executing the power, or to the selection of the objects of the trust, as where the trust fund is directed to be applied, paid, or distributed, "when," or "in such manner,"[5] or "in such proportions,"[6] or to such person[7] or persons,[8] within a certain class or otherwise, as the trustees shall determine. So the discretion may be implied, as where the execution of the power calls for judgment and discretion in the trustee, or for his approbation or consent to a settlement, or sale, or marriage;[9] or

[1] Nelson v. Callow, 15 Sim. 353; Cresson v. Ferree, 70 Penn. St. 446.

[2] Maddison v. Andrew, 1 Ves. 53.

[3] Crossling v. Crossling, 2 Cox, 396; Kemp v. Kemp, 5 Ves. 849; Longmore v. Broom, 7 Ves. 124; Pink v. De Thuisey, 2 Madd. 157.

[4] Morice v. Bishop of Durham, 9 Ves. 399; Keates v. Burton, 14 Ves. 434; Potter v. Chapman, Amb. 98; Gibbs v. Rumsey, 2 V. & B. 294; Naglee's Est., 52 Penn. St. 154.

[5] Cassidy v. Hynton, 44 Ohio St. 532.

[6] Downer v. Downer, 9 Vt. 231; Marlborough v. Godolphin, 2 Ves. 61; Walsh v. Wallinger, 2 R. & M. 78.

[7] Brown v. Higgs, 4 Ves. 708.

[8] Grant v. Lyman, 4 Russ. 292; Loring v. Blake, 98 Mass. 253.

[9] Brereton v. Brereton, 2 Ves. 87, n.; Clarke v. Parker, 19 Ves. 12; Mortlock v. Buller, 10 Ves. 314.

where he is called upon to decide upon the conduct of a party,[1] or upon the necessity or expediency of any payment or other act;[2] or where he is directed to pay an annuity, "unless circumstances should render it unnecessary, inexpedient, or impracticable."[3] All such matters must be mere matters of opinion and discretion.

§ 508. Discretionary powers of trustees are usually divided into four principal classes, as follows: (1) Where it is left to the discretion of the trustees to make or withhold a gift or appointment of the trust property to a specified donee, or *cestui que trust*, or class of donees. In this class, if it is a condition precedent to the gift, legacy, or other interest, that the trustees shall exercise their power in favor of the donee, whether of appointment or assent, no interest will vest in the donee until the power is exercised; and if the trustees refuse to exercise it, the gift cannot be enforced.[4] The court cannot decide upon the propriety or impropriety of the refusal of the trustees to give their assent,[5] unless it proceed from selfish, corrupt, or improper motives; and the burden is upon the donee to prove such motives, and not upon the trustees to show good reasons for their action.[6] The court will, however, always strive to construe this class of powers into trusts, which will give the donee a vested interest, and the trustee only the power of selection, apportionment, and distribution.[7] (2) Where the dis-

[1] Walker *v.* Walker, 5 Madd. 424; Robinson *v.* Smith, 6 id. 194; Eaton *v.* Smith, 2 Beav. 236.

[2] Gower *v.* Mainwaring, 2 Ves. 87.

[3] French *v.* Davidson, 3 Madd. 396.

[4] Pink *v.* De Thuisey, 2 Madd. 157; Weller *v.* Weller, id. 160, n.; French *v.* Davidson, 3 id. 396; Walker *v.* Walker, 5 id. 424; Brown *v.* Higgs, 4 Ves. 719; 5 Ves. 508; 8 Ves. 568; Marlborough *v.* Godolphin, 2 Ves. 61; Lyman *v.* Parsons, 26 Conn. 493; 28 Barb. 564; reversing 4 Bradf. 268. See s. c., 20 N. Y. 103; N. Y. Rev. St. part 2, c. 1, tit. 2, art. 3, § 9; Grace *v.* Phillips, 2 Phill. 701; Leavitt *v.* Beirne, 21 Conn. 1. [See *supra*, § 248 and note.]

[5] Pink *v.* De Thuisey, 2 Madd. 162, n.

[6] Clarke *v.* Parker, 19 Ves. 11; French *v.* Davidson, 3 Madd. 402.

[7] Wainwright *v.* Waterman, 1 Ves. Jr. 311; Keates *v.* Burton, 14 Ves. 434; *ante*, §§ 248–258; Cochran *v.* Paris, 11 Grat. 356.

cretionary power is confined to the selection from, or apportionment to, or distribution among, the objects of the trust. This class of powers is held to create trusts. The beneficial interest is generally vested in the whole class of objects from which the trustees have the power of selection, to be divested out of those who are not selected by the trustees in the exercise of the power; and if the trustees die, or refuse to execute the powers, the whole class takes the property.[1] (3) Where the discretion applies to some ministerial act connected with the estate, such as powers of leasing, selling, appointing new trustees, felling timber, and the like. This class of powers is much more under the control of courts than powers depending upon the exercise of opinion and judgment.[2] The court can enter into all matters in relation to those things that are beneficial to the estate, and into the motives of the trustees for exercising or refusing to exercise these powers; and the courts will not allow the trustees to exercise their powers in this respect in an arbitrary or capricious manner;[3] but if the court has acquired jurisdiction of the case by bill or decree, the trustees must act under the sanction of the court in appointing new trustees, making investments, sales, leases, and in varying the securities,[4] unless the instrument of trust declares that their discretion is to be uncontrolled.[5] And (4) where the discretion to be exercised is a mere matter of personal judgment, as where the consent or approbation of the trustees is required to a mar-

---

[1] Loring v. Blake, 98 Mass. 253. The whole matter of powers as trusts is discussed, ante, §§ 248–258, and the cases are cited, which see.

[2] Milsington v. Mulgrave, 4 Madd. 491; Hewit v. Hewit, Amb. 508; Mortimer v. Watts, 14 Beav. 616.

[3] Ibid.; Webb v. Shaftesbury, 7 Ves. 480; Att. Gen. v. Clack, 1 Beav. 467; De Manneville v. Crompton, 1 V. & B. 359; Druid Park Heights Co. v. Oettinger, 53 Md. 63. [Infra, § 511, note a.]

[4] Ibid.; Booth v. Booth, 1 Beav. 125; Pocock v. Reddington, 5 Ves. 794; Parry v. Warrington, 6 Madd. 155; Lord v. Godfrey, 4 id. 459; Brice v. Stokes, 11 Ves. 324; Broadhurst v. Balguy, 1 Younge & C. Ch. 28. And see Cafe v. Bent, 3 Hare, 245, and Hitch v. Leworthy, 2 Hare, 405.

[5] Milsington v. Mulgrave, 3 Madd. 403; Lee v. Young, 2 Younge & C. Ch. 536.

riage, or to the conduct of an individual. The trustees alone can exercise these powers, and courts cannot generally interfere to control these mere personal judgments upon personal matters.[1] But the trustees must exercise a reasonable discretion; thus they ought not to pay money into the hands of a lunatic or drunkard to be wasted.[2] If they have power to make advances to set up children in business, they may make advances to a married daughter to set up her husband in business, but not to pay off his debts.[3] And if they have once executed the power by naming a sum to be paid, they cannot reduce it,[4] but in some cases they may make a further advance.[5] And it is always a question for the courts to determine whether the action of the trustees in a given case is within the discretionary powers given them by the instrument of trust.[6]

§ 509. A general power in trustees to vary securities confers upon them power to do all the acts incidental or essential to the performance of that duty; and therefore they may sell and give receipts to purchasers for the purchase-money.[7] This is a power given for the security of the estate and benefit of the trust property; [8] and it ought not to be exercised except when required by necessity or convenience,[9] and upon proper inquiry and circumspection.[10] Therefore trustees ought always

[1] Cole v. Wade, 16 Ves. 47; Walker v. Walker, 5 Madd. 424; Eaton v. Smith, 2 Beav. 236; Cochran v. Paris, 11 Grat. 356; French v. Davidson, 3 Madd. 396; Brereton v. Brereton, 2 Ves. 87, n.; Clarke v. Parker, 19 Ves. 11; Weller v. Ker, 1 Macq. H. L. Sc. Cas. 11. [Infra, § 511, note a.]

[2] Gott v. Cook, 7 Paige, 538; Mason v. Jones, 2 Barb. S. C. 248.

[3] Talbot v. Marshfield, L. R. 4 Eq. 661.

[4] Mason v. Mason, 4 Sandf. Ch. 631; Weller v. Ker, 1 Macq. H. L. Sc. Cas. 11.

[5] Webster v. Boddington, 16 Sim. 177.

[6] Trustees of Smith v. Northampton, 10 Allen, 498. [Infra, § 511, note a.]

[7] Wood v. Harman, 5 Madd. 368. See ante, § 466.

[8] Lord v. Godfrey, 4 Madd. 459.

[9] Broadhurst v. Balguy, 1 Younge & C. Ch. 28.

[10] Hanbury v. Kirkland, 3 Sim. 271; Wormley v. Wormley, 1 Brock. 330; 8 Wheat. 421.

to have an immediate and advantageous investment in view before they sell the existing securities.[1]   A sale for the mere purpose of converting real estate into personal, or *vice versa*, or without some well-defined and proper purpose in view, would render them responsible for any loss.[2]   Each trustee must be satisfied by inquiries of the propriety of the act, and he must not trust to the representations of his cotrustee.[3]   This power is necessarily left in a large degree to the sound discretion of the trustees;[4] and if any check is imposed upon their discretion, as if the consent, or the consent in writing, of the *cestui que trust*, or any other formalities are required before the trustees can act, they must strictly comply with all such requirements.[5] If the trustees have a discretionary power of changing the investments with the consent of the tenant for life, the court cannot compel them to exercise the power at the request of the tenant for life, if they refuse to do so in the *bona fide* exercise of their discretion.[6]   But where the power is imperative on the trustees to invest in any particular securities, at the request of the *cestuis que trust*, the court will compel them to exercise the power.[7]   But if the power is *imperative*, and there has been a great change of circumstances, as where the *cestuis que trust*, or their connections, to whom the trustees were required to loan the trust fund, have become bankrupt, the court will not compel the trustees to exercise the power.[8]   The exercise of the power of varying the securities cannot alter or change the rights of the *cestuis que trust;* on the other hand, the rights of

[1] Ibid.; Watts *v.* Girdlestone, 6 Beav. 188.

[2] Brice *v.* Stokes, 11 Ves. 324; Meyer *v.* Montriou, 5 Beav. 146.

[3] Hanbury *v.* Kirkland, 3 Sim. 265; Broadhurst *v.* Balguy, 1 Younge & C. Ch. 16.

[4] De Manneville *v.* Crompton, 1 V. & B. 354.

[5] Ibid.; Cocker *v.* Quayle, 1 R. & M. 535; Greenwood *v.* Wakeford, 1 Beav. 579; Kellaway *v.* Johnson, 5 Beav. 319.

[6] Prendergast *v.* Prendergast, 3 H. L. Cas. 195; Lee *v.* Young, 2 Younge & C. Ch. 532.

[7] Ross *v.* Goodsall, 1 N. C. C. 618; Beauclerk *v.* Ashburnham, 8 Beav. 322.

[8] Ibid.

the *cestuis que trust* will be the same whether the trustees invest the fund in real or personal estate.[1] Power to vary the securities is a *usual* power, to be inserted in settlements with the *usual* powers.[2]

§ 510. In early times, courts assumed jurisdiction and control over discretionary powers in trustees, and compelled trustees to execute them, or the court itself executed the powers in such manner as it judged most beneficial for the *cestuis que trust;*[3] but this jurisdiction is now repudiated, and courts will not exercise a mere discretionary power, either during the lifetime of the trustees, or after their death or refusal to execute it.[4] But if the power is in the nature of a trust for a class, with a power of selection in the trustees of particular persons of the class, and the trustees die or refuse to make the selection, the courts will still execute the trust for the whole class.[5] In one case a distinction was attempted to be established between a discretion in the trustee to be exercised upon matters of

[1] Lord *v.* Godfrey, 4 Madd. 455; Walter *v.* Maunde, 19 Ves. 424. [Gray *v.* Whittemore, 192 Mass. 367; Hovey *v.* Dary, 154 Mass. 7; Henszey's Estate, 220 Pa. St. 212. On the doctrine of equitable conversion, see *supra*, § 448, note.]

[2] Sampayo *v.* Gould, 12 Sim. 426.

[3] Flanders *v.* Clarke, 1 Ves. 10; Wainwright *v.* Waterman, 1 Ves. Jr. 311; Clarke *v.* Turner, 2 Freem. 198; Gower *v.* Mainwaring, 2 Ves. 87, 110; Hewit *v.* Hewit, Amb. 508; Carr *v.* Bedford, 2 Ch. R. 77; Warburton *v.* Warburton, id. 420; 1 Bro. P. C. 34; Wareham *v.* Brown, 2 Vern. 153. Where one is unable to execute the trust given him, the courts will execute it; and where a widow, named coexecutrix of a will which directed that so much of the estate be sold as may be necessary for her support, has been supported on the understanding that the support should be paid out of the property, the party furnishing such support is entitled to be subrogated to the rights of the widow, and to have the court exercise the power in that behalf. Terve *v.* Am. Board, 53 Vt. 171.

[4] Maddison *v.* Andrew, 1 Ves. 60; Alexander *v.* Alexander, 2 Ves. 640; Kemp *v.* Kemp, 5 Ves. Jr. 849; Keates *v.* Burton, 14 Ves. 437; 2 Sugd. Pow. 190; Gower *v.* Mainwaring, 2 Ves. 88; Brereton *v.* Brereton, id. 88, n.; Potter *v.* Chapman, Amb. 98; Lee *v.* Young, 2 Younge & C. Ch. 522; Caplin's Will, 11 Jur. (N. S.) 383; Prendergast *v.* Prendergast, 3 H. L. Cas. 195; Coe's Trust, 4 K. & J. 199; Eldredge *v.* Head, 106 Mass. 582.

[5] *Ante*, §§ 255–258, and cases cited.

opinion and judgment, and a discretion to be exercised upon *matters of fact;* as where the trustees were to exercise certain powers over the estate, if the conduct of one of the beneficiaries was such as to gain their confidence and approval, the court seemed to distinguish between matters of judgment and matters of fact, and directed an inquiry.[1] Lord Hardwicke seemed to give some countenance to this distinction,[2] but the distinction is not established and acted upon; and, in the nature of things, such a distinction cannot be applied to the execution of powers by trustees. It is sufficient to hold them to good faith and fair intentions in the conduct of the trust. It was held, however, in Holcomb *v.* Holcomb, that a discretion entirely beyond the control of courts of equity could not be conferred upon trustees, and that courts could set aside acts done by trustees under a power so unlimited.[3] The discretion of the trustee will not be controlled or questioned so long as he is not guilty of bad faith or abuse of his power and trust; but it is difficult if not impossible to create in the trustee such unbounded power as to preclude a court of equity from controlling him when he acts fraudulently, or palpably abuses his power, as by unreasonably refusing to exercise it, or undertaking to exercise it in an unreasonable manner.[4] As where a discretionary trustee refuses to pay for proper medical attendance upon the *cestui,* the court will interfere.[5] If a trustee having arbitrary power dies and there is no provision for a successor, equity will appoint a new trustee to act under equitable principles in place of the arbitrary discretion.[6]

[1] Walker *v.* Walker, 5 Madd. 424.
[2] Gower *v.* Mainwaring, 2 Ves. 87–110.
[3] Holcomb *v.* Holcomb, 3 Stockt. 281.
[4] Cromie *v.* Bull, 81 Ky. 646. [Dickson *v.* N. Y. Biscuit Co., 211 Ill. 468; Kimball *v.* Blanchard, 101 Me. 383; Patterson *v.* Lanning, 62 Neb. 634; Angell *v.* Angell, 28 R. I. 592; Dubois *v.* Barbour, 27 R. I. 281; Givens *v.* Clem, 107 Va. 435; Whelan *v.* Palmer, 39 Ch. Div. 648; *Re* Stanger, 64 L. T. 693; *Re* Burrage, 62 L. T. 752.]
[5] Pole *v.* Pietsch, 61 Md. 570. [See also *In re* Hodges, 7 Ch. Div. 754.]
[6] Weiland *v.* Townsend, 33 N. J. Eq. 393.

§ 511. If the trustees exercise their discretionary powers in *good faith* and without fraud or collusion, the court cannot review or control their discretion.[1] Nor will a bill be entertained to compel the execution of a mere discretionary power.[2] The refusal of a trustee to exercise such a power is no breach of trust for which he can be removed, though he gives no reason for his refusal, and though the execution of the power would appear to be proper and beneficial to the estate.[3] But while the court cannot interfere with a discretion honestly exercised, a party interested in property subject to the discretion of a trustee has a right to institute a bill for a discovery of the property, and also of all the acts of the trustee, and the reasons for the acts, in order that it may be seen whether the discretion of the trustee is honestly exercised or not. And if the administration of the trust is thus rightfully brought within the jurisdiction of the court, the power may be required to be exercised under the eye of the court, though the exercise of it must still remain in the discretion of the trustee, and not in that of the court.[4] And so if the exercise of a discretionary power entirely miscarries, the court may take jurisdiction of the administration of the trust.[5] It has been ruled, however,

---

[1] Smith *v.* Wildman, 37 Conn. 384; Potter *v.* Chapman, Amb. 98; Cowley *v.* Hartsonge, 1 Dow, 378; Prendergast *v.* Prendergast, 3 H. L. Cas. 195; Att. Gen. *v.* Moseley, 12 Jur. 889; 2 De G. & Sm. 398; Clarke *v.* Parker, 19 Ves. 11; Pink *v.* De Thuisey, 2 Madd. 157; French *v.* Davidson, 3 id. 396; Wood *v.* Richardson, 4 Beav. 177; Morton *v.* Southgate, 28 Maine, 41 ; Littlefield *v.* Cole, 33 Me. 552; Leavitt *v.* Beirne, 21 Conn. 2; Hawley *v.* James, 5 Paige, 485; Arnold *v.* Gilbert, 3 Sandf. Ch. 556; Mason *v.* Mason, 4 id. 623; Bunner *v.* Storm, 1 id. 357; Gochenauer *v.* Froelich, 8 Watts, 19; Chew *v.* Chew, 28 Penn. St. 17; Cowles *v.* Brown, 4 Call, 477; Cochran *v.* Paris, 11 Grat. 356; Cloud *v.* Martin, 1 Dev. & Bat. 397; Aleyn *v.* Belchier, 1 Lead. Cas. Eq. 304. And see Berry *v.* Hamilton, 10 B. Mon. 135; O'Bannon *v.* Musselman, 2 Dev. 523; Eldredge *v.* Head, 106 Mass. 582; Pulpress *v.* African Church, 48 Penn. St. 204. [Kimball *v.* Blanchard, 101 Me. 383.]

[2] Brereton *v.* Brereton, 2 Ves. 87 n.; Pink *v.* De Thuisey, 2 Madd. 157; Green *v.* McBeth, 12 Rich. Eq. 254.

[3] Lee *v.* Young, 2 Younge & C. Ch. 532; Matter of Vanderbilt, 20 Hun (N. Y.), 520.

[4] Costabadie *v.* Costabadie, 6 Hare, 410.

[5] Feltham *v.* Turner, 23 L. T. (N. S.) 345.

that the trustees might exercise their discretionary powers, although a bill had been filed for the purpose of having the trusts declared and carried into effect.[1] The trustee cannot, however, exercise his discretion for any fraudulent, selfish, or improper purposes, nor can he refuse to exercise a discretionary power for any such purposes; nor can the power be executed in an illusory or collusive manner.[2] (a) And if he acts,

[1] Sillibourne v. Newport, 1 K. & J. 603.
[2] Carson v. Carson, 1 Wins. (N. C.) 24. [Whelan v. Palmer, 39 Ch. Div. 648.]

(a) In case of discretionary powers given to trustees the courts will usually assume that the creator of the trust intended the discretion to be exercised not only with an honest intention of carrying out the purposes of the trust but in a manner which might reasonably be expected to accomplish the purpose for which the power was given. Accordingly the courts will interfere to prevent or to correct a dishonest or a capricious exercise of such a power. Dingman v. Beall, 213 Ill. 238; Keeler v. Lauer, 73 Kan. 388; Cromie v. Bull, 81 Ky. 646; Lovett v. Farnum, 169 Mass. 1; Price v. Bassett, 168 Mass. 598; Read v. Patterson, 44 N. J. Eq. 211; Collister v. Fassitt, 163 N. Y. 281; Jones v. Jones, 30 N. Y. S. 177; Angell v. Angell, 28 R. I. 592; Barbour v. Cummings, 26 R. I. 201; Trout v. Pratt, 106 Va. 431, 8 L. R. A. (N. S.) 398, note; Stephenson v. Norris, 128 Wis. 242, 259; Bound v. So. Car. Ry. Co., 50 Fed. 853; Rowlls v. Bebb, [1900] 2 Ch. 107; In re Hodges, 7 Ch. Div. 754; Re Stanger, 64 L. T. 693; Re Burrage, 62 L. T. 752. See Cal. Civ. Code (1907), § 2269; Rev. Codes of So. Dak. (1903), § 1644.

Thus where property was left in trust with directions to the trustee to make payments out of the income and principal to certain beneficiaries, "the times, amounts, and methods of such payments being left absolutely in the discretion of the trustee," it was held the trustee's discretion must be exercised reasonably and would always be subject to the control of the court in case of unreasonable detention of income. Angell v. Angell, 28 R. I. 592. In Cromie v. Bull, 81 Ky. 646, the trustee was empowered "in his discretion" to pay to life beneficiaries out of profits "the whole or a part of their portion of the same, as he shall deem proper, in view of their necessities or capacity to use the same advantageously in business." The court was of opinion that it could interfere to prevent an improper exercise of the discretionary power or to compel a proper exercise of it: "If the trustee acts fraudulently, abuses the power confided to his discretion, by refusing to execute the trust, or, in the attempt to exercise it, does that which is unreasonable and calculated to defeat the purpose of its creation, the chancellor will interfere . . . for the preser-

or refuses to act, upon such grounds, the court will interfere and give a remedy to the parties injured by the fraudulent act, or refusal to act, not for the purpose of controlling the discretion of the trustee, but to relieve the parties from the consequences of an improper exercise of the discretion;[1] and if the trustee refuses to exercise his discretion from selfish and interested motives, as where he declines to give his consent to a

[1] Clarke v. Parker, 19 Ves. 12; Peyton v. Bury, 2 P. Wms. 628; French v. Davidson, 3 Madd. 396; Dashwood v. Bulkeley, 10 Ves. 245; D'Aguilar v. Drinkwater, 2 V. & B. 225; Kemp v. Kemp, 5 Ves. 849; Mesgrett v. Mesgrett, 2 Vern. 580; 10 Ves. 243; Topham v. Portland, L. R. 5 Ch. 40.

vation of the trust estate, and will see that the trustee discharges his duties as such. . . . It is difficult, in fact, to create a trust where the trustee has such unlimited power over the trust property as to preclude the chancellor from controlling his action, when his conduct is such as to indicate a palpable or fraudulent abuse of his power to the injury of the parties in interest."

Where trustees have been authorized in their discretion to postpone the conversion of wasting or unproductive investments or to continue the testator's business, the English courts incline to take the view that the power was given for the purpose of getting the best possible bargain for the estate as a whole, and not for the purpose of allowing the trustee to vary the relative interests of life beneficiaries and remainder-men. Rowlls v. Bebb, [1900] 2 Ch. 107; In re Smith, [1896] 1 Ch. 171; Porter v. Baddeley, 5 Ch. Div. 542; Blake v. O'Reilly, [1895] 1 Ir. R. 479; In re Courtier, 34 Ch. Div. 136. As to the adjustment of income in such cases see infra, § 549, note. But if the testator's clear intention was to

give the trustees the right to exercise such a power for the benefit of one or the other of two classes of beneficiaries, the courts will not interfere with an honest exercise of the discretion for such a purpose. In re Crowther, [1895] 2 Ch. 56; In re Chancellor, 26 Ch. Div. 42; In re Pitcairn, [1896] 2 Ch. 199; Re Leonard, 43 L. T. 664; Yates v. Yates, 28 Beav. 637.

The courts will not substitute their own discretion for that of the trustee unless it appears in view of all the circumstances, that he has abused or is about to abuse the discretion confided in him. Dickson v. N. Y. Biscuit Co., 211 Ill. 468; Kimball v. Blanchard, 101 Me. 383; Proctor v. Heyer, 122 Mass. 525; Patterson v. Lanning, 62 Neb. 634; Read v. Patterson, 44 N. J. Eq. 211; Dubois v. Barbour, 27 R. I. 281; Givens v. Clem, 107 Va. 435; Trout v. Pratt, 106 Va. 431, 8 L. R. A. (N. S.) 398; Matthews v. Capshaw, 109 Tenn. 480; In re Bryant, [1894] 1 Ch. 324; Tabor v. Brooks, 10 Ch. Div. 273; Re Atkins, 81 L. T. 421; Re Stanger, 64 L. T. 693; Re Burrage, 62 L. T. 752.

sale, marriage, or settlement, the court may compel him to assent.[1] In a Kentucky case, where the deed gave the trustee power to sell, on written request of the lady who was the *cestui*, if he deemed it to be for her interest, it was held that he had no right to refuse to sell when he admitted it was necessary, and that the written request had been made. And the court remarked that although the chancellor could not compel a trustee to exercise a naked power, or a power coupled with a trust, if his refusal was a *bona fide* exercise of the discretion placed in him, yet if he perverts the trust or refuses without excuse to exercise the power, the chancellor's authority to compel him to execute his duties is unrestricted.[2]

§ 511 *a*. It is proper further to say, that courts do not favor constructions that confer upon trustees absolute and uncontrollable powers. The donee of the power is not the absolute owner of the property; most frequently he has no beneficial or other interest in it, but simply a power over it for the benefit of third persons.[3] The owner of property may of course confer upon another an absolute and uncontrollable power over it; but it is the policy of the law to limit irresponsible power as much as possible, and to subject the conduct of every person having the rights and interests of others in his power, to the regulations and control of the rules of law.[4] Wherever the law can control the exercise of a discretionary power, it will do so; as where a trustee had power to expend the principal of an estate for the benefit of a poor woman, "if urgent necessity should require," it was held that the court could compel the execution of the power.[5] So, also, courts can interfere and prevent, by

---

[1] Norcum *v.* D'Oench, 2 Bennett, Mo. 98.

[2] Walker *v.* Smyser's Ex'rs, 80 Ky. 620.

[3] Topham *v.* Duke of Portland, 1 De G., J. & S. 568; Haydel *v.* Hurck, 5 Mo. App. 267.

[4] *Ante*, § 249. [Compare *In re* Hodges, 7 Ch. Div. 754, and Tabor *v.* Brooks, 10 Ch. Div. 273.]

[5] Erisman *v.* Directors of Poor, 47 Penn. St. 509. [See Elias *v.* Loeb, 65 S. E. 724 (S. C. 1909).]

injunction or decree, an abusive, fraudulent, collusive, illusive, or other improper exercise of a discretionary power.[1] To determine what is an abuse of a discretionary power, or what is a fraudulent or improper execution of it, is frequently a matter of great difficulty. In the nature of things, only very general rules can be laid down upon a subject where so much must depend upon the facts of each individual case. Some general propositions have, however, been stated. It has been said, (1) That where a power of electing is given to trustees, as to the rights of third persons, they are bound to exercise such power most beneficially for the *cestuis que trust.*[2] (2) Reference must always be had, in the execution of a power, *to the end or purpose intended* by the creator of the power, and this end or purpose must be gathered from a construction of the written instrument; and a power must always *be executed bona fide for the end and purpose designed.*[3] (3) A power cannot be executed in favor of the donee of the power, or of his family, unless the instrument specially authorized him so to do.[4] (4) The donee of a power cannot execute it for any pecuniary gain, directly or indirectly, to himself.[5] Nor (5) can he exer-

---

[1] *Ante,* § 511; McFarland's App., 37 Penn. St. 205; Pulpress *v.* African Church, 48 id. 210.

[2] Haynesworth *v.* Cox, Harp. Eq. R. 149.

[3] Aleyn *v.* Belchier, 1 Eden, 132; 1 Lead. Cas. in Eq. 304, and cases cited. [See Dubois *v.* Barbour, 27 R. I. 281; *supra,* § 511, note.]

[4] *Ante,* § 254, and cases cited.

[5] Lord Sandwich's Case, referred to in McQueen *v.* Farquhar, 11 Ves. 480, and in Kcily *v.* Keily, 4 Dr. & War. 55; Lady Wellesley *v.* Earl of Mornington, 2 K. & J. 143; *In re* Marsden's Trust, 4 Drew. 594; Fearon *v.* Desbrisay, 14 Beav. 635; Beere *v.* Hoffmister, 23 id. 101; Birley *v.* Birley, 25 id. 299; Daubeny *v.* Cockburn, 1 Mer. 640; Watt *v.* Creyke, 3 Sm. & Gif. 362; Lee *v.* Fernie, 1 Beav. 483; Vane *v.* Dungannon, 2 Sch. & Lef. 118; Horne *v.* Askham, 12 Beav. 503; Rowley *v.* Rowley, Kay, 242, 262; Lysaght *v.* Royse, 2 Sch. & Lef. 151; Lane *v.* Page, Amb. 233; Butcher *v.* Johnson, 14 Sim. 444; Wright *v.* Goff, 22 Beav. 207; Campbell *v.* Home, 1 Y. & C. Ch. 664; Wheete *v.* Hall, 17 Ves. 80; Carver *v.* Bowles, 2 Russ. & My. 301; *Re* Beloved Wilkes's Charity, 3 Mac. & G. 440; 7 Eng. L. & Eq. 85; Henchinbroke *v.* Seymour, 1 Bro. Ch. 394; Huguenin *v.* Baseley, 14 Ves. 273; Ring *v.* Hardwick, 2 Beav. 352; Lassence *v.* Tierney, 1 Mac. & G. 551; Saunders *v.* Vautier, 1 Cr. & Phill. 240; Sadler *v.* Pratt, 5 Sim.

cise it for any other purposes personal to himself.¹ A distinction is made between the *motives* which lead to the execution of a power, and *the purpose or end* for which it is executed. Thus, a power may be properly executed according to the true purpose and intent of the creator of the power, but the motives which led the donee to such execution may have been corrupt. On the other hand, a power may have been improperly executed by the donee of the power, induced thereto by motives commendable in themselves, as by filial obedience, or affection.² A trust is always to be discharged in the most faithful and conscientious manner, and equity takes care to guard and protect a trustee in the discharge of his duties, while by its strict rule it shields him from temptation so far as possible, by rendering it difficult for him to gain any advantage to himself by his dealings with the trust fund. More especially is this the rule in the exercise, by a trustee, of so many and so great discretionary powers over the rights and interests of persons who are in no position to protect themselves. In the exercise of such powers, the trustee should act with purity of purpose, and with a single view to carry out the exact purpose of the power, and the intention of the settlor. If the execution of a power of appointment fails, or if the appointment is set aside as improperly made, the donee may make a new appointment; ³ but if an appointment is set aside by reason of what has taken place between the donee of the power and the appointee, a second ap-

632; Sugd. on Powers, 606 (8th ed.); Agassiz *v.* Squire, 18 Beav. 431; Farmer *v.* Martin, 2 Sim. 502; Wallgrave *v.* Tebbs, 2 K. & J. 313; Tee *v.* Ferris, id. 357; Lomax *v.* Ripley, 3 Sm. & Gif. 48; Stroud *v.* Norman, Kay, 313; Alexander *v.* Alexander, id. 242; White *v.* St. Barbe, 1 Ves. & B. 399; Scroggs *v.* Scroggs, Amb. 272. And when the purpose becomes unattainable the power ceases. Hetzel *v.* Hetzel, 69 N. Y. 1; Brown *v.* Meigs, 11 Hun (N. Y.), 203. [Degman *v.* Degman, 98 Ky. 717; *In re* Perkins, [1893] 1 Ch. 283; Whelan *v.* Palmer, 39 Ch. Div. 648; *In re* Kirwan's Trusts, 25 Ch. Div. 373; Tempest *v.* Camoys, 21 Ch. Div. 571.]

¹ Dummer *v.* Chippenham, 14 Ves. 245; *Re* Beloved Wilkes's Charity, 3 Mac. & G. 440; 7 Eng. L. & Eq. 85.

² Topham *v.* Portland, L. R. 5 Ch. 57; 1 De G., J. & S. 571.

³ Topham *v.* Portland, 11 H. L. Cas. 32; L. R. 5 Ch. 40.

pointment by the same donee to the same appointee cannot be sustained otherwise than by clear proof, on the part of the appointee, that the second appointment is perfectly free from the original taint which attached to the first appointment.[1]

[1] Topham *v.* Portland, L. R. 5 Ch. 60, 61; Birley *v.* Birley, 25 Beav. 299; Carver *v.* Richards, 27 Beav. 488, 1 De G., F. & J. 548.

The great case of Topham *v.* Duke of Portland involved most of the learning upon the subject of appointment under powers. The great question was whether an appointment, which excluded Lady Mary Bentinck from the enjoyment of certain property, was made in accordance with the intent and purpose of the power, or whether the appointment was made under the influence of personal reasons, she having married Colonel Topham contrary to the wishes of her family. It was first heard by Sir John Romilly, Master of the Rolls, and reported 31 Beav. 525. The Master of the Rolls decided that the appointment was void. The duke appealed, and the case was heard by the Lord Justices Turner and Knight Bruce. 1 De G., J. & S. 517. The decree of the Master of the Rolls was affirmed. An appeal was taken to the House of Lords, where the decree was again sustained. 11 H. L. Cas. 32. The Duke of Portland then made a new appointment of the same appointee, and Lady Mary again brought her bill to set aside the second appointment. It was heard before the Vice-Chancellor, Sir William M. James, and the second appointment set aside. See L. R. 5 Ch. 49. An appeal was again taken, which was heard before the Lord Justices, and the decree setting aside the second appointment was sustained. See Topham *v.* Portland, L. R. 5 Ch. 40. Lord Justice Sir George M. Gifford concluded his opinion as follows: "If the object of the appointment in this case had been simply the benefit of the Duke of Portland himself, I am persuaded he would never have come into court. The real object, though morally speaking far different, must, legally speaking, be considered on precisely the same principles as though he sought a benefit for himself; or the object is to bring about a state of things not warranted by the powers. It may be that, on consideration, the Duke of Portland will concur in the opinion that the matter may from henceforth be well left at rest." And it has rested.

In Library Co. of Philadelphia *v.* Williams, 30 Legal Intel. 177 (May 20, 1873), 73 Penn. St. 249, the exercise of a discretionary power by a trustee was much discussed. Dr. Rush gave to his trustee a large amount of property in trust for the Library Company, and gave the trustee power to select a parcel of land, and construct a library building for the company. Dr. Rush afterwards negotiated for the purchase of a lot of land, and procured a pledge or promise from the trustee that he would select that particular lot for the purpose of the library building. Having made the selection, after the death of Dr. Rush, the Library Company brought a bill to correct the execution of the power, on the ground that the trustee had incapacitated himself from exercising the power with a sound judgment

§ 511 *b*. The execution of a power requires careful consideration. If the manner of its execution is not pointed out, it must be executed in good faith, in the usual manner of doing the business to be done under the power; and there must be a strict adherence, not only to the substance of the power, but also to all the formalities required in its execution by the instrument. These formalities and solemnities are required for the protection of those persons whose rights may be defeated by the exercise of the power, and to prevent the donee of the power from acting with haste and without proper consideration.[1] If a writing is required, a parol disposition would be void, although the property might otherwise be disposed of by parol at law.[2] If it is to be by deed, nothing but a deed will execute the power, even though it is to be executed by a married woman; and it must be signed, sealed, acknowledged, delivered, and recorded.[3] If the number of witnesses is named, that number must witness to the instrument that purports to execute the power.[4] If the

and a free discretion, for the reason that he had bound his judgment and discretion by his promise and pledge to the testator. This view of the case was sustained in an able opinion in the court below; but, upon appeal to the Supreme Court of Pennsylvania, the judges, without expressly affirming or disaffirming the law as claimed by the Library Company, found the facts to be, that the trustee was not incapacitated, and that he had made a full and free exercise of his judgment and discretion in the execution of his power, and that the power was properly executed. The court, however, seemed to be of the opinion that the donee of a power might pledge himself to the creator of the power to execute it in a certain manner, and that an execution of the power in pursuance of the pledge might still be good.

[1] Hawkins *v*. Kemp, 3 East, 410; Rex *v*. Anstrey, 6 M. & Sel. 324; Holmes *v*. Coghill, 7 Ves. 506; Day *v*. Thwaites, 3 Ch. Cas. 69, 107; Ferry *v*. Laible, 31 N. J. 566.

[2] Thruxton *v*. Att. Gen., 1 Vern. 340.

[3] Digges's Case, 1 Rep. 73; Dundas *v*. Biddle, 2 Barr, 160.

[4] Bath *v*. Montague's Case, 3 Ch. Cas. 55; 2 Freem. 193; Kibbett *v*. Lee, Hob. 312; Ch. Cas. 90; Doe *v*. Keir, 4 Man. & Ry. 101; Wright *v*. Wakeford, 17 Ves. 459. It was formerly held that the attestation of the witnesses must be noticed in the deed itself. Wright *v*. Wakeford, 17 Ves. 459; Wright *v*. Barlow, 3 Mau. & Sel. 512. But the rule is now relaxed, and it is sufficient that the witnesses in fact attest the writing. Vincent *v*. Beshopre, 5 Exch. 683; Burdett *v*. Spilsbury, 6 Man. & G. 386; Ladd *v*. Ladd, 8 How. 30–40.

consent of any third person must be had to the execution, such consent must appear;[1] so if the deed is to be sealed.[2] If it is to be signed, it must be signed by the donee of the power.[3] If notice is to be given of the execution of the power, such notice must be shown,[4] and so of the slightest formality prescribed. If the power is to be executed by deed, it cannot be executed by will.[5] The converse of the proposition is also true, and a power to be executed by a will cannot be executed by a deed, or any instrument to take effect during the lifetime of the donee of the power.[6] Whether the execution of the power is to be by will or deed, or either, depends upon the words of the instrument. If the trustee is "to will it," the power must be executed by will;[7] and so if "afterwards to leave it," *i. e.* after the life-estate; but after the death of a tenant for life, *then* "to be at the disposal of A." does not imply a will.[8] If a power is to be executed by a will, all the solemnities of making a will, according to the statutes in force, must be observed, in order that the will may be duly probated;[9] but if the creator of the power point out all the formalities to be used in executing the will, a will executed according to the formalities prescribed in the power will be a valid execution of the power, although the

[1] Hawkins *v.* Kemp, 3 East, 410; Mansell *v.* Mansell, Wilm. 36.

[2] Dormer *v.* Thurland, 2 P. Wms. 506.

[3] Bird *v.* Stride, Bridg. 21; Thayer *v.* Thayer, Palm. 112; Blackville *v.* Ascott, 2 Eq. Cas. Abr. 654.

[4] Ward *v.* Lenthal, 1 Sid. 143.

[5] Woodward *v.* Halsey, 1 Sugd. on Pow. 255 (3d Am. ed.); Earl of Darlington *v.* Putney, Cowp. 260; Doe *v.* Cavan, 5 T. R. 567; 6 Bro. P. C. Taml. 175; Bushell *v.* Bushell, 1 Rep. t. Redesdale, 96; 4 Taunt. 297; Follett *v.* Follett, 2 P. Wms. 469; Alley *v.* Lawrence, 12 Gray, 373; Moore *v.* Demond, 5 R. I. 130.

[6] Whaley *v.* Drummond, 1 Sugd. on Pow. 257 (3d Am. ed.); Reid *v.* Shergold, 10 Ves. 370; Anderson *v.* Dawson, 15 Ves. 532. But see Heatly *v.* Thomas, 15 Ves. 596. [Hood *v.* Haden, 82 Va. 588.]

[7] Paul *v.* Heweston, 2 Myl. & K. 434.

[8] Anon. 3 Lev. 71; Thomlinson *v.* Dighton, 1 Com. 194; 1 P. Wms. 149; *Ex parte* Williams, 1 J. & W. 89; Doe *v.* Thorley, 10 East, 488; Walsh *v.* Wallinger, 2 Russ. & My. 78; Taml. 425; Brown *v.* Chambers, 1 Hayes, 597; Archibald *v.* Wright, 9 Sim. 161.

[9] 1 Sugd. on Pow. 257. [See *In re* Broad, [1901] 2 Ch. 86.]

instrument is invalid as a will.[1] (*a*)   The general rule is rigidly adhered to, that powers can be executed only in the mode, and at the time, and upon the conditions prescribed in the instrument creating the power or trust.[2]   A power to sell and to change investments gives no power to pledge some investments in order to raise money to enter upon hazardous enterprises for

[1] Eyre *v.* Fitton, 1 Sugd. on Pow. 155; Day *v.* Thwaites, 3 Ch. Cas. 69, 92; 2 Vern. 80; Wilkes *v.* Holmes, 9 Mod. 485; 16 Ves. 237, 268; Goodhill *v.* Brigham, 1 Bos. & Pul. 198; Longford *v.* Eyre, 1 P. Wms. 740; Habergham *v.* Vincent, 2 Ves. Jr. 204.

[2] See *ante*, § 254, and *post*, §§ 778, 779, 783–785. If in executing the power something is also stipulated which is not authorized to be done, but which can be clearly distinguished from the rightful execution of the power, the execution so far as authorized is valid, and void for the excess. Laskey *v.* Perrysburg Board, &c., 35 Ohio St. 519.

(*a*) When the creator of the power has directed that it be executed by will of the donee, the validity of the will is to be determined by the law of the donee's domicile at the time of the latter's death. Ward *v.* Stanard, 81 N. Y. S. 906, 82 App. Div. 386. See also Barretto *v.* Young, [1900] 2 Ch. 339. But as the appointment takes effect under the will or other instrument creating the power, the sufficiency of the execution in other respects is to be determined by the law of the domicile of the donor, *e. g.*, whether or not a general residuary clause without reference to the power is a sufficient execution. Lane *v.* Lane, 4 Pennewill (Del.) 368, 64 L. R. A. 849, 892; Cotting *v.* De Sartiges, 17 R. I. 668. The legality of the disposition attempted in an appointment which conforms to the terms of the power is to be determined by the law of the jurisdiction where the property is situated. Thrasher *v.* Ballard, 33 W. Va. 285; Pouey *v.* Hordern, [1900] 1 Ch. 492; Newton *v.* Hunt, 112 N. Y. S.

573. A will executing a power is revoked *in toto*, including the exercise of the power, by general words of revocation in a subsequent will, even although the subsequent will is not a good execution of the power. *In re* Kingdon, 32 Ch. D. 604. But if a subsequent will, insufficient as an execution of power, makes no reference to it and does not expressly revoke the first will, there is no revocation of the appointment. Cadell *v.* Wilcocks, [1898] P. 21.

As a married woman can execute a power of appointment over property belonging to another without the concurrence of her husband, marriage of a woman appointor after appointing by will does not revoke the appointment. Osgood *v.* Bliss, 141 Mass. 474; Heath *v.* Withington, 6 Cush. 497. Although the will may not be valid as a disposition of her own property, it should be probated, and the allowance should be qualified and limited. Ibid.

the possible profit of the trust estate.[1] In Maryland, the intention to execute a power of appointment by will must appear by reference to the power or the subject of it in the will, or from the fact that the will would be inoperative without the aid of the power (a); but in Massachusetts, a general devise or bequest is construed to include all property of which the testator had the general power of appointment, unless the contrary intent appears by his will, and where the power was created by the will of one domiciled in Massachusetts and in respect to property situated in that State, a will made in Maryland will operate as an execution of the power just as if made here.[2]

§ 511 c. The donee of a power may execute it without expressly referring to it, or taking any notice of it, provided that it is apparent from the whole instrument that it was intended as an execution of the power.[3] The execution of the power, however, must show that it was intended to be such execution; for if it is uncertain whether the act was intended to be an execution of the power, it will not be construed as an execution. The intention to execute a power will sufficiently appear, — (1) When there is some reference to the power in the instrument of execution; (2) where there is a reference to the property which is the subject-matter on which execution of the power is to operate; and (3) where the instrument of execution would have no operation, but would be utterly insensible and

[1] Loring v. Brodie, 134 Mass. 453, 466.
[2] Sewall v. Wilmer, 132 Mass. 131, 134.
[3] Gindrat v. Montgomery Gaslight Co., 82 Ala. 596, 606. [Young v. Sheldon, 139 Ala. 444; Gulf Red Cedar Lumber Co. v. O'Neal, 131 Ala. 117, 130; Guarantee & Trust Co. v. Jones, 103 Tenn. 245, 255; Kent v. Kent, L. R. [1902] Prob. 108; In re Mayhew, [1901] 1 Ch. 677; In re Sharland, [1899] 2 Ch. 536; In re Milner, [1899] 1 Ch. 563; In re Adams, 54 Weekly Rep. 42; Lee v. Giles, 124 Ga. 494.]

(a) This has been changed by a statute enacted in 1888. Pub. Gen. Laws of Md. (1904), Art. 93, § 323. As to execution of a power of sale or of appointment without specific reference to it, see infra, § 511 c and notes.

833

absurd, if it was not the execution of a power. (a) Thus, if a donee of a power to sell land have also an interest in his own right in the same land, his deed of the land, making no reference to the power, will convey only his own interest; for there is a subject-matter for the deed to operate upon, excluding the power, and, therefore, as it does not conclusively appear that the deed was intended to be an execution of the power as well as a conveyance of the grantor's interest in the land, it will be held not to be an execution of the power: but if the grantor has no interest in the land, his deed will be insensible and a mere absurdity, if not intended as an execution of the power; therefore, it will be held to be an execution of the power, if it refers to the subject-matter of the power, or describes the land over which his power extends.[1] It will be seen that this last conclu-

[1] Bingham's App., 64 Penn. St. 349; Drusadow v. Wilde, 63 id. 172; Coryell v. Dunton, 7 id. 530; Wetherell v. Wetherell, 18 id. 265; Meconkey's App., 13 id. 259; Keefer v. Schwartz, 47 id. 503; Allison v. Kurtz, 2 Watts, 185; Thompson v. Garwood, 3 Whart. 287; Commonwealth v. Duffield, 2 Jones, 280; Hefferman v. Addams, 7 Watts, 116; Cler's Case, 6 Rep. 17 b; Mo. 476, 577; Cro. Eliz. 877; Cro. Jac. 31; Brooke v. Turner, 2 Bing. N. C. 422; Wykham v. Wykham, 18 Ves. 419; Scrope's Case, 10 Rep. 143 b; Frampton v. Frampton, 6 Rep. 144 b; Snape v. Turton, Cro. Car. 472; Deg v. Deg, 2 P. Wms. 413; Sel. Cas. 44; Fitzgerald v. Fauconberge, Fitz, 107; Roscommon v. Fowke, 4 Bro. P. C. 523; George v. Lansley, 8 East, 13; Guy v. Dormer, Raym. 295; 3 Ch. Cas. 91; Udal v. Udal, Al. 81; Att. Gen. v. Brackenbury, 1 Hurl. & Colt. 782; Baton v. Jacks, 6 Rob. (N. Y.) 166; Collins v. Will, 40 Mo. 28; Hamilton v. Crosby, 32 Conn. 342; White v. Hicks, 43 Barb. 64; 33 N. Y. 383; Davis v. Vincent, 1 Houst. 416; Parcher v. Daniel, 12 Rich. Eq. 349; Myers v. McBride, 13 Rich. L. 178; Pease v. Pilot Knob Co., 49 Mo. 124; Blagge v. Miles, 1 Story, 426; Amory v. Meredith, 7 Allen, 397; Owen v. Switzer, 5 Mo. 322; Clark v. Hornthal, 47 Miss. 434. [Middlebrooks v. Ferguson, 126 Ga. 232; Kirkman v. Wadsworth, 137 N. C. 453; Walke v. Moore, 95 Va. 729.]

(a) Papin v. Piednoir, 205 Mo. 521; Farlow v. Farlow, 83 Md. 118. Thus where persons who were both executors and trustees and in their capacity of trustees had power of sale, executed a deed which they inadvertently signed as executors, it was held that the deed transferred the title. Philbin v. Thurn, 103 Md. 342. See also Renner v. Marshall, 58 S. W. 863, 870 (Tenn.). But see Clarke v. East Atlanta Land Co., 113 Ga. 21.

sion is a presumption of law; this presumption may be more or less strong, according to all the circumstances of the case and the condition of the property. If all the words of a deed or will can have an effect given to them, and an operation upon property or rights, without being taken as the execution of a power, they will not be an execution of such power.[1] (a)   If a man has

[1] Bingham's Appeal, 64 Penn. St. 350. [Weinstein v. Weber, 178 N. Y. 94. See Daniel v. Felt, 100 Fed. 727.] A mere quitclaim deed contains no apt words to indicate an intent to sell under a power, and only the beneficial interest of the grantor will pass by deed in that form. Towle v. Erving, 23 Wis. 336; Griswold v. Bigelow, 6 Conn. 258; Johnson v. Stanton, 30 Conn. 297; Mory v. Mitchell, 18 Mo. 227.

(a) When the donee of the power has executed an instrument which is otherwise sufficient to execute the power, but has failed to refer to the power, the whole question for the court is whether or not the donee intended to execute the power. Cooper v. Haines, 70 Md. 282; Lee v. Simpson, 134 U. S. 572; Scott v. Bryan, 194 Pa. St. 41.

The fact that he has no interest of his own in the property described in the deed or will is usually sufficient evidence that he intended to execute the power. Kirkman v. Wadsworth, 137 N. C. 453, 457; Walke v. Moore, 95 Va. 729.

When the donee of the power has also an individual interest of his own in the property which he has described in the deed and fails to refer to the power, the conveyance will be presumed to have been intended to pass only his own interest unless a contrary intention appears. Merolla v. Lane, 107 N. Y. S. 439, 122 App. Div. 535; Weinstein v. Weber, 178 N. Y. 94; Kirkman v. Wadsworth, 137 N. C. 453, 457; N. E. Mortgage Co. v. Buice, 98 Ga. 795; Ridgely v. Cross, 83 Md. 161. Thus where a husband and wife

who had equitable life estates in certain land and also a power to sell, executed a deed of "all the right, title, or interest we may have either severally or jointly" in the land, it was held that the deed conveyed merely their equitable life interests and was not an execution of the power. Ridgely v. Cross, 83 Md. 161. To a similar effect is Weinstein v. Weber, 178 N. Y. 94, where a life tenant with power to sell executed a quitclaim deed of all her right, title, and interest. But a quitclaim deed by a life tenant does not necessarily have this limited effect. Goff v. Pensenhafer, 190 Ill. 200; Ladd v. Chase, 155 Mass. 417.

If the deed of conveyance, though making no reference to the power, purports to convey an interest greater than or different from the individual interest of the donee of the power, this fact is usually strong evidence that an execution of the power was intended. Scott v. Bryan, 194 Pa. St. 41; Walke v. Moore, 95 Va. 729, 738. Thus if the deed of a life tenant with power to sell the fee purports to convey the fee, courts will usually inter-

several powers, and refers to some and not to others, the execution will exclude those not referred to.[1] From these propositions it may be seen why a conveyance of specific property, or a specific devise of property, will generally operate at the execution of a power, if the grantor or testator has no other interest in the property but the power, although he makes no reference to the power in his deed or will.[2] On the other hand, the student will understand why it was so long held that a general conveyance or assignment of all a grantor's property which named no particular property, or a general devise of all a testator's property, without referring to any particular property, and without referring to any power to be executed, did not operate to execute a power the grantor or testator might have.[3]

[1] Att. Gen. v. Vigor, 8 Ves. 256; Maundrell v. Maundrell, 10 Ves. 246; Trollope v. Linton, 1 S. & S. 477; Bailey v. Lloyd, 5 Russ. 330; Pidgely v. Pidgely, 1 Col. C. C. 255; Hougham v. Sandys, 2 Sim. 95; Roach v. Haynes, 6 Ves. 153; 8 Ves. 584; Monk v. Mawdesly, 1 Sim. 286; Lawson v. Lawson, 3 Bro. Ch. 272. [See note a, supra, p. 835.]

[2] See 1 Sugd. Pow. 356, 383 (3d Am. ed.)

[3] 1 Sugd. Pow. 383 et seq. (3d Am. ed.); Doe v. Roake, 2 Bing. 497; Blagge v. Miles, 1 Story, 426; 4 Kent, 336; Jones v. Tucker, 2 Mer. 533; Doe v. Vincent, 1 Houst. 416, 427; Hughes v. Turner, 3 Myl. & K. 688. But the English statutes, 7 Will. IV and 1 Vict. c. 26, § 27, have altered the rule; and at the present day a general devise of real or personal estate operates as an execution of all the power that a testator may have over such property, unless it appears to have been the intention not to execute such power. See Collard v. Sampson, 16 Beav. 543; 4 De G., M. & G. 224; Lake v. Currie, 2 De G., M. & G. 536; West v. Ray, 1 Kay, 385; Orange v. Pickford, 4 Drew. 363; Wilson v. Eden, 16 Beav. 153; Enniss v. Smith, 2 De G. & Sm. 722; Wisden v. Wisden, 2 Sm. & Gif. 396; Blagge v. Miles,

pret the deed as an execution of the power. Grace v. Perry, 197 Mo. 550; Rinkenberger v. Meyer, 155 Ind. 152; McMillan v. Deering, 139 Ind. 70; Vines v. Clarke, 97 N. Y. S. 532, 111 App. Div. 12; Underwood v. Cave, 176 Mo. 1, 18; Matthews v. Capshaw, 109 Tenn. 480; Young v. Mutual Life Ins. Co., 101 Tenn. 311.

The size of the consideration may help to determine the intention of the grantor, McMillan v. Deering, 139 Ind. 70; Ladd v. Chase, 155 Mass. 417; or the age of the life tenant, Morffew v. S. F. & S. R. R. Co., 107 Cal. 587; or the fact that the life tenant signs the deed as executrix. Thomas v. Wright, 66 S. W. 993 (Ky. 1902). See also McCreary v. Bomberger, 151 Pa. St. 323; Hill v. Conrad, 91 Tex. 341.

In the one case, a specific reference to the property indicates an intention to execute a power, if the act can have no other sense,

1 Story, 426. [See *In re* Marten, [1902] 1 Ch. 314.] The court in Massachusetts has adopted the rule of the English statute. See Amory *v.* Meredith, 7 Allen, 400. (*a*)

(*a*) The English statute has been interpreted to refer only to general powers of appointment and to have no application to limited or special powers. Doyle *v.* Coyle, [1895] 1 Ir. R. 205; *In re* Huddleston, [1894] 3 Ch. 595; *In re* Hayes, [1900] 2 Ch. 332. With regard to powers of the latter class, general residuary words are not sufficient execution, unless it appears from the whole will that the donee intended thereby to execute his power of appointment. But it has been held that the donee's use of the word "appoint" in a residuary clause, when she had no other power of appointment may be sufficient evidence of her intention to execute a limited power, and that the fact that she had no other power of appointment is admissible as evidence. *In re* Mayhew, [1901] 1 Ch. 677. In general, however, the intention of the testator must be gathered from the will. *In re* Huddleston, [1894] 3 Ch. 595; *In re* Marsh, 38 Ch. Div. 630.

Several States have enacted statutes similar to the 27th section of the English Wills Act. See Pub. Gen. Laws of Md. (1904) Art. 93, § 323; IV N. Y. Consol. Laws (1909), p. 2846, § 18, p. 3408, § 176; Brightly's Purdon's Digest Pa., p. 1205, § 26; Safe Dep. & Trust Co. *v.* Friend, 201 Pa. St. 429. In several States it has become established law without legislation, that a general disposition of the residue of a testator's estate will operate

as an execution of a general power of appointment unless the testator's purpose appears to have been otherwise. Tudor *v.* Vail, 195 Mass. 18, 26; Stone *v.* Forbes, 189 Mass. 163, 168; Talbot *v.* Field, 173 Mass. 188; Hassam *v.* Hazen, 156 Mass. 93; Cumston *v.* Bartlett, 149 Mass. 243, 248; Emery *v.* Haven, 67 N. H. 503; Johnston *v.* Knight, 117 N. C. 122. In Stone *v.* Forbes, 189 Mass. 163, 168, the court intimated that it would follow the sam reule in regard to limited or special powers of appointment. See also Johnston *v.* Knight, 117 N. C. 122.

Other jurisdictions have abided by the common-law rule, that a general devise or bequest by the donee of a power of appointment is not sufficient evidence of an intention of the donee to execute the power. Hollister *v.* Shaw, 46 Conn. 248; Lane *v.* Lane, 4 Pennewill (Del.), 368, 64 L. R. A. 849 and note; Wooster *v.* Cooper, 59 N. J. Eq. 204, 223; Harvard College *v.* Balch, 171 Ill. 275; Mason *v.* Wheeler, 19 R. I. 21.

Under the English statute, a residuary clause in a will executed prior to the creation of the power of appointment is a good execution of a general power unless the court is satisfied that the donee could not have intended his will to have that effect. This rule is based upon . the doctrine that a will is a continuing instrument, and speaks from

as if the donee of the power has no other interest in the property; but a general devise or conveyance, which neither refers to specific property nor to the power to be executed, indicates no intention to execute a power. It will be understood that there is a wide distinction between executing a special or discretionary power, and a simple devise of the trust estate; for it will be remembered that a trust estate passes under general words in a will to the devisee, but the devisee takes the trust estate subject to the same trusts under which the original trustee held them.[1] It will also be remembered, that there is a difference between a trustee's executing a power of appointment, or otherwise, in his last will, and a *cestui que trust* devising his beneficial interest in a trust estate. It has been considerably discussed, whether general words in the will of a *cestui que trust* devises all his interest in a trust fund, as well as all the estate to which he may have the legal title. It is established by statute in England, that general words in a will shall convey the *cestui que trust's* legal and beneficial estates, and this rule is followed in Massachusetts.[2]

§ 512. A *personal* power is sometimes given to trustees to consent to or approve the marriage of the *cestui que trust;* and the enjoyment of the bounty of the testator by the beneficiaries is sometimes made to depend upon the exercise of this power by trustees. These powers, if exercised in restraint of mar-

---

[1] See *ante*, §§ 335–345.
[2] Amory *v.* Meredith, 7 Allen, 397.

the death of the testator. Boyes *v.* Cook, 14 Ch. Div. 53. See also *In re* Hayes, [1900] 2 Ch. 332; Phillips *v.* Cayley, 43 Ch. Div. 222; *In re* Tarrant's Trust, 58 L. J. Ch. 780. The same view has been taken in Massachusetts. Stone *v.* Forbes, 189 Mass. 163, 168. See also Burkett *v.* Whittemore, 36 S. C. 428.

But see Estate of Vaux, 11 Phila. 57; Estate of Fry, 11 Phila. 305.
The fact that the will of the donee of the power speaks of the property as if it were his own property will not prevent his disposition of it from being a valid execution of his power. Loring *v.* Wilson, 174 Mass. 132, 141.

riage, are not favored in equity.[1] Therefore, if an interest is *vested* in a beneficiary, subject to be divested in case the beneficiary marries without the consent or approbation of the trustee, and there is *no gift over* to take effect upon the marriage without such consent, the power or condition will be treated as void, and will not be enforced.[2] But this rule will not apply to a charge on real estate.[3] If the condition is *subsequent*, and the interest is given over on the failure of the donee to comply with it, the court will enforce the gift over if the first donee marry without the consent of the trustees.[4] (a) It is said to be doubtful, whether a general gift of the residue will be a sufficient gift over to give validity to such power;[5] but if the direction is, that the particular gift shall fall into the residue, in case the donee marries without the consent of the trustees, it is a good gift over.[6]

§ 513. If the property once vests absolutely in the donee, and there is a general and unlimited condition that he shall not marry without the consent of the trustees, the necessity of the consent ceases as soon as the interest vests; as where a legacy is given to a child at twenty-one, provided, if he marry without the consent of the trustees, he should forfeit it. The legacy vests at twenty-one, and if he marry afterwards without

---

[1] Stackpole v. Beaumont, 3 Ves. Jr. 89; Long v. Dennis, 4 Burr. 2052; Daley v. Desbouverie, 2 Atk. 261.

[2] Semphill v. Hayley, Pr. Ch. 562; Garrett v. Pritty, 2 Vern. 293; 3 Mer. 120; Jervoise v. Duke, 1 Vern. 20; Harvey v. Aston, 1 Atk. 378; Wheeler v. Bingham, 3 Atk. 364; Lloyd v. Branton, 3 Mer. 117; 1 Rop. Leg. 715; W. v. B., 11 Beav. 621; Poole v. Bate, 11 Hare, 33; Marples v. Bainbridge, 1 Madd. 590; McIlvaine v. Gether, 3 Whart. 575; Hooper v. Dundas, 10 Barr, 75; Maddox v. Maddox, 11 Grat. 804.

[3] Ibid.; Reynish v. Martin, 3 Atk. 333; Berkely v. Ryder, 2 Ves. 535.

[4] Ibid.; Stratton v. Grimes, 2 Vern. 357; Dashwood v. Bulkeley, 10 Ves. 230; Scott v. Tyler, 2 Bro. Ch. 431; 2 Lead. Cas. Eq. 105, and notes.

[5] Harvey v. Aston, 1 Atk. 375; *contra*, Wheeler v. Bingham, 3 Atk. 364; Lloyd v. Branton, 3 Mer. 118; Scott v. Tyler, 2 Lead. Cas. Eq. 396.

[6] Wheeler v. Bingham, 3 Atk. 368; Lloyd v. Branton, 3 Mer. 118.

(a) See *In re* Moore, 39 Ch. D. 116, 123, 131.

consent, the condition, being subsequent, is gone, and there is no forfeiture;[1] and where a child marries in the testator's lifetime, with his consent, but after the date of the will, such conditions, as to consent of trustees, are of no effect; and they do not apply to a second marriage.[2]

§ 514. Where power is given to a trustee to consent to a marriage, as a condition precedent to the gift's taking effect, nothing will vest in the donee until the condition is complied with; as where there is a gift in trust for a party *upon his marriage*, or *upon his marriage with the proper consent of the trustee*, the gift will not vest in the beneficiary until his marriage with the consent of the trustee.[3] Under such form of gift, it is immaterial whether there is a gift over or not.[4] The rule will apply, whether the consent to the marriage is required until a certain age, or during the whole life.[5] Where there was a gift in trust to a party, if he should marry with the consent of the

[1] Pullen *v.* Ready, 2 Atk. 587; Desbody *v.* Boyville, 2 P. Wms. 547; Knapp *v.* Noyes, Amb. 662; Osborn *v.* Brown, 5 Ves. 527; Stackpole *v.* Beaumont, 3 Ves. Jr. 89; Malcolm *v.* O'Callaghan, 2 Madd. 354; Lloyd *v.* Branton, 3 Mer. 108; Graydon *v.* Hicks, 2 Atk. 18; Garrett *v.* Pritty, 2 Vern. 293; 3 Mer. 120, n.

[2] Clarke *v.* Berkely, 2 Vern. 720; Crommelin *v.* Crommelin, 3 Ves. Jr. 227; Parnell *v.* Lyon, 1 V. & B. 479; Wheeler *v.* Warner, 1 S. & S. 304; Smith *v.* Cowdery, 2 S. & S. 358; Coventry *v.* Higgins, 8 Jur. 182.

[3] Reeves *v.* Herne, 5 Vin. Abr. 343, pl. 41; Reynish *v.* Martin, 3 Atk. 330; Frye *v.* Porter, 1 Ch. Cas. 138; 1 Mod. 300; Bertie *v.* Falkland, 3 Ch. Cas. 129; Holmes *v.* Lysight, 2 Bro. P. C. 261; Hemmings *v.* Munckley, 1 Bro. Ch. 303; Scott *v.* Tyler, 2 Bro. Ch. 489; 2 Lead. Cas. Eq. 105, notes; 2 Dick. 712; Knight *v.* Cameron, 14 Ves. 289; Creagh *v.* Wilson, 2 Vern. 572; Gillett *v.* Wray, 1 P. Wms. 284; Harvey *v.* Aston, 1 Atk. 375; Newton *v.* Marsden, 2 John. & H. 356; Hotz's Est., 38 Penn. St. 422; Cornell *v.* Lovett, 35 id. 100; Taylor *v.* Mason, 9 Wheat. 350; Collier *v.* Slaughter, 2 Ala. 263; Stratton *v.* Grymes, 2 Vern. 357; Barton *v.* Barton, id. 308; Hawkins *v.* Skeggs, 10 Humph. 31; Bennett *v.* Robinson, 10 Watts, 348; Com'th *v.* Stauffer, 10 Penn. St. 350; McCullough's App., 2 Jones, 197; Phillips *v.* Medbury, 7 Conn. 568.

[4] Ibid.; Clarke *v.* Parker, 19 Ves. 8; Malcolm *v.* O'Callaghan, 2 Madd. 349; Long *v.* Ricketts, 2 S. & S. 179; Stackpole *v.* Beaumont, 3 Ves. Jr. 89; 1 Rop. Leg. 658.

[5] Ibid.; Lloyd *v.* Branton, 3 Mer. 108.

trustees, and *over*, if he should marry *against* their consent, it was held, that *against* was equivalent to *without*, and that the gift went over, although it did not appear that the trustees opposed the marriage.[1] The trustees' powers are exhausted by consent to one marriage; if, therefore, they consent to one marriage, the beneficiary may marry a second time without their consent.[2] But the rule in relation to a first marriage without consent, and a second marriage with consent, is uncertain.[3]

§ 515. A general restraint of marriage, with or without the consent of trustees, or with any person, is illegal and void, as contrary to the policy of the law. Therefore, a gift, in trust, upon the condition that the beneficiary shall not marry at all, will vest in the donee, and the condition is void.[4] So all conditions, leading to a probable prohibition of marriage, are void.[5] But a condition, restraining marriage under the age of twenty-one, or before a reasonable age without consent, is valid.[6] So conditions that restrain marriage with a particular person, or with natives of a particular country, or of a particular religion, or conditions that prescribe the ceremonies of the marriage, are valid, and may be enforced in relation to the property.[7]

[1] Long *v.* Ricketts, 2 S. & S. 179; and see Harvey *v.* Aston, 1 Atk. 375; Pollock *v.* Croft, 1 Mer. 184.

[2] Hutcheson *v.* Hammond, 3 Bro. Ch. 128; Crommelin *v.* Crommelin, 3 Ves. Jr. 227; Low *v.* Manners, 5 B. & Ald. 967; 1 Rop. Leg. 709.

[3] Malcolm *v.* O'Callaghan, 2 Madd. 349.

[4] Waters *v.* Tazewell, 9 Ind. 291; Maddox *v.* Maddox, 11 Grat. 804; Keily *v.* Monck, 3 Ridgw. P. C. 205, 244, 249, 261; Harvey *v.* Aston, Comyn, 726; 1 Atk. 361; 1 Eq. Cas. Ab. 110, pl. 2, n. (a); Rishton *v.* Cobb, 9 Sim. 615; Morley *v.* Rennoldson, 2 Hare, 570; Connelly *v.* Connelly, 7 Moore, P. C. 438.

[5] Ibid.; Long *v.* Dennis, 4 Burr. 2052.

[6] Sutton *v.* Jewke, 2 Ch. R. 9; Creagh *v.* Wilson, 2 Vern. 573; Ashton *v.* Ashton, Pr. Ch. 226; Chauncy *v.* Graydon, 2 Atk. 616; Hemmings *v.* Munckley, 1 Bro. Ch. 304; Dashwood *v.* Bulkely, 10 Ves. 230; Stackpole *v.* Beaumont, 3 Ves. Jr. 96; Pearce *v.* Loman, 3 Ves. 139; Yonge *v.* Furse, 3 Jur. (N. S.) 603.

[7] Jervois *v.* Duke, 1 Vern. 19; Randall *v.* Payne, 1 Bro. Ch. 55; Perrin *v.* Lyon, 9 East, 170; Duggan *v.* Kelly, 10 Ir. Eq. 295; 1 Eq. Cas. Ab. 110, pl. 2, n. (a); Haughton *v.* Haughton, 1 Moll. 611.

§ 516. Where there is a limitation of property to a person until marriage, and, upon marriage *over* to some other person, or during widowhood, or while single, or where there is an annuity, payable to a person until such time, or during such time, and then to cease, the limitation is valid. Such a gift is upon no condition at all, but is a clear limitation, that marks the duration and continuance of the interest.[1] But where a testator devised lands to trustees in trust for B. for life, provided she does not marry, and, after her decease or marriage, over to other persons, and the testator afterwards married B. himself, and republished his will, with the same proviso in it, it was held that B. was entitled to the property notwithstanding her marriage.[2]

§ 517. Where such powers of consent are given to trustees, the marriage of the *cestui que trust*, during the testator's lifetime with his consent or subsequent approval, renders them inapplicable, and they cannot be executed.[3] The assent of the trustees, when necessary, may be implied, as where they allow a courtship and marriage to take place, and make no objection.[4] In this case no particular form of consent was prescribed. Even where a written consent was prescribed, and the trustees negotiated the settlement and the marriage, it was held suffi-

---

[1] Jordan v. Holkam, Amb. 209; Barton v. Barton, 2 Vern. 308; Scott v. Tyler, 2 Lead. Cas. Eq. 396; Lowe v. Peers, Wilm. 369; Bird v. Hunsdon, 2 Swanst. 342; Marples v. Bainbridge, 1 Madd. 590; Webb v. Grace, 2 Phill. 701, reversing 15 Sim. 394; Richards v. Baker, 2 Atk. 321; Sheffield v. Orrery, 3 Atk. 282; Gordon v. Adolphus, 3 Bro. P. C. 306; Heath v. Lewis, 3 De G., M. & G. 954. The early case of Parsons v. Winslow, 6 Mass. 169, is not in accordance with the authorities, nor can it be sustained on principle.

[2] Cooper v. Cooper, 6 Ir. Ch. 217; Corkers v. Minons, 1 Ir. Jur. 316; West v. Kerr, 6 id. 141.

[3] Clarke v. Berkely, 2 Vern. 720; Coffin v. Cooper, cited 1 Ves. & B. 481; Parnell v. Lyon, id. 479; Wheeler v. Warner, 1 S. & S. 374; Coventry v. Higgins, 14 Sim. 30; Crommelin v. Crommelin, 3 Ves. Jr. 227; Smith v. Cowdery, 2 S. & S. 358.

[4] Mesgrett v. Mesgrett, 2 Vern. 580; Clarke v. Parker, 19 Ves. 12; Harvey v. Aston, 1 Atk. 375; O'Callaghan v. Cooper, 5 Ves. 126.

cient: [1] they should be estopped to deny their consent to a marriage of their own procurement. There need be no consent to a particular marriage, if the *cestui que trust* has a general consent or license to marry whom she chooses.[2] If the consent is required to be in writing, very loose and general expressions of consent in letters, if acted upon, will be construed into assent.[3] If the consent is required to be in writing, any fraud or procurement, on the part of the trustees, will estop them from insisting upon the forfeiture; [4] but if there is no collusive conduct, and consent is required to be in writing, an implied or verbal consent cannot satisfy the condition.[5] A deed is not necessary, unless specially required by the will.[6] The consent must be given previously to the marriage, and the approbation of the trustees afterwards is immaterial, because no subsequent approbation could be a performance of the condition, or avoid a forfeiture for a breach of it.[7] If the time is stated for the exercise of the power, the consent cannot be three years before the time named.[8] If, however, the trustees gave their consent to the marriage at the proper time, but were prevented by accident from executing the formal writings until after the solemnization of it, it was held to be a compliance with the condition, as courts of equity may at all times relieve from accidents and

[1] Strange *v.* Smith, Amb. 263; Worthington *v.* Evans, 1 S. & S. 165.

[2] Mercer *v.* Hall, 4 Bro. Ch. 328; Pollock *v.* Croft, 1 Mer. 181.

[3] Daley *v.* Desbouverie, 2 Atk. 261; D'Aguilar *v.* Drinkwater, 2 V. & B. 225; Merry *v.* Ryves, 1 Eden, 1; Worthington *v.* Evans, 1 S. & S. 165; Le Jeune *v.* Budd, 8 Sim. 441. [*In re* Smith, 44 Ch. Div. 654.]

[4] Strange *v.* Smith, Amb. 263; Clarke *v.* Parker, 19 Ves. 18; Farmer *v.* Compton, 1 Ch. R. 1.

[5] D'Aguilar *v.* Drinkwater, 2 V. & B. 225; Clarke *v.* Parker, 19 Ves. 12.

[6] Worthington *v.* Evans, 2 S. & S. 165.

[7] Reynish *v.* Martin, 3 Atk. 331; Clarke *v.* Parker, 19 Ves. 21; Berkley *v.* Ryder, 2 Ves. 532; Long *v.* Ricketts, 2 S. & S. 179; Malcolm *v.* O'Callaghan, 2 Madd. 349; Hemmings *v.* Munckley, 1 Bro. Ch. 304; Frye *v.* Porter, 1 Ch. Cas. 138; 1 Mod. 300. In Burleton *v.* Humphrey, Amb. 256, Lord Hardwicke held a different doctrine; but it has not been acted upon, and is not the law.

[8] Weller *v.* Ker, 1 Macq. H. L. Sc. App. Cas. 11.

mistakes.[1] If the trustees have once given their full consent to the marriage, with a knowledge of all the facts, they cannot withdraw it; for they have allowed the affections and feelings of the parties to become entangled, and it would be in the nature of a fraud to withdraw their consent.[2] But if any new facts should come to the knowledge of the trustees, which would render the marriage an improper one, they may withdraw their consent, and they ought to do so.[3]

§ 518. The consent of the trustees may be given conditionally, if the condition is not unreasonable. Thus an assent, *if a proper settlement is made*, or *if the cotrustees consent*, is conditional;[4] and if the parties fail or refuse to perform the condition, the consent may be withdrawn;[5] but if, in pursuance of the condition, a settlement is made after marriage, it will save the forfeiture.[6] All the trustees who accept the trust must consent,[7] unless the dissenting trustee is influenced by selfish and improper motives;[8] for if the testator has named the parties who are to assent, although he has used words to indicate that he attached no particular importance to the assent of all, yet the court cannot change the condition, and deprive those of their interest, to whom there is an express devise over.[9] A trustee may, however, authorize his cotrustee to consent for him, for that would be his own consent.[10] In general, the power

[1] Worthington v. Evans, 2 S. & S. 172; O'Callaghan v. Cooper, 5 Ves. 117.

[2] Le Jeune v. Budd, 6 Sim. 441; Farmer v. Compton, 1 Ch. R. 1; Strange v. Smith, Amb. 263; Merry v. Ryves, 1 Edm. 1; Dashwood v. Bulkely, 10 Ves. 242.

[3] D'Aguilar v. Drinkwater, 2 V. & B. 234; 1 Rop. Leg. 699.

[4] O'Callaghan v. Cooper, 5 Ves. 517; Dashwood v. Bulkely, 10 Ves. 230; D'Aguilar v. Drinkwater, 2 V. & B. 235.

[5] Dashwood v. Bulkely, 10 Ves. 230.

[6] O'Callaghan v. Cooper, 5 Ves. 117; 10 Ves. 230.

[7] Clarke v. Parker, 19 Ves. 12. The *dictum* in Harvey v. Aston, 1 Atk. 375, has not been followed.

[8] Peyton v. Bury, 2 P. Wms. 626; Mesgrett v. Mesgrett, 2 Vern. 580.

[9] Clarke v. Parker, 19 Ves. 12, 15.

[10] Daley v. Desbouverie, 2 Atk. 261; Clarke v. Parker, 19 Ves. 12; D'Aguilar v. Drinkwater, 2 V. & B. 225, 235, 236.

to assent is given to the executors or trustees, *in that character*, and not *personally*, and those who renounce the trust have no power;[1] yet the power may be conferred upon an executor or trustee *personally*, so that his assent may be required, although he renounce the trust.[2] And a power may be so given to executors to sell lands that they may execute the power of selling the lands although they renounce the executorship.[3] If the power becomes impossible by the death of one or more of the trustees, it will be dispensed with so far as it is impossible to execute it literally;[4] and if all the trustees die, the power is absolutely gone. So, if the condition is subsequent, and the consent of the executors or trustees in the plural number is required, and one dies, the condition is gone;[5] but if the death of the original trustee is provided for by the appointment of a new one, and the power extends to him, then the consent of the trustees must be had.[6] After a considerable lapse of time, and no action taken to disturb the possession of the property, the consent of the trustees will be presumed to have been given in proper form.[7]

§ 519. The exercise of this discretionary power, of assenting to the marriage of the *cestui que trust*, is of so peculiar a nature that courts of equity will exercise a control over it, and will not suffer the power to be abused; they will examine into the conduct and motives of the persons refusing their assent, and ascertain whether the refusal proceeds from a corrupt, selfish, or improper motive; and if it does, the court will relieve from a forfeiture incurred by a marriage without consent.[8]

[1] Worthington *v.* Evans, 1 S. & S. 165.
[2] Graydon *v.* Graydon, 2 Atk. 16, explained in 1 Rop. Leg. 695.
[3] Moody *v.* Fulmer, 3 Grant, 17.
[4] 1 Rop. Leg. 691.
[5] Peyton *v.* Bury, 2 P. Wms. 626; Jones *v.* Suffolk, 1 Bro. Ch. 528; Graydon *v.* Hicks, 2 Atk. 16–18; Aislabie *v.* Rice, 3 Madd. 256; 8 Taunt. 459; Grant *v.* Dyer, 2 Dow. 93.
[6] Clarke *v.* Parker, 19 Ves. 15.
[7] *Re* Birch, 17 Beav. 358.
[8] 1 Rop. Leg. 697.

Lord Eldon said, this was a "dangerous power" in the court, and one delicate and difficult to exercise.[1] But there is no question that the courts will exercise it in a proper case, as where the trustees refuse their assent from anger, pique, resentment, or from interested motives, as where some interest in the property would come to them or their families, in case of a marriage without their assent, or the death of the *cestui que trust* before marriage, or where the trustees have themselves promoted and procured the marriage.[2] So, where a trustee refused to assent or dissent to a proposed marriage of the beneficiary, the court sent the case to a master to inquire whether the marriage was a proper one, and to receive proposals for a settlement.[3]

---

[1] Dashwood *v.* Bulkely, 10 Ves. 245; Clarke *v.* Parker, 19 Ves. 12.

[2] Mesgrett *v.* Mesgrett, 2 Vern. 580; 10 Ves. 243; Strange *v.* Smith, Amb. 264; Merry *v.* Ryves, 1 Eden, 6; Peyton *v.* Bury, 2 P. Wms. 328; Daley *v.* Desbouverie, 2 Atk. 261; Clarke *v.* Parker, 19 Ves. 19.

[3] Goldsmid *v.* Goldsmid, 19 Ves. 368; Coop. 225.

CHAPTER XVII.

TRUSTEES OF THE DRY LEGAL TITLE; TO PRESERVE CONTINGENT
REMAINDERS; OF TERMS ATTENDANT; OF FREEHOLDS; AND OF
LEASEHOLDS.

§ 520.   It is a *simple* or dry trust, when property is vested
in one person in trust for another, and the nature of the trust,
not being prescribed by the donor, is left to the construction
of law.[1]   In such case the *cestui que trust* is entitled to the actual
possession and enjoyment of the property, and to dispose of
it, or to call upon the trustee to execute such conveyances of

---

[1] Abolished in Alabama.   The *cestui* takes at once the estate given to
the trustee (Code of 1876, § 2185).   [Code of 1907, § 3408.]   See Wilkinson *v.*
May, 69 Ala. 33; Webb *v.* Crawford, 77 Ala. 440; Gosson *v.* Ladd, id. 224;
see also Sutton *v.* Aiken, 62 Ga. 733; Elliot *v.* Deason, 64 id. 63.   The same
thing is held in Illinois.   Witham *v.* Brooner, 63 Ill. 344; Lynch *v.* Swayne, 83
id. 336; Kirkland *v.* Cox, 94 id. 600; Long *v.* Long, 62 Md. 33; Owens *v.*
Crow, 62 Md. 491; Farmers' Nat'l Bank *v.* Moran, 30 Minn. 165.   But if
the *cestuis* are are not *sui juris*, the estate vests in the trustee.   Dean *v.*
Long, 122 Ill. 458.

the legal estate as he directs.[1] In short, the *cestui que trust* has an absolute control over the beneficial interest, together with a right to call for the legal title, and the person in whom the legal title vests is a *simple* or *dry trustee*.[2] (*a*) Settlors sometimes convey estates in this manner for an ulterior purpose; or an active trust having been accomplished, the legal title and the beneficial interest may have fallen into this condition. The duties and powers of such dry trustees of the legal estate are few and simple. They are usually said to be threefold, and similar to those of the old feoffees to uses: (1) To permit the *cestui que trust* to occupy and receive the incomes and profits of the estate. (2) To execute such conveyances, or make such disposition of the estate as the *cestui que trust* may direct. In such case, if the trustee has made advances to the *cestui que trust* upon the credit of the land, the decree to convey should provide for the repayment of them.[3] The *cestui que trust* cannot, however, call for a conveyance, if such conveyance is inconsistent with all the agreements and purposes of the trust.[4] (*b*) If a trustee is to convey to children, he cannot be compelled to convey before all the children who may take under gift are born.[5] (3) To protect and defend the title, or to allow their names to be used for that purpose.[6] At law they are the legal

[1] Lewin on Trusts, 18.
[2] Hill on Trustees, 316.
[3] Robles *v.* Clarke, 25 Cal. 317.
[4] Thompson *v.* Galloupe, 100 Mass. 435. [See *infra*, § 920 and notes.]
[5] Dial *v.* Dial, 21 Tex. 529.
[6] Cruise, Dig. tit. 12, c. 4, § 6.

(*a*) As to when the courts will decree the termination of an express trust because it is or has become a dry or passive trust, see *infra*, § 920, and notes.

(*b*) When the trust instrument provides that the property is to be sold by the trustee and that the proceeds are to be divided, the beneficiaries have no right to a partition of the property itself.

Gerard *v.* Buckley, 137 Mass. 475; 1 Ames' Cases on Trusts, (2d ed.) 452, 453, 455; Brown *v.* Miller, 45 W. Va. 211; Story *v.* Palmer, 46 N. J. Eq. 1. But if all the beneficiaries unite in asking partition in specie, courts of equity will usually order partition if no material purpose of the trust will thereby be defeated. Brown *v.* Miller, 45 W. Va. 211.

owners of the estate, and their names must be used in all suits at law affecting the legal title;[1] but in equity the *cestui que trust* is the owner, and the trustees will be restrained by injunction from using their power over the legal title to the injury of the *cestui que trust.*[2] If such trustees refuse from improper motives to convey the dry legal title when required by a person clearly entitled to the equitable interest, the court will decree a conveyance, and impose costs upon the trustees for their refusal.[3] (a) Even in an action at law, in the name of the trustee for the benefit of the *cestui que trust*, the trustee cannot release or discontinue the action, without the consent of the beneficiary; and if he does so, courts of law will set aside the release;[4] but where a trustee's name is thus used for the benefit of the *cestui que trust*, he is entitled to be indemnified against the costs, and the *cestui que trust* may be restrained in equity from proceeding until he has furnished such security.[5]

[1] Goodtitle *v.* Jones, 7 T. R. 47; Wake *v.* Tinkler, 16 East, 36; Cox *v.* Walker, 26 Me. 504; Methodist Soc. of Georgetown *v.* Bennett, 39 Conn. 293; First Bap. Soc. in Andover *v.* Hazen, 100 Mass. 322; Beach *v.* Beach, 14 Vt. 28; Matthews *v.* Ward, 10 G. & John. 443; Moore *v.* Burnet, 11 Ohio, 334; Wright *v.* Douglass, 3 Barb. 559; Mordecai *v.* Parker, 3 Dev. 425. In Pennsylvania, however, the action of ejectment is an equitable action, and the *cestui que trust* can maintain it for the possession even against the trustee.(b)

[2] Balls *v.* Strutt, 1 Hare, 146.

[3] Boteller *v.* Allington, 1 Bro. Ch. 73; Willis *v.* Hiscox, 4 Myl. & Cr. 197; Jones *v.* Lewis, 1 Cox, 199; Lyse *v.* Kingdom, 1 Coll. 184; Penfold *v.* Bouch, 4 Hare, 471; Watts *v.* Turner, 1 R. & M. 634; Buttanshaw *v.* Martin, Johns. V. C. 89; Boskerck *v.* Herrick, 65 Barb. 250.

[4] Manning *v.* Cox, 7 Moore, 617; Barker *v.* Richardson, 1 Yo. & Jer. 362; Chitty, Contr. 605; McClurg *v.* Wilson, 43 Penn. St. 439. [See Bizzell *v.* McKinnon, 121 N. C. 186; Chicago, etc., Land Co. *v.* Peck, 112 Ill. 408; Pearce *v.* Bryant Coal Co., 121 Ill. 590.]

[5] Annesley *v.* Simeon, 4 Madd. 390; Chambersburg Ins. Co. *v.* Smith, 11 Penn. St. 120. [Falmouth Bank *v.* Cape Cod Canal Co., 166 Mass. 550, 567.]

(a) If the trustee is properly before the court, it may order him to transfer to the *cestuis* the legal title of real estate situated in another State, if the purposes of the trust have been accomplished or have become impossible of accomplishment. Donaldson *v.* Allen, 182 Mo. 626.

(b) See *supra*, § 328.

§ 521. In a simple trust of this nature, the dry trustee has no power of managing, or disposing of the estate, even although the *cestui que trust* is an infant, married woman, lunatic, or other person incapable of the management or control. Nor can he alter the nature of the property, by changing real estate into personal, or *vice versa*.[1] But there is this qualification of the rule, — if a trustee, having the legal title, and being in possession, makes a conveyance for a valuable consideration to a purchaser who has no notice of the trust, the title of the purchaser will prevail.[2] Such a transaction, however, under our registry laws is almost impossible, for the recording of the settlement or other deeds of the property is notice to all the world of the trust. So impersonal are the relations of dry trustees to the *cestui que trust*, that it is said they may purchase the estate of the beneficiary.[3] It is further to be remarked, that there can be but few of these dry trusts; for where there is no control, and no duty to be performed by the trustee, it becomes a simple use, which the statute of uses executes in the *cestui que trust;* and he thus unites both the legal and beneficial estate in himself.[4]

§ 522. Trusts to preserve contingent remainders are less frequent in this country than in England; and they are less frequent in England since the statute of 8 & 9 Vict. c. 106, which enacted that a contingent remainder should be deemed capable of taking effect, notwithstanding the determination by forfeiture, surrender, or merger of any preceding estate of freehold, in the same manner and in all respects as if such determination had not happened. In consequence of this act, there is no necessity for any machinery to preserve contingent

---

[1] Furiam v. Saunders, 7 Bac. Abr. Uses and Trusts, E.; Witter v. Witter, 3 P. Wms. 100.

[2] Millard's Case, 2 Freem. 43; Bovey v. Smith, 1 Vern. 149.

[3] Parker v. White, 11 Ves. 226. [See also Heckscher v. Blanton, 66 S. E. 859 (Va. 1910).]

[4] Peck v. Brown, 2 Rob. (N. Y.) 119; Davis v. Rhodes, 39 Miss. 152. [Everts v. Everts, 80 Mich. 222. See *supra*, § 299 *et seq.*]

remainders. Previous to the act, where there were no trustees to preserve them, they could be destroyed in two ways: First, contingent remainders were extinguishable by the surrender or merger of the particular estate in the inheritance; as, if lands were limited to A. for life, with remainder to his unborn children, with remainder to B., A. might surrender his life-estate to B., or B. might release his remainder to A., or both A. and B. might join in a conveyance of the fee; and thus in each case the contingent remainder was squeezed out, and if children were afterwards born to A. they had no remedy in law or equity. Second, they could be extinguished by the tenant for life with the concurrence of the person who stood next in the series of limitations; as, where the oldest son or heir of the tenant for life, being of age and next in the series, could unite with his father in making a tenant to the *præcipe* to bar all subsequent remainders. Thus the estate became the absolute property of the father and son, and the subsequent interests in remainder were sacrificed, except so far as father and son might choose to give them effect.[1]

§ 523. To obviate these results, settlements were drawn in one of two modes: First, the legal estate was limited to the use of the parent for ninety-nine years, if he should live so long, with remainder to the use of trustees and their heirs, during the life of the termor upon trust to preserve the contingent limitations, and on his death to other uses in remainder; or to the use of trustees and their heirs, during the life of the parent in trust for him, and on his death to the other uses in remainder. Secondly, the use was to the parent for life, with remainder to trustees and their heirs, during the life of the parent, in trust to preserve the contingent limitations, and on his death to other uses in remainder. In the first form of settlement, the object in view, by vesting the freehold in trustees, was to preserve the contingent limitations from being destroyed by the surrender or merger of the particular estate, which would have been prac-

[1] Lewin on Trusts, 308.

ticable had the freehold been limited to the parent himself, and also to prevent the barring of the entail and the alienation of the estate for purposes not authorized by the spirit of the settlement. In the second form, it was the duty of the trustees, as before, to preserve the contingent limitations; but, as the freehold in possession was vested in the parent, the trustees had no power to prevent a recovery by the father and son as soon as the son came of age; but if the tenant for life committed a forfeiture, as by a feoffment in fee in order to defeat the contingent remainders, it was then the duty of the trustees to enter and so vest the possession of the freehold in themselves; and it was their further duty, as in the first form, though the settlor himself might not have contemplated such a purpose, not to concur in putting an end to the settlement, except where such interference was prudent and proper.[1]

§ 524. Where a term for years is created by mortgage or by will for securing jointures or portions, or where a term is carved out of the inheritance for any particular purpose, and there is no condition in the instrument that the term shall cease when

---

[1] Lewin on Trusts, 309 (5th Lond. ed.), 404 (2d Amer. ed.). There is a very considerable amount of learning in the books upon the duty of trustees under these circumstances: when they should concur in determining the contingent estates, when they should concur in changing the uses and the limitations for the accommodation and benefit of families, and when they should apply to the court for instruction and direction in the performance of their duties. The statute 8 & 9 Vict. c. 106 renders the machinery of trustees to preserve contingent remainders no longer necessary in England, and Mr. Lewin has left all the learning upon the subject out of the last edition of his valuable treatise on Trusts. The reader will find it in the second American edition, and in Hill on Trustees, 318. It is not thought necessary to pursue the subject further, as, in nearly all the American States, statutes similar to the statute of 8 & 9 Vict. render trustees unnecessary to preserve such remainders. Mr. Washburn cites the statutes of the various States. 2 Wash. Real Prop., pp. 202, 262, 263, 266 (1st ed.). See also Hill on Trustees, 318, n.; 2 Green. Cruise, 270, and n.; 285, n.; 4 Kent, Com. 255. In Pennsylvania, however, trustees may still be necessary for this purpose. Dunwoodie v. Reed, 3 Serg. & R. 435; Toman v. Dunlop, 8 Penn. St. 72. The case of Vanderheyden v. Crandall, 2 Denio, 9, was decided before the change by the statutes in New York.

the purposes of its creation are satisfied, although the term or time for which it was carved out has not elapsed, the holder of the term for the remainder of the time holds it in trust for the owner of the inheritance, and it is said to be a term attendant upon the legal title. It is sometimes convenient in English conveyancing to keep these terms outstanding in the hands of a trustee, as the owner has the right to call at any time for a conveyance of them to himself; and such term may give the owner of the inheritance a legal title to the possession, anterior to some possible incumbrances that may have been put upon the estate prior to his purchase of the inheritance. In the same manner, purchasers in America sometimes take assignments of mortgages made long before their purchase, in order, by foreclosure or otherwise, to gain a title prior to other possible incumbrances, anterior to their purchase of the fee.

§ 525. Trustees of these dry terms hold them in trust for the owners of the inheritance. The rights and duties of the trustees of such terms are very similar to the rights and duties of trustees of the dry legal estate.[1]

§ 526. Trustees of freeholds are the legal owners of the estate, and they alone can be recognized in a court of law.[2] Their right to the possession will depend entirely upon the construction of the instrument of trust, and the nature of the duties required.[3] If their duties are such that they cannot perform them without the possession, the court will give it to them.[4] The situation and condition, therefore, of the *cestuis que trust* may be important on the question of the possession

---

[1] These terms are now abolished in England by stat. 8 & 9 Vict. c. 112, and have ceased to be important. They never prevailed to any great extent in this country, and it is not necessary to enlarge upon the subject. The reader who desires to see the learning upon this matter will find it in Hill on Trustees, 324, 329; 1 Green. Cruise, 414, 418, 424, 442, 443; 2 Green. Cruise, 63, 170.

[2] *Ante*, § 523; Wickhem *v.* Berry, 55 Penn. St. 70.

[3] *Ante*, § 329.

[4] Ibid.; Tidd *v.* Lister, 5 Madd. 433.

and control of the trustee; as, if the *cestui que trust* is a married woman, an infant, or a lunatic, incapable of managing or controlling the estate, the trustee must of necessity have the possession and management.[1] If the trustees have the possession, control, and management, they may make necessary repairs;[2] but, without some general or special authority, they cannot enter upon large improvements.[3] If they are trustees for the sale of land they will not be allowed for improvements,[4] and no allowance can be made for cultivating such lands;[5] nor will the trustees be responsible for not renting land that comes to them in trust for sale.[6]

§ 527. Where trustees are in possession, and have the management of the estate, they must pay all rates and taxes,[7] and protect the estate from tax sales; they may, therefore, insure, and good management would demand it, but they are not

[1] Tidd *v.* Lister, 5 Madd. 433.

[2] Fontaine *v.* Pellet, 1 Ves. Jr. 337; Green *v.* Winter, 1 Johns. Ch. 26. A trustee, having authority to make repairs, may by express agreement make the expenditure for repairs a charge upon the estate, but he cannot, by a subsequent promise to pay out of the estate, give a lien upon it. New *v.* Nicoll, 73 N. Y. 127; Stanton *v.* King, 8 Hun (N. Y.), 4; Austin *v.* Munro, 47 N. Y. 360. [See *supra,* § 479 and notes.]

[3] Ibid.; Cogswell *v.* Cogswell, 4 Edw. Ch. 231; L'Amoureux *v.* Van Rensselaer, 1 Barb. Ch. 34; Wykoff *v.* Wykoff, 3 Watts & S. 481; Ames *v.* Downing, 1 Bradf. 321; Dickinson *v.* Conniff, 65 Ala. 581. [*In re* Cole's Estate, 102 Wis. 1.] The cost of improvements made in reliance on the trust estate with a promise by trustee to pay for them, may be a charge upon the estate to the extent that the value of the estate is enhanced thereby, at least in cases where the trustee resides abroad, and so cannot be personally reached by the persons making the improvements. Field *v.* Wilbur, 49 Ver. 157. But the general rule is that the trustee must be looked to, and it is clear that an administrator has no power to borrow money and charge the trust estate. Bank *v.* Weeks, 53 Vt. 115. A general power of management may give a power to make permanent improvements. Bowes *v.* Strathmore, 8 Jur. 92. [See *supra,* § 479 and notes.]

[4] Green *v.* Winter, 1 Johns. Ch. 28; Thompson *v.* Thompson, 16 Wis. 91.

[5] Ibid.

[6] Burr *v.* McEwen, Baldw. C. C. 154; Griffin *v.* Macaulay, 7 Grat. 476.

[7] Burr *v.* McEwen, Baldw. C. C. 154; Lovat *v.* Leeds, 31 L. J. Ch. 503. [See *infra,* § 554 and notes.]

bound to do so.¹ Where they have the management, they must use due diligence in collecting rents. If they are directed to accumulate the rents, or to receive them for any other purpose, they will become personally liable if they allow the tenants to fall in arrear, and a loss is thus imposed upon the estate.²

§ 528. When trustees are charged with the payment of annuities, debts, or legacies, or any other sums out of the estate, but have no power of sale, they have an implied power of leasing upon the ordinary terms or custom of the State or town in which the land is situated.³ (a) If the trust consists of farming lands, the trustees can grant ordinary farming leases; if of houses in a city, they can grant the ordinary leases of such property.⁴ But they will not be justified in granting any unusual leases; as building-leases (b), or leases for a long term,⁵ or of un-opened mines.⁶ If, under such circumstances, a trustee uses due diligence in granting a lease at a proper rent, and for a proper term, he will not be responsible, although a much larger sum may be obtained, before the lease expires, by reason of an increase or rise in rents.⁷ It is said that the neglect must approximate fraud to impose such a liability upon a trustee.⁸ If, however, the estate consists of a plantation and slaves, or of a farm fully stocked, the trustee may not lease it at all, but he

¹ Ibid. [See *supra*, § 487, and *infra*, § 553.]
² Tebbs *v.* Carpenter, 1 Madd. 290.
³ Naylor *v.* Arnitt, 1 R. & M. 501; Newcomb *v.* Keteltas, 19 Barb. 608; Hedges *v.* Riker, 5 Johns. Ch. 163; Black *v.* Ligon, Harp. Eq. 205.
⁴ Ibid.; Greason *v.* Keteltas, 17 N. Y. 491; Pearse *v.* Baron, Jac. 158.
⁵ Greason *v.* Keteltas, 17 N. Y. 491; Pearse *v.* Baron, Jac. 158.
⁶ Clegg *v.* Rowland, L. R. 2 Eq. 160.
⁷ Ferraby *v.* Hobson, 2 Phill. 255.
⁸ Ibid.

(a) As to powers of trustees to lease in general, see *supra*, § 484 and notes.

(b) Where trustees of city property were given power of sale and power to lease "upon such terms and conditions as they may consider most advisable," it was held that they had power to give building leases. *In re* James, 64 L. J. Ch. 686.

may employ the personal property upon the estate in its culti- vation.[1] If the tenant for life in occupation of the lands be- comes insolvent, and his rent is largely in arrear, the trustees will be reimbursed for all the necessary expenses of ejecting him, and they will be justified in releasing to him the arrears of rent, and in paying a *bonus* as among the expenses of obtaining the possession. These expenses are for the benefit of the es- tate.[2] Under the general implied powers of leasing, trustees can only grant a lease in possession, and cannot grant a lease in reversion;[3] and it is doubted if they can make a lease to com- mence at a future day.[4] If the trust is only for a life, the trus- tees cannot bind the remainder-men by a covenant to renew in a lease executed by them.[5] (a)

§ 529. If special powers of leasing are conferred upon trustees, they must follow the powers strictly. Any deviation from the manner of leasing pointed out in the trust instrument would be a breach of the trust. Thus, where leases are to be in possession and not in reversion, or where the lessor is not to take any fine or premium from the lessee, a lease made contrary to these powers is improper and would be set aside.[6] Where there is power to lease for a certain number of years, a lease for a less number is good,[7] but a lease for a longer term than that prescribed is bad, as contrary to the power;[8] although it is

[1] Dennis v. Dennis, 15 Md. 73.

[2] Blue v. Marshall, 3 P. Wms. 381.

[3] Sussex v. Worth, Cro. Eliz. 5; 2 Sugd. on Pow. 370. [See *supra,* § 484, note.]

[4] Sinclair v. Jackson, 8 Cow. 581.

[5] Bergengren v. Aldrich, 139 Mass. 259.

[6] Bowes v. East London Water Works Co., 3 Madd. 375; Jac. 324.

[7] Isherwood v. Oldknow, 3 M. & S. 382.

[8] Sinclair v. Jackson, 8 Cow. 581.

(a) But if the trustee has been given power to bind the remainder- man by leases to begin in *futuro*, or by covenants to renew, equity will enforce specific performance by the remainder-man of a valid contract to lease, especially if the lessor is in possession and has improved the property in reliance on the contract. Taussig v. Reel, 134 Mo. 530.

said, that such a lease may be sustained in equity for the proper number of years, and that the excess only is void.[1] It has been held, however, where there was a direction to keep mines constantly leased upon leases not exceeding five years, and it was found that good tenants could not be obtained for so short a term, and that leases for such a term would destroy the mines, that a court of equity could direct leases to be made for a longer term, as for fifteen years.[2] Under a power to lease for twenty-one years, a lease for twenty-one years, determinable at the option of the lessee, is a good execution of the power;[3] but where lands, not within the authority to lease, are joined in the same lease at one rent with lands within the power, the whole lease is without authority, for there can be no apportionment of the rent.[4] If the lease is not strictly within the terms of the special power, the receiving of rent by the *cestui que trust* for several years will not confirm the lease, unless they are aware of the defective execution of the power.[5] It seems to be in accordance with sound principle, that a lease, which is void for want of power in the trustee to execute it, is incapable of confirmation by the *cestuis que trust*, who have no power either to make or confirm leases;[6] but perhaps a long acquiescence by them in occupation under the lease, accompanied by valuable improvements made by the lessee, might estop them from setting up a claim to avoid the lease.[7] (a) If the freehold is vested in the trustees, the lease will take effect out of their legal interest, and will be valid in law, though it may be a breach of the trust;

[1] Pawcey *v.* Bowen, 1 Ch. Cas. 23; 3 Ch. R. 11.

[2] Matter of Philadelphia, 2 Brews. 426. [See Donegre *v.* Walker, 214 Ill. 113; Marsh *v.* Reed, 184 Ill. 263, where the court authorized leases for 99 years upon a showing of necessity.]

[3] Edwards *v.* Millbank, 4 Drew. 606.

[4] Doe *v.* Stevens, 6 Q. B. 208.

[5] Bowes *v.* East London Water Works Co., 3 Madd. 375; Jac. 324.

[6] Sinclair *v.* Jackson, 8 Cow. 581.

[7] Black *v.* Ligon, Harp. Eq. 205. But see 4 Kent, 107.

(a) A lease by a mere naked trustee, when assented to by the beneficiary, is practically the act of the latter, who has the rights of the landlord. White *v.* Cannon, 125 Ill. 412.

but a court of equity can in all cases set aside any conveyance or lease which is a breach of the trust.[1] If there is any fraud or collusion in the trustee, the lease will be set aside, or the lessee may be converted into a trustee; as, where the trustee and a third person by collusion suffered a lease to be forfeited, in order that such person might obtain the lease to himself, he was held to be a constructive trustee.[2] (a)

§ 530. Where the special power is to lease lands usually let, or upon the usual rent, it will apply *prima facie* to such lands only as have been generally let, and to the ordinary adequate rent;[3] but where the general scope of the whole instrument involves an intention that all the lands shall be let, the words will be construed to embrace all;[4] and the joining of several parcels of land in one lease, which have been *usually* let separately, will not vitiate the execution of the power.[5] The *usual* rent means the old and uniform custom, and not the rent reserved on a single lease, executed just before the creation of the power.[6] Where the power is to make a lease containing "usual and reasonable covenants," the rule is to follow a lease of the lands in existence at the time of the creation of the power, if there is such a lease.[7] Where a widow was to have the right to cultivate as much land as she pleased, and the executors were to lease the balance, the power of leasing was held to extend to the whole estate, upon the death of the widow.[8]

---

[1] Bowes *v.* East London Water Works Co., 3 Madd. 375; Jac. 324. [Gomez *v.* Gomez, 147 N. Y. 195; *In re* Hubbell Trust, 135 Iowa, 637.]

[2] Aspinall *v.* Jones, 2 Bennett (Mo.), 209.

[3] Cardigan *v.* Montague, 2 Sugd. Pow. App. 14, 339; Orbey *v.* Mohun, 2 Vern. 531; Pr. Ch. 257; 2 Roll. Ab. 261, pl. 11, 12.

[4] Goodtitle *v.* Funucan, Doug. 565; 2 Sugd. Pow. 349.

[5] Doe *v.* Stephens, 6 Q. B. 208; Doe *v.* Williams, 11 Q. B. 688.

[6] Doe *v.* Hole, 15 Q. B. 848.

[7] Doe *v.* Stephens, 6 Q. B. 208.

[8] Hoyle *v.* Stowe, 2 Dev. 318.

(a) As to effect of leases for a term which extends beyond the duration of the trust, see *supra*, § 484, note.

If the trustees have a fee, determinable upon a contingent event, they nevertheless have power to make a lease to extend beyond their interest in the land.[1] A power to lease for lives will not authorize a lease for years; but under a power to lease not exceeding twenty-one years, or three lives, a lease for years may be granted.[2] So a lease for two lives will be good under a power to lease for three lives.[3] In granting a lease for lives, it must be during lives in being, and all must be running at the same time;[4] if some of the lives have expired, there is authority to grant a lease during the life of the survivor.[5] A power to lease land generally will not authorize a lease of unopened mines, but a general power will authorize a lease of opened mines.[6] (a) Trustees should not grant leases of mines without impeachment of waste.[7] In deciding the length of the term for which the lease may be granted, trustees must be guided by the best interests of the estate; at law they may exercise the power by granting the longest term;[8] but in equity they are subject to the supervision of the court.[9] If they enter into covenants in leases, they will be personally bound.[10] Whether the heirs of the testator, the trustee having refused to act, can execute the power of leasing depends upon the terms of the power, whether it is a personal confidence, or is a trust that goes with the estate and office of the trustee.[11]

[1] Greason v. Keteltas, 17 N. Y. 491. [But see *supra*, § 484, note a.]
[2] Whitlock's Case, 8 Co. R. 69 b; 1 Sugd. Pow. 514; 2 id. 354.
[3] 2 Sugd. Pow. 365.
[4] Doe v. Halcombe, 7 T. R. 13; 2 Sugd. Pow. 364; Raym. 263.
[5] Doe v. Hardwicke, 10 East, 549.
[6] Clegg v. Rowland, L. R. 2 Eq. 160.
[7] Campbell v. Leach, Amb. 740; Daly v. Beckett, 6 C. B. 114; Lee v. Balcarras, id. 849.
[8] Muskerry v. Chinnery, Llo. & Goo. 185; 1 Sugd. Pow. 548.
[9] Sutton v. Jones, 15 Ves. 587; Black v. Ligon, Harp. Eq. 205; 4 Kent, 107. [*In re* Hubbell Trust, 135 Iowa, 637; *supra*, § 484, note a.]
[10] Greason v. Keteltas, 17 N. Y. 491.
[11] Robson v. Flight, 10 Jur. (N. S.) 1228; 11 Jur. (N. S.) 147; 5 N. R. 344; 34 Beav. 110.

(a) As to whether rent or royalties from mines or oil-wells belong to income or to principal, see *infra*, § 546, note.

§ 531. Where the trust property consists of leasehold estates, questions often arise respecting the duty of the trustees
to renew, and on whom the expense shall fall. These estates
are not so common in the United States as in England; but it
may be important to state the law on the subject, together with
the American authorities. It has before been stated, that where
a leasehold is limited in the instrument of trust to a tenant for
life with remainder over, and is rapidly diminishing in value
through the expiration of the term, it is the duty of the trustee
to sell the lease and invest the proceeds, and to pay the income of such investment to the tenant for life, and the principal
to the remainder-man. Where there is a *specific* gift of the leasehold, or other depreciating property, the tenant is entitled to
receive the income *in specie.*

§ 532. It is the duty of the trustees to renew all leases at
the regular periods, where an *express* trust is created for that
purpose.[1] In the absence of such trust, the duty may be *implied* from the expressions used by the settlor, or from the
whole scope of the instrument.[2] In the absence of such guides,
it has been held that where a leasehold interest is settled in
trust for life with remainders over, it must be the general intention that the interest should continue, and be preserved for
the benefit of all who take under the limitations of the trust;
and that it is the duty of the trustees to renew, although there
are no particular or general expressions directing a renewal.[3]
So in the case of marriage articles, if renewable leaseholds are
part of the estates to be settled, the court will order a direction

[1] Montford *v.* Cadogan, 17 Ves. 485; 19 Ves. 635; 2 Mer. 3; Colegrave
v. Manby, 6 Madd. 72; 2 Russ. 238; Bennett *v.* Colley, 5 Sim. 181; 2 Myl.
& K. 235.

[2] Curtis *v.* Lukin, 5 Beav. 147; Lock *v.* Lock, 2 Vern. 666; Hulkes *v.*
Barrow, Taml. 264.

[3] Verney *v.* Verney, Amb. 88; 1 Ves. 428; White *v.* White, 4 Ves. 33;
Montford *v.* Cadogan, 17 Ves. 485; 19 Ves. 638; Lock *v.* Lock, 2 Vern. 666;
Milsington *v.* Mulgrave, 3 Madd. 491; 5 Madd. 471; Hulkes *v.* Barrow,
Taml. 264.

to the trustees to renew to be inserted in the settlement.[1] If the trustees have a power of renewal in the form of a *discretionary* power, it will generally be construed as an absolute direction to renew, but the manner and time may be optional; for where trustees are appointed to preserve estates for those who are to take in succession, it can hardly be supposed that it would be left discretionary with them to destroy the interests of those who are to take in the future.[2]

§ 533. The mere fact that renewable leaseholds are settled upon persons to take in succession does not *per se* give the remainder-man a right to call upon the tenant for life to pay the expenses of a renewal.[3] In such case it is within the discretion of the tenant for life to renew. And even where a devise was made to a tenant for life, subject to all fines as they became due yearly and for every year, the tenant for life was not obliged to renew.[4] But if the tenant for life does renew, he cannot use his renewal to deprive the remainder-man of his rights, but such remainder-man will be entitled to the interest given him under the settlement, upon paying the proportional part of the expenses of renewal;[5] nor will the mere fact of the *interposition of a trustee* in the settlement indicate an intention that the tenant for life shall renew;[6] but such duties may be imposed directly, or by implication that ar enewal must be made.[7]

[1] Graham *v.* Londonderry, cited Stone *v.* Theed, 2 Bro. Ch. 246; Pickering *v.* Vowles, 1 id. 197.

[2] Milsington *v.* Mulgrave, 3 Madd. 491; 5 id. 472; Mortimer *v.* Watts, 14 Beav. 616; Verney *v.* Verney, 1 Ves. 430; Harvey *v.* Harvey, 5 Beav. 134; Luther *v.* Bianconi, 10 Ir. Eq. 203.

[3] White *v.* White, 4 Ves. 32; 9 Ves. 561; Nightingale *v.* Lawson, 1 Bro. Ch. 443; Stone *v.* Theed, 2 id. 248; Capel *v.* Wood, 4 Russ. 500.

[4] Capel *v.* Wood, 4 Russ. 500.

[5] Stone *v.* Theed, 2 Bro. Ch. 248; Coppin *v.* Fernyhough, id. 241; Nightingale *v.* Lawson, 1 id. 440; Fitzroy *v.* Howard, 3 Russ. 225. [Bradford *v.* Brownjohn, 37 L. J. Ch. 198. See *infra*, § 538, note.]

[6] O'Ferrall *v.* O'Ferrall, Llo. & Goo. t. Plunk. 79; French *v.* St. George, 1 Dr. & Wals. 417; Lawrence *v.* Maggs, 1 Eden, 453.

[7] Verney *v.* Verney, 1 Ves. 429; White *v.* White, 4 Ves. 33; Hulkes *v.* Barrow, Taml. 264; Lock *v.* Lock, 2 Vern. 666.

§ 534. If trustees neglect to renew leases, they will be liable to the *cestuis que trust* for all the loss and damage that accrue by reason of the neglect. Thus, if a remainder-man subsequently effects a renewal at an increased cost and expense, they must reimburse him, or they may be ordered to renew at their own expense.[1] If the tenant for life has received an increased income by reason of the non-renewal, the trustees may withhold income from him to equalize what they may have been obliged to pay. If there are two successive tenants for life, they must contribute according to the duration of their respective interests.[2] The same principles are applicable where estates are settled without the intervention of a trustee, and the tenant for life is directed to renew. The remainder-man may renew in case of neglect by the tenant for life, and call upon his estate for reimbursement; and if the lease has expired and is lost, so that it cannot be renewed, the remainder-man may have compensation in damages.[3] But if the remainder-man pays an unreasonable sum for the renewal, the estate of the tenant for life will not be compelled to pay the whole, but the court will refer it to a master to determine a reasonable amount.[4] A purchaser from the tenant for life is not, however, compelled to make these payments, although he has notice of the settlement, unless the assignment to him expressly provides that the interest taken by him is subject to a trust for renewal.[5]

§ 535. Trustees, however, will not be liable for not renewing, where the trust for renewal cannot be carried into effect on account of its illegality, or their covenant to renew cannot be fulfilled because of the termination of their trust.[6] If there is an illegal direction to accumulate rents and profits,

---

[1] Montford *v.* Cadogan, 17 Ves. 485; 19 Ves. 635; 2 Mer. 3; Colegrave *v.* Manby, 6 Madd. 87; 2 Russ. 238; Milsington *v.* Mulgrave, 2 Madd. 491; 5 Madd. 472. [2] Ibid.

[3] Colegrave *v.* Manby, 6 Madd. 87; 2 Russ. 238; Bennett *v.* Colley, 5 Sim. 181; 2 Myl. & K. 225. [4] Ibid.

[5] Montford *v.* Cadogan, 19 Ves. 635. [6] See § 528.

for the purpose of renewal, the trustee cannot be called upon to renew, for the reason that the fund, from which he is to pay the expenses of renewal, cannot legally exist.[1] So a lessor is not obliged to renew a lease unless it contains covenants to that effect. Therefore, if the lessor refuses to renew, or if he demands unreasonable terms, the trustees are not liable for not renewing.[2] In such case, however, the tenant for life cannot be allowed the exclusive benefit of the non-renewal; but so much of the expenses as would have come out of his interest will be invested for the benefit of the *cestuis que trust*, including the remainder-men.[3] If a leasehold is a loss to the estate, by calling for the payment of more rent than is received, the trustees must get rid of the leasehold by assignment, and they have been held responsible for not doing so.[4]

§ 536. The trustee in whom the leasehold interest vests, by the settlement or will, is liable, as assignee of the lease, to perform all its covenants during the continuance of his interest. Therefore, if he ceases to be trustee or assigns the lease, he will be liable for no covenants, unless they are broken while it was held by him.[5] But an executor of a lessee is liable upon the covenants, by reason of the privity of estate;[6] and so a trustee will be liable, if he has bound himself personally. On this account, an executor or trustee cannot be required by the *cestuis que trust* to assign over the estate before he is indemnified for such liability.[7] (a)

---

[1] Curtis v. Lukin, 5 Beav. 147.

[2] Colegrave v. Manby, 6 Madd. 82; Tardiff v. Robinson, id. 83, n.

[3] Ibid.; Bennett v. Colley, 2 Myl. & K. 231; 5 Sim. 181.

[4] Rowley v. Adams, 4 Myl. & Cr. 534.

[5] Onslow v. Corrie, 2 Madd. 330; Valliant v. Dodemede, 2 Atk. 546; Pitcher v. Toovey, 1 Salk. 81; 2 Ventr. 228; Taylor v. Shum, 1 B. & P. 21; Rowley v. Adams, 4 Myl. & Cr. 532; Trevele v. Coke, 1 Vern. 165.

[6] Brett v. Cumberland, Cro. Jac. 521.

[7] Simmonds v. Borland, 3 Mer. 567; Marsh v. Wells, 2 S. & S. 90.

(a) As to the option of a trustee under a voluntary assignment for creditors, to abandon assignable leases or to accept them, see *infra*, § 598, note.

863

§ 537. By the law of tenures, as established under the feudal system, the tenant was obliged to pay a fee or fine to his superior lord, upon every alienation of his land, whether in fee, or for life or for years. Hence, to this day in England, upon every renewal of a lease, there is a fine or a fee, considerable in amount, to be paid.[1] In the United States, all such restraints upon the alienation of lands are inconsistent with the spirit of our laws and institutions, and are absolutely void, even if annexed as terms or conditions in the instruments under which the lands are held.[2] Therefore, one great head of equity jurisdiction, in the matter of trust in leasehold estates, is obsolete in the United States. In England, it is frequently a matter of doubt and construction to determine whose estate and interest shall pay the fine and expenses of the renewal.[3]

§ 538. The right to renew a lease is a valuable right, and may be sold and conveyed.[4] Courts recognize this right, and protect it for the benefit of the trust estate. If trustees are deprived of this right by the acts of third persons, they are entitled to compensation; as where the land is taken for public works, by virtue of some statute, trustees, having a right by custom or by covenant to renew a lease, will have the right to compensation for the land taken.[5] Nor can a trustee renew a lease, in his individual name and for his private benefit, even if the lessor utterly refuses to renew the lease for the benefit of the *cestui que trust;*[6] for the reason that the trustee cannot

---

[1] 2 Black. Com. 72.

[2] Livingston *v.* Stickles, 8 Paige, 398; De Peyster *v.* Michael, 6 N. Y. 467; Overbagh *v.* Petrie, id. 510; 8 Barb. 28.

[3] For the reasons stated in the text, it is not important in this country to notice all the rules and distinctions which have been established by the authorities in England. If important, they may be found in Lewin on Trusts, 295–308, and Hill on Trustees, 434–439.

[4] Phyfe *v.* Wardwell, 5 Paige, 268; Anderson *v.* Lemon, 8 N. Y. 236.

[5] Jones *v.* Powell, 4 Beav. 96.

[6] Keech *v.* Sandford, Sel. Cas. Ch. 61; 1 Lead. Cas. Eq. 36, notes; Holt *v.* Holt, 1 Cas. Ch. 190; Fitzgibbon *v.* Scanlan, 1 Dow. P. C. 269; James *v.* Dean, 11 Ves. 392; 15 Ves. 236; Parker *v.* Brooke, 9 Ves. 583; Rowe *v.*

avail himself of his situation to make any advantage or profit to himself, and if he makes a profit by renewing a lease in his own name, it inures to the benefit of the trust estate, or he shall continue to hold it as trustee.[1] The same rule extends to ·· all persons who hold any position of influence and confidence in respect to others, as tenants for life, (a) tenants in common,

Chichester, Amb. 719; Killick v. Flexney, 4 Bro. Ch. 161; Griffin v. Griffin, 1 Sch. & Lef. 352; Holdridge v. Gillespie, 2 Johns. Ch. 33; McClanahan v. Henderson, 2 A. K. Marsh. 388; Galbraith v. Elder, 8 Watts, 81; Heager's Ex'rs, 15 Serg. & R. 65; Fisk v. Sarber, 6 Watts & S. 18.

[1] Nesbitt v. Tredennick, 1 B. & B. 29; James v. Dean, 11 Ves. 396.

(a) The principle on which the courts have in the main proceeded is stated as follows in Robinson v. Jewett, 116 N. Y. 40: "Those who are in possession of lands under a lease have an interest therein beyond the subsisting term usually called the tenant's right of renewal. Between the landlord and the tenant this interest cannot strictly be denominated a right or estate, but is merely a hope or expectation, there being in the absence of contract, no way, legal or equitable, of compelling a renewal. But, as between third persons, the law recognizes this interest as a valuable property right, and the renewal as a reasonable expectancy of the tenants in possession." The new lease is said to be a "graft," upon the old one and a trustee, partner, agent or even cotenant will not be allowed to retain it for his own benefit. Mitchell v. Reed, 61 N. Y. 123; Sneed v. Deal, 53 Ark. 152; Leach v. Leach, 18 Pick. 68, 76. See also Bevan v. Webb, [1905] 1 Ch. 620; Longton v. Wilsby, 76 L. T. 770; Phillips v. Phillips, 29 Ch. Div. 673; In re Biss, [1903] 2 Ch. 40; Johnson's Appeal, 115 Pa. St. 129; Lacy v. Hall, 37 Pa. St. 360, 365. See supra, § 196.

In regard to a cotenant or a life tenant, who is not strictly a fiduciary, the basic principle is that "all persons interested in a lease have something in the nature of a special advantage over others, which the Court of Equity will recognize; and if one of those persons tries to avail himself of that interest by getting the benefit of a renewal for himself, the court will say that he must hold it for the benefit of all." Lord Romer in In re Biss, [1903] 2 Ch. 40, 53. On this principle a mere cotenant cannot renew for his own sole benefit and thus appropriate to himself the whole "expectancy" of renewal, unless he is able to show that the others had no expectancy of renewal. In re Biss, [1903] 2 Ch. 40; In re Lulham, 53 L. J. Ch. 928, 931. But if he shows that the landlord without solicitation on his part has refused to renew in favor of the others, there seems to be no reason why he should not take a new lease for himself provided he has taken no undue advantage of the others. In re Biss, [1903] 2 Ch. 40. Likewise when the others have announced that they do not intend to renew. Tygart v. Wilson, 39 App. Div. (N. Y.) 58. See also

and partners. All such persons, if they obtain the renewal of a lease, hold it for the benefit of those interested with them in the estate.[1] The parties, however, who undertake to enforce this trust, must do equity by repaying their proportion of the expenses incurred in the renewal.[2]

[1] Palmer v. Young, 1 Vern. 276; Pickering v. Bowles, 1 Bro. Ch. 197; Fitzgerald v. Raynsford, 1 B. & B. 37, n.; Giddings v. Giddings, 3 Russ. 241; Featherstonhaugh v. Fenwick, 17 Ves. 298; Rowe v. Chichester, Amb. 715; Eyre v. Dolphin, 2 B. & B. 290; Foster v. Marriott, Amb. 658; Tanner v. Elworthy, 4 Beav. 487; Randall v. Russell, 3 Mer. 196; Vanhorn v. Fonda, 5 Johns. Ch. 388; Smiley v. Dixon, 1 Pa. 439. [Sneed v. Deal, 53 Ark. 152; Leach v. Leach, 18 Pick. 68, 76; Mitchell v. Reed, 61 N. Y. 123; Johnson's Appeal, 115 Pa. St. 129.]

[2] Randall v. Russell, 3 Mer. 196; James v. Dean, 11 Ves. 396; Miller v. Stanley, 2 De G., J. & S. 185.

Chittenden v. Witbeck, 50 Mich. 401; Phillips v. Reeder, 18 N. J. Eq. 95.

In regard to a trustee or agent, and usually a partner, there is the additional principle that the fiduciary shall not be allowed to avail himself of his position to make a profit for himself. Accordingly, a fiduciary, especially a trustee, whose duty required him to renew for the benefit of others, will not usually be permitted to hold the new lease for his own benefit, even when the landlord has refused to renew the lease with him in his fiduciary capacity. See In re Biss, [1903] 2 Ch. 40; Mitchell v. Reed, 61 N. Y. 123.

The purchase of the reversion, or of the premises subject to the lease, stands on different ground; and it has been held to be settled law in England that a life tenant of leasehold property who purchases the reversion expectant on the ter-

mination of the lease is not a trustee for the remainder-men, when the leaseholds are not renewable by contract or custom. Longton v. Wilsby, 76 L. T. 770. And the same has been held true of a trustee purchasing the reversion, since it is a matter of indifference to the lessees, who owns the reversion. Bevan v. Webb, [1905] 1 Ch. 620; Randall v. Russell, 3 Mer. 190. See Anderson v. Lemon, 8 N. Y. 236.

But it has been held that where the leaseholds are renewable by custom, a life tenant who purchases the reversion comes within the principle applied to the renewal of leaseholds. Phillips v. Phillips, 29 Ch. Div. 673.

Doubtless the courts would prevent a trustee who purchased for himself the premises of which he holds a lease as trustee, from using his position as landlord to the injury of the trust. See Mitchell v. Reed, 61 N. Y. 123, 143.

CHAPTER XVIII.

POWERS AND DUTIES OF TRUSTEES AS BETWEEN TENANT FOR LIFE AND REMAINDER-MAN.

§ 539. WHERE property is settled upon a trustee to hold in trust for one person for life, and the remainder over for some other person or persons, it is the duty of the trustee to consult the interest of both the tenant for life and the remainder-man. The trustee must act impartially, and not give either an advantage at the expense, or to the prejudice, of the other.[1] The

---

[1] Mortlock v. Buller, 10 Ves. 308; Cowgill v. Oxmantown, 3 Y. & C. 369; Watts v. Girdlestone, 6 Beav. 188; Langston v. Ollivant, Coop. 33;

867

principal of the trust fund must not be converted to the use of the life cestu.[1] (a)   A court of equity can correct any mismanagement between the trustee and either the tenant for life or the remainder-man; it has even set aside a decree obtained by collusion between the trustee and tenant for life.[2]   The court will not allow property to be sold if the interests of remainder-men, known or unknown, would be thereby imperilled.[3] And when the remainder takes effect, equity will compel the trustee to fulfil his last duty to the remainder-men by turning over the property to them.[4]

§ 540.   The right of the tenant for life to the possession has already been stated.[5]   Where property is devised specifically, and the right of the trustees to convert it is excluded, and the tenant for life can have no beneficial enjoyment without possession, the trustees must allow him such possession.[6]   As was before said, if the title of the tenant for life is a legal and not an equitable title, he is, of course, entitled to the possession;[7]

Stuart v. Stuart, 3 Beav. 430; Pechel v. Fowler, 2 Anst. 550; Mahon v. Stanhope, cited 2 Sugd. Pow. 512; Marshall v. Sladden, 4 De G. & Sm. 468; Moseley v. Marshall, 22 N. Y. 200; McNeil v. McDonald, 22 Ark. 477.   [Rowlls v. Bebb, [1900] 2 Ch. 107.]

[1] Woodburn v. Woodburn, 23 Ill. App. 289; Mitchell v. Colburn, 61 Md. 244.

[2] Wright v. Miller, 4 Seld. 9; Clerke v. Devereux, 1 S. C. 172; Cunningham v. Schley, 41 Ga. 476.

[3] Dunham v. Milhous, 70 Ala. 606.

[4] Haddock v. Perham, 70 Ga. 576.

[5] Ante, § 329.

[6] Tidd v. Lister, 5 Madd. 432; 10 B. Mon. 290.

[7] Ante, § 328; Moseley v. Marshall, 22 N. Y. 200.

(a) In an exceptional case, where the chief purpose of the trust was to provide for the comfortable support of the testator's daughters, but there was an express provision that no part of the principal should be paid to them, the court authorized the trustee to encroach upon the principal for the support of the daughters, unforeseen circumstances having swept away so much of the principal that the income was insufficient for the purpose.   Offutt v. Devine's Ex'r, 49 S. W. 1065 (Ky. 1899).   To the same effect see Brown v. Berry, 71 N. H. 241.

but the tenant for life is, in such case, an implied or *quasi* trustee for the remainder-man, and a court of equity can enjoin him from injuring the inheritance.[1] (a) But if the title is equitable merely, the trustees must see that the equitable tenant for life does not commit waste of any kind;[2] and if he is tenant without impeachment for waste, the trustees must see that the estate is not materially lessened in value by the use made of it.[3] But the trustees cannot compel the tenant for life to repair; and neither the court nor the trustees can interfere with the possession on such grounds.[4] It has been held, however, in the United States, that the tenant for life is obliged to keep the buildings in which he lives from going to decay, by using

[1] Joyce *v.* Gunnels, 2 Rich. Eq. 259; Horrey *v.* Glover, 2 Hill, Ch. 515; Clarke *v.* Saxon, 1 id. 69; Shibley *v.* Ely, 2 Halst. Ch. 181; Wilson *v.* Edmonds, 4 Fost. 545; Broom *v.* Curry, 19 Ala. 805.

[2] Tidd *v.* Lister, 5 Madd. 432; Freeman *v.* Cook, 6 Ired. Eq. 376; Woodman *v.* Good, 6 Watts & S. 169.

[3] Waldo *v.* Waldo, 7 Sim. 261; Leeds *v.* Amherst, 14 Sim. 357; 2 Phill. 117; Burge *v.* Lambe, 16 Ves. 174; Marker *v.* Marker, 9 Hare, 1; 4 Eng. L. & Eq. 95; Newdigate *v.* Newdigate, 1 Sim. 131; Wykham *v.* Wykham, 19 Ves. 14; Smythe *v.* Smythe, 2 Swanst. 251; Morris *v.* Morris, 15 Sim. 510; Brydges *v.* Brydges, 2 Sim. 150; Davies *v.* Lee, 6 Ves. 786; Chamberlain *v.* Dummer, 3 Bro. Ch. 549; Woodman *v.* Good, 6 Watts & S. 169; Briggs *v.* Oxford, 19 Jur. 817; 1 De G., M. & G. 363; Whitfield *v.* Burnett, 2 P. Wms. 242.

[4] Powis *v.* Blagrave, 1 Kay, 495; 4 De G., M. & G. 448; Gregg *v.* Coates, 23 Beav. 33. [*In re* Courtier, 34 Ch. Div. 136; *In re* Hotchkys, 32 Ch. Div. 408; *In re* Cartwright, 41 Ch. Div. 532.]

(a) Even when the legal title is given for life to a widow by her husband's will, with full possession and power to use, dispose of, and consume the estate for her life-support, a duty rests upon her, in the nature of a trust, to have due regard to the rights of the remainder-men, and not to recklessly squander or give away the estate, and such trust is enforceable against purchasers with knowledge of the trust. Johnson *v.* Johnson, 51 Ohio St. 446; Cox *v.* Wills, 49 N. J. Eq. 130, 573; Hoxie *v.* Finney, 147 Mass. 616; Stocker *v.* Foster, 178 Mass. 591; Garland *v.* Smith, 164 Mo. 1; Terry *v.* Rector, etc., 81 N. Y. S. 119, 79 App. Div. 527; Gardner *v.* Whitford, 23 R. I. 396; Phillips *v.* Wood, 16 R. I. 274; Sires *v.* Sires, 43 S. C. 266. See O'Brien *v.* Flint, 74 Conn. 502. As to whether the limited estate is raised to a fee by powers of disposal, see *supra*, § 252, note.

ordinary care, but that he is not obliged to expend any extraordinary sums.[1] Although the rules as to waste are the same
in this country and in England, yet it has been said that there
should be a different application of them here, on account of
the difference of circumstances, and that tenants for life are
encouraged to open mines and cut timber, for the reason that
such acts are rather improvements than waste, in America.[2]
This may be true in some parts of the country, where it is important to clear the land and develop its resources, but it is
not true in the older States. (a)

[1] Wilson v. Edmonds, 11 Fost. 545. [Murch v. Smith M'f'g Co., 47 N.
J. Eq. 193; Kearney v. Ex'r of Kearney, 17 N. J. Eq. 504; Clemence v.
Steere, 1 R. I. 272; See Pratt v. Douglas, 38 N. J. Eq. 516, 542; Caldecott
v. Brown, 2 Hare, 144.]

[2] Williams on Real Prop., 23 n.; Lynn's App., 31 Penn. St. 44. [See
Smith v. Smith, 105 Ga. 106, 111; Drown v. Smith, 52 Me. 141; King v.
Miller, 99 N. C. 583; Sayers v. Hoskinson, 110 Pa. St. 473; Owen v. Hyde,
6 Yerg. 334; Wilkinson v. Wilkinson, 59 Wis. 557, 561; Keeler v. Eastman,
11 Vt. 293. See *contra*, Clark v. Holden, 7 Gray, 8.]

(a) In Stonebraker v. Zollickoffer,
52 Md. 154, a wind-storm having
blown down a large quantity of timber on an estate held in trust, the
trustee converted part of the fallen
trees into cooper-stuff and sold it.
He sold the remainder, consisting
of the tops and smaller branches,
for firewood. It was held that the
proceeds of the cooper-stuff belonged to principal but that the
proceeds of the firewood belonged
to income of the life beneficiary.
The court applied the general rule
applicable to life-tenant and remainder-man, that the former is
entitled to old trees which cannot
be used as timber, and to the tops
and smaller branches of trees which
are felled for timber, and to the
regular thinnings and trimmings of
trees in the woods.

In Keniston v. Gorrell, 74 N. H.
53, where timber was damaged by
fire for which a railroad was responsible and paid damages amounting
to $600, and the damaged tim-
ber was sold for $600, it was held
that the $1200 should be apportioned
between life tenant and remainder-
man, according to the mortality
tables, as a fund of which the life
tenant was entitled to the income.

The rights of the tenant for life
as to proceeds of timber may be
modified by the custom of the testator in his treatment of the timber,
it being presumed that he intended
the life tenant to have the customary
use of the property. Findlay v.
Smith, 6 Munf. 134; Williard v.
Williard, 56 Pa. St. 119; Eley's
Appeal, 103 Pa. St. 300; Bedford's
Appeal, 126 Pa. St. 117.

§ 541.   Where the tenant for life is entitled to the beneficial use of movable articles, heirlooms, furniture, plate, pictures, and similar things, the trustees must take in the first instance a schedule of the articles delivered to such tenant for life signed by him;[1] but if there is any danger that the articles will be wasted, secreted, or carried away, security may be insisted upon and the trustees or the *cestui que trust* in remainder may apply to the court for an injunction, and a decree that the tenant for life be required to give proper security for their safety.[2] But where trustees under a will were directed to hold property for a certain term, and then to pay it over to persons named, to be held by them during their own lives, security cannot be required from the tenants for life for its preservation for the remainder-men, if no such security is required by the terms of the will.[3] In Pennsylvania, there is special legislation authorizing the executor to take security.[4] In case of a legacy

---

[1] Leeke v. Bennett, 1 Atk. 471; Bill v. Kynaston, 2 Atk. 82; Cheshire v. Cheshire, 2 Ired. Eq. 590; Westcott v. Cady, 5 Johns. Ch. 334; Henderson v. Vaulx, 10 Yerg. 30; Covenhoven v. Shuler, 2 Paige, 122; De Peyster v. Clendining, 8 Paige, 295; Spear v. Tinkham, 2 Barb. Ch. 211; Emmons v. Cairnes, 3 Barb. 243; Langworthy v. Chadwick, 13 Conn. 42; Hudson v. Wadsworth, 8 Conn. 363; Nance v. Coxe, 16 Ala. 125; Mortimer v. Moffatt, 4 Hen. & Munf. 503; Slanning v. Style, 3 P. Wms. 336.

[2] Woodman v. Good, 6 Watts & S. 169; Swann v. Ligan, 1 McCord, Ch. 227; Henderson v. Vaulx, 10 Yerg. 30; Covenhoven v. Shuler, 2 Paige, 122; Braswell v. Morehead, 1 Busb. Eq. 26; Lippincott v. Warder, 14 Serg. & R. 118; Ramey v. Green, 18 Ala. 771; Kinnard v. Kinnard, 5 Watts, 108; Westcott v. Cady, 5 Johns. Ch. 334; Langworthy v. Chadwick, 13 Conn. 42; Bill v. Kynaston, 2 Atk. 82; Frazer v. Beville, 11 Grat. 9; Foley v. Burnell, 1 Bro. Ch. 279; Hudson v. Wadsworth, 8 Conn. 363; Holliday v. Coleman, 2 Munf. 162; Mortimer v. Moffatt, 4 Hen. & Munf. 503; Chisholm v. Starke, 3 Call, 25; McLemore v. Good, 1 Harp. Eq. 272; Cheshire v. Cheshire, 2 Ired. Eq. 569; Sutton v. Cradock, 1 id. 134; Howell v. Howell, 3 Ired. Eq. 522; Clarke v. Saxon, 1 Hill, Ch. 75; Condy v. Adrian, id. 154; Spear v. Tinkham, 2 Barb. Ch. 211. A purchaser from the tenant for life may be compelled to give security. Pringle v. Ellen, 1 Hill, Ch. 135; Cordes v. Adrian, id. 154; Howe v. Dartmouth, 2 Lead. Cas. Eq. 262.

[3] Waldo v. Cummings, 43 Ill. 421.

[4] Act, 1834, [Purdon's Digest, (1903) p. 1123, § 165]; Dunlop, 528; Rodgers v. Rodgers, 7 Watts, 19; Lippincott v. Warder, 14 Serg. & R. 118; and Kinnard v. Kinnard, 5 Watts, 108, were decided before this legislation.

for life of money or stocks, the tenant for life cannot have possession of them without giving security for the protection of the remainder-man.[1] But the right of possession by the tenant for life, even in such a case, may depend upon the terms of the will.[2] When the trustee holds funds and there is no evidence that part of it is income, it is presumed to be capital.[3]

§ 542. Personal chattels, like furniture and other articles, may be used by the tenant for life, if he is entitled to the possession in any house or place; or he may let them out for hire,[4] but he cannot pawn or sell them beyond the extent of his interest;[5] but articles in a house, in the nature of heirlooms, are annexed to the house, and go with it, therefore they cannot be removed.[6]

§ 543. Where the trust property consists of stocks and other personal securities, the trustee must retain possession for the benefit of the remainder-man; but he may put the tenant for life in possession of the dividends, interest, or income, by giving him a power of attorney to collect them as they become due. The power should be restricted to the collection of the income; for if he gave the tenant for life power to sell the securities, he would commit a breach of trust. Nor should it be used after the death of the tenant for life; for the trustee would be responsible to the remainder-man for all income received by the representatives of the tenant, accruing after his death. Care must be taken by the trustee, after giv-

---

[1] Patterson v. Devlin, 1 McMul. Eq. 459; Freeman v. Cooke, 6 Ired. 679; Eichelberger v. Barnitz, 17 Serg. & R. 293; Rodgers v. Rodgers, 7 Watts, 19; Kinnard v. Kinnard, 5 Watts, 108. [Scott v. Scott, 137 Iowa, 239; Reed v. Reed, 80 Conn. 411; Maguire v. Maguire, 110 La. 279; McKee v. McKee's Ex'r, 82 S. W. 451 (Ky. 1904); Wilkinson v. Rosser's Ex'r, 104 S. W. 1019 (Ky. 1907); Matter of McDougall, 141 N. Y. 21; In re Roffo, 64 N. Y. S. 455, 51 App. Div. 35.]

[2] De Graffenreid v. Green, 1 Cold. 109.

[3] Peirce v. Burroughs, 58 N. H. 302.

[4] Marshall v. Blew, 2 Atk. 217.

[5] Hoare v. Parker, 2 T. R. 376.

[6] Cadogan v. Kennett, Cowp. 432.

ing the power, himself not to receive the dividends; for that would be a revocation of the power, and a new one would be necessary. So the death of the trustee, or of one of several trustees, would be a revocation.[1] If, at any time, the tenant for life obtains more than belongs to him, the trustee may withhold, or recoup from, subsequent income.[2]

§ 544. Considerable difference of opinion and practice has existed respecting the rights of the tenant for life, and of the remainder-man, to extraordinary dividends or bonuses from corporations. The early English rule held that *extra* dividends paid in cash, and *a fortiori* if they were declared or paid in capital stock, went to the capital of the trust fund, and were held by the trustee for the remainder-man; and that the income only from such extra dividends belonged to the tenant for life.[3] This rule, applied to extra-cash dividends from the earnings of the capital stock of corporations, worked a great hardship upon the tenant for life, and it is unreasonable. In Barclay *v.* Wainwright, Lord Eldon first threw a doubt over the cases, by decreeing an increased or extra dividend to the tenant for life.[4] It was afterwards said, that wherever the increased dividend was made clearly and distinctly as a dividend only, the tenant for life should have it; but where it was not clearly given as a dividend, it was considered as an accretion to the capital, and went to the remainder-man.[5] Thus cash dividends, extra dividends, or bonuses declared from the earnings of corporations, are now held to be income and to belong to the tenant for life.[6] So also

---

[1] Sadler *v.* Lee, 6 Beav. 324; Hill on Trustees, 386; Lewin, 485.

[2] Williams *v.* Allen, 32 Beav. 650; Barratt *v.* Wyatt, 30 Beav. 442. [But see *In re* Horne, [1905] 1 Ch. 76.]

[3] Brander *v.* Brander, 4 Ves. 801; Paris *v.* Paris, 10 Ves. 184; Witts *v.* Steele, 13 Ves. 363; Clayton *v.* Gresham, 10 Ves. 288; Hooper *v.* Rossiter, 13 Price, 774; 1 McClel. 527; Preston *v.* Melville, 16 Sim. 163.

[4] Barclay *v.* Wainwright, 14 Ves. 66; Norris *v.* Harrison, 2 Madd. 279.

[5] Hooper *v.* Rossiter, 1 McClel. 527.

[6] Price *v.* Anderson, 15 Sim. 473; Bates *v.* Mackinlay, 31 Beav. 280; Johnson *v.* Johnson, 15 Jur. 714; 5 Eng. L. & Eq. 164; Murray *v.* Glasse, 17 Jur. 816; Cuming *v.* Boswell, 2 Jur. (N. S.) 1005; Clive *v.* Clive, Kay, 600;

dividends and bonuses earned before the testator's death, but declared afterwards, are held to be income and to belong to the tenant for life.[1] (a)   But the enhanced price for which

Plumbe v. Neild, 6 Jur. (N. S.) 529; Wright v. Tucket, 1 Johns. & H. 266; Cogswell v. Cogswell, 2 Edw. Ch. 231; Ware v. McCandlish, 10 Leigh, 595; Read v. Head, 6 Allen, 174.

[1] Bates v. Mackinlay, 31 Beav. 280. [In re Alsbury, 45 Ch. Div. 237.]

(a) With regard to extra dividends paid from earnings accumulated wholly or partly before the legal or equitable life interest in the stock came into existence, there is a well defined difference of authority. 19 Am. Law Rev. 571, 737; 26 id. 1; 36 Cent. L. J. 452. Massachusetts and several other American jurisdictions abide by the common-law rule that the whole dividend in such a case, if it is a cash dividend, belongs to the life tenant, because he is the person entitled to the income at the time the dividend is declared. It is reasoned that earnings of a corporation do not become income of a stockholder until they are declared as dividends and that it is impracticable to go deeply enough into the affairs of the corporation, in a collateral inquiry, to determine justly when the basis of the dividend accrued. Minot v. Paine, 99 Mass. 101; Hemenway v. Hemenway, 181 Mass. 406; Adams v. Adams, 139 Mass. 449, 452; Gifford v. Thompson, 115 Mass. 478; Rand v. Hubbell, 115 Mass. 461; Richardson v. Richardson, 75 Me. 570; Waterman v. Alden, 42 Ill. App. 294, 144 Ill. 90; De Koven v. Alsop, 205 Ill. 309; Hite's Devisees v. Hite's Ex'r, 93 Ky. 257; Second Universalist Church v. Colegrove, 74 Conn. 79; Bulkeley v. Worthington Ecc. Soc., 78 Conn. 526, 530; Matter of Kernochan,

104 N. Y. 618; Gibbons v. Mahon, 136 U. S. 549. See also Gen. Statutes Conn. (1902), § 377; Millen v. Guerrard, 67 Ga. 284; In re Alsbury, 45 Ch. Div. 237.

It has also been held, as a corollary of this doctrine, that if a corporation comes to a final liquidation with a surplus of undivided earnings which have not been capitalized, and makes a distribution of the property of the corporation in a large final dividend without a separation of earnings from capital, the whole dividend should be treated as belonging to principal, because there has been no declaration of a dividend from earnings as earnings. Gifford v. Thompson, 115 Mass. 478; Second Univ. Church v. Colegrove, 74 Conn. 79; In re Armitage, [1893] 3 Ch. 337; Curtis v. Osborn, 79 Conn. 555. See also Brownell v. Anthony, 189 Mass. 442.

But the courts of New York will in such a case give to income so much of the final dividend as is based upon accumulated earnings which have not been put into the working capital of the corporation. Matter of Rogers, 161 N. Y. 108. See also In re Stevens, 98 N. Y. S. 28, 111 App. Div. 773; 187 N. Y. 471; Robertson v. De Brulatour, 188 N. Y. 301; 111 App. Div. 882.

Pennsylvania and several other jurisdictions hold that a dividend

stocks sell, by reason of dividends earned, but not declared, belongs to the remainder-man and not to the tenant for life.[1] Where a tenant for life is entitled to the income, a year or more after the testator's death having expired, and stocks are sold before the day of the dividend, in order to complete a purchase of land which was directed by the will, the tenant for life is entitled to compensation for the loss of his income.[2] So if, under a gift in a will to an executor of so much stock or other property as will produce $2,000 per year, which is to be paid over to a tenant for life, property is set apart in good faith, with the consent of all parties, sufficient to produce $2,000, and afterwards the property produces much more, and there is no provision in the will for such a contingency, the tenant for life will be entitled to the whole income, and may maintain a bill in equity for it.[3]

§ 545.   Another question has lately arisen, upon which there is much diversity of opinion and practice.   The question

[1] Scholfield v. Refern, 32 L. J. Ch. 627. [Connolly's Estate No. 1, 198 Pa. St. 137.]   [2] Londesborough v. Somerville, 19 Beav. 295.
[3] Russell v. Loring, 3 Allen, 126.

based upon earnings should be apportioned so that the life-tenant should get no more than the portion earned during the period when he was entitled to income; the balance of the dividend is given to the *corpus* of the estate. Earp's Appeal, 28 Pa. St. 368; Smith's Estate, 140 Pa. St. 344; Thomas v. Gregg, 78 Md. 545; Van Doren v. Olden, 19 N. J. Eq. 176; Lang's Ex'r v. Lang, 56 N. J. Eq. 603; Cobb v. Fant, 36 S. C. 1; Goodwin v. McGaughey, 108 Minn. 248 (*semble*). See also Conn. Gen. Stats. (1902), § 377; Pritchitt v. Nashville Trust Co., 96 Tenn. 472. It is reasoned in these jurisdictions that earnings accumulated during the life of a testator, or before the stock was bought by the trustee or life tenant, are represented in the value of the stock at the time the life tenant's right to income began, and that to give him the whole dividend would seriously impair the *corpus*. It is urged with great force that when testators speak of "profits and income," they mean only such as are made by the corporation after the trust has been established. Cases cited *supra*. See also Quinn v. Safe Dep. & Tr. Co., 93 Md. 285.

In all jurisdictions the clear intention of the creator of the trust as expressed in the will or other trust instrument will control, and the rule established in any jurisdiction is merely one of interpretation of probable intention.

is, to whom stock dividends, so called, belong. Are they income, and belong to the tenant for life; or capital, and belong to the remainder-man? By the early English rule, they went with all extra-cash dividends of *bonuses* to the remainder-man.[1] This rule has been so far changed, that dividends in money which come from the earnings of the capital invested belong to the tenant for life.[2] But this question has arisen where a corporation has capitalized a part of its earnings, by using them to enlarge its property, or to improve its value. In such cases, corporations sometimes vote to issue and apportion among their stockholders new certificates of stock, which certificates (in whole or in part) represent the amount of earnings that have been capitalized, as some of the books call it. On one side of this question, it is urged that nothing is income from the stock of a corporation until the corporation itself has set it apart as income, and declared it to be payable in money as a dividend; that a corporation may in good faith determine whether it will declare a dividend or not, and it may also declare whether any part of its earnings shall be turned into capital or not; that if a corporation in good faith uses a part of its earnings in enlarging and improving its works, and thereby increases the value of its stocks, such increased value belongs to the remainder-man; that it is immaterial whether a corporation allows the old shares to stand at this increased value, or whether it issues new certificates of shares to represent this new and increased value of its capital stock; that nothing is a dividend, in the legal sense of the word, which is not a division of money from what the corporation has determined to be in-

[1] Brander *v.* Brander, 4 Ves. 800; Paris *v.* Paris, 10 Ves. 185; Witts *v.* Steele, 13 Ves. 363; Clayton *v.* Gresham, 10 Ves. 288; Hooper *v.* Rossiter, 13 Price, 774; 1 McClel. 527; Preston *v.* Melville, 16 Sim. 163.

[2] Barclay *v.* Wainwright, 14 Ves. 66; Norris *v.* Harrison, 2 Madd. 279; Hooper *v.* Rossiter, 1 McClel. 527; Price *v.* Anderson, 15 Sim. 473; Bates *v.* Mackinlay, 31 Beav. 280; Johnson *v.* Johnson, 5 Eng. L. & Eq. 164; 15 Jur. 714; Murray *v.* Glasse, 17 Jur. 816; Cuming *v.* Boswell, 2 Jur. (N. S.) 1005; Clive *v.* Clive, Kay, 600; Plumbe *v.* Neild, 6 Jur. (N. S.) 529; Wright *v.* Tucket, 1 John. & H. 266; Cogswell *v.* Cogswell, 2 Edw. Ch. 231; Ware *v.* McCandlish, 11 Leigh, 595; Lord *v.* Brooks, 52 N. H. 77.

come; that if a corporation determines to apply a certain sum of money in its hands to purposes for which capital is usually applied, and to issue new certificates of stock to its shareholders, in the proportion of their number of shares, to represent such sum, it is in no legal sense a dividend, but an apportionment of capital, and although such proceedings are in popular language and in corporate votes often called stock dividends, they are not dividends in law, but are accretions to the capital, and go to the remainder-man. (a)   It is further urged, in illustration, that if the trust fund is invested in land, and the land rises in value from its situation, or from the use and necessary improvements made by the tenant for life, such increased value becomes capital and belongs to the remainder-man.   Chief-Baron Alexander, Vice-Chancellor Wood, now the Lord Chancellor, and the Supreme Court of Massachusetts, have adopted this view, and have determined that such appropriations of earnings and the new certificates of stock, representing additions to the capital stock, whether declared under the name of stocks, dividends, or however appointed or apportioned by the corporation or its directors, are capital, and belong to the remainder-man.[1]   The rule laid down in these several cases seems

[1] Hooper v. Rossiter, 1 McClel. 527; In re Barton's Trust, L. R. 5 Eq. 238; Minot v. Paine, 99 Mass. 101; Balch v. Hallett, 10 Gray, 408. [D'Ooge v. Leeds, 176 Mass. 558; Daland v. Williams, 101 Mass. 571; Adams v. Adams, 139 Mass. 449, 452; Rand v. Hubbell, 115 Mass. 461; Second Univ. Church v. Colegrove, 74 Conn. 79; Spooner v. Phillips, 62 Conn. 62; De Koven v. Alsop, 205 Ill. 309; Richardson v. Richardson, 75 Me. 570; Greene v. Smith, 17 R. I. 28; Brown & Larned, Petitioners, 14 R. I. 371; Bouch v. Sproule, 12 App. Cas. 385; Gibbons v. Mahon, 136 U. S. 549, 558; Billings v. Warren, 216 Ill. 281.]

(a) This view of stock dividends is set forth as follows in Gibbons v. Mahon, 136 U. S. 549, 558, by Gray, J.: "A stock dividend really takes nothing from the property of the corporation, and adds nothing to the interests of the shareholders. Its property is not diminished, and their interests are not increased.   After such a dividend, as before, the corporation has the title in all the corporate property; the aggregate interests therein of all the shareholders are represented by the whole number of shares representing the same proportional interest that the original shares represented before the issue of new ones."

to be this, that where the apportionment of shares, or stock dividend, so called, creates new capital, in addition to that already existing, thereby enlarging and increasing the value of the property, whether it comes from earnings or from other sources, as from rise in value, it belongs to the remainder-man; while all dividends paid in cash or otherwise, not in addition to or in diminution of the capital, go to the tenant for life. These courts, observing this general distinction, range all cases under one or the other head, without so much regard to the name given to the dividend as to the actual character of the transaction. (a)   Thus, *In re* Barton's Trust, and in Minot *v.* Paine,[1] where the earnings were not divided as cash, but were expended on the property, the capital increased, and a stock dividend declared, it was held to go to the remainder-man; while in Leland *v.* Hayden,[2] the corporation having purchased its own stock with its earnings, and then divided it among its stockholders, it was held that it went to the tenant for life, it

[1] Hooper *v.* Rossiter, 1 McClel. 527; *In re* Barton's Trust, L. R. 5 Eq. 238; Minot *v.* Paine, 99 Mass. 101; Balch *v.* Hallett, 10 Gray, 408.

[2] Leland *v.* Hayden, 102 Mass. 550.

(a) A dividend in the form of interest-bearing bonds, based upon a fund of accumulated earnings which are put in trust by the company, has been held to belong to the principal of a trust fund, because no property was taken out of the business or was changed in its relation to the business. D'Ooge *v.* Leeds, 176 Mass. 558.

In passing upon precisely the same question, the Connecticut court lays stress upon the fact that the bonds were in form the unlimited obligations of the company and might ultimately have to be paid out of the capital of the company, although the property set aside in trust as a provision for the payment of both interest and principal was evidently designed to provide amply for the bonds without such resort to the fundamental capital. Bishop *v.* Bishop, 81 Conn. 509. See Mills *v.* Britton, 64 Conn. 4.

An interesting inquiry might be made as to the distribution of the principal of these bonds if ultimately paid by the company out of the fund of surplus earnings set apart for the purpose. As the time for payment was set far in advance the courts did not feel called upon to discuss that point.

In Thayer *v.* Burr, 119 N. Y. S. 755, 134 App. Div. 889, the Supreme Court of New York held this bond dividend to be a division of earnings and therefore income of a life beneficiary.

not being an accretion to the capital. But in Daland v. Williams, the court, looking to the substance of the transaction, held that, although the dividend was declared in stock or cash at the option of the stockholder, yet if he, being a trustee, elected to take the stock, and it was for the interest of the estate that he should, and all the parties so agreed, it then belonged to the remainder-man and not to the tenant for life.[1] On the other hand, it has been claimed in behalf of the tenant for life, that, as nothing but profits can be divided, all dividends declared, whether in stock or cash, being the produce, proceeds, or result of the property, belong to the tenant for life. Cases involving this question have been decided in several States, contrary to the decisions in Massachusetts and the courts in England; and it has been decreed that stock dividends, in whole or in part, belong to the tenant for life, and not to the remainder-man. In Pennsylvania, it was held that all accumulations in stock, after the death of a testator, are as much a part of the income of the principal as current dividends, and as such belong to the tenant for life; and that no action whatever of the corporation could deprive the tenant for life of them and give them to the remainder-man; that the value of stock held by the testator at the time of his death is the capital of the trust, and must remain subject to the trusts in the will; that all income of such capital, whether in the form of other certificates or not, must be regarded as income.[2] (a) While in New York

[1] Daland v. Williams, 101 Mass. 571. [See Hyde v. Holmes, 198 Mass. 287; In re Northage, 60 L. J. Ch. 488, cases where the new stock was worth more than par. See notes infra this section.]

[2] Earp's App., 28 Penn. St. 368. [Smith's Estate, 140 Pa. St. 344.] The question stated at length in this section is important to tenants for life and to remainder-men; and from the character of the decisions in the various States, and from the great number of States in which no decision has yet been had, it may be considered an open question, [in many] of the States. There is no doubt of the doctrine in England. Beginning with the rule, that all extra dividends or "bonuses," even if paid in cash, should go to the

(a) Several other jurisdictions that stock dividends based upon have adopted the Pennsylvania rule, earnings should be given to income

and New Jersey, masters were appointed to inquire and determine how much of the stock divided was capital, or made to

remainder-man [see cases before cited], it gradually came about that all such dividends made as "dividends" from the earnings, produce, proceeds, interest, or income of the corporation, should be considered income, and should belong to the tenant for life. But while such was the rule in regard to all dividends, made as dividends, it became equally well settled that all appropriations from the earnings made to the capital, or stock dividends, as they are sometimes called, belong to the remainder-man. Thus in Hooper v. Rossiter, 1 McClel. 536, (1824) Ch. Baron Alexander said: "All the cases proceed upon the same principle. It seems from all of them, from the first to the last, that wherever the addition was made clearly and distinctly, as dividend only, the tenant for life was to have it; but wherever it was not clearly given as a dividend, it was considered as an accretion of capital, divisible among the proprietors. I have looked into all the cases with great care, and that seems to be the result of them. Whether the testator makes use of the expression, 'dividends,' or 'dividends and profits,' or 'dividends, interest, and profits,' or (as in this case) 'interest, dividends, profits, and proceeds,' I look upon all of them to come to the same thing, and that this is too nice a circumstance to found any distinction on. This disposes of the claim of the plaintiff, as tenant for life." And see Maclaren v. Stainton, 3 De G., F. & J. 202; Kinmonth v. Brigham, 5 Allen, 270. Again, in 1868, In re Barton's Trusts, L. R. 5 Eq. 244, Vice-Chancellor Wood, in answer to the argument and the observation of Lord Eldon, that the corporation has the power to give the property to the tenant for life, or to the

when, and to the same extent as, a cash dividend resting upon the same basis. Kalbach v. Clark, 133 Iowa, 215; Atlantic Coast Line Dividend Cases (Safe Deposit Co. v. White), 102 Md. 73; Thomas v. Gregg, 78 Md. 545; Goodwin v. McGaughey, 108 Minn. 248; Lang's Ex'r v. Lang, 56 N: J. Eq. 603; Ballantine v. Young, ˙70 A. 668 (N. J. Ch. 1908); Ashhurst v. Field's Adm'r, 26 N. J. Eq. 1, 11; Van Doren v. Olden, 19 N. J. Eq. 176; Brown v. Brown, 72 N. J. Eq. 667; Smith's Estate, 140 Pa. St. 344; Pritchitt v. Nashville Tr. Co., 96 Tenn. 472. See also Holbrook v. Holbrook, 74 N. H. 201; Peirce v. Burroughs, 58 N. H. 302; Lord v. Brooks, 52 N. H. 72; Cobb v.

Fant, 36 S. C. 1. In some jurisdictions also where extraordinary cash dividends are not apportioned, the entire stock dividend is given to income if based upon earnings, regardless of when the earnings were accumulated by the corporation. Hite v. Hite, 93 Ky. 257; Lowry v. Farmers' L. & Tr. Co., 172 N. Y. 137; McLouth v. Hunt, 154 N. Y. 179; Robertson v. De Brulatour, 98 N. Y. S. 15, 188 N. Y. 301. See also Millen v. Guerrard, 67 Ga. 284. But the language of the New York decisions indicates that the court would not give to a life tenant a stock dividend based upon earnings accumulated mostly during the life of the testator.

represent an increase in the value of the property, and how much came from income or earnings, and also how much of the

remainder-man, said: "The dividend to which the tenant is entitled is the dividend which the company chooses to declare. And when the company meet and say, that they will not declare a dividend, but will carry over some portion of the half-year's earnings to the capital account, and turn it into capital, it is competent for them to do so; and when this is done everybody is bound by it, and the tenant for life of those shares cannot complain. . . . If a man has his shares placed in settlement, he gives his trustees, in whose names they stand, a power of voting, and he must use his influence to get them to vote as he wishes. But where the company, by a majority of their votes, have said, that they 'will not divide' this money, but turn it into capital, capital it must be from that time. I think that is the true principle." The meaning of this is, that where a corporation votes "not to divide" its earnings, but to turn it into capital, it becomes capital to the corporation, and that what is capital to the corporation must be capital to its shareholders; and although the corporation may vote that such increased capital shall be apportioned or divided among its shareholders pro rata, it is not a "dividend" of "profits," or "interest," or "income," or "proceeds," or "produce," within the meaning of the testator in his will, or within the meaning of the law. The same principle was reiterated by V. C. Malins, in December, 1870, in Ricketts v. Harling, Weekly Notes, Dec. 17, 1870, p. 260. The Supreme Court of Massachusetts, in Minot v. Paine, 99 Mass. 101, probably intended to establish this general doctrine; but the opinion went somewhat further, and laid down a rule which is not properly guarded, and as a rule it has been modified or abandoned in the later decisions. The rule, as stated, is "to regard cash dividends, however large, as income, and stock dividends, however made, as capital." [The rule has been taken to apply only to dividends which are based upon earnings. See *infra*, § 546, note.] In Simpson v. Moore, 30 Barb. 637, there was a cash dividend of eighteen per cent., which embraced a part of the capital of the corporation, it being a bank in process of liquidating and winding up its affairs. This manner of declaring a dividend would not prejudice where the same person was entitled to the whole sum beneficially, but where a tenant for life was entitled to the income, and a remainder-man was entitled to have the capital reinvested, it became necessary, of course, to determine the proportions belonging to each. And so in Leland v. Hayden, 102 Mass. 550, where a dividend was made of the stock of the corporation, which stock had been bought in by the corporation itself with its earnings, and the dividend so made did not represent any increase of the capital stock, the court decreed it to be income and to belong to the tenant for life. If the court had been content to reaffirm the principle of the later English cases, such as Hooper *v.* Rossiter, and *In re* Barton's Trusts, and had not laid down the rule as quoted above from Minot *v.* Paine, it would have saved some misapprehension. This rule, in the broad terms in which it is stated, has been thus

stock dividend was made up of accumulations of earnings before, and how much from earnings after, the investment.[1] (a)

[1] Clarkson v. Clarkson, 18 Barb. 646; Simpson v. Moore, 30 id. 638; Van Doren v. Olden, 19 N. J. 117. [Brown v. Brown, 72 N. J. Eq. 667.]

---

modified in Leland v. Hayden, and the rule as stated in the text seems to be the result of the Massachusetts decisions on this subject.

Earp's App., 28 Penn. St. 368, is a leading case against the authority of the English and Massachusetts cases. In that case a testator had 541 shares of stock in a corporation, the par value of which was $50, but which at the time of his death, in 1848, were worth $125 per share. The shares went on increasing in value, in addition to regular dividends, so that, in 1854, the corporation called in the old certificates, and issued certificates for 1350 shares of the value of $80 per share, in place of the 541 held by the testator at his death. Or, by another mode of calculating, the shares were worth $67,500 at the time of the testator's death, and $108,000 in 1854. The question arose whether this increase of $40,500 belonged to the tenants for life or the remainder-men. The action of the corporation, in making this change of certificates, does not very clearly appear; nor does it very clearly appear whether the increased value was wholly from accumulation of profits, or whether any part of it was from the rise of the value of the property. Perhaps this is not material, from the view taken by the court. Chief Justice Lewis in the opinion says: "It is equally clear, that the profits, arising since the death of the testator, are 'income' within the meaning of the will, and should be distributed among the appellants (tenants for life). The profits amounted at the time of the issue of new certificates of stock, to the sum of $40,500, exclusive of the current semi-annual dividends which have been previously declared and paid. That sum is the rightful property of the appellants. The managers might withhold the distribution of it for a time, for reasons beneficial to the interests of the parties entitled. But they could not, by any form of procedure whatever, deprive the owners of it, and give it to others not entitled. The omission to distribute it semi-annually, as it accumulated, makes no change in its ownership. The distribution of it among the stockholders, in the form of new certificate, has no effect whatever upon the equitable right to it. It makes no kind of difference whether this fund is secured by 541 or by 1350 certificates. Its character cannot be changed by the evidence given to secure it. Part of it is 'principal,' the rest is 'income' within the meaning of the will. The principal must remain unimpaired during the lives of the appellants, and the 'income' arising since the death of the testator is to be distributed among them. Standing upon principle, and upon the intent of the testator plainly ex-

(a) When stockholders are given an option to take their dividend, declared from earnings, either in cash or in new stock of the same

Where new certificates of stock are issued to one who already holds shares as trustee, if the new certificates represent earn-

pressed in his will, we have no difficulty whatever in making this disposition of the fund." In regard to this case, it may be said that it goes too

value, courts which adhere to the Massachusetts rule in regard to stock dividends have held that the dividend should be treated as a cash dividend to the extent of its par value and should go to income, even though it is actually taken in the form of new stock. The transaction is treated as in substance the declaration of a cash dividend and a simultaneous sale by the company of new stock at par. Hyde v. Holmes, 198 Mass. 287; Lyman v. Pratt, 183 Mass. 58: Davis v. Jackson, 152 Mass. 58; Waterman v. Alden, 42 Ill. App. 294, 144 Ill. 90. See also In re Malam, [1894] 3 Ch. 578; In re Northage, 60 L. J. Ch. 488.

But if the new stock is worth more than par value the difference, being the value of the rights to subscribe for the new stock at par, will belong to the principal. Hyde v. Holmes, 198 Mass. 287; In re Northage, 60 L. J. Ch. 488.

A division by a corporation of its own stock which it has bought or taken in satisfaction of a debt after it has been issued, is equivalent to a cash dividend, and should be treated as such even though it is improperly described as a "stock dividend." Leland v. Hayden, 102 Mass. 542; Green v. Bissell, 79 Conn. 547, 8 L. R. A. (N. S.) 1011. But if the corporation has paid for such stock with money raised by an issue of bonds, and the distribution of the stock actually impairs its fundamental capital, the dividend should be credited to principal.

Gilkey v. Paine, 80 Me. 319. To the same effect, see Pabst v. Goodrich, 133 Wis. 43.

A distinction has been made between extraordinary dividends and large dividends which are delayed payments of guaranteed regular dividends. In Meldrim v. Trustees of Trinity Church, 100 Ga. 479, lessees of a railroad had agreed with the lessor corporation to declare and pay to the latter's stockholders, semi-annual dividends of seven per cent, but for several years had failed to do it. A successor under the lease later paid over a portion of these back dividends. A life tenant of stock had meanwhile died, but it was held that his estate was entitled to these back dividends which should have been paid during his life. It was said that the dividends were not undeclared during the ownership of the life tenant, but had been predeclared by the contract between the two corporations. It is important to note that the delayed dividends were not to be paid by the corporation in which the life tenant held stock, but by a lessee corporation which, under its contract, might be considered a debtor of the stockholder without having declared the guaranteed dividends, whether it had earned them or not. For this reason the decision cannot be considered authority for cases of delayed payments of guaranteed dividends when the guaranty is between the corporation and its own stock-

ings or income of the corporation, they belong to the *cestui*, but if they are issued simply to equalize the value of the inter-

far. It cannot be sustained in all its broad assertions, whether they are necessary for the decision of the case or not. For instance, it has

holders. Doubtless such dividends would not be income until declared, or at least until the basis for them has been earned. See *In re* Taylor's Trusts, [1905] 1 Ch. 734.

Rights given to stockholders to subscribe at par for new shares of stock in a corporation whose stock is worth more than par do not belong to income even in jurisdictions which give to income stock dividends which are based upon earnings. Brinley *v.* Grou, 50 Conn. 66; De Koven *v.* Alsop, 205 Ill. 309; Hite's Devisees *v.* Hite's Ex'r, 93 Ky. 257; Hyde *v.* Holmes, 198 Mass. 287; Atkins *v.* Albree, 12 Allen, 359; Robertson *v.* De Brulatour, 188 N. Y. 301, 98 N. Y. S. 15; Eisner's Appeal, 175 Pa. St. 143; Biddle's Appeal, 99 Pa. St. 278; Moss's Appeal, 83 Pa. St. 264; Greene *v.* Smith, 17 R. I. 28; Richmond *v.* Richmond, 108 N. Y. S. 298, 123 App. Div. 117.

This disposition of rights is not inconsistent with the Pennsylvania rule that stock dividends based upon earnings should be given to those entitled to income during the time when the earnings were accumulated, for they are not dividends in any sense. Although the value of the rights may be due to the existence of a fund of undivided earnings, and although the issue of new stock increases the number of shares which may at some time become entitled in a division of these earnings, there is no division of these

earnings and no change in the manner in which the corporation holds them. There is no certainty that the earnings will ever be divided and usually no way of determining accurately how much of the value of the rights is due to their existence and how much to other causes. Moss's Appeal, 83 Pa. St. 264.

But in Holbrook *v.* Holbrook, 74 N. H. 201, it was held that rights should be apportioned on the same principle as extraordinary dividends, and that income is entitled to them in so far as they stand for increase of value due to earnings accumulated during the time when the life beneficiary was entitled to income. See also Wiltbank's Appeal, 64 Pa. St. 256 (compare Eisner's Appeal, 175 Pa. St. 143).

It has also been held in Pennsylvania that, where rights are given to stockholders to subscribe for shares in another company, so that there is no resulting decrease in the value of the shares held in trust, the rights should be treated as a product or earnings of the shares and should be given to income. Eisner's Appeal, 175 Pa. St. 143.

The mere accumulation of earnings by a corporation and a consequent increase of the value of its stock does not give the life beneficiary a right to have the shares sold and the increase of value paid to him as income. No court would hold that earnings of the corporation are available as income of the stock-

ests of stockholders in two corporations about to be consolidated, they belong to the *corpus* of the estate.[1] (*a*)

[1] Goldsmith *v.* Swift, 25 Hun, 201.

---

never been supposed that a stockholder in a corporation had any ownership in the earnings of a corporation before the corporation itself had set apart a sum as earnings, and declared and divided it as a dividend. Crawford *v.* North Eastern Railw., 3 K. & J. 744; Williston *v.* Michigan, &c. Railw., 13 Allen, 400. If, therefore, a corporation, acting in good faith, uses its earnings in improving its property, and neglects to apportion or divide them, how can a tenant for life enforce his ownership? Can a court of equity compel a corporation, acting in good faith, to declare a dividend? Further, it has generally been supposed, that if a corporation does not declare a dividend, and the value of the stock increases from the use of the earnings, as capital in its business, or if the value of its stock rises from any reason, and the stock is sold by the trustee for an enhanced price, all the increased value over the original appraised value belongs to the trust fund, and the income thereof only goes to the tenant for life, and the fund to the remainder-men. But if this is not so, and the increased value of the stock goes to the tenant for life, as held by Chief Justice Lewis, is the converse of his proposition true; and if stock sells for less than its appraised value at the time of the institution of the trust, can the trustee withhold dividends or income from the tenant for life until the original appraised value is made good? The authority of a corporation to apply any part of its earnings to the permanent improvement of its property, and thus to deprive the tenant for life of his share of the income or earnings of the corporation, is denied in this case, at least so far as the rights of a tenant for life are concerned. In short, the proposition or assertion of this case, that the earnings are the rightful property of the tenant for life, and that no action of the corporation can alter his rights to them, cannot be sustained in practice, for the simple reason that nothing belongs to the stockholder until a dividend is made; and, until a dividend is made, the tenant for life has no rights or ownership to be altered or affected by the action of the corporation. Coleman *v.* Columbia Oil Co., 51 Penn. St. 74; Granger *v.* Bassett, 98 Mass. 462; March *v.* Eastern R. R. Co., 43 N. H. 515; Crawford *v.* North Eastern Railw., 3 K. & J. 744. But see Johnson *v.* Bridgewater Co., 14 Gray, 274; Taft *v.* Providence, &c. Railw., 8 R. I. 310; McLaughlin *v.* Detroit, &c., 8 Mich. 100; Williston *v.* Michigan, &c., 13 Allen, 400; Foote's App.,

holder until a dividend of some kind had been declared. Tubb *v.* Fowler, 118 Tenn. 325; Boardman *v.* Boardman, 78 Conn. 451.

(*a*) Dividends, whether regular or extraordinary, which are paid out of the "fundamental" capital of the corporation are not income, but

§ 546. A different rule seems to apply to the gift of a farm and stock of cattle for life. In such cases, all improvements

22 Pick. 299. It was said by Lord Eldon, that the corporation has it in its power to give the benefit to the tenant for life or not; and this he said, not as a proposition of law, but as a statement of the practice of the courts. The corporation cannot alter any of the rights of the tenant for life, nor can it invest any of his money in a manner not agreeable to him, for the simple reason that until the corporation has declared the dividend, the tenant for life has no rights to be altered, and no money to be invested. It is only after the corporation has made a dividend, and the trustee has it in hand, that the tenant for life has any right, or is in any position to claim anything. The corporation must deal with its stockholders as absolute owners. If, therefore, the corporation has a right to turn any part of its "income" into capital, as against the absolute owner, who has not only the life-interest, but the whole interest in himself, it must have the same right as against the trustee, who, so far as the corporation is concerned, is the absolute owner of the stocks. The corporation, then, would seem to have the right, acting in good faith, to apply its income as capital to its business, especially if the corporation itself, or its directors, acting within the scope of their authority, vote to do so. If the corporation votes to do so, and thus increases the value of the shares in the hands of the trustees, but creates no new shares, can the tenant for life call for this increased value? If he can, and the case in Pennsylvania seems so to decide, a new principle will be established in the government of corporations and in the administration of trusts. It is apparent from these observations, that the opinion in the case of Earp's Appeal cannot be carried to the logical conclusions to which it leads. It is proper to say, however, that the nature of the acts by the corporation does not very clearly appear. Whether the corporation intended to make a stock dividend or not, or whether the accumulations were used in the legitimate business of the corporation as capital, or whether it remained accumulated income not divided, and not applied to capital, does not certainly appear; perhaps for the reason that the court treats such considerations as immaterial.(a) In New York, the

should be preserved as part of the principal of the trust in the absence of a contrary intention manifested in the instrument creating the trust. This would be true of dividends from a mining company which provided no fund for the purchase of new mines. In such a case the declaration of a dividend by the corporation, although giving the stockholders a right to cash payments, does not make these cash payments income. They are distributions of capital and part of

---

(a) An answer to the foregoing criticisms of the doctrine enunci-

ated in Earp's Appeal and followed in later cases in Pennsylvania and

made upon the real estate by the tenant for life will accrue to the remainder-man as of course. (a)   But any increase in the

case of Simpson v. Moore, 31 Barb. 638, has little to do with the question, for the reason that the cash dividend made in that case was partly composed

(a) Pratt v. Douglas, 38 N. J. Eq. 516, 541; Caldecott v. Brown, 2 Hare, 144.

the corpus of the investment, whatever the directors may call them. Heard v. Eldredge, 109 Mass. 258; Walker's Ex'r v. Walker, 68 N. H. 407; Wheeler v. Perry, 18 N. H. 307; Vinton's Appeal, 99 Pa. St. 434; Gilkey v. Paine, 80 Me. 319; Mercer v. Buchanan, 132 Fed. 501.   By fundamental capital is meant that on which the capital stock is based, being the original investment of the stockholders with such additions from earnings as were made to repair waste and such other additions to working capital as have formed the basis for new issues of shares. It is immaterial that the property thus distributed is no longer needed in the business of the company (cases cited *supra*), or that it has been taken from the company by right of eminent domain. Heard v. Eldredge, 109 Mass. 258.

For a case of this kind where the regular dividends, although wasting, were given to the equitable life tenant because the testator evidently intended that they should belong to him, see Reed v. Head, 6 Allen, 174.

As the officers of a corporation usually have no right to use up the capital of the corporation in divi-dends, a dividend is presumed to be from earnings unless the contrary is shown. Walker's Ex'r v. Walker, 68 N. H. 407; Smith v. Dana, 77 Conn. 543. This is especially true of the regular dividends, and trustees would usually be safe in treating them as income, unless it clearly appears that they were paid from capital.

As the vote declaring an extraordinary dividend usually specifies the source, the trustee may be called upon to decide whether this source is income of the corporation or part of the capital. But it has been held that in the absence of evidence to the contrary the court will presume that an extraordinary dividend, whether in cash or in stock, is based upon earnings.   Kalbach v. Clark, 133 Iowa, 215.

It is also immaterial that the value of the property remaining in the capital of the corporation is as large as or even many times larger than the sum total of the capital stock at par,   Smith v. Hooper, 95 Md. 16; Wheeler v. Perry, 18 N. H. 307; Matter of Rogers, 161 N. Y. 108; for the increase in value of property in which the capital is invested is not income

in several other jurisdictions, is that a stockholder does have a cer-tain equitable interest in the earnings of the corporation as they ac-

farming stock will belong to the tenant for life. He is under
no obligation to increase the stock upon the farm; and if he

of earnings, and partly of capital of a corporation that was winding up its
affairs. But the case of Clarkson v. Clarkson, 18 Barb. 646, is a direct decision upon the point, that, if a corporation makes a stock dividend from its
gains, profits, income, and proceeds, such stock dividend must be considered
as income from the original investment, and belongs to the tenant for life;
but if anything is given to the trustee, not as interest, dividend, or proceeds,
but as part of the capital, it is capital, and belongs to the remainder-man.
The court sent the case to a referee to determine the facts. In New Jersey,
in the case of Van Doren v. Olden, 19 N. J. Eq. 117, the chancellor approved
of the reasoning of the courts in New York and Pennsylvania, and sent
the case to a master to inquire and report how much of the stock dividend
was capital, and how much income, and also how much of the stock dividend
was made up of accumulations before the investment of the trust fund in
the stock of the corporation, and how much of it came from earnings after
the investment. The court of Massachusetts notices a difficulty in making
satisfactory inquiries on these points, as corporations might refuse to expose
their business, or they might be out of the jurisdiction of the court, and
situated so that it would be impossible to arrive at a satisfactory result. It
is quite important that a principle should be established to guide trustees
in the performance of their duties, as in many cases the remainder-men
are infants, or they are not even in existence when the question arises, and
should be settled. Generally, the rights of such *cestuis que trust* cannot be
definitely adjusted until they are competent to act for themselves, and call
for a settlement of the accounts. Thus trustees may be compelled to rectify
any mistake they may make in this matter years after the event. See the
question further discussed by Mr. Justice Ladd in Lord v. Brooks, 52 N. H. 77.

In Read v. Head, 6 Allen, 174, it was decided that dividends of a land
company, whose income was made from sales of its land or capital in
business, belonged to the tenant for life under the will of a testator, although
such sales might exhaust the capital of the corporation and entirely defeat
the remainder-man. This decision went upon the ground that it was the
intention of the testator when he devised the income of such stock to one
for life, that, as the tenant for life could have no income except from such
dividends as came from capital, he must take the dividends as made. All
the cases profess to go upon the intention of the testator. Therefore a
testator may foreclose this question in his will by giving such directions

---

(cases cited *supra*) except where the
business of the corporation is specu-

lation. Thus the increase in value of
land on which a manufacturing cor-

---

crue. Although he cannot as a
mere stockholder compel a dis-

tribution of them, they are held
for the ultimate benefit of all the

CHAP. XVIII.] FARM STOCK AND TOOLS. [§ 546.

does so, the increase will not be capital, but will inure to the benefit of the tenant for life or his representatives.[1] A different

as to leave no question as to his intention. And see Balch v. Hallett, 10 Gray, 403; Heard v. Eldredge, 109 Mass. 258.

The great argument in Massachusetts, which does not seem yet to have been considered by the court, is this: Corporations are forbidden to make dividends except from profits; if, therefore, a corporation declares a dividend, whether payable in stock or in money, such dividend must accrue from profits upon the capital invested, and, it being profit upon the capital stock invested, it must belong to the tenant for life.

[1] Robertson v. Collier, 1 Hill, Eq. 370; Calhoun v. Furgeson, 3 Rich. Eq. 170; Woods v. Sullivan, 1 Swanst. 507; Horrey v. Glover, 2 Hill, Eq.

poration has its factory does not belong to income, but a profit due to the increase in value of land of a corporation engaged in buying and selling land for profit is properly income. Thomson's Estate, 153 Pa. St. 332; Oliver's Estate, 136 Pa. St. 43; Balch v. Hallet, 10 Gray, 402.

Dividends from capitalized earnings, that is, earnings which have been made the basis of a new issue of stock, belong to principal, even in jurisdictions where the new issue of stock is not treated as income. Hemenway v. Hemenway, 181 Mass. 406; Smith v. Dana, 77 Conn. 543.

Dividends from earnings which have been made part of the "floating capital" of the corporation are not divisions of *corpus*, and in States where extraordinary cash dividends are not apportioned, belong entirely to income. Hemenway v. Hemenway, 181 Mass. 406; Matter of Rogers, 161 N. Y. 108; *In re* Stevens, 98 N. Y. S. 28. See also Quinn v. Safe Dep. & Tr. Co., 93 Md. 285; Robertson v. De Brula-

tour, 188 N. Y. 301. "Floating capital" is meant to include accumulated earnings invested to produce income outside of the corporation's regular business: for example, an investment of a fund of accumulated earnings in stocks, bond, and securities of other companies, Hemenway v. Hemenway, 181 Mass. 406; Matter of Rogers, 161 N. Y. 108; see also Stewart v. Phelps, 173 N. Y. 621, 71 App. Div. 91; or in the purchase of the company's own stock, Leland v. Hayden, 102 Mass. 542.

Dividends out of earnings which have been temporarily added to the "working capital" of the corporation, have been held to belong to income for the same reason. Smith v. Dana, 77 Conn. 543. See Bouch v. Sproule, 12 App. Cas. 385, 402; *In re* Stevens, 98 N. Y. S. 28; Weschler's Estate, 212 Pa. St. 508. These temporary additions of earnings to the "working capital" are meant to include the investments of earnings in the main business of the corporation, which go beyond

stockholders, and their accumulation adds to the market value of

each share of stock. If they are distributed in the form of a cash

889

rule was applied in the Southern States in relation to the gift of negro slaves for life. In Virginia, Alabama, North Carolina,

515; Patterson v. High, 8 Ired. Eq. 52; Scott v. Dobson, 1 H. & McH. 160; Wooten v. Burch, 2 Md. Ch. 191; Holmes v. Mitchell, 4 id. 163; Patterson v. Devlin, 1 McMul. 459; Evans v. Inglehart, 6 G. & J. 172; Poindexter v. Blackburn, 1 Ired. Eq. 286; Saunders v. Houghton, 8 id. 217; Hunt v. Watkins, 1 Humph. 498.

the mere repairing of waste and depreciation, and with respect to which there has been no action of the corporation definitely and formally making them part of the fundamental capital. The language of the opinion in Hemenway v. Hemenway, 181 Mass. 406, 411, may indicate that the Massachusetts court will take a different view, because of its holding that extraordinary cash dividends cannot be apportioned.

Dividends in liquidation. In jurisdictions which hold that it is the declaration of the dividend which makes it income as between life tenant and remainder-man, a division in liquidation of the property of the corporation without any separation of income from capital by the corporation, belongs entirely to principal, even though a large part of the assets consisted of accumulated earnings in the form of

floating capital. Curtis v. Osborn, 79 Conn. 555; Second Universalist Church v. Colegrove, 74 Conn. 79; Brownell v. Anthony, 189 Mass. 442; Gifford v. Thompson, 115 Mass. 478; In re Armitage, [1893] 3 Ch. 337; Bulkeley v. Worthington Ecc. Soc., 78 Conn. 526. See Hemenway v. Hemenway, 181 Mass. 406. But the courts of New York will in such a case give to income so much of the final dividend as is based upon accumulated earnings which have not been put into the working capital of the corporation. Matter of Rogers, 161 N. Y. 108. See Robertson v. De Brulatour, 188 N. Y. 301; In re Stevens, 98 N. Y. S. 28, 111 App. Div. 773. There seems to be no reason why courts of jurisdictions, where extraordinary dividends are usually apportioned, should make any exception in a case of a dividend in liquidation. See Weschler's Estate, 212 Pa. St. 508.

---

dividend while a life tenant is entitled to income, all courts regard them as income, at least to the extent that they were earned by the corporation during the time when the life tenant was entitled to the income. If, instead of being distributed, they are added to the permanent capital of the corporation and new stock is issued based entirely upon them, why should not

the new stock be classed as income? As between persons equitably entitled, should the courts distinguish between a distribution of actual earnings and a distribution of salable stock based upon the earnings? If the corporation votes a cash dividend out of surplus earnings and contemporaneously votes increase of its capital stock to the same amount, with the design that

and South Carolina, the increase of such slaves was added to the capital, and went to the remainder-man.[1] In ·Maryland, the general rule was applied, and the tenant for life took the increase of the slaves;[2] but where the *income* of a farm, on which there were slaves, was given to one for life, the increase was allowed to the remainder-man.[3] In Pennsylvania, it was held that the remainder-men were entitled to farm stock and implements purchased by the tenant for life to keep up the stock and tools; but this was under the special words of a will.[4] The general rule is, that the tenant for life is under no obligation to replace those things given for life, which are consumed by the using, and, if he purchases other articles in the place of them, such articles are his own.[5] Underbrush and timber cut

---

[1] Ellison *v.* Woody, 6 Munf. 368; Calhoun *v.* Furgeson, 3 Rich. Eq. 160; Covington *v.* McEntire, 2 Ired. Eq. 316; Patterson *v.* High, 8 id. 52; Milledge *v.* Lamar, 4 Des. 616; Strong *v.* Brewer, 7 Ala. 713; Robertson *v.* Collier, 1 Hill, Eq. 370; Patterson *v.* Devlin, 1 McMul. 459; Horrey *v.* Glover, 2 Hill, Eq. 515.

[2] Scott *v.* Dobson, 1 H. & McH. 160; Holmes *v.* Mitchell, 4 Md. Ch. 163; Wooten *v.* Burch, 2 id. 191; Evans *v.* Inglehart, 6 G. & J. 172.

[3] Holmes *v.* Mitchell, 4 Md. Ch. 263; 4 Md. R. 532.

[4] Flowers *v.* Franklin, 5 Watts, 265.

[5] Patterson *v.* Devlin, 1 McMul. 459; Calhoun *v.* Furgeson, 3 Rich. Eq. 160; Black *v.* Ray, 1 Dev. & B. Eq. 443; Covenhoven *v.* Shuler, 2 Paige, 131.

---

the stockholders may pay for new stock with their dividends, the Massachusetts courts treat the dividend as income to the extent of its par value. In such a case the stockholder is given the money with the privilege of turning it into new stock; in the case of a stock dividend he is given new stock which he has the undoubted right to turn into money by sale. It seems hard to justify on equitable principles a rule of law which gives the life tenant in one case and to the remainder-man in the other case.

Although it is true that a stock dividend does not turn over any property from the corporation to its stockholders, nevertheless, it is a definite appropriation of undivided earnings to the permanent capital of the corporation and a declaration of the share of this new capital to which each stockholder is entitled. The treatment of the new shares of stock as income to the extent of their par value is no more an impairment of the principal of a stockholder's investment than would be the treatment of a cash dividend of equal amount as income.

periodically in the regular course of thinning forests, are to be treated as income, and belong to the tenant for life; but timber not cut in the regular course of thinning, but to improve the growth of the remaining trees, belongs to the capital of the trust. (a)   Gravel sold from land is income, and the proceeds belong to the tenant for life; (b) but the expense of fencing waste lands given for the general benefit of the trust must be paid out of the capital.[1] The share of the testator in the profits of a partnership which is to continue after his death belongs to the life *cestui*.[2] (c)   But any accretion to the fund itself which is to be invested as by the rise in value of securities goes to the remainder-man. The life tenant also derives advantage from this increased value through the larger income resulting, but

---

[1] Cowley v. Wellesley, L. R. 1 Eq. 657; 35 Beav. 637; and see Honywood v. Honywood, L. R. 18 Eq. 306.

[2] Heighe v. Littig, 63 Md. 301.

(a) Honywood v. Honywood, 18 Eq. 306; Dashwood v. Magniac, [1891] 3 Ch. 306; *In re* Harrison's Trusts, 28 Ch. Div. 220; Noyes v. Stone, 163 Mass. 490; Smith v. Smith, 105 Ga. 106, 111; Stonebraker v. Zollickoffer, 52 Md. 154; Keniston v. Gorrell, 74 N. H. 53; Modlin v. Kennedy, 53 Ind. 267; Lester v. Young, 14 R. I. 579; Morehouse v. Cotheal, 22 N. J. Law, 521; Williard v. Williard, 56 Pa. St. 119. *Supra*, § 540, note a, p. 870.

(b) The product of mines, oil wells, and quarries which are opened by a trustee belongs to principal and should be invested to produce income, which alone belongs to the life beneficiary. McFadden's Estate, 224 Pa. St. 443; Blakley v. Marshall, 174 Pa. St. 425; Wilson v. Youst, 43 W. Va. 826; Swayne v. Lone Acre Oil Co., 98 Tex. 597; *In re* Ridge, 31 Ch. Div. 504. 508. See also Ohio

Oil Co. v. Daughetee, 240 Ill. 361. But the product of mines, oil wells, or quarries which were open when the trust was established, or which the trust instrument gave the trustee the right to open, belongs entirely to income. Woodburn's Estate, 138 Pa. St. 606; Eley's Appeal, 103 Pa. St. 300; McClintock v. Dana, 106 Pa. St. 386; Wentz's Appeal, 106 Pa. St. 301; Bedford's Appeal, 126 Pa. St. 117; *In re* Ridge, 31 Ch. Div. 504, 508.

(c) But not if it is a case of delay in converting into the permanent trust investments. Kinmonth v. Brigham, 5 Allen, 270; Westcott v. Nickerson, 120 Mass. 410; Mudge v. Parker, 139 Mass. 153; Willard's Ex'r v. Willard, 21 A. 463 (N. J. Ch. 1891). As to what should go to the life beneficiary as income in such a case, see *infra*, § 548, note a.

if the securities mature or are sold, the increased value belongs to the remainder.[1]

§ 547. Where there is a *specific* gift for life of things which are consumed in the using, the tenant for life must have the possession and the use, according to the gift.[2] But if the gift of such articles, or of perishable articles, is *residuary* or *general*, the trustee must sell the articles and invest the proceeds, so that the tenant for life may receive the interest or income, and the principal sum may remain for the remainder-man.[3] If the property consists of leaseholds, annuities, or other interests, which grow less valuable by lapse of time, they must be sold, and the proceeds invested in some permanent form, so that the interest can be paid to the tenant for life, and the remainder-man can receive a proper sum as principal.[4] If the trustee does not con-

---

[1] *In re* Gerry, 103 N. Y. 450. [Boardman *v.* Boardman, 78 Conn. 451; Tubb *v.* Fowler, 118 Tenn. 325.]

[2] Tyson *v.* Blake, 22 N. Y. 558; Shaw *v.* Huzzey, 41 Maine, 495; Scott *v.* Perkins, 28 id. 22; McDonnald *v.* Walgrove, 1 Sandf. Ch. 275; McLane *v.* McDonald, 2 Barb. S. C. 537; Wright *v.* Miller, 8 N. Y. 25.

[3] Clark *v.* Clark, 8 Paige, 152; Williamson *v.* Williamson, 6 Paige, 298; Randall *v.* Russell, 3 Mer. 194; Porter *v.* Tournay, 3 Ves. Jr. 314; Andrew *v.* Andrew, 1 Col. C. C. 690; Spear *v.* Tinkham, 2 Barb. Ch. 211; Emmons *v.* Cairns, 3 Barb. 243; Cairns *v.* Chaubert, 9 Paige, 160; Woods *v.* Sullivan, 1 Swanst. 507; Covenhoven *v.* Shuler, 2 Paige, 122; Eichelberger *v.* Barnitz, 17 Serg. & R. 293; Booth *v.* Ammerman, 4 Bradf. 132; Bradner *v.* Falkner, 2 Kern. 472; Patterson *v.* Devlin, 1 McMul. Eq. 459; Robertson *v.* Collier, 1 Hill, Eq. 373; Horrey *v.* Glover, 2 Hill, Eq. 515; Calhoun *v.* Furgeson, 7 Rich. Eq. 165; Saunders *v.* Houghton, 8 Ired. Eq. 217; Taylor *v.* Bond, 1 Busb. Eq. 25; Homer *v.* Shelton, 2 Met. 194. In Maryland, however, under the act of 1798, c. 101, it was held that the general rule as to conversion was not in force in that State, and that the tenant for life under a *general* residuary clause was entitled to enjoy the articles of property that fell into the residue *in specie.* Evans *v.* Inglehart, 6 G. & J. 192. But if the residue consists of money, or property, the use of which is a conversion into money, the executor or trustee must convert it into money and invest it. Evans *v.* Inglehart, 6 G. & J. 192; Wooten *v.* Burch, 2 Md. Ch. 199.

[4] *Ante,* §§ 449, 450; Minot *v.* Thompson, 106 Mass. 584; Howe *v.* Dartmouth, 7 Ves. 137; Mills *v.* Mills, 7 Sim. 501; Lichfield *v.* Baker, 2 Beav. 481; Alcock *v.* Sloper, 2 Myl. & K. 701; Fearns *v.* Young, 9 Ves. 552; Pickering *v.* Pickering, 2 Beav. 57; 4 Myl. & Cr. 298; Dimes *v.* Scott, 4 Russ. 200; Cairns *v.* Chaubert, 9 Paige, 160; Clark *v.* Clark, 8 Paige, 152; Benn *v.*

vert such property within a reasonable time, the remainder-man can proceed against him as for a breach of trust. The tenant for life will be compelled to refund whatever he has received beyond his equitable proportion, and the trustees, in the event of the failure or inability of the tenant for life to refund, must make good the difference.[1] If, however, the remainder-man acquiesces for a long time in the receipt of the whole actual income by the tenant for life, or does not claim any relief for such payments, the court will confine its decree to conversion. So, if all parties consent that annuities and other rights may not be sold, the court will sanction their retention by the trustees.[2] The rights of tenant for life and remainder-man will depend very much upon the construction of the will and the directions contained in it.[3] If leaseholds and terminable annuities are rapidly growing less valuable, or if other property is perishing, and they are given *specifically* in the will for the tenant for life, he is entitled to them, although the remainder-man will be

---

Dixon, 10 Sim. 636; Eichelberger *v.* Barnitz, 17 Serg. & R. 293; Covenhoven *v.* Shuler, 2 Paige, 132; Wooten *v.* Burch, 2 Md. Ch. 190; Kinmonth *v.* Brigham, 5 Allen, 270. [*In re* Game, [1897] 1 Ch. 881. But see *Re* Leonard, 433 L. T. 664. *Infra*, § 548, note.] Farming stock is not within the rule. Groves *v.* Wright, 2 K. & J. 347.

[1] Ibid.; Kinmonth *v.* Brigham, 5 Allen, 270. In Meyer *v.* Simonson, 5 De G. & Sm. 726, Vice-Chancellor Parker stated the rules which govern the court on the subject as follows: The personal estate of a testator may be considered as divided into three different classes: (1) Property which is found at the testator's death invested in such securities as the court can adopt, as money in the funds or on real securities. The tenant for life is entitled to the whole income of this. (2) Property which can be converted into money without sacrificing anything by a forced sale. As to this the rule is clear: It must be converted, and the produce must be invested in securities which the court allows, and the tenant for life is entitled to the income of such investment. (3) Property which, according to a reasonable administration, is not capable of an immediate conversion, and which cannot be sold immediately without involving a sacrifice of both principal and interest. In this case the rule is to take the value of the testator's interest, and to give the tenant for life the income of that present value. Kinmonth *v.* Brigham, 5 Allen, 270.

[2] Lichfield *v.* Baker, 2 Beav. 481; Pickering *v.* Pickering, 4 Myl. & Cr. 298; Glengall *v.* Barnard, 5 Beav. 245.

[3] Moseley *v.* Marshall, 22 N. Y. 205.

entirely excluded; for the reason that the testator himself had the right to make such disposition of his estate as he saw fit, and if he conferred upon the remainder-man only the possible chance of taking what might be left by the tenant for life un-exhausted, the remainder-man will receive all that was intended for him, and he has no right to complain.[1] So where discretion was given to trustees, to pay the income to a tenant for life, or to purchase an irredeemable annuity, and there was a gift over, and the trustees did not purchase the annuity, but paid the *cestui que trust* from time to time more than the income, but less than the principal, it was held to be a proper exercise of the discretion.[2] In England, whenever a fund is held on an authorized permanent investment, the life tenant is to receive the entire actual income, and no part of it is to be set aside to indemnify the remainder-men for the disadvantage resulting to them from the purchase above par of stock that has only a short time to run, and for which they will receive only par. Massachusetts follows the English law though refusing to lay down any universal rule, preferring to deal with each case as it arises.[3] The case cited is a very strong one; the court covers the ground thoroughly, and goes to the pith of the matter, remarking that substantial justice between life tenant and remainder-men is the object, that the object of investment in stocks that are above par is not alone the increased interest, but the higher security of the capital, and that if the interest

---

[1] Howe *v.* Dartmouth, 7 Ves. 149; 2 Wh. & T. L. C. 321; Lord *v.* Godfrey, 4 Madd. 455; Vaughan *v.* Buck, 1 Phill. 80; Bethune *v.* Kennedy, 1 Myl. & Cr. 116; Pickering *v.* Pickering, 4 id. 299; Phillips *v.* Sargent, 7 Hare, 33, where it was held that, if the trustees wrongfully converted such property, the tenant for life was entitled to the whole fund to the exclusion of the remainder-man. Beaufoy's Est., 1 Sm. & Gif. 22; *Re* Steward's Est., 1 Dru. 636; Howe *v.* Howe, 14 Jur. 359; Cotton *v.* Cotton, id. 950; Morgan *v.* Morgan, 14 Beav. 72; Pickup *v.* Atkinson, 4 Hare, 628; Prendergast *v.* Prendergast, 3 H. L. Cas. 195. [See *infra*, § 548, note *a*.]

[2] Messena *v.* Carr, L. R. 9 Eq. 260, and see Miller *v.* Miller, L. R. 13 Eq. 267.

[3] Hemenway *v.* Hemenway, 136 Mass. 447. [But see note *a*, *infra*, pp. 896–898.]

is to be divided between life tenant and remainder-men, a prob-
lem of infinite difficulty arises in the question, how, upon what
line or principle, shall the division be made?   In a later case
in Massachusetts, however, the majority of the court held that
if a trustee holding a fund to pay the income to a certain person
for life, with remainder over, makes an investment at a premium
in bonds payable at a day certain, he may retain from the income enough to make good to the capital the amount of premium paid.   The court notices Hemenway v. Hemenway, and
seeks, not to seem to overrule, but to avert its force, and distinguish it.   The effort does not seem successful, and the dissent of Morton, C. J., and Allen and Holmes, JJ., contains far
the weightier argument.[1] (a)   Where a trustee buys at the fore-

[1] New England Trust Co. v. Eaton, 140 Mass. 532.

(a) Bonds bought at a premium
are ordinarily a wasting investment
if the whole interest on the bonds
is treated as income, because if the
bonds are held until maturity the
premium will be entirely lost, and
even if they are not held until
maturity, other things being equal,
the premium will gradually grow
smaller as maturity approaches.
For this reason it has been held in
some jurisdictions that a trustee
who has purchased bonds at a
premium should deduct from the
various collections of interest, and
add to the principal, such sums as
will replace the premium if the
bonds are held until maturity. That
is to say, he should establish a sort
of sinking fund to repair the yearly
waste of principal. N. Y. Life Ins.
Co. v. Baker, 165 N. Y. 484; Matter
of Stevens, 187 N. Y. 471; Curtis v.
Osborn, 79 Conn. 555; In re Allis's
Estate, 123 Wis. 223 (even though
the bonds will not mature until after
the termination of the trust);
Ballantine v. Young, 70 A. 668

(N. J. Ch. 1908). See Matter of
Johnson, 57 N. Y. App. Div. 494,
502, modified in 170 N. Y. 139.

If after this has been done the
bonds should be sold at a larger
premium than was paid for them,
it has been held that the increase
of premium belongs to the principal,
and also such of the sinking fund as
has already been accumulated, the
increase of premium being regarded
as an increase in the value of the
corpus. N. E. Trust Co. v. Eaton,
140 Mass. 532.

Although the premium on bonds
frequently varies from month to
month in the bond market, these
fluctuations should have no effect
upon the amount of deductions
from the interest payments, but
the purpose of the trustee should
be to regulate his sinking fund so
that the total at the time of maturity shall exactly replace the premium he has paid. If the bonds are
held until maturity, it is certain that
this premium will be entirely wiped
out, and the original principal will be

closure sale of his mortgage and afterwards sells the land at a profit, this belongs to the *corpus* of the estate, and not to the life tenant.[1] (*a*)

---

[1] Parker *v*. Johnson, 37 N. J. Eq. 366.

---

reduced by the amount of the premium which he had previously paid, unless there is some such provision to repair the loss. This view of such investments is well stated in the majority opinion, written by Devens, J., in N. E. Trust Co. *v*. Eaton, 140 Mass. 532: "There can ordinarily be no better test of the true income which a sum of money will produce, having regard to the rights of both the tenant for life and the remainder-man, than the interest which can be received from a bond which sells above par and is payable at the termination of a fixed time, deducting from such interest, as it becomes due, such sums as will at maturity efface the premium. If such a bond has increased in value since its purchase, assuming it to have been an entirely safe investment, and none other should be made, it is because a change in the rates of interest, or some similar cause, has altered market values."

In some other jurisdictions it has been held that no part of the interest on the bonds should be used to replace a premium. Hite's Devisees *v*. Hite's Ex'r, 93 Ky. 257; Penn-Gaskell's Estate (No. 2), 208 Pa. St. 346. Whitridge *v*. Williams, 71 Md. 105 (*semble*). It is pointed out that premiums are not paid to

secure greater income, but usually represent safety and permanency of investment and facility of transfer and use, and in fact usually accompany a low rate of interest. It is argued from this fact that the premium is paid more for the benefit of the remainder-man than for the benefit of the life tenant, and should therefore be considered as a payment that the fund itself ought to ⁎endure, as a charge for the benefit of the whole fund. See dissenting opinion of Holmes, J., in N. E. Trust Co. *v*. Eaton, 140 Mass. 532, 545.

In Massachusetts, notwithstanding the strong language of the majority opinion in N. E. Trust Co. *v*. Eaton, 140 Mass. 532, there is considerable doubt as to whether a trustee is obliged to repair a premium paid by him. The actual decision goes no further than to hold that a trustee who had done so had acted properly. Moreover, there was a strong dissent by three of the seven judges and the decision of Hemenway *v*. Hemenway, 134 Mass. 446, was not expressly overruled, although the minority considered that case inconsistent with the majority opinion. In the last cited case, which was a bill for instructions by trustees under a will, the trustees had bought a comparatively few railroad bonds at a small

---

(*a*) But it has been held that part of this profit should be ap-

portioned to income where there has been default in the payment of

§ 548.   If there is a *positive direction* in a will that the trustees shall convert the personal property into government or

premium. The court refused to lay down any general rule which would control all cases of bonds bought at a premium, but said, "The trustee, who has the fund always in his hands and under his eyes, must take reasonable care to hold the balance even between opposing interests." It was found as a fact in this case that the balance had been evenly held, and the court refused to hold that the fact of payment of a small premium was not, of itself alone, enough to prevent those entitled to income from receiving the entire net interest on the bonds. In view of these two cases, the safe course for trustees to follow in Massachusetts seems to be, to set aside a proportional part of each interest payment to replace the premium paid by them.

If the intention of the creator of the trust appears to have been that wasting premiums should not be replaced out of current interest, of course that intention controls. Shaw *v.* Cordis, 143 Mass. 443; Matter of Hoyt, 160 N. Y. 607. But it has been held in a recent New York case that the premiums must be repaired unless an intention to the

contrary appears in the very clearest manner. The purpose of the court was to furnish a rule which trustees could safely follow. Matter of Stevens, 187 N. Y. 471.

Where bonds which are rated at a premium are part of the identical property left by the testator and the trustees have properly allowed the investment to remain, deductions should not be made from current interest to replace the wasting premium, unless it appears that the creator of the trust intended that such provision should be made. Conn. Trust, etc., Co.'s Appeal, 80 Conn. 540; Sargent *v.* Sargent, 103 Mass. 297; Robertson *v.* De Brulatour, 188 N. Y. 301; Matter of Stevens, 187 N. Y. 471. See also Reed *v.* Head, 6 Allen, 174; Lynde *v.* Lynde, 99 N. Y. S. 283, 113 App. Div. 411.

If bonds are sold at a larger premium than was paid for them, all the increase belongs to the principal. Matter of Gerry, 103 N. Y. 445; Matter of Proctor, 85 Hun, 572; N. E. Trust Co. *v.* Eaton, 140 Mass. 532; Graham's Estate, 198 Pa. St. 216. But see Park's Estate, 173 Pa. St. 190.

---

income. Parker *v.* Seeley, 56 N. J. Eq. 110. See Fanning *v.* Main, 77 Conn. 94. But see Park's Estate, 173 Pa. St. 190. This is upon the theory that part of the purchase money on foreclosure sale must be taken to be unpaid interest to which the life beneficiary was entitled. Accordingly, in Parker *v.* Seeley, the

profit was apportioned between income and principal in the ratio that the unpaid interest bore to the principal of the mortgage debt.

Where, however, a trustee bought in real estate at a receiver's sale in order to protect the interest of the estate in a partnership and later realized a profit on the sale of the

real securities, and hold them in trust for one for life and remainder over, the *cestui que trust* for life is entitled to receive only so much income as would have arisen from the personal estate if converted and invested at the date of the testator's death. If, therefore, a security bearing a much higher rate of interest remains undisposed of, they cannot pay the whole interest so arising to the tenant for life; and if they pay to him the whole extra interest, they would be liable to make good to the remainder-man the difference between what should have been paid under the above rule, and the sum actually paid.[1] If they afterwards dispose of the security, thus bearing a higher rate of interest, more advantageously than they could have done within the year, they will not be allowed to reimburse themselves for the sums they are liable to pay to the remainder-man; but they will be charged with all the interest they received,

[1] Dimes *v.* Scott, 4 Russ. 195.

property, no part of the profit was given to income. Neel's Estate, 207 Pa. St. 446. See also Slocum *v.* Ames, 19 R. I. 401. The two cases are not inconsistent, because in the latter case no income was invested in the purchase.

In cases where there has been a default in the payment of both principal and interest of a debt due the trustee, *e. g.*, a debt secured by mortgage, and the sum realized on foreclosure is insufficient to make good both principal and interest, the net sum realized must be apportioned between principal and income in the ratio that the principal of the debt bears to the unpaid interest on it at the agreed rate. Hagan *v.* Platt, 48 N. J. Eq. 206; Tuttle's Case, 49 N. J. Eq. 259; Trenton Trust, etc., Co. *v.* Donnelly, 65 N. J. Eq. 119; Meldon *v.* Devlin, 31 App. Div. (N. Y.) 146; Parsons *v.* Winslow, 16 Mass. 361; *In re* Hubbuck, [1896] 1 Ch. 754; *In re* Alston, [1901] 2 Ch. 584. See also Greene *v.* Greene, 19 R. I. 619. But the life tenant's claim to any part of the sum ultimately realized is absolutely dependent upon the default in the payment of interest on income that was due him. See *In re* Taylor's Trusts, [1905] 1 Ch. 734; Slocum *v.* Ames, 19 R. I. 401.

The expense of carrying the property after foreclosure should be paid in the first instance from principal of the trust fund if the property itself is unproductive. *In re* Pitney, 99 N. Y. S. 588, 113 App. Div. 845. But this expense should be deducted from the gross proceeds realized upon a sale of the property. Neel's Estate, 207 Pa. St. 446; Trenton Trust, etc., Co. *v.* Donnelly, 65 N. J. Eq. 119.

and with the full amount for which they sold the securities, and will be credited only with the amount that they should have paid the tenant for life.[1]   It is said, however, that if there is no express direction in the will for conversion, the trustees will be justified in paying over to the tenant for life all the income received from the securities, whatever the rate of interest,[2] for trustees have a discretion to convert or not as they see fit.[3] (a)

[1] Dimes v. Scott, 4 Russ. 195.

[2] Howe v. Dartmouth, 7 Ves. 150; Williamson v. Williamson, 6 Paige, 303; Prendergast v. Prendergast, 3 H. L. Cas. 195; Meyer v. Simonson, 5 De G. & Sm. 726.

[3] Yates v. Yates, 28 Beav. 637.

(a) When there has been an express or implied direction to convert the property into a certain kind of investment or when conversion is necessary because the fund is not properly invested, the question frequently arises as to what income the life beneficiary should receive during the period between the testator's death and the actual conversion. The actual income is frequently more, and sometimes less, than the income of the trust funds when properly invested. When the testator has indicated his intention that all of the actual income, and no more, during the period of delay shall go to the life beneficiaries, there is no reason why that intention should not be carried out, if the delay has been a proper one. See Rowlls v. Bebb, [1900] 2 Ch. 107; Re Leonard, 43 L. T. 664.

But when there is nothing in the will to show his intention one way or the other, the well established rule of the courts is to treat the fund as equitably converted into the proper investments as of the date of the testator's death, and to give the life beneficiaries the equitable income, i. e., income at the rate which the converted fund would have earned if invested at that date. Any excess of actual income is treated as part of the principal and any deficiency of actual income is to be made up from the *corpus* of the fund unless there is a sufficient reason for making the trustee pay it. Edwards v. Edwards, 183 Mass. 581; Kinmonth v. Brigham, 5 Allen, 270; Westcott v. Nickerson, 120 Mass. 410; Mudge v. Parker, 139 Mass. 153; Minot v. Thompson, 106 Mass. 583; Healey v. Toppan, 45 N. H. 243; Willard's Ex'r v. Willard, 21 A. 463 (N. J. Ch. 1891); Brown v. Gellatly, 2 Ch. 751; Greene v. Greene, 19 R. I. 619.

The method of finding the amounts which should belong respectively to principal and income is to treat the total amount of the proceeds upon actual conversion and the actual net income received less the expenses of conversion, as the principal and income of a sum invested at the testator's death at

§ 549. The trustee must exert himself equally to protect the tenant for life and the remainder-man. Therefore, if there

a rate of interest which it would have earned if then invested in the authorized manner. Thus, suppose the converted property realizes $100,000 net at the end of one year, and that the actual net income received before conversion amounts to $6,000; assuming that the equitable rate of income is 4 per cent, the equitable *corpus* at the time of conversion will be found by dividing $106,000 by $1.04, giving $101,923.08 as the equitable principal and $4,076.92 as the equitable income. If the conversion has been delayed for a period of more than a year and nothing has been paid as income, the equitable income should be reckoned at compound interest. Edwards *v.* Edwards, 183 Mass. 581; Greene *v.* Greene, 19 R. I. 619.

Mr. Lewin has suggested that where the income of the life tenant remains in the business after the first year a proportion of the actual profits should be given the equitable life tenant to the extent that the profits are attributable to his share of income remaining in the business. Lewin (11th ed.), 337; *In re* Hill, 50 L. J. Ch. 551. Possibly the Massachusetts court had this in mind when in several cases it reckoned equitable interest of the life beneficiary at 6 per cent, the *corpus* having been tied up in business and earning more than 6 per cent. Westcott *v.* Nickerson, 120 Mass. 410; Kinmonth *v.* Brigham, 5 Allen, 270.

In England where the original property was unproductive of income, *e. g.*, was a reversionary interest, the courts used to reckon

the equitable income at 4 per cent, but in recent cases, they have reduced the rate to 3 per cent. *In re* Goodenough, [1895] 2 Ch. 537; Rowlls *v.* Bebb, [1900] 2 Ch. 107.

Recent cases in England have held that the rule does not apply to income producing real estate when the sale has not been improperly postponed, even when the trustee is not authorized by the will to postpone conversion; and the life tenant is given the full income. *In re* Oliver, [1908] 2 Ch. 74; *In re* Searle, [1900] 2 Ch. 829; *In re* Darnley, [1907] 1 Ch. 159. See also Hope *v.* D'Hédouville, [1893] 2 Ch. 361; Casamajor *v.* Strode, 19 Ves. 390, n.; Lewin (11th ed.), 339. But in these cases the actual income was apparently as large as the equitable income would have been. None of them was a case like Edwards *v.* Edwards, 183 Mass. 581, where the unconverted property was unproductive land and conversion was delayed because of inability to find a purchaser at the proper price. It is doubtful if many jurisdictions in America will follow the English decisions in making this distinction between personalty and real estate.

It has also been held in England that the rule of Howe *v.* Dartmouth has no application to trusts established by deed. Re Van Straubenzee, [1901] 2 Ch. 779.

When it appears that the testator intended that until the trust property should actually be converted, the actual income, and that only, should be paid to the life beneficiary, his intention controls. *In re* Hab-

are reversionary interests or rights that may not fall in during the life of the tenant for life, so that he can enjoy a benefit

buck, [1896] 1 Ch. 754; Mackie *v.* Mackie, 5 Hare, 70; Hope *v.* D' Hédouville, [1893] 2 Ch. 361; Jordan *v.* Jordan, 192 Mass. 337, 344. If he has given his trustees or executors authority to continue the investments unconverted at their discretion, this fact is considered by some courts a strong indication that he intended the actual income to be paid to the life beneficiary. Buckingham *v.* Morrison, 136 Ill. 437; Hite's Devisees *v.* Hite's Ex'r, 93 Ky. 257; Heighe *v.* Littig, 63 Md. 301; Green *v.* Crapo, 181 Mass. 55; Outcalt *v.* Appleby, 36 N. J. Eq. 73; *In re* Thomas, [1891] 3 Ch. 482. See Patterson *v.* Vivian, 117 N. Y. S. 504. But this fact is not usually conclusive as to his intention. Brown *v.* Gellatly, 2 Ch. 751; Westcott *v.* Nickerson, 120 Mass. 410; Mudge *v.* Parker, 139 Mass. 153.

The effect of the Englsh decisions on this point seems to be that authority to delay conversion will be presumed to have been given for the benefit of the whole estate, and not for the purpose of enabling the trustee to vary the rights of the life tenant and remainder-man. In the absence of an apparent intention that the discretion to postpone conversion was given to be exercised for the benefit of either of the parties in interest and in the absence of a positive direction, that pending conversion the actual income was to be paid to the life tenant, the rule seems to be to adjust the rights of the parties in interest as if the conversion had been made at the

date of the testator's death. Thus it has been held that authority to trustees to postpone conversion without naming any particular investment does not entitle the life tenant to the actual income of wasting investments such as leaseholds and annuities. Porter *v.* Baddeley, 5 Ch. Div. 542; Blake *v.* O'Reilly, [1895] 1 Ir. R. 479; Rowlls *v.* Bebb, [1900] 2 Ch. 107. See Walker *v.* Shore, 19 Ves. 387.

But where the testator has authorized his trustees to postpone conversion as long as they think fit and pending conversion to pay the actual income to the tenant for life, it has been held that the entire profits of the testator's business should go to the life tenant, the trustees having delayed conversion for two years for the purpose of selling it profitably as a going concern. *In re* Chancellor, 26 Ch. Div. 42. See also *In re* Crowther, [1895] 2 Ch. 56; *In re* Smith, [1896] 1 Ch. 171. It was, however, intimated that it would have been otherwise if they had continued the business for the purpose of earning profits since that would not have been a proper exercise of their discretion.

Where trustees have been given the absolute discretion whether or not to convert at all, as well as discretion as to time, the actual income, and that only, would usually, if not always, be given to the life tenant. *Re* Leonard, 43 L. T. 664; *In re* Pitcairn, [1896] 2 Ch. 199; Yates *v.* Yates, 28 Beav. 637.

In a recent English decision where a trustee had improperly

from them, the trustee must sell and convert them into money
if they have a value and admit of conversion.[1] As the tenant
for life, if entitled to the possession, is a *quasi* or implied trustee
for the remainder-man, and is accountable for the highest good
faith,[2] so the trustee and the remainder-man must exercise the
like good faith towards the tenant for life; and if they join in
evicting him from the possession, they will be compelled to
make good the rent, whether they received any or not, and that
without any equitable allowances.[3] (*a*)

§ 550.   In Sitwell *v.* Bernard, the testator directed his personal estate to be laid out in lands to be settled upon A. for life
with remainder over, and that "the interest of his personal
estate," meaning interest upon debts due that could not be
collected immediately, "should be accumulated and laid out
in lands to be settled to the same uses." Of course, if the
collections of some outstanding debts were deferred for a considerable time, and the interest accumulated as directed, the
tenant for life would lose the income of all the estates to be
purchased with the accumulated interest. To obviate this
hardship upon the tenant for life, the court confined the accumu-

---

[1] Howe *v.* Dartmouth, 7 Ves. 150; Fearns *v.* Young, 9 Ves. 549; Dimes
v. Scott, 4 Russ. 200; *ante*, § 450. [*Supra*, § 548, note.]

[2] *Ante*, § 540.

[3] Kaye *v.* Powell, 1 Ves. Jr. 408.

used trust funds in his own business,
paying 5 per cent interest and later
repaying the principal, it was held
that none of the 5 per cent should
be given to the principal, although
the fund if properly invested would
not have yielded so large an investment. Slade *v.* Chaine, [1908]
1 Ch. 522.

The doctrine set forth in the
foregoing note is confined to cases
of delayed conversion and has not
been extended to cases of improper
investments by the trustee.

(*a*) If trustees have a discretion
as to the manner of raising a charge,
and the remainder is prejudiced by
their postponing the raising of the
charge from a wasting security, the
court may adjust the burden of the
charge according to the parties' interests and require the tenant for
life to contibute. Blake *v.* O'Reilly,
[1895] 1 Ir. R. 479; *In re* Harrison,
43 Ch. D. 55; *In re* Muffett, 39 Ch.
Div. 534.

lation to one year from the testator's death, on the ground that one year was allowed for settling estates and collecting debts, and that, at the expiration of that time, the trustees should be presumed to be ready to make the investment as directed; and if it was not made at that time, that the tenant for life would be entitled to the interest received upon the personal estate, in the place of the income that he would receive from the real estate if the investment was made at the end of one year.[1] On the other hand, if a testator devises his real estate to be sold, and the proceeds thereof, and the rents and profits in the meantime, to be laid out in securities to be settled on A. for life, with remainders over, the accumulation of the rents and profits will be allowed for only one year; that is, there will be one year allowed for the sale of the estate, and the rents and profits may accumulate for that time. If the investment is not then made, the tenant for life is entitled to the rents and profits, as if the sale and investment had been made, and until it is made.[2] From the expressions used by Lord Eldon, in the case of Sitwell *v.* Bernard, it was supposed that in no case could the tenant for life receive any part of the income, where there was a direction to convert personalty into land, or land into personalty; and it was so determined in two cases,[3] but it is now settled that the tenants for life shall have the first year's income, where there is no express direction to accumulate.[4] (*a*)

[1] Sitwell *v.* Bernard, 6 Ves. 520; Entwistle *v.* Markland, and Stuart *v.* Bruere, cited 6 Ves. 528, 529; Griffith *v.* Morrison, cited 1 J. & W. 311; Tucker *v.* Boswell, 5 Beav. 607; Kilvington *v.* Gray, 2 S. & S. 396; Parry *v.* Warrington, 6 Madd. 155; Stair *v.* Macgill, 1 Bligh (N. s.), 662; Walker *v.* Shore, 19 Ves. 387; Taylor *v.* Clark, 1 Hare, 167; Cassamajor *v.* Pearson, 8 Cl. & Fin. 69.

[2] Noel *v.* Henley, 7 Price, 241; Vickers *v.* Scott, 3 Myl. & K. 500; Vigor *v.* Harwood, 12 Sim. 172; Greisley *v.* Chesterfield, 13 Beav. 288; Beauland *v.* Halliwell, 1 C. P. Coop. t. Cott. 169, note (a).

[3] Sitwell *v.* Bernard, 6 Ves. 520; State *v.* Hollingworth, 3 Madd. 161; Taylor *v.* Hibbert, 1 J. & W. 388.

[4] Angerstein *v.* Martin, T. & R. 238; Hewitt *v.* Morris, id. 244; Mac-

(*a*) The general rule is now well established that when property is devised or bequeathed in trust to pay the income to a person for life

§ 551.   The rule, that a tenant for life has an interest in the first year's income, varies according to the circumstances of

pherson v. Macpherson, 16 Jur. 847; Green v. Blackwell, 32 N. J. Eq. 773; Van Blarcom v. Dager, 31 id. 783.

or for a limited time, he is entitled to either actual or equitable income from the date of the testator's death, unless the testator has indicated an intention that the enjoyment of income shall not begin until some later date. Cal. Civ. Code (1903), §§ 1366, 1368; Mass. Rev. Laws (1902), c. 141, § 24; Jordan v. Jordan, 192 Mass. 337, 345; Sargent v. Sargent, 103 Mass. 297; Keith v. Copeland, 138 Mass. 303; Weld v. Putnam, 70 Me. 209; Doherty v. Grady, 72 A. 869 (Me. 1908); Wethered v. Safe Dep. & Tr. Co., 79 Md. 153; Matter of Stanfield, 135 N. Y. 292; Bank of Niagara v. Talbot, 110 App. Div. (N. Y.) 519 (affirmed 184 N. Y. 576); Flickwir's Estate, 136 Pa. St. 374; Eichelberger's Estate, 170 Pa. St. 242; Baker v. Fooks, 8 Del. Ch. 84; Bishop v. Bishop, 81 Conn. 509; Macpherson v. Macpherson, 16 Jur. 847; Lewin (11th ed.), 333. See also In re Whitehead, [1894] 1 Ch. 678.

In a case where a certain share of income was directed to be paid to A. "quarterly during his natural life," and A. died three days before the end of the first quarter, it was held that his estate was nevertheless entitled to the income up to the time of his death. Union Safe Dep., etc., Co. v. Dudley, 104 Me. 297. To the same effect see Welch v. Apthorp, 203 Mass. 249; In re Hoyt, 116 N. Y. App. Div. 217 (189 N. Y. 511); In re Keogh, 98 N. Y. S. 433, 112 App. Div. 414.

Any income which accumulates in the hands of executors before the principal is turned over to trustees should be treated by the trustees as income, if the life beneficiary is entitled to it under the rules of law. Cushing v. Burrell, 137 Mass. 21; Smith v. Fellows, 131 Mass. 20. And if for any reason income to which the life beneficiary is entitled has meantime been invested, its earnings also belong to him. Lovering v. Minot, 9 Cush. 151.

When the trust principal is a residue which cannot be exactly ascertained until after the payment of debts and legacies which do not bear interest during the first year after the testator's death, it has been held, and seems to be the rule in England, that the life tenant should be given, not the income of the whole estate, but the income only of so much of the estate as is ultimately to constitute the trust fund. This principal of the residuary estate is to be determined by deducting from the entire fund out of which debts and legacies are to be paid, the sum which, "together with the income of such part for a year, will be wanted for the payment of debts, legacies, and other charges, during the year; and the proper and necessary fund must be ascertained by including the income for one year which may arise upon the fund which may be so wanted." Allhusen v. Whittell, 4 Eq. 295.

In making these adjustments as

each case. Mr. Lewin[1] states the following propositions and distinctions, gathered from the cases: (1) The tenant for life of a residue is not entitled to the income accruing, during the delay allowed for the payment of the legacies, on so much of the testator's property as is subsequently applied in paying them.[2] (2) If a testator desires that his personal estate shall be laid out and invested either in government or real securities in trust for one for life, with remainders over; or in a purchase of lands, with a direction, express or implied, for the investment thereof in the meantime in government or real security, and that the lands to be purchased shall be in trust for A. for life, with remainders over, — the income of the "government and real securities," of which the testator was possessed at the time of his death, these being the very investments contemplated by his will, belongs from the time of the death to the tenant for life.[3] (3) If the sale and investment, or conversion, is made immediately, during the first year, the tenant for life is entitled to the produce of the property in the converted form "from the time of the conversion," although the trustee had the whole year to convert it.[4] (4) Where, at the death of the testator, the property is not in the state in which it is directed to be, the tenant for life, before the conversion, is entitled, as the court has decided, not to the actual produce, but to a reasonable fruit of the property, from the death of the

[1] Lewin on Trusts, 247, 248, 249 (5th ed.). [11th ed., 337–349.]

[2] Holgate v. Jennings, 24 Beav. 623; Crawley v. Crawley, 7 Sim. 427; Crawley v. Dixon, 23 Beav. 512; Fletcher v. Stevenson, 9 Hare, 371. [See In re Whitehead, [1894] 1 Ch. 678; Allhusen v. Whittell, 4 Eq. 295; supra, § 550, note a.]

[3] Hewitt v. Morris, T. & R. 241; La Terriere v. Bulmer, 2 Sim. 18; Angerstein v. Martin, T. & R. 232; Caldicott v. Caldicott, 1 Y. & C. Ch. 337. [See supra, § 548, note a.]

[4] La Terriere v. Bulmer, 2 Sim. 18; Gibson v. Bott, 7 Ves. 89; Angerstein v. Martin, T. &. R. 240. [See supra, § 548, note a.]

between principal and income, interest upon such debts as bear interest should be treated as payable from income. Marshall v. Crowther, 2 Ch. Div. 199.

testator up to the time of the conversion, whether made in the course of the first year or subsequently; as, if personal estate is directed to be laid out in government or real securities, and part of the personal estate consists of bonds, stocks, &c., not being government or real securities, the tenant for life is entitled to the dividends from the death of the testator, or so much three per cent consolidated bank annuities as such part of the personal estate, not being government or real securities, would have purchased at the expiration of one year from the testator's death.[1]   (5) Where the non-conversion is attended with any risk to the property, as in case of bonds, &c., the remainder-man, whose interest is thus imperilled, has a right to share in the extra profit of the annual produce;[2] but suppose land to have yielded a rental beyond what would have been the annual produce of the purchase-money, and there has been no depreciation, can the remainder-man call back the extra rent received by the tenant for life; or, as the remainder-man gets all that was ever intended for him, viz., the undepreciated property, may the tenant for life keep the full rent? (a) If not, then conversely, if the land yields no annual fruit, or less than what the purchase-money would yield, the tenant for life should have a claim against the remainder-man.[3]   But if the tenant for life is also a trustee for sale, and neglects to sell, he cannot be allowed to put into his own pocket the higher annual produce which has arisen "from his own" laches; for no trustee can derive a profit from the exercise or non-exercise of his own

[1] Dimes v. Scott, 4 Russ. 495; Douglass v. Congreve, 1 Keen, 410; Taylor v. Clark, 1 Hare, 161; Morgan v. Morgan, 14 Beav. 72; Holgate v. Jennings, 24 Beav. 623; Llewellyn's Trust, 29 id. 171; Hume v. Richardson, 8 Jur. (N. S.) 686. [See *supra*, § 548, note *a*.]

[2] Dimes v. Scott, 4 Russ. 495; Stroud v. Gwyer, 28 Beav. 130.

[3] Yates v. Yates, 28 Beav. 637. [Edwards v. Edwards, 183 Mass. 581.]

(a) It has been held that he can, but on the ground that the rule of Howe v. Dartmouth does not apply to land. *In re* Oliver, [1908] 2 Ch. 74; *In re* Searle, [1900] 2 Ch. 829; *In re* Darnley, [1907] 1 Ch. 159. See Hope v. D'Hédouville, [1893] 2 Ch. 361; Casamajor v. Strode, 19 Ves. 390, n.

office.[1] (6) In Gibson v. Bott,[2] leaseholds from a defect of title could not be sold, and the court gave the tenant for life interest at four per cent on the value from the death of the testator. It does not appear from the report at what time the value was to be taken; but according to recent cases it should have been ascertained at the expiration of one year from the testator's death.[3] (7) If a testator's estate comprises funds not immediately convertible, but receivable by instalments, such as a testator's share in a partnership, assessed at a certain sum and payable by instalments, carrying interest at five per cent, the tenant for life is allowed four per cent, from the death of the testator, on the value taken at the expiration of one year from the testator's death.[4] (8) If it appears from the terms of the will, that the testator intended to give his trustees a discretion as to the time of conversion, which discretion has been fairly exercised, and that the tenant for life was to have the actual income until conversion, the case must be governed by the testator's intention, and not by the general rule.[5]

[1] Wightwick v. Lord, 6 H. L. Cas. 217.

[2] 7 Ves. 89.

[3] Caldicott v. Caldicott, 1 Y. & C. Ch. 312; Sutherland v. Cook, 1 Col. C. C. 503. [See supra, § 550, note a.]

[4] Llewellyn's Trust, 29 Beav. 171; Meyer v. Simonson, 5 De G. & Sm. 723. [See Rowlls v. Bebb, [1900] 2 Ch. 107; In re Goodenough, [1895] 2 Ch. 537; Wentworth v. Wentworth, [1900] A. C. 163.]

[5] Mackie v. Mackie, 5 Hare, 70; Wrey v. Smith, 14 Sim. 202; Sparling v. Parker, 9 Beav. 524; Johnstone v. Moore, 4 Jur. (N. S.) 356; Murray v. Glasse, 17 Jur. 816. [See Blake v. O'Reilly, [1895] 1 Ir. R. 479; Rowlls v. Bebb, [1900] 2 Ch. 107, to the effect that merely giving trustees discretion as to the time of conversion is not usually sufficient to show an intention that they have the right to vary the interests of the life tenants and the remainder-men. See also § 548, note a.]

Mr. Hill says, that "the interest which the tenant for life will take during the first year after the testator's death is yet an unsettled question. This question admits of four possible solutions, and the decisions of very eminent judges may be urged in support of each: (1) First, the tenant for life may be entitled to nothing until the expiration of a twelvemonth from the testator's death, according to the opinion of Sir John Leach in Scott v. Hollingworth, 3 Madd. 161; Vickers v. Scott, 3 Myl. & K. 509, and of Sir Thos. Plumer in Taylor v. Hibbert, 1 J. & W. 308 (see Tucker v. Boswell, 5 Beav. 607); and the income in the meantime is to be added

§ 552. The liability of the equitable tenant for life in respect to repairs and waste is substantially the same as the

to and form a part of the capital of the residue. Both those learned judges
appear to have assumed that this opinion was in accordance with the established rule of the court, and Sir Thos. Plumer treats this general rule as
having been so settled by Lord Eldon in the case of Sitwell *v.* Bernard,
6 Ves. 522. However, in the subsequent case of Angerstein *v.* Martin, T.
& R. 238, and see Hewitt *v.* Morris, id. 244, that great judge himself dis-
claimed any intention of establishing any such general rule by his decision
in Sitwell *v.* Bernard, 6 Ves. 522, — a decision which he stated to have been
founded on the direction to accumulate, which formed an ingredient in
that case; and his lordship's further observations on the decisions in Sitwell
v. Bernard and Scott *v.* Hollingworth have materially weakened the authority
of those cases, if indeed they do not expressly overrule them. The case of
Vickers *v.* Scott, 3 Myl. & K. 500, arose upon real estate, which was directed
to be sold, and the point in question does not seem to have been much argued
in that case. (2) According to the decision of A. Hart, V. C., in La Terriere
v. Bulmer, 2 Sim. 18, the *cestui que trust* for life during the first year after
the testator's death will take the income of such parts of the estate as are
properly invested at the testator's death, or may become so invested during
that year. Lord Eldon's decisions in Gibson *v.* Bott, 7 Ves. 95; Hewitt *v.*
Morris, T. & R. 241, are also in favor of this doctrine, which is also strongly
supported by the observations of Sir J. Wigram, V. C., in the recent case of
Taylor *v.* Clark, 1 Hare, 173. See also Caldicott *v.* Caldicott, 1 Younge &
C. Ch. 312. (3) The tenant for life may be entitled to the income arising
from the property in its existing state during the first year from the testator's
death. And this view of the law is supported by Lord Eldon's decision in the
case of Angerstein *v.* Martin, T. & R. 232, and that of Lord Langdale, M. R.,
in Douglass *v.* Congreve, 1 Keen, 410. It has been observed by Vice-
Chancellor Wigram, 1 Hare, 172, 1 Younge & C. Ch. 318, that it might be
a question whether Lord Eldon's decree in Angerstein *v.* Martin was intended to impeach the law as laid down in La Terriere *v.* Bulmer; and even
if such were Lord Eldon's intentions, it must have been considered as overruled in Lord Lyndhurst's decision in Dimes *v.* Scott, 4 Russ. 209. The
later case of Douglass *v.* Congreve, 1 Keen, 410, which is clearly inconsistent with Dimes *v.* Scott, was also strongly questioned by Vice-Chancellor
Wigram in the recent case of Taylor *v.* Clark, 1 Hare, 172, in which all
the authorities on this subject are collected and reviewed, and his honor's
decision, in which he followed Dimes *v.* Scott in preference to Douglass *v.*
Congreve, is directly at variance with the latter case. (4) According to
the determination of Lord Lyndhurst in Dimes *v.* Scott, the tenant for
life will take, not the interest actually arising from the property during
the first year after the testator's death, but the amount of the dividends
on so much three per cent stock as would have been produced by the conversion of the property at the end of that year. And this solution of the

liability of a legal tenant for life,[1] except that the trustee cannot interfere with the possession of the equitable tenant for
life if he neglects to repair; nor for permissive waste,[2] if there is
nothing in the settlement that gives him the management or
control of the estate.   A legal tenant for life may cut timber
for repairs,[3] though he cannot cut timber for sale, or to pay for
repairs.[4]   So a trustee may cut timber for repairs, if the tenant
for life will furnish the means for using the timber in repairing;

question has recently been adopted by Vice-Chancellor Wigram in the
case of Taylor *v.* Clark, 1 Hare, 161." Hill on Trustees, pp. 388, 389.

Mr. Hill further observes, "that, in this conflict of authority, the question can be put to rest only by the decision of the court of the highest authority. And that in the mean time the fourth alternative, as established by
Lord Chancellor Lyndhurst in Dimes *v.* Scott, 4 Russ. 299, and adopted in
Taylor *v.* Clark, 1 Hare, 172, must be considered as carrying with it the
greatest authority in its favor." Mr. Spence, Eq. Jur. 564, fully discusses
the authorities, and approves of Dimes *v.* Scott. That case was also followed in Morgan *v.* Morgan, 14 Beav. 72, in which the case of Douglass
v. Congreve was overruled. Holgate *v.* Jennings, 24 Beav. 623; *Re* Llewellyn's
Trust, 29 Beav. 171; Hume *v.* Richardson, 8 Jur. (N. S.) 686, followed Dimes
v. Scott. And see Robinson *v.* Robinson, 1 De G., M. & G. 247; Scholefern
v. Redfen, 2 Dr. & Sm. 173; 32 L. J. Ch. 627; Meyer *v.* Simonson, 5 De G.
& Sm. 726.

In the United States, the question has not been largely discussed, but
in Evans *v.* Inglehart, 6 G. & J. 191, and Williamson *v.* Williamson, 6 Paige,
303, the court assumed that the law was correctly stated in the third alternative, or in Angerstein *v.* Martin, 2 Sim. 18. In Massachusetts, the
matter is regulated by statute, that the tenant for life shall be entitled to
the income for the first year upon the fund given for his use. Gen. Stat.
c. 97, § 23 [R. L. (1902) c. 141, § 24]; Sohier *v.* Eldredge, 103 Mass. 351;
Sargent *v.* Sargent, id. 297; Brown *v.* Gellaty, L. R. 2 Ch. 751; Lamb *v.*
Lamb, 11 Pick. 371; Minot *v.* Amory, 2 Cush. 377, 388; Lovering *v.*
Minot, 9 id. 151. [For recent American decisions to the same effect,
see *supra*, § 550, note *a*.]

[1] Powys *v.* Blagrave, 4 De G., M. & G. 458, and cases cited; Harnett
v. Maitland, 16 M. & W. 257.

[2] Powys *v.* Blagrave, Kay, 495; 4 De G., M. & G. 448; *Re* Skingley,
3 M. & G. 221; Gregg *v.* Coates, 23 Beav. 33. [*In re* Courtier, 34 Ch. Div.
136; *In re* Hotchkys, 32 Ch. Div. 408; *In re* Cartwright, 41 Ch. Div. 532.]

[3] Co. Litt. 54 b.

[4] Co. Litt. 53 b; Gower *v.* Eyre, G. Coop. 156; Marlborough *v.* St. John,
5 De G. & Sm. 181. [Armstrong *v.* Wilson, 60 Ill. 226; Noyes *v.* Stone, 163
Mass. 490; McKee *v.* Dail, 1 Tenn. Ch. App. 689.]

for the trustee can sell no timber for repairs, nor can he use any other trust funds for the purpose, unless specially authorized by the instrument of trust. Nor can the trustees raise any sum out of, or make any charge upon, the *corpus* of the estate itself for repairs, however the want of such repairs may be occasioned.[1] (*a*) The equitable tenant for life must defray the expenses of such repairs out of his own income, or the trustee must defray them out of the interest of the tenant for life. The repairs of the tenant for life are his own voluntary act; and, however substantial and beneficial to the estate and the remainder-man, he can make no claim for them upon the inheritance. Nor would a court, upon his application, direct any repairs to be made at the expense of the remainder-man;[2] though it was said in one case that the rule might not be without exception; as where an estate was settled to certain uses, and a fund was directed to be applied to the purchase of an estate to be settled to the same uses, it might be more beneficial to the remainder-man that part of the fund should be applied to the repair and preservation of the estate already settled.[3] (*b*) It would be an extraordinary case, however, to

[1] *Ante*, § 477; Bostock *v.* Blakeney, 2 Bro. Ch. 653; Hibbert *v.* Cooke, 1 S. & S. 552; Nairn *v.* Majoribanks, 3 Russ. 582; Caldicott *v.* Brown, 2 Hare, 144; Thurston *v.* Dickinson, 2 Rich. Eq. 317; Cogswell *v.* Cogswell, 2 Edw. Ch. 231; Jones *v.* Dawson, 19 Ala. 672; Thurston *v.* Thurston, 6 R. I. 296; Martin's App., 23 Penn. St. 438. In this case it was doubted if it was constitutional for the legislature to authorize such an expenditure by the trustee.

[2] Amory *v.* Lowell, 104 Mass. 265; Hibbert *v.* Cooke, 1 S. & S. 552; Caldicott *v.* Brown, 2 Hare, 144; Bostock *v.* Blakeney, 2 Bro. Ch. 653; Hamer *v.* Tilsley, Johns. (Eng.) 486; Dent *v.* Dent, 30 Beav. 363; Nairn *v.* Marjoribanks, 3 Russ. 582; Corbett *v.* Laurens, 5 Rich. Eq. 301; Sharshaw *v.* Gibbs, 1 Kay, 333.

[3] Caldicott *v.* Brown, 2 Hare, 145; *Re* Barrington's Est., 1 John. & H. 142.

(*a*) But see note (*b*), *infra* this section.

(*b*) The strict rule that a life tenant cannot make the remainder-man pay for permanent improvements and alterations which benefit the estate in remainder ought not to be applied to trustees who have the duty of managing the trust property for the interests of both;

Justify such a proceeding.[1] But where trustees are directed to purchase, or invest in real estate, they may put such estate

[1] Dunne v. Dunne, 3 Sm. & Gif. 22; 7 De G., M. & G. 207; Dent v. Dent, 30 Beav. 363.

and cases frequently arise where the trustee has the authority to use the trust principal to pay for outlay upon the trust property which he cannot properly pay, from income. See *supra*, § 477, and notes.

Repairs of the ordinary kind, such as are made to keep the property in as good condition as when it became part of the trust estate, should be paid out of income. Little v. Little, 161 Mass. 188; Abell v. Brady, 79 Md. 94; Jordan v. Jordan, 192 Mass. 337, 343; Smith v. Keteltas, 70 N. Y. S. 1065, 62 App. Div. 174; *In re* Tracy, 83 N. Y. S. 1049, 87 App. Div. 215.

But the expense of permanent improvements, such as are likely to outlast the life estate, or of permanent alterations should not be charged to income, but should be paid from the *corpus* if the trustee had the right to use *corpus* for this purpose. Abell v. Brady, 79 Md. 94, 101; *In re* Parr, 92 N. Y. S. 990; Boon v. Hall, 78 N. Y. S. 557, 76 App. Div. 520; Smith v. Keteltas, 70 N. Y. S. 1065, 62 App. Div. 174; Stevens v. Melcher, 152 N. Y. 551; Greene v. Greene, 19 R. I. 619. Thus the cost of changing into stores the lower story of buildings which had been used as dwelling houses has been held to have been properly charged to principal, as was also the cost of changing an apartment hotel into an office building. But the cost of entirely re-plumbing a house, repapering, paint-

ing, and putting in a new elevator to replace an old one, all amounting to nearly double the annual rent, has been held to have been properly charged to income. Little v. Little, 161 Mass. 188. New construction, such as entirely rebuilding, would usually come out of principal, although the result is to increase the income. Stevens v. Melcher, 152 N. Y. 551; Smith v. Keteltas, 70 N. Y. S. 1065, 62 App. Div. 174. And the duty to pay for repairs and to repair waste out of income does not usually oblige a trustee to set aside a sinking fund out of income for the purpose of rebuilding when structures on the property shall become antiquated. Smith v. Keteltas, 70 N. Y. S. 1065, 62 App. Div. 174.

Where alterations and additions benefit both the life tenant and the remainder-man, the courts will not usually set aside or revise the trustee's apportionment unless it is clearly wrong. Little v. Little, 161 Mass. 188 ; Jordan v. Jordan, 192 Mass. 337.

Where trustees with power to sell property left by the testator and to reinvest, choose to retain the property and expend considerable sums in repairs and alterations, it has been held that the expense might be properly charged to principal as a new investment of trust funds. Sohier v. Eldredge, 103 Mass. 345. But this is not necessarily true of all repairs needed at the

in tenantable repair, and the expense of such repair will be chargeable to the trust fund as part of the purchase-money.[1] A testator may be under such obligations in his leases or lease-holds which he devises for life to one, with remainder over, that the trustees must make repairs, and charge the expense to the *corpus* of the estate.[2] So it has been held, that where a tenant for life makes large and permanent repairs, and subsequently the trustee sells the estate for the accommodation of all parties, the tenant for life may have a fair proportion for his repairs out of the *corpus* of the proceeds of the sale.[3] And in one case the court ordered the trustee to apply a sum from the personal estate to the construction of warehouses, and provided for a reservation from the rents of interest upon the sum expended during the continuance of the life-estate.[4] Where a testator directs that the "net proceeds" after paying charges and expenses shall go to the life tenants, all ordinary repairs and improvements and replacement of articles worn out are chargeable to the income; but probably a different rule would apply to a large and unusual expenditure, as for additional buildings.[5]

§ 553. Both the equitable tenant for life and the remainder-man have an insurable interest in the trust estate; and if one insures his own interest in the buildings, and they are burned, neither can call upon the other for any part of the insurance money. (a) The trustee also has an insurable interest in the

[1] Parsons *v.* Winslow, 16 Mass. 361. [Greene *v.* Greene, 19 R. I. 619. See Sohier *v.* Eldredge, 103 Mass. 345.]

[2] Harris *v.* Poyner, 1 Drew. 174. And see a distinction in Hickling *v.* Boyer, 1 De G., M. & G. 762. [*In re* Courtier, 34 Ch. Div. 136.]

[3] Gambril *v.* Gambril, 3 Md. Ch. 259.

[4] Cogswell *v.* Cogswell, 2 Edw. 231.

[5] *In re* Jones, 103 N. Y. 621.

death of the testator. Little *v.* Little, 161 Mass. 188.

In England the Settled Estates Acts have greatly enlarged the powers of trustees in respect to re-pairs and improvements. See *supra,* § 477 and notes.

(a) A life tenant usually has no duty of insuring the interest of the remainder-man, and insurance

buildings upon the trust estate; and if he insures, and the buildings are entirely destroyed by fire, the insurance money received is so far a conversion of the property into personalty that the trustee cannot rebuild, unless he is specially directed by the instrument of trust to do so; but the money so received must remain personal property, and the tenant for life and the remainder-man will receive their respective rights and interests according to the terms of the settlement.[1] If a building is partially burned or injured, and the trustees have an insurance policy, they should apply the money to the repair of the building.[2] Of course the repair of trust property is frequently the

[1] See *ante*, § 487; Graham *v.* Roberts, 8 Ired. Eq. 99; Haxall *v.* Shippen, 10 Leigh, 536; Lerow *v.* Wilmarth, 9 Allen, 382. [See *In re* Miller, 62 N. J. Eq. 764, 67 N. J. Eq. 431.]

[2] Brough *v.* Higgins, 9 Grat. 408.

money received upon his own interest belongs entirely to him. Spalding *v.* Miller, 103 Ky. 405; Harrison *v.* Pepper, 166 Mass. 288; De Witt *v.* Cooper, 18 Hun, 67.

It has been held in one or two cases that a life tenant as a *quasi* trustee for the remainder-man can insure, not merely his own life interest, but the whole estate, and that, where he has insured the whole estate in his own name and there has been a total loss, he may recover from the insurance company the whole amount as trustee for himself and the remainder-man. Welch *v.* London Assurance Co., 151 Pa. St. 607; Green *v.* Green, 50 S. C. 532; Clyburn *v.* Reynolds, 31 S. C. 118. But it has also been held, and it seems the better reasoning, that where he insures in his own name and carries the policy at his own expense, the contract and the rights under it are wholly his, and if he succeeds in collecting from the insurance company the value of

more than his insurable interest, the remainder-man has no interest in it. Gaussen *v.* Whatman, 93 L. T. 101. See also Spalding *v.* Miller, 103 Ky. 405.

Insurance by a trustee who represents both life beneficiaries and remainder-men naturally goes to the whole estate, and insurance money received by him in case of loss is held upon the same trust as the property itself. Bridge *v.* Bridge, 146 Mass. 373.

A trustee who holds the legal title for both life tenant and remainder-man usually has the duty of insuring; and accordingly insurance premiums paid by a trustee would probably be universally treated as an ordinary expense of holding and managing the property, and therefore payable out of income. Bridge *v.* Bridge, 146 Mass. 373; Stevens *v.* Melcher, 152 N. Y. 551. As to the practice of trustees, see Loring's Trustee's Handbook, (3d ed.) 140.

subject of express provisions in wills and settlements, and trustees must be governed by the directions contained in the instrument of trust. So there are frequent directions in instruments of trust respecting insurance of property, and the use and application of the insurance money in case of loss or damage by fire. Trustees will be governed by such directions in all cases. In Pennsylvania, there are express enactments by which repairs can be made upon trust property at the mutual expense of the tenant for life and the remainder-man; the manner of the repairs and the proportion of the expenses are to be determined by a court upon the application of any party in interest.[1]

§ 554. The ordinary taxes, and expenses in the care and management of the capital, are charges on the life estate, to be paid out of the [income].[2] (a) But in some cases where an ar-

---

[1] Act May 3, 1855, § 3; Purdon's Dig. 973. [4 Purdon's Digest (13th ed.), p. 4885, § 42.]

[2] Peirce v. Burroughs, 58 N. H. 302.

(a) A life tenant enjoying the income of property must keep it free from incumbrance by paying the ordinary yearly taxes; and a trustee must pay such taxes out of income of the property taxed. Hagan v. Varney, 147 Ill. 281; Varney v. Stevens, 22 Me. 331; Bridge v. Bridge, 146 Mass. 373; Holmes v. Taber, 9 Allen, 246; Dufford v. Smith, 46 N. J. Eq. 216; Cairns v. Chabert, 3 Edw. Ch. 312; Matter of Tracy, 87 N. Y. App. Div. 215, 218; Peirce v. Burroughs, 58 N. H. 302.

The same is true of water rates. Bridge v. Bridge, 146 Mass. 373.

It has been held that an annual tax assessed on trust property on May first for the year following is payable out of income of a life beneficiary who died before the end of the year, and is not apportionable. Holmes v. Taber, 9 Allen, 246. But it seems to be the practice in Pennsylvania to apportion the tax in such cases. Crump's Estate, 13 Pa. Co. Ct. R. 286.

Taxes assessed on an estate before the death of a testator constitute a liability of his estate, even though they are for a period which begins only a few days before his death. Matter of Babcock, 52 Hun, 142.

Taxes assessed because of betterments in the form of permanent improvements in the locality or in the property itself, such as laying out a new street or putting in a new sewer, should be borne by both life tenant and remainder-man. Moore v. Simonson, 27 Or. 117; Plympton v. Boston Dispensary,

rangement which gives rise to taxes is entered into for the benefit of both capital and income, the taxes may be divided between them.[1] The *income* of a trust estate must bear the expense of administering it.[2] It is the duty of the trustee to see that the equitable tenant for life, in rightful possession of the estate, pays all rates and taxes; but if the trustee pays them he cannot charge them in his account with other parties in interest.[3] If, however, an assessment is made against the estate for something in the nature of permanent improve-

---

[1] Barger's App., 100 Penn. St. 239.

[2] Butterbaugh's App., 98 Penn. St. 351.

[3] Amory v. Lowell, 104 Mass. 265; Fountaine v. Pellett, 1 Ves. Jr. 342; Tupper v. Fuller, 7 Rich. Eq. 170; Cairns v. Chalbert, 2 Edw. Ch. 312; Jones v. Dawson, 19 Ala. 672; Varney v. Stevens, 22 Maine, 331. In case of a widow being tenant for life, one-third of the taxes and repairs were charged to her, Cochran v. Cochran, 2 Des. 521; but no general principle can be stated upon this case.

---

106 Mass. 544; Estate of Miller, 1 Tuck. (N. Y. Sur.) 346. Where such a tax is assessed upon an estate held in trust, the trustee has simply to pay the whole tax out of the principal in which both life tenant and remainder-man are interested. Plympton v. Boston Dispensary, 106 Mass. 544.

Taxes assessed because of lasting improvements which, however, are likely to wear out during the probable existence of the life estate, should be paid out of income or by the life tenant. Reyburn v. Wallace, 93 Mo. 326; Hitner v. Ege, 23 Pa. St. 305; Delker v. Owensboro, 98 S. W. 1031 (Ky. 1907). If the betterments, though not permanent, are likely to last beyond the probable life of the life tenant, the tax should be equitably apportioned according to the benefit likely to be received by each estate. Wordin's Appeal, 71 Conn. 531;

Huston v. Tribbetts, 171 Ill. 547; Bobb v. Wolff, 54 Mo. App. 515; Pratt v. Douglas, 38 N. J. Eq. 516; 542; Pack v. Sherwood, 56 N. Y. 615; Fleet v. Dorland, 11 How. Pr. 489.

Taxes upon unimproved property which produces no income should be paid out of the *corpus* of the estate. Patterson v. Johnson, 113 Ill. 559, 576; Clark v. Middlesworth, 82 Ind. 240; Stone v. Littlefield, 151 Mass. 485; Murch v. Smith M'f'g Co., 47 N. J. Eq. 193; In re Martens' Estate, 39 N. Y. S. 189.

Inheritance taxes upon the interest of a life tenant or a life beneficiary are payable out of income. Such a tax upon the interest of the remainder-man is payable out of the *corpus*. Sohier v. Eldredge, 103 Mass. 345; Brown's Estate, 208 Pa. St. 161.

ment or betterment of the whole estate, the assessment may be ratably and equitably divided between the tenant for life and the remainder-man.[1] (a)   And if a third person with consent of the executor advances money to pay the taxes, neither the executor nor the life *cestui* having means to pay them, such advances become a charge on the estate.[2]   The equitable tenant for life must pay the interest upon all incumbrances upon the estate,[3] to the extent of the rents and profits.[4]   If a tenant pays off, and takes an assignment of an incumbrance to himself, his representatives may claim from the remainder-man the difference between the rents and profits of the estate and the interest upon the incumbrance, if he notifies the remainder-man that the rents and profits are insufficient to pay the interest;[5] in such cases, the tenant for life cannot be charged with wilful default, like a mortgagee in possession, except upon some very peculiar ground.[6]   A second tenant for life is not under any obligation to apply the rents and profits accruing to him to pay off arrears of interest which accrued during the life of the preceding tenant for life; but such arrears become, as between the second tenant for life and the remainder-man, a

[1] Plympton *v.* Boston Dispensary, 106 Mass. 546. [Moore *v.* Simonson, 27 Or. 117; Estate of Miller, 1 Tuck. (N. Y.) 346.]

[2] Griffin *v.* Fleming, 72 Ga. 703.

[3] Jones *v.* Sherrard, 2 Dev. & Bat. Eq. 187; Hinves *v.* Hinves, 3 Hare, 609; Caulfield *v.* Maguire, 2 Jo. & La. 141; Cogswell *v.* Cogswell, 2 Edw. Ch. 231; 4 Kent, 74.

[4] Kensington *v.* Bouverie, 7 De G M. & G. 134; 19 Beav. 39.

[5] Ibid.; Kensington *v.* Bouverie, 7 H. L. Cas. 557. [See Tindall *v.* Peterson, 71 Neb. 166.]

[6] Ibid. See Campbell *v.* Campbell, 27 Mich. 454; Swaine *v.* Perine, 5 Johns. Ch. 482; Van Vronker *v.* Eastman, 7 Met. 157.

(a) In the absence of statute provisions to the contrary, personal property held in trust is taxable in the city or town where the trustee resides; and if there are two or more trustees not residing in the same city or town, the tax is divided, the trustees being treated as equal owners. Trustees *v.* Augusta, 90 Ga. 634, 20 L. R. A. 151 and note. But the matter of taxation of trust property has been largely dealt with by statute. See Mass. R. L. (1902), c. 12, § 23, cl. 5.

charge upon the inheritance.[1] The expenses of cultivating a farm or plantation, or of running a manufacturing establishment, must be wholly defrayed by the tenant for life, or the person entitled to the income arising from such operations.[2] If the land under incumbrance is sold, the proceeds may be invested, and the tenant for life may take the income for life, or the net proceeds may be divided according to the annuity tables. The tables, however, are not to be taken absolutely; for reference must be had to the health of the tenant for life, and also to the condition of the land and its annual income, and whether the land is so situated that the price is rising or falling, and whether it can be easily improved.[3] (a)

[1] Sharshaw v. Gibbs, 1 Kay, 333. Penrhyn v. Hughes, 5 Ves. 99, appears to be overruled.

[2] Tupper v. Fuller, 7 Rich. Eq. 170; Jones v. Dawson, 19 Ala. 672; North Amer. Coal Co. v. Dyett, 7 Paige, 9.

[3] Niemcewicz v. Gahn, 3 Paige, 652; Atkins v. Kron, 8 Ired. Eq. 1; Gambril v. Gambril, 3 Md. Ch. 259; Chesson v. Chesson, 8 Ired. Eq. 141; Williams' Case, 3 Bland, 186; Jones v. Sherrard, 2 Dev. & Bat. 189; 4 Kent, 74.

(a) A trustee who places an incumbrance on the trust property or allows one to remain, should pay the interest out of income. If he pays off the principal of the incumbrance, he should pay it all out of the trust fund of which both life tenant and remainderman are beneficiaries. Martin v. Martin, 146 Mass. 517; Plympton v. Boston Dispensary, 106 Mass. 544. See In re Muffett, 39 Ch. Div. 534; In re Harrison, 43 Ch. Div. 55.

If a remainder-man pays off the incumbrance, the life tenant must continue to pay interest to the remainder-man, or must pay to the remainder-man the present worth of an annuity equal to the annual interest running during the number of years which constitute the expectancy of life of the tenant. Moore v. Simonson, 27 Or. 117; Plympton v. Boston Dispensary, 106 Mass. 544.

There is not much authority upon the question of whether brokerage charges upon the sale of trust property should be paid from income or from principal. Much doubtless depends upon the purpose of the sale. If the purpose is to convert the property into the form of investment authorized or directed by the trust instrument it would seem that the expense of making the conversion ought to be paid from the *corpus* of the property unless a different intention is apparent. If the sale is made merely for the purpose of

§ 555. If an equitable tenant for life becomes bankrupt or insolvent, all his interest goes to his assignees, and the trustee must hold it subject to their disposition;[1] unless the property is so given that it goes over upon the bankruptcy of the *cestui que trust*. And although it is held that a general provision that a *cestui que trust* shall not alienate his interest, or that it shall not go to his creditors or to his assignees, if the interest is an absolute one, is void, as contrary to the rule of law, that when an estate is given to a man no restrictions inconsistent with the gift are valid,[2] yet a gift made in such form that it is to go over upon alienation or bankruptcy of the *cestui que trust* is good.[3] And if the limitations are interwoven into the gift

[1] *Ante,* § 386; Wells *v.* Ely, 3 Stockt. 172.

[2] Rockford *v.* Hackman, 9 Hare, 475; 10 Eng. L. & Eq. 67; Co. Litt. 223 a; Hallett *v.* Thompson, 5 Paige, 583; Heath *v.* Bishop, 4 Rich. Eq. 46; Dick *v.* Pitchford, 1 Dev. & Bat. 480; Rider *v.* Mason, 4 Sandf. Ch. 352; Co.Litt. 223 a; Blackstone Bank *v.* Davis, 21 Pick. 43; Bramhall *v.* Ferris, 14 N. Y. 44; Etches *v.* Etches, 3 Drew. 441; Tillinghast *v.* Bradford, 5 R. I. 205; Sparhawk *v.* Cloon, 125 Mass. 263; Daniels *v.* Eldridge, id. 350; Smith *v.* Moore, 37 Ala. 327; McIllvaine *v.* Smith, 42 Mo. 45; Bremer *v.* Bremer, 18 Hun (N. Y.), 147. But see *per contra* in the United States, *ante,* § 386 *a, et seq.*

[3] Dommett *v.* Bedford, 3 Ves. 149; Cooper *v.* Wyatt, 5 Madd. 482; Shee *v.* Hale, 13 Ves. 404; Brandon *v.* Aston, 2 N. C. C. 24; Twopenny *v.* Peyton, 10 Sim. 487; Page *v.* Way, 3 Beav. 20; Lewes *v.* Lewes, 6 Sim. 304; Rock-

changing an investment, the expense of the change would usually be one of the ordinary expenses of management, and as such payable from income. See R. I. Hospital Trust Co. *v.* Waterman, 23 R. I. 342. Thus it has been held in Massachusetts that brokerage on the sale and purchase of shares of stock was payable from income. Heard *v.* Eldredge, 109 Mass. 258. In Jordan *v.* Jordan, 192 Mass. 337, it was held that the same rule applied to the large commissions payable upon the sale of real estate. Soon after the last decision, the legislature of Massachusetts provided by statute that "trustees' and brokers' commissions and other expenses properly incurred and paid by trustees for or in connection with the sale, exchange, or purchase of property shall be charged to capital." Acts of 1907, c. 371. This statute obviates all necessity in Massachusetts of distinguishing between sales and purchases for the purpose of converting to the authorized form of investment and mere changes of investment in the course of management.

itself, they are valid; as if an estate is given to A. until he becomes bankrupt, the limitation is part of the gift, and the estate will go over upon the happening of the event.[1] If, however, any interest remains in the *cestui que trust* for life, it must
go to his assignees.[2] If it is in the discretion of the trustees
whether the *cestui que trust* shall have an interest or not, the
assignees will take nothing;[3] but if the trustees have exercised
their discretion, the assignees will take the interest conferred
by it.[4] If the limitation is to take effect only upon alienation
by the *cestui que trust*, it will not take effect upon bankruptcy,
and the assignees will be entitled.[5] The law does not permit a
man to settle his property on himself, with a limitation over in
case of bankruptcy.[6] (*a*) If the income is given to the *cestui*

ford *v.* Hackman, 9 Hare, 475; Dickson's Trust, 1 Sim. (N. s.) 37; *Ex parte*
Baddam, 2 De G., F. & J. 625; Muggridge's Trusts, John. (Eng.) 625; Dorsett *v.* Dorsett, 31 L. J. Ch. 122; Joel *v.* Mills, 3 K. & J. 458; *In re* Stultz,
17 Jur. 615. [See *supra*, § 388, note *a*.]
    [1] Stagg *v.* Beekman, 2 Edw. Ch. 89; Ashhurst *v.* Given, 5 Watts & S.
323; Vaux *v.* Parke, 7 id. 19; Eyrick *v.* Hetrick, 13 Penn. St. 491; Girard
Ins. Co. *v.* Chambers, 46 id. 485; Norris *v.* Johnston, 5 id. 289; Fisher *v.*
Taylor, 2 Rawle, 33; Shee *v.* Hale, 13 Ves. 404; Cooper *v.* Wyatt, 5 Madd.
482; *Ex parte* Oxley, 1 B. & B. 257; Sharpe *v.* Cosserat, 20 Beav. 470; Yarnold *v.* Moorhouse, 1 R. & M. 364; Lockyer *v.* Savage, 2 Strange, 947;
Stevens *v.* James, 4 Sim. 499; Kearsly *v.* Woodcock, 3 Hare, 185; Churchill
v. Marks, 1 Coll. C. C. 441; Large's Case, 2 Leon. 82. As to other limitations
see Grace *v.* Webb, 2 Phil. 701; Lloyd *v.* Lloyd, 2 Sim. (N. s.) 255; Heath
v. Lears, 1 Eq. R. 55; Potts *v.* Richards, 24 L. J. Ch. 488; Hooper *v.* Dundass,
10 Barr, 75; Com'th *v.* Stauffer, id. 350; Maddox *v.* Maddox, 11 Grat. 804.
    [2] Rippon *v.* Norton, 2 Beav. 63; Younghusband *v.* Gisborne, 1 Coll.
N. C. C. 400; Piercy *v.* Roberts, 1 Myl. & K. 4; Lord *v.* Bunn, 2 Younge
& C. Ch. 98; Green *v.* Spicer, 1 R. & M. 395; Snowden *v.* Dales, 6 Sim. 524;
Rockford *v.* Hackman, 9 Hare, 475.
    [3] Godden *v.* Crowhurst, 10 Sim. 642; Kearsley *v.* Woodcock, 3 Hare,
185; Lord *v.* Bunn, 2 Younge & C. Ch. 98; Twopenny *v.* Peyton, 10 Sim.
487; 1 Col. C. C. 400; 10 Jur. 419. [Stone *v.* Westcott, 18 R. I. 685; *In re*
Coleman, 39 Ch. Div. 443.]   [4] Ibid.
    [5] Lear *v.* Leggett, 2 Sim. 479; 1 R. & M. 690; Whitfield *v.* Pricket, 2
Keen, 608; Wilkinson *v.* Wilkinson, G. Coop. 259; 3 Swanst. 528. [*Re*
Harvey, 60 L. T. 710.]
    [6] Mackason's App., 42 Penn. St. 330; Higginbottam *v.* Holmes, 19 Ves.

(*a*) The objection to such a   creditors when the limitation over
provision is that it is a fraud upon   is voluntary, even though the

que trust for a particular purpose which would be defeated, the property interest may not go to the assignees.[1] (*a*)

§ 556. At common law rent could not be apportioned; and if a tenant for life died near the end of a quarter, his representatives could receive no part of the rent for the term.(*b*) Statutes have now changed that rule in England; [2] and there are statutes in many of the United States making rent apportionable.[3] In States where there are such statutes the trustees must pay so much of the rent as accrued before the death of the tenant for life to his representatives, and the balance to the remainder-man.[4] (*c*) But an annuity to a tenant for life

98; *Ex parte* Hill, 1 Cooke, Bank. Law, 291; Murphy *v.* Abraham, 15 Ir. Ch. 371; *In re* Murphy, 1 Sch. & Lef. 44.

[1] See *ante*, §§ 386 *a*, 386 *b*, 387, 388.

[2] 11 Geo. II. c. 19; 4 Wm. IV. c. 22; St. Aubin *v.* St. Aubin, 1 Dr. & Sm. 611; Longworth's Est., 23 L. J. Ch. 104. [Apportionment Act of 1870, 33 and 34 Vict. c. 35.]

[3] 3 Kent, Com. 471; 3 Green. Cruise, Dig. 117, note. [Ark. St. (1894) § 4453; Laws of Del. (1893) c. 120, § 15; Ill. R. S. (1903) c. 80, § 35; Ind. St. (1901) § 7104; Ind. Terr. St. (1899) § 2837; Iowa Code (1897), § 2988; Ky. St. (1909) § 3896; Mass. Rev. Laws (1902), c. 141, §§ 24, 25; Miss. Code (1892), § 2543; Mo. R. S. (1899) § 4098; N. J. Gen. St. (1893) II. p. 1915, § 2; N. Y. Code Civ. Pro. § 2870; N. C. Code (1908), § 1988; Pa. St. 1 Brightly's Purdon, (12th ed.) p. 584, §§ 71, 72; R. I. Gen. Laws (1909), c. 254, §§ 38, 39; S. C. Civ. Code (1902), §§ 2408, 2409; Tenn. Code 1896, § 4184; Va. Code (1904), §§ 2809, 2810; W. Va. Code (1899), c. 94, § 1; c. 95, § 1; Wis. St. (1898) § 2193.]

[4] Price *v.* Pickett, 21 Ala. 741.

settlor was not indebted at the time of making the settlement. Mackintosh *v.* Pogose, [1895] 1 Ch. 505. The provision is valid as against the settlor, and when in case of bankruptcy the creditors have been satisfied, the limitation over takes effect, so that creditors in a second bankruptcy have no rights. *In re* Johnson Johnson, [1904] 1 K. B. 134. See Godefroi on Trusts (3d ed.), p. 919.

(*a*) The various points touched upon in this paragraph are dealt with more fully in § 386 *et seq.* and notes.

(*b*) See Dexter *v.* Phillips, 121 Mass. 178; Sohier *v.* Eldredge, 103 Mass. 345.

(*c*) These statutes do not usually change the common-law rule as to rent which is not due at the death of a testator, but are limited to rent as between life tenant and re-

is not apportionable; and if the tenant dies within three days of the day of payment, his representatives are not entitled to any proportion of the annuity.[1] But where an annuity is given to a widow in lieu of dower, or for maintenance of an infant, or for the separate maintenance of a married woman, an apportionment is made on the ground that such annuity is necessary for support till the death of the annuitant.[2] (a) [Regular] dividends upon shares in corporations and upon stocks are not

---

[1] Wiggin v. Swett, 6 Met. 194; Tracy v. Strong, 2 Conn. 659; Earp's Will, 1 Pars. Eq. 468; Mannings v. Randolph, 1 Southard, 144; Waring v. Purcell, 1 Hill, Eq. 199; Gheen v. Osborn, 17 Serg. & R. 171; McLemore v. Goode, Harp. Eq. 275. [Nehls v. Sauer, 119 Iowa, 440; Chase v. Darby, 110 Mich. 314.]

[2] Hay v. Palmer, 2 P. Wms. 581; Pearly v. Smith, 3 Atk. 260; Howell v. Hanforth, 2 Bl. R. 1016; Gheen v. Osborn, 17 Serg. & R. 171. [Henry v. Henderson, 81 Miss. 743; Quinn v. Madigan, 65 N. H. 8; In re Lackawanna Co., 37 N. J. Eq. 26; Parker v. Seeley, 56 N. J. Eq. 110; Blight v. Blight, 51 Pa. St. 420; R. I. Hospital Trust Co. v. Harris, 20 R. I. 160; In re Cushing's Will, 58 Vt. 393.] But see Tracy v. Strong, 2 Conn. 659; Fisher v. Fisher, 4 Am. Law Jour. (N. S.) 539.

---

mainder-man. Sargent v. Sargent, 103 Mass. 297; Dexter v. Phillips, 121 Mass. 178; Marshall v. Moseley, 21 N. Y. 280; Huff v. Latimer, 33 S. C. 255; Rowan v. Riley, 6 Bax. (Tenn.) 67.

(a) Some States have refused to include in the exception, annuities given in lieu of dower. Mower v. Sanford, 76 Conn. 504; Chase v. Darby, 110 Mich. 314. See note to Henry v. Henderson, 63 L. R. A. 616 (81 Miss. 743). Other States have extended the exception to include all annuities which seem to have been intended for the support of the annuitant. Quinn v. Madigan, 65 N. H. 8; In re Lackawanna Co., 37 N. J. Eq. 26; In re Cushing's Will, 58 Vt. 393. In England and several States statutes have made annuities apportionable

up to the death of the annuitant. English Apportionment Act of 1870, 33 & 34 Vict. c. 35; Ky. Statutes (1909), § 3846; Mass. R. L. (1902) ch. 141, § 25; N. Y. Code Civ. Pro. § 2720; Code of N. C. (1908) § 1988; Va. Code (1904), § 2810; W. Va. Code (4th ed. 1899), ch. 95, § 1; Gen. Laws R. I. (1909) ch. 254, § 39 (confined to annuities given by testamentary instruments).

When no different intention is apparent in the instrument creating the annuity, it is taken to be payable yearly on the anniversary of the date of the instrument, or, in case of a will, on the anniversary of the date of testator's death. Henry v. Henderson, 81 Miss. 743; Kearney v. Cruikshank, 117 N. Y. 99; Gibson v. Bott, 7 Ves. 89 and note.

apportionable, and nothing is earned for the shareholders until the dividends are declared.[1] (a)   But interest-money upon notes, bonds, mortgages, and similar securities accrues from day to day, although it is not payable until a fixed day; it is therefore apportionable, and trustees must pay the proportion accruing during the life of the tenant for life to his representatives.[2] (b)   In Massachusetts, annuities, rent, interest, and in-

[1] *Ante*, § 545, n.; Earp's Will, 1 Pars. Eq. 453; Earp's Appeal, 28 Penn. St. 368; Wilson *v.* Harman, 2 Ves. 672; Rashleigh *v.* Master, 3 Bro. Ch. 99. [Greene *v.* Huntington, 73 Conn. 106, 115; Mann *v.* Anderson, 106 Ga. 818; Hyatt *v.* Allen, 56 N. Y. 553; Clapp *v.* Astor, 2 Edw. Ch. 379; Ross's Estate, 2 Kulp, 472; Union Safe Dep. etc. Co. *v.* Dudley, 104 Me. 297.] But see *Ex parte* Rutledge, Harp. Eq. 65; Foote's App., 22 Pick. 299; Moseley *v.* Eastern R. R. Co., 43 N. H. 558; Granger *v.* Bassett, 98 Mass. 462; Johnson *v.* Bridgewater, 14 Gray, 274; Crawford *v.* North Eastern Ry., 3 K. & J. 744; Coleman *v.* Columbia Oil Co., 51 Penn. St. 74. [See *supra*, §§ 544, 545 and notes, as to extraordinary dividends.]

[2] Earp's Will, 1 Pars. Eq. 453; Sweigart *v.* Berks, 8 Serg. & R. 299; Roger's

(a) The same reasoning applies to profits of a partnership between the days of accounting. Profits of a business do not accrue at a steady rate from day to day, and are therefore incapable of apportionment. Browne *v.* Collins, 12 Eq. 586; Jones *v.* Ogle, 8 Ch. 192; McKeen's Appeal, 42 Pa. St. 479. The important dates are the dates marking the beginning and the end of the period for which the profits are ascertained, not the date on which they are ascertained. For example, profits of a partnership for a period of accounting ending May 1 would belong to the person entitled to income on that date, although the profits were not ascertained until several months after his interest had ceased. Browne *v.* Collins, 12 Eq. 586; Jones *v.* Ogle, 8 Ch. 192. This same rule has been applied to a dividend declared by a corporation during the life of the

life tenant, but payable on a date before which he dies. Hill *v.* Newichawanick Co., 8 Hun, 459, 71 N.Y. 593. And it has been held that a corporation dividend expressly declared for a period ending May 31 belonged to a life tenant who died on June 12, although the dividend was not declared until June 23, after his death. Johnson *v.* Bridgewater, etc., Co., 14 Gray, 274. See Bates *v.* Mackinley, 31 Beav. 280; Londesborough *v.* Somerville, 19 Beav. 295.

Under the English Apportionment Act, regular dividends of corporations are apportioned as if the earnings accrued from day to day. This seems to be true under the North Carolina statute. N. C. Code (1908), § 1988. For a different interpretation of the New York statute, see Matter of Kane, 64 App. Div. (N. Y.) 566.

(b) The English courts used to distinguish between interest on

923

come are made apportionable in all cases by statute, unless the instrument of trust manifests a different intention.[1] (a)

Trust, 1 Dr. & Sm. 611. [Dexter v. Phillips, 121 Mass. 178; Riggs v. Cragg, 26 Hun, 89, 98; Banner v. Lowe, 13 Ves. 135; Union Safe Dep. & Tr. Co. v. Dudley, 104 Me. 297, 312.]

[1] Gen. St. c. 97, § 24; [Rev. Laws (1902), c. 141, § 25;] Sohier v. Eldredge, 103 Mass. 345.

debts or notes and interest on the public funds, holding that the latter is not apportionable at common law, being within the class of payments coming due at fixed times. Pearly v. Smith, 3 Atk. 260; Wilson v. Harman, 2 Ves. Sen. 671. See also Warden v. Ashburner, 2 De G. & Sm. 366.

The Massachusetts court has followed the English rule as to interest on the public debt, except in cases coming within the Massachusetts statute of apportionment, and has applied the rule to interest on coupon bonds, including those of private corporations. The court reasons that each coupon is a separate contract to pay a definite amount at a certain time, and represents an obligation distinct from the bond and from every other coupon. Dexter v. Phillips, 121 Mass. 178. To the same effect, see Union Safe Dep. etc. Co. v. Dudley, 104 Me. 297, 312. In Pennsylvania and New York a different view seems to have been taken. Wilson's Appeal, 108 Pa. St. 344 (overruling Earp's Will, 1 Pars. Eq. 453); U. S. Trust Co. v. Tobias, 21 Abb. N. C. 393.

Semi-annual dividends paid to depositors in savings banks, though often spoken of as interest, are in the class of dividends of corporations, and as such are not ap-

portionable except by statute provisions. Green v. Huntington, 73 Conn. 106, 114. But interest on deposits which are subject to check has been held to be apportionable. Union Safe Dep. etc. Co. v. Dudley, 104 Me. 297, 312.

(a) It is important to note that the Massachusetts statute (R. L. (1902) c. 141, § 25) applies only to cases where the limited estate is created by will or other instrument, and so does not apply where a widow or husband acquires a life estate under statute. Moreover, the statute applies only as between life tenants or persons whose estate or enjoyment of income is to terminate on the happening of some contingency, and the persons entitled after them. As it applies only at the termination of such limited estate, it has no application to apportionment on changes of investment. Sargent v. Sargent, 103 Mass. 297; Hemenway v. Hemenway, 134 Mass. 446. The Rhode Island statute is similar in this respect. R. I. Gen. Laws (1909), ch. 254, §§ 38, 39. See also Huff v. Latimer, 33 S. C. 255; Rowan v. Riley, 6 Bax. (Tenn.) 67.

Dividends on shares of stock are not apportionable even under the statute, and probably not profits of a business. Granger v. Bassett, 98 Mass. 462.

§ 556 *a*.   Where a trustee died largely indebted to his trust estate by a breach of the trust, the income of which trust estate was payable to a tenant for life, and the principal sum went over, and, several years after the trustee's death, a compromise was effected, by which a part of the original sum was received, it was held that, as between the tenant for life and the remainder-man, the sum paid was to be treated as composed of a principal debt due at the date of the transaction out of which the claim originated, or the date of the breach of the trust, and of interest from that day up to the day of the testator's death, and of interest upon said aggregate of principal and interest from the testator's death to the day of settlement and payment; and that the principal sum thus ascertained, and the interest thereon up to the testator's death, were chargeable against the *corpus* of the trust fund, and the interest since the testator's death was to be charged as income.[1]   The administrator of a tenant for life can maintain a bill for an account against the trustee for income accruing before the death of the tenant.[2]

[1] Maclaren *v.* Stainton, L. R. 4 Eq. 448; L. R. 11 Eq. 382; Turner *v.* Newport, 2 Phill. 14; Cox *v.* Cox, L. R. 8 Eq. 343; *In re* Grabowski's Settlement, L. R. 6 Eq. 12.   [See Parsons *v.* Winslow, 16 Mass. 361; Cook *v.* Lowry, 95 N. Y. 103.]

[2] Brown *v.* Hicks, 30 Ga. 777.   [Union Safe Dep. etc. Co. *v.* Dudley, 104 Me. 297.]

CHAPTER XIX.

TRUSTS UNDER A WILL FOR THE PAYMENT OF DEBTS; FOR THE PAYMENT OF LEGACIES; AND FOR RAISING PORTIONS.

§ 557. AT common law, the personal estate only of a deceased person was liable for his debts, unless they were debts by specialty or matter of record. However large his real estate might be, no recourse could be had to it to pay simple-contract debts, although his personal property was utterly insufficient to meet them.[1] The common law has been changed, and it is

---

[1] Kidney v. Coussmaker, 1 Ves. Jr. 436, Mr. Sumner's notes.

now provided by statute that copyhold and freehold estates shall be assets for the payment of simple-contract and other debts. The operation of the act is confined to those estates where no provision is made by will for payment of debts, or to those which the person dying has not by his last will charged with, or devised subject to, the payment of his debts.[1]

§ 558. The law in England stands thus: personal estate always has been liable for debts, and is now primarily liable, so far as it will go. All creditors have the right to proceed for payment of their claims out of such personalty, and the deceased person can make no provision, or trust by will, which shall in any way change, alter, postpone, or defeat the rights of creditors in personal property; that is to say, a trust created by will in personal property was and is wholly inoperative in relation to creditors.[2] But real estate, being wholly exempt from simple-contract debts of the deceased person, may be devised in trust for their payment. Courts favored these trusts, for the reason that it was just and equitable that a man's debt should be paid; and if he charged his lands in any way for their payment, or created a trust for that purpose, such trust would be so carried into effect as to answer the purposes for which they were created, and the ends of justice. By the statute above cited, real estate in England is now made assets for the payment of debts; but if the deceased person in his will has charged the whole or a particular part of his real estate, or created a trust in the whole or any part of it, creditors must have recourse to such real estate for the payment of their claims in the manner pointed out in the will.[3] Thus, in England, a trust created by a will in real estate, unlike a trust in

[1] 3 & 4 Wm. IV. c. 104.

[2] Evans v. Tweedy, 1 Beav. 55; Freake v. Cranefeldt, 4 Myl. & Cr. 499; Scott v. Jones, 4 Cl. & Fin. 398, overruling Lord Brougham in same case, 1 R. & M. 255.

[3] Collis v. Robins, 1 De G. & Sm. 139; Hunt v. Bateman, 10 Ir. Eq. 371; Francis v. Gower, 5 Hare, 39; Young v. Wilton, 10 Ir. Eq. 10.

chattels, is valid and of controlling effect for the payment of debts. (a)

§ 559.   In the United States, both real and personal property are liable for the debts of a deceased person; and no valid trust can be created by will for the payment of debts in either personal or real estate to the injury of the rights of creditors. The statutes of the several States point out how estates shall be administered for the payment of debts.   Creditors in all cases have the right to demand payment, according to the provisions of the statutes.   Thus trusts, charges, or other directions in wills for the payment of debts have no legal operation, so far as creditors are concerned.   If a testator gives to A. his real estate in trust to pay his debts, creditors may still claim that the estate shall be settled in a probate court, and the land sold under a license, and the proceeds applied according to law, and not according to the terms of the will.   So absolute is this rule that creditors do not hold the relation of *cestuis que trust* to the trustees, or other persons appointed under a will to apply the property to the payment of debts.   It is well understood, that the statute of limitations does not run against a *cestui que trust* so long as the relation of trustee and *cestuis que trust* is acknowledged to exist; but a trust or charge in a will upon certain property for the payment of debts creates no such relation, between the trustee and creditor, that the statute of limitations ceases to operate.   On the contrary, the claims of a creditor against the estate of a deceased person will be barred by the statute of limitations, notwithstanding certain property is given in trust, or charged with the payment of such claims.[1] (b)   The princi-

[1] Carrington v. Manning, 13 Ala. 628; Lewis v. Bacon, 3 Hen. & Mun. 106; Bull v. Bull, 8 B. Mon. 332; Agnew v. Fetterman, 4 Penn. St. 62; Cornish v. Wilson, 6 Gill, 318; Hines v. Spruill, 2 Dev. & Bat. Eq. 93; Man v. Warner, 4 Whart. 455; Jones v. Scott, 4 Cl. & Fin. 398; Freake v. Cranefeldt, 3 Myl. & Cr. 499; Evans v. Tweedy, 1 Beav. 55; Hall v. Bumstead, 20 Pick. 2; Smith v. Porter, 1 Binn. 209; Rooseveldt v. Mark, 5 Johns. Ch.

(a) See *In re* Stephens, 43 Ch. D. 39, 44.

(b) It has been held that where a will provides that the executor

ple is, that the statutes having limited the time within which claims against a deceased person's estate must be presented, the mere fact that he designates certain property to pay his debts (which the creditors are not obliged to resort to) shall not avail to prolong the time for presentation of claims. But if the creditors assent to the trust thus created in a will, and an executor settles the estate accordingly, the creditors will be estopped from claiming a legal settlement of the estate; and the executor will become a trustee to settle the estate, as directed in the will and assented to by the creditors.[1] And it is said that a trust thus created to pay debts will prevent the lien of a judgment from expiring without being renewed, unless the creditor has neglected to renew the judgment within the statute period.[2] So it has been held that if a testamentary trustee to pay debts sells the land which he is directed to sell for their payment, and applies the money to the purposes named, the land will be discharged from the lien of the other creditors.[3]

§ 560. But while the creation of a trust by will, in personal or real estate, is wholly without legal operation so far

266; Rogers v. Rogers, 3 Wend. 503; Dundas v. Blake, 11 Ir. Eq. 138; Steele v. Steele's Adm'r, 64 Ala. 460.

[1] Bank of U. S. v. Beverly, 1 How. 134.

[2] Baldy v. Brady, 15 Penn. St. 111; Alexander v. McMurry, 8 Watts, 504; Trinity Church v. Watson, 50 Penn. St. 518; Pettingill v. Pettingill, 60 Maine, 412. To have this effect, the will must clearly show an intention to create such a trust and to take the estate out of pale of the law. Steele v. Steele's Adm'r, 64 Ala. 460.

[3] Cadbury v. Duval, 10 Penn. St. 267.

hold the property in trust to pay debts, the creditors must at least present their claims to the executor within the time provided by the statute; that otherwise their claims will be barred by the statute. Foley v. McDonnell, 48 Wash. 272. But if a creditor manifests his acceptance of such a provision for his benefit before his claim has been barred by the statute of limitations, there seems no reason why the tentative lien provided in the will should not become fully operative and take the place of the lien which the law gives him. McKinley v. Coe, 66 N. J. Eq. 70; Gordon v. McDougall, 84 Miss. 715. See In re Stephens, 43 Ch. Div. 39.

as creditors are concerned, it may be of the utmost consequence, as between heirs, legatees, devisees, and other persons interested in the estate. Thus, where a testator gave
two-thirds of a farm and all the stock and property connected
with it to a son, in fee, with an express order and direction that
the son should pay all his just debts out of the estate so given,
and then gave all the residue, both real and personal, to his
wife in fee, and made her executrix of the will, the debts not
being paid by the son, the creditors brought suits at law against
the executrix. The son had sold the farm, but part of the
purchase-money had been applied to pay a debt due to the
purchaser from the son, and part was unpaid, the purchaser
having notice of the terms of the bequest to the son. The executrix brought a bill against the son and the purchaser, who had
the purchase-money in his hands, to compel the performance
of the trust, and the payment of the debts out of the farm thus
bequeathed to the son. It was held that the debts were not a
mere charge on the devisee, but also a charge on the lands
devised.[1]

---

[1] Gardner v. Gardner, 3 Mason, 178. See Sands v. Champlin, 1 Story,
376; In re Butler, [1894] 3 Ch. 250; Turner v. Laird, 68 Conn. 198; Creesy
v. Willis, 159 Mass. 249; Mitchell's Estate, 182 Penn. St. 530; Hattersley
v. Bissett, 52 N. J. Eq. 693; Bergman v. Bogda, 46 Ill. App. 351; Kelly v.
Richardson, 100 Ala. 584; Nash v. Ober, 2 App., D. C. 304; Deering v. Kerfoot, 89 Va. 491. Mr. Justice Story said, in Gardner v. Gardner: "It
remains only to advert to the objection that the present plaintiffs are not
competent to maintain the present suit, because they have not yet paid
the testator's debts. The argument is, that the creditors alone have a right
to maintain a suit to enforce the charge, unless they have been paid by
the executrix or the devisees. The right of the creditors to enforce the
charge in equity cannot be doubted. Green v. Lowe, 3 Bro. Ch. 218. But I
am also of the opinion, that the executrix, who, by the law of the State, is
responsible for the payment of the debts, where there are real or personal
assets, has also a right to enforce the charge. She might procure a license
from the proper authority to sell the real estate, upon the deficiency of the
personal assets, pursuant to the statute. She might in this way, perhaps,
reach the estate charged with the debts, but the remedy would be circuitous,
and might be inadequate to all the purposes of equity. She is not com-
pellable to adopt that course; but may directly, by the assistance of a court
of equity, reach the fund which, in the eyes of such a court, is appropriated

§ 561. This case of Gardner *v.* Gardner, and Mr. Justice Story's opinion, sufficiently explain the effect of a testator's attempting to create a trust or charge upon a portion of his property for the payment of his debts. Though the creditors may reach the property directly through the executor, and seize that which the testator has charged, or any other property, those of the testator's heirs, legatees, or devisees, who have been disappointed or may be disappointed and deprived of their rights by being compelled to part with the property given to them, may bring a process against the devisee or trustee who has received the property charged with the payment of debts, and compel him to execute the trust imposed upon him, or charged upon the property given to him.

§ 562. The general rule of the English and American courts is, that the personal property of a deceased person is primarily liable for the payment of his debts. It has been seen that, at common law, personal assets were exclusively liable for simple-contract debts. When real estate in England became subject to debts, the same rule applied as was always held in the United States, — that real estate should not be called upon for payment until the personal property was exhausted. This rule extends to the payment of debts secured by mortgage, so that the heir to whom the mortgaged property has descended has a

for the payment of the debts. If she can do this after payment of the debts, there is no reason why she may not do it before, since she is entitled to avert an impending mischief, and is not bound to advance her own money to pay the creditors. Besides, the testator has disposed of all his real and personal estate by his will; and the executrix, who is a residuary legatee and devisee, has no right to apply the personal estate bequeathed to other legatees to the payment of the debts where there are other funds appropriated to the purpose; and she has a direct interest to relieve property devised to herself from the burden of the debts. The like remark equally applies to the other plaintiffs, who are devisees exonerated by the will from any contribution or lien. I entertain no doubt, therefore, that the plaintiffs are competent to maintain the present suit. It is the common case of a party subjected to a burden chargeable upon her in law, but from which she is entitled to be relieved in equity by a paramount obligation on another to exonerate her from the whole burden."

right to call upon the executor to apply the personal assets to the discharge of the mortgage.[1] But if a testator purchases land subject to a mortgage, his personal estate is not bound to pay off and discharge such mortgage, unless an intention to that effect can be gathered from his will.[2]

§ 563. The next fund in order for the payment of debts is that portion of the real estate specially set apart in the will, or charged with, or given in trust for, the payment of debts. Of course, where a testator has indicated what part of his real estate shall be devoted to the payment of debts, it is just and equal between those interested in his estate, aside from creditors, that his will should be carried out. A distinction is drawn between a particular and specific charge upon a particular parcel or portion of land, and a general charge of debts.[3]

---

[1] McCampbell v. McCampbell, 5 Lit. 95; Wyse v. Smith, 4 G. & J. 295; M'Dowell v. Lawless, 6 Monr. 141; Haleyburton v. Kershaw, 3 Des. 105; Dunlop v. Dunlop, 4 Des. 305; Stuart v. Carson, 1 Des. 500; Garnet v. Macon, 6 Call, 608; 2 Brock. 185; Rogers v. Rogers, 1 Paige, 188; Livingston v. Livingston, 3 Johns. Ch. 148; Hoye v. Brewer, 3 G. & J. 153; Stevens v. Gregg, 10 G. & J. 143; Tessier v. Wyse, 3 Bland, 185; Lewis v. Thornton, 6 Munf. 87; Hawley v. James, 5 Paige, 318; Ancaster v. Mayer, 1 Bro. Ch. 454; McKay v. Green, 3 Johns. Ch. 56; Livingston v. Newkirk, id. 312; Stroud v. Barnett, 3 Dana, 394; Schemerhorn v. Barhydt, 9 Paige, 29; Chase v. Lockerman, 11 G. & J. 185; Seaver v. Lewis, 14 Mass. 83; Adams v. Brackett, 4 Met. 280; Gore v. Brazier, 4 Mass. 354; Brydges v. Phillips, 6 Ves. 570; Kelsey v. Western, 2 Comst. 500; Gibson v. McCormick, 10 G. & J. 65; Holman's App., 24 Penn. St. 174; Dandridge v. Minge, 4 Rand. 397; Lupton v. Lupton, 2 Johns. Ch. 614; Morris v. Mowatt, 2 Paige, 587; Mollan v. Griffith, 3 Paige, 402; Hancock v. Minot, 8 Pick. 29; Ruston v. Ruston, 2 Yeates, 54; Todd v. Todd, 1 Serg. & R. 453; Martin v. Frye, 17 Serg. & R. 426; Miller v. Harwell, 3 Murph. 195; McLoud v. Roberts, 4 Hen. & M. 443; Foster v. Crenshaw, 3 Munf. 514; Waring v. Waring, 2 Bland, 673; Marsh v. Marsh, 10 B. Mon. 360; Leavitt v. Wooster, 14 N. H. 551; Sims v. Sims, 2 Stock. Ch. 158; Clinefetter v. Ayers, 16 Ill. 329; Hayes v. Jackson, 6 Mass. 149; 4 Kent, 421; Hewes v. Dehon, 3 Gray, 206.

[2] Andrews v. Bishop, 5 Allen, 490; Cumberland v. Codrington, 2 Johns. Ch. 229, 257, 272; Rogers v. Rogers, 1 Paige, 188; Hewes v. Dehon, 3 Gray, 206, 208.

[3] Manning v. Spooner, 3 Ves. 114; Donne v. Lewis, 3 Bro. Ch. 257; Milnes v. Slater, 8 Ves. 295; Davies v. Topp, 1 Bro. Ch. 524; Powis v. Corbet,

§ 564. Next in order for the payment of debts is land which descends to the heir. There being no intention expressed concerning this land, it comes next after the personalty, which is always first, and that part of the land which by an express direction is made liable for debts. If these two funds are not sufficient, that part of the testator's land which had descended to his heirs, without any intention whatever expressed in regard to them, must, if necessary, be taken to discharge his debts.[1]

§ 565. The last fund to be resorted to for the payment of debts is land specifically devised, although there may be a general charge of debts upon all the lands. The testator may be supposed to have expressed a particular intention that the specific devisees of land shall have it at any rate, unless all other funds for the payment of his debts have been exhausted, and it is necessary to resort to the specifically devised land, in order that his debts may be paid.[2]

§ 566. Thus the general rule is, that a deceased person's estate is to be applied to the payment of his debts in the following order: (1) The general personal estate; (2) Estates specifically devised for the payment of debts; (3) Estates descended; (4) Estates specifically devised, though charged generally with the payment of debts. And it requires express words, or the clear intent of the testator, to disturb this order.[3] Therefore,

3 Atk. 556; Harmood v. Oglander, 8 Ves. 131; Martin v. Frye, 17 Serg. & R. 426.

[1] Oneal v. Mead, 1 P. Wms. 693; Cope v. Cope, 2 Salk. 449; Howell v. Price, 1 P. Wms. 291; White v. White, 2 Vern. 43; Johnson v. Milksopp, id. 112; Evelyn v. Evelyn, 2 P. Wms. 659; Gray v. Gray, 1 Ch. Cas. 296; Gower v. Mead, Pr. Ch. 2; Commonwealth v. Shelby, 13 Serg. & R. 348; Warley v. Warley, 1 Bail. Eq. 398; Robards v. Wortham, 2 Dev. Eq. 173; Livingston v. Livingston, 3 Johns. Ch. 148. [Scott v. Cumberland, 18 Eq. 578.]

[2] Livingston v. Livingston, 3 Johns. Ch. 148; Chase v. Lockerman, 11 G. & J. 186; Ruston v. Ruston, 2 Yeates, 54.

[3] Stephenson v. Heathcote, 1 Ed. 38; Inchquin v. French, 1 Cox, 1; Webb v. Jones, id. 245; Bootle v. Blundell, 1 Mer. 193; Barnwell v. Cawdor,

while creditors are not generally confined to this order for the payment of their claims, legal representatives, heirs, legatees, and devisees have rights against each other for relief in case this order is disarranged; for instance, if land, specifically devised, is taken for the payment of debts, the specific devisee may call upon the legal representatives to make up his loss from the personal estate in their hands; if that has been already exhausted, he may call upon the land that was specifically devised for the payment of debts; if that has been applied, he may call upon the heir to whom any portion of the land has descended; if such land has already been taken, then the specific devisees shall contribute ratably to each other.[1] (a)

§ 567. This order of payment or contribution among those interested in an estate is called the marshalling of assets. Of course, it is subject to the will of the testator, for he may direct out of what part of his estate his debts shall be paid; but it requires a direct expression, or a manifest intent, to change this order. It might be supposed, that, if a testator gave away his personal property, and charged his debts upon his real estate, it would be a plain manifestation of an intention to change the order. But such is not the case; for when a testator gives his personal estate, he is supposed to give it subject to the payment of his debts, that being the first fund available for the purpose; and when he charges his real estate with the payment of his debts, he is supposed to charge his real estate with the payment of such debts as may remain unpaid after his personal estate is exhausted. Merely giving away personal estate and

3 Madd. 453; Watson v. Brickwood, 9 Ves. 447; Livingston v. Newkirk, 3 Johns. Ch. 312; Livingston v. Livingston, id. 148; Stroud v. Barnett, 3 Dana, 394; Warley v. Warley, 1 Bail. Eq. 397; Schemerhorn v. Barhydt, 9 Paige, 29; Chase v. Lockerman, 11 G. & J. 185; Cook v. Dawson, 29 Beav. 123; Seaver v. Lewis, 14 Mass. 83; Hewes v. Dehon, 3 Gray, 205; Plympton v. Fuller, 11 Allen, 140.

[1] Livingston v. Livingston, 3 Johns. Ch. 148; Gen. Stat. Mass. c. 92, §§ 29–36 [R. L. (1902), c. 135, §§ 26, 27]; Blaney v. Blaney, 1 Cush. 107.

(a) See 1 Ames on Trusts (2d ed.), 438, n.

charging debts upon the real estate is not inconsistent with the application of the personal estate to the payment of debts, so far as it will go, and of calling upon the real estate only when the personal estate is exhausted. Therefore the rule is, that there must not only be a giving away of the personalty, and a charging of debts on the realty, but there must be something further to show that the testator intended to exonerate the whole personalty from the payment of the debts, and to charge all the debts upon the realty, and not simply what debts may remain after exhausting the personal estate.[1] (a)

§ 568. Legacies, whether specific or general, are payable out of the personal assets of a testator, and the duty of paying them devolves upon the executor in the due course of his administration. If all the personal assets are exhausted in the payment of debts, specific legatees have a claim for compensation out of some other fund, if in law they have a higher equitable claim in the marshalling of the assets; or for contribution, if they stand upon the same equitable equality. If, however, the personal assets are exhausted in the payment of debts, general legacies must fail, unless the testator has charged the

[1] Ancaster v. Mayer, 1 Bro. Ch. 454; 1 Lead. Cas. Eq. 505, with English and American notes; Aldrich v. Cooper, 8 Ves. 382; 2 Lead. Cas. Eq. 56, English and American notes; Silk v. Prime, 1 Bro. Ch. 138, n.; 1 Dick. 384, 2 Lead. Cas. Eq. 82, and notes; Allan v. Gott, L. R. 4 Ch. 439; Tench v. Cheese, 6 De G., M. & G. 453. The purpose of this work, in treating of trusts for the payment of debts, does not call for a more particular statement of the rules that govern the marshalling of assets among all the persons who may call for such marshalling by reason of some interest being taken from them or endangered. The reader will find the cases, both English and American, collected in the notes to the leading cases above referred to, and the rules of law stated and illustrated with a clearness and affluence of learning rarely equalled.

(a) Mere authority to pay debts does not, it seems, create a charge upon real estate. *In re* Head's Trustees, 45 Ch. D. 310, 315. McGlaughlin v. McGlaughlin, 43 W. Va. 226. And even a direction to pay debts out of real estate has been held insufficient to show an intention to exonerate the personalty. Kilford v. Blaney, 31 Ch. Div. 56; *In re* Banks, [1905] 1 Ch. 547.

payment of them upon his real estate. If there is a charge for the payment of legacies out of the real estate, the devisee or the heir, as the case may be, will hold the real estate as a trustee for their payment.[1] (a)

§ 569. If the trust is created in express words, or if the payment of the legacy is directly charged upon a particular part, or the whole of the real estate, there can be no question as to the trust, or liability of the estate to pay the legacy;[2] but where the trust depends upon the construction to be put upon general words, or upon implication from the use of certain phrases, it has been a question of considerable doubt whether expressions and words sufficient to charge the payment of debts upon real estate are also adequate to charge it with legacies. The ground of the doubt is this, that the payment of

---

[1] Stevens v. Gregg, 10 G. & J. 143.
[2] Schnure's App., 70 Penn. St. 400.

(a) It seems more accurate to describe such a charge upon the devised or descended property as an equitable lien rather than a technical trust. The lien is merely the legatee's security for payment of his legacy when it becomes due. Gee v. Gee, 204 Ill. 588; Spangler v. Newman, 239 Ill. 616; Merchants' Nat. Bank v. Crist, 140 Iowa, 308; Holt's Ex'r v. Deshon, 126 Ky. 310; Whitehouse v. Cargill, 86 Me. 60; Stringer v. Gamble, 155 Mich. 295; Conkling v. Weatherwax, 173 N. Y. 43; In re Taber, 116 N. Y. S. 960; Hunt v. Wheeler, 116 N. C. 422; Dodge v. Hogan, 19 R. I. 4; Isner v. Kelley, 51 W. Va. 82; Merton v. O'Brien, 117 Wis. 437. Upon failure of payment after the legacy has become due, equity will enable the legatee to foreclose the lien, even against a purchaser for value unless he has purchased without notice. Conkling v. Weatherwax, 173 N. Y. 43; Dodge v. Hogan, 19 R. I. 4; Korn v. Friz, 128 Wis. 428; Smith v. Jackman, 115 Mich. 192. Until the legacy has fallen due and there has been a failure to pay it, the only fiduciary duty of the owner of the property seems to be not to destroy the lien by transferring to a purchaser without notice and not to commit waste which would impair the value of the security. Merton v. O'Brien, 117 Wis. 437. Where the legatee's lien is foreclosed by a judicial sale of the property, he is entitled only to payment of his legacy with interest from the time it ought to have been paid. Bowen v. True, 74 S. C. 486.

debts is a duty, and courts will construe very general and loose expressions into an intention to pay such debts out of the real estate, in case of the failure of the personal estate, but that legacies are mere voluntary gifts, and they will not be charged upon real estate, unless there is a manifest intent to do so.[1] In the late cases, however, the doubt is not referred to, and the general tendency is to charge the real estate with the payment of legacies by the same words that would charge the payment of debts upon real estate.[2] Whether legacies are charged upon lands or not is in all cases a matter of intention, to be gathered from the whole will.[3] Thus a mere direction that all debts and legacies are to be paid is not a charge of legacies upon the real estate; nor is a devise of all the rest of his real and personal estate, not before devised, a charge of legacies upon land, — there being no other words tending to show that the legacy is first to be paid from the land. But if real estate is devised, after the payment of debts and legacies, there is no question; for the *residue*, after the payment of the legacies, is devised.[4]

§ 570.   Where a testator gives several legacies, and blends both his real and personal estate into one fund for the pay-

[1] Davis *v.* Gardner, 2 P. Wms. 187, 190; Kightley *v.* Kightley, 2 Ves. Jr. 328; Williams *v.* Chitty, 3 id. 551; Kneeling *v.* Brown, 5 Ves. 362.

[2] Williams *v.* Chitty, 3 Ves. 551; Trott *v.* Vernon, Pr. Ch. 430; 1 Vern. 708; Tompkins *v.* Tompkins, Pr. Ch. 397; Elliot *v.* Hancock, 2 Vern. 143; Lypet *v.* Carter, 1 Ves. 499; Ellison *v.* Airey, 2 Ves. 568; Mirehouse *v.* Scaife, 2 Myl. & Cr. 708; Patterson *v.* Scott, 1 De G., M. & G. 531; Sherman *v.* Sherman, 4 Allen, 392.

[3] Jones *v.* Selby, Pr. Ch. 288; Trent *v.* Trent, 1 Dow, 102; Austen *v.* Halsey, 6 Ves. 475; Miles *v.* Leigh, 1 Atk. 574; Minor *v.* Wicksteed, 3 Bro. Ch. 627; Webb *v.* Webb, Barn. 86; Downman *v.* Rust, 6 Rand. 587; Van Winkle *v.* Van Houten, 2 Green, Ch. 191; Lupton *v.* Lupton, 2 Johns. Ch. 618; Paxson *v.* Potts, 2 Green, Ch. 322; Harris *v.* Fly, 7 Paige, 421; Logan *v.* Deshay, 1 Clarke, Ch. 209; Brandt's App., 8 Watts, 198; Wright's App., 12 Pa. St. 256; Ripple *v.* Ripple, 1 Rawle, 386; Montgomery *v.* McElroy, 3 Watts & S. 370; Hoes *v.* Van Hoesen, 1 Comst. 122; Gridley *v.* Andrews, 8 Conn. 1; Stevens *v.* Gregg, 10 G. & J. 143; Simmons *v.* Drury, 2 G. & J. 32.

[4] Ibid.; Newman *v.* Johnson, 1 Vern. 45; Harris *v.* Ingledew, 3 P. Wms. 91; Trott *v.* Vernon, 2 Vern. 708; Bench *v.* Biles, 4 Madd. 187; Tompkins *v.* Tompkins, Pr. Ch. 397; Kentish *v.* Kentish, 3 Bro. Ch. 257.

937

ment of his debts and legacies, and devises the residue, the legacies are charged upon the real estate, if the personal estate is insufficient to pay both debts and legacies; for a devise of the *residue* can only refer to what is left after satisfying all previous gifts.[1] But whatever may be the disposition made of the property, or however the legacies may be given, there must be a manifest intent, clearly deducible from the will, that legacies are to be paid from the real estate upon failure of the personal estate, or they cannot be charged upon the land.[2] Thus, where the devisee of real estate is appointed executor, and he is expressly directed to pay debts and legacies, he will be held to be a trustee for the legatee, or the land in his hands will be subject to the charge or trust for the debts and legacies.[3] (*a*) But

---

[1] Cornish v. Willson, 6 Gill, 299; Kirkpatrick v. Rogers, 7 Ired. Eq. 44; Tracy v. Tracy, 15 Barb. 503; Canfield v. Bostwick, 21 Conn. 550; Aubrey v. Middleton, 2 Eq. Cas. Ab. 479; Hassel v. Hassel, 2 Dick. 256; Bright v. Larcher, 3 De G. & J. 148; Kidney v. Coussmaker, 1 Ves. Jr. 436; Bench v. Biles, 4 Madd. 187; Brudenell v. Boughton, 2 Atk. 268; Mirehouse v. Scaife, 2 Myl. & Cr. 695; Cole v. Turner, 4 Russ. 376; Edgell v. Haywood, 3 Atk. 358; Greville v. Brown, 7 H. L. Cas. 689; Field v. Peckett, 29 Beav. 568; Hassanclever v. Tucker, 2 Binn. 525; Witman v. Norton, 6 Binn. 395; Nichols v. Postlethwaite, 2 Dall. 131; McLanahan v. Wyant, 1 Pa. R. 111; McGlaughlin v. McGlaughlin, 24 Pa. St. 22; Gallagher's App., 48 Pa. St. 121; Adams v. Brackett, 5 Met. 280; Downman v. Rust, 6 Rand. 587; Van Winkle v. Van Houten, 2 Green, Ch. 172; Carter v. Balfour, 19 Ala. 815; Lewis v. Darling, 16 How. 10; Buckley v. Buckley, 11 Barb. 43. [Hill v. Bean, 86 Me. 200; Walker v. Follett's Estate, 73 A. 1092 (Me. 1909); Lacey v. Collins, 134 Iowa, 583; Willcox v. Willcox, 106 Va. 626; Paterson Gen. Hosp. Ass'n v. Blauvelt, 72 N. J. Eq. 725; Simonsen v. Hutchinson, 231 Ill. 508; Moerlein v. Heyer, 100 Tex. 245; Sloan's Appeal, 168 Pa. St. 422.]

[2] Adams v. Brackett, 5 Met. 282; Lupton v. Lupton, 2 Johns. Ch. 614; Stevens v. Gregg, 10 G. & J. 143; Gridley v. Andrews, 8 Conn. 1; and see Paxson v. Potts, 2 Green, Ch. 320; Francis v. Clemow, 1 Kay, 435; Wheeler v. Howell, 3 K. & J. 198; Gyett v. Williams, 2 John. & H. 429; Owing's Case, 1 Bland, 290. [Tyler v. Tallman, 29 R. I. 57; Simonsen v. Hutchinson, 231 Ill. 508; Getchell v. Rust, 8 Del. Ch. 284; *In re* Will of Newcomb, 98 Iowa, 175.]

[3] Henvell v. Whittaker, 3 Russ. 343; Dober v. Gregory, 10 Sim. 393;

(*a*) This rule applies whether the executor takes the whole bene-   ficial interest, or only a life estate, or no beneficial interest at all. *In*

if land is devised to an executor, and there is no direction to pay legacies, they cannot be charged upon the land in his hands.[1] If, however, the personalty is grossly insufficient to pay the debts and legacies, very slight indications in the will will be laid hold of by the court to raise an implied intention that the executor is to pay the legacies out of the real estate given to him.[2] (a) The use of the word "devise," in giving the legacies, has been relied upon as some evidence that the testator intended to charge them upon his real estate;[3] and so stress has been laid upon the fact that the heir-at-law was appointed residuary legatee, devisee, and executor;[4] and so the fact that the legacy

Alcock v. Sparhawk, 2 Vern. 228; Doe v. Pratt, 6 Ad. & El. 180; Elliot v. Hancock, 2 Vern. 143; Cross v. Kennington, 9 Beav. 150; Downman v. Rust, 6 Rand. 587; Van Winkle v. Van Houten, 2 Green, Ch. 172. But see Parker v. Fearnley, 2 S. & S. 592; Paxson v. Potts, 2 Green, Ch. 313; Nyssen v. Gretton, 2 Y. & C. Exch. 222.

  [1] Stevens v. Gregg, 10 G. & J. 143.
  [2] Harris v. Fly, 7 Paige, 421; Luckett v. White, 10 G. & J. 480. [Irwin v. Teller, 188 N. Y. 25.]
  [3] Trott v. Vernon, 2 Vern. 708; Hassel v. Hassel, 2 Dick. 526.
  [4] Aubrey v. Middleton, 2 Eq. Cas. Ab. 497; Alcock v. Sparhawk, 2 Vern.

re Tanqueray-Willaume, 20 Ch. D. 465, 476.

(a) Although an insufficiency of personal property to pay legacies may oftentimes be strong evidence of an intention that real estate shall be used so far as necessary, McQueen v. Lilly, 131 Mo. 9; Price v. Price, 52 N. J. Eq. 326; the mere fact that the personalty proves to be insufficient is ordinarily not enough to show such an intention. Heathcote's Estate, 209 Pa. St. 522; Moerlein v. Heyer, 100 Tex. 245; Burns v. Allen, 89 Hun, 552; Wentworth v. Read, 166 Ill. 139. It is otherwise by statute in California and Maryland. Estate of Ratto, 149 Cal. 552; Pearson v. Wartman, 80 Md. 528. Thus where the deficiency of per-sonalty which may be used for the purpose has been caused by waste or misappropriation by the executor, the intention to charge the real estate cannot be implied. Allen v. Mattison, 39 A. 241 (R. I. 1898). But when it is clear that the testator intended to charge the real estate with payment of legacies, the lien is not extinguished by the mere fact that enough personalty comes into the hands of the executor to pay the legacies. Paterson Gen. Hosp. Ass'n v. Blauvelt, 72 N. J. Eq. 725. In the last cited case it was held to be immaterial that the executor had wasted or misappropriated personalty which, if properly used, would have exonerated the real estate.

was to a child, or other person whom the testator was under some moral obligation to support, has been considered as some evidence that the testator intended the legacy to be paid out of his real estate, if the personal estate was insufficient.[1]

§ 571. Where there is a general direction given to the executor to pay debts and legacies, he is to pay them out of the personal estate only.[2] If there is a deficiency of personal assets, they must be first applied to the payment of debts, and the legacies fail in the absence of a manifest intention to pay them out of the real estate.[3] Where real estate is devised, subject to the payment of debts and legacies, the real estate is to be resorted to in aid of the personal; and the personal must be first exhausted before the real estate can be called upon, unless there is a plain intention that the personal estate is to be entirely exonerated.[4] There is a distinction, however, between a general charge of legacies on land, and a devise of land subject to the payment of a specific sum of money, or upon condition that the devisee pays a certain sum, or in trust to pay a certain sum.[5] In such cases, the gift of the sum is contained in the devise of the land; and such sum is not to come out of the personalty at all, but is confined to the land *exclusively*.[6] There is a

238; Downman *v.* Rust, 6 Rand. 5b7; Van Winkle *v.* Van Houten, 2 Green, Ch. 191.

[1] Lypet *v.* Carter, 1 Ves. 499.

[2] Parker *v.* Fearnley, 2 S. & S. 592; Warren *v.* Davies, 2 Myl. & K. 49.

[3] Hoover *v.* Hoover, 5 Penn. St. 351.

[4] Amesbury *v.* Brown, 1 Ves. 481; Holford *v.* Wood, 4 id. 76; Hancock *v.* Minot, 8 Pick. 29; Leavitt *v.* Wooster, 14 N. H. 550; Hassanclever *v.* Tucker, 2 Binn. 525; Ruston *v.* Ruston, 2 Yeates, 65; Fenwick *v.* Chapman, 9 Pet. 466; Bank of U. S. *v.* Beverly, 1 How. 134; Lewis *v.* Darling, 16 How. 10; Hoes *v.* Van Hoesen, 1 Comst. 122; Buckley *v.* Buckley, 11 Barb. 43; Chase *v.* Lockerman, 11 G. & J. 186.

[5] Clery's App., 35 Penn. St. 54.

[6] Whaley *v.* Cox, 2 Eq. Cas. Ab. 549; Amesbury *v.* Brown, 1 Ves. 481; Noel *v.* Henley, 7 Price, 241; Phipps *v.* Annesley, 2 Atk. 57; Wood *v.* Dudley, 2 Bro. Ch. 316; Holford *v.* Wood, 4 Ves. 89; Read *v.* Lichfield, 3 Ves. 479; Fowler *v.* Willoughby, 2 S. & S. 354; Spurway *v.* Glynn, 9 Ves. 483; Gitting *v.* Steele, 1 Swanst. 24; Hoover *v.* Hoover, 5 Barr, 351; Halliday *v.* Summerville, 2 Pa. R. 533.

great difference between this class of legacies and debts; for debts are a charge upon the personalty at all events, and independent of the will, while general legacies are given by will voluntarily, and are confined to payment out of the personalty, unless an intention can be found in the will to charge them on the real estate upon failure of the personal; but these gifts out of the real estate have no existence except in the gift of the real estate, and can in no event be made a charge upon the personal estate.[1]

§ 572. As the charge of legacies upon real estate is wholly a matter of intention in the testator, it may happen that some of the legacies given in a will are charged upon the real estate, and some are not. Thus, where a testator devised lands subject to certain legacies mentioned, and then gave *other* legacies, and devised the residue of his lands, it was held by Lord Thurlow, that the last-named legacies were not charged upon the real estate.[2] So the testator may direct that certain portions of his real estate shall be exempt from the payment of legacies, although he charges the legacies generally upon his real estate.[3]

§ 573. If a testator charges some legacies on his land, and leaves others not so charged, and the legacies payable out of the land are paid out of the personal estate, those legacies not payable out of the land have a right to stand in the place of the legacies that were expressly charged upon the land. For although there is generally no marshalling in favor of general legatees or annuitants, yet if legatees who can resort to the real estate exhaust the personal, the legatees who have only the personal shall be subrogated, and their legacies become a

[1] Bickham *v*. Cruttwell, 3 Myl. & Cr. 763; Noel *v*. Henley, 7 Price, 241; 2 Jarm. Pow. Dev. 708.

[2] Howe *v*. Medcroft, 1 Bro. Ch. 261; Masters *v*. Masters, 1 P. Wms. 421; Strong *v*. Ingraham, 6 Sim. 197; Radburn *v*. Jervis, 3 Beav. 450. But see Rooke *v*. Worrell, 11 Sim. 216.

[3] Birmingham *v*. Kirwin, 2 Sch. & Lef. 448.

charge upon the real estate.[1] So if debts are expressly charged upon real estate, legatees shall be paid out of the personal estate, as against the heir or devisee.[2]

§ 574. Where an executor, who is also appointed trustee for the investment and holding of legacies, has set apart and invested the legacies, he will cease to be executor as to those particular legacies, but will be holden as trustee; and the testator's estate will no longer be holden for the payment of the legacy, if it is afterwards lost.[3] (a) In the United States, it is

[1] Hanby v. Roberts, Amb. 127; Masters v. Masters, 1 P. Wms. 421; Bligh v. Darnley, 2 id. 619; Bonner v. Bonner, 13 Ves. 379.

[2] Patterson v. Scott, 1 De G., M. & G. 531; Conron v. Conron, 7 H. L. Cas. 168; Bardwell v. Bardwell, 10 Pick. 19; Mollan v. Griffith, 3 Paige, 402; Smith v. Wyckoff, 11 Paige, 49; Loomis's App., 10 Penn. St. 390. Mirehouse v. Scaife, 2 Myl. & Cr. 695, is overruled. This rule does not apply, in England, to legacies for charitable purposes, as the statutes of mortmain might thereby be eluded. Mogg v. Hodges, 2 Ves. 62; Williams v. Kershaw, note to Hobson v. Blackburn, 1 Keen, 273; Philanthropic Soc. v. Kemp, 4 Beav. 581; Sturge v. Dimsdale, 6 Beav. 462; Robinson v. Geldard, 3 Mac. & Gor. 735. It is not within the purpose of this work to trace the rules in regard to the marshalling of assets. See Aldrich v. Cooper, 2 Lead. Cas. Eq. 56, for an able review of the cases and statement of all the rules; and see Teas's App., 23 Penn. St. 228; Miller v. Harwell, 3 Murph. 194; Toombs v. Roch, 2 Col. C. C. 494; Fleming v. Buchanan, 3 De G., M. & G. 976.

[3] Page v. Leapingwell, 18 Ves. 463; Jenkins v. Wilmot, 1 Beav. 401; Tyson v. Jackson, 30 Beav. 384; Byrchall v. Bradford, 6 Madd. 13, 235;

(a) As to the liability of the executor in such a case where the property set apart proves insufficient to satisfy the trust legacies and he has meanwhile paid out the remainder of the estate to other legatees, some of whom were merely residuary legatees, see Re Hurst; Addison v. Topp, 67 L. T. 96. It is there said, on the authority of Fenwick v. Clark, 4 De G., F. & J. 240, and Frere v. Winslow, 45 Ch. Div. 249, that the executor is not liable for a deficiency due to a depreciation in value of the property set apart by him unless he was negligent, and is not responsible for having paid too much to the other legatees. But on the facts of the principal case he was held liable for having unnecessarily paid residuary legatees, where the only property held for the trust legacies was a compulsory investment upon somewhat risky security.

usual for the executor in such cases to receive an appointment
as trustee, and give a bond to the judge of probate for the performance of the trust; but the executor may act as trustee, and
the sureties on his bond as executor will be holden for his acts.[1]
The estate of the testator will not be holden for any loss, if the
executor has clearly set aside any fund as payment of a legacy,
although he holds the same in his own hands as trustee for the
legatee. If, however, the executor has not settled an account
in probate court, and charged off the amount of the legacy paid
to him as trustee, he must show some act, such as setting apart
and payment, or the legatee will still be entitled to receive the
legacy out of the estate of the testator. The mere mental determination of the executor to set aside a certain fund as payment of a legacy, and to hold the same thereafter as trustee, is
not sufficient.[2]

§ 575. If the testator names any time for the payment of
legacies, they will bear interest from that time. It has already been seen, that the tenant for life is entitled to income
upon the estate given for his use, after the expiration of one
year from the testator's death, on the ground that the executor
or trustee has one full year to reduce the estate to possession,
and to convert and invest it.[3] (a) So if a testator names no

Ex parte Chadwin, 3 Swanst. 380; Philippo *v.* Munnings, 2 Myl. & Cr. 309;
Newman *v.* Williams, 10 L. J. (N. S.) Ch. 106.

[1] Dorr *v.* Wainwright, 13 Pick. 388; Brown *v.* Kelsey, 2 Cush. 248;
Hubbard *v.* Lloyd, 6 Cush. 524; Prior *v.* Talbot, 10 Cush. 1; Hall *v.* Cushing,
9 Pick. 395.

[2] Miller *v.* Congdon, 14 Gray, 114; Newcomb *v.* Williams, 9 Met. 534;
Conkey *v.* Dickinson, 13 Met. 63; *ante*, §§ 263, 281.

[3] *Ante*, § 548.

(a) It has become a general
rule that the life beneficiary in
such a case is entitled to income
from the date of the testator's
death in the absence of a contrary
intention, although the executor
cannot be compelled to actually
pay it over until the expiration of
a year. Wethered *v.* Safe Dep. &
Tr. Co., 79 Md. 153; Union Safe
Dep., etc., Co. *v.* Dudley, 104 Me.
297, 312; Doherty *v.* Grady, 105
Me. 36; Weld *v.* Putnam, 70 Me.
209; Jordan *v.* Jordan, 192 Mass.

time for the payment of legacies, they will be payable in one
year after his death, and will bear interest from that time,[1] unless a contrary intention is shown in the will.

§ 576. Where an express trust is created in lands for the
payment of legacies, or they are devised to an executor, trustee,
or other person beneficially, and he is to pay the legacies charged,
and such trustee, executor, or other person accepts the devise
and the trust, he will become personally liable to execute the
trusts and pay the legacies.[2] (a) The lands so charged with the
trust of paying legacies may be followed into whosesoever hands
they come; for the title of the devisee or trustee being by will
and recorded, purchasers will be charged with constructive

---

[1] 2 Rop. Leg. 222; 2 Kent, 417; Hite v. Hite, 2 Rand. 409; Birdsall v.
Hewlett, 1 Paige, 32; Glen v. Fisher, 6 Johns. Ch. 33; Trippe v. Frazier,
4 H. & J. 446; 2 Redf. on Wills, 465–475.

[2] Lockwood v. Stockholm, 11 Paige, 387; Dodge v. Manning, id. 334;
Bank of United States v. Beverly, 1 How. 134; Mahar v. O'Hara, 4 Gilm.
424; Solliday v. Gruver, 7 Penn. St. 452; Mittenberger v. Schlegel, id. 241;
Bugbee v. Sargent, 23 Maine, 269; Glen v. Fisher, 6 Johns. Ch. 33; Larkin
v. Mason, 53 Barb. 267.

337, 345; Ayer v. Ayer, 128 Mass.
575; Sargent v. Sargent, 103 Mass.
297; Baker v. Fooks, 8 Del. Ch.
84; Bishop v. Bishop, 71 A. 583
(Conn. 1909); Matter of Stanfield,
135 N. Y. 292; Bank of Niagara v.
Talbot, 110 App. Div. (N. Y.) 519
(affirmed 184 N. Y. 576); Eichelberger's Estate, 170 Pa. St. 242;
Flickwir's Estate, 136 Pa. St. 374.
See supra, § 550 and notes.

(a) A devise or bequest to a
person "upon condition" that he
pay a certain legacy or an annuity,
or provide for the support and
proper maintenance of another is
usually held to create a personal
obligation of such devisee or legatee,
arising upon his acceptance, to-

gether with a lien upon the property as security for the performance of this personal obligation.
Spangler v. Newman, 239 Ill. 616;
Stringer v. Gamble, 155 Mich.
295; Merchants' Nat. Bank v.
Crist, 140 Iowa, 308; Cunningham v. Parker, 146 N. Y. 29. See
Spearman v. Foote, 126 Ill. App.
370; In re Taber, 116 N. Y. S.
960; Waddell v. Waddell, 68 S. C.
335. The ordinary statute of
limitations will run against the personal obligation from the time of
its breach. Merton v. O'Brien, 117
Wis. 437. But it does not necessarily follow that the lien, if it is
an interest in land, is lost. See
McKinley v. Coe, 66 N. J. Eq. 70.

notice.[1] A payment of the legacy by the note of the trustee or devisee, and a receipt in full signed by the legatee, will not discharge the lien upon the land, if the legatee cannot collect a judgment on the note against the devisee.[2] This rule, however, would probably be confined to the original parties; for if, after the note and receipt, there should be a sale of the land, a purchaser would not probably be holden. So the statute of limitations will not bar the claim of the legatee or *cestui que trust* to receive his legacy from the devisee or trustee;[3] but the lapse of twenty years will create a presumption of payment.[4]

§ 577. In marriage and family settlements, whether by deed or will, provisions are sometimes inserted that the trustee shall raise portions for children at certain times or upon certain events, as upon their marriage, or arrival at the age of twenty-one. In England, a term of years is generally carved out of the estate, and limited to the trustees to secure the payment of such portions as are directed to be raised. In the United States, it is more usual to direct the portions to be raised from the rents and profits of the estate, or by sale or mortgage of some part of it. These directions are in the nature of charges upon the real estate, and although there may be a covenant in the deed of settlement that the settlor will pay the amount, yet the charge on the real estate is generally the *primary* fund, and the covenants of the settlor or his personal estate are merely

[1] Harris *v.* Fly, 7 Paige, 421; Aston *v.* Galloway, 3 Ired. Eq. 126; Wallington *v.* Taylor, Saxton, 314; Howard *v.* Chaffee, 2 Dr. & Sm. 236; Dodge *v.* Manning, 11 Paige, 334; Mahar *v.* O'Hara, 3 Gilm. 424; Mittenberger *v.* Schlegel, 7 Penn. St. 241; Solliday *v.* Gruver, id. 452; Bank of U. S. *v.* Beverly, 1 How. 134; Hallett *v.* Hallett, 2 Paige, 15; Owing's Case, 1 Bland, 290; Kemp *v.* McPherson, 7 H. & J. 320; Phillips *v.* Gutteridge, 3 De G., J. & S. 332.

[2] Terhune *v.* Colton, 2 Stockt. 21; Schanck *v.* Arrowsmith, 1 id. 314.

[3] Watson *v.* Saul, 1 Gif. 188. [See Merton *v.* O'Brien, 117 Wis. 437; McKinley *v.* Coe, 66 N. J. Eq. 70.]

[4] Henderson *v.* Atkins, 28 L. J. Ch. (N. S.) 913. As to the duty of purchasers to look to the application of the purchase-money of lands sold for the payment of legacies, see chapter upon that subject.

auxiliary to the charge upon the land.[1] If the charge or trust is created by will, it is of course to be executed precisely as created, and the land only is liable for the amount to be raised.[2] (a)

§ 578. It sometimes happens, that trustees are directed to hold an estate for the life of parents, for their use, and to pay the parents the rents during their lives, or to permit them to use, occupy, and improve the same; and they are directed to raise portions for the children, to be paid them upon the happening of certain events, as their marriage, or arrival at twenty-one, which events frequently happen during the lifetime of the parents, or tenants for life. Under such directions, very vexatious questions have arisen: whether the trustees are to raise the portions *immediately* on the happening of the event upon which the children are to be paid, or whether the raising of the money should be postponed to the end of the life-estate of the parents. A vast number of conflicting decisions have been made upon this question.[3] In one class of cases, it has been held that the portions should be raised, during the life-estate of the parents, by a sale or mortgage of the reversion; [4] in other cases, that the sale or mortgage should be postponed until the determination of the life-estate.[5] "The raising or not raising

[1] Lanoy v. Athol, 2 Atk. 444; Lechmere v. Charlton, 15 Ves. 193.

[2] Burgoyne v. Fox, 1 Atk. 576; Edwards v. Freeman, 2 P. Wms. 437; 1 Story's Eq. Jur. § 575.

[3] 4 Kent, 149, 150; 2 Story's Eq. Jur. § 1003.

[4] Hillier v. Jones, 1 Eq. Cas. Ab. 337; Smith v. Evans, Amb. 533; Mitchell v. Mitchell, 4 Beav. 549; Staniforth v. Staniforth, 2 Vern. 460; Gerrard v. Gerrard, id. 458; Hebblethwaite v. Cartwright, Forr. 30; Sandys v. Sandys, 1 P. Wms. 707; Codrington v. Foley, 6 Ves. 364; Hall v. Carter, 2 Atk. 354; Smith v. Foley, 3 Y. & C. 142; Mills v. Banks, 3 P. Wms. 9.

[5] Reresby v. Newland, 2 P. Wms. 94; 6 Bro. P. C. 75; Verney v. Verney, 2 Eden, 25; Stanley v. Stanley, 1 Atk. 545; Conway v. Conway, 3 Bro. Ch. 267; Clinton v. Seymour, 4 Ves. 440; Stevens v. Dethick, 3 Atk. 39;

(a) In a case where, for the purpose of paying debts, it became necessary to resort to real estate charged with the payment of portions, it was held that nothing was to be deducted from the amount of the portions. *In re* Saunders-Davies, 34 Ch. Div. 482.

will depend upon the particular penning of the trust and the intention of the instrument;"[1] and the court will have no leaning one way or the other.[2]

§ 579. The general rule is now established, that where there is a direction to raise the portion by sale or mortgage, and to pay the same at a particular time or on the happening of a particular event, as on marriage, or at twenty-one, and there is nothing in the will or settlement to indicate a different intention, the portions must be raised by the trustees by an immediate sale or mortgage;[3] but if there are any expressions from which it may be inferred that the portions are not to be raised during the continuance of the life-estate of the parents, effect will be given to such expressions. Thus where the parents were to appoint the portions, by deed or *will ;*[4] or where the trustee was to raise the portions from and after the end of the life-estate,[5] it was held that these expressions were conclusive that the portions were not to be raised during the lifetime of the parents. The intention must be sought in the instrument only, and no extraneous evidence can be used.[6]

§ 580. At the present day, it is the usual practice to insert in settlements a clause to the effect that portions shall not be raised during the continuance of the life-estate, or during the lifetime of the parents.[7] Upon the happening of the

Wynter *v.* Bold, 1 S. & S. 507; Corbett *v.* Maydwell, 2 Vern. 640; Brome *v.* Berkley, 2 P. Wms. 484; Butler *v.* Duncomb, 1 id. 448.

[1] Lord Talbot in Hebblethwaite *v.* Cartwright, Forr. 32, and Lord Eldon in Codrington *v.* Foley, 6 Ves. 379.

[2] Codrington *v.* Foley, 6 Ves. 380; contrary to Stanley *v.* Stanley, 1 Atk. 549, and Clinton *v.* Seymour, 4 Ves. 460, where it was said that the court would lean against the raising.

[3] Codrington *v.* Foley, 6 Ves. 380.

[4] Wynter *v.* Bold, 1 S. & S. 507. But see Gough *v.* Andrews, 1 Coll. 69.

[5] Butler *v.* Duncomb, 1 P. Wms. 448.

[6] Corbett *v.* Maydwell, 2 Vern. 641.

[7] Hall *v.* Carter, 2 Atk. 356.

event upon which the portion is payable, the child takes a vested interest in the portion; and if he dies before it is paid, the right to the portion will vest in his representatives, to be paid when the portion is raised. Courts adopt this construction wherever it is possible to sustain it,[1] though they never do violence to the express words of the instrument in order to uphold it.[2] Thus, if it is manifest on the face of the instrument that no child was intended to take a portion unless he survived his parents, the expressed intention will prevail.[3] So, in the case of a voluntary settlement, the children of a deceased child, for whom a portion was to be raised, will take such portion, and the consideration of love and affection extended to grandchildren will be a sufficient consideration to uphold the settlement, though voluntary, so far as the settlor has placed himself *in loco parentis*.[4] Therefore it is now the usual practice to insert a clause in the settlement to the effect, that such portion shall, or shall not, be payable to such child's representatives in case he dies before his parents, or before the portion is payable to him. (*a*)

§ 581. If the portions to be raised are effectually charged upon the land, the trustees will take, by implication, the power

[1] Clayton *v.* Glengall, 1 Dr. & W. 1; Howgrave *v.* Cartier, 3 V. & B. 86; Coop. 66; Whatford *v.* Moore, 2 Myl. & Cr. 291; Emperor *v.* Rolfe, 1 Ves. 208; Powis *v.* Burdett, 9 Ves. 428; Frye *v.* Shelbourne, 3 Sim. 243; Combe *v.* Combe, 2 Atk. 185; Hope *v.* Clifden, 6 Ves. 499; Woodcock *v.* Dorset, 3 Bro. Ch. 569; King *v.* Hake, 9 Ves. 438.

[2] Whatford *v.* Moore, 7 Sim. 574; 3 Myl. & Cr. 274; Fitzgerald *v.* Field, 1 Russ. 430; Hotchkin *v.* Humphrey, 2 Madd. 65.   [3] Ibid.

[4] Swallow *v.* Binns, 1 K. & J. 417; 19 Jur. 843; Henderson *v.* Kennicott, 12 Jur. 848; Jones *v.* Jones, 13 Sim. 568; Evans *v.* Scott, 1 Cl. & Fin. (N. S.) 57.

(*a*) In construing a marriage settlement, there is a presumption that the settlor, in providing for his unborn children, intends that their portions shall become vested at twenty-one or marriage. Wakefield *v.* Maffet, 10 A. C. 422, 435. The rule that that construction is to be favored which will give portions to all of a class of children who may live to require them, applies both to settlements and to wills. *In re* Knowles, 21 Ch. D. 806.

of selling or mortgaging it for the purpose, although that
power is not given to them in the instrument; for that is the
most natural way of carrying out the intention of the parties
in raising the portions.[1] Even where the trust is to raise the
portion from rents and profits, if a *particular time* is named
for the payment so near that it is impossible to raise the sum
before the appointed time, it will be considered that it was
inconsistent that the settlor intended that the whole sum
should be raised from the annual rents and profits, and a mortgage or sale will be ordered.[2] (*a*) So if the directions to the
trustees are to raise the portions "as soon as conveniently
may be," or "as soon as possible." [3] The rule has been carried
to the extent, that where the trustees were directed to raise
a gross sum for portions from the *rents and profits*, and there
were no words restricting the authority to *annual* rents and
profits, they have been held to be authorized to raise the required sum at once by sale or mortgage.[4] The intention of
the settlor, however, must prevail, and if the portions are
to be raised from *annual* rents and profits, or if any words
are used implying such an intention, there can be no sale or
mortgage.[5] In cases where the portions are to be raised from
rents and profits, and a power of sale or mortgage is also given
by implication or in express words, the rents and profits must

[1] Backhouse *v.* Middleton, 1 Ch. Cas. 175; Sheldon *v.* Dormer, 2 Vern.
310; Ashton *v.* ——, 10 Mod. 401; Maynel *v.* Massey, 2 Vern. 1.

[2] Sheldon *v.* Dormer, 2 Vern. 310; Okeden *v.* Okeden, 1 Atk. 551; Backhouse *v.* Middleton, 1 Ch. Cas. 175; Allan *v.* Backhouse, 2 V. & B. 65.

[3] Trafford *v.* Ashton, 2 P. Wms. 416; Ashton *v.* ——, 10 Mod. 401;
Bloom *v.* Waldron, 3 Hill, 367.   n

[4] Ivy *v.* Gilbert, 2 P. Wms. 19; Evelyn *v.* Evelyn, id. 669; Baines *v.*
Dixon, 1 Ves. 42; Green *v.* Belcher, 1 Atk. 505; Shrewsbury *v.* Shrewsbury,
1 Ves. Jr. 234; Warburton *v.* Warburton, 2 Vern. 420; Mills *v.* Banks, 3
P. Wms. 7; Hall *v.* Carter, 2 Atk. 358; Anon., 1 Vern. 104; Schermerhorne
v. Schermerhorne, 6 Johns. Ch. 70; 1 Story's Eq. Jur., § 1063 *et seq.*

[5] Garmstone *v.* Gaunt, 9 Jur. 78.

(*a*) A direction in a will to pay
debts out of rents and profits of
realty *prima facie* charges the debts
on the *corpus.* Metcalfe *v.* Hutchinson, 1 Ch. D. 591; *In re* Green,
40 id. 610.

first be applied so far as they will go, in order to sell as small a part of the estate as possible.[1] The trustees may also raise portions by selling the wood and timber upon an estate, or the minerals and mines may be worked for the raising of portions.[2]

§ 582. If a *gross* sum is directed to be raised for the portions of several children, to be paid at twenty-one or any other appointed time, and the shares of each are vested, though not payable, the gross sum should be raised as soon as the first portion becomes payable;[3] and the portions not then payable should be invested in the securities allowed by law, or in safe securities, where there are no investments pointed out by statutes or orders of court. It is not a proper administration to incumber an estate with as many different mortgages as there are portions, when one gross sum is directed to be raised.[4] But if *several distinct sums* are directed to be raised and paid at different times, the several portions cannot be raised until they become payable; and if the trustees raise them before, and lose or misapply the money, the land would still be liable to the charge, although some of the portions were payable.[5]

§ 583. Where trustees are directed to apply the rents and profits of an estate for a certain period to the maintenance and education of children or other persons, such direction will constitute a charge upon the estate in the hands of the trustees.[6] If the trustees are directed to raise a portion or portions out of the rents and profits, at or before a certain

[1] Okeden v. Okeden, 1 Atk. 552; Warter v. Hutchinson, 1 S. & S. 276; Hall v. Carter, 2 Atk. 358.
[2] Offley v. Offley, Pr. Ch. 27.
[3] Gillbrand v. Goold, 5 Sim. 149.
[4] Ibid.
[5] Dickinson v. Dickinson, 3 Bro. Ch. 19; Breedon v. Breedon, 1 R. & M. 413; Sowarsby v. Lacy, 4 Madd. 142; Lavender v. Stanton, 6 Madd. 46.
[6] Robinson v. Townshend, 3 G. & J. 413; Fox v. Phelps, 17 Wend. 393; 20 Wend. 437.

time, and they suffer the term to expire without raising the portions, the court can direct them to be raised out of the rents and profits on hand, or it can order those persons to whom such rents and profits have been distributed, to refund or contribute to the raising of the portions.[1]

§ 584. Interest is payable upon portions from and after the time named for their payment, although nothing is said in the settlement upon that subject.[2] If, however, there are any provisions in the will or settlement upon the subject of interest, or for the payment of any particular sum in place of interest, such provisions must be carried into effect.[3] So the directions of the settlement must be followed in relation to the expenses of raising the portions; but if there are no such directions, the expenses must be paid out of the estate.[4] Trusts for accumulations to raise portions for children are specially excepted from the operation of the Thellusson Act,[5] (a) so called, regulating trusts for accumulation; but such trusts are not excepted in the statutes of New York[6] and Pennsylvania[7] against accumulations.

[1] Hawley v. James, 5 Paige, 318.

[2] Beal v. Beal, Pr. Ch. 405; Bagenal v. Bagenal, 6 Bro. P. C. 81; Roseberry v. Taylor, id. 43; Hall v. Carter, 2 Atk. 358; Pomfret v. Winsor, 2 Ves. 472; Boycott v. Cotton, 1 Atk. 552; Leech v. Leech, 2 Dr. & W. 568, overruling Hays v. Bayley, 3 Sugd. V. & P. (10th ed.); Guillam v. Holland, 2 Atk. 343; Trimlestown v. Colt, 1 Ves. Sr. 277.

[3] Clayton v. Glengall, 1 Dr. & W. 1; Boycott v. Cotton, 1 Atk. 553; Mitchell v. Bower, 3 Ves. 286.

[4] Mitchell v. Mitchell, 4 Beav. 549.

[5] 39 & 40 Geo. III. c. 98; Edwards v. Tuck, 3 De G., M. & G. 40; Barrington v. Liddell, 2 De G., M. & G. 480; Jones v. Maggs, 9 Hare, 605; Evans v. Hellier, 5 Cl. & Fin. 114; Burt v. Sturt, 10 Hare, 415; Beech v. Vincent, 3 De G. & Sm. 678; 19 L. J. Ch. 131; Morgan v. Morgan, 20 L. J. Ch. 109; Halford v. Stains, 16 Sim. 488.

[6] R. S. pt. 2, tit. 2, c. 1, art. 1, § 37. [IV Consol. Laws (1909), pp. 2844 & 3384.]

[7] Purd. L. 507; 1853, April 18, § 9. [4 Purdon's Digest (13th ed.), p. 4036, § 65.]

(a) See Re Walker, 54 L. T. 322; In re Heathcote, [1904] 1 Ch. 792; In re Stephens, [1904] 1 Ch. 826; supra, § 394, et seq.

CHAPTER XX.

§ 585. A DEBTOR may convey or assign both his real and personal estate to trustees for the payment of his debts; and such trust may be limited to the payment of one particular debt due to the trustees [1] or some third person,[2] or of several debts specified in the deed or schedule annexed to it.[3] This trust may be extended generally for the benefit of all the

[1] Foster *v*. Latham, 21 Ill. App. 165.

[2] Page *v*. Broom, 4 Russ. 6; De Wol *v*. Chapin, 4 Pick. 59; Cooper *v*. Whitney, 3 Hill, 95; Chaplin *v*. Maglaughlin, 65 Penn. St. 492.

[3] Boazman *v*. Johnson, 3 Sim. 377; Hamilton *v*. Houghton, 2 Bligh,169; Garrard *v*. Lauderdale, 3 Sim. 1; Walwyn *v*. Coutts, 3 Mer. 707; 3 Sim. 14; Shirly *v*. Ferrers, 1 Bro. Ch. 41; Purefoy *v*. Purefoy, 1 Vern. 28.

debtor's or grantor's creditors,[1] or to all who execute the deed or otherwise assent thereto.[2] (*a*) The trust may be further limited to pay equally without distinction;[3] or at common law, it may be limited to make certain priorities and preferences in the payments.[4] The deed may direct the debts to be paid in full,[5] or a certain proportion or composition may be determined to be paid.[6] The deed may contain a trust for creditors, and also a settlement upon a wife and children.[7] An arrangement of this kind, fairly made by a contract with the creditors, or accepted or acted upon by them, is valid and binding upon all parties;[8] even a creditor not concurring but only standing by and without objection seeing the trustee act under the

[1] Carr *v.* Burlington, 1 P. Wms. 228; Boswell *v.* Parker, 2 Ves. 364; Hinde *v.* Blake, 3 Beav. 234; Acton *v.* Woodgate, 2 Myl. & K. 492.

[2] Dunch *v.* Kent, 1 Vern. 260; *Ex parte* Richardson, 14 Ves. 184; Spottiswoode *v.* Stockdale, Coop. 102; Hatch *v.* Smith, 5 Mass. 42.

[3] Carr *v.* Burlington, 1 P. Wms. 228.

[4] Lanning *v.* Lanning, 2 Green, Ch. 228; McColghan *v.* Hopkins, 17 Md. 395; Purefoy *v.* Purefoy, 1 Vern. 28; Cunningham *v.* Freeborn, 11 Wend. 241; Stevenson *v.* Agry, 7 Ham. (2d pt.) 247; Pearson *v.* Rockhill, 4 B. Mon. 296; Niolon *v.* Douglas, 2 Hill, Ch. 443; Moffatt *v.* McDowall, 1 McCord, Ch. 434; Tompkins *v.* Wheeler, 16 Pet. 106; McCollough *v.* Sommerville, 8 Leigh, 415; Hickley *v.* Farmers' & Merch. Bank, 5 Gill & J. 377; Williams *v.* Brown, 4 Johns. Ch. 427; Brashear *v.* West, 7 Pet. 608; Spring *v.* South Carolina Ins. Co., 8 Wheat. 268; Hatch *v.* Smith, 5 Mass. 42; Stevens *v.* Bell, 6 Mass. 339; Lippincott *v.* Barker, 2 Binn. 174; Wilkes *v.* Ferris, 8 Johns. 335; Rankin *v.* Loder, 2 Ala. 380; How *v.* Camp, Walk. Ch. 427; Holbrook *v.* Allen, 4 Fla. 87.

[5] Ibid.

[6] Stephenson *v.* Hayward, Pr. Ch. 310; Tatlock *v.* Smith, 6 Bing. 339; Constantein *v.* Blache, 1 Cox, 287; Vernon *v.* Morton, 8 Dana, 247.

[7] Johnson *v.* Malcomb, 6 Jones, Eq. 120.

[8] Small *v.* Marwood, 9 B. & Cr. 300.

(*a*) The scope of this book does not premit a full examination of all the recent decisions upon the topic of assignments for the benefit of creditors. As the text has dealt with the topic only in outline, the editor of the sixth edition has tried to confine his notes and new cita-tions to the original purpose of the chapter. The citation of authorities is, therefore, not exhaustive, but is designed only to indicate the various questions that have arisen and the various differences of authority.

trust may be bound by tacit acquiescence;[1] and courts will enjoin or restrain any act in violation of this trust by any of the parties.[2] Such a trust deed for the payment of debts is favorably regarded in equity; and it will be supported, if possible, without regard to the strict technicalities of the law;[3] as, where a party, with power of leasing in possession, made a lease to commence in the future, in trust for the payment of his debts, or where a party covenanted to stand seized of land to the use of another, in consideration of his paying the debts of the covenantor out of the profits of the land, the transactions were upheld in equity as trusts for the payment of debts, though they would not have been good at law.[4] In such a deed the recital of debts raises a presumption of indebtedness, but it may be rebutted.[5] Where one creates a trust, making himself the *cestui* for life, and then assigns his beneficial interest as security for debt, he cannot, as against the creditor, subsequently alter the terms of the trust so as to make the payment of the income discretionary with the trustee.[6]

§ 586. At common law, an insolvent debtor has the right to prefer any of his creditors. He may prefer one to all, or all to one, for the reason that it is not illegal to pay debts; and as creditors may sue and obtain judgment, and levy executions, each one for himself, and obtain as much advantage as possible by gaining priority of time, so the debtor may voluntarily do what each of his creditors may do by law, that is, obtain a preference.[7] Under the bankrupt law of the United States now in force, all conveyances and assignments

---

[1] Condict *v.* Flower, 106 Ill. 105.

[2] Spottiswoode *v.* Stockdale, Coop. 102; Mackenzie *v.* Mackenzie, 16 Ves. 372; *Ex parte* Sadler, 15 Ves. 52; Beck *v.* Parker, 65 Pa. St. 262.

[3] Dunch *v.* Kent, 1 Vern. 260; Spottiswoode *v.* Stockdale, Coop. 102; Turner *v.* Jaycox, 40 Barb. 164.

[4] Pollard *v.* Greenville, 1 Ch. Cas. 10; Lord Paget's Case, 1 Leon. 194; 4 Cruise, Dig. tit. 32, c. 9, §§ 25, 26.

[5] Graham *v.* Anderson, 42 Ill. 514.

[6] Pacific Nat'l B'k *v.* Windram, 133 Mass. 175.

[7] *Ante*, § 585, and cases cited.

made within six months of filing a petition of bankruptcy, which give a preference to any creditor, are fraudulent and void, if the debtor knows himself to be insolvent, and there is an intent to prefer.[1] (a) Substantially the same provisions are enacted in the English statutes of bankruptcy.[2] In some of the States preferences are prohibited, and an assignment containing a preference is fraudulent and void; but in others, as in Ohio and Pennsylvania, the assignment is not void, but the provision only containing the preference is void, and the assignment enures to all creditors equally in proportion to their demands:[3] but if the assignment is in trust for such creditors as release, no releasing creditors are excluded.[4] In States where preferences have not been prohibited by statute, courts lean strongly against them, and will not support them if they can be avoided for any good reason.[5] But these statutes against preferences apply only to general assignments, and not to *bona fide* sales to a creditor to pay a valid debt, or partial assignments for particular purposes.[6] While the general bankrupt law is in force, assignments will be infrequent; but, as they may still be made, a general outline of the law only will be stated. (b)

[1] Stat. 1867, March 2, §§ 81, 82, 83.

[2] 24 & 25 Vict. c. 134.

[3] Law v. Mills, 18 Penn. St. 185; Wiener v. Davis, id. 331; Hulls v. Jeffrey, 8 Ohio, 390; Harshman v. Lowe, 9 id. 92; Wilcox v. Kellogg, 11 id. 394; Mitchell v. Gazzam, 12 id. 315. [See note b.]

[4] Lea's App., 9 Barr, 504.

[5] Boardman v. Halliday, 10 Paige, 224; Cram v. Mitchell, 1 Sandf. 251; Webb v. Daggett, 2 Barb. 10; Nicholson v. Leavitt, 4 Sandf. 279.

[6] McWhorter v. Wright, 5 Ga. 555; Bates v. Coe, 10 Conn. 281; Mer. Man. Co. v. Smith, 8 N. H. 347; Beard v. Kimball, 11 N. H. 471; Barker v. Hall, 13 N. H. 298; Henshaw v. Sumner, 23 Pick. 446. [Maloney v. Gonhue, 152 Mich. 325, 336; Morriss v. Blackman, 179 Ill. 103; United Rys. & Elec. Co. v. Rowe, 97 Md. 656. See Walker v. Ross, 150 Ill. 50; Grimes Dry Goods Co. v. Malcolm, 164 U. S. 483; Adler-Goldman Co. v. Phillips, 63 Ark. 40.]

(a) Under the U. S. Bankruptcy Law of 1898, § 60, the period within which the petition must be filed is four months. See *infra*.

(b) In some States statutes have been enacted which deal specifically with preferences in voluntary assignments. These statutes, how-

§ 587. If a debtor assigns his whole property, he becomes insolvent and bankrupt. The bankrupt laws require a bank-

ever, usually provide that the attempted preference, not the assignment itself, shall be void. See Shillito Co. v. McConnell, 130 Ind. 41; Sturtevant v. Sarbach, 58 Kan. 410; Dwight v. Scranton, etc., Lumber Co., 67 Mich. 507, 513; Pollock v. Sykes, 74 Miss. 700, 713; Royster v. Stallings, 124 N. C. 55. It does not seem to be within the scope of this book to state the various provisions of these statutes. For a comprehensive examination of them see Burrill on Assignments (6th ed.), Appendix I.

Provisions in the insolvency statutes of the various States to the effect that preferences shall be void were usually limited to preferences made within a limited period, usually six months or less, before the beginning of the proceedings in insolvency. For a typical statute of this kind see Mass. R. L. (1902), c. 163, § 110. Steel Edge, etc., Co. v. Manchester Bank, 163 Mass. 252; Nat. Mechanics' & Traders' Bank v. Eagle Sugar Ref., 109 Mass. 38.

Under the United States Bankruptcy Law of 1898, which has superseded the various insolvency statutes though apparently not the assignment statutes, a mere preference is not fraudulent unless made within four months before the filing of a petition in bankruptcy. Even then it is only constructively fraudulent. This kind of fraud is essentially different from the fraud which taints a conveyance made for the purpose of "hindering, de-

laying or defrauding creditors." The payment or the creation of a trust for the payment of one or more creditors in full when the debtor has insufficient to pay all, is not fraud of the latter kind, and is not fraud under the United States Bankruptcy Law unless made within four months before a petition in bankruptcy is filed by or against the insolvent debtor. Although the Federal Bankruptcy Law expressly provides that a general assignment for the benefit of creditors, even without preferences, is an act of bankruptcy, if the petition is filed within four months after the assignment, this provision does not affect assignments made more than four months before the petition. The validity of such assignments is dependent upon the local law, and it is only when they are in violation of some local statute or are fraudulent under the principles of the Statute of Elizabeth that the trustee in bankruptcy can have them set aside. Randolph v. Scruggs, 190 U. S. 533; Cohen v. Am. Surety Co., 192 N. Y. 227.

The effect of the Bankruptcy Act upon general assignments is stated as follows in Cohen v. Am. Surety Co., *ubi supra:* "A general assignment, even though without preferences, is now, if made within four months of the filing of the petition, a constructive fraud on the Bankruptcy Act and in itself without either insolvency or intent an available act of bankruptcy. This does not mean that

rupt's estate to be under the control of commissioners or assignees appointed by and amenable to a court of law, and not under the control of persons appointed by the debtor.[1] Therefore every general assignment is an act of bankruptcy; if there are preferences, it is a fraud upon the other creditors.[2] If it is an assignment for an equal distribution, it is a fraud upon the policy of the law.[3] Such deed will be fraudulent and an act of bankruptcy, although it contains a proviso that it shall be void if the trustees think fit, or a proviso that, if the creditor or creditors to a certain amount do not execute within

[1] Dutton v. Morrison, 17 Ves. 199; Worsley v. Demattos, 1 Burr. 476; Simpson v. Sikes, 6 M. & S. 312; Hobson v. Markson, 1 Dillon, 420; In re Burt, id. 439.

[2] Wilson v. Day, 2 Burr. 827; Alderson v. Temple, 4 Burr. 2240; Lewin on Trusts, 375 (5th ed.).

[3] Kettle v. Hammond, 1 Cook's B. L. 108; Tappenden v. Burgess, 4 East, 239; Lewin on Trusts, 375. [See *supra*, § 586, note.]

general assignments are no longer lawful, rather that the assignor and his counsel thereby set the door of the court of bankruptcy ajar for such creditors as may choose to bid them enter." For a good discussion of the Massachusetts decisions in reference to the effect upon general assignments in that State of a similar provision in the state bankruptcy statute, see 8 Harvard L. Rev. 270.

In England under the provisions of the Bankruptcy Act, 1883, it has been held that a voluntary assignment which becomes void by reason of bankruptcy proceedings within the time fixed by the act, is void, not from the time it was made, but only from the time when the title of the trustee in bankruptcy accrued, with the result that a *bona fide* sale for value by the assignee in the interim is valid. *In re* Carter and Kender-

dine's Contract, [1897] 1 Ch. 776, overruling *In re* Briggs and Spicer, [1891] 2 Ch. 127. See *In re* Poppleton and Jones' Contract, 74 L. T. 582. But in the United States the title of the voluntary assignee is tentative from the beginning until four months have elapsed without the filing of a petition in bankruptcy. The assignee, however, is given a preferred claim upon the assets for his services and necessary disbursements in collecting and preserving the assets, in so far as his services and disbursements have been beneficial to the estate in his hands, even if the assignment is rendered void by a petition in bankruptcy within the four months. Randolph v. Scruggs, 190 U. S. 533. See also Louisville Tr. Co. v. Columbia Finance & Tr. Co., 59 S. W. 867 (Ky. 1900); Clark v. Sawyer, 151 Mass. 64.

a certain time, a decree of bankruptcy shall be entered; or if the trustees did not accept the deed or intend to act; or if the trustees induced the debtor to execute the deed.[1] The same general principles prevail in the United States under the national bankrupt law. A general assignment for the benefit of creditors is an act of bankruptcy, and so is the sale or mortgage of a stock of goods or property out of the usual and ordinary course of the debtor's business.[2] But, in order to avoid the deed of assignment, there must be a debt due at the time of its execution;[3] and the deed, though voidable by creditors and assignees in bankruptcy, is good between the parties themselves.[4]

§ 588. A corporation has the same right as a natural person to make assignments for the benefit of its creditors;[5] and it may make preferences among its creditors[6] though grave doubts have been raised whether it can do anything but make an equal division of its property among its creditors in case of insolvency.[7] A general assignment by a corporation of all the

---

[1] Tappenden v. Burgess, 4 East, 230; Back v. Gooch, 4 Camp. 232; Holt, 13; Dutton v. Morrison, 17 Ves. 193; Lewin on Trusts, 376.

[2] See Brightly's Annotated Bankrupt Law of the United States, pp. 72–74, 78–80, and the cases cited by him. [See U. S. Bankruptcy Law of 1898, § 3.]

[3] Ex parte Taylor, 5 De G., M. & G. 392; Ex parte Louch, 1 De G. 612; Oswald v. Thompson, 2 Exch. 215.

[4] Bessey v. Windham, 6 Q. B. 166.

[5] Catlin v. Eagle Bank, 6 Conn. 233; Savings Bank v. Bates, id. 506; Dana v. Bank of the United States, 5 Watts & S. 224; Hopkins v. Gallatin Turnpike, 4 Humph. 403; Tower v. Bank of River Raisin, 2 Doug. 530; 6 Humph. 532; State of Maryland v. Bank of Maryland, 6 Gill & J. 205; Bank of U. S. v. Huth, 4 B. Mon. 423; Ex parte Conway, 4 Pike, 305; Ringo v. R. E. Bank, 13 Ark. 575; Arthur v. Commercial, &c. Bank of Vicksburg, 9 Sm. & M. 396; De Ruyter v. St. Peter's Church, 3 Barb. Ch. 119; 3 Comst. 238; Union Bank of Tennessee v. Ellicott, 6 Gill & J. 363. In New York a corporation has no such right. Loring v. United States Co., 30 Barb. 644.

[6] Ibid.

[7] Robins v. Embry, 1 Sm. & M. Ch. 207; Montgomery v. Commercial Bank, id. 632; Bean v. Bullis, 57 Penn. St. 221.

property with which it does its business is a good cause for taking away its charter and ending its existence.[1]

§ 589. No formalities are required in an assignment in trust for creditors, if the instrument is so constructed that the intention of the parties can be inferred from it.[2] In those States where there are statutes regulating such assignments, the instrument must be substantially according to the statute: thus a lease reserving rent in trust for creditors may be an assignment;[3] and a power of attorney to collect money and pay it to creditors, in an order named, is an assignment;[4] and a letter sent to an absent creditor, assigning personal property for the benefit of himself and other creditors, is valid as an assignment.[5] But an assignment directly to creditors to pay their own debts does not come within the rules respecting assignments in trust, although the surplus may go to the debtor.[6] Nor is a judgment confessed to a creditor in trust an assignment;[7] nor is a mortgage in trust to pay debts, with or without a power of sale, an assignment.[8]

§ 590. A conveyance of all a debtor's property in trust, for the payment of all or any number of his creditors, is not within the statute of 13 Eliz. c. 5, or 29 Eliz. c. 5, which makes void all conveyances made to hinder, delay, or defraud creditors; although the assignment may operate to change the rights of a creditor, and may result in delaying him.[9] But all such

---

[1] State v. Real Estate Bank, 5 Pike, 596.

[2] Harvey v. Mix, 24 Conn. 406.

[3] Lucas v. Sunbury & Erie R. R. Co., 32 Penn. St. 458; Bittenger v. R. R. Co., 40 id. 269.

[4] Watson v. Bagaley, 12 Penn. St. 164.

[5] Dargan v. Richardson, 1 Cheves, L. 197; Shubar v. Winding, id. 218.

[6] Henderson's App., 31 Penn. St. 502; Chaffees v. Risk, 24 id. 432; Vallance v. Miners' Life Ins. Co., 42 id. 441.

[7] Guy v. McIlree, 26 Penn. St. 92; Lord v. Fisher, 19 Ind. 7.

[8] Barker v. Hall, 13 N. H. 298; Manuf. and Mech. Bank v. Bank of Pa., 7 Watts & S. 335; Harkrader v. Leiby, 4 Ohio St. 602.

[9] Meux v. Howell, 4 East, 9; Estwick v. Callaud, 5 T. R. 424; Wilt v.

assignments will be void if affected by *actual fraud:* [1] as if the purpose is to hinder, delay, and defraud the creditors,[2] or any one or more of them;[3] or if a fictitious debt is preferred;[4] or there is the reservation of a power of revoking the assignment, or the reservation of any other right and power which gives the debtor the control of the property;[5] or if a clause is introduced which exempts the assignees from the ordinary duties affixed by law to the office of assignee, as that the assignees shall not be liable for any loss not happening from their own gross negligence or misfeasance.[6] So the selection of a sick, weak, or incapable assignee, or of one at a distance from the locality, or of an insolvent person, or of one of such moral or pecuniary character as to evince a purpose on the part of the debtor to keep the control of the property, or to render it unprofitable to the creditors, will be strong evidence of fraud in fact, and will avoid the assignment.[7] The postponement, for an unreasonable length of time, of the sale of the property, and of the settlement of the accounts and payment of the creditors

Franklin, 1 Binn. 514. [Billings *v.* Parsons, 17 Utah, 22; Roberts *v.* Norcross, 69 N. H. 533; Geer *v.* Traders' Bank, 132 Mich. 215.]

[1] Twyne's Case, 3 Co. 80 a; Dutton *v.* Morrison, 17 Ves. 197; Wilson *v.* Day, 2 Burr. 827; Hungerford *v.* Earle, 2 Vern. 261; Tarback *v.* Marbury, id. 510; Pickstock *v.* Lyster, 3 M. & S. 371; Law *v.* Skinner, W. Black. 996; Stone *v.* Grantham, 2 Buls. 218; Worsley *v.* Demattos, 1 Burr. 467; Wilson *v.* Gray, 2 Stock. 233; Jessup *v.* Hulse, 29 Barb. 539; Gazzam *v.* Poyntz, 4 Ala. 374.

[2] Sheldon *v.* Dodge, 4 Denio, 218; Bodley *v.* Goodrich, 7 How. 277; Hart *v.* McFarland, 13 Penn. St. 185.

[3] Knight *v.* Packer, 1 Beasley, 214.

[4] Waters *v.* Comly, 3 Harr. 117; Webb *v.* Daggett, 2 Barb. 10; Planck *v.* Schermerhorn, 3 Barb. Ch. 644; Irwin *v.* Keen, 3 Whar. 347. But if a creditor extinguishes his claim by fraud, his share goes into the residue for the other creditors. Hardcastle *v.* Fisher, 24 Mo. 70.

[5] Whallon *v.* Scott, 10 Watts, 237; Riggs *v.* Murray, 2 Johns. Ch. 565; 15 Johns. 571; Grover *v.* Wakeman, 11 Wend. 187.

[6] Litchfield *v.* White, 3 Sandf. Ch. 547; Olmstead *v.* Herrick, 1 E. D. Smith, 310; Hutchinson *v.* Lord, 1 Wis. 286.

[7] Currie *v.* Hart, 2 Sandf. Ch. 251; Reede *v.* Emery, 8 Paige, 417; Connah *v.* Sedgwick, 1 Barb. 211; Cram *v.* Mitchell, 1 Sandf. 251; Hayes *v.* Doane, 3 Stock. 84.

961

by the trustees, is evidence of fraud.[1] (*a*)   So is the assignment
of property which, on the face of the paper, the assignee is
not authorized to distribute.[2]   So any unusual powers given
to the trustees that may prejudice the claims of the creditors
and favor the debtor, will render the settlement fraudulent;
as a power given to the trustees to compound with the creditors, or a right reserved either to the grantor or trustee to
make preferences or to alter them.[3] (*b*)   In some States a power

[1] Adlum *v.* Yard, 1 Rawle, 163; Mitchell *v.* Beal, 8 Yerg. 134.   Three
years is an unreasonably long time.   Adlum *v.* Yard, *ut supra*.   The length
of time which will be reasonable depends upon the nature and situation
of the property.   Hafner *v.* Irwin, 1 Ired. L. 490; Hardy *v.* Skinner, 9 id.
191; Browning *v.* Hart, 6 Barb. 91; Robins *v.* Embry, 1 Sm. & M. Ch. 205;
Rundlett *v.* Dale, 10 N. H. 458; Hardy *v.* Simpson, 13 Ired. L. 138;
Grover *v.* Wakeman, 11 Wend. 187; Bennett *v.* Union Bank, 5 Humph.
612; Farmer's Bank *v.* Douglass, 11 Sm. & M. 472; Arthur *v.* Com. &
Railw. Bank of Vicksburg, 9 Sm. & M. 396; Henderson *v.* Downing 24 Miss.
119.   A year's suspension was deemed fraudulent in one case.   Ward *v.*
Trotter, 3 Mon. 1; Johnson *v.* Thweatt, 18 Ala. 745.   In Pennsylvania a
year was deemed a proper time, and a longer time was deemed fraudulent.
Sheener *v.* Lautzerbeizer, 6 Watts, 543; Dana *v.* Bank of U. S., 5 Watts &
S. 224; Abercrombie *v.* Bradford, 16 Ala. 560; Hodge *v.* Wyatt, 10 Ala. 271;
Hindman *v.* Dill, 11 Ala. 689; Lockhart *v.* Wyatt, 10 Ala. 231.   Three
months in most cases would not be unreasonably long.   Christopher *v.*
Covington, 2 B. Mon. 357.   But if the trustee may use his own discretion,
it is void.   D'Invernois *v.* Leavitt, 23 Barb. 63.

[2] Hooper *v.* Tuckerman, 3 Sandf. 316.

[3] Wakeman *v.* Grover, 4 Paige, 24; 11 Wend. 187; Hudson *v.* Maze,
3 Scam. 579; Sheldon *v.* Dodge, 4 Denio, 218; Mitchell *v.* Stiles, 13 Penn.
St. 306; Barnum *v.* Hampstead, 7 Paige, 569; Boardman *v.* Halliday, 10
Paige, 224; Strong *v.* Skinner, 4 Barb. 547; Averill *v.* Loucks, 6 Barb. 471;
Gazzam *v.* Poyntz, 4 Ala. 374; D'Invernois *v.* Leavitt, 23 Barb. 63.   But
the assignees may compromise claims due to the debtor.   White *v.* Monsar-
rat, 18 B. Mon. 809; Dow *v.* Platner, 16 N. Y. 562; Robins *v.* Embry, 1

(*a*) A provision that the assignee
shall continue the business for a
reasonable time does not render
the assignment void for fraud.
Hurst *v.* Leckie, 97 Va. 550; Bow-
ling *v.* Davidson, 107 Va. 389.
But a power to continue the business for a longer time than is
reasonably necessary for realizing
on the assets would usually be
considered an attempt to hinder
and delay creditors, unless there
is a provision that the power is
dependent upon consent of the
creditors.

(*b*) But a power given to the

to sell on credit is considered evidence of fraud;[1] and so is a power to mortgage, or lease, or incumber the estate.[2] The trust may be to sell at either public or private sale.[3]

§ 591. So the reservation of a use or benefit to the grantor will render a general assignment void. It is a settled principle that a reservation to the grantor or his family, or to any one not a creditor, of any trust, profit, or benefit out of the property, or of a credit on account of any part of it, or

Sm. & M. Ch. 207; Bellows v. Partridge, 19 Barb. 176; Meacham v. Sternes, 9 Paige, 398.

[1] Mussey v. Noyes, 26 Vt. 426; Sutton v. Hanford, 11 Mich. 513; Pierce v. Brewster, 32 Ill. 268; Page v. Olcott, 28 Vt. 465; Barney v. Griffin, 2 Comst. 366; Nicholson v. Leavitt, 2 Seld. 510, overruling 4 Sandf. 366; Billings v. Billings, 1 Cal. 113; Swoyer's App., 5 Penn. St. 317; Estate of Davis, 5 Whart. 530; Kellogg v. Slauson, 1 Kern. 305; American Exch. Bank v. Inloes, 7 Md. 380; Porter v. Williams, 5 Seld. 142; Hutchinson v. Lord, 1 Wis. 286; Keep v. Sanderson, 2 Wis. 42; Booth v. McNair, 11 Mich. 19; Mower v. Hanford, 6 Minn. 535. In other States a power to sell on credit is good. Grinell v. Adams, 11 Humph. 85; Shackleford v. Bank of Mobile, 2 Ala. 238; Abercrombie v. Bradford, 16 Ala. 560; Neally v. Ambrose, 21 Pick. 185; Hopkins v. Ray, 1 Met. 79. A power to convert the estate into money, in such convenient time as to the assignees should seem meet, is a power to sell on credit, and is void. Woodburn v. Mosher, 9 Barb. 255; Murphy v. Bell, 8 How. Pr. Cas. 468. So a power to complete the manufacture of stock in such manner as, in the judgment of the assignees, to obtain the most money, was void. Dunham v. Waterman, 17 N. Y. 9. But to sell for the best interests of the parties is not a power to sell on credit. Whitney v. Krows, 11 Barb. 200; Kellogg v. Slauson, 1 Kern. 302; Maennel v. Murdock, 13 Md. 164; Clark v. Fuller, 21 Barb. 128; Nichols v. McEwen, 21 id. 65; Ely v. Hair, 16 B. Mon. 230. If there is no power in the assignment to sell on credit, but the trustee sells on credit, the assignment is not void. Small v. Ludlow, 20 N. Y. 155.

[2] Planck v. Schermerhorn, 3 Barb. Ch. 644; Barnum v. Hempstead, 7 Paige, 568.

[3] Bellows v. Partridge, 19 Barb. 176.

assignee to accept the assent and release of a creditor after the time limit fixed by the deed of assignment does not render the assignment fraudulent, since he will not be allowed to delay the settlement of the estate by means of the power. National Union Bank v. Copeland, 141 Mass. 257.

of any control by the grantor,[1] is a fraud in law, and avoids the whole assignment.[2] So a stipulation that the grantor should retain the possession avoids the assignment.[3] But in many States the possession by the assignor of the property after the assignment is only evidence, more or less stringent, of fraud under the circumstances of each case, and may be explained.[4] A stipulation for the maintenance of the grantor or his family, or that the grantor shall be employed to manage and dispose of the property at a fixed salary,[5] or the reservation of a fixed sum of money, or of so much a year, avoids the assignment.[6] (a) An express reservation of the surplus

[1] Smith v. Conkwright, 28 Minn. 23.

[2] Thomas v. Jenks, 1 Amer. Lead. Cas. 69; Mackie v. Cairns, 5 Cow. 549; Jackson v. Parker, 9 Cow. 73; Byrd v. Bradley, 2 B. Mon. 239; Kissam v. Edmundson, 1 Ired. Eq. 180; Goodrich v. Downs, 6 Hill, 438; Farmer v. Lesley, 6 Penn. St. 121; Shaffer v. Watkins, 7 Watts & S. 219; Leadman v. Harris, 3 Dev. 144; Mead v. Phillips, 1 Sandf. 83; Anderson v. Fuller, 1 McMul. Eq. 27; McAllister v. Marshall, 6 Binn. 338; Peacock v. Tompkins, Meigs, 317; Austin v. Johnson, 7 Humph. 191.

[3] Twyne's Case, 3 Co. 80 b; 1 Smith Lead. Cas. 1, and notes; Dewey v. Adams, 4 Edw. Ch. 21; Connah v. Sedgwick, 1 Barb. 210; Rogers v. Vail, 16 Vt. 329; Caldwell v. Williams, 1 Cart. 405.

[4] In Massachusetts, such stipulations are not fraudulent. Baxter v. Wheeler, 9 Pick. 21; Foster v. Saco Manuf. Co., 12 Pick. 451. If the assignment is good on its face, it is not void for an illegal act done afterwards, as the assignor's carrying away a bag of $5,000 in gold, unless the assignment was executed with a fraudulent intent. Wilson v. Forsyth, 24 Barb. 105. Perhaps, in most States, the retention of the possession by the assignor is only evidence of fraud, and not in itself fraud. Brooks v. Marbury, 11 Wheat. 82; Vernon v. Morton, 8 Dana, 247; Pike v. Bacon, 8 Shep. 280; Osborne v. Fuller, 14 Conn. 530; Strong v. Carrier, 17 Conn. 239; Klapp v. Shurk, 13 Penn. St. 589; Fitler v. Maitland, 5 Watts & S. 307; Dallam v. Fitler, 6 Watts & S. 323; Dewey v. Littlejohn, 2 Ired. Eq. 495; Christopher v. Covington, 2 B. Mon. 357; Hardy v. Skinner, 9 Ired. L. 191; Ravisies v. Allston, 5 Ala. 297; Darwin v. Handley, 3 Yer. 502; Barker v. Hall, 13 N. H. 298; Shackleford v. Bank of Mobile, 22 Ala. 238; Lockhart v. Wyatt, 10 Ala. 231.

[5] Johnson v. Harvey, 2 Pen. & Watts, 82; McClug v. Lecky, 3 Pen. & Watts, 83; Henderson v. Downing, 24 Miss. 117.

[6] Mackie v. Cairns, 5 Cow. 549; Butler v. Van Wyck, 1 Hill, 463; Good-

(a) But the actual employment of the assignor without a previous stipulation therefor, and payment for his services does not render the

to the grantor, upon a partial assignment for a portion of the creditors, renders the assignment void.[1] So it is said that an express reservation of the surplus in a general assignment renders it void.[2] On the other hand, it has been held that the reservation of the surplus, after paying all the creditors, is only what the law implies, and is therefore not void.[3] But

rich v. Downs, 6 Hill, 440, overruling Riggs v. Murray, 2 Johns. Ch. 565, 15 Johns. 571, and Austin v. Bell, 20 Johns. 442; Harris v. Sumner, 2 Pick. 129; Richards v. Hazzards, 1 Stew. & Por. 139. A reservation of so much as is allowed by law avoids the deed in Tennessee, Sugg v. Tillman, 2 Swanst. 210; but not in Pennsylvania, Mulford v. Shurk, 28 Pa. St. 473. But the courts will be governed by circumstances and the intent of the parties, in determining whether certain reservations are fraudulent, as if the sum is small and reasonable. Canal Bank v. Cox, 6 Maine, 395; Skipwith v. Cunningham, 8 Leigh, 272; Kevan v. Branch, 1 Grat. 275. The trustees may employ the assignor, at reasonable compensation, to assist in disposing of the property. Shattuck v. Freeman, 1 Met. 10; Vernon v. Morton, 8 Dana, 247; Pearson v. Rockhill, 4 B. Mon. 296; Bank of Mobile v. Clark, 7 Ala. 765; Jones v. Whitbread, 11 C. B. 406; Fitler v. Maitland, 5 Watts & S. 307; Nicholson v. Leavitt, 4 Sandf. 270; Mulford v. Shurk, 28 Penn. St. 473. So the trustees may employ other agents in managing the property. Hennessey v. Western Bank, 6 Watts & S. 300; Kelly v. Lank, 7 B. Mon. 220; Coates v. Williams, 7 Exch. 208; Peck v. Whiting, 21 Conn. 206. The trustee may act and convey by attorney. Blight v. Schenck, 10 Penn. St. 285; Maennel v. Murdock, 13 Md. 164; Gillespie v. Smith, 22 Ill. 473.

[1] Doremus v. Lewis, 8 Barb. 124; Suidam v. Martin, Wright, 698; Goodrich v. Downs, 6 Hill, 438; Strong v. Skinner, 4 Barb. 547; Cole v. Jessup, id. 307; Griffin v. Barney, 2 Comst. 365; Leitch v. Hollister, 4 Comst. 214; Dana v. Lull, 17 Vt. 390.

[2] Ibid.

[3] Hall v. Denison, 17 Vt. 311; Ely v. Cook, 18 Barb. 612; Beatty v. Davis, 9 Gill, 213; Rahn v. McElrath, 6 Watts, 151; Hindman v. Dill, 11 Ala. 689; Austin v. Johnson, 7 Humph. 191. [See Farnsworth v. Doom, 109 Ky. 794; Bole v. McKelvy, 189 Pa. St. 505; Ralston's Appeal, 169 Pa. St. 254; Early v. Early, 75 S. C. 15; Provident Life & Tr. Co. v. Fidelity Ins., etc., Co., 203 Pa. St. 82.]

assignment fraudulent. Hurst v. Leckie, 97 Va. 550. A reservation by the assignor of property which by statute is exempt from being taken on execution does not render the assignment fraudulent. Thompson v. Shaw, 104 Me. 85; 2 Bigelow on Fraud, 214; Bump on Fraudulent Conveyances (4th ed.), § 220.

all secret reservations are fraudulent.[1] If the assignor secretly, and without the knowledge of the general creditors, pays extra money, or gives a special advantage to some particular creditor to procure his assent to the assignment, or to secure his influence with the other creditors in gaining their assent or discharge, such assignment will be illegal and void, as a fraud upon the general creditors; and if the general creditors have signed a release of their claims, such release will be no bar to an action against the debtor.[2] If such creditor has taken notes or other securities from the debtor, as an extra consideration for assenting to such assignment, such notes and securities are void.[3] A deed may be fraudulent by reason of delaying creditors in the collection of their debts; but a conveyance for the benefit of creditors cannot be impeached for fraud by a creditor who assents with knowledge of the facts;[4] otherwise as to one who, though present at the proceedings and expressing no dissent, yet took no part and gave no assent.[5]

§ 592. A condition in a deed of assignment, requiring the creditors to release the assignor from all claims before receiving any benefit under the deed, the surplus returning to the debtor and not to the non-releasing creditors, renders the deed fraudulent and void; and such a stipulation, as a condition of preference, although the only effect is to postpone the non-releasing creditors to a share of the surplus, renders the assignment void. The principle is, that although preferences are allowed, yet the appropriation of the property to the creditors must be absolute and unconditional, and a trust which coerces the creditors into a relinquishment of part of their

[1] M'Cullock v. Hutchinson, 7 Watts, 434; Smith v. Lowell, 6 N. H. 67; Smith v. Smith, 11 N. H. 460.

[2] Mare v. Sandford, 1 Gif. 288; Case v. Gerrish, 15 Pick. 50; Ramsdell v. Edgarton, 8 Met. 227; Lothrop v. King, 8 Cush. 382; Partridge v. Messer, 14 Gray, 180.

[3] Ibid.

[4] Greene v. Sprague, Manuf. Co., 52 Conn. 330.

[5] Waterman v. Sprague Manuf. Co., 55 Conn. 554.

claims, in order to enjoy any benefit under the deed, is fraudulent and void, although no portion of the surplus may go to
the grantor.[1] (a)   An assignment to a trustee of *part* of a

[1] Doe v. Scribner, 41 Maine, 277; Owen v. Arvis, 2 Dutch. 23; Miller v.
Conklin, 17 Ga. 430; Goddard v. Hapgood, 25 Vt. 351; Green v. Trieber,
3 Md. 13; Hysloop v. Clarke, 14 Johns. 458; Austin v. Bell, 20 Johns. 442;
Wakeman v. Grover, 4 Paige, 24; 11 Wend. 187; Goodrich v. Downs, 6
Hill, 438; Hafner v. Irwin, 1 Ired. L. 490; Robins v. Embry, 1 Sm. & M.
Ch. 208; Whallom v. Scott, 10 Watts, 237; Hastings v. Belknap, 1 Denio,
197; Atkinson v. Jordan, 5 Ham. 293; Woolsey v. Verner, Wright, 606;
Barrett v. Reids, id. 701; Brown v. Knox, 6 Mo. 302; Drake v. Rogers, id.
317; Ingraham v. Wheeler, 6 Conn. 277; Howell v. Edgar, 3 Scam. 417;
Ramsdell v. Sigerson, 2 Gill, 78; Swearingin v. Slicer, 5 Mo. 241; The
Watchman, Ware, 232; Todd v. Buckman, 2 Fairf. 41; Pearson v. Crosby,
23 Maine, 261; Hurd v. Silsbee, 10 N. H. 108; Jacot v. Corbett, 1 Cheves,
Ch. 71; Grimshaw v. Walker, 12 Ala. 101; Brown v. Lyon, 17 Ala. 659;
West v. Snodgrass, id. 549; Fox v. Adams, 5 Maine, 245; Ashurst v. Martin,
9 Porter, 567; McCall v. Hinkley, 4 Gill, 129. In the early cases in Alabama,
such a condition was held not to vitiate the assignment. Gazzam v. Poyntz,
4 Ala. 374; Wiswall v. Ticknor, 6 Ala. 179. In Pennsylvania, Virginia,
South Carolina, Massachusetts, and Rhode Island, such conditions have
been held to be good, and not to vitiate the deeds of assignments. Lippincott v. Barker, 2 Binn. 174; Livingston v. Ball, 3 Watts, 198; Bayne v.
Wylie, 10 Watts, 309; Mechanics' Bank v. Gorman, 8 Watts & S. 304;
Pierpont v. Graham, 4 Wash. 232; Skipwith v. Cunningham, 8 Leigh, 272;
Kevan v. Branch, 1 Grat. 275; Niolon v. Douglas, 2 Hill, Ch. 443; Le Prince
v. Guillemont, 1 Rich. Eq. 187; Brashear v. West, 7 Pet. 609; Dana v. Bank
of U. S., 5 Watts & S. 224; Borden v. Sumner, 4 Pick. 265; Andrew v. Ludlow, 5 Pick. 28; Nostrand v. Atwood, 19 Pick. 281; Canal Bank v. Cox, 6
Maine, 395; Curtis v. Leavitt, 15 N. Y. 9; Halsey v. Whitney, 4 Mason,
207. A release by a separate deed, not part of the assignment, does not
avoid the assignment. Renard v. Graydon, 39 Barb. 548; Nightingale v.
Harris, 6 R. I. 321; Livermore v. Jenckes, 21 How. 126.

(a) A common provision is that
the assignment shall be for the
benefit only of those creditors who
shall become parties to the deed
and shall release the assignor from
personal liability for the balance of
his debt to each of them. The
better opinion is that this kind of
a preference is valid, in the absence of statute provisions to the
contrary, if a reasonable opportunity is given to all creditors to
accept, and if the assignment includes all the property of the
debtor except his statutory exemp-
tions. Thompson v. Shaw, 104
Me. 85; Reddy v. Raymond, 194
Mass. 367; Moulton v. Bartlett,
195 Mass. 33; National Bank of
Commerce v. Bailey, 179 Mass.
415; Hurst v. Leckie, 97 Va. 550;
Davis Co. v. Augustus, 105 Va.

debtor's property, on condition of a full release, is fraudulent everywhere.[1] A void assignment may be remedied by an additional assignment,[2] but it cannot be helped by parol evidence.[3]

§ 593. In England, a voluntary assignment to a trustee for creditors, not communicated to them, and they not being parties thereto and privy to its execution, conveys a mere power or agency to the trustees, which may be altered or revoked at the will of the assignor. (a) The creditors, though

---

[1] Seaving v. Brinkerhoff, 5 Johns. Ch. 329; Skipwith v. Cunningham, 8 Leigh, 272; Le Prince v. Guillemont, 1 Rich. Eq. 187; Jacot v. Corbett, 1 Cheves, Ch. 71. This question was left open in Nostrand v. Atwood, 19 Pick. 284; Fassit v. Phillips, 4 Whart. 399; Thomas v. Jenks, 5 Rawle, 221; 1 Am. Lead. Cas. 70; Hennessey v. Western Bank, 6 Watts & S. 301; Sangston v. Gaither, 3 Md. 41; Greene v. Trieber, id. 11. [Hurst v. Leckie, 97 Va. 550; Long v. Meriden Britannia Co., 94 Va. 594; Davis Co. v. Augustus, 105 Va. 843.]

[2] Merrill v. Englesby, 2 Vt. 150.

[3] Inloes v. American Ex. Bank, 11 Ind. 173; Groschen v. Page, 6 Cal. 138; Hampstead v. Johnston, 18 Ark. 123.

843; Long v. Meriden Britannia Co., 94 Va. 594; McElwee v. McGill, 57 S. C. 6 (semble). See also Boston v. Turner, 201 Mass. 190; Hudson v. Parker Machine Co., 173 Mass. 242; Andrews v. Tuttle-Smith Co., 191 Mass. 461. But see Ralston's Appeal, 169 Pa. St. 254.

Where the assignment contains such a provision, it is essential that the assignor shall have included in the assignment all the property which creditors could have reached by legal process for the satisfaction of their demands. If he has failed to do this, the assignment is a fraudulent attempt to hinder and delay creditors. Hurst v. Leckie, 97 Va. 550; Long v. Meriden Britannia Co., 94 Va.

594. But an accidental omission of a small part of his unexempt property will not have this effect. Davis Co. v. Augustus, 105 Va. 843; Long v. Meriden Britannia Co., 94 Va. 594.

In regard to the effect of such an assignment before assented to by creditors whose claims are sufficient to absorb the whole estate, it has been said that the surplus is held in trust for the assignor and that non-assenting creditors can reach it by trustee process. Thompson v. Shaw, 104 Me. 85; Reddy v. Raymond, 194 Mass. 367; Avery v. Monroe, 172 Mass. 132; Weston v. Nevers, 72 N. H. 65. See Ralston's Appeal, 169 Pa. St. 254.

(a) In England the rule is, as

named in the deed, cannot enforce the trust against the assignor or trustee;[1] but it is said that the communication of the trust by the trustees to the creditors takes away the power to revoke it,[2] and if the trustees have made payments or advances, they are entitled to possession of the property until they are reimbursed.[3] If the deed declares that it shall be void unless executed by all the creditors within a certain time, yet it is not void in equity if the creditors accept and act under it, though it is not signed by them.[4]   And even though one of the trustees

[1] La Touch v. Lacom, 7 Cl. & Fin. 772; Walwyn v. Coutts, 3 Mer. 707; 3 Sim. 14; Page v. Broom, 4 Russ. 6; Garrard v. Lauderdale, 3 Sim. 1; 2 R. & M. 451; Bill v. Cureton, 2 Myl. & K. 511; Simmonds v. Pallas, 2 Jo. & Lat. 489, 8 Ir. Eq. 335, 489; Griffiths v. Ricketts, 7 Hare, 307; Siggers v. Evans, 22 Eng. L. & Eq. 139; Nicholson v. Tutin, 2 K. & J. 18; Wilding v. Richards, 1 Col. C. C. 659; Kirwan v. Daniel, 5 Hare, 499; Evans v. Bagwell, 2 Con. & Law. 616; 4 Dru. & War. 398; Brown v. Cavendish, 1 Jo. & Lat. 635; Synnot v. Simpson, 5 H. L. Cas. 141.

[2] Acton v. Woodgate, 2 Myl. & K. 495. [Lewin on Trusts (11th ed.), p. 598; Johns v. James, 8 Ch. Div. 744.]

[3] Hind v. Blake, 3 Beav. 234.

[4] Spottiswoode v. Stockdale, G. Coop. 104; Dunch v. Kent, 1 Vern. 260; Whitmore v. Turquand, 3 De G., F. & J. 110; Re Baber, L. R. 10 Eq. 554. The creditor must put himself in the same relation as if he had signed the deed. Forbes v. Limond, 4 De G., M. & G. 298. And within the time fixed, if there is a limit of time within which he must execute the assignment, or assent thereto. Halsey v. Whitney, 4 Mason, 206; Aston v. Woodgate, 2 Myl. & K. 492; Phœnix Bank v. Sullivan, 9 Pick. 410; De Caters v. Chaumont, 9 Paige, 490. The creditors are not necessarily excluded if they do not come in within the prescribed time, as they may show reasons why they should not be excluded. See cases before cited. Tennant v. Stoney, 1 Rich. Eq. 222; Hosack v. Rogers, 6 Paige, 415; Nicholson v. Tutin, 2 K. & J. 18; Watson v. Knight, 19 Beav. 369; Pierpont v. Graham, 4 Wash. C. C. 232; Stoddart v. Allen, 1 Rawle, 258; Dedham Bank v. Richards, 2 Met. 105; Furman v. Fisher, 4 Cold. 626. But if the time within which creditors are to come in is unreasonably short, the assignment will be fraudulent and void. Brashear v. West, 7 Pet. 609; Vaughn v. Evans, 1 Hill,

stated by Kekewich, J., in Priestley v. Ellis, [1897] 1 Ch. 489, 500: "A debtor, minded to provide for his creditors, and to that intent vesting the property in another with directions to apply it in payment of his debts, does not thereby constitute an irrevocable trust, at all events during his life. The trustee is only his agent for effecting his wishes, and is responsible only to him."

does not sign the deed, it is good at law as well as in equity.[1]
If the deed itself declares that it is made for those *only* who
become parties to it, only those who become parties can claim
anything under it;[2] though it has been held that they need not
sign it, if they perform all its conditions, and take no step
inconsistent with it.[3]   In the United States the rule is different.
If an assignment, not fraudulent, is made to trustees for the
benefit of creditors, their assent is not necessary; or their
assent will be presumed in all cases, if it is for their benefit,
and contains no unusual clauses or restrictions.[4] (a)   A debtor

Ch. 414; Vernon v. Morton, 8 Dana, 447; Skipwith v. Cunningham, 8
Leigh, 272; Biron v. Mount, 24 Beav. 642; Lancaster v. Elce, 31 id. 325. If
a *third party* conveys property in trust for a debtor's liabilities, only those
creditors can avail themselves of the fund who come strictly within the
terms of the trust, and execute the assignment and comply with all its
conditions.   Williams v. Moslyn, 33 L. J. Ch. 54.

[1] Small v. Marwood, 9 B. & Cr. 360; Good v. Cheesman, 2 B. & Ad. 328.
[2] Garrard v. Lauderdale, 3 Sim. 1; Balfour v. Welland, 16 Ves. 151.
[3] Field v. Donoughmore, 1 Dr. & War. 227.
[4] Nicoll v. Mumford, 4 Johns. Ch. 523; Cunningham v. Freeborn, 11
Wend. 241; Houston v. Nowland, 7 Gill & J. 480; Bank of U. S. v. Huth,
4 B. Mon. 423; Smith v. Leavitt, 10 Ala. 93; Kinnard v. Thompson, 12
Ala. 487; Governor, &c. v. Campbell, 17 Ala. 566; Rankin v. Duryer, 21
Ala. 392; Klapp v. Shurk, 13 Penn. St. 539; Harland v. Binks, 15 Ad. &
E. (N. S.) 721; Brooks v. Marbury, 11 Wheat. 78; Brown v. Minturn, 2
Gall. 557; Wheeler v. Sumner, 4 Mason, 183; Halsey v. Whitney, id. 206;
New England Bank v. Lewis, 8 Pick. 113; Ward v. Lewis, 4 Pick. 518;
North v. Turner, 9 Serg. & R. 244; Wiley v. Collins, 2 Fairf. 193; Wilt v.
Franklin, 1 Binn. 502; Reinhard v. Bank of Kentucky, 6 B. Mon. 252;
Moses v. Murgatroyd, 1 Johns. Ch. 129; Neilson v. Blight, 1 Johns. Cas.
205; Weston v. Barker, 12 id. 281; 4 Kent, 307; Marigny v. Remy, 15
Martin, 607; Gray v. Hill, 10 Serg. & R. 436; De Forrest v. Bacon, 2 Conn.

(a) This must necessarily be
otherwise where the deed contains
a valid provision expressly limiting the benefit of the assignment to
those creditors who shall sign the
deed and release the assignor from
his personal liability for so much of
their demands as shall not be paid
out of the assigned property.
Thompson v. Shaw, 104 Me. 85;
Reddy v. Raymond, 194 Mass.
367; Avery v. Monroe, 172 Mass.
132; Weston v. Nevers, 72 N. H.
65 (*semble*).   See Kingman v.
Cornell-Tebbetts Co., 150 Mo. 282
(*semble*); Gonzales v. Batts, 20
Tex. Civ. App. 421.

cannot revoke the assignment where the property has vested in the trustees, or the creditors have had notice of it, or any of the trusts have been performed.[1] The English rule prevailed in Massachusetts before the court had jurisdiction in equity over such assignments;[2] but after the Act of 1836, c. 238, the assent of creditors was not necessary.[3] (*a*)   If the conveyance is made *directly to the creditors*, in consideration of the debts due them, their assent to the conveyance is necessary; but it may be presumed under some circumstances.[4] If the assignment is made to a trustee not present, his assent will be presumed; and the deed will take effect from its delivery, subject to be defeated by the refusal of the trustee.[5]

633; Rankin *v.* Lodor, 21 Ala. 380; Stewart *v.* Hall, 3 B. Mon. 218. [Robinson *v.* Thomason, 113 Ala. 526; Smith *v.* Herrell, 11 App. D. C. 425; Fearey *v.* O'Neill, 149 Mo. 467; Kingman *v.* Cornell-Tebbetts Co., 150 Mo. 282; McClain *v.* Pittsburg Stock Exch., 219 Pa. St. 435; Gonzales *v.* Batts, 20 Tex. Civ. App. 421; Billings *v.* Parsons, 17 Utah, 22; Zell Guano Co. *v.* Heatherly, 38 W. Va. 409; Burrill on Assignments (6th ed.), §§ 257, 258.   But see Robertson *v.* Desmond, 62 Ohio St. 487.]

[1] Robinson *v.* Sublett, 6 Humph. 313; Lawrence *v.* Davis, 3 McLean, 177; Petriken *v.* Davis, 1 Morris, 296.

[2] Russell *v.* Woodward, 10 Pick. 408; Stephens *v.* Bell, 6 Mass. 339; Widgery *v.* Haskell, 5 Mass. 144.

[3] Shattuck *v.* Freeman, 1 Met. 10.

[4] Tompkins *v.* Wheeler, 16 Pet. 106; Nicoll *v.* Mumford, 4 Johns. Ch. 522.

[5] Wilt *v.* Franklin, 1 Binn. 502; McKinney *v.* Rhoades, 5 Watts, 343; Skipwith *v.* Cunningham, 8 Leigh, 272; Merrill *v.* Swift, 18 Conn. 257; Ward *v.* Lewis, 4 Pick. 518; Moore *v.* Collins, 3 Dev. 126; Read *v.* Robinson, 6 Watts & S. 329; Dargan *v.* Richardson, 1 Cheves, L. 197; Shubar *v.* Winding, id. 218. [See McClain *v.* Pittsburg Stock Exch., 219 Pa. St. 435.]

(*a*) This statute has been repealed. See Burrill on Assignments (6th ed.), § 258; 8 Harvard Law Rev. 270. The usual form of assignment for creditors in Massachusetts contains a provision requiring the express assent of creditors as a condition of their becoming entitled to its benefits. See note (*a*), *supra*, p. 970.   But see Boston *v.* Turner, 201 Mass. 190.

Where the assignee himself is a creditor, his signature to the deed of assignment will be taken as both an acceptance of the legal title and trust, and an assent as creditor. Reddy *v.* Raymond, 194 Mass. 367.

But if there is any doubt concerning the trustee's acceptance, all liens put upon the property during such delay, and before the trustee actually accepts, will take preference of the deed of assignment.[1]

§ 594. As soon as an assignee accepts a general assignment for the payment of debts to creditors, either directly or by implication, he becomes a trustee for them; and, as soon as they have notice, they may compel the execution of the trust in a court of equity.[2] Failure of the trustee to execute the trust within the time named in the deed will not divest the rights of the beneficiaries. The court may remove the trustee or compel him to do his duty.[3] (a) But the assign-

---

[1] Crosby v. Hillyer, 24 Wend. 280.

[2] Moses v. Murgatroyd, 1 Johns. Ch. 119; Shepherd v. McEvers, 4 Johns. 136; Hulse v. Wright, Wright, 61; Pingree v. Comstock, 18 Pick. 46; Weir v. Tannehill, 2 Yerg. 57; Nicoll v. Mumford, 4 Johns. Ch. 523; Ward v. Lewis, 4 Pick. 518; New Eng. Bank v. Lewis, 8 Pick. 113; Robertson v. Sublett, 6 Humph. 313; Pearson v. Rockhill, 4 Mon. 296; Kelley v. Babcock, 49 N. Y. 320.

[3] Clark v. Wilson, 77 Ind. 176.

(a) In some States statutes have especially provided for oversight and control of such trusts by the courts, and sometimes the assignee must qualify by giving bond. Matter of Sheldon, 173 N. Y. 287. In the absence of such statutes, courts of equity have general jurisdiction to enforce the proper performance. Brockett v. Lewis, 144 Mich. 561.

They have jurisdiction to remove a trustee for misconduct or incapacity and to appoint a new trustee in his place upon complaint of the creditors for whose benefit the trust exists. Haven v. Sibbald, 41 A. 371 (N. J. Ch. 1898); Assigned Estate of Ahl, 192 Pa. St. 370; Taylor v. Mahoney, 94 Va.

508; Bryson v. Wood, 187 Pa. St. 366; State v. Johnson, 105 Wis. 164, 178; Morgan v. So. Milwaukee, etc., Co., 100 Wis. 465. But if the trust is valid the courts have no power to take the property out of the hands of a trustee and appoint a receiver except upon proof of misconduct or other cause which justifies his removal. Dozier v. Logan, 101 Ga. 173; Pollard v. Southern Fertilizer Co., 122 Ala. 409; Baltimore Bargain House v. St. Clair, 58 W. Va. 565.

Courts of equity have jurisdiction to permit the assignee to resign, Andrews v. Wilson's Assignee, 114 Ky. 671, and to appoint a new trustee to carry out the trust where the office becomes vacant by

ment must be accepted according to its terms, and within the time named.¹ In bringing a bill to seek the benefit of such an assignment, all the creditors must join in the suit, or one may sue in behalf of the others, who may come in and join him. Such bill must be brought for the enforcement of the trust generally, and for a sale of the property, the settlement of the accounts, and the payment of all the debts: a decree for the payment of a single debt would be erroneous.² But if the bill is to set aside the assignment for any reason, a single creditor may maintain it.³ As a general rule, if the assignment

¹ First Nat'l Bank of Easton v. Smith, 133 Mass. 26.
² Atherton v. Worth, 1 Dick. 375; McDougald v. Dougherty, 11 Ga. 570; Wakeman v. Grover, 4 Paige, 24; Bryant v. Russell, 23 Pick. 523; Edmeston v. Lyde, 1 Paige, 637; Hamilton v. Houghton, 2 Bligh, P. C. 169; Reynolds v. Bank of Va., 6 Grat. 174; Fisher v. Worth, 1 Busb. Eq. 63. But where one creditor filed a bill when no claim had been made for twenty years, and the trustee had stated that all the other creditors had been satisfied, he was allowed to maintain his bill. Mumford v. Murray, 6 Johns. Ch. 1.
³ Russell v. Lasher, 4 Barb. 233; Wakeman v. Grover, 4 Paige, 24;

failure of the assignee to accept or to qualify, or upon his death, resignation, or removal. Claflin Co. v. Middlesex Banking Co., 113 Fed. 958; Brown v. Parker, 97 Fed. 446; Tuttle v. Merchants' Nat. Bank, 19 Mont. 11; Rogers v. Pell, 166 N. Y. 565.

A creditor has no standing to petition for the removal of the assignee or for the enforcement of the trust, until he has brought himself within the class of those for whose benefit the assignment was made. Loucheim v. Casperson, 61 N. J. Eq. 529. There is an important difference between such a proceeding and a proceeding by a creditor to have the assignment declared invalid, and the two proceedings are inconsistent. Brockett v. Lewis, 144 Mich. 561.

It has been held in Massachusetts that a creditor who has failed to accept the terms of the assignment within the time limited in the deed cannot compel the assignee to exercise his discretionary power to accept the assent after the time has expired, unless possibly upon a showing that his refusal to accept the assent was not justified. Moulton v. Bartlett, 195 Mass. 33; National Bank of Commerce v. Bailey, 179 Mass. 415.

Where the deed of assignment does not provide that the assignee shall have power to accept the assent of a creditor after the time fixed by the deed, he cannot extend the time even for a day. McElwee v. McGill, 57 S. C. 6.

is set aside and a receiver appointed, or the court orders the estate to be settled, claims will be paid *pari passu;* but some creditors may have obtained legal preferences at law, and in such case the court will order them to be paid according to their priority.[1]

§ 595.   In a suit to enforce the trust under an assignment, the trustee must be brought before the court; and a proceeding without notice to him would be erroneous.[2]   If the assignment is unconditional, the assignor, his heirs or representatives, need not be made parties;[3] but if there is an express stipulation that the surplus shall be paid to the assignor, he or his representatives must be parties.[4]   So if the trust to pay debts is created under a will, the heir of the testator must be made a party to a suit.[5]   A creditor may maintain a suit in behalf of such creditors as may join him against the assignees, for an administration of the trust; and, upon public notice being given for creditors to come in and prove their claims, all creditors will be barred, although they may have had no actual notice.[6] But a single creditor cannot sue a trustee for neglect or default, the remedy is by bill in equity on behalf of all the creditors; nor can an individual creditor sue at law to recover any larger part of his debt than is ascertained or admitted to be due from the trustee.[7]

Stout *v.* Higbee, 4 J. J. Marsh. 632.   In Ohio, the creditor that procures the assignment to be set aside obtains a priority in the distribution of the assets.   Atkinson *v.* Jordan, Wright, 247.   The Rev. Statutes of N. Y. are to the same effect.   Corning *v.* White, 2 Paige, 567; Burrall *v.* Leslie, 6 Paige, 445; Lucas *v.* Atwood, 2 Stew. 378.

[1] Gracey *v.* Davis, 3 Strob. Eq. 58; Austin *v.* Bell, 20 Johns. 442; McDermutt *v.* Strong, 4 Johns. Ch. 687; McMeekin *v.* Edmonds, 1 Hill, Eq. 293; Codwise *v.* Gelston, 10 Johns. 519; Le Prince *v.* Guillemont, 1 Rich. Eq. 220.

[2] Hamilton *v.* Houghton, 2 Bligh, 169; Routh *v.* Kinder, 3 Swanst. 144, n.

[3] Hobart *v.* Andrews, 21 Pick. 532.

[4] Houghton *v.* Davis, 23 Maine, 28.

[5] Harris *v.* Ingledew, 3 P. Wms. 93.

[6] Kerr *v.* Blodgett, 48 N. Y. 62.

[7] Bouvé *v.* Cottle, 143 Mass. 313.

§ 596. As a matter of course, mortgagees, judgment creditors, and all others having a lien upon the trust property prior to the assignment, are not affected by it. Their rights remain as before the assignment; and an attachment or any lien that is fastened upon the property after the assignment is made, but before it is accepted by the trustee, takes preference of the assignment.[1] (a) A creditor as one of the *cestuis que trust* may be a trustee;[2] in such case he has no power to prefer his own claim, but must take equally with the others, unless by the terms of the deed a preference is given him.[3] By accepting the trust according to its terms, a creditor trustee waives all claims and liens upon the property inconsistent with the deed.[4] But it is said, that the rule which prohibits

[1] Crosby *v.* Hillyer, 24 Wend. 280; Codwise *v.* Gelston, 10 Johns. 517; Hayes *v.* Heidelberg, 9 Penn. St. 203; Hogan *v.* Strayhorn, 65 N. C. 279; Bloomer *v.* Waldron, 3 Hill, 367.

[2] Balfour *v.* Welland, 16 Ves. 151; Boazman *v.* Johnston, 3 Sim. 377; Acton *v.* Woodgate, 2 Myl. & K. 49; Siggers *v.* Evans, 32 Eng. L. & Eq. 139; Hobson *v.* Thelluson, L. R. 2 Q. B. 642. [State *v.* Johnson, 105 Wis. 164, 182. But see Farrar *v.* Powell, 71 Vt. 247.]

[3] Boazman *v.* Johnston, 3 Sim. 382; Anon., 2 Ch. Cas. 54; Child *v.* Stephens, 1 Eq. Cas. Ab. 141; 1 Vern. 102; Garrard *v.* Lauderdale, 3 Sim. 1; Miles *v.* Bacon, 4 J. J. Marsh. 468; Harrison *v.* Mock, 10 Ala. 185.

[4] Harrison *v.* Mock, 10 Ala. 185.

(a) In some States it is provided by statute that the assignee under a voluntary assignment for the benefit of creditors may proceed, as the representative of creditors, to set aside a previous transfer of property by the assignor in fraud of creditors. Dickson *v.* Kittson, 75 Minn. 168, 173; Swedish-Am. Bank *v.* First Nat. Bank, 89 Minn. 98; Huey *v.* Prince, 187 Pa. St. 151. It has been held even in the absence of statute provisions that the assignee has this right and duty to the extent that the property fraudulently transferred is needed to satisfy the claims of creditors. Wimpfheimer *v.* Perrine, 67 N. J. Eq. 597; Taylor *v.* Lauer, 127 N. C. 157. But the sounder view seems to be that he acquires by the assignment only such rights and interests as the assignor himself could have enforced. First Nat. Bank *v.* Menke, 128 Cal. 103; Maiders *v.* Culver's Assignee, 1 Duv. (Ky.) 164; Jacobi *v.* Jacobi, 101 Mo. 507; Babcock *v.* Maxwell, 29 Mont. 31, 34; Murchie *v.* Wentworth, 74 N. H. 3; Smith *v.* Equitable Trust Co., 215 Pa. St. 418.

a trustee from acquiring an interest adverse to his *cestui que trust* does not apply to a *bona fide* creditor who has become trustee; and that such trustee may purchase a judgment against his *cestui que trust*.[1] But the fact that the trustee is a *bona fide* creditor, ignorant of any fraud, will not prevent the assignment from being declared void, if it is fraudulent upon any legal grounds.[2] So creditors who accept the benefits conferred under such deed, and receive dividends or other advantages thereby, cannot set up rights inconsistent with the deed; nor can they, after receiving such advantages, impeach it, and procure it to be set aside, but they must comply with its provisions.[3] The assignee of an insolvent affirms a fraudulent sale made by his assignor by suing the fraudulent purchaser for the price.[4] A creditor, before he can commence process to set aside a fraudulent assignment or conveyance, must first obtain judgment on his claim.[5] If the debtor B. is unwilling to give a mortgage directly to one of his creditors A., but executes one to another creditor C., to secure C. in regard to what is owing to C. directly, and in respect to any liabilities incurred by C. on B.'s account, and C. guarantees to A. the payment of B.'s debt to him, A. can enforce the trust thus created against C. to the full extent of the mortgage, if necessary in order to pay debts to A. not otherwise secured.[6]

§ 597. When an assignment is made and executed, and all parties assent that the estate shall be managed and settled by trustees, the deed that vests the estate in the trustees for the payment of the debts, may prescribe the manner of carry-

[1] Prevost *v.* Gratz, Peters, C. C. 373.

[2] Rathburn *v.* Platner, 18 Barb. 272.

[3] Adlum *v.* Yard, 1 Rawle, 163; Gutzwiller *v.* Lackman, 23 Miss. 168; Pratt *v.* Adams, 7 Paige, 615; Burrows *v.* Alter, 7 Miss. 424; Jewett *v.* Woodward, 1 Edw. Ch. 195; Lanahan *v.* Latrobe, 7 Md. 268.

[4] Butler *v.* Hildreth, 5 Met. 49.

[5] Neustadt *v.* Joel, 2 Duer, 532. [Loucheim *v.* Casperon, 61 N. J. Eq. 529.]

[6] Parsons *v.* Clark, 132 Mass. 569.

ing the trust into execution, and paying the debts.[1] These directions may be contrary to law, and may be set aside on proceedings had for that purpose, yet if all parties proceed under the deed, the trustees must find their power in the deed of assignment or settlement, and they must proceed in accordance with it in selling the property and in paying the debts; if preferences are made, the trustees must pay them;[2] if all are to be paid equally, the trustees must pay in that manner.[3] If the trust is to pay only a certain class of debts, or a certain number of debts named, the trustees must confine themselves to their power.[4] The principle on which this rests is, that the assignor was the owner of the property, and he could give such directions as to the disposal of it as he pleased; and, so long as the law does not interfere to set aside the assignment, the assignee must follow the only power given to him, to wit, the deed of assignment. In England, the deed generally specifies the mode of raising the money for the purpose of the trust, by directing a sale or mortgage. In the absence of such direction, the intention is to be gathered from the scope of the whole deed, whether a sale or mortgage was intended; for the intention is to govern.[5] If the property is conveyed in trust to pay debts generally, the trustees can make a good title to the purchaser, either in fee or in mortgage, and the purchaser is not bound to see whether there are debts, or whether a sale is necessary, or to see to the application of the purchase-money:

[1] Boazman v. Johnston, 3 Sim. 381; Carr v. Burlington, 1 P. Wms. 229.

[2] Garrard v. Lauderdale, 3 Sim. 1; Douglass v. Allen, 2 Dr. & War. 213; Pearce v. Slocombe, 3 Y. & Col. 84.

[3] Ibid.; Anon. 3 Ch. Cas. 54; Wolestoncroft v. Long, 1 id. 32; Child v. Stevens, 1 Vern. 102; Hamilton v. Houghton, 2 Bligh, 169.

[4] Purefoy v. Purefoy, 1 Vern. 28; Loddington v. Kime, 3 Lew. 433; Pratt v. Adams, 7 Paige, 615; Stoddart v. Allen, 1 Rawle, 258; Brainard v. Dunning, 30 N. Y. 211.

[5] Spalding v. Shalmer, 1 Vern. 301; Ball v. Harris, 8 Sim. 485; Sheldon v. Dormer, 2 Vern. 310; Shrewsbury v. Shrewsbury, 1 Ves. Jr. 234; Ivy v. Gilbert, 2 P. Wms. 13; Mills v. Banks, 3 id. 1; Allen v. Backhouse, 2 V. & B. 65; Wilson v. Halliley, 1 R. & M. 590; 1 Sugd. Pow. 116; Stroughill v. Anstey, 1 De G., M. & G. 635.

the creditors must look to the trustees.[1] But if the trust is to
pay one particular debt, or debts named in a schedule, the
purchaser must see to the necessity of the sale, and to the
application of the purchase-money,[2] unless the trustees are
authorized to give receipts, or there is a clause in the trust-
deed discharging the purchaser from such obligations.[3]

§ 598. In the United States, a deed of assignment to pay
debts necessarily implies a power to sell; and if it is an insolvent estate, a power to mortgage contained in the deed would
render it fraudulent and void;[4] therefore all deeds of assignment for the payment of debts generally, without any limitations or directions, confer upon the trustees a right to sell.[5]
But if there are special directions given as to the time, manner,
and conditions of sale, they must be followed as given.[6] Thus
a conveyance of land in trust to pay out of the rents and profits
the grantor's debts, and to support the grantor, his wife, and
children, and at his death divide it among his children, gave
no right to sell for payment of debts, or for any purpose.[7] An
unsealed writing purporting to convey land in trust to pay

[1] Johnson v. Kennett, 3 Myl. & K. 631; Shaw v. Borrer, 1 Keen, 559;
Eland v. Eland, 4 Myl. & Cr. 428; Forbes v. Peacock, 11 Sim. 152; Page v.
Adam, 4 Beav. 269; Culpepper v. Aston, 2 Ch. Cas. 115; Anon., Salk. 153;
Dunch v. Kent, 1 Vern. 260; Jenkins v. Hiles, 6 Ves. 654, n.; Williamson
v. Curtis, 3 Bro. Ch. 96; Doran v. Wiltshire, 3 Swanst. 699; Jones v. Price,
11 Sim. 558; Glyn v. Locke, 3 Dr. & War. 11; 2 Sugd. V. & P. 32; Doe v.
Hughes, 6 Exch. 223; Lock v. Lomas, 21 L. J. Ch. 503; Robinson v. Lowater,
17 Beav. 601; 5 De G., M. & G. 277.

[2] Doran v. Wiltshire, 3 Swanst. 701; Elliott v. Merryman, Barn. 78;
1 Keen, 573; 2 Atk. 41; Spalding v. Shalmer, 1 Vern. 301; Lloyd v. Baldwin,
1 Ves. 73; Balfour v. Welland, 16 Ves. 151.

[3] Binks v. Rokeby, 2 Madd. 227; Roper v. Hallifax, 2 Sugd. Pow. 501,
App. 3; Jones v. Price, 11 Sim. 557; Culpepper v. Aston, 2 Ch. Cas. 115;
Spalding v. Shalmer, 1 Vern. 301; Braybroke v. Inskip, 8 Ves. 417.

[4] Planck v. Schermerhorn, 3 Barb. Ch. 644.

[5] Goodrich v. Proctor, 1 Gray, 567; Purdie v. Whitney, 20 Pick. 25;
Gould v. Lamb, 11 Met. 84; Williams v. Otey, 8 Humph. 563. [Lumbering
Co. v. Powell, 120 Mich. 51.]

[6] Walker v. Brungard, 13 Sm. & M. 723.

[7] Mundy v. Vawter, 3 Grat. 518.

one debt, does not confer a power of sale, but creates a simple lien to be enforced in equity.[1] If a trustee sells, however, without power, and all parties are present, acquiescing in the sale, they are estopped in equity to deny the title of the purchaser.[2] (a)   An assignment that does not purport to convey land in trust will not give the trustees power to sell.[3] If the trustee has power to sell land to pay debts generally, it is impossible for the purchaser to know what the debts are, or whether there is a necessity for the sale.   This is a part of the trust and duty confided in the trustee, and a purchaser is not obliged to look to the application of the purchase-money.[4] The English rules upon this subject are not favored in this country, and they will not be applied if any circumstance can be found to take the case out of their operation.   But if the trust is to pay a particular debt, or certain debts named in a schedule, the purchaser must see to the necessity of the sale, and to the application of the purchase-money, unless there is some circumstance or power to take the case out of the rule.[5] If there is collusion or fraud between the trustee and purchaser, or knowledge in the purchaser that there are no debts, or that the sale is unnec-

[1] Linton v. Boly, 12 Mo. 567.

[2] Spencer v. Hawkins, 4 Ired. Eq. 288.

[3] Baker v. Crookshank, 1 Whart. Dig. (6th ed.) Debt. & Cred. pl. 370.

[4] Goodrich v. Proctor, 1 Gray, 670; Andrews v. Sparhawk, 13 Pick. 393; Gardner v. Gardner, 3 Mason, 178; Williams v. Otey, 8 Humph. 568; Garnett v. Macon, 2 Brock. 185; 6 Call, 308; Grant v. Hook, 13 Serg. & R. 259; Bruch v. Lantz, 2 Rawle, 392; Coombs v. Jordan, 3 Bland, 284; Redheimer v. Pyron, Spears, Eq. 134; Cadbury v. Duval, 10 Penn. St. 267; Dalzell v. Crawford, 1 Pars. Eq. 57; Hannum v. Spear, 1 Yeates, 553; 2 Dall. 291; Hauser v. Shore, 5 Ired. Eq. 357; Sims v. Lively, 14 B. Mon. 433; Lining v. Peyton, 2 Des. 378; Wilson v. Davisson, 2 Rob. (Va.) 385; Nicholls v. Peak, 12 N. J. Eq. 69; Rutledge v. Smith, 1 Busb. Eq. 283.

[5] Gardner v. Gardner, 3 Mason, 178; Duffy v. Calvert, 6 Gill, 487; Wormley v. Wormley, 8 Wheat. 422; Cadbury v. Duval, 10 Penn. St. 267; Dalzell v. Crawford, 1 Pars. Eq. 57; Elliott v. Merryman, 1 Lead. Cas. Eq. 45, n. [See infra, § 790, note.]

(a) When there is no chance of a surplus over the claims of creditors, it is not necessary to have the assent of the assignor to an advantageous sale for other than cash. Whitman v. McIntyre, 199 Mass. 436.

essary or not authorized, it is all void as fraudulent.[1] Although there is fraud, or a misapplication of the purchase-money with the knowledge of the purchaser, he will take a good *title at law;* but equity will convert him into a trustee, and make him accountable to the creditors or *cestuis que trust.*[2] (a)

[1] Potter *v.* Gardner, 12 Wheat. 498; Garnett *v.* Macon, 2 Brock. 185; Redheimer *v.* Pyron, Spears, Eq. 134. [See *infra,* § 800, note.]

[2] D'Oyley *v.* Loveland, 1 Strob. L. 46. A sale by a trustee holding the legal title, though unauthorized or collusive, will generally pass the legal title; but the grantee will take the estate charged with the same trusts that the original trustee was charged with. [See *supra,* § 789 *et seq.*]

(a) When a large part of the assigned estate consists of goods in the process of manufacture or when a large part of the value of the estate depends upon the ability to sell the assignor's business as a going concern, the assignee is sometimes justified in continuing the business for a short time. But if he does so without the previous consent of creditors or authority ·from court and a loss results, he runs great danger of being held liable for the loss, even though the deed of assignment purports to give him power to continue the business. Cooper *v.* Lankford, 117 Ky. 792; Hill *v.* Cornwall, 95 Ky. 526; Brown's Assigned Estate, 193 Pa. St. 281; Quimby *v.* Uhl, 130 Mich. 198, 211; Wilhelm *v.* Byles, 60. Mich. 561, 567. Under the common form of assignment in Massachusetts which requires creditors to become parties to the deed, a provision in the deed authorizing the assignee to continue the business for a reasonable time would seem to be sufficient authority from the creditors who become parties to it.

Even when the continuance of the business has been expressly authorized by the creditors, they are not liable as proprietors upon the trustee's contracts. The trustee is neither an agent nor a partner, but is primarily liable upon his contracts. A right to reach the trust assets or the beneficiaries must be worked out through the trustee's right to indemnity. Wells-Stone Co. *v.* Grover, 7 N. D. 460; Smith *v.* Williams, 178 Ill. 420; Sterns Paper Co. *v.* Williams, 178 Ill. 626. See *contra,* Wright *v.* Caney River Ry. Co., 66 S. E. 588 (N. C. 1909). As to the trustee's right to reimbursement from creditors who have received dividends, when the trust estate is insufficient, see Wells-Stone Co. *v.* Aultman, 9 N. D. 520.

When the assigned assets include the unexpired term of a lease which is not forfeited by the assignment, the assignee has a reasonable time in which to decide whether he will accept the lease and assume the burdens of its covenants on behalf of the estate, or abandon it. Walton *v.* Stafford,

980

§ 599.   As a general rule, the assets of a partnership are holden to pay partnership debts, and the separate property of each individual partner is holden, first, to pay his private debts; so, if an insolvent partnership make an assignment, the trustee must apply the joint property to the joint debts, and the separate property to private debts.[1] So a partnership assignment that prefers private debts is void; and a general assignment by an individual partner that preferred partnership debts, would be void.[2] But where it is legal to make preferences, an assignment may probably prefer either class.[3] So it is said that provisions in a partnership assignment that

[1] Pearce v. Slocombe, 3 Y. & Col. 84; Merrill v. Neill, 8 How. 414.
[2] Jackson v. Cornell, 1 Sandf. Ch. 348.
[3] Kirby v. Schoonmaker, 3 Barb. Ch. 46.

162 N. Y. 558; Wilder v. McDonald, 63 Ohio St. 383; Trust Co. v. Wabash Ry. Co., 150 U. S. 299; N. H. Trust Co. v. Taggart, 68 N. H. 557; Rand v. Francis, 168 Ill. 444.

Like other trustees, the assignee is entitled to reasonable compensation for his services. McDougal v. Fuller, 148 Cal. 521; Branch v. Am. Nat. Bank, 57 Kan. 282; Pickerell v. Thompson, 109 Ky. 498; Nat. Bank v. Dulaney, 96 Md. 159, 171; Hay v. Bacon, 80 Minn. 188; Sliker v. Fisher, 45 N. J. Eq. 132; Matter of Assignment of Hulburt, 89 N. Y. 259; Re Assignment of Woodall, 33 Or. 382; Re Assignment of Bank of Oregon, 32 Or. 84; Tustin's Appeal, 176 Pa. St. 382; Coleman's Assigned Estate, 200 Pa. St. 29; Real Estate Inv. Co.'s Estate, 212 Pa. St. 304; Mann v. Poole, 48 S. C. 154; Woodcock v. Reilly, 16 S. D. 198; German Bank v. Haller, 103 Tenn. 73; Morris v. Ellis, 62 S. W. 250 (Tenn. Ch. Ap. 1901); Beecher

v. Foster, 51 W. Va. 605, 621. And he is entitled to employ counsel where reasonably necessary, and to pay reasonable counsel charges out of the assigned estate. National Bank v. Dulaney, 96 Md. 159, 171; Berkeley v. Green, 102 Va. 378, 381; Courier-Journal Co. v. Columbia Fire Ins. Co., 54 S. W. 966 (Ky. 1900).

Like other trustees, he is chargeable with losses due to his failure to use the care and prudence of an ordinarily prudent man. Matter of Leventritt, 58 N. Y. S. 256, 40 App. Div. 429; Wright's Estate, 182 Pa. St. 90.

He is not allowed to make a profit for himself by his dealings with reference to the trust estate, and is not allowed to purchase, either directly or indirectly, the trust property without the assent of those beneficially interested. Allison's Estate, 183 Pa. St. 555; Nabours v. McCord, 97 Tex. 526; McCord v. Nabours, 101 Tex. 495.

do not go beyond the provisions of the law will not avoid it though releases are stipulated for.[1] But a partnership assignment that provides for a release, must convey all the property, joint and separate, held by the firm;[2] and the deed must be signed and sealed by all the members of the firm; for a general assignment by one partner will not pass the partnership assets;[3] nor will a general assignment by a single member of a limited partnership pass the property of the firm.[4] By statutes in nearly all the States, all preferences by limited partnerships are forbidden.[5]

§ 600. If by the terms of an assignment no debts are to be paid until they have been examined by the trustees, a creditor can claim no benefit under the deed, until he has submitted his claim to the trustees.[6] If the trustees are clothed with absolute power to allow or reject all claims, the court cannot interfere with their discretion;[7] but such a power in a general assignment by an insolvent debtor would render the assignment void. So a power given to the trustees to prefer such debts as they please would render the assignment void.[8] A general power to pay debts will not justify the trustees in paying fictitious debts;[9] nor will it include debts founded upon a usurious consideration:[10] but, where such debts are specially named and directed to be paid, the trustee cannot

[1] Andress v. Miller, 15 Penn. St. 318.
[2] Hennessey v. Western Bank, 6 Watts & S. 300.
[3] Ibid.; Moddewell v. Keever, 8 Watts & S. 63.
[4] Merritt v. Wilson, 29 Maine, 58.
[5] Mills v. Argall, 6 Paige, 577.
[6] Wain v. Egmont, 3 Myl. & K. 445; Drever v. Mawdesley, 16 Sim. 511; Nunn v. Wilsmore, 8 T. R. 521; Cosser v. Radford, 1 De G., J. & Sm. 585.
[7] Ibid.
[8] Wakeman v. Grover, 4 Paige, 24; 11 Wend. 187; Hudson v. Maze, 3 Scam. 579. But a power given to the trustees to compromise claims due to the estate does not avoid it. Bellows v. Partridge, 19 Barb. 178.
[9] Irwin v. Keen, 3 Whart. 347; Webb v. Daggett, 2 Barb. 10; Hardcastle v. Fisher, 24 Mo. 70.
[10] Pratt v. Adams, 7 Paige, 617; Beach v. Fulton Bank, 3 Wend. 584.

refuse to pay them, deducting the usurious excess.[1] If a debt is specially directed to be paid, and afterwards a bill is sustained to set aside such debt as illegal or fraudulent, the trustees cannot pay it.[2] So a general direction in a will to pay debts applies only to legal debts, due upon good consideration, and enforceable against the testator's estate.[3] A trust to pay debts named in the schedule does not convert such debts into interest-bearing debts if they did not bear interest before. Even if the direction is to pay certain debts with interest, debts that do not bear interest will not be thus converted into interest-bearing debts.[4] But debts that bear interest, by the contract proving them, must be paid with interest.[5] If interest is realized by trustees upon funds in their hands, interest must be paid.[6] If the trustees permit a creditor to sign the deed for a specified sum, they cannot afterwards contest the debt.[7] But if there is gross fraud, they can apply to the court to set it aside.[8] If

[1] Green v. Morse, 4 Barb. 332; Pratt v. Adams, 7 Paige, 641.

[2] Morse v. Crofoot, 4 Comst. 114.

[3] Rogers v. Rogers, 3 Wend. 503; Chandler v. Hill, 2 Hen. & M. 124. Chancellor Kent, in an opinion, printed 6 Humph. 532, advised that a preference given by a bank to pay notes illegally issued for borrowed money was valid, and that the trustees should pay them. The bank should be liable for money had and received, though the issuing of its bills was illegal. It had had the consideration and ought to pay, though it had done such acts as to forfeit its charter.

[4] Carr v. Burlington, 1 P. Wms. 229; Bothomly v. Fairfax, id. 334; Maxwell v. Wettenhall, 2 id. 27; Lloyd v. Williams, 2 Atk. 111; Barwell v. Parker, 2 Ves. 364; Creuze v. Hunter, 2 Ves. Jr. 157; 4 Bro. Ch. 316; Tait v. Northwick, 4 Ves. 816; Shirley v. Ferrers, 1 Bro. Ch. 41; Hamilton v. Houghton, 2 Bligh, 169.

[5] Hamilton v. Houghton, 2 Bligh, 187; Tait v. Northwick, 4 Ves. 816; Bath v. Bradford, 2 Ves. 588; Stewart v. Noble, Vern. & Scriv. 528, 536; Anon. 1 Salk. 154; Burke v. Jones, 2 V. & B. 284; Hughes v. Wynne, 1 Myl. & K. 20; Pearce v. Slocombe, 3 Y. & Col. 84; Bryant v. Russell, 23 Pick. 508; Winslow v. Ancrum, 1 McCord, Ch. 100. But it has been held, that, in cases of preferred debts, the preference applied only to the principal debt, and that the interest was to be paid *pro rata* with the unpreferred debts. Morris's App., 1 Am. Law Reg. 631.

[6] Pearce v. Slocombe, 3 Y. & Coll. 84.

[7] Lancaster v. Elce, 31 Beav. 335.

[8] Ibid.

a creditor repudiates the deed and sues the debtor, the trustee cannot allow him to retrace his steps and sign the deed; and if he should allow it to be done, the other creditors may procure it to be set aside.[1]

§ 601. It has been held in some cases that a devise for the payment of debts will prevent the statute of limitations from running against such debts as are not barred at the time of the testator's death; but it will not revive a debt already barred [2] upon the principle that, as soon as a trust is created for the payment of a debt, the statute of limitations ceases to apply, as it does not run against trusts generally. Mr. Hill inclines to the opinion, that the same principle would apply to trusts under deeds for the payment of debts; [3] but it is held in the United States, that an assignment by deed for the benefit of creditors, or an assignment in insolvency, does not prevent the statute from running, and it would be a good plea in bar at law, although the debts were specially named in the deeds or schedules.[4] But the creditors may enforce their claims in equity against the assets in the hands of the trustees.[5]

[1] Field v. Donoughmore, 1 Dr. & War. 227; reversing 2 Dru. & Walsh, 630.

[2] Fergus v. Gore, 1 Sch. & Lef. 107; Hughes v. Wynne, T. & R. 307; Culton v. Oughton, 3 Beav. 1; Burke v. Jones, 2 V. & B. 275; Hargreave v. Mitchell, 6 Madd. 326; Harcourt v. White, 28 Beav. 303; Jones v. Scott, 1 R. & M. 225; 4 Cl. & Fin. 382; O'Connor v. Haslam, 5 H. L. Cas. 177. [See In re Tanqueray-Willaume, 20 Ch. Div. 465; Foley v. McDonnell, 48 Wash. 272; Gordon v. McDougall, 84 Miss. 715; McKinley v. Coe, 66 N. J. Eq. 70.]

[3] Hill on Trustees, 341.

[4] Reed v. Johnson, 1 R. I. 81; Christy v. Flemington, 10 Penn. St. 129.

[5] Gary v. May, 16 Ohio, 66. And this must be upon the principle of Mr. Hill's opinion above cited. As soon as a trust is created for the payment of a debt, and the relation of trustee and *cestui que trust* is established, the statute of limitations does not run so long as the relation exists, but that does not prevent the statute from running at law against the original debtor; though how far the execution of the deeds or schedules naming a debt would be a memorandum in writing acknowledging the debt, and thus taking it out of the statute, is not very well settled.

§ 602. In settling an estate under an assignment, the preferred debts will first be paid. The remainder is then distributed to the unpreferred debts due at the date of the assignment, *pro rata*, if there is a deficiency of assets.[1] If there is a residue, after paying all the creditors who come in under the deed, it results to the assignor.[2] If there are non-assenting creditors who have no rights under the deed, they can reach the surplus in the hands of the trustee, by the process of foreign attachment, garnishment, or trustee process.[3]

§ 602 *a.* Intimately connected with general assignments in trust for creditors, thus far treated of in this chapter, are trusts created by deeds to secure the payment of particular debts, — deeds which give the grantee certain powers over the estate, but do not exhaust the entire interest of the grantor in it. Such a trust was the subject of discussion in a recent case, in which the will of the trustee discharged the land from liability for the debts to cover which the trust had been created.[4] In an Illinois case A. took title to certain land to secure a debt due him, and to pay any surplus to B. and equity enforced the trust.[5] These deeds of trust and mortgage-deeds containing powers of sale create a peculiar kind of trust, which it is proper to discuss in this connection.

[1] Purefoy *v.* Purefoy, 1 Vern. 28.

[2] 3 P. Wms. 251, n.; Poole *v.* Pass, 1 Beav. 600; Dubose *v.* Dubose, 7 Ala. 235; Hall *v.* Denison, 17 Vt. 311; Rahn *v.* McElrath, 6 Watts, 151; Stevens *v.* Earles, 25 Mich. 41. [Farnsworth *v.* Doom, 109 Ky. 794; Bole *v.* McKelvy, 189 Pa. St. 505; Early *v.* Early, 75 S. C. 15. See also Ralston's Appeal, 169 Pa. St. 254; Provident Life and Trust Co. *v.* Fidelity Ins., etc., Co., 203 Pa. St. 82.] So if there is a residue in the hands of an assignee in bankruptcy.

[3] Hastings *v.* Baldwin, 17 Mass. 558; Hearn *v.* Crutcher, 4 Yerg. 461; Wright *v.* Henderson, 7 How. (Miss.) 539; Todd *v.* Bucknam, 2 Fairf. 41; Dubose *v.* Dubose, 7 Ala. 235; Vernon *v.* Morton, 8 Dana, 247. [Avery *v.* Monroe, 172 Mass. 132; Reddy *v.* Raymond, 194 Mass. 367; Thompson *v.* Shaw, 104 Me. 85; Weston *v.* Nevers, 72 N. H. 65.]

[4] Damon *v.* Bibber, 135 Mass. 458.

[5] Gillett *v.* Hickling, 16 Brad. (Ill.) 392.

§ 602 b. There are several forms of mortgages: (1) A mortgage in the common form of a conveyance of the estate, with a
defeasance inserted which provides, that if a certain sum of
money shall be paid within a certain time the deed shall be void.
(2) A mortgage in the form of a deed absolute on its face, but
which was made to pay or secure a debt, and the grantor takes
back from the grantee an agreement that when the debt is paid,
or when a certain sum of money is paid to the grantee, he will
sell and convey the premises to the grantor. The parties sometimes resort to ingenious devices to disguise the transaction;
but if the substance of the transaction is the security of an ante-
cedent debt, it will be decreed to be a mortgage, whatever may
be the form of the writings, or whatever may be their recitals;
and even parol evidence is admissible in some States under
some circumstances to prove that a deed absolute on its face is
in fact a mere security for a debt or a mortgage.[1] Both these
forms of mortgage can be foreclosed only by proceedings in
equity for a foreclosure, or by an entry and taking possession
according to the law or the statutes in force where the land is
situated, and by the expiration of three years or other limit of
time fixed to bar the mortgagor's equity of redemption. (3) A
mortgage may be in the form of a deed of trust from the grantor
to the grantee, providing that if the grantor shall not pay a certain sum of money at a certain time, the grantee may sell the
estate in a certain manner, or do whatever other thing the deed
of trust points out to be done. (4) A fourth form of mortgage
is a deed of conveyance with a defeasance inserted as in ordinary
mortgages, and with a power of sale superadded to enable the
grantee or mortgagee to sell the property at any time after default of payment, according to the terms of the power contained
in the mortgage. It is quite apparent that many questions peculiar to the law of trusts must arise under deeds and mortgages
which contain such powers and provisions.

---

[1] *Ante*, § 226; Campbell *v.* Dearborn, 109 Mass. 130, where the cases
are reviewed. [Potter *v.* Kimball, 186 Mass. 120; Weiseham *v.* Hocker, 7
Okla. 250; *supra*, § 76, note *a*, p 70.]

§ 602 c. In the civil law a power of sale was implied in every mortgage upon default of payment according to the terms of the pledge, and an express agreement did not deprive the mortgagee of this right.[1] By the common law, at first, mortgages became absolute deeds, if the terms of the defeasance were not strictly performed at the day; but courts of equity succeeded in establishing an equity of redemption in the mortgagor in the land, which remained an equity in him until the mortgage was duly foreclosed by process of law. Courts were astute in protecting this equity of redemption, and leaned strongly against all agreements between the mortgagor and mortgagee which abridged it. "Once a mortgage always a mortgage" became a maxim. Therefore, when provisions began to be inserted in deeds which enabled the mortgagee to destroy at once this equity of redemption, courts looked upon them with suspicion, if not with aversion, as devices intended to oppress and injure mortgagors, who are, from the nature of the case, more or less in the power of mortgagees. Perhaps, where the rights of the mortgagor were not properly guarded, the fears of Lord Eldon and others, who opposed the introduction of these forms and trusts, were not unreasonable or groundless. But, notwithstanding all opposition, the use of them has steadily increased, until they are common in England and in nearly all the States. They are regulated by statutes, and are under the jurisdiction of courts of equity, which can interfere, by injunctions, prohibitions, orders, and decrees, to prevent oppression and remedy abuses. A large proportion of the mortgage-deeds of real estate now contain powers of sale in case of default, and the laws regulate and protect them.[2]

[1] 1 Domat, 360.

[2] Croft v. Powell, 1 Comyn, 603 (1729); 2 Cruise, Dig. 90; Clay v. Sharpe, Sugd. V. & P. App. 21; Corder v. Morgan, 18 Ves. 344; 2 Call, 465, 568; Curling v. Shuttleworth, 6 Bing. 121; Forster v. Hoggart, 15 Q. B. 155; Clay v. Willis, 1 B. & C. 364; 4 Kent's Com. 146; 2 Story, Eq. Jur. § 1027; Longwith v. Butler, 3 Gilm. 32; Slee v. Manhattan Co., 1 Paige, 57; Lawrence v. Farmer's Loan & Trust Co., 3 Kern. 200; Bronson v. Kinsie, 1 How. 321; Fogarty v. Sawyer, 17 Cal. 589; Bradley v. Phil. R. R. Co., 36 Penn. St. 141; Hyde v. Warren, 46 Miss. 13.

§ 602 *d.* Mortgages containing powers of sale and deeds of trust to secure a debt due to a creditor are as a rule substantially the same thing in law and equity; but a deed of trust may be made so as to contain no forfeiture (no limit to the right to redeem so long as the land remains in the hands of the trustee), but merely a power in the trustees to enter on default and manage, sell, etc., as agents of the grantor for the purpose of paying his debts and handing over any surplus to the grantor, and in such case it is very different from a mortgage. No foreclosure by entry and lapse of time is possible under such a deed, for foreclosure can exist only where there is an equity of redemption to foreclose, and there can be no equity·of redemption where there is no forfeiture agreed upon, for equities of redemption came into existence and live in the law only to relieve against forfeitures.[1] At law, both kinds of deeds purport to convey the legal title to the grantee, or creditor, or trustee; but in equity the land, the title, and the deeds stand for security of the debt. The debt is the principal thing, and the conveyance of the land is collateral to the debt. The mortgagor in both cases has an estate in the land called an equity of redemption; if he fails to pay the debt, his equity of redemption is barred upon due proceedings had; but if the debt is paid at any time before his equity is defeated by the steps appointed to be taken, it becomes absolute, and he is entitled to a reconveyance or a discharge of the mortgage, as the case may be. In some circumstances a discharge of the mortgage upon payment or a reconveyance is not material, as by the terms of the mortgage and by the law it becomes null and void. A mortgage is a pledge‎or security for a debt, whatever may be the form which the transaction takes, whether a simple mortgage-deed in form, or a mortgage with a power of sale, or a deed in trust, or a deed absolute on its face, accompanied by an agreement in writing to reconvey, or to sell, or to do any other thing upon the payment of a certain sum of money; courts of equity look upon it as a mortgage, and deal with it as such. The test in all these forms is this, Does

[1] Shepard *v.* Richardson, 145 Mass. 32, 36.

the transaction resolve itself into a security for the payment of a sum of money or a debt; and until a default in the payment of a sum of money or a debt, has the grantor any right to pay the money and keep or receive back the title to his property?[1] And it is immaterial that the conveyance is made to a third person, and not to the creditor himself. In such case the grantee is a trustee by an express or a resulting trust, as the case may be, to the amount of the debt, and the grantor has an equity in all beyond, or if the deed is absolute on its face, or a deed of trust, the grantee is a trustee for the grantor for what remains over and above the debt.[2] Thus a bank authorized to hold lands mortgaged for security may take deeds of trust to themselves or to trustees for their use;[3] and a railroad company authorized to mortgage its property was held to have authority to make a deed of trust;[4] and where there are special statutes in relation to the recording of mortgages, it has been held that these statutes embrace deeds of trust made as security for debts;[5] and so the statutes relating to the satisfaction and discharge of mortgages embrace deeds of trust,[6] and it has been held that an agent, having a general power to execute a mortgage in the name of his principal, may execute a mortgage containing a power of sale.[7]

---

[1] 4 Kent's Com. 136, 146; 2 Story, Eq. Jur. § 1018; Cotterell *v*. Long, 20 Ohio, 464, 472; Wilcox *v*. Morris, 1 Murph. (N. C.) 116; Eaton *v*. Whiting, 3 Pick. 484; Bloom *v*. Rensselaer, 15 Ill. 505; Woodruff *v*. Robb, 19 Ohio, 217; Sargent *v*. Howe, 21 Ill. 149; Fanning *v*. Kerr, 7 Iowa, 450; Crocker *v*. Robertson, 8 Iowa, 404; Flagg *v*. Mann, 2 Sumn. 533; Jackson *v*. Blount, 2 Dev. Eq. 555; Rogan *v*. Walker, 1 Wis. 527; Johnson *v*. Clark, 5 Ark. 321. A judgment against the grantor who remains in possession after default with the acquiescence of the mortgagee, is a lien on the premises subject to the mortgage, or trust-deed in the nature of a mortgage. Martin *v*. Aliter, 42 Ohio St. 94.

[2] Woodruff *v*. Robb, 19 Ohio, 217; Sargent *v*. Howe, 21 Ill. 450.

[3] Bennett *v*. Union Bank, 5 Humph. 612.

[4] Wright *v*. Bundy, 11 Met. 398, 404.

[5] Magee *v*. Carpenter, 4 Ala. 469; Fogarty *v*. Sawyer, 23 Cal. 570.

[6] McGregor *v*. Hall, 3 Stew. & Por. 397; Woodruff *v*. Robb, 19 Ohio, 212; Wolfe *v*. McDowell, 13 Sm. & M. 103; Smith *v*. Doe, 26 Miss. 291; Crosby *v*. Huston, 1 Tex. 239.

[7] Wilson *v*. Troup, 7 Johns. Ch. 25; 2 Cowen, 195; 4 Kent, Com. 147.

There are incidental differences between mortgages with or without powers of sale and deeds of trust, as there are differences in mortgage-deeds themselves in the special stipulations that may be inserted. Parties can make their own contracts; and the contracts must be performed according to the special stipulations;[1] but both mortgages and deeds of trust are alike in their great characteristics. They both stand as security for the payment of money or the performance of some other obligation; under both the grantor has an equitable right of redemption, or to have the property again upon the performance of his obligation, and this equity of redemption can only be barred by regular proceedings according to the law, or according to the provisions and conditions contained in the respective deeds.

§ 602 *e*. Mortgages with power of sale and deeds of trust are executed like all other instruments of trust. They need not be signed by the grantee, trustee, or *cestuis que trust*. Acceptance of the trusts created under them may be proved by parol, whether such acceptance was manifested by words or acts.[2] The assent of the creditors to be secured by such deeds will be presumed, if they are beneficial to them; but if the effect of the deeds is to hinder and delay the creditors, their assent must be shown,[3] and such deeds cannot be revoked after the assent of the parties to be benefited.[4]

§ 602 *f*. Such deeds may be executed for the payment of debts, or for the performance of any kind of a legal obligation, whether of the grantor or of a third person. So they may be

---

[1] Elliott *v.* Wood, 45 N. Y. 71.

[2] *Ante*, §§ 589, 593, 594; Scull *v.* Reeves, 2 Green, Ch. 84; Flint *v.* Clinton Co., 12 N. H. 432; Spencer *v.* Ford, 1 Rob. (Va.) 648; Liffler *v.* Armstrong, 4 Iowa, 482; Pope *v.* Brandon, 2 Stew. (Ala.) 401; Skipwith *v.* Cunningham, 8 Leigh, 271; Hipp *v.* Hutchell, 4 Tex. 20; Field *v.* Arrowsmith, 3 Humph. 442; Robertson *v.* Sublett, 6 id. 313; Brevard *v.* Neely, 2 Sneed, 164; Mayer *v.* Pullam, 2 Head, 347.

[3] *Ante*, § 593; Shearer *v.* Loften, 26 Ala. 703; Wiswall *v.* Ross, 4 Porter (Ala.), 328; Mauldin *v.* Armstead, 14 Ala. 702.

[4] *Ante*, §§ 593, 594; Gate *v.* Debrett, 10 Yerg. 146.

given to indemnify one against contingent obligations. Thus a trust-deed to indemnify sureties upon a bond or note or endorser of notes will be upheld;[1] and so mortgages with power of sale, made by a married woman to pay the debt or note of her husband, have been upheld in law and equity.[2]

§ 602 *g*.   The powers of trustees under deeds of trust, and of mortgagees under mortgages with power of sale, depend entirely upon the terms of the deeds. Such powers are created by, and exist in the deeds, and of course they exist in the terms in which they are created, and in no others. They are to be exercised by the trustees *in pais*. They are wholly matters of convention and contract between the parties, and not of law or jurisdiction. They can be exercised because they are conferred by one party upon another, and not because the law or the courts have conferred or authorized them. Statutes in some of the States have regulated their execution, but such statutes do not create the powers themselves.[3] (*a*)   Therefore it is that purchasers of land under powers take under the deed in which the powers are created; it is as if the purchaser's name was inserted in that deed. It follows that the purchaser must look carefully to the intention and purpose of the power as well as to its extent, for if it is executed contrary to its intent or purpose, or outside of its true scope, or not in the manner in which it is provided that it should be executed, the purchaser will take no title. The purchaser is bound to know the full particulars and purpose of the power under which he purchases; and·if he makes any mistake in the construction of the power, or if he does not

[1] Griffin *v.* Doe, 12 Ala. 783; Hawkins *v.* May, id. 673; Thurston *v.* Prentiss, 1 Mich. 194, Walk. Ch. 529; Graham *v.* King, 15 Ala. 563, 5 Port. 191; Boden *v.* Jaco, 17 Ala. 344. But see Jackson *v.* Hampton, 8 Ind. 457.

[2] Young *v.* Graff, 28 Ill. 20; Bartlett *v.* Bartlett, 4 Allen, 440.

[3] Doolittle *v.* Lewis, 7 Johns. Ch. 45; Beatie *v.* Butler, 21 Mo. 313; Turner *v.* Johnson, 7 Ohio, 216, 220; Elliott *v.* Wood, 45 N. Y. 71; Hyde *v.* Warren, 46 Miss. 13; Richmond *v.* Hughes, 9 R. I. 228.

(*a*) See Jones on Mortgages, *passim; supra*, § 199, n.

fully inform himself and acts in ignorance, he will take no title if the power is not properly executed.[1] The power to sell need not be contained in the same instrument with the conveyance of the title. Thus a simple mortgage may be made without a power of sale to secure debt, and at the same time the mortgagor may give a power to the mortgagee or to a third person to sell the land upon default of payment, and to pay the debt from the proceeds, and to account for the balance, if any; and such power will be valid, and the execution of it will bar the equity of redemption of the mortgagor;[2] and so the power may be changed by consent of parties, by a writing under seal of equal solemnity with the original instrument.[3] The power of sale should be expressed in plain terms, but no particular form is necessary, and a power of sale may arise by implication, as where a duty is imposed upon a trustee which he cannot perform without selling;[4] and the right to sell implies the right to convey.[5] So the mortgagee may bind himself to execute any other power or perform some other act, as to convey the land to some other person or to the mortgagor's wife upon the payment of the mortgage debt.[6] The power to sell may be made to depend upon almost any circumstance, as upon default in payment of the taxes by the mortgagor.[7] A condition may be annexed to the power that the mortgagor shall concur in the sale, and join in the deed.[8]

---

[1] Wallis *v.* Thornton, 2 Brock. 422; Demall *v.* Morgan, 5 Call, 417; Wilson *v.* Troup, 7 Johns. Ch. 25; Ormsby *v.* Tarascon, 3 Litt. 410; Williams *v.* Otey, 8 Humph. 518; Walker *v.* Brungbad, 13 Sm. & M. 723. See *ante*, §§ 511 *a*, 511 *b*, 511 *c*, and *post*, §§ 764–787.

[2] Brisbane *v.* Stoughton, 17 Ohio, 482.

[3] Baldridge *v.* Walton, 1 Mo. 520.

[4] *Post*, § 766; Purdie *v.* Whitney, 20 Pick. 25; Williams *v.* Otey, 8 Humph. 563; Munday *v.* Vattier, 3 Grat. 518; Linton *v.* Boly, 12 Mo. 567; Goodrich *v.* Proctor, 1 Gray, 567. See Wing *v.* Cooper, 37 Vt. 169; Hyman *v.* Devereux, 63 N. C. 624.

[5] Williams *v.* Otey, 8 Humph. 563 ; Fogarty *v.* Sawyer, 17 Cal. 589.

[6] Blount *v.* Carroway, 67 N. C. 396.

[7] Pope *v.* Durant, 26 Iowa, 233.

[8] Kissam *v.* Dierkes, 49 N. Y. 602.

§ 602 *h*. It is a universal rule that a power coupled with an interest is irrevocable; and as a power of sale inserted in a mortgage or contained in a deed of trust to a creditor to secure a debt or to a third person for his benefit, is a power coupled with an interest, it cannot be revoked by any act of the grantor or donor of the power. Not even the death or insanity of the grantor or donor will annul the power or suspend its exercise. The debt remains, the right or lien on the property remains, and the power is coupled with them. In other words, the power is annexed to the property, and is an irrevocable part of the security, and goes with it.[1] The mortgagor cannot disseize the mortgagee by an exclusive possession in such manner as to defeat the power of sale.[2] A mere power of attorney, however, from a debtor to a creditor, authorizing him to sell property, and, after deducting the amount due to himself, to account for the balance, is a naked power, revocable at the will of the donor. Such a power is not connected with the estate, and is no part either of the estate or the debt due.[3]

§ 602 *i*. The mortgagee in a deed of mortgage and the trustee in a deed of trust take the *legal* title and estate for the purposes of their security. In all cases the legal title is in the trustee under the trust-deed, if the deed purports to convey the

---

[1] *Ante*, § 593; Wiswall *v*. Ross, 4 Port. (Ala.) 328; Bergen *v*. Bennett, 1 Caines, Cas. in Er. 1; Wilson *v*. Troup, 7 Johns. Ch. 25; Wilbur *v*. Spofford, 4 Sneed, 698; Hyde *v*. Warren, 46 Miss. 13; Berry *v*. Skinner, 30 Md. 567; Collins *v*. Hopkins, 7 Clarke (Iowa), 463; Bancroft *v*. Ashhurst, 2 Grant's Cas. 513; Hannah *v*. Carrington, 18 Ark. 104; Beattie *v*. Butler, 21 Mo. 313; Walker *v*. Crowder, 2 Ired. Eq. 478; Stimpson *v*. Fries, 2 Jones, Eq. 156; Doe *v*. Duval, 1 Ala. 745. In Robertson *v*. Paul, 16 Tex. 472, and 26 Tex. 205, the court admitted these general principles, but thought that powers of sale to be executed after the death of a donor were inconsistent with the statutes authorizing the settlement of the estates of deceased persons. Buchanan *v*. Monroe, 22 Tex. 587; Brewer *v*. Winchester, 2 Allen, 389; and see Encking *v*. Simmons, 28 Wis. 272, where a sale was set aside for the reason that the mortgagor was insane and the price very low.

[2] Sheridan *v*. Welch, 8 Allen, 166.

[3] Mansfield *v*. Mansfield, 6 Conn. 559.

estate.[1] (a) Such a title, however, is defeasible upon the performance by the grantor of the obligations undertaken by him. Performances of the condition of the deed on the part of the grantor, or tender of performance before the sale, will defeat the power of sale in a mortgage or deed of trust. Such performance or tender extinguishes the power; and a sale afterwards under the power, even to an innocent purchaser, will be void.[2]

§ 602 *j*. In law, a mortgage is considered, as between the mortgagor and mortgagee, and so far as it is necessary to give full effect to the mortgage as a security for the performance of

[1] White *v.* Whitney, 3 Met. 81; Greenleaf *v.* Queen, 1 Pet. 138; Morris *v.* Way, 16 Ohio, 469; Anderson *v.* Holloman, 1 Jones, L. 169; Thornhill *v.* Gilmer, 4 Sm. & M. 153; Brown *v.* Bartie, 10 Sm. & M. 268, 275; Sargent *v.* Howe, 21 Ill. 148; Hannah *v.* Carrington, 18 Ark. 85; Taylor *v.* King, 6 Munf. 358; Newman *v.* Jackson, 12 Wheat. 570.

[2] Cook *v.* Dillon, 9 Iowa, 407; King *v.* Merchants' Ex. Co., 1 Seld. 547; Cameron *v.* Irwin, 5 Hill, 272; Deyo *v.* Van Valkenburg, id. 246; Wood *v.* Colvin, 2 id. 566.

(a) There is a wide-spread conflict of authority as to whether prior to breach of condition such a deed passes the legal title to a mortgagee or trustee who has no right to possession until breach of condition. In some States it is held that, notwithstanding the language of the deed, the legal title remains in the grantor. Benton Land Co. *v.* Zeitler, 182 Mo. 251, 272; Clark *v.* Wilson, 53 Miss. 119; Driskill *v.* Rebbe, 117 N. W. 135 (S. D. 1908). See Wood *v.* Grayson, 22 App. D. C. 432, 445; McNutt *v.* Life Ins. Co., 181 Mo. 94. In other States it is established that the deed passes the bare legal title. See Weber *v.* McCleverty, 149 Cal. 316, 320; Collier *v.* Alexander, 142 Ala. 422. The rule of each State is set forth in detail in Jones on Mortgages (6th ed.), § 17 *et seq.*

The tendency of the American courts seems to be to treat the legal interest of a mortgagee or trustee under such a deed as an inchoate title only, an interest to vest in future on the happening of certain contingencies, *viz.*, breach of condition and foreclosure proceedings. Under this view, until entry to foreclose the mortgagor's interest is such a legal title that he may maintain ejectment, and his interest may be attached and levied upon as a legal estate. Benton Land Co. *v.* Zeitler, 182 Mo. 251, 272.

A full discussion of this point and of the decisions bearing upon it belongs to the subject of mortgages and seems outside the scope of this book.

the condition, as a conveyance in fee. But for all other purposes it is considered, especially until entry for condition broken, as a mere charge or incumbrance, which does not divest the estate of the mortgagor. He is deemed seized so far that he can convey it subject to the mortgage; he may make a second mortgage; it may be attached for his debts; he is considered as having all the rights and powers of an owner, except so far as it is necessary to hold otherwise in order to give effect to the mortgage. The interest of a mortgagor is therefore regarded as an estate; though, in legal strictness and as against the mortgagee, it is an equity of redemption. It may be levied upon and seizin delivered by the officer; in which case the creditor will hold in fee subject to the mortgage. The same principles apply to the rights and title of the grantor in deeds of trust.[1]

§ 602 *k*. The legal estate being thus in the mortgagee or trustee for the purpose of the security, the power of sale is a power appendant to the estate itself, and takes effect out of it.[2] If the mortgagee or trustee ceases in any way to have an interest in the estate, he ceases to have any power over it. If, therefore, they totally alienate the estate to which the power is appendant, they extinguish the power.[3] If a trustee conveys the property, even in breach of the trust, he extinguishes his power, and a subsequent sale will be void.[4] But a court of equity can give relief from fraud and breaches of trust. If, however, a

[1] White *v.* Whitney, 3 Met. 81; Harrison *v.* Battle, 1 Dev. Eq. 541; Poole *v.* Glover, 2 Ired. L. 129; Anderson *v.* Jones, 1 Jones, Law, 169. The text states the prevailing rule in the majority of States. McGregor *v.* Hall, 3 Stew. & Por. 397; 4 Kent, 160, 161, 195, n. If the trustee make a sale, and there is a surplus, the wife of the grantor is entitled to dower in it as in an equity of redemption. In a few States, — Mississippi, Ohio, Arkansas, and perhaps others, — this equity of the grantor in a deed of trust cannot be reached at law. A creditor is compelled to have resort to a proceeding in equity.

[2] *Post*, § 765; Alger *v.* Fay, 12 Pick. 322.

[3] Sugd. Pow. 54.

[4] Huckabee *v.* Billingsby, 16 Ala. 414; Hogan *v.* Lepretre, 1 Port. 392; Doe *v.* Robinson, 24 Miss. 688.

trustee has sold the property in breach of the trust, and he afterwards obtains the legal title, the old trust will reattach to it in his hands, and he may again have a power of sale as a part of the terms of the trust.[1]

§ 602 *l.* The trustee, or mortgagee with a power of sale, holds the lands in trust for the purposes for which the deeds are made, which purposes are generally specified in the deeds themselves. The trusts are, generally, (1) to sell the lands upon default of payment in the manner pointed out in the deed; (2) to apply so much of the proceeds of the sale as is necessary to the payment of the debts secured by the deeds; and (3) to account for and pay over the balance, after paying the expenses of the trust and the sale to the grantor or mortgagor, his legal representatives or assigns. The interest of the mortgagee with a power of sale is the same as the interest of the other mortgagees under the old form of mortgage; and the *cestuis que trust* under deeds of trust have a mere equitable interest, which can only be enforced in equity. Neither the interests of mortgagees nor of *cestuis que trust* can be reached at law by the levy of execution; but proceedings must be in equity for such purposes.[2]

§ 602 *m.* The trustee, in a deed of trust for security, is subject to the same rules that govern all trustees. He may refuse the office, as no one is compelled to accept a trust;[3] but if he once accepts the trust, or does any acts, he cannot abandon it without the consent of all parties in interest or the decree of the court.[4] In all cases of a trust or power coupled with an interest, the power survives so long as the interest survives, and

---

[1] Salisbury *v.* Bigelow, 20 Pick. 174.

[2] 4 Kent, Com. 159, 160; McIntire *v.* Agricultural Bank, 1 Freem. Ch. 105; Harrison *v.* Battle, 1 Dev. Eq. 541; Jenks *v.* Alexander, 11 Paige, 619, 624; Leonard *v.* Ford, 8 Ired. L. 418; McGregor *v.* Hale, 3 Stew. & Por. 408.

[3] *Ante,* § 259.

[4] *Ante,* §§ 94, 268; Drane *v.* Gunter, 19 Ala. 731; 3 Yerg. 307; 21 Ill. 148.

it goes with the interest and the estate.[1] If a part of the trustees named in a deed refuse to accept, or die or resign, those who accept the trust and survive can execute the trust, even to the last one.[2] Upon the death of the last trustee, the estate descends to his heirs,[3] but the court can appoint new trustees; and in many States there are statutes that vest the estate and all powers that are appendant to the estate in the new trustee ; [4] if there are no such statutes, courts can order the heirs to convey the estate to the new trustees.[5] The same rules apply to the appointment of new trustees under deeds of trust that apply to the removal and appointment of trustees in any other case.[6] So, the same rules apply in relation to the concurrence of all the trustees in the execution of the trust,[7] and to the liabilities of the trustees for the acts of their cotrustees.[8] Nor can they delegate their power.[9] The creditors are the *cestuis* and may sue for waste or mismanagement.[10] (*a*)

§ 602 *n*. Powers of sale contained in a mortgage deed stand upon somewhat different principles. A mortgage is personal

[1] *Ante*, §§ 502, 503, 505.

[2] Williams *v.* Otey, 8 Humph. 562; Taylor *v.* Benham, 5 How. 233; Scull *v.* Reeves, 2 Green, Ch. 84; Hannah *v.* Carrington, 18 Ark. 104; Parsons *v.* Boyd, 20 Ala. 118; Franklin *v.* Osgood, 14 Johns. 527; Robertson *v.* Gaines, 2 Humph. 367; In Matter of Stevenson, 3 Paige, 420; Hawkins *v.* May, 12 Ala. 672; Peters *v.* Beverly, 10 Peters, 532.

[3] *Ante*, §§ 273, 341; Mauldin *v.* Armstead, 14 Ala. 708.

[4] *Ante*, § 284; Woolridge *v.* Planters' Bank, 1 Sneed, 297; Goss *v.* Singleton, 2 Head, 67; Duffy *v.* Calvert, 6 Gill, 487; Gibbs *v.* Marsh, 2 Met. 243, 253.

[5] *Ante*, § 284; Greenleaf *v.* Queen, 1 Pet. 138.

[6] See *ante*, § 275 *et seq.* [Sulphur Mines Co. *v.* Thompson, 93 Va. 293; Converse *v.* Davis, 90 Tex. 462; Clark *v.* Wilson, 53 Miss. 119.]

[7] *Ante*, § 411.

[8] *Ante*, § 405.

[9] *Ante*, § 401. [Grover *v.* Hale, 107 Ill. 638; Fuller *v.* O'Neil, 69 Tex. 349.]

[10] Cohen *v.* Morris, 70 Ga. 313.

(*a*) After the trustee has taken possession, the mortgagor also is a *cestui*. Charles Green R. E. Co. *v.* Building Co., 196 Mo. 358.

assets, and goes to the administrator or executor; the right to foreclose the mortgage goes to the administrator, with the debt, and also the power of sale contained in the mortgage. Therefore the administrator or executor of a deceased mortgagee with a power of sale may or must execute the power of sale if it is necessary to resort to the power to collect the debt or enforce the mortgage.[1] And it is said that this power of sale is in an administrator by virtue of his being named in the deed of mortgage, and by virtue of an appointment in any jurisdiction; so that, if the mortgagee was a non-resident, and his administrator is appointed by a court foreign to the State in which the land is situated, the administrator may execute the power and convey the land.[2] Powers of sale differ from deeds of trust in another respect. Ordinarily a trustee cannot assign or delegate his trust, or its duties or powers, to another, and it is a breach of the trust to attempt to do so; but powers of sale in a mortgage may be assigned with the debt and the mortgage, and such assignee of the mortgage may execute the power of sale.[3] If the mortgagee assigns the debt for which the mortgage is security, but does not assign the mortgage deed, in equity he holds the security and the power of sale in trust for the assignee of the debt, and the assignee may call upon him to execute the power;[4] and if he assigns a part of the debts, or a part of the notes secured by the mortgage, he holds the security and the power in trust *pro tanto*.[5] But the partial assignee of a mortgage cannot execute the power of sale, as the power is not divisible.[6]

[1] *Ante*, §§ 338, 495; Doolittle *v.* Lewis, 7 Johns. Ch. 45; Collins *v.* Hopkins, 7 Iowa, 463; Turner *v.* Johnson, 7 Ohio, 216, 220; Brewer *v.* Winchester, 2 Allen, 389; Varnum *v.* Meserve, 8 id. 158; Anderson *v.* Austin, 34 Barb. 319; Harnickell *v.* Orndorff, 35 Md. 341.

[2] Doolittle *v.* Lewis, 7 Johns. Ch. 45; Baldwin *v.* Allison, 4 Minn. 25.

[3] *Ante*, §§ 338, 495; Strother *v.* Law, 54 Ill. 413.

[4] Sargent *v.* Howe, 21 Ill. 148; Keyes *v.* Wood, 21 Vt. 331, 550; Anderson *v* Baumgartner, 27 Mo. 80; Wood *v.* Snow, 1 Mich. 128; Slee *v.* Manhattan Co., 1 Paige, 48; Wilson *v.* Troup, 1 Johns. Ch. 25; 2 Cowen, 195; Lacas *v.* Harris, 20 Ill. 165; Trustee, &c. *v.* Prentiss, 29 Miss. 46; Hinds *v.* Mooers, 11 Iowa, 211; Sangster *v.* Love, id. 580.   [5] Ibid.

[6] Wilson *v.* Troup, 7 Johns. Ch. 25; 2 Cow. 195.

§ 602 o. Trustees and mortgagees, in the execution of their powers, must use the utmost good faith toward all parties in interest. This proposition cannot be too strongly stated and enforced. They must act impartially for every person who has any rights in the estate. If they allow the debtor to take the rents and profits of the estate they hold for the benefit of creditors, they will become personally liable to the creditors.[1] They must use every effort to sell the estate under every possible advantage of time, place, and publicity. They must exercise their discretion, so far as they have any, in an intelligent and reasonable manner. A mortgagee is bound, in the exercise of his power, not to use it to oppress the debtor, nor to sacrifice the estate. If he unfairly or unnecessarily prejudices the rights or interests of the mortgagor, or any other party, the sale may be set aside, or he may be made personally responsible for the injury.[2] The creditors cannot make the trustee their agent to purchase the property to the best advantage, for he owes a duty to the debtor and those claiming through him any residue after the debts are satisfied. The creditors may, however, send the trustee their bid, and he may sell the land to them if no one else bids more.[3] After the power has been exercised, the mortgagee may bring a suit to recover any balance due to him after applying the proceeds of the sale; but the mortgagor may defend such suit, if he can show that the sale was unfairly or fraudulently conducted,[4] and this he may do although he may still have a right to redeem.[5]

[1] Ely v. Turpin, 75 Mo. 83.

[2] See *post*, § 770, and cases cited; Howard v. Ames, 3 Met. 311; Matthie v. Edwards, 2 Coll. 465; Hobson v. Bell, 2 Beav. 17; Goldsmith v. Osborne, 1 Edw. Ch. 561; Driver v. Fortner, 2 Port. (Ala.) 9; Prewett v. Laud, 36 Miss. 495; Richards v. Holmes, 18 How. 143; Lane v. Tidhall, 1 Gilm. (Va.) 132; Quarles v. Lacy, 4 Munf. 251; Singleton v. Scott, 11 Iowa, 589, 597; Jenks v. Alexander, 11 Paige, 619; Hunt v. Ball, 2 Dev. Eq. 292; Johnson v. Eason, 3 Ired. Eq. 330; Rossett v. Fisher, 11 Grat. 492; Outwater v. Berry, 2 Halst. Eq. 63. [Cassady v. Wallace, 102 Mo. 575; Givens v. McCray, 196 Mo. 306; Hinton v. Pritchard, 120 N. C. 1; Preston v. Johnson, 105 Va. 238.]

[3] Seesel v. Ewan, 35 Ark. 127. [Easton v. German-Am. Bank, 127 U.S. 532.]

[4] Howard v. Ames, 3 Met. 311; Sabin v. Stickney, 9 Vt. 164.

[5] Lowell v. North, 4 Min. 32.

§ 602 *p*. It must be constantly borne in mind that the power of sale given in the deed or mortgage must be strictly followed in all its details. The power of transferring the property of one man to another must be followed strictly, literally, and precisely. Such a power admits of no substitution and of no equivalent, even in unimportant details. If the power contains the details, the parties have made them important; and no change can be made even if the mortgagor would be benefited thereby, nor if a statute provides a different manner. If the power is not executed as it is given in all particulars, it is not executed at all, and the mortgagor still has his equity of redemption. And so, if a statute of a State regulates the execution of these powers of sale, they must be executed as they are created in the deed and as they are regulated by the statute. When one mode of executing such powers is pointed out in the deed, and such mode is regulated by statute, all other modes of executing the power are negatived and excluded.[1] If, however, the power is a general power, and no modes of executing it are pointed out in the power, it is an authority to execute the power in any legal mode.[2] Thus a power to *sell* on default will not authorize a lease or mortgage.[3] If the trustee is to sell partly for cash and partly on credit, he cannot sell wholly for credit.[4] If the power is to sell for the amount then due at the time of the sale, a sale for more will be void.[5] But a sale to be made in default of payment of interest when due, may be made for the whole amount of

---

[1] *Ante*, §§ 511 *a*, 511 *b*, 511 *c ; post*, §§ 770–785; Greenleaf *v*. Queen, 1 Pet. 138; Waldron *v*. Chastney, 2 Blatchf. 62; Gunter *v*. Jones, 10 Cal. 643; Taylor *v*. Atkins, 1 Burr. 60; Ormsby *v*. Tarascon, 3 Litt. 405; Hawkins *v*. Kemp, 3 East, 410; Crosby *v*. Heston, 1 Tex. 225; Bush *v*. Stamps, 26 Miss. 463; Gray *v*. Howard, 14 Mo. 341; Foster *v*. Goree, 4 Ala. 428; Beebe *v*. De Baum, 3 Eng. 510; Stine *v*. Wilkson, 10 Mo. 75; Baldridge *v*. Walton, 1 Mo. 520; Smith *v*. Provin, 4 Allen, 514; Griffin *v*. Marine Co., 52 Ill. 130; Elliott *v*. Wood, 53 Barb. 285; Hall *v*. Towne, 45 Ill. 493.

[2] Foster *v*. Goree, 4 Ala. 428; 1 Sugd. Pow. 266.

[3] *Post*, §§ 768, 769; Walker *v*. Brungard, 13 Sm. & M. 723; 4 Kent, Com. 148; Sparks *v*. Kearney, 2 Jones, Eq. 481.

[4] Norman *v*. Hill, 2 Pat. & H. 676.

[5] Ormsby *v*. Tarascon, 3 Litt. 405.

the debt.[1] If the sale is to be at public auction, a private sale will be set aside.[2] If the power authorizes sureties to sell before they have paid the debt or have been damnified, they can do so; but if they become the purchasers, they will hold the property upon the original trust or mortgage, and the mortgagor may redeem:[3] and powers of sale may be executed to secure future advances, but the exact terms of the mortgage and the power must be complied with, and the rights of intervening parties or interests cannot be defeated.[4] If there are conditions precedent, they must all be strictly complied with and performed before a sale can be made.[5] So the execution of the deed under the power must correspond to the power. If the trustee is to execute the deed as the attorney of the debtor, he cannot execute in his own name.[6] The original purchaser under the power will be held to have notice of all the irregularities of the proceedings of sale, and his deed will be void; but remote purchasers will take a good title, unless they can be affected with notice of the irregularities attending the sale.[7]

§ 602 q. Powers may authorize sales to be public or private, and they must be executed as they are given. In the absence of any directions upon the subject, the sale may be either public or private, as circumstances render it for the advantage of the estate,[8] unless there are statutes that require all sales under

[1] Richards v. Holmes, 18 How. 143.

[2] Greenleaf v. Queen, 1 Pet. 138.

[3] Thurston v. Prentiss, 1 Mich. 194, Walker Ch. 529; Hawkins v. May, 12 Ala. 673, 5 Porter, 191; Roden v. Jaco, 17 Ala. 344; Wheeler v. Stone, 4 Gill, 38.

[4] Curling v. Shuttleworth, 6 Bing. 121.

[5] Post, §§ 784, 785; Roarty v. Mitchell, 7 Gray, 243; Dutton v. Cotton, 10 Iowa, 408. Where the power was that, in case of default in payment, the mortgagor might enter and take possession and sell, it was held that he could not sell without making an entry and taking possession. Roarty v. Mitchell, 7 Gray, 243.

[6] Speer v. Hadduck, 31 Ill. 439. As to the forms of executing powers in general, see ante, §§ 511 a, 511 b, 511 c.

[7] Hamilton v. Lubukee, 51 Ill. 415.

[8] Post, §§ 780–782.

powers to be at public auction.[1] If the form of notice, and the manner of giving it, whether by posting in public places or by advertising in a newspaper, are prescribed in the power, they must be strictly followed; and if the particular place of notice is named, notice must be posted in that place; if the newspaper is named, publication of notice must be made in that paper. It is not necessary to give other notice of the sale than that prescribed in the power, but it is necessary to follow the power in good faith.[2] If the notice named in the power cannot be given, as if the newspaper named has ceased to be published, the mortgagee cannot sell without recourse to a court of equity.[3] If the form of notice and manner of giving it are not prescribed, the mortgagee must give a proper notice in a reasonable manner; and if he fails to do so, the sale will be set aside.[4] If no particular form is prescribed, no particular form is required.[5] But it should be sufficient to identify the land and to invite competition.[6] In Massachusetts, it has been held that the notice should state the name of the owner of the land, or of the equity of redemption, and also of the holder of the mortgage, especially if the original mortgagor has sold his equity of redemption, or if the original mortgagee has assigned the mortgage; and a sale under a notice which did not give this full information was set aside.[7] If no specific directions are given in the power as to where notices are to be posted, or in what newspapers publication is to be made, the mortgagee must use a fair and honest discretion in posting the notices, or in selecting the newspaper in which to insert notice of the sale. If the notices of sale were posted in remote or isolated places, where they would be seen by few persons and where they could give no

[1] Lawrence *v.* Farmers', &c. Co., 3 Kern. 200, 210.

[2] Ormsby *v.* Tarascon, 3 Litt. 405, 411; Crocker *v.* Robertson, 8 Clarke (Iowa), 404.

[3] Dutton *v.* Cotton, 10 Iowa, 408.

[4] 4 Kent. Com. 490; Anon. 6 Madd. 15.

[5] *Post*, § 782.

[6] Ibid.

[7] See Hoffman *v.* Anthony, 6 R. I. 282.

publicity to the sale and invite little competition, or if they were inserted in an obscure newspaper, in an obscure manner, or if they were inserted in a remote newspaper, it would be strong evidence of fraud, and the sale would be set aside.[1] If several lots in different counties are embraced in the same deed, notice of the sale must be given in different counties.[2]

§ 602 r. The notice of the sale must be certain as to *time* and *place* of sale,[3] and the description must be sufficient to apprise the public of what property is to be sold.[4] Mere clerical errors or inaccuracies or omissions in a notice, which do not mislead or which correct themselves on their face, will not vitiate a sale.[5] Notice of sale on the "28th of December next," omitting the year, was held good;[6] notice of a sale "at the town of St. Joseph" was held good, the town being small, and no injury having been done;[7] notice of sale at "City Hall," or "Merchants' Exchange," or any other public place, is good, if the sale is actually made in that part of such buildings or place where sales are usually made.[8] If the power provides that the sale shall be on the premises, or names any other place, of course the sale must be notified for that place, and it must be made at that place. Notice for sale on the 23d of May was changed to the 25th, without the debtor's knowledge. He attended on the 23d; but the sale was made on the latter day, and it was held to

---

[1] Singleton v. Scott, 11 Iowa, 589; Newman v. Jackson, 12 Wheat. 570; Johnson v. Eason, 3 Ired. Eq. 530; Jenks v. Alexander, 11 Paige, 619; 2 Am. L. Rev. (N. S.) 719.

[2] Wells v. Wells, 47 Barb. 416. But see Berthold v. Holmes, 12 Minn. 335.

[3] Burnett v. Denniston, 5 Johns. Ch. 35; Gray v. Howard, 14 Mo. 341; Dana v. Farrington, 4 Minn. 437.

[4] Newman v. Jackson, 12 Wheat. 570; Fitzpatrick v. Fitzpatrick, 6 R. I. 64.

[5] Ibid.; White v. Malcomb, 15 Md. 529; Rathburn v. Clark, 9 Abbott, Pr. (N. Y.) 12, 66, n.

[6] Gray v. Howard, 14 Mo. 341.

[7] Beatie v. Butler, 21 Mo. 313.

[8] Harmon v. Carver, 12 How. Pr. (N. Y.) 490.

be void.[1] It is usual to specify the precise hour of the sale, and probably a notice that did not state the hour of the sale would be bad;[2] but a notice specifying a day, between twelve and five of the clock, in the absence of any unfair practice, was held good.[3] Where a notice of sale was given for Friday the 17th, but Friday was the 16th, and the correction was made on Friday the 16th, it was held to be void.[4] In Massachusetts, a sale upon notice to be published three weeks successively in a newspaper, is good, although made less than three weeks from the time of the first publication, provided there has been a publication of the notice three successive weeks before the sale.[5] In New York, if a notice is to be given once in each week for twelve successive weeks, the first publication must be eighty-four days, or twelve full weeks, before the day of the sale.[6] If thirty days' notice is required, there need not be thirty days between the first and last publication, but thirty days between the first publication and the day of the sale. The publication of the notice must be continued for the requisite time.[7] Where twenty days' notice in two daily newspapers was required, it was held not to be necessary that daily notice should be given in each newspaper.[8]

§ 602 *s*. All the statements made in the notice, or required to be stated in a notice, must be stated truly and according to the facts. Thus, where the notice stated that the premises were to be sold for default upon three mortgages, and there were but

---

[1] Dana *v.* Farrington, 4 Minn. 433. And so where a mistake was made in the year. Fenner *v.* Tucker, 6 R. I. 557.

[2] Fitzpatrick *v.* Fitzpatrick, 6 R. I. 64.

[3] Cox *v.* Halstead, 1 Green, Ch. 311.

[4] Wellman *v.* Lawrence, 15 Mass. 326; Fenner *v.* Tucker, 6 R. I. 551.

[5] Frothingham *v.* March, 1 Mass. 247.

[6] Bunce *v.* Reed, 16 Barb. 350; Early *v.* Doe, 16 How. 610; Howard *v.* Hatch, 29 Barb. 297; Worley *v.* Naylor, 6 Minn. 192.

[7] Bunce *v.* Reed, 16 Barb. 350; Stine *v.* Wilkson, 10 Mo. 75; Leffer *v.* Armstrong, 4 Iowa, 482.

[8] White *v.* Malcomb, 15 Md. 529. See also Johnson *v.* Dorsey, 7 Gill, 286; Gibbs *v.* Cunningham, 1 Md. Ch. 44.

two, the equity of redemption was not bound.[1] The power is to sell the estate, not the equity of redemption, although the sale operates as a foreclosure; and the notice must state that it is to be a sale of the estate, and not of the mere equity of redemption,[2] but the mortgagee in a junior power of sale mortgage cannot sell the entire estate, free from incumbrances of prior mortgages, without consent of the holders of such prior mortgages.[3] If neither the power nor any statute requires the amount of the claim or debt, for which the sale is made, to be stated, it need not be stated in the notice, and the sale will not be affected by such omission;[4] but if such statement in the notice is required by the power or by a statute, the amount of the debt must be stated with substantial accuracy;[5] or if, not being required, a greatly exaggerated claim should be fraudulently stated in the notice, the sale would not bar the equity of redemption.[6] So, if the sale is proposed to be made for more than is due to the creditor, equity will restrain the sale;[7] and, if actually made, it will be set aside.[8]

§ 602 *t*. If the notices of sale are not made and published according to the power, the sale is absolutely void, not merely voidable, and no title passes to the purchasers. This is upon the ground that the power was not executed according to the terms of it upon its face;[9] and so if a sale is made upon a wrong

[1] Bennett *v.* Denniston, 5 Johns. Ch. 35; Johnson *v.* Turner, 7 Ohio, 216; Matthie *v.* Edwards, 2 Coll. 465.

[2] Merrill *v.* Fowle, 10 Allen, 350.

[3] Donohue *v.* Chase, 130 Mass. 139.

[4] Wiswall *v.* Ross, 4 Port. (Ala.) 321.

[5] Burnett *v.* Denniston, 5 Johns. Ch. 35; Johnson *v.* Turner, 7 Ohio, 216.

[6] Klock *v.* Cronkhite, 1· Hill, 107; Jenks *v.* Alexander, 11 Paige, 619; Bunce *v.* Reed, 16 Barb. 347; Spencer *v.* Anon., 4 Minn. 544; Ramsey *v.* Merriam, 6 Minn. 168.

[7] Ibid.

[8] Ibid.

[9] Bunce *v.* Reed, 16 Barb. 350; Baldridge *v.* Walton, 1 Mo. 520; Gibson *v.* Jones, 5 Leigh, 370; Jackson *v.* Clark, 7 Johns. 217, 226; Bigler *v.* Walker, 14 Wall. 297.

day or at a wrong place.[1]   After the lapse of a long time, however, courts will presume that everything was correctly done
which the power or the law required to be done,[2] and the mortgagor or grantor and his privies in blood or estate, or the parties
having a right in the estate, can alone object to any defects in
the proceedings.   Strangers have no rights in the estate, and
cannot take advantage of such informalities for any purpose.[3]

§ 602 *u*.   If an adjournment of the sale is not prohibited
by the power, the donee of the power may adjourn the sale to
another time and to another place.   Such power is implied.
Of course it is a discretionary power, and must be exercised
in good faith; it may be the clear *duty* of the trustee to adjourn the sale, and evidence of bad faith not to adjourn; as if
there are few or no purchasers present, and the bids are very
low and inadequate to the value of the property.[4]   The adjournment should regularly be made at the time and place of sale;
public proclamation should be made of it at the time; and if
there is nothing in the power or in any statute, the same notice
of sale should be given as was given in the first instance,[5] except
that it need not be for the same length of time;[6] but the adjournment made on the premises and the published notice of it
should correspond.[7]   If notice of an intended adjournment should

[1] Miller *v.* Hull, 4 Denio, 104; Dana *v.* Farrington, 4 Minn. 433.

[2] Bergen *v.* Bennett, 1 Caines' Cas. 1; Demarest *v.* Wynkoop, 3 Johns.
Ch. 129.

[3] Edmondson *v.* Walsh, 27 Ala. 578; Wightman *v.* Doe, 24 Miss. 675;
Casy *v.* Colvin, 11 Ala. 514; Hellegas *v.* Hellegas, 5 Barr, 97; Franklin *v.*
Greene, 2 Allen, 519.

[4] Richard *v.* Holmes, 18 How. 143; Jackson *v.* Clark, 7 Johns. 217, 225;
Sayles *v.* Smith, 12 Wend. 57; Miller *v.* Hall, 4 Denio, 104; Baldridge *v.*
Walton, 1 Mo. 520.

[5] Richard *v.* Holmes, 18 How. 147; Johnson *v.* Eason, 3 Ired. Eq. 366.
If a postponement is duly proclaimed at the time and place advertised for
the sale, new notices need not be given in any State.   Cox *v.* Halstead, 1
Green, Ch. 311; 1 Stockt. 287.   But a postponement may be made before
the day of sale arrives.   Bennett *v.* Brundage, 8 Minn. 432.

[6] Jackson *v.* Clark, 7 Johns. 217, 225; Dana *v.* Farrington, 4 Minn. 433.

[7] Miller *v.* Hull, 4 Denio, 104; Cole *v.* Moffit, 2 Barb. 18; Sayles *v.*
Smith, 12 Wend. 57; Westgate *v.* Handlin, 7 How. Pr. (N. Y.) 372.

be published, and the sale should notwithstanding be made on that day originally appointed, it would be void.[1]

§ 602 v. It is necessary to repeat, on every occasion, that a trustee for sale, and a mortgagee with a power of sale, or the assignee cannot execute the trust or the power in favor of themselves.[2] A trustee cannot purchase the trust property directly or indirectly, nor can the mortgagee, under a power of sale mortgage, purchase directly or indirectly. He cannot purchase for himself, nor can any one purchase for him, nor can he purchase as agent for any third person. Nor can any agent, auctioneer, attorney, or other person employed in the selling of the estate, purchase it for the mortgagee or for themselves or for any other person.[3] (a) There is so much danger of fraud or

[1] Jackson v. Clark, 7 Johns. 217.

[2] Ante, §§ 254, 511 a, 511 b, 511 c ; post, § 787; Allen v. Chatfield, 8 Minn. 455 ; Mapps v. Sharpe, 32 Ill. 13; Griffin v. Marine Co., 52 Ill. 130.

[3] Ante, §§ 195, 199, and cases cited; Arnot v. McClure, 4 Denio, 41; Hall v. Towne, 45 Ill. 493; Jackson v. Calden, 4 Cow. 266; Huff v. Earle, 3 Port. (Ind.) 306; Nichols v. Baxter, 5 R. I. 491; Parmenter v. Walker, 9 R. I. 225; Hyndman v. Hyndman, 19 Vt. 9; Pettibone v. Perkins, 6 Wis. 616; Bailey v. Robertson, 1 Grat. 4; Robinson v. Butler, 24 Ill. 387; Saltmarsh v. Burn, 4 Port. 283; Blackley v. Fowler, 21 Cal. 326; Jeffersonville Assoc. v. Fisher, 7 Port. (Ind.) 699; Bunce v. Reed, 16 Barb. 347; Sabin v. Stickney, 9 Vt. 164; Field v. Arrowsmith, 3 Humph. 442; Hunt v. Bass, 2 Dev. Eq. 292; Hester v. Hester, 3 Ired. Eq. 330; Scott v. Gamble, 1 Stockt. 218; Remick v. Butterfield, 11 Foster, 70; Winter v. Geroe, 1 Halstead, Ch. 319; Armstrong v. Campbell, 3 Yerger, 201; Ringgold v. Ringgold, 1 Har. & Gill, 11. But it is said that such sale by the mortgagee to himself is not void, but voidable only, at the instance of the mortgagor. Robinson v. Cullom, 41 Ala. 693; Thornton v. Irwin, 43 Mo. 153.

(a) That a mortgagee with power of sale cannot purchase on his own account either directly or indirectly, see Douthit v. Nabors, 133 Ala. 453; Payton v. McPhaul, 128 Ga. 510, 517; Nichols v. Otto, 132 Ill. 91; Patten v. Pearson, 57 Me. 428; Korns v. Shaffer, 27 Md. 83; Houston v. National Mut. B'ld'g Ass'n, 80 Miss. 31; McNees v. Swaney, 50 Mo. 388; Very v. Russell, 65 N. H. 646; Rich v. Morisey, 149 N. C. 37. But it is common to insert in power of sale mortgages a provision that the mortgagee may himself be a purchaser. Mutual Loan & Banking Co. v. Haas, 100 Ga. 111; Hall v. Bliss, 118 Mass. 554.

The principle applies with greater

collusion, and it is so difficult to trace and expose them, in the execution of such powers, that the law has placed almost an absolute prohibition in the front of such an execution of trusts or powers.[1] If, however, a trustee or mortgagee buys in a prior mortgage, he will hold it in trust for the *cestui que trust* or mortgagor, with the right of being reimbursed for so much as he fairly paid for such mortgage.[2] If a trustee or mortgagee purchases the property thus within his power to sell, and the title is conveyed to him, either directly or indirectly, through a third person, he will continue to hold the property upon the old trust, or the mortgagor may redeem. The execution of the trust or the foreclosure of the mortgage has not been advanced.[3] The *cestui que trust* may, however, buy in the property.[4] And so the power itself may authorize the mortgagee to purchase, or the statutes of a State upon that subject may authorize such purchase.[5]

§ 602 w. This distinction must be carried along. If a trustee or mortgagee with a power of sale should execute a deed under the trust or power directly to himself, the deed would be simply void, and would pass nothing or make no change in the situa-

[1] *Ante*, §§ 195–197.

[2] Critchfield v. Haynes, 14 Ala. 49; Gunter v. Jones, 9 Cal. 643; Jones v. Dawson, 9 Ala. 672. [*Supra*, § 195, note *a*, p. 318.]

[3] Hyndman v. Hyndman, 19 Vt. 1; Benham v. Rowe, 2 Cal. 387.

[4] Lyons v. Jones, 6 Humph. 533; Wade v. Harper, 3 Yerger, 383; Walker v. Brungard, 13 Sm. & M. 723; Lucas v. Oliver, 34 Ala. 626; Richards v. Holmes, 18 How. 143. [Easton v. German-Am. Bank, 127 U. S. 532.]

[5] Ramsey v. Merriam, 6 Minn. 168; Griffin v. Marine Co., 52 Ill. 130; Elliott v. Wood, 53 Barb. 285. [Wygal v. Bigelow, 42 Kan. 477; Galvin v. Newton, 19 R. I. 176.]

force to a trustee under a deed given for security, since he is trustee for both creditor and debtor when he exercises his power of sale. Lass v. Sternberg, 50 Mo. 124; Harrison v. Manson, 95 Va. 593; Parks v. Worthington, 101 Tex. 505. Not only is he not allowed to purchase for himself either directly or indirectly, but he is not allowed to purchase as a representative and on behalf of either debtor or creditor or of a third party. Smith v. Downey, 38 Colo. 165.

tions and relations of the parties, on the ground that no man can contract with himself, or make a deed to himself, or from himself in one capacity to himself in another;[1] (a) but if a mortgagee or trustee execute deeds to third persons, and take back the title to themselves, such deeds are not void, but voidable only; and the *cestui que trust* or mortgagor can avoid them, or compel the purchaser to keep the property and pay the money.[2] And such deeds are voidable by the *cestuis que trust* alone: third persons cannot interfere.[3](b) It follows that, if the *cestuis que trust* are *sui juris*, they must elect to avoid the deed within a reasonable time after the facts come to their knowledge.[4] The deed being voidable only, an innocent purchaser from the trustee, for value and without notice, will take an indefeasible title.[5]

§ 602 x. Sales under powers in deeds of trust or mortgage are a harsh mode of foreclosing the rights of the mortgagor. They are scrutinized by courts with great care, and will not be sustained unless conducted with all fairness, regularity, and scrupulous integrity.[6] Upon very slight proof of fraud or unfair conduct, or of any departure from the terms of the power, they will be set aside.[7] If proper notices of the sale

---

[1] *Ante*, § 207, 1 Sugd. V. & P. 97 (8th ed. Am.).

[2] *Ante*, § 198, and cases; Pitt v. Pitnay, 12 Ired. L. 69; Brothers v. Brothers, 7 Ired. Eq. 150; Parmenter v. Walker, 9 R. I. 225. [Houston v. National Mutual Building, etc. Ass'n, 80 Miss. 31; Payton v. McPhaul, 128 Ga. 510, 517; Nichols v. Otto, 132 Ill. 91; Very v. Russell, 65 N. H. 646.]

[3] Edmondson v. Walsh, 27 Ala. 578.

[4] Scott v. Freeland, 7 Sm. & M. 409; Smith v. Frost, 70 N. Y. 65.

[5] Robbins v. Bates, 4 Cush.' 104; Cranston v. Crane, 97 Mass. 459; Montague v. Dawes, 12 Allen, 397.

[6] Bloom v. Rensselaer, 15 Ill. 507.

[7] Longwith v. Butler, 3 Gilm. 32, 44; Dana v. Farrington, 4 Minn. 433; Spencer v. Anon., id. 542.

(a) But it has been held in Massachusetts that a mortgagee expressly authorized to purchase at his own foreclosure sale may do so directly and make the deed to himself. Hall v. Bliss, 118 Mass. 554.

(b) But a junior mortgagee may avoid the sale. Douthit v. Nabors, 133 Ala. 453; Elrod v. Smith, 130 Ala. 212.

1009

are not given, or if the proceedings are in any way contrary
to justice and equity, the sale will not be allowed to stand.[1]
And so, as the trustee cannot delegate his power or duty, if
the power is not executed by the proper person, or in good
faith, or with due diligence, or if proper notices have not been
given, or if the power has been extinguished, sales under it
will be set aside.[2] Thus, if the mortgagee should deceive the
debtor by a promise to extend the time of payment, and the
debtor, relying on such promise, should go away temporarily,
a sale made in his absence would be set aside.[3] So also of a
sale made in violation of an agreement to extend the time.[4]
So a sale will be set aside if the creditor is guilty of any fraud or
collusion, or if he pursues a course calculated to prevent competition.[5] So the sale will be set aside if made after the full
amount of the debt is paid [6] or tendered.[7] A sale ought not to
be made when the debt is uncertain or in dispute; and, if made,
it may be set aside.[8] But the expression of an erroneous opinion
at the sale, upon any subject, by third persons, is not a ground
for setting the sale aside; [9] nor will an innocent purchaser be
affected by private agreements to extend the time of payment
not recorded and not notified to him.[10]

§ 602 *y*. The directions of the power must be complied
with in selling the property as a whole or in lots or parcels.

[1] Bronson *v.* Kinsie, 1 How. 321; Singleton *v.* Scott, 10 Iowa, 408;
King *v.* Duntz, 11 Barb. 191.

[2] Rowan *v.* Lamb, 4 G. Greene, 468; Johnson *v.* Eason, 3 Ired. 330;
Jenks *v.* Alexander, 11 Paige, 619.

[3] Schoonhoven *v.* Pratt, 25 Ill. 457.

[4] Ibid.

[5] Longwith *v.* Butler, 3 Gilman, 32.

[6] Wade *v.* Harper, 3 Yerg. 383; Cameron *v.* Irwin, 5 Hill, 272; Ledyard
v. Chapin, 6 Port. (Ind.) 320; Sherman *v.* ——, 3 Port. (Ind.) 320. See
Montague *v.* Dawes, 12 Allen, 397; Cranston *v.* Crane, 97 Mass. 369.

[7] Burnett *v.* Denniston, 5 Johns. Ch. 35.

[8] Gibson *v.* Jones, 5 Leigh, 370; Lane *v.* Tidhall, 1 Gilm. 230. [See
Hartman *v.* Evans, 38 W. Va. 669, 679.]

[9] Bloom *v.* Rensselaer, 15 Ill. 503.

[10] Beatie *v.* Butler, 21 Mo. 313.

If a sale in either mode is excluded, the sale must not be made in that mode. If nothing is said about the manner of selling, whether by parcels or not, the donee of the power must exercise a sound and wise discretion for the purpose of procuring the largest price for the property, and if he exercises such discretion with due diligence and without fraud or collusion or for improper purposes, the sale will be good whether he sell in parcels or the whole.[1] A sale may be made in parcels, although the property is advertised as a whole, if a proper exercise of the trustee's discretion points out such mode.[2] It has been said that if the purchaser is ignorant of any abuse in the exercise of the discretion of the trustee he will take a good title, although the trustee abused his power; but this may be doubted.[3] If the value of the property is greatly above the amount of the mortgage, and the creditor sells in lots, he cannot sell after he has sold enough to satisfy his debts, and the court may decree a sale by lots or of part of the estate.[4]

§ 602 z. The sale will not be set aside for mere inadequacy of price, if due diligence was used by the donee of the power to sell under every possible advantage.[5] But there may be cases where the price is so grossly inadequate that the mere statement of it demonstrates that there must have been some mismanagement or collusion, as if land worth $500 should be sold for $50.[6] In such case, if the bidders are few, and the sum offered low, the trustee should exercise his discretion to adjourn the sale, and not to do so might be fraud, which would demand that the sale should be avoided.[7] If, however, the price is rendered inade-

---

[1] Post, § 774, and cases cited. Quarles v. Lacy, 4 Munf. 25; Singleton v. Scott, 11 Iowa, 589; Turner v. Johnson, 10 Ohio, 204; 7 id. 216; Lamerson v. Morvin, 8 Barb. 9.

[2] Gray v. Howard, 14 Mo. 341.

[3] Singleton v. Scott, 11 Iowa, 597.

[4] Johnson v. Williams, 4 Minn. 260.

[5] See ante, § 187; Singleton v. Scott, 11 Iowa, 589.

[6] See ante, § 187; Wright v. Wilson, 2 Yerg. 294.

[7] Ante, § 602, n.; Runkle v. Gaylord, 1 Nev. 123; Encking v. Simmonds, 28 Wis. 272; Horsey v. Hough, 38 Md. 130; Marfield v. Ross, id. 85.

quate by any action of the *cestui que trust*, as by his forbidding the sale, or by any other conduct, the sale will be good if the trustee acted in good faith.[1]

§ 602 *aa.* In a conveyance to a trustee or mortgagee, the title as between the grantor or mortgagor and the trustee, passes to the trustee or mortgagee. A trustee who has the fee in himself may convey it even if the conveyance is a breach of the trust, and his grantee takes a title upon which he can maintain actions at law. And so it is said that, although a trustee may convey the legal title in breach of the trust, and without complying with the power, yet the grantee will take a title good at law.[2] But such a purchaser in equity will still hold the property upon the same trusts upon which the trustee held it, for the reason that the purchaser will be held to know the record title of his vendor. He will have notice of the trust and of the power, and must be treated in equity as a trustee.[3] The law regards only the legal title; if that passes, it will prevail at law; but if a trustee

---

[1] Jones *v.* Neale, 2 Pat. & H. (Va.) 339; Forde *v.* Herron, 4 Munf. 316.

[2] *Ante*, §§ 321, 328, 334; Reece *v.* Allen, 5 Gilm. 236; Taylor *v.* King, 6 Munf. 356; Harris *v.* Harris, id. 367; Carrington *v.* Goddin, 13 Grat. 600; Gibson *v.* Jones, 5 Leigh, 370; Christian *v.* Yancey, 2 Pat. & H. 240; Skepworth *v.* Cunningham, 8 Leigh, 271; 10 Leigh, 183; Stimpson *v.* Fries, 2 Jones, Eq. 136; Newman *v.* Jackson, 12 Wheat. 270; Rowan *v.* Lamb, 4 G. Greene, 468; Conoy *v.* Troutman, 7 Ired. L. 418; Singleton *v.* Scott, 11 Iowa, 589; Gale *v.* Mensing, 20 Mo. 461; Bank *v.* Benning, 4 Cranch, C. C. 81; Jackson *v.* Clark, 7 Johns. 217; Miller *v.* Hull, 4 Denio, 104; King *v.* Buntz, 11 Barb. 192; Sherwood *v.* Reed, 7 Hill, 431; Dana *v.* Davenport, 4 Munf. 433; Huntley *v.* Buckner, 6 Sm. & M. 7; Brown *v.* Bartee, 10 Sm. & M. 268. This rule is founded upon a general principle, and prevails in all the States; see *ante*, § 334; except in New York, which converts the title of a trustee into a power by forbidding and making void all sales in breach of the trust.

[3] Norman *v.* Hill, 2 Pat. & H. 676; Rowan *v.* Lamb, 4 G. Greene, 468; Singleton *v.* Scott, 11 Iowa, 589; Newman *v.* Jackson, 12 Wheat. 570; Waldron *v.* Chastney, 2 Blatchf. 62; Bayard *v.* Colefax, 4 Wash. C. C. 38. In equity a purchaser of a trustee under a power must show that the sale was regular, that due notices were given, and he must prove all the facts that make a good title. Gibson *v.* Jones, 5 Leigh, 370; Norman *v.* Hill, 2 Pat. & H. 676.

has not the legal title but only a naked power over it, the legal title does not pass unless the power is strictly executed according to its terms. A trustee cannot bind the trust fund in his hands by entering into covenants in respect to it, and he is not authorized so to do. Therefore courts will not compel him to covenant except against his own acts. If, however, he enters into covenants, he will only bind himself personally. It is his duty, however, to make a good title, and if in his proposal for sale he states that the title is good, or that there is to be a good title, he cannot compel the purchaser to complete the sale if it is otherwise.[1] If the trustee once executes the power by a sale and deed, his power is extinguished, and he cannot afterwards give a new deed or make any recitals or admissions binding upon the parties.[2]

§ 602 *bb*. The execution of the power of sale in a deed of trust or mortgage conveys the title to the mortgaged land to the purchaser, and deprives the mortgagee of all interest in the premises,[3] and it bars the rights of all persons claiming under the mortgagor by conveyances made subsequent to the creation of the power or in other ways.[4] The purchaser's title, if the power has been properly and regularly executed, is absolute and irredeemable, and the sale bars infants, heirs, and married women of their dower.[5] The purpose of the power is to extinguish the equity of redemption of the mortgagor;[6] and, after its regular execution, his only right is to the surplus that may remain after

[1] *Post*, §§ 784, 787; Ennis *v.* Leach, 1 Ired. Eq. 416.

[2] Doe *v.* Robinson, 24 Miss. 688.

[3] Clay *v.* Sharp, Sugd. V. & P. Appendix No. 14; Corder *v.* Morgan, 18 Ves. 344; Sims *v.* Huntley, 2 How. (Miss.) 896; Tuthill *v.* Tracy, 31 N. Y. 157.

[4] Corder *v.* Morgan, 18 Ves. 344; Eaton *v.* Whiting, 3 Pick. 484; Turner *v.* Johnson, 10 Ohio, 204; Brisbane *v.* Stoughton, 17 id. 482; Bloom *v.* Rensselaer, 15 Ill. 506; Bancroft *v.* Ashhurst, 2 Grant, Cas. 513.

[5] Demarest *v.* Wynkoop, 3 Johns. Ch. 129; Burnett *v.* Denniston, 7 id. 45; Johnson *v.* Turner, 10 Ohio, 204; 7 Ohio, 216; Brackett *v.* Baum, 50 N. Y. 8.

[6] Calkins *v.* Ishell, 20 N. Y. 147.

the liquidation of the debt for which the property was sold. If he remains in possession of the premises, he is a mere tenant at sufferance,[1] and the purchaser is entitled to the crops growing upon the land at the time of the sale.[2] The statutes of the States that provide for redemption upon sales by license of courts, or upon executions, have no application to sales under powers.[3] But if there are statutes in any State broad enough to give a right of redemption for a certain time after a sale under a power, the sale confers an inchoate title upon the purchaser, subject to be defeated if redeemed within the time, and to become absolute, if not redeemed, and it then relates back to the time of purchase. When the title becomes thus perfected, the purchaser may maintain an action for injury to the premises by the mortgagor or others after the purchase, and before the title becomes irredeemable.[4] A sale under such prior power cuts off all subsequent mortgages, attachments, judgments, and liens,[5] even although the sale should be made to the mortgagor.[6] But a sale under a junior power of sale mortgage conveys only the equity of redemption. It cuts off all liens, attachments, and judgments subsequent to the power under which it was made, but does not affect prior ones.[7] A sale under a power which does not pass the title may yet operate as an assignment of the mortgage debt or a part of it.[8] The same rules apply to the enforcement of sales and purchases under these powers as apply to other sales by trustees.[9] After a sale has been made under a

---

[1] Kinsley *v.* Ames, 2 Met. 29; Bank *v.* Guttschlick, 14 Pet. 19.

[2] Shepherd *v.* Philbrick, 2 Denio, 174.

[3] Bloom *v.* Rensselaer, 15 Ill. 503.

[4] Stone *v.* Keyes, 2 Doug. 184; Reil *v.* Baker, 2 Denio, 79; Smith *v.* Colvin, 7 Barb. 157.

[5] Wiswall *v.* Ross, 4 Port. (Ala.) 321; Brown *v.* Bartee, 10 Sm. & M. 268; Bodine *v.* Moore, 18 N. Y. 347; Pahlman *v.* Shumway, 24 Ill. 127; Collyer *v.* Collins, 9 Iowa, 127.

[6] Brown *v.* Bartee, 10 Sm. & M. 268.

[7] Graham *v.* King, 15 Ala. 568.

[8] Gilbert *v.* Cooley, Walk. Ch. 494; Grosvenor *v.* Day, 1 Clark, 109; Jackson *v.* Bowen, 7 Cow. 13.

[9] Hem *v.* Rushowski, 18 Mo. 216.

power, a tender of the amount of the debt will not revest the title in the mortgagor even when there is a right to redeem, but recourse must be had to a court of equity.[1] It follows that the creditor, in making the sale, is absolutely accountable for the proceeds of the sale; if he gives any credit, or the money is lost in any way, he must still account for it.[2]

§ 602 cc. If a power of sale in a mortgage or deed of trust in the nature of a mortgage is not regularly executed, the right of redemption is not foreclosed or barred; but the mortgagor may still redeem the estate of the purchaser. Therefore, it is said that a bill in equity cannot be sustained to set aside such sale, but that the bill should be framed as for a bill to redeem. If the sale is relied upon as a bar to redemption, its regularity according to the power must be shown.[3]

§ 602 dd. The provisions in the power limiting and regulating the sale are for the benefit of the debtor. They are for his protection, and they may be waived by him, or his conduct may estop him from taking advantage of any irregularities, as if being present at the sale and knowing of the irregularity he should make no objection, but permit the sale to proceed, or if he should procure some one to purchase the property under such circumstances. Any conduct of the debtor that would render it inequitable for him to take advantage of such defects would debar him from setting them up.[4] And so, if the debtor has acquiesced in the sale for a long time, and has seen the property resold to innocent purchasers, or has seen valuable improvements made upon the land, or has in any way been guilty of

---

[1] Smith v. Anders, 21 Ala. 728.

[2] Bailey v. Ætna Ins. Co., 10 Allen, 286.

[3] Goldsmith v. Osborne, 1 Edw. Ch. 560; Schwarz v. Sears, Walk. Ch. 170. This may be the rule to avoid circuity of action. The opposite doctrine was held in Driver v. Fortner, 5 Port. (Ala.) 9.

[4] Lamb v. Goodwin, 10 Ired. Eq. 320; Chowning v. Cox, 1 Rand. 306; 3 Leigh, 654; Beebe v. De Baum, 3 Eng. 510; Hall v. Harris, 1 Tex. 300; Gift v. Anderson, 5 Humph. 577; Echols v. Dimik, 2 Stew. 144; Greenleaf v. Queen, 1 Pet. 138; Foster v. Gover, 5 Ala. 428.

negligence or laches in claiming his rights, equity will not interfere in his favor.[1] Nor will equity interfere at the suggestion
of strangers who show no interest in the property,[2] nor when the
sale is in accordance with the agreement of all the parties in
interest, entered into for the protection of all their interests.[3]

§ 602 *ee.* It may be stated as a general proposition, that
where the proceedings are so irregular that a sale would be
nugatory or void, equity would enjoin it, if application was
made.[4] If the trustee or creditor acts in bad faith, or exceeds
his power, or proceeds in an irregular or oppressive manner,
equity will enjoin the sale. This must be the rule, for the reason that if a debtor knows of the irregularity or of the fraud,
and stands by and allows the proceedings to go on, he may be
estopped from afterwards taking advantage of it.[5] If there is
a dispute or doubt concerning the title, which would injure the
sale of the property and greatly reduce the price of it, it is the
duty of the trustee to clear up the title before the sale, and equity
will enjoin the sale until it is done, and if there is doubt or dispute as to how much is due, or if the debt is unliquidated, a
sale will be enjoined. The amount of the debts must be certain;[6] and if it is not so, the creditor must file a bill to ascer-

[1] Chowning *v.* Cox, 3 Leigh, 654; Cresop *v.* McLean, 5 Leigh, 391;
Caldwell *v.* Chapline, 11 Leigh, 342.

[2] Hannah *v.* Carrington, 18 Ark. 85; Foster *v.* Gover, 5 Ala. 428; Bayard
v. Colefax, 4 Wash. C. C. 38; Drake *v.* Moore, 18 Ala. 597; Franklin *v.*
Greene, 2 Allen, 519.

[3] Pollock *v.* Keasley, 24 N. J. Eq. 94.

[4] York, &c. Railw. Co. *v.* Myers, 4 Maine, 109; Van Berghen *v.* Demarest, 4 Johns. Ch. 37, 38; Platt *v.* McClure, 3 Wood. & Minot, 151; Matthie
v. Edwards, 2 Coll. 465.

[5] Doolittle *v.* Lewis, 7 Johns. Ch. 45, 50; Johnson *v.* William, 4 Minn.
260; Johnson *v.* Henry, 10 Johns. 185, 186.

[6] Peck *v.* Peck, 9 Yerg. 301; Cole *v.* Savage, Clark (N. Y.), 361; Johnson
v. Eason, 3 Ired. Eq. 330; Wilkins *v.* Gordon, 10 Leigh, 547; Ord *v.* Noel,
5 Madd. 440; Lane *v.* Tidball, 1 Gil. (Va.) 130; Gibson *v.* Jones, 5 Leigh,
370; Bassett *v.* Fisher, 11 Grat. 499; Hunt *v.* Bass, 2 Dev. Eq. 292; James
v. Gibbs, 1 Pat. & H. 277; Miller *v.* Argyle, 5 Leigh, 460; Fisher *v.* Bassett,
9 Leigh, 119; Guy *v.* Hancock, 1 Rand. 72; Sandford *v.* Flint, 24 Mich. 26.

tain the amount, and pray for leave to sell to pay the amount found due. And it is said that equity will enjoin a sale when new and further litigation would be prevented.[1] So when the whole debt is disputed, as for usury, or for any other defence to the claim made in good faith.[2] If, however, any amount is admitted to be due, or appears to the court to be due, that sum must be brought into court or tendered to the creditor before an injunction would be granted.[3] Nor would the court grant an injunction in order that different debtors might settle their individual rights among themselves; the sale must be made, and they can settle their own relations among themselves.[4] And equity will not interfere to give the mortgagor a further time to pay the debt.[5]

§ 602 *ff*. The trust of the creditor under his deed or mortgage, if not otherwise expressed in the deed, is to sell the property, and after deducting the amount of his debt and the expenses of the sale, to pay the balance, if any, to the debtor, his heirs, executors, administrators, or assigns, and the surplus must be paid according to the terms of the trust.[6] If there are subsequent liens, mortgages, judgments, or assignments, the creditor must pay the surplus to the persons holding such liens or assignments, in the order in which they attach to the property.[7] No subsequent lien or assignment can displace a pre-

[1] Echliff *v.* Baldwin, 16 Ves. 267; Curtis *v.* Buckingham, 3 Ves. & B. 168.

[2] Marks *v.* Morris, 3 Munf. 407.

[3] Sloan *v.* Coolhaugh, 10 Iowa, 30; Stringham *v.* Brown, 7 id. 33; Casady *v.* Bosler, 11 id. 242.

[4] Brinckerhoff *v.* Lansing, 4 Johns. Ch. 65; Cooper *v.* Stevens, 1 id. 425; Gill *v.* Lyon, id. 447.

[5] Hyman *v.* Devereux, 63 N. C. 624.

[6] Goulden *v.* Buckelew, 4 Cal. 107; Pierce *v.* Robinson, 13 Cal. 116; Russell *v.* Duflon, 4 Lans. 399.

[7] Bodine *v.* Moore, 18 N. Y. 347; Calkins *v.* Isbell, 20 N. Y. 152; Bartlett *v.* Gage, 4 Paige, 503; Averill *v.* Loucks, 6 Barb. 470; Eddy *v.* Smith, 13 Wend. 488; Waller *v.* Harris, 7 Paige, 167; 20 Wend. 555; White *v.* Watkins, 23 Mo. 429; Doniphan *v.* Paxton, 19 Mo. 288; Kennedy *v.* Hammond, 16 Mo. 341; Cook *v.* Dillon, 9 Iowa, 407; Chase *v.* Parker, 14 id.

vious lien, and although a debtor can assign any surplus that may be coming to him, yet such assignment cannot defeat a prior lien on the property.[1] To entitle a judgment creditor to follow or claim the surplus, he must have made his judgment a lien on the property or upon the equity of redemption. If there are no liens or assignments of the surplus by the debtor, creditors can reach the surplus in the mortgagor's hands by attachment,[2] trustee process, or garnishment, or, in some cases, by a creditor's bill. If there are no subsequent claims upon the surplus, it goes to the debtor; if he is dead, it goes as real estate to his heirs, for a conversion under a deed of trust or mortgage with a power of sale extends to so much only as is necessary to pay the debt, and the widow is entitled to dower in the surplus, as in an equity of redemption, or she is entitled to dower in the whole estate if she has not released it by joining in the deed.[3] If the sale is made under a second deed of trust or mortgage, nothing is to be paid to the prior mortgagee, as such sale does not affect such prior lien, but it cuts off all subsequent mortgages, liens, judgments, or assignments; therefore they are to be paid as before stated.[4] Whether the trustee is to search for such subsequent liens upon the property, or whether he can dispose of the surplus in the absence of notice of subsequent liens with safety to himself, is not entirely settled; but it would

207; Pahlman *v.* Shumway, 24 Ill. 127; Presnell *v.* Landers, 5 Ired. Eq. 251; Palmer *v.* Yarborough, 1 id. 310; Harrison *v.* Battle, 1 Dev. Eq. 541; Marlow *v.* Johnson, 31 Miss. 128; Russell *v.* Duflon, 4 Lans. 399. A mortgagee who sells property subject to his mortgage and other liens becomes trustee for the benefit of all concerned, and if he acts in good faith and within the scope of his authority, the court will not hold him responsible for mere errors of judgment, however unfortunate, which he could not reasonably have anticipated. Mackay *v.* Langley, 92 U. S. 142.

[1] Doniphan *v.* Paxton, 19 Mo. 288; Palmer *v.* Yarborough, 1 Ired. 310.

[2] Bailey *v.* Merritt, 7 Minn. 159.

[3] Wright *v.* Rose, 2 S. & S. 323; Moses *v.* Murgatroyd, 1 Johns. Ch. 119; Tabele *v.* Tabele, id. 45; Hinchman *v.* Stiles, 1 Stockt. 454. But see Pahlman *v.* Shumway, 24 Ill. 127; and see Varnum *v.* Meserve, 8 Allen, 158, where the mortgagor had died, leaving a will.

[4] Helmey *v.* Heitcamp, 20 Mo. 569; Graham *v.* King, 15 Ala. 563.

appear that a mortgagee is not compelled to search the record for liens subsequent to the date of his own deed.[1]

§ 602 *gg*. These powers of sale in mortgage-deeds do not change their character as mortgages, but the powers of sale are superadded to mortgages. It is a cumulative power of foreclosure; and if the mortgagee does not choose to exercise the power, he may foreclose the mortgage by any of the other methods provided by law,[2] and the power need not be coextensive with the mortgage or its conditions;[3] and so, if the mortgagee has once entered to foreclose, he may afterwards exercise the power of sale.[4]

[1] Cook *v*. Dillon, 9 Iowa, 407.

[2] Cormerais *v*. Genella, 22 Cal. 116; Thompson *v*. Houze, 48 Miss. 445; Merriott *v*. Givens, 8 Ala. 694; Morrison *v*. Bean, 15 Tex. 257.

[3] Butler *v*. Ladue, 12 Mich. 173; Montgomery *v*. McEwen, 9 Minn. 103.

[4] Montague *v*. Dawes, 12 Allen, 397.

CHAPTER XXI.

TRUSTEES FOR INFANTS.

§ 603. INFANTS and their property are, in an especial manner, under the protection of courts of equity. The court has an inherent jurisdiction, which extends to the care of the persons

of infants, so far as it is necessary for their protection and education, and also of their property, real and personal, and its
due management, preservation, and proper application to their
maintenance.[1] The court is their general guardian, and upon
the institution of proceedings therein, involving their personal
or pecuniary rights, they are regarded as wards of the court, and
under its special cognizance and protection, and no act can be
done affecting either their persons, property, or condition, except under the express .or implied direction of the court itself;
and everything done without such direction is treated as a
violation of the authority of the court, and the offending party
is deemed guilty of a contempt, and treated accordingly.[2] (a)

§ 604. In England it is a settled rule of the court that money,
in trust for an infant must be laid out in three per cent consols;
and the court will not even refer it to a master to inquire whether
it would be for the benefit of the infant that the trustee should
invest the sum in real or any other security, unless there is
something very special in the case to induce the court to relax
the rule.[3] In the United States, there is no such general rule,
and there are no statutes directing how trustees shall invest the
trust funds; but in some States there are statutes directing how
savings-banks shall invest money deposited with them, and

[1] Hope v. Hope, 4 De G., M. & G. 328; Dawson v. Jay, 3 id. 764; Stuart
v. Bute, 9 H. L. Cas. 440; Johnson v. Beattie, 10 Cl. & Fin. 440; Nugent
v. Vetzera, L. R. 2 Eq. 704; Spring v. Woodworth, 4 Allen, 326; Anderson v.
Mather, 44 N. Y. 229.

[2] Per Nelson, J., Williamson v. Berry, 8 How. 555; 2 Story, Eq. Jur.
§§ 1341, 1352, 1353; Smith v. Smith, 3 Atk. 304; Eyre v. Shaftesbury, 2 P.
Wms. 103; Gilb. 172; 2 Eq. Cas. Ab. 710, pl. 3; 755, pl. 4; 3 Lead. Cas.
Eq. 538–600; Aymar v. Roff, 3 Johns. Ch. 49; In Matter of Whittaker, 4
Johns. Ch. 378; Garr v. Drake, 2 Johns. Ch. 542; Van Duzer v. Van Duzer,
6 Paige, 366; De Manneville v. De Manneville, 10 Ves. 52.

[3] Norbury v. Norbury, 4 Mod. 191.

(a) The foregoing statement in
the text seems not to have been
intended to apply to a trustee's
exercise of powers expressly or
impliedly given him by the instrument of trust, unless the exercise
of the powers was made dependent
upon the consent of the infant
cestuis.

courts have sometimes directed trustees to invest the trust funds in those securities that have been legalized for savings-banks.

§ 605. In England, trustees or guardians are not ordinarily permitted to change the nature of the infant's property by converting personalty into realty, or *vice versa;* [1] as, where the trustees of an infant had saved £3,000 out of the profits of real estate, and laid it out in lands adjoining the infant's estate, with the consent of the guardian, and the infant died under age, the trustees were held not justified in making such an investment, and were ordered to account to the infant's executors.[2] The rule originated in the fact that formerly an infant at seventeen might make a will of personalty, and to convert his personalty into real estate took away a power that the law gave him; on the other hand, to convert his real estate into personalty gave him a power contrary to the policy of the law.[3] (*a*) This reason ceased with the statute of wills, which takes away the right of infants to make wills, either of real or personal estate, before they are twenty-one. Lord Eldon seemed to think that the rule was established for the protection of the relative interests of the real and personal representatives of the infant;[4] but it is now established that the court will not regard the interests of an infant's representatives, nor interfere to protect them, but will look only to the best interest of the

[1] 1 Madd. Ch. Pr. 269; 2 Story, Eq. Jur. § 1357; *Ex parte* Phillips, 19 Ves. 122; Witter *v.* Witter, 3 P. Wms. 101; Rook *v.* Worth, 1 Ves. 461; Tullett *v.* Tullett, Amb. 370.

[2] Winchelsea *v.* Norcliffe, 1 Vern. 341; Gibson *v.* Scudmore, 1 Dick. 45.

[3] Ware *v.* Polhill, 11 Ves. 278; *Ex parte* Phillips, 19 Ves. 122; Ashburton *v.* Ashburton, 6 Ves. 6; Sergeson *v.* Sealey, 2 Atk. 413; Rook *v.* Worth, 1 Ves. 461; Witter *v.* Witter, 3 P. Wms. 99; Inwood *v.* Twyne, 2 Eden, 152; *Ex parte* Bromfield, 1 Ves. Jr. 461; Pierson *v.* Shore, 1 Atk. 480; *Ex parte* Grimstone, Amb. 708.

[4] Ware *v.* Polhill, 11 Ves. 278.

(*a*) See Att. Gen. *v.* Ailesbury, 12 A. C. 672, 682, 694; 16 Q. B. D. 439.

infant.[1] There seems now to be no principle at the bottom of
the rule; and therefore it has been said in some cases, that where
the advantage or convenience of the infants called for a change
in the nature of the property, the court would order it.[2] In other
and later cases, the jurisdiction and power of the court to change
the nature of an infant's property have been denied; and it
seems now to be the established rule, that such change cannot
be made even for the advantage of the infant.[3]

§ 606. In the United States, a guardian or trustee cannot
convert an infant's personalty into real estate.[4] If such conversion is made, the wards, on coming of age, may elect to receive their personal property, and the trustee or guardian must
account and pay it over to them;[5] or they may acquiesce in
the purchase after becoming of age, and if they so acquiesce for
a long time, they cannot afterwards claim the money, although
the original conversion into real estate was wrongful.[6] So to
use any part of the ward's personal property in making permanent improvements upon his real estate, is a conversion of personalty into real estate, and is unauthorized, and will not be
allowed to the trustee or guardian.[7] Where a guardian used
his own money in constructing buildings upon the ward's land,
it was held that he could not recover the money back from the

[1] Pierson v. Shore, 1 Atk. 480; Oxenden v. Compton, 2 Ves. Jr., 69; 4
Bro. Ch. 201; Ex parte Grimstone, Amb. 706; 4 Bro. Ch. 235, n.; In Matter
of Salisbury, 3 Johns. Ch. 347; Lloyd v. Hart, 2 Penn. St. 477.

[2] Inwood v. Twyne, Amb. 419; 2 Eden, 147; Terry v. Terry, Ch. Pr. 273.

[3] Taylor v. Phillips, 2 Ves. 23; Simpson v. Jones, 2 R. & M. 365; Calvert v. Godfrey, 6 Beav. 97; Peto v. Gardner, 12 L. J. (N. S.) Ch. 371; 2
Y. & C. Ch. 312; Garmstone v. Gaunt, 1 Col. C. C. 577; Anderson v. Mather,
44 N. Y. 249.

[4] Eckford v. De Kay, 8 Paige, 89; Rogers v. Paterson, 4 Paige, 409;
Ex parte Crutchfield, 3 Yerg. 335; Moore v. Moore, 12 B. Mon. 651; Bon-
sall's App., 1 Rawle, 273; Wolf v. Eichelberger, 2 Pen. & W. 346; Royer's
App., 11 id. 36. [Manternach v. Studt, 240 Ill. 464.]

[5] Eckford v. De Kay, 8 Paige, 89; Rogers v. Paterson, 4 Paige, 409.

[6] Moore v. Moore, 12 B. Mon. 651.

[7] Hassard v. Rowe, 11 Barb. 22; Bellinger v. Shafer, 2 Sandf. Ch. 297;
Alexander v. Alexander, 8 Ala. 796; Copely v. O'Neil, 39 How. (N. Y.) 41.

infant.[1] But where the enlargement of a tenement upon the ward's land greatly increased the rents, the trustee was allowed a credit for the expenditure.[2] In one case, it was referred to a master to report whether it was for the interest of the infant to spend money in repairs upon real estate of which he was tenant in tail in expectancy ;[3] and in another case it was said that an allowance for permanent improvements may be made where it is obviously for the ward's interest.[4] But a trustee or guardian should not venture to expend the ward's personalty in that manner without first obtaining the sanction of the court; for if an unauthorized act is first done, the court will not sanction it, though in the particular case it might be proper if first sanctioned by the court; for the principle is that trustees and guardians of infants should take no important step without leave of the court, and the court will punish such action taken on their own responsibility, by refusing to sanction the expenditures.[5]

§ 607. It is said that, in case of necessity, the guardian or trustee may purchase land with the personalty of an infant.[6] No rules can be laid down to govern the conduct of the guardian or trustee as to such necessity, and the safest course is to apply to the court having jurisdiction of the ward's estate. In a proceeding to divide an estate, in which the infant owned a third, it was held that a guardian might purchase the interest of other heirs to prevent a sacrifice of the estate and the ward's property.[7] A guardian may relieve his ward's real estate from

---

[1] Hassard v. Rowe, 11 Barb. 22.

[2] Miller's Estate, 1 Penn. St. 326.

[3] Hood v. Bridport, 11 Eng. L. & Eq. 271.

[4] Jackson v. Jackson, 1 Grat. 143.

[5] Worth v. Curtis, 3 Shep. 228; Miller's Estate, 1 Penn. St. 326; Mason v. Wait, 4 Scam. 127.

[6] Bonsall's App., 1 Rawle, 273; Royer's App., 11 Penn. St. 36; Billington's App., 3 Rawle, 55.

[7] Bowman's App., 3 Watts, 369. This was held not to be a conversion of personalty into real estate, but simply the expenditure of such money as was necessary to preserve the estate.

an elegit, extent, mortgage, or lien, which, if left unredeemed, would probably destroy the ward's interest.[1] If a guardian purchases real estate for his ward, he cannot convey it again without the leave and sanction of the court; as where a guardian purchased real estate in trust for his wards, and upon their marriage he conveyed it to their husbands, the fee was held to be still in the wards.[2]

§ 608. There can be no doubt that it is the duty of the trustees or guardians of infants to lease the lands of their wards, as the wards are incapable of acting for themselves; and they must collect the rents and account for them:[3] but they cannot execute leases extending beyond the majority of the infants; if they do, the infants, on coming of age, can disaffirm the lease and take the possession.[4]

§ 609. Reference thus far has been made only to the power of trustees or guardians to convert their ward's personalty into real estate, for the reason that under no circumstances can a trustee or guardian of an infant convert the ward's real estate into personalty by a sale, without the order, decree, or license of a court. If such sale is already made, and an application is made to have it sanctioned, the court will refuse.[5] (a)

§ 610. Whether a court of general equity powers has an inherent jurisdiction, without some enabling statute, to decree a

[1] Ronald v. Buckley, 1 Brock. 356.

[2] Kauffman v. Crawford, 9 Watts & S. 131; Robinson v. Robinson, 22 Iowa, 427.

[3] Field v. Schieffelin, 7 Johns. Ch. 150; Byrne v. Van Hoesen, 5 Johns. 66; Ross v. Gill, 4 Call, 250; Genet v. Talmadge, 1 Johns. Ch. 561; Emerson v. Spicer, 55 Barb. 418.

[4] Ross v. Gill, 4 Call, 250; Emerson v. Spicer, 55 Barb. 428.

[5] Worth v. Curtis, 3 Shep. 228; Miller's Estate, 1 Penn. St. 326; Mason v. Wait, 4 Scam. 127.

(a) This, of course, is not intended to apply to sales by a trustee in execution of a power given him in the instrument of trust.

conversion of an infant's property, is a matter of doubt and
much conflict of opinion. The jurisdiction to decree such conversion has been sustained in some cases,[1] and denied in others.[2]
The reasoning of the cases where the jurisdiction is denied is,
that where statutes have been enacted, giving power to surrogates or probate courts to authorize the sale of lands belonging
to infants and minors by their guardians, trustees, or other
persons, such statutes are to be followed; that they give an exclusive jurisdiction, and prescribe all the rules of the sale, and
enact what securities shall be taken for the protection of the
ward; and that courts of equity can have no jurisdiction where
such formal proceedings and such adequate remedies are given
by statute. Nearly all the States have statutes giving guardians, or other persons appointed by the court, power to sell
the real estate of infants, on applying in due form, and showing

[1] William's Case, 3 Bland, 186; *Ex parte* Jewett, 16 Ala. 409; Troy *v.*
Troy, 1 Busb. Eq. 87; Williams *v.* Harrington, 11 Mod. 616; Huger *v.* Huger,
3 Des. 18; Stapleton *v.* Langstaff, id. 22; Matter of Salisbury, 3 Johns. Ch.
347; Wood *v.* Mather, 38 Barb. 573. [Thorington *v.* Thorington, 82 Ala.
489; Goodman *v.* Winter, 64 Ala. 410, 434; Gorman *v.* Mullins, 172 Ill.
349; Hale *v.* Hale, 146 Ill. 227, 249; Downin *v.* Sprecher, 35 Md. 474, 483
(*semble*); Johns *v.* Smith, 56 Miss. 727, 731; Houston *v.* Houston, 62 N. C.
95; Sutton *v.* Schonwald, 86 N. C. 198; Marsh *v.* Dellinger, 127 N. C. 360;
Ricardi *v.* Gaboury, 115 Tenn. 484; Lenow *v.* Arrington, 111 Tenn. 720;
Holt *v.* Hamlin, 120 Tenn. 496. See Pennington *v.* Met. Museum, 65
N. J. Eq. 11.]

[2] In Baker *v.* Lorillard, 4 Comst. 257, the court said that it had no
jurisdiction to order a sale of an infant's real estate, except by the statute
giving it that power. Rogers *v.* Dill, 6 Hill, 415, decided that a title taken
under a decree of sale by a court of equity, contrary to the testator's will,
was bad. Forman *v.* Marsh, 1 Kern. 547, was the exercise of the jurisdiction under the statute. Nelson, J., denied the jurisdiction in Williamson *v.* Berry, 8 How. 531; 3 Lead. Cas. in Eq. 269 (3d Amer. ed.). In Anderson *v.* Mather, 44 N. Y. 249, it was held that chancery has an inherent
power over an infant's lands held in trust, not derived from the statute;
that the statute relates to lands owned in fee by the infant, and not to his
equitable estates; and that the prohibitions of the statute are restrictions
upon trustees, and not limitations upon the power of courts. [For cases
holding that the courts have no such inherent power, see Elliott *v.* Fowler,
112 Ky. 376; Liter *v.* Fishback, 75 S. W. 232 (Ky. 1903); Messner *v.* Giddings, 65 Tex. 301; Rhea *v.* Shields, 103 Va. 305; Hoback *v.* Miller, 44
W. Va. 635.]

that it will be advantageous to the infant to convert his real
estate into some other kind of property.(a)   The authority or
license given by the court to the guardian, trustee, or other person who may be appointed to sell and convey the estate, confers
upon them the same power that is given to executors and administrators to sell the real estate of a deceased person for payment of debts.[1]   Legislatures, in the absence of general statutes
authorizing courts to act, may authorize the sale and conversion
of an infant's real estate, and such legislation in particular
cases, or generally in enabling courts to grant authority, is constitutional.[2]   In addition to these statutes, there are statutes
in several of the States authorizing trustees to apply to the court,

[1] Field v. Schieffelin, 7 Johns. Ch. 150; Bank of Va. v. Clegg, 6 Leigh,
399; Garland v. Loring, 6 Rand. 396; Matter of Wilson, 2 Paige, 412;
Pope v. Jackson, 11 Pick. 113; Talley v. Starke, 6 Grat. 339; Duckett v.
Skinner, 11 Ired. 431; Brown's Case, 8 Humph. 200; Peyton v. Alcorn,
7 J. J. Marsh. 500; Dow's Pet., Walk. Ch. 145; Young v. Keogh, 11 Ill.
642; Harding v. Larned, 4 Allen, 426; Dalrymple v. Taneyhill, 4 Md. Ch.
171; Joor v. Williams, 9 George, 546; Ex parte Jewett, 16 Ala. 409; Morris
v. Morris, 2 McCarter, 239; Beal v. Harman, 36 Mo. 435; Wood v. Mather,
38 Barb. 473.

[2] Snowhill v. Snowhill, 2 Green, Ch. 20; Norris v. Clymer, 2 Penn. St.
277; Davis v. Johannot, 7 Met. 388; Spotswood v. Pendleton, 4 Call, 514;
Dorsey v. Gilbert, 11 G. & J. 87; Powers v. Bergen, 2 Seld. 358; Nelson v.
Lee, 10 B. Mon. 495; In Matter of Bull, 45 Barb. 524.   For other cases of
sale and conversion of trust estates authorized by legislatures, see Leggett
v. Hunter, 19 N. Y. 445; Clark v. Van Surley, 15 Wend. 436; Cochran v. Van
Surley, 20 id. 365; Bambaugh v. Bambaugh, 14 Serg. & R. 191; Blagge v.
Miles, 1 Story R. 426; Matthew v. Holman, 16 Pet. 25; Wilkson v. Leland,
2 Pet. 627; Ward v. Screw Co., 1 Cliff. 565; Florentine v. Barton, 2 Wall.
210; Thurston v. Thurston, 6 R. I. 296; Sohier v. Mass. General Hospital,
3 Cush. 483; and Ervin's App., 16 Penn. St. 256, where a sale made under
an act of the legislature, but before the time prescribed in the instrument
of trust, was held invalid. [See Estate of Hamilton, 120 Cal. 421; Elliott
v. Fowler, 112 Ky. 376; Rhea v. Shields, 103 Va. 305; Hoback v. Miller,
44 W. Va. 635; Beauchamp v. Bertig, 90 Ark. 351; Baker v. Lane, 118
S. W. 963 (Ky. 1909); Commonwealth v. Lee, 120 Ky. 433.]

(a) The power of a court of
equity to fully administer a trust
is not curtailed, so as to give the
probate court jurisdiction pro tanto,
by the fact that infants are parties
interested in the sale, mortgage or
lease which it authorizes.   Mayall
v. Mayall, 63 Minn. 511.

by petition or bill, for license to sell real estate held in trust, whether for infants or adults, although there may be interests that may devolve upon persons not yet in being. The statutes authorize the courts to appoint some one to appear for and represent minors and persons not in being; and if, upon the hearing of all parties interested, it appears to be for the interest of all that the real estate should be sold, a sale is decreed, and the trustees are ordered to invest the proceeds in safe securities upon the same trusts.[1] If, however, there is any particular privilege conferred upon an infant, of which he would be deprived by a sale of the estate, a sale will be denied; as where a testator gave his mansion-house and farm to a son for life, and his mansion-house and a portion of his farm to such one of his grandsons, by this or another son, in remainder, as should elect the mansion-house and land as his share. Upon a petition setting forth that it was for the interest of all parties that the estate should be sold, the court held that it was a specific devise to such grandson in remainder as should elect to take the mansion-house; that to decree a sale would defeat the intention of the testator; that if the mansion-house was going to decay and the income was insufficient to repair it, so that the devise over would be substantially defeated, a sale might be ordered, but, no such case appearing, a sale was denied.[2] If, however, a power of conversion is given in the instrument of trust, the trustee may exercise all the powers of conversion given him.[3] In such cases, the trustee for an infant may exercise even larger powers than a trustee for a person *sui juris;* for such person's signature to receipts may be required,[4] but as an infant can do

---

[1] Public Stat. Mass. [R. L. (1902), c. 146, § 4 *et seq.*] It has been said, however, that the court ought to retain the title to the land for security of the purchase-money.

[2] Davis's Pet., 14 Allen, 24. In Rogers *v.* Dill, 6 Hill, 415, the court went further, and declared that a purchaser, under a decree of sale that ought not to have been made by the court, took no title. See Matter of Heaton, 21 N. J. Eq. 221.

[3] Ashburton *v.* Ashburton, 6 Ves. 6; Terry *v.* Terry, Pr. Ch. 273; Rogers *v.* Dill, 6 Hill, 415.

[4] 2 Sugd. V. & P. 45.

no valid act, a trustee for sale of his property takes by implication the power to sign receipts and receive the purchase-
money.[1]

§ 611. If an infant's lands are sold by order of the court the
proceeds remain real estate, so far as the guardian and infant
are concerned, until he is of age;[2] but if he dies after coming
of age the proceeds are treated as personalty.[3] Timber cut
upon an infant's estate, and the proceeds and the accumulation
of the proceeds, remain real estate, if the infant is tenant in
fee;[4] but if he is tenant in tail, they are considered personalty,
to prevent them from going to the remainder-man.[5] If an infant's personal property is used to pay off incumbrances on
the estate, it is still looked upon as part of the personalty.[6]
But necessary expenses for keeping up the estate, as ordinary
repairs, are thrown upon the personalty;[7] and so where an
estate was devised to an infant, in consideration of his paying
off the original cost, such payment was held to be a necessary

[1] Lavender v. Stanton, 2 Madd. 46; Sowarsby v. Lacy, 4 Madd. 142;
Breedon v. Breedon, 1 R. & M. 413.

[2] Genet v. Talmadge, 1 Johns. Ch. 564; Snowhill v. Snowhill, 2 Green,
Ch. 20; Lloyd v. Hart, 2 Pa. St. 473; March v. Berrier, 6 Ired. Eq. 524;
Shumway v. Cooper, 16 Barb. 556; Sweezy v. Thayer, 1 Duer, 286; Forman
v. Marsh, 1 Kern. 544; Fidler v. Higgins, 21 N. J. Eq. 138. [Matter of
McMillan, 110 N. Y. S. 622, 126 App. Div. 155; Wetherill v. Hough, 52
N. J. Eq. 683; Merriam v. Dunham, 62 N. J. Eq. 567; Major v. Hunt, 64
S. C. 97; Findley v. Findley, 42 W. Va. 372.]

[3] Snowhill v. Snowhill, 2 Green, Ch. 20.

[4] Tullet v. Tullet, 1 Dick. 352; Amb. 370; Mason v. Mason, cited Amb.
371; Ex parte Phillips, 19 Ves. 124; Rook v. Worth, 1 Ves. 461; Ex parte
Bromfield, 1 Bro. Ch. 516.

[5] Ibid.; Dyer v. Dyer, 34 Beav. 504.

[6] Ibid.; Seys v. Price, 9 Mod. 220; Dowling v. Belton, 1 Flan. & Kelly,
462; 2 Freem. 114, 126; Ex parte Grimstone, Amb. 708; Palmes v. Danby,
Pr. Ch. 137; Zoach v. Lloyd, cited Awdley v. Awdley, 2 Vern. 192; Dennis
v. Badd, — see Winchelsea v. Norcliffe, 1 Vern. 436; Mason v. Dry, Pr.
Ch. 319; Pierson v. Shore, 1 Atk. 480. [See Matter of Bolton, 159 N. Y.
129.]

[7] Ex parte Grimstone, cited Oxenden v. Compton, 4 Bro. Ch. 235, n.;
Amb. 708.

expense and to fall upon the personalty.[1] Generally, the proceeds of an estate, as timber, go with the estate;[2] but in a late case, an infant dying under age, the proceeds of timber cut during his life was held to be personalty.[3] These distinctions are quite immaterial in the United States, as in most of them, if not all, both real and personal estate descend to the same persons as heirs, and both real and personal estates are equally liable for debts.

§ 612. A father is bound to maintain his infant children, if he has sufficient ability; therefore a trustee cannot apply any part of the income of an infant's estate to its maintenance[4] without an order of court.[5] If the father has the means to maintain his children, the trustee cannot apply income to their support, although there is a provision for their maintenance in the instrument of trust.[6] (a) But if there is an agreement in a

[1] Vernon v. Vernon, cited Ex parte Bromfield, 1 Ves. Jr. 456.

[2] Field v. Brown, 27 Beav. 90.

[3] Dyer v. Dyer, 34 Beav. 504.

[4] Fawkner v. Watts, 1 Atk. 408; Jackson v. Jackson, id. 513; Butler v. Butler, 3 Ark. 60; Darley v. Darley, id. 399; Stocken v. Stocken, 4 Myl. & Cr. 98; Cruger v. Heyward, 2 Des. 94; Matter of Kane, 2 Barb. Ch. 375; Bethea v. McColl, 5 Ala. 312; Sparhawk v. Buell, 9 Vt. 41; Walker v. Crowder, 2 Ired. Eq. 478; Chaplin v. Moore, 7 Mon. 173; Dupont v. Johnson, 1 Bail. Eq. 279; Myers v. Myers, 2 McCord, Ch. 214. [Kinsey v. State, 98 Ind. 351; Burke v. Turner, 85 N. C 500; Stigler's Ex'x v. Stigler, 77 Va. 163, 171; Windon v. Stewart, 43 W. Va. 711, 718.]

[5] McKnight v. Walsh, 23 N. J. Eq. 136.

[6] Mundy v. Howe, 4 Bro. Ch. 224; Hughes v. Hughes, 1 id. 387; Andrews v. Partington, 3 id. 60; 2 Cox, 223; Hamley v. Gilbert, Jac. 354; Thompson v. Griffin, 1 Cr. & Ph. 317. To apply the income of an infant's property in the hands of a trustee to the maintenance of the infant is to convert it into a gift to the father, which the donor does not generally intend. Addison v. Bowie, 2 Bland, 606; Spear v. Spear, 9 Rich. Eq. 188.

(a) Unless it is clear that the intention was to relieve the father from the burden of maintenance and education, as where the property was left to a father in trust for the express purpose of applying the income to the support and education of infant children. Camden Safe Dep. & Tr. Co. v. Ingham, 40 N. J. Eq. 3.

That the duty of a father to supply necessaries for his minor

marriage settlement that the father shall have maintenance out of the trust property, the trustee must apply the income to the support of the children, without reference to the father's ability to support them.[1] If, however, the trustees have a discretionary power in that respect, the father cannot compel them to exercise it in his favor;[2] nor will the court interfere if they choose to exercise their discretion.[3] (a) But where the income is expressly given to the father for the maintenance of his children, these rules do not apply; for such gift is in some sort a gift to the father.[4] If income is directed to be paid to a parent "for" or "towards" the maintenance of children, and, in case of their death under twenty-one, the share of each with all accumulations is to go to the survivors, the father having maintained the children is entitled to the income without an account.[5] (b)

---

[1] Mundy v. Howe, 4 Bro. Ch. 224; Meachey v. Young, 2 Myl. & K. 490; Stocken v. Stocken, 4 Myl. & Cr. 95; 4 Sim. 152; Stephens v. Lawry, 2 N. C. C. 87; White v. Grane, 18 Beav. 571; Ransome v. Burgess, L. R. 3 Eq. 773.

[2] Thompson v. Griffin, 1 Cr. & Ph. 322.

[3] Brophy v. Bellany, L. R. 8 Ch. 798.

[4] Brown v. Casamajor, 4 Ves. 498; Hammond v. Neame, 1 Swanst. 35; Blackburn v. Byne, 26 Beav. 41. [Camden Safe Dep. & Tr. Co. v. Ingham, 40 N. J. Eq. 3.]

[5] Browne v. Paull, 1 Sim. (N. S.) 92; 15 Jur. 5; Hadow v. Hadow, 9 Sim. 438; Rainsford v. Rainsford, Rice, Eq. 343.

children is a legal as well as a moral duty, see Porter v. Powell, 79 Iowa, 151; 30 Am. L. Reg. (N. S.) 20, 28; 30 Cent. L. J. 286, 288, note.

(a) Although the court will not interfere with a reasonable and honest exercise of discretion of the trustees either in paying over or in withholding income in such cases, In re Bryant, [1894] 1 Ch. 324; Read v. Patterson, 44 N. J. Eq. 211; if it appears that the father is unable to maintain and educate the infant beneficiary in a manner suitable to the latter's station in life and expectations, the court will order a sufficient allowance to the father, or other guardian, for the purpose. King-Harman v. Cayley, [1899] 1 Ir. 39; In re Lofthouse, 29 Ch. Div. 921; In re Birch's Trusts, 15 L. R. Ir. 380. See Wilson v. Turner, 22 Ch. Div. 521.

(b) This does not apply when the income is not given to the father, but he is clothed only with a power to use it for the support and education of the beneficiary. Neal v. Bleckley, 51 S. C. 506, 531.

Where the income of a life-estate under a marriage settlement was given to parents for the support of their children, and they became bankrupt, the court ordered the whole income to be applied to the support of the children.[1] But where there is a provision to parents for the maintenance of their children, and a third person voluntarily supports one of the children, the parents being ready to render such support, they cannot be called upon to reimburse such third person, nor can the fund be charged.[2] Where a testatrix devised her property, in trust to apply the income to the maintenance of the children of her daughter M., who at that time had four children, and who afterwards married again and had five other children, it was held that the maintenance must be applied to the support of all the children, and that it commenced with their birth, and continued during their minority, or until the females were married.[3] If the trustee has a discretion, he cannot apply the whole income, if the infant can be properly maintained on a less sum.[4]

§ 613. A stepfather is not compelled to maintain his wife's children, and he will be entitled to receive maintenance out of the income, if the trustee can pay it for that purpose;[5] (a) but if the support of the infant costs the stepfather nothing,

[1] Dalton's Settlement, 1 De G., M. & G. 265.

[2] Crawford v. Patterson, 11 Grat. 364.

[3] Connor v. Ogle, 4 Md. Ch. 425.

[4] McKnight v. Walsh, 24 N. J. Eq. 498. [See Wilson v. Turner, 22 Ch. Div. 521.]

[5] Freto v. Brown, 4 Mass. 675; Gay v. Ballou, 4 Wend. 403. [Livingston v. Hammond, 162 Mass. 375; In re Besonby, 32 Minn. 385; Dissenger's Case, 39 N. J. Eq. 227; Ela v. Brand, 63 N. H. 14; Wilson's Guardianship, 40 Or. 353; Gerber v. Bauerline, 17 Or. 115.]

(a) But where he has taken them into his family and assumed the relation of parent to them without evidence of an intention to charge them for maintenance, his subsequent claim for an allowance for *past* maintenance stands upon practically the same basis as would such a claim by the infant's father. Ela v. Brand, 63 N. H. 14; Dissenger's Case, 39 N. J. Eq. 227. See Livingston v. Hammond, 162 Mass. 375.

though the ward lives with him, he will not be allowed anything.[1] So a mother is not legally obliged to support her children, whether she is living with the husband by whom she had the children, or is a widow, or is married to a second husband; therefore she is entitled to maintenance out of the income of the trust fund.[2] If a father makes application for maintenance out of the income of his children in the hands of trustees, it will be referred to a master to inquire and report respecting the father's ability to support them.[3] (a) But no inquiry is made when the mother makes application for maintenance, as her ability is immaterial, she not being obliged to maintain her children.[4] (b) If the fact of the poverty of the father is apparent,

[1] Booth v. Sineath, 2 Strob. Eq. 31.

[2] Haley v. Bannister, 4 Mod. 275; Hodgson v. Hodgson, 4 Cl. & Fin. 323; 11 Bligh (N. S.) 62; Llo. & Goo. Sugd. 259; Llo. & Goo. Plunk. 137; Lanoy v. Athol, 2 Atk. 447; Ex parte Petre, 7 Ves. 403; Beasley v. Magrath, 2 Sch. & L. 35; Greenwell v. Greenwell, 5 Ves. 194; Douglass v. Andrews, 12 Beav. 310; Heyward v. Cuthbert, 4 Des. 445; Matter of Bostwick, 4 Johns. Ch. 100; Whipple v. Dow, 2 Mass. 415; Dawes v. Howard, 4 Mass. 97; Bruin v. Knott, 1 Phil. 573; Anderton v. Yates, 5 De G. & Sm. 202; Smee v. Martin, 1 Bunb. 131. [See note b, infra.]

[3] Hughes v. Hughes, 1 Bro. Ch. 386; Lucknow v. Brown, 12 Jur. 1017; McKnight v. Walsh, 23 N. J. Eq. 136.

[4] Billingsley v. Critchett, 1 Bro. Ch. 268; Douglass v. Andrews, 12 Beav. 311, n. [In re Beisel, 110 Cal. 267; Perkins v. Westcoat, 3 Colo. App. 338; In re Besondy, 32 Minn. 385.]

(a) The necessity for an allowance from the estate of an infant and the amount must depend upon the circumstances of each case; and the court will be guided entirely by a consideration of what is best for the infant in view of his station in life and his prospects. In the case of a father, the purpose of the allowance is to furnish to him what he lacks to enable him to bring up the child and educate him in the manner calculated to fit him for the station in life which in view of his means and natural aptitudes he will probably occupy. In some of the English cases the parent has been allowed sufficient to maintain a suitable family establishment. King-Harman v. Cayley, [1899] 1 Ir. 39; In re Walker, [1901] 1 Ch. 879. See Brown v. Smith, 10 Ch. Div. 377. But in America different social conditions render the English cases on this point of but little help. See McKnight's Ex'rs v. Walsh, 23 N. J. Eq. 136; Stephens v. Howard's Ex'r, 32 N. J. Eq. 244.

(b) In some recent cases it has

the court will not send the matter for inquiry,[1] nor if the property is small,[2] or no allowance is asked for.[3] If the children are taken from the custody of a father on account of his misconduct, the court must order maintenance for them out of the income in the hands of the trustees, as there is no principle upon which a court can take children from a father, and then order him to support them from his own means, in a manner dictated by the court.[4]

§ 614. In inquiring into the ability of a father to support his children, no account will be made of the fortune of his wife settled to her own use, as the property of the wife is in no way bound for the maintenance of the children.[5] In making the inquiry, reference will be had to the position of the children in society, their expectations, and the relative style and expense in which they ought to live; as where a father had £6,000 per year, maintenance was allowed to enable him to educate his children properly for the position which they would probably fill.[6] In all these matters, the best interests of the children are

---

[1] *Ex parte* Mountford, 15 Ves. 449; *In re* England, 1 R. & M. 499; Payne *v.* Low, id. 223.

[2] Walker *v.* Shore, 15 Ves. 387; *Ex parte* Swift, 1 R. & M. 575; Payne *v.* Low, id. 223; *Ex parte* Dudley, 1 J. & W. 254, n.

[3] *In re* Neale, 15 Beav. 250.

[4] Wellesley *v.* Beaufort, 2 Russ. 29; 2 Bligh N. S. 124.

[5] *Ante*, § 613.

[6] Jervoise *v.* Silk, 1 Geo. Cooper, 52; *Ex parte* Williams, 2 Col. C. C. 740; Moulton *v.* De M'Carty, 6 Rob. (N. Y.) 533.

---

been held that a widowed mother has the same obligation to support her children that the father had, and that she should be allowed to use the estate of her infant children for their maintenance and education only when she has insufficient means of her own. Ellis *v.* Soper, 111 Iowa, 631; Alling *v.* Alling, 52 N. J. Eq. 92 (disapproving of a dictum to the contrary in Pyatt *v.* Pyatt, 46 N. J. Eq. 285). See Melanefy *v.* O'Driscoll, 164 Mass. 422. But even when the circumstances are such that the court would grant her an allowance, her creditors cannot compel her to ask for it. Hanford *v.* Prouty, 133 Ill. 339.

consulted, rather than mere pecuniary considerations;[1] as where two infant daughters were entitled to a large fortune on coming of age, and had an income of $4,000 per year, their father not being able to keep a house in accordance with their expectations and future prospects, an allowance of $2,500 per year was made to him, that he might keep up an establishment proper for his daughters, and educate them at home, although the expense of sending them to a boarding-school would not have been more than $1,200 per year.[2] Such an allowance will be made, that the wards may have the means of bestowing charity, where the fortune is ample, and such an expenditure reasonable.[3] Regard will be had to all the circumstances of the family, as where there was a large number of young children, and all were destitute, a liberal allowance was made for the maintenance of an older boy, in order that the younger children might be better maintained and educated.[4] So a liberal maintenance will be allowed to relieve the distress of the parents,[5] even where the indigence arises from their own misconduct.[6]

§ 615. Upon these principles, courts will order maintenance for infants out of their income, where the father is unable to support them. (a) This inability does not mean absolute pov-

[1] *Ex parte* Burke, 4 Sandf. Ch. 617; Owens *v.* Walker, 2 Strob. Eq. 289. But see McKnight *v.* Walsh, 23 N. J. Eq. 136. [See *In re* Walker, [1901] 1 Ch. 879; Brown *v.* Smith, 10 Ch. Div. 377; King-Harman *v.* Cayley, [1899] 1 Ir. 39.]   [2] Ibid.

[3] Langton *v.* Brackenburgh, 2 Col. C. C. 446.

[4] Pierpont *v.* Cheney, 1 P. Wms. 493; Harvey *v.* Harvey, 2 P. Wms. 22; Lanoy *v.* Athol, 2 Atk. 447; *Ex parte* Petre, 7 Ves. 403; Tweddell *v.* Tweddell, T. & R. 13; *Ex parte* Williams, 2 Col. C. C. 740; Petre *v.* Petre, 3 Atk. 511; Bradshaw *v.* Bradshaw, 1 J. & W. 647. [See King-Harman *v.* Cayley, [1899] 1 Ir. 39; *In re* Walker, [1901] 1 Ch. 879; Brown *v.* Smith, 10 Ch. Div. 377. But see *contra*, McKnight's Ex'rs *v.* Walsh, 23 N. J. Eq. 136; Stephens *v.* Howard's Ex'r, 32 N. J. Eq. 244.]

[5] Roach *v.* Gavan, 1 Ves. 160; Hill *v.* Chapman, 2 Bro. Ch. 231; Heysham *v.* Heysham, 1 Cox, 179.

[6] Allen *v.* Coster, 1 Beav. 202.

(a) Perkins *v.* Westcoat, 3 Colo. App. 338; McGeary *v.* McGeary, 181 Mass. 539; Stephens *v.* Howard's Ex'r, 32 N. J. Eq. 244.

erty, but an inability to give the child an education suitable to his fortune and expectations.[1] The allowance will be made, although the settlement contains no directions for maintenance, and although there is a direction to accumulate the income.[2] (a) Generally, application should be made to the court for leave to apply the income in that way, but the trustees may apply the income for maintenance without an express decree, taking the risk of having it disallowed by the court.[3] (b) There is a difference between past expenses and an allowance for future maintenance. If a trustee takes the risk of supporting the

[1] Buckworth v. Buckworth, 1 Cox, 80; Jervoise v. Silk, 1 G. Coop. 52; Matter of Burke, 4 Sandf. Ch. 617; Rice v. Tonnele, id. 568; Heyward v. Cuthbert, 4 Des. 445; Wilkes v. Rogers, 6 Johns. 566; McKnight v. Walsh, 24 N. J. Eq. 498. [Bedford v. Bedford, 136 Ill. 354, 360.]

[2] Ibid.; Greenwell v. Greenwell, 5 Ves. 194, 195, n.; 197, n.; Evans v. Massey, 1 Y. & J. 196; Stretch v. Watkins, 1 Madd. 253. [In re Walker, [1901] 1 Ch. 879; Read v. Patterson, 44 N. J. Eq. 211; Pitts v. R. I. Hospital Trust Co., 21 R. I. 544.]

[3] Rice v. Tonnele, 4 Sandf. Ch. 568; Bethea v. McColl, 5 Ala. 312; Corbin v. Wilson, 2 Ashm. 178; Newport v. Cook, id. 337.

(a) The express intention of a testator should not, of course, be interfered with. In Havelock v. Havelock, 17 Ch. D. 807, where there was a direction to accumulate, the court felt justified in making an allowance for the benefit of infants, on the ground of want; and this was followed in Re Collins, 32 Ch. D. 229. But in Kemmis v. Kemmis, 13 L. R. Ir. 372; 15 id. 90, this decision was disapproved, and it was held that when there is an imperative trust to accumulate, the court cannot make an allowance for maintenance. See also Re Smeed, 54 L. T. 929.

(b) Doubtless courts will usually ratify a payment by the trustee or guardian to the parent for the purpose of maintenance and education upon the same facts upon which it would have authorized the allowance in advance. Melanefy v. O'Driscoll, 164 Mass. 422; Wilson's Guardianship, 40 Or. 353; Alling v. Alling, 52 N. J. Eq. 92; Brown v. Smith, 10 Ch. Div. 377. See also Pfefferle v. Herr, 71 A. 689 (N. J. Prerog. 1909); Bellamy v. Thornton, 103 Ala. 404; Gott v. Culp, 45 Mich. 265, 273; Boyd v. Hawkins, 60 Miss. 277. Even when the father himself is the guardian or trustee, upon proof of his own inability to support and educate the child in a manner suitable to the latter's station and prospects, reasonable expenditures of the child's funds have been ratified. McGeary v. McGeary, 181 Mass. 539.

infant, he will be allowed only for actual expenses;[1] but if an application is made for future maintenance, a liberal allowance is made according to the circumstances of the case.[2] And the court has power to order trustees to anticipate the time of payment upon a case made showing the necessity of maintenance.[3] In England, a father cannot have an allowance for past expenses, except under peculiar circumstances.[4] And the court may disallow all the payments for maintenance, if they were made improperly and without leave first obtained.[5] If, however, the circumstances are such that the court would have made the allowance if asked, they will be allowed.[6] If the annual amount to be paid for the infant's support is named in the instrument of trust, the trustee of his own motion cannot exceed that amount,[7] unless he is clothed with a discretion; [8] but if the fund goes absolutely to the infant, the *court* can increase the amount if the circumstances require it.[9] If the exigencies are very pressing, the court will increase the amount although there is a direction for accumulation, and the infant's interest is contingent.[10] If there are two funds from which main-

[1] Bruin *v.* Knott, 1 Phil. 572, overruling 12 Sim. 436; *Ex parte* Bond, 2 Myl. & K. 439; Stephens *v.* Lawry, 2 Y. & Col. Ch. 87; Corbin *v.* Wilson, 2 Ashm. 178; Newport *v.* Cook, id. 337; Matter of Bostwick, 4 Johns. Ch. 100.

[2] Ibid.

[3] Rhoades *v.* Rhoades, 43 Ill. 239.

[4] Reeves *v.* Brymer, 6 Ves. 425; Sherwood *v.* Smith, id. 454; Presley *v.* Davis, 7 Rich. Eq. 109; See Carmichael *v.* Hughes, 20 L. J. Ch. 396; Ransome *v.* Burgess, L. R. 3 Eq. 773.

[5] Andrews *v.* Partington, 3 Bro. Ch. 60; Cotham *v.* West, 1 Beav. 381; Bridge *v.* Brown, 2 Y. & C. Ch. 187.

[6] Lee *v.* Brown, 4 Ves. 369; Barlow *v.* Grant, 1 Vern. 255; Franklin *v.* Green, 2 Vern. 137; 1 Rop. Leg. 768; Sisson *v.* Shaw, 9 Ves. 288; Maberly *v.* Turton, 14 Ves. 499; *Ex parte* Darlington, 1 B. & B. 241.

[7] Hearle *v.* Greenbank, 2 Atk. 697, 716; Long *v.* Long, 3 Ves. 286, n.

[8] Rawlins *v.* Goldfrap, 5 Ves. 440.

[9] Aynsworth *v.* Pratchett, 13 Ves. 321; Allen *v.* Coster, 1 Beav. 202; Josselyn *v.* Josselyn, 9 Sim. 63; Stretch *v.* Watkins, 1 Madd. 253; Newport *v.* Cook, 2 Ashm. 332; Corbin *v.* Wilson, id. 178; Evans *v.* Massey, 1 Y. & J. 196.

[10] Ibid.

tenance may be ordered, it will be ordered from that fund from which it will be most beneficial for the infant to take it.[1] If maintenance is directed for the infant until twenty-one, its marriage does not determine the maintenance;[2] and if the maintenance is directed during the life of A., the allowance will continue during the life of A., although the children are more than twenty-one years of age.[3] If maintenance is directed, but no time is limited, it will cease when the infants are of age.[4] In making the allowance the trustee is not confined to the income of the year; but he may set off the gross amount of the maintenance against the gross amount of income.[5] If maintenance is directed by will during minority, and the property is given over in case the infant dies under age, the court will not permit the infant to be deprived of proper maintenance for the benefit of the remainder-man, nor will it permit a wasteful maintenance in disregard of the contingent rights of others.[6]

§ 616. A distinction is made between property coming to a child from a parent, or from a person in the place of a parent, and property given in trust for an infant by a stranger. When the gift comes from parents, or persons in the place of parents, whose duty it is to support the children, maintenance will be ordered where the subject of the trust is residuary personal estate, or a contingent interest only, although there was no power in the will, and there was an express direction for an accumulation, and although there was a gift over to other children,

[1] Bruin v. Knott, 1 Phil. 572; Lygon v. Lord, 14 Sim. 41; Rawlins v. Goldfrap, 5 Ves. 440; Foljambe v. Willoughby, 2 S. & S. 165; Re Ashley, 1 R. & M. 371; Winch v. Winch, 1 Cox, 433; Methold v. Turner, 20 L. J. Ch. 201; Chisolm v. Chisolm, 4 Rich. Eq. 266.

[2] Chambers v. Goldwin, 11 Ves. 1.

[3] Badham v. Mee, 1 R. & M. 631.

[4] Ibid.

[5] Carmichael v. Wilson, 3 Moll. 79; Edwards v. Grove, 2 De G., F. & J. 210. [In re Wise, [1896] 1 Ch. 281; Robinson v. Bonaparte, 102 Md. 63.]

[6] Curtis v. Smith, 6 Blatch. 537.

if the chance of survivorship is equal.[1] (a) If the chance of survivorship is not equal, maintenance will not be allowed;[2] nor will it, if the interest is real estate and contingent or residuary.[3] But maintenance will be refused out of a contingent interest, or where the fund is given over; or where the gift proceeds from a stranger, or from a grandfather; or where'the infant is a natural child not adopted by the father.[4]

[1] Aherley v. Vernon, 1 P. Wms. 783; Rogers v. Soutten, 2 Keen, 598; Incledon v. Northcote, 3 Atk. 433; Harvey v. Harvey, 2 P. Wms. 22; Lambert v. Parker, Coop. 143; Brown v. Temperly, 3 Russ. 263; Mills v. Robarts, 1 R. & M. 555; Ex parte Chambers, id. 577; Boddy v. Dawes, 1 Keen, 362; Rhoades v. Rhoades, 43 Ill. 239; Fairman v. Green, 10 Ves. 45; Lomax v. Lomax, 11 Ves. 48; Mole v. Mole, 1 Dick. 310; Greenwell v. Greenwell, 5 Ves. 194; Cavendish v. Mercer, id. 195; Collis v. Blackburn, 9 Ves. 470; McDermot v. Kealy, 3 Russ. 264; Stretch v. Watkins, 1 Madd. 253; Seibert's App., 19 Penn. St. 49; Corbin v. Wilson, 2 Ashm. 208; Newport v. Cook, id. 342; Matter of Ryder, 11 Paige, 185; Ex parte Kebble, 11 Ves. 604; Turner v. Turner, 4 Sim. 434.

[2] Errat v. Barlow, 14 Ves. 202; Kime v. Welpitt, 3 Sim. 533; Turner v. Turner, 4 Sim. 430; Cannings v. Flower, 7 Sim. 523.

[3] Green v. Ekins, 2 Atk. 476; Bullock v. Stones, 2 Ves. 521; Leake v. Robinson, 2 Mer. 384.

[4] Errington v. Chapman, 12 Ves. 24; Lowndes v. Lowndes, 15 Ves.

(a) By section 43 of the English Conveyancing, etc., Act of 1881 (44 & 45 Vict. c. 41), it is provided that: — "Where any property is held by trustees in trust for infants, either for life, or for any greater interest, and whether absolutely, or contingently on his attaining the age of twenty-one, or on the occurrence of any event before his attaining that age, the trustees may, at their sole discretion, pay to the infant's parent or guardian, if any, or otherwise apply for or towards the infant's maintenance, education, or benefit, the income of that property, or any part thereof, whether there is any other fund applicable to the same purpose or any person bound by law to provide for the infant's maintenance or education, or not," — except where a contrary intention is expressed in the instrument under which the interest of the infant arises.

This is a modification of a similar provision in Lord Cranworth's Act (23 & 24 Vict. c. 145). For decisions on questions involved in these statutes, see In re Dickson, 28 Ch. Div. 291; In re Judkin's Trusts, 25 Ch. Div. 743; In re George, 5 Ch. Div. 837; In re Cotton, 1 Ch. Div. 232; In re Moody, [1895] 1 Ch. 101; In re Woodin, [1895] 2 Ch. 309; Best v. Donmall, 40 L. J. Ch. 160. See also In re Greaves' Settled Estates, [1900] 2 Ch. 683, as to allowances to children out of portions.

§ 617. If the fund goes absolutely to the infant, and no conflicting interests can arise, the order for maintenance will be
made on petition and without suit.[1] But if there are opposing
and complicated interests, the court will not act without a
regular suit and notice to all parties.[2]

§ 618. It is a settled rule, that trustees for infants should
never, on their own authority, break in upon the capital of the
trust fund for the maintenance, and seldom for the advancement of their ward. This is a rule for the protection of children, and if trustees break it, their accounts will be disallowed,
although the particular case is a hardship; as it is better that
a single individual should suffer a hardship which he might have
avoided, than that the interests of all infants should be endangered.[3] Sir William Grant expressed a doubt whether the court
itself had power to authorize the expenditure of the trust fund
for the infant's support and advancement.[4] It is now, however,
well established, that the court has such power, and will exer-

301. But see Greenwell v. Greenwell, 5 Ves. 194. In Seibert's App., 19
Penn. St. 49, maintenance was allowed, though the gift came from a grand-
father not in *loco parentis*. See Chisolm v. Chisolm, 4 Rich. Eq. 266, and
Corbin v. Wilson, 2 Ashm. 208.

[1] *Ex parte* Whitfield, 2 Atk. 315; *Ex parte* Kent, 3 Bro. Ch. 88; *Ex
parte* Salter, id. 500; *Ex parte* Mountford, 15 Ves. 445; *Ex parte* Starkie,
3 Sim. 399; *Ex parte* Chambers, 1 R. & M. 577; *Ex parte* Green, 1 J. & W.
253; *Ex parte* Myercough, id. 151; *Ex parte* Hayes, 13 Jur. 765; 3 De G. &
Sm. 485; Matter of Bostwick, 4 Johns. Ch. 100; Rice v. Tonnele, 3 Sandf.
Ch. 571; Cross v. Bevan, 2 Sim. (N. S.) 53.

[2] Fairman v. Green, 10 Ves. 45.

[3] *Per* Sir R. P. Arden, Walker v. Wetherell, 6 Ves. 473; Davis v. Austen,
1 Ves. Jr. 247; Lee v. Brown, 4 Ves. 362; Anon., Moseley, 41; Davis v.
Harkness, 1 Gilm. 173; Prince v. Logan, Spears, Eq. 29; McDowell v.
Caldwell, 2 McCord, Ch. 43; Davis v. Roberts, 1 Sm. & M. Ch. 543; Hesters
v. Wilkinson, 6 Humph. 219; Frelick v. Turner, 26 Miss. 393; Martin's
App., 23 Penn. St. 438; Petit's App., 39 id. 324; Villard v. Chovin, 2 Strob.
Eq. 40; Bybee v. Thorp, 4 B. Mon. 313; Carter v. Rolland, 11 Humph.
339; Cornwise v. Bourgum, 2 Ga. Dec. 15; Haigood v. Wells, 1 Hill, Eq.
59; Swinnock v. Crisp, Freem. 78; Caffey v. McMichael, 64 N. C. 507;
Matter of Bostwick, 4 Johns. Ch. 101.

[4] Walker v. Wetherell, 6 Ves. 474.

cise it with caution in a proper case.[1] But if the trustee exercises the power by breaking in upon the trust fund for mere maintenance, without leave of the court, he will be compelled to replace it.[2] It has been said, that a trustee may pay from the capital fund upon his own authority in case of necessity;[3] but it would not be safe to follow this. The burden would be on the trustee to prove a case of necessity, and that it was impossible to apply to a court for direction; for courts look with disfavor upon the assumption of such authority by guardians and trustees.[4] (a) When such a case can be made, the trustee will

[1] Barlow v. Grant, 1 Vern. 255; Ex parte Green, 1 J. & W. 253; Ex parte Chambers, 1 R. & M. 577; Ex parte Knott, id. 499; Ex parte Swift, id. 575; Evans v. Massey, 1 Y. & J. 196; Bridge v. Brown, 2 N. C. C. 181; Williams's Case, 3 Bland, 186; Ex parte Potts, 1 Ashm. 340; Ex parte Bostwick, 4 Johns. Ch. 100; Long v. Norcom, 2 Ired. Eq. 354; Haigood v. Wells, 1 Hill, Eq. 79; Maupin v. Dulany, 5 Dana, 593; Worthington v. McCreer, 23 Beav. 81; Prince v. Hine, 26 id. 634; Ex parte Hayes, 3 De G. & Sm. 485; 13 Jur. 762; Ex parte Allen, 3 De G. & Sm. 485; Withers v. Hickman, 6 B. Mon. 293; Prince v. Logan, 1 Spears, Eq. 29; Teague v. Dendy, 2 McCord, Ch. 207.

[2] Davis v. Austen, 3 Bro. Ch. 178; Lee v. Brown, 4 Ves. 362; Walker v. Wetherell, 6 Ves. 473.

[3] Davis v. Austen, 3 Bro. Ch. 178; Barlow v. Grant, 1 Vern. 255; Carmichael v. Wilson, 3 Moll. 79; Bridge v. Brown, 2 Y. & Col. Ch. 181.

[4] Prince v. Logan, Spears, Eq. 29; Teague v. Dendy, 2 McCord, Ch. 207; McDowell v. Caldwell, id. 43; Davis v. Roberts, 1 Sm. & M. Ch. 543; Myers v. Wade, 6 Rand. 444; Davis v. Harkness, 1 Gilm. 173; Holmes v. Joslin, 5 Strob. 31; Downey v. Bullock, 7 Ired. Eq. 102; Villard v. Chovin, 2 Strob. Eq. 40.

(a) When the infant's income is insufficient for his support and maintenance and his parents are unable to supply the deficiency, the courts will authorize reasonable encroachments on the principal, but do so with considerable reluctance and only when satisfied of the necessity. Bellamy v. Thornton, 103 Ala. 404; Gott v. Culp, 45 Mich. 265, 273; Alling v. Alling, 52 N. J. Eq. 92; Pfefferle v. Herr, 71 A. 689 (N. J. Prerog. 1909); Wilson's Guardianship, 40 Or. 353.

Usually the courts will ratify an unauthorized use of principal for this purpose, if on the facts it would have authorized the use beforehand. Bellamy v. Thornton, 103 Ala. 404; Gott v. Culp, 45 Mich. 265, 273; Pfefferle v. Herr, 71 A. 689 (N. J. 1909); Wilson's Guardianship, 40 Or. 352. But it has been held that under the Mississippi statute previous authority is essential. Boyd v. Hawkins, 60 Miss. 277.

No allowance from principal

be allowed the amount paid out, in his accounts.[1] Courts are much more willing to authorize an expenditure of the capital fund of the trust to establish the minor in life, or to pay his entrance fee as an apprentice, or to educate him properly for business and life, than for mere maintenance. In such cases courts look upon the capital, not as consumed and extinguished, but as converted into another and useful form.[2] This allowance from the capital fund is confined to cases where the trust fund is small: if the capital consists of several thousand pounds, and the income is sufficient to educate and support the infant, the court will not allow nor justify any expenditure of the principal.[3]

§ 619. Where there is a limitation over to a stranger on the death of the infant, neither the trustee nor the court can expend any part of the capital fund for the maintenance or advancement of the ward. As where £100 was given to trustees to apply the income to the support and education of an infant, and to transfer the principal to him at twenty-one; but if he

[1] Long v. Norcom, 2 Ired. Eq. 354; Sparhawk v. Buell, 9 Vt. 41; Withers v. Hickman, 6 B. Mon. 203; Matter of Bostwick, 4 Johns. Ch. 100.

[2] Williams's Case, 3 Bland, 186; Hanson v. Chapman, id. 198; Matter of Bostwick, 4 Johns. Ch. 100; Barlow v. Grant, 1 Vern. 255; Franklin v. Green, 2 Vern. 137; In re England, 1 R. & M. 499; Ex parte Chambers, id. 577; Re Welch, 23 L. J. Ch. 344; Nunn v. Harvey, 2 De G. & Sm. 301; Re Clarke, 17 Jur. 362; Re Lane, id. 219; Worthington v. McCreer, 23 Beav. 81; Ex parte Swift, 1 R. & M. 575; Ex parte Green, 1 J. & W. 253; Bridge v. Brown, 2 Y. & Col. Ch. 181; Davies v. Davies, 2 De G., M. & G. 53; Walsh v. Walsh, 1 Drew. 64; Ex parte Hayes, 3 De G. & Sm. 485; Swinnock v. Crisp, Freem. 78; Ex parte McKey, 1 B. & B. 405; Sisson v. Shaw, 9 Ves. 285; Prince v. Hine, 26 Beav. 634.

[3] Barlow v. Grant, 1 Vern. 255; Davis v. Austen, 1 Ves. Jr. 247; 3 Bro. Ch. 178; Beasley v. Magrath, 2 Sch. & Lef. 35; Deen v. Cozzens, 7 Rob. (N. Y.) 178.

can be made when the infant's interest in the principal is only contingent, unless all the others who are interested consent, for the court cannot take away the prop- erty of another person for the pur- pose. Pitts v. R. I. Hospital Trust Co., 21 R. I. 544; In re Smeed, 54 L. T. 929. See In re Jobson, 44 Ch. Div. 154.

died under that age, the said sum was to be paid over to other persons, the court refused leave to expend any part of the capital.[1] Where an infant, upon a certain contingency, was to lose certain rights, and the trustee made an advancement before the contingency happened, and it afterwards happened in the ward's favor, the advancement was allowed to the trustee.[2] So where a legacy is given to a class of children, with a limitation over to the others in case of the death of one before marriage or twenty-one, an allowance may be made, on the ground that all have an equal chance of surviving, before their particular proportions are vested so that they cannot be divested.[3] An advancement may be made if all the parties in remainder are competent to consent, and do consent to the allowance.[4] But advancements cannot be made where the gift is to a class of children, though not absolutely to them, but in certain events to go over to a stranger.[5] If the limitation over is to the issue of a deceased child, such issue is a stranger, and no allowance can be made.[6] So where the children in being are not all the persons interested in the fund, as where another child may be born.[7] If a legacy is given to children when they become twenty-one, the court cannot anticipate the time and make an allowance,[8] as it may not come to them at all. If, however,

---

[1] Lee v. Brown, 4 Ves. 362; Van Vechten v. Van Vechten, 8 Paige, 104; Dean v. Cozzens, 7 Rob. (N. Y.) 178.

[2] Worthington v. McCreer, 23 Beav. 81.

[3] Franklin v. Green, 2 Vern. 137; Greenwell·v. Greenwell, 5 Ves. 194, and notes; Brandon v. Aston, 2 Y. & Col. Ch. 30; Marshall v. Holloway, 2 Swanst. 436.

[4] Evans v. Massey, 1 Y. & J. 196; Cavendish v. Mercer, 5 Ves. 195, n. [Pitts v. R. 1. Hospital Trust Co., 21 R. I. 544.]

[5] Ex parte Kebble, 11 Ves. 604, overruling Greenwell v. Greenwell, 6 Ves. 194; Errington v. Chapman, 12 Ves. 20. [In re Smeed, 54 L. T. 929.]

[6] Ex parte Kebble, 11 Ves. 606; Turner v. Turner, 4 Sim. 430; Errington v. Chapman, 12 Ves. 20; Ex parte Whitehead, 2 Y. & J. 243; Fendall v. Nash, 5 Ves. 197, n.; contra, but disapproved by Lord Eldon, 14 Ves. 203.

[7] Ex parte Kebble, 11 Ves. 604.

[8] Lomax v. Lomax, 11 Ves. 48. See Haley v. Bannister, 4 Madd. 275; Errat v. Barlow, 14 Ves. 202; Cannings v. Flower, 7 Sim. 253; Turner v. Turner, 4 Sim. 430. [See In re Jobson, 44 Ch. Div. 154.]

there is a clear intention, to be gathered from the whole will, that the children are to have a maintenance, the court will order it, although there is a gift over.[1]

§ 620. When a trust is created, and the trustees are directed to pay the income to a person for the support of his children, he will be entitled to receive the income so long as he continues to maintain them.[2] Where the income was directed to be paid by the trustees to M. H. H. for the maintenance of her children, the fund to be divided among her children at twenty-one, and, in default of issue, over to another person, it was held that the income was payable to M. H. H., although she had no child.[3] Where a widow was to receive the income from trustees for the support of herself and children, and she eloped, she was held entitled only to a part of the income.[4] So where a trustee was to pay the income to the testator's son for the support of himself and children, and the son misapplied the income, the court said that he took the income as a subtrustee for his wife and children, and that the court had power to regulate and control it, by directions to the original trustee, in such manner as to accomplish the purpose for which it was given.[5] The fund is in some sort payable to the father, but the trustee will be held accountable for its proper application.[6] In paying

[1] Lambert v. Parker. G. Coop. 143. [Dockins v. Vass, 124 S. W. 290 (Ky. 1910).]

[2] Hadow v. Hadow, 9 Sim. 438; Jubber v. Jubber, id. 503; Berkely v. Swinburne, 6 Sim. 613; Thurston v. Essington, Jac. 361, n.; Longmore v. Elcum, 2 Y. & Col. Ch. 363; Leach v. Leach, 13 Sim. 304; Hart v. Tribe, 19 Beav. 149; Brown v. Paull, 1 Sim. (N. S.) 92; Hammond v. Neame, 1 Swanst. 35; Raikes v. Ward, 1 Hare, 445; Crockett v. Crockett, 2 Phil. 553; Chase v. Chase, 2 Allen, 104; Loring v. Loring, 100 Mass. 340.

[3] Hammond v. Neame, 1 Swanst. 35; Loring v. Loring, 100 Mass. 340.

[4] Castle v. Castle, 3 Jur. (N. S.) 723; 1 De G. & J. 352; Loring v. Loring, 100 Mass. 340. [In re G., [1899] 1 Ch. 719.]

[5] Chase v. Chase, 2 Allen, 104; Loring v. Loring, 100 Mass. 340.

[6] Andrews v. Partington, 2 Cox, 223; Robinson v. Tickell, 8 Ves. 142; Woods v. Woods, 1 Myl. & Cr. 409; Raikes v. Ward, 1 Hare, 445; Crockett v. Crockett, 2 Phil. 553; Webb v. Wool, 2 Sim. (N. S.) 267; Joddrell v. Joddrell, 14 Beav. 397; Biddles v. Biddles, 16 Sim. 1; Wetherell v. Wetherell, 1

the income for maintenance, the trustee must exercise a sound discretion. He may apply it himself, or he may place it in the hands of parents or guardians; but he must not place it in the hands of a beneficiary, who mentally or morally is incapable of using it properly or profitably; and he must not allow the income to be thrown away, or perverted from its purpose.[1]

§ 621. In most respects, the relation between the trustee and an infant *cestui que trust* is the same as between trustees and other *cestuis que trust*. An infant has the same remedies for a breach of trust as if of full age. If a trustee employs the infant's money in his own business, the infant has an election to take the profits or the interest;[2] or if an improper investment is made by the trustee, the infant can enforce compensation for the loss.[3] If, by any neglect or violation of duty by a trustee, a loss happens to the infant, the trustee must make it up; as if a trustee should allow the statute of limitations to run without suit on a claim in favor of an infant, the trustee would be held to account for the loss.[4] So if he should suffer five years to elapse without claim, after a stranger had entered upon the infant's estate and levied a fine.[5] In all such cases the trustees will be responsible for all the loss that occurs from their negligence or mismanagement.

§ 622. It is the duty of trustees to accumulate all the income of a trust for infants which is not employed in mainte-

Keen, 80; Brown *v.* Casamajor, 4 Ves. 498; Hamley *v.* Gilbert, Jac. 354; Collier *v.* Collier, 3 Ves. 33.

[1] Mason *v.* Jones, 2 Barb. 248; Gott *v.* Cook, 7 Paige, 538; Van Vechten *v.* Van Vechten, 8 id. 104.

[2] Anon., 2 Ves. 630.

[3] Holmes *v.* Dring, 2 Cox, 1; Terry *v.* Terry, Pr. Ch. 273.

[4] Williams *v.* Otey, 8 Humph. 563; Smilie *v.* Biffle, 2 Barr, 52; Wyck *v.* East India Co., 3 P. Wms. 309; Wooldredge *v.* Planters' Bank, 1 Sneed, 297; Worthy *v.* Johnson, 10 Ga. 358; Long *v.* Cason, 4 Rich. Eq. 60; Blake *v.* Allman, 5 Jon. Eq. 407.

[5] Huntington *v.* Huntington, 3 P. Wms. 310, n.; Allen *v.* Sayer, 2 Vern. 368, is the other way, but it is not considered the true exposition of the law. Pentland *v.* Stokes, 2 B. & B. 75.

nance and education as before stated, whether a direction for such accumulation is contained in the instrument of trust or not. (a) This rule applies where the subject of the trust is a *residue* of the testator's personal estate, and the interest of the infant is *contingent*, as where the trust is for a child, " if " or "when" it becomes twenty-one.[1] But the rule will not apply where a *sum certain* is to be paid to the infant when twenty-one;[2] nor to the income of real estate where such estate is given to the infant if he shall reach twenty-one;[3] unless there is a direction that the income in the mean time shall be used for the infant's benefit.[4] Without such direction the income in the first case would fall into the residue,[5] and in the second case it would go to the heirs-at-law.[6] If the infant takes a vested interest in the trust fund, and the payment only is postponed, and an accumulation is directed until he is twenty-four, he is absolutely entitled to the fund at twenty-one, and will be entitled to receive the income at that time, and the *corpus* of the trust at the time fixed, so that accumulation will cease at twenty-one.[7]

§ 623. The court has power to apply the income in support of the infant although he is abroad, or out of the jurisdiction of the court. In such cases the court may require a guardian [8]

[1] Green *v.* Ekins, 2 Atk. 473; Studholme *v.* Hodgson, 3 P. Wms. 299; Trevanion *v.* Vivian, 2 Ves. 430; Bullock *v.* Stones, id. 521.

[2] Leake *v.* Robinson, 2 Mer. 363, 384.

[3] Green *v.* Ekins, 2 Atk. 473; Studholme *v.* Hodgson, 3 P. Wms. 299; Bullock *v.* Stones, 2 Ves. 521.

[4] Bullock *v.* Stones, 2 Ves. 521.

[5] Ibid.

[6] Ibid.

[7] Saunders *v.* Vautier, 4 Beav. 115; Cr. & Ph. 240. [*In re* Wrey, 30 Ch. Div. 507.]

[8] Logan *v.* Fairlee, Jac. 193.

(a) The accumulation of unexpended income to which the infant is absolutely entitled is held for his benefit until he attains majority and is not added to the principal unless there is a direction to that effect in the trust instrument. *In re* Wells, 43 Ch. Div. 281. See *Re* Martin, 57 L. T. 471.

or attorney [1] to be appointed within the jurisdiction to receive the income; or the court may appoint a guardian who resides in the same jurisdiction with the infant, and who has been appointed guardian by the courts in that jurisdiction.[2] In some instances where the fund is small, the court has ordered not only the income, but the whole *corpus* of the trust, to be paid to the parents residing abroad,[3] or who were about emigrating.[4] If the trustee is within the jurisdiction, the court can take administration of the trust fund, and compel a proper application of the income to the purposes for which it was given; [5] and it may use its power to compel the parents residing abroad to bring the infants within the jurisdiction, by refusing any allowance from the income for maintenance.[6]

§ 624. If a trustee holds in his hands a sum of money to be paid absolutely to an infant, he must not pay it to the infant, nor to his father or other person, without the sanction of the court.[7]   Should he do so, he may be compelled to pay it again to the infant when he comes of age.[8] Even a receipt or release taken from the infant under age is worthless; [9] but an infant, after coming of age, can confirm such payments by acts, clearly intended to sanction and confirm them.[10] If the infant fraudulently represents himself to be of age, and thus procures payments from the trustees, he will be estopped to claim the fund

[1] De Weever *v.* Rockport, 6 Beav. 391; *In re* Morrison, 16 Sim. 42; Hart *v.* Tribe, 19 Beav. 149.

[2] Daniel *v.* Newton, 8 Beav. 485.

[3] Volans *v.* Carr, 2 De G. & Sm. 242.

[4] Walsh *v.* Walsh, 1 Drew, 64; *Ex parte* Hayes, 3 De G. & Sm. 485.

[5] Chase *v.* Chase, 2 Allen, 101.

[6] Lockwood *v.* Fenton, 1 Sm. & G. 73.

[7] Furman *v.* Coe, 1 Caines's Cas. 96; Sparhawk *v.* Buell, 9 Vt. 41.

[8] Dagley *v.* Tolferry, 1 P. Wms. 285; Phillips *v.* Paget, 2 Atk. 80; Davis *v.* Austen, 3 Bro. Ch. 178; Lee *v.* Brown, 1 Ves. 369.

[9] Overton *v.* Bannister, 3 Hare, 503; 8 Jur. 996.

[10] Dagley *v.* Tolferry, 1 P. Wms. 285; Lee *v.* Brown, 4 Ves. 362; Cooper *v.* Thornton, 3 Bro. Ch. 97; Cory *v.* Gertcken, 2 Madd. 40.

again.[1] (a)   In the United States, guardians are appointed by probate courts to take charge of infants' estates. Such guardians are required to give bonds for the security of such estates, and payments may safely be made to them.[2]   In some instances where the sums are small, courts have directed them to be paid directly to the persons maintaining the children, to save the expenses of obtaining guardianship.[3]   Where the instrument of trust directs the manner of paying over the money, the trustee will be safe in following the directions.[4]

[1] Cory v. Gertcken, 2 Madd. 40; Overton v. Bannister, 3 Hare, 503. [Hayes v. Parker, 41 N. J. Eq. 630.]

[2] Furman v. Coe, 1 Caines's Cas. 96; Sparhawk v. Buell, 9 Vt. 41; Hoyt v. Hilton, 2 Edw. Ch. 202.

[3] Farrance v. Viley, 21 L. J. Ch. 313; Ker v. Buxton, 16 Jur. 491.

[4] 2 Wms. Ex'rs, 866; 1 Rop. Leg. 771; Cooper v. Thornton, 3 Bro. Ch. 96, 186; Robinson v. Tickell, 8 Ves. 142.

(a) On the question of estoppel of an infant when he has made false representations that he is of age, there is some conflict of authority. See Bigelow on Estoppel, (5th ed.) pp. 605–607; Beauchamp v. Bertig, 90 Ark. 351; Rowe v. Allison, 87 Ark. 206, 213; Tobin v. Spann, 85 Ark. 556; Slayton v. Barry, 175 Mass. 513; Brooks v. Sawyer, 191 Mass. 151; Pace v. Cawood, 110 S. W. 414 (Ky. 1908); Pemberton B'ld'g, etc., Ass'n v. Adams, 53 N. J. Eq. 258.